Revenue Statistics in Africa 2020

Statistiques des recettes publiques en Afrique 2020

1990-2018

Please cite this publication as:
OECD/AUC/ATAF (2020), *Revenue Statistics in Africa 2020*, OECD Publishing, Paris, *https://doi.org/10.1787/14e1edb1-en-fr.*

Merci de citer cet ouvrage comme suit :
OCDE/CUA/ATAF (2020), *Statistiques des recettes publiques en Afrique 2020*, Éditions OCDE, Paris, *https://doi.org/10.1787/14e1edb1-en-fr.*

ISBN 978-92-64-95200-3 (print/imprimé)
ISBN 978-92-64-63164-9 (pdf)

Revenue statistics in Africa/*Statistiques des recettes publiques en Afrique*
ISSN 2617-6521 (print/imprimé)
ISSN 2617-653X (online/en ligne)

Photo credits/Crédits photo: Cover/Couverture © some of the graphic elements in the main cover illustration were adapted from Freepik.com./certains des éléments graphiques de l'illustration de la couverture principale ont été adaptés de Freepik.com

Corrigenda to publications may be found on line at: *www.oecd.org/about/publishing/corrigenda.htm.*
Les corrigenda des publications sont disponibles sur : www.oecd.org/about/publishing/corrigenda.htm.

Foreword

Revenue Statistics in Africa *is a joint publication by the OECD Centre for Tax Policy and Administration, the OECD Development Centre, the African Tax Administration Forum and the African Union Commission, with the technical support of the African Development Bank and the Cercle de réflexion et d'échange des dirigeants des administrations fiscales and with the financial support of the governments of Ireland, Japan, Luxembourg, Norway, Sweden and the United Kingdom.*

The report presents detailed, internationally comparable data on both tax and non-tax revenues for 30 African countries. Its approach is based on the well-established methodology of the OECD Revenue Statistics *database, which has become an essential reference source for OECD member countries and many more. Comparisons are also made with the average for OECD economies and for the economies featured in* Revenue Statistics in Latin America and the Caribbean.

The term "taxes" in this publication is confined to "compulsory, unrequited payments to general government". As outlined in the Interpretative Guide to the Revenue Statistics, taxes are "unrequited" in the sense that benefits provided by government to taxpayers are not normally in proportion to their payments. The OECD methodology classifies a tax according to its base: income, profits and capital gains (classified under heading 1000), payroll (heading 3000), property (heading 4000), goods and services (heading 5000) and other taxes (heading 6000). Compulsory social security contributions paid to general government are treated as taxes and classified under heading 2000. The tax concept and the classification of taxes are set out in much greater detail in the OECD Interpretative Guide in Annex A.

The term "non-tax revenue" includes all general government revenue that does not meet the OECD definition of taxation. Revenues that do not constitute taxation include grants (e.g. foreign aid), returns on government market investments, rents on the extraction of resources from public lands, sales of government-produced goods and services, and the collection of fines and forfeits. More details on these types of revenues in Annex B.

Chapter 1 and Chapter 2 of this report provide an overview of the main trends in tax- and non-tax revenues respectively in the 30 participating countries from 2010 to 2018. A special feature on the future of domestic revenue mobilisation in Africa in light of both the COVID-19 pandemic and the implementation of the African Continental Free Trade Area (AfCFTA) is contained in Chapter 3. Chapter 4 explores the level of tax revenues by main tax category and how the respective tax structures of the 30 countries have evolved since 1990. Chapters 5 and 6 contain detailed information on tax- and non-tax revenues respectively on a country-by-country basis as well as a comparison of the non-tax revenues mix over time in the 30 countries.

Avant-propos

Les Statistiques des recettes publiques en Afrique *est une publication conjointe du Centre de politique et d'administration fiscales de l'OCDE, du Centre de développement de l'OCDE, du Forum sur l'administration fiscale africaine (ATAF), et de la Commission de l'Union Africaine, avec l'assistance technique de la Banque africaine de développement et du Cercle de réflexion et d'échange des dirigeants des administrations fiscales et le soutien financier des gouvernements d'Irlande, du Japon, du Luxembourg, de la Norvège, de la Suède et du Royaume-Uni.*

Le rapport fournit des données détaillées et comparables à l'échelle internationale, sur les recettes fiscales et non fiscales de 30 pays africains. Son approche repose sur la méthodologie bien établie des Statistiques des recettes publiques de l'OCDE, *devenue une source de référence essentielle pour les pays membres de l'Organisation et au-delà. Des comparaisons sont également effectuées avec la moyenne des économies de l'OCDE et avec celle des économies couvertes par les* Statistiques des recettes publiques en Amérique latine et dans les Caraïbes.

Dans cette publication, le terme « impôts » fait référence uniquement aux « versements obligatoires sans contrepartie aux administrations publiques ». Comme indiqué dans le Guide d'interprétation pour les Statistiques des recettes publiques, les impôts sont « sans contrepartie » en ce sens que les prestations fournies par les administrations aux contribuables ne sont pas normalement proportionnelles à leurs paiements. La méthodologie de l'OCDE consiste à classer les impôts en fonction de l'assiette : le revenu, les bénéfices et les gains en capital (rubrique 1000), les salaires et la main-d'œuvre (rubrique 3000), le patrimoine (rubrique 4000), les biens et les services (rubrique 5000) et autres impôts (rubrique 6000). Les cotisations obligatoires de sécurité sociale versées aux administrations publiques sont aussi traitées comme des impôts et classées dans la rubrique 2000. Des informations plus détaillées sur la notion d'impôt et sur la classification des impôts sont présentées dans le Guide d'interprétation de l'OCDE figurant à l'annexe A.

Le terme « recettes non fiscales » recouvre toutes les recettes des administrations publiques qui ne sont pas considérées comme des « impôts » selon la définition de l'OCDE. Les recettes non fiscales incluent les dons (comme l'aide extérieure), les rendements d'investissements publics, les rentes tirées de l'extraction de ressources du domaine public, la vente de biens et de services produits par le secteur public, et les amendes et confiscations. On trouvera, à l'annexe B, des informations plus détaillées sur ces catégories de recettes.

Le chapitre 1 et le chapitre 2 du rapport offrent une vue d'ensemble des grandes tendances de 2010 à 2018, dans les 30 pays participants, des recettes fiscales et non fiscales respectivement. Une étude spéciale sur la mobilisation des recettes publiques en Afrique à la lumière de la pandémie COVID-19 et de la mise en œuvre de la Zone de libre-échange continentale africaine (ZLECAf) est incluse dans le chapitre 3. Le chapitre 4 examine le niveau des recettes fiscales par principaux types d'impôts et l'évolution des structures fiscales des 30 pays depuis 1990. Les chapitres 5 et 6 fournissent respectivement des données détaillées sur les recettes fiscales et non fiscales par pays ainsi qu'une comparaison des structures des recettes non fiscales dans le temps dans les 30 pays.

Acknowledgements

Revenue Statistics in Africa has been jointly produced by the Organisation for Economic Co-operation and Development (OECD) Centre for Tax Policy and Administration (CTP), the OECD Development Centre (DEV), the African Tax Administration Forum (ATAF) and the African Union Commission (AUC), with the technical support of the African Development Bank (AfDB) and the Cercle de réflexion et d'échange des dirigeants des administrations fiscales (CREDAF) and with the financial support of the governments of Ireland, Japan, Luxembourg, Norway, Sweden and the United Kingdom. The staff from these organisations with responsibility for producing the publication were: Emmanuelle Modica, Leonie Cedano, Talita Yamashiro Fordelone, Michael Sharratt and Michelle Harding of CTP under the supervision of the Director Pascal Saint-Amans, the Deputy Director Grace Perez-Navarro and the Head of the Tax Policy and Tax Statistics Division David Bradbury; Sébastien Markley, Arthur Minsat and Alexander Pick of DEV under the supervision of the Director of the Development Centre and Special Advisor to the OECD Secretary-General on Development Mario Pezzini, the Deputy Director Federico Bonaglia and the Senior Communications Manager Henri-Bernard Solignac-Lecomte; Nara Monkam, Director of Research at ATAF, Frankie Mbuyamba, African Tax Outlook & Tax Statistics Programme Specialist at ATAF, Ezera Madzivanyika, Research Manager at ATAF; Ndinaye Sekwi Charumbira, Rumbidzai Treddah Manhando, Edwin Kofi Owusu-Ansah, and Mary Menta under the supervision of Dossina Yeo, Head of Economic Policy and Research Division, Leila Ben Ali, Head of Statistics Division, Jean Bertrand Azapmo, Regional Trade Adviser and Jose Awong Alene, Senior Statistician at the AUC; Chaouch Anouar, Statistician at AfDB under the Director of Statistics Department Charles Leyeka Lufumpa, and Koua Louis Kouakou at AfDB, Manager of Economic and Social Statistics Division; Secretary General Jean-Marc Niel of CREDAF. The special feature (Chapter 3) was written by Ndinaye Sekwi Charumbira and Yeo Dossina (AUC), Ezera Madzivanyika and Nara Monkam (ATAF), and Leonie Cedano, Michelle Harding, Sébastien Markley, Emmanuelle Modica, Alexander Pick and Talita Yamashiro Fordelone (OECD). Elizabeth Nash and Delphine Grandrieux at DEV and Alexandra Le Cam and Marie-Aurélie Elkurd at CTP assisted with the production and publication of this report and Stephanie Coic produced the cover.

The authors would like to thank the officials at the finance ministries, national tax agencies and national statistical institutes of the countries participating in this project who gathered and compiled the national data and provided their invaluable knowledge and expertise on their country's revenue collection systems and data. In particular, the authors would like to thank the focal points appointed for each country and their colleagues who facilitated the technical work: Seitebaleng Fologang and Winstern Kabo for Botswana; Mariame Dabo and Michel Yaméogo for Burkina Faso; Carlos José Oliveira Bentub and Hamilton Cabral Fortes for Cabo Verde; Rogangoum Kodindouma Hervé and Hassan Adoum Mbodou Mbami for Chad; Nkom Ndum Dorothy Agbor, Edouard Kalawa, and Stéphane Nepetsoun for Cameroon; Yacouba Fofana and Alex Koula Pouhe for Côte d'Ivoire; Christophe Bitasimwa Bahii, Liliane Bilonda, Elisabeth Dikisha Dietu, Dieudonné

Bukasa Kabongo, Floribert Masuku Mambambu, Yvette Barhashishwa Shabani Mwangu, Richard Kabila Mutshi and Popol Mukoko Akabuele for the Democratic Republic of the Congo; Aya Abdel-Aziz, Alaa Abdel-Rahman, and Yomna Khattab for Egypt; Bindang Ndong Okiri and Santiago Obama Benga for Equatorial Guinea; Eric Thembinkosi Dlamini, Mvuselelo B. Mdluli, Khulekani Innocent Mncina, and Yvonne Ntfombiyenkhosi Mthombo for Eswatini; Asuo Afram and Francis Bright Mensah for Ghana; Alex Mwangi for Kenya; Vololonirina Léa Randrianarisoa and Donah for Madagascar; Mokete Khobotle and Katiso Ramalebo for Lesotho; Laurent Kalonga and Alick Wella for Malawi; Siaka Samaké and Boubacar Diakité for Mali; Mohamed Falilou Gueye for Mauritania; Meeshrani Balgobin and Roshan Oree for Mauritius; El Moustapha Bennani and Abderrahim Mezroui for Morocco; Idi Itope and Nelago Ekandjo for Namibia; Mahamadou Djibrilla for Niger; Sunusi Gwaram Shuaibu for Nigeria; Frédéric Ngolele for the Republic of the Congo; Roy Valence Gasangwa and Agnes Kanyangeyo for Rwanda; Cheikh Ahmed Tidiane Ba, Ndèye Louise Mbissine Camara Tine, Pape Malick Diallo, Banta Magassouba, Papa Diouf and Mamadou Cissé for Senegal; Yvette Campanella-Rumbos, Dick Labonte, and Ayda Noel for Seychelles; Mampho Baholo, Paul Dreyer, Lawrence Gqesha, Mamiky Leolo, Tshepo Makgoro, Denis Marais, Nontokozo Mnqayi, Vivienne Smithdorf, and Darlington Zhou for South Africa; Ouro-Adoï Abdelganiou and Imrane Moussa for Togo; Saoussen Boumaiza, Raja Hadj Khalifa and Rihab Ben Challadia for Tunisia; and Ronald Nyenje Makumbi and Milly Isongoma Nalukwago for Uganda. *Revenue Statistics in Africa* benefited from the financial support of the European Union between 2017 and 2019 and the authors would like to thank Policy Officer Gaëlle Doléans, Team Leader - Panafrican Programme Fabio Di Stefano, and Head of Domestic Revenue Mobilisation Sector Benedikt Madl at the European Commission (DEVCO) for their continued support and contributions to the report.

This document was produced with the financial assistance of the governments of Ireland, Japan, Luxembourg, Norway, Sweden and the United Kingdom. The views expressed herein can in no way be taken to reflect the official opinion or policies of the governments of Ireland, Japan, Luxembourg, Norway, Sweden and the United Kingdom.

Remerciements

La publication des *Statistiques des recettes publiques en Afrique* a été produite conjointement par le Centre de politique et d'administration fiscales (CPAF) de l'Organisation de coopération et de développement économiques (OCDE), le Centre de développement de l'OCDE (DEV), le Forum sur l'administration fiscale africaine (ATAF), et la Commission de l'Union Africaine (CUA), avec l'assistance technique de la Banque africaine de développement (BAfD), du Cercle de réflexion et d'échange des dirigeants des administrations fiscales (CREDAF), et avec le soutien financier des gouvernements d'Irlande, du Japon, du Luxembourg, de la Norvège, de la Suède et du Royaume-Uni. Les agents de ces organisations auxquels la responsabilité de la publication a été confiée sont : Emmanuelle Modica, Leonie Cedano, Talita Yamashiro Fordelone, Michael Sharratt et Michelle Harding du CPAF sous la supervision du Directeur du Centre Pascal Saint-Amans, de Grace Perez-Navarro, Directrice adjointe du CPAF et de David Bradbury, Chef de la Division des politiques fiscales et statistiques ; Sébastien Markley, Arthur Minsat et Alexander Pick de DEV sous la supervision du Directeur du Centre de développement et Conseiller spécial auprès du Secrétaire général de l'OCDE sur le développement Mario Pezzini, du Directeur adjoint Federico Bonaglia et de Henri-Bernard Solignac-Lecomte, Chef de la communication ; Nara Monkam, Directrice de recherche à l'ATAF, Frankie Mbuyamba, Spécialiste du programme Perspectives fiscales en Afrique et statistiques fiscales à l'ATAF, Ezera Madzivanyika, Responsable de recherche à l'ATAF ; Ndinaye Sekwi Charumbira, Rumbidzai Treddah Manhando, Edwin Kofi Owusu-Ansah, et Mary Menta sous la supervision de Dossina Yeo, Directeur de la division de la politique économique et de la recherche, Leila Ben Ali, Chef de la division des statistiques, Jean Bertrand Azapmo, Conseiller pour le commerce régional et Jose Awong Alene, Principal statisticien de la CUA ; Chaouch Anouar, statisticien à la BAfD, sous la supervision de Charles Leyeka Lufumpa, Directeur du département des statistiques et Koua Louis Kouakou, de la BAfD, Chef de la Division des statistiques économiques et sociales ; Jean-Marc Niel, Secrétaire général du CREDAF. L'étude spéciale a été rédigée par Ndinaye Sekwi Charumbira et Dossina Yeo (CUA), Ezera Madzivanyika et Nara Monkam (ATAF) et Leonie Cedano, Michelle Harding, Sébastien Markley, Emmanuelle Modica, Alexander Pick et Talita Yamashiro Fordelone (OCDE). Elizabeth Nash et Delphine Grandrieux de DEV et Alexandra Le Cam et Marie-Aurélie Elkurd du CPAF ont aidé à la production de la publication et Stephanie Coic a produit la couverture.

Les auteurs souhaitent remercier les responsables des ministères des finances, des administrations fiscales nationales et des instituts nationaux de statistique des pays participant au projet qui ont collecté et rassemblé les données nationales et ont partagé leur connaissance et expertise inestimable sur les systèmes de collecte de recettes et les données de leur pays. Les auteurs souhaitent en particulier remercier les points focaux désignés pour chaque pays et leurs collègues qui ont facilité le travail technique : Seitebaleng Fologang et Winstern Kabo pour le Botswana ; Mariame Dabo et Michel Yaméogo pour le Burkina Faso ; Carlos José Oliveira Bentub et Hamilton Cabral Fortes pour le Cabo Verde ; Nkom Ndum Dorothy Agbor, Edouard Kalawa et Stéphane Nepetsoun pour le Cameroun ;

Yacouba Fofana et Alex Koula Pouhe pour la Côte d'Ivoire ; Christophe Bitasimwa Bahii, Liliane Bilonda, Elisabeth Dikisha Dietu, Dieudonné Bukasa Kabongo, Floribert Masuku Mambambu, Yvette Barhashishwa Shabani Mwangu, Richard Kabila Mutshi et Popol Mukoko Akabuele pour la République démocratique du Congo ; Aya Abdel-Aziz, Alaa Abdel-Rahman et Yomna Khattab pour l'Égypte ; Bindang Ndong Okiri et Santiago Obama Benga pour la Guinée équatoriale ; Eric Thembinkosi Dlamini, Mvuselelo B. Mdluli, Khulekani Innocent Mncina et Yvonne Ntfombiyenkhosi Mthombo pour l'Eswatini ; Asuo Afram et Francis Bright Mensah pour le Ghana ; Alex Mwangi pour le Kenya ; Mokete Khobotle et Katiso Ramalebo pour le Lesotho ; Vololonirina Léa Randrianarisoa et Donah pour Madagascar ; Laurent Kalonga et Alick Wella pour le Malawi ; Siaka Samaké et Boubacar Diakité pour le Mali ; Mohamed Falilou Gueye, pour la Mauritanie ; Meeshrani Balgobin et Roshan Oree pour Maurice ; El Moustapha Bennani et Abderrahim Mezroui pour le Maroc ; Idi Itope et Nelago Ekandjo pour la Namibie ; Mahamadou Djibrilla pour le Niger ; Sunusi Gwaram Shuaibu pour le Nigéria ; Frédéric Ngolele pour la République du Congo ; Roy Valence Gasangwa et Agnes Kanyangeyo pour le Rwanda ; Cheikh Ahmed Tidiane Ba, Ndèye Louise Mbissine Camara Tine, Pape Malick Diallo, Banta Magassouba, Papa Diouf et Mamadou Cissé pour le Sénégal ; Yvette Campanella-Rumbos, Dick Labonte, et Ayda Noel pour les Seychelles ; Mampho Baholo, Paul Dreyer, Lawrence Gqesha, Mamiky Leolo, Tshepo Makgoro, Denis Marais, Nontokozo Mnqayi, Vivienne Smithdorf et Darlington Zhou pour l'Afrique du Sud ; Rogangoum Kodindouma Hervé et Hassan Adoum Mbodou Mbami pour le Tchad, Ouro-Adoï Abdelganiou et Imrane Moussa pour le Togo ; Saoussen Boumaiza, Raja Hadj Khalifa et Rihab Ben Challadia pour la Tunisie ; et Ronald Nyenje Makumbi et Milly Isongoma Nalukwago pour l'Ouganda. La publication *Statistiques des recettes publiques en Afrique* a bénéficié du soutien financier de l'Union européenne entre 2017 et 2019 et les auteurs tiennent à remercier Gaëlle Doléans, Chargée de mission ; Fabio Di Stefano, Chef d'équipe programme panafricain; Benedikt Madl, Chef du secteur de la mobilisation des ressources intérieures à la Commission européenne (DEVCO) pour leur soutien continu et leurs contributions au rapport.

Ce document a été produit avec le soutien financier des gouvernements d'Irlande, du Japon, du Luxembourg, de la Norvège, de la Suède et du Royaume-Uni. Les opinions exprimées dans ce présent rapport ne peuvent en aucun cas refléter l'opinion ou politique officielle des gouvernements d'Irlande, du Japon, du Luxembourg, de la Norvège, de la Suède et du Royaume-Uni.

Table of contents

Table des matières

LIST OF TABLES/LISTE DE TABLEAUX

Chapter 3/Chapitre 3

COVID-19 and AfCFTA: Risks and opportunities for domestic revenue mobilisation in Africa/COVID-19 et ZLECAf : Risques et opportunités liés à la mobilisation des ressources intérieures en Afrique

Chapter 4/Chapitre 4

Tax levels and tax structures, 1990-2018/ Niveaux et structures des impôts, 1990-2018

Chapter 5/Chapitre 5

Country tables, tax revenues, 1998-2018/ Tableaux pays, recettes fiscales, 1998-2018

Chapter 6/Chapitre 6

Non-tax revenue levels and structures, 1998-2018/ Tableaux des recettes non fiscales, 1998-2018

LIST OF FIGURES/LISTE DE GRAPHIQUES

Chapter 1/Chapitre 1

Tax revenue trends, 2010-2018/ Tendances des recettes fiscales, 2010-2018

Chapter 2/Chapitre 2

Non-tax revenue trends, 2000-2018/ Tendances des recettes non fiscales, 2000-2018

Revenue Statistics in Africa 1990-2018/Statistiques des recettes publiques en Afrique 1990-2018

Executive summary

Achieving the United Nations' Sustainable Development Goals (SDGs) and implementing the Addis Ababa Action Agenda and the African Union's Agenda 2063 require mobilising additional finance, in particular domestic resources, to fund public goods and services. This report presents internationally comparable indicators on tax and non-tax revenues that can be used to track progress on domestic resource mobilisation (DRM) and to inform tax policy analysis and future reform. Additionally, it provides an important backdrop in understanding the fiscal capacity of the African region to respond to the COVID-19 crisis. The report and its data also contribute to the implementation of the Pan-African Statistics Programme, a joint effort between the European Union and the African Union to support statistical capacity in Africa.

Revenue Statistics in Africa 2020 provides data on 30 countries: Botswana, Burkina Faso, Cabo Verde, Cameroon, Chad, the Republic of the Congo, the Democratic Republic of the Congo, Côte d'Ivoire, Equatorial Guinea, Egypt, Eswatini, Ghana, Lesotho, Kenya, Madagascar, Malawi, Mali, Mauritania, Mauritius, Morocco, Namibia, Niger, Nigeria, Rwanda, Senegal, the Seychelles, South Africa, Togo, Tunisia and Uganda. It includes a special feature discussing factors likely to affect the future of DRM in Africa in the aftermath of the COVID-19 pandemic, including the impact of the African Continental Free Trade Area (AfCFTA) on trade and public revenues.

Tax revenues

In 2018, the unweighted average tax-to-GDP ratio for the 30 countries in this publication (the "Africa (30) average") was 16.5%. The tax-to-GDP ratio refers to total tax revenue, including social security contributions, as a percentage of gross domestic product (GDP). The Africa (30) average in 2018 was below the Latin America and the Caribbean (LAC) average of 23.1% and the OECD average of 34.3% in the same year. Tax-to-GDP ratios in Africa ranged from 6.3% in Equatorial Guinea and Nigeria to 32.4% in the Seychelles, with 21 countries having ratios between 10% and 25%. The tax-to-GDP ratio exceeded 25% in four countries (Morocco, Seychelles, South Africa and Tunisia) and was less than 10% in five countries (Chad, the Republic of the Congo, the Democratic Republic of the Congo, Equatorial Guinea and Nigeria).

The increase in the Africa (30) average tax-to-GDP ratio between 2010 and 2018 was 1.4 percentage points (p.p.), although since 2014, the average has remained relatively constant at between 16.4% and 16.5% of GDP. The increase since 2010 is lower than the increase in the LAC and the OECD averages over the same period (1.9 p.p. and 2.0 p.p. respectively). The main changes in the Africa (30) average tax-to-GDP ratio between 2010 and 2018 were increases in revenues from value-added tax (VAT) (1.0 p.p.) and personal income taxes (0.7 p.p.). VAT and income tax revenues increased mostly between 2010 and 2014 (0.9 p.p. and 0.5 p.p. respectively).

Taxes on goods and services were the main source of tax revenues among the countries included in this publication, accounting for 51.9% of total tax revenues on average in 2018, with VAT alone accounting for 29.7%. Taxes on income and profits accounted for 38.7% of tax revenues. Africa's average tax structure was similar to that of the LAC region in 2018, except in relation to social security contributions, which were on average more than twice as high in LAC than in Africa. Labour taxes remain low in Africa and LAC compared to the OECD: personal income taxes and social security contributions amounted to 24.7% of total tax revenues for the Africa (30) average and 26.7% in the LAC region, whereas in the OECD these revenues represented on average 49.9% of tax revenues.

Taxes on goods and services were the principal source of tax revenues for 21 African countries in 2018, ranging from 39.7% of tax revenues in Tunisia to 76.3% in Togo. For the nine other countries (Chad, the Democratic Republic of the Congo, Equatorial Guinea, Nigeria and all countries that constitute the Southern African Customs Union (SACU) i.e. Botswana, Eswatini, Lesotho, Namibia and South Africa), taxes on income and profits accounted for the principal share of total tax revenue.

Environmentally related taxes are a key tool for countries wanting to decarbonise their economies and raise revenues. In Africa, revenues from these taxes amounted to 1.1% of GDP in 2018, on average, the same level as the LAC region and lower than the OECD unweighted average of 2.3% of GDP. In 2018, energy taxes generated 70% of these revenues in Africa on average, followed by motor vehicle and transport taxes. The Africa (30) average rose by 0.2 p.p. between 2010 and 2018. The largest increases in environmentally related tax revenue (over 1.0 p.p.) between 2010 and 2018 were observed in Eswatini, Ghana and Mauritania and were due to increases in fuel and petroleum tax revenues.

This report also presents data on the VAT revenue ratio (VRR) for each country, calculated as the difference between VAT revenues that would be expected if standard rates were uniformly applied to the entire potential tax base and what was actually collected. These differences could be a result of exemptions and reduced rates, fraud, evasion and tax planning, as well as weaknesses in tax administration. In 2018, Cabo Verde and South Africa had the highest VRR (0.73 and 0.61 respectively) whereas Chad, the Democratic Republic of the Congo and Equatorial Guinea had the lowest, below 0.15.

Non-tax revenues

In 2018, average non-tax revenues were equivalent to 6.5% of GDP in Africa. Non-tax revenues were below 5% of GDP in 16 of the 30 African countries and above 10% in six, ranging from 0.6% of GDP in South Africa to 25.2% of GDP in Lesotho. Four of the six countries (Lesotho, Botswana, Namibia and Eswatini) receiving non-tax revenues exceeding 10% of GDP were net recipients of funds from the SACU Common Revenue Pool into which all SACU members pay their customs and excise revenues for the purposes of redistribution. The other two countries were the Republic of the Congo and Equatorial Guinea, which both received oil revenues exceeding 15% of GDP. Non-tax revenues were lower than tax revenues in all countries except Botswana, the Republic of the Congo, Equatorial Guinea and Lesotho.

In contrast with the Africa (30) average tax-to-GDP ratio, average non-tax revenues in these countries fell from 8.3% of GDP in 2010 to 6.5% in 2018, including a sharp decline of 3.2 p.p. between 2012 and 2016. This was driven mainly by declines in rents and royalties and in grant revenues.

The sources of non-tax revenues vary across the countries in the report. For 12 countries (in descending order Rwanda, Togo, Niger, Chad, Burkina Faso, Senegal, the Democratic Republic of the Congo, Madagascar, Malawi, Mali, Côte d'Ivoire and Uganda), grants were the principal source of non-tax revenues. Six countries (the Republic of the Congo, Equatorial Guinea, Mauritania, Cameroon, Tunisia and Nigeria) received their highest share of non-tax revenues from rents and royalties. The eight remaining countries, excluding the four net recipient SACU countries, collected their highest share of non-tax revenues from other non-tax revenues, such as interest and dividends, fees for goods and services, or miscellaneous sources.

COVID-19 and AfCFTA: Risks and opportunities for domestic revenue mobilisation in Africa

The special feature in this year's edition discusses factors likely to affect DRM in Africa in the aftermath of the COVID-19 pandemic. As in other regions, the pandemic will have heavy socio-economic impacts in Africa and is likely to severely affect public revenues, potentially endangering progress made in DRM over the past decades. Although there is considerable uncertainty about how the COVID-19 crisis will evolve, fiscal policies will be an essential tool for all countries in the economic and fiscal recovery process over the longer term. DRM will be an important part of this discussion, as countries seek to restore public finances in a fair and sustainable way, to boost resources to reduce inequalities and promote development, and to allow a greater degree of fiscal space to respond to future shocks. This includes exploring new avenues of raising domestic resources to offset the financing gap created by the pandemic, due to resources being diverted to minimise the effects of an emerging humanitarian and economic crisis. The implementation of the AfCFTA can contribute to this process: in the short term, it has the potential to mitigate the effects of COVID-19 by deepening intra-African trade and accelerating the post-pandemic economic recovery; over the longer term, it will likely play an important role in building greater resilience and insulating the continent against future shocks.

Résumé

Pour atteindre les Objectifs de développement durable (ODD) des Nations Unies et mettre en œuvre le Programme d'action d'Addis-Abeba et l'Agenda 2063 de l'Union africaine, il est nécessaire de mobiliser des moyens financiers supplémentaires, et notamment des ressources intérieures, afin de financer l'offre de biens et de services publics. Le présent rapport contient un ensemble d'indicateurs internationalement comparables sur les recettes fiscales et non fiscales qui peuvent servir à mesurer les progrès en matière de mobilisation des ressources intérieures et à éclairer les politiques et les réformes fiscales à l'avenir. En outre, il apporte une contribution importante à la compréhension de la capacité budgétaire des pays d'Afrique à surmonter la crise du COVID-19. Ce rapport et les données qu'il contient contribuent aussi à la mise en œuvre du Programme statistique panafricain, une initiative conjointe de l'Union européenne et de l'Union africaine qui vise à renforcer les capacités statistiques en Afrique.

L'édition 2020 des *Statistiques des recettes publiques en Afrique* livre des données sur 30 pays d'Afrique : Afrique du Sud, Botswana, Burkina Faso, Cabo Verde, Cameroun, Côte d'Ivoire, Guinée équatoriale, Égypte, Eswatini, Ghana, Kenya, Lesotho, Madagascar, Malawi, Mali, Maroc, Maurice, Mauritanie, Namibie, Niger, Nigéria, Ouganda, République démocratique du Congo, République du Congo, Rwanda, Sénégal, Seychelles, Tchad, Togo et Tunisie. Elle contient une étude spéciale qui examine les facteurs susceptibles d'influer sur l'avenir de la mobilisation des ressources intérieures en Afrique à la suite de la pandémie de COVID-19, notamment l'impact de la Zone de libre-échange continentale africaine (ZLECAf) sur le commerce et les recettes publiques.

Recettes fiscales

En 2018, le ratio moyen non pondéré impôts/PIB dans les 30 pays d'Afrique couverts par cette publication [désigné ci-après « moyenne des pays d'Afrique (30) »] s'est établi à 16.5 %. Le ratio impôts/PIB correspond aux recettes fiscales totales (y compris les cotisations de sécurité sociale) exprimées en pourcentage du produit intérieur brut (PIB). En 2018, la moyenne des pays d'Afrique (30) était inférieure à celle de la région Amérique latine et Caraïbes (ALC), de 23.1 %, et à celle de la zone OCDE (34.3 %). Les ratios impôts/PIB en Afrique s'échelonnaient entre 6.3 % en Guinée équatoriale et au Nigéria et 32.4 % aux Seychelles, et 21 pays affichaient des ratios compris entre 10 % et 25 %. Le ratio impôts/PIB dépassait 25 % dans quatre pays (Afrique du Sud, Maroc, Seychelles et Tunisie), mais était inférieur à 10 % dans cinq pays (Guinée équatoriale, République démocratique du Congo, République du Congo, Nigéria et Tchad).

La hausse du ratio moyen impôts/PIB des 30 pays d'Afrique entre 2010 et 2018 s'établissait à 1.4 point de pourcentage, bien que depuis 2014, la moyenne soit restée relativement constante, oscillant entre 16.4 % et 16.5 % du PIB. La progression depuis 2010 est inférieure à la hausse des moyennes de la région ALC et de la zone OCDE au cours de la même période (respectivement 1.9 et 2.0 points). Les principales variations du ratio impôts/PIB moyen de l'Afrique (30) entre 2010 et 2018 concernaient l'augmentation des recettes de la taxe sur la valeur ajoutée (TVA) (1.0 point) et des impôts sur le revenu des personnes physiques (0.7 point). Les recettes générées par la TVA et par l'impôt sur le revenu ont surtout progressé entre 2010 et 2014 (de respectivement 0.9 et 0.5 point).

Les impôts sur les biens et services constituaient la principale source de recettes fiscales dans les pays couverts par cette publication, puisqu'ils ont généré 51.9 % du total des recettes fiscales en moyenne en 2018, la TVA à elle seule contribuant à 29.7 % du total. Les impôts sur le revenu et sur les bénéfices ont procuré 38.7 % des recettes fiscales. En 2018, la structure fiscale moyenne des pays d'Afrique (30) était comparable à celle de la région ALC, sauf pour les cotisations de sécurité sociale qui, dans la région ALC, étaient en moyenne plus de deux fois supérieures au niveau enregistré en Afrique. Les impôts sur le travail restent faibles en Afrique et dans la région ALC par rapport à la zone OCDE : l'impôt sur le revenu des personnes physiques et les cotisations de sécurité sociale représentaient 24.7 % du total des recettes fiscales pour la moyenne de l'Afrique (30) et 26.7 % dans la région ALC, alors que dans la zone OCDE, ces recettes généraient en moyenne 49.9 % des recettes fiscales.

En 2018, les impôts sur les biens et services constituaient la principale source de recettes fiscales pour 21 pays africains, allant de 39.7 % du total des recettes fiscales en Tunisie à 76.3 % au Togo. Dans les neuf autres pays (Guinée équatoriale, Nigéria, République démocratique du Congo, Tchad et tous les pays qui constituent l'Union douanière d'Afrique australe (SACU), à savoir l'Afrique du Sud, le Botswana, l'Eswatini, le Lesotho et la Namibie), les impôts sur le revenu et sur les bénéfices généraient la majeure partie des recettes fiscales totales.

Les taxes liées à l'environnement représentent un outil essentiel pour les pays qui souhaitent décarboner leur économie et accroître leurs recettes. En Afrique, les recettes tirées de ces taxes s'élevaient en moyenne à 1.1 % du PIB en 2018, soit le même niveau que dans la région ALC et moins que la moyenne non pondérée de l'OCDE de 2.3 % du PIB. En 2018, les taxes sur l'énergie ont généré 70 % de ces recettes en moyenne, suivies des taxes sur les transports et sur les véhicules à moteur. La moyenne de l'Afrique (30) s'est accrue de 0.2 point entre 2010 et 2018. Les plus fortes augmentations des recettes fiscales liées à l'environnement (plus de 1.0 point) entre 2010 et 2018 ont été observées en Eswatini, au Ghana et en Mauritanie, et étaient dues à l'accroissement des recettes tirées des taxes sur les carburants et sur le pétrole.

Ce rapport présente également des données sur le ratio des recettes de TVA (RRT) pour chaque pays, qui correspond à l'écart entre les recettes de TVA qui seraient perçues si les taux normaux étaient uniformément appliqués à l'ensemble de la base d'imposition potentielle et les recettes effectivement collectées. Cet écart peut résulter des exemptions, des taux réduits, des pratiques de fraude et d'optimisation fiscales, ainsi que des défaillances de l'administration fiscale. En 2018, l'Afrique du Sud et le Cabo Verde enregistraient le RRT le plus élevé (respectivement 0.61 et 0.73), tandis que la Guinée équatoriale, la République démocratique du Congo et le Tchad affichaient le RRT le plus bas (inférieur à 0.15).

Recettes non fiscales

En 2018, les recettes non fiscales moyennes équivalaient à 6.5 % du PIB en Afrique. Les recettes non fiscales étaient inférieures à 5 % du PIB dans 16 des 30 pays africains et supérieures à 10 % dans 6 pays, allant de 0.6 % du PIB en Afrique du Sud à 25.2 % du PIB au Lesotho. Quatre des six pays (Lesotho, Botswana, Namibie et Eswatini) dont les recettes non fiscales dépassaient 10 % du PIB étaient les bénéficiaires nets des recettes du fonds commun de la SACU, qui regroupe les droits de douane et les accises payés par l'ensemble des membres de la SACU avant d'être redistribués. Les deux autres pays étaient la République du Congo et la Guinée équatoriale, qui ont tous deux perçu des recettes provenant du pétrole, supérieures à 15 % du PIB. Le total des recettes non fiscales était inférieur à celui des recettes fiscales dans l'ensemble des pays à l'exception du Botswana, de la Guinée équatoriale et de la République du Congo.

Contrairement au ratio impôts/PIB moyen de l'Afrique (30), les recettes non fiscales moyennes de ces pays ont fléchi de 8.3 % du PIB en 2010 à 6.5 % en 2018, avec une forte baisse de 3.2 points entre 2012 et 2016. Ce recul s'explique principalement par une érosion des loyers et des redevances ainsi que des recettes provenant des dons.

L'origine des recettes non fiscales diffère selon les pays. Les dons en constituent la principale source dans douze des pays couverts par la publication (par ordre décroissant : Rwanda, Togo, Niger, Tchad, Burkina Faso, Sénégal, République démocratique du Congo, Madagascar, Malawi, Mali, Côte d'Ivoire et Ouganda). Six autres pays (République du Congo, Guinée équatoriale, Mauritanie, Cameroun, Tunisie et Nigéria) tirent quant à eux la majeure partie de ces recettes de loyers et de redevances. Les pays restants, à l'exception des quatre pays bénéficiaires nets de la SACU, ont tiré l'essentiel de leurs recettes non fiscales d'autres sources telles que les intérêts et dividendes, les frais administratifs et frais au titre de la vente de biens et services ou de recettes diverses.

COVID-19 et ZLECAf : risques et opportunités liés à la mobilisation des ressources intérieures en Afrique

L'étude spéciale du rapport de cette année examine les facteurs susceptibles d'avoir une incidence sur la mobilisation des ressources intérieures en Afrique, dans le sillage de la pandémie de COVID-19. Comme dans d'autres régions, la pandémie aura d'importantes conséquences socio-économiques en Afrique et risque de peser lourdement sur les recettes publiques, ce qui pourrait mettre en péril les progrès accomplis en matière de mobilisation des ressources intérieures au cours des dernières décennies. En dépit des nombreuses incertitudes qui entourent l'évolution de la crise du COVID-19, les politiques budgétaires joueront un rôle essentiel dans tous les pays dans le processus de reprise économique et le redressement des finances publiques à plus long terme. La mobilisation des ressources intérieures représentera un volet important de cette stratégie, car les pays s'efforcent de rétablir leurs finances publiques de manière équitable et durable, d'accroître leurs recettes pour réduire les inégalités et promouvoir le développement, et de ménager une plus grande marge de manœuvre budgétaire pour faire face aux chocs futurs. Il s'agit notamment d'explorer de nouvelles voies pour mobiliser des ressources intérieures afin de compenser le déficit de financement créé par la pandémie, en raison du détournement des ressources pour minimiser les effets d'une crise humanitaire et économique naissante. L'impact de la Zone de libre-échange continentale africaine (ZLECAf) peut contribuer à ce processus : à court terme, il peut atténuer les effets de la crise du COVID-19 en intensifiant les échanges entre pays africains et en accélérant la reprise économique après la pandémie. À plus longue échéance, il jouera probablement un rôle important pour renforcer la résilience et protéger le continent face aux chocs futurs.

Chapter 1

Tax revenue trends, 2010-2018

Chapitre 1

Tendances des recettes fiscales, 2010-2018

Chapter 1

Tax revenue trends, 2010-2018

Achieving the United Nations' Sustainable Development Goals (SDGs), and implementing the Addis Ababa Action Agenda and the African Union's Agenda 2063 requires mobilising additional finance, in particular domestic resources, to fund public goods and services. Taxation provides a predictable and sustainable source of government revenue, in contrast with the volatility of other important sources of public revenues, such as official development assistance and mineral royalties.

This report presents an internationally comparable set of indicators on tax and non-tax revenues which can be used to track progress on domestic resource mobilisation (as envisaged in Agenda 2063, the SDGs, the Addis Ababa Action Agenda as well as related-initiatives such as the Addis Tax Initiative) and to inform tax policy and reform. The report and its data also contribute to the Pan-African Statistics Programme, a joint effort between the European Union and the African Union to support statistical capacity in Africa, by providing quality revenue statistics data that can inform decision-making processes and policy monitoring towards Africa integration. The report provides critical information on tax systems in the region and their revenue performance in recent years as well as an important backdrop in understanding the fiscal capacity of the region to respond to the COVID-19 pandemic.

This chapter discusses trends in the tax-to-GDP ratio, tax structure and share of tax revenue by level of government in 30 African countries from 1990 (where available) until 2018: Botswana, Burkina Faso, Cabo Verde, Cameroon, Chad, the Republic of the Congo, the Democratic Republic of the Congo, Côte d'Ivoire, Equatorial Guinea, Egypt, Eswatini, Ghana, Lesotho, Kenya, Madagascar, Malawi, Mali, Mauritania, Mauritius, Morocco, Namibia, Niger, Nigeria, Rwanda, Senegal, the Seychelles, South Africa, Togo, Tunisia and Uganda. It also compares the averages of the 30 African countries with the average of 25 Latin American and Caribbean (LAC) countries (OECD et al., 2020[1]) and the average of 36 OECD countries (OECD, 2019[2]). The discussion supplements the detailed country information on tax revenue in Chapter 5.

Tax-to-GDP ratios

Tax-to-GDP ratios in 2018

The average tax-to-GDP ratio in the 30 African countries in this publication (referred to as the "Africa (30) average") was 16.5% in 2018 (Figure 1.1). The tax-to-GDP ratio is measured as tax revenues (including social security contributions paid to general government) as a proportion of gross domestic product (GDP).[1] In comparison, the average tax-to-GDP ratios in LAC and the OECD were 23.1% and 34.3% respectively in 2018.

In 2018, tax-to-GDP ratios varied widely across the countries included in this publication, ranging from 6.3% in Equatorial Guinea and Nigeria to 32.4% in the Seychelles. The countries in this publication with the highest incomes per capita, Morocco, the Seychelles, South Africa and Tunisia had tax-to-GDP ratios above 25%. Twenty-one countries recorded tax-to-GDP ratios between 11.0% and 22.0% while Chad, the Republic of the Congo, the Democratic Republic of the Congo, Equatorial Guinea and Nigeria had tax-to-GDP ratios below 9%.

Figure 1.1. **Tax-to-GDP ratios and total tax revenue (excluding social security contributions) as a percentage of GDP, 2018**

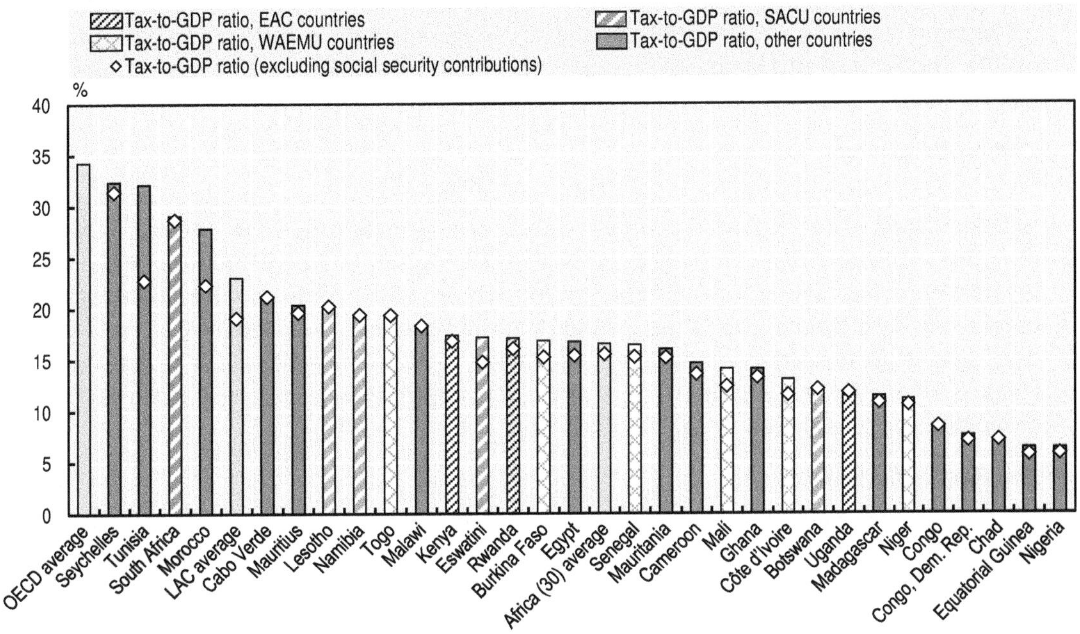

Note: Data include sub-national government tax revenues for Eswatini, Mauritania, Mauritius, Morocco, Nigeria (state revenues only) and projected values for South Africa for 2018.

The Africa (30) average, the averages for LAC (25 countries) and the OECD (36 countries) are unweighted.

The Africa (30) average should be interpreted with caution as data on social security contributions are not available for Chad, the Republic of the Congo, the Democratic Republic of the Congo (prior to 2012), Madagascar (prior to 2011), Namibia, Togo and Uganda and are only partially available for Cameroon and Senegal. Social security contributions for Botswana, Lesotho and Malawi are deemed to be null as they do not meet the criteria to be classified as social security contributions set out in the OECD classification of taxes in the Interpretative Guide. See the country tables in Chapter 5 for further information.

The tax-to-GDP ratio for South Africa includes payments made by South Africa to the Southern African Customs Union (SACU) pool.

Source: Tables 4.1 and 4.2 in Chapter 4 and (OECD/ATAF/AUC, 2020[3]), "Revenue Statistics in Africa: Comparative tables", *OECD Tax Statistics* (database), *https://doi.org/10.1787/be755711-en*.

StatLink *https://doi.org/10.1787/888934181299*

Many of the countries in this publication belong to regional organisations whose members adopt common tax and external tariff rules and form a customs union.

- The average tax-to-GDP ratio of the three East Africa Community (EAC)[2] countries included in this publication was 15.5% in 2018, which was below the Africa (30) average. Tax-to-GDP ratios in Kenya and Rwanda exceeded 17.0% in 2018 and amounted to 11.8% in Uganda.
- The West African Economic and Monetary Union (WAEMU)[3] has set a goal for member countries to achieve tax-to-GDP ratios of at least 20% (Diallo, 2018[5]). The tax-to-GDP ratio for the six WAEMU countries included in this publication averaged 15.2% in 2018. Ratios varied across member countries from 11.1% in Niger to 19.4% in Togo; two of the six WAEMU countries (Burkina Faso and Togo) had tax-to-GDP ratios above the Africa (30) average.
- The average tax-to-GDP ratio for the Southern African Customs Union (SACU)[4] countries was 19.6% in 2018. Tax-to-GDP ratios in SACU countries varied from 12.1% of GDP in Botswana to 29.1% of GDP in South Africa. Eswatini and Namibia had tax-to-GDP ratios below 20% of GDP (17.2% and 19.4%, respectively), while Lesotho had a tax-to-GDP ratio of 20.2% in 2018. The evolution of tax-to-GDP ratios of SACU countries since 2010 is discussed in Box 1.2.

Box 1.1. **Methodology: the tax-to-GDP ratio**

The tax ratios shown in this publication express aggregate tax revenues as a percentage of GDP. The value of this ratio depends on its denominator (GDP) as well as its numerator (tax revenue).The denominator, GDP, is subject to historical revision.

The numerator (tax revenue)

For the numerator, this publication uses revenue figures that are submitted annually by focal points from national Ministries of Finance, tax administrations or statistics offices. Historical tax revenue data are subject to revisions each year, with more important revisions in latest years. Past figures may also change from one edition to the next when new data are obtained by focal points. This is the case for Mauritania, which provided local tax revenue data and social security contributions paid to the CNAM (Caisse Nationale d'Assurance Maladie) for the first time in this edition, and in Equatorial Guinea, which provided data on social security contributions.

The denominator (GDP)

For the denominator, the GDP figures used for the series *Revenue Statistics in Africa* are sourced from the *World Economic Outlook* (WEO) published by the IMF. Using these GDP figures ensures maximum consistency across countries, as well as international comparability. GDP figures are also revised and updated to reflect better data sources and improved estimation procedures, or to move towards new internationally-agreed guidelines to measure the value of GDP.

The most recent available figures from WEO were published in April 2020 (IMF, 2020[4]) and include GDP revisions made by some countries to align with the most recent System of National Accounts (SNA2008). In this edition, Burkina Faso, Côte d'Ivoire, Madagascar, Mauritania, Niger and Uganda have revised their GDP data, resulting in lower tax-to-GDP ratios in these countries, and on average, than in the previous edition. The difference in tax-to-GDP ratios in 2017 between this year's and last year's editions ranged from 2.1 p.p. in Uganda to 4.6 p.p. in Côte d'Ivoire; and the average for African countries in the publication is 0.6 p.p. lower in 2017 in this edition than in last year's edition.

Changes in tax-to-GDP ratios between 2017 and 2018

The average tax-to-GDP ratio for African countries increased by just under 0.1% of GDP between 2017 and 2018. Tax-to-GDP ratios increased in 19 countries, decreased in 10 and remained unchanged in one country. Ratios in seven countries grew by more than one percentage point (p.p.) whereas they decreased by more than one p.p. in four countries. The largest increases between 2017 and 2018 occurred in Lesotho (1.9 p.p.), Niger (1.6 p.p.) and Mauritania (1.5 p.p.). The Republic of the Congo had the largest decrease in the tax-to-GDP ratio in 2018, of 5.1 p.p., followed by Mali (2.6 p.p.) and Togo (1.6 p.p.).

In Lesotho, the higher tax-to-GDP ratio in 2018 followed two years of declining tax revenues as a percentage of GDP. The rise between 2017 and 2018 was driven by increases equivalent to 0.9% of GDP in both VAT revenues and income tax revenues. Lesotho has introduced a new strategy to address compliance issues for all tax types and taxpayers and declining revenue by improving the quality of Lesotho Revenue Authority services and easing processes. The strategy includes initiatives such as the simplified business tax system, a voluntary compliance programme, and a tax lottery to win cars (Lesotho Times, 2019[6]). In addition, Lesotho raised its standard VAT rate from 14% to 15% as well as raising other VAT rates (e.g. electricity and telecommunications) in April 2018 (LRA, 2018[7]). Besides these reforms, Lesotho benefitted in 2018 from a significant increase in income tax revenue from the mining and quarrying industry that more than doubled compared to the previous year (Lesotho Times, 2019[8]; Lesotho Times, 2018[9]). These factors contributed to an increase of 1.9 percentage points between 2017 and 2018.

Figure 1.2. **Change in tax-to-GDP ratios between 2017 and 2018 (percentage points)**

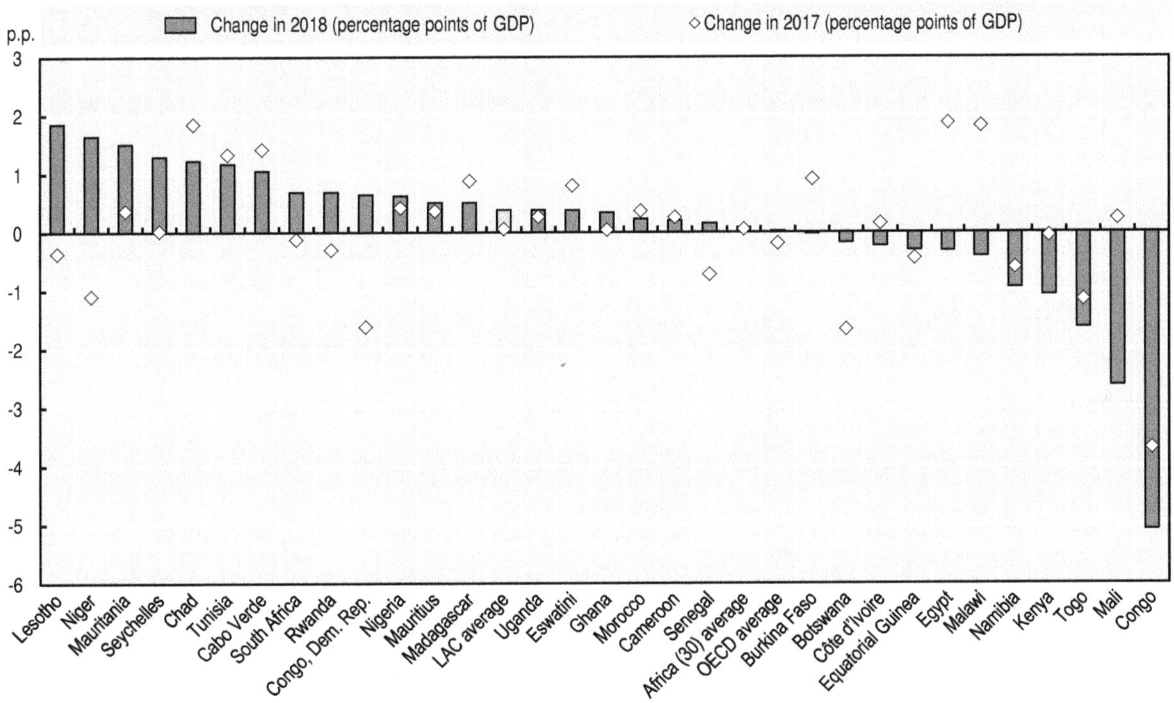

Notes: The figures include sub-national government tax revenues for Eswatini, Mauritania, Mauritius, Morocco, Nigeria (state revenues only) and projected values for South Africa for 2018.

The Africa (30) average, the averages for LAC (25 countries) and the OECD (36 countries) are unweighted.

The change in the Africa (30) average should be interpreted with caution as data for social security contributions are not available or are partial in a few countries. See the country tables in Chapter 5 for further information.

Source: Authors' calculations based on data in Table 4.1 in Chapter 4 and (OECD/ATAF/AUC, 2020[3]), "Revenue Statistics in Africa: Comparative tables", *OECD Tax Statistics* (database), *https://doi.org/10.1787/be755711-en.*

StatLink *https://doi.org/10.1787/888934181318*

In Niger, the tax-to-GDP ratio increased by 1.6 p.p. between 2017 and 2018, driven principally by VAT revenues, which increased by 1.9 p.p. Revenues from domestic VAT more than doubled during this time. Niger adopted measures from the 2018 Budget to increase domestic revenue collection after two years of declining tax revenues (by 2.0 p.p. and 1.1 p.p. in 2016 and 2017, respectively). The 2018 budget included a tax administration reform to reinforce audits and controls, introduced new taxes, and expanded the VAT base for certain transport sectors. Niger also experienced robust economic growth in 2018 (real GDP growth was 6.5% in 2018) (IMF, 2019[10]).

The increase of tax revenues in Mauritania between 2017 and 2018 was mainly driven by higher revenues from VAT (0.7% of GDP) and from other taxes on goods and services (0.6% of GDP). Although heavily dependent on the mining sector, Mauritania recorded GDP growth of 3.6% in 2018 from the non-extractive sector (agriculture, construction and telecommunications) (Direction générale du Trésor France, 2020[11]) (Jeune Afrique, 2019[12]).

Figure 1.3. **Change in tax-to-GDP ratios by main tax heading between 2017 and 2018 and by country (percentage points)**

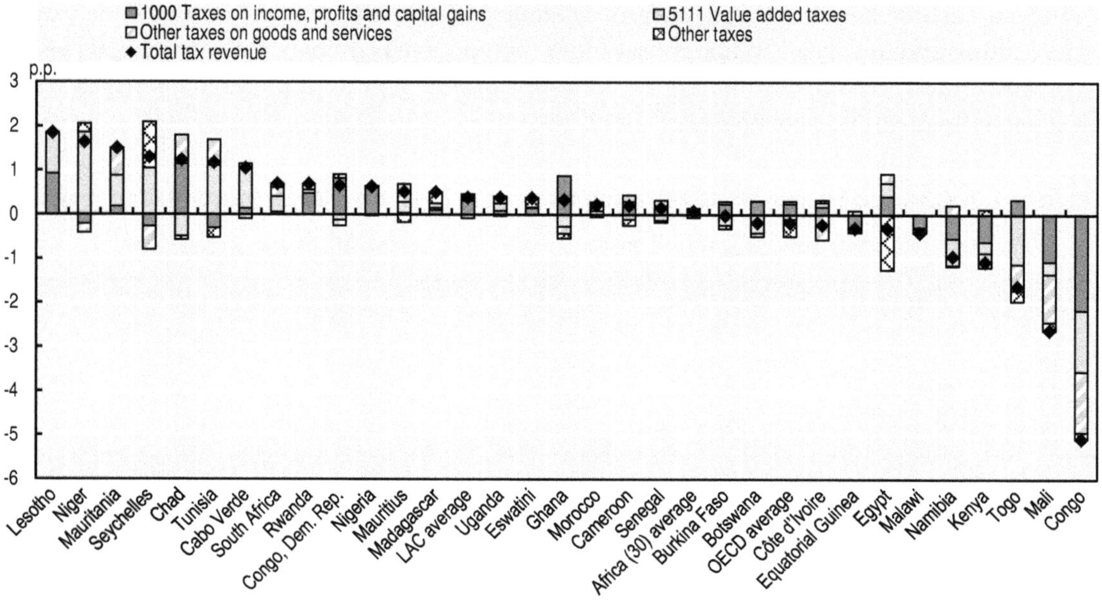

Notes: The figures include sub-national government tax revenues for Eswatini, Mauritania, Mauritius, Morocco, Nigeria (state revenues only) and projected values for South Africa for 2018.

The Africa (30) average, the averages for LAC (25 countries) and the OECD (36 countries) are unweighted.

The Africa (30) average should be interpreted with caution as data for social security contributions are not available or are partial in a few countries. See the country tables in Chapter 5 for further information.

Source: Authors' calculations based on data in (OECD/ATAF/AUC, 2020[3]), "Revenue Statistics in Africa: Comparative tables", *OECD Tax Statistics* (database), *https://doi.org/10.1787/be755711-en*.

StatLink *https://doi.org/10.1787/888934181337*

The two largest decreases in tax-to-GDP ratios between 2017 and 2018 were observed in the Republic of Congo and Mali. Congo's tax-to-GDP ratio decreased by 5.1 p.p. in 2018 due to decreases in revenues from all the main tax categories (2.2 p.p. for income taxes and 1.4 p.p. for both VAT and taxes on other goods and services). Nominal GDP in Congo increased by 25% in 2018 (driven by the recovery of oil prices) whereas nominal tax revenues declined by 22% between 2017 and 2018. The decrease in tax revenues in 2018, caused by a contraction of the non-oil economy, was the third consecutive annual decrease. The mobilisation of non-oil revenues remains a challenge in the Republic of the Congo. The IMF noted that "there was substantial potential to increase non-oil revenues in the short-term given the large stock of tax arrears and the plans to curb tax exemptions" (IMF, 2020[13]).

Mali experienced the second-largest decrease in the tax-to-GDP ratio between 2017 and 2018, due to declines in all the main tax categories (1.1 p.p. for income taxes, 1.1 p.p. for taxes on other goods and services and 0.3 p.p. for VAT revenues). The decrease in tax revenues in 2018 occurred after three consecutive years of higher tax revenue collection attributable to tax policy and administration reforms (including increases in tax rates, broadening of tax bases and strengthening of tax administrations) (IMF, 2018[14]). The decrease in tax revenues in 2018 can be explained by a variety of factors including an economic slowdown, an increase in fraud due to rising insecurity, recurrent terrorist attacks and administrative challenges.[5]

Across the 30 countries, the changes in tax-to-GDP ratios between 2017 and 2018 were mainly driven by changes in VAT revenues and income taxes (Figure 1.3). The changes in VAT revenue ranged from a decrease of 1.4 p.p. in the Republic of the Congo to an increase of 1.9 p.p. in Niger over the same period; with respect to income tax, the changes between

2017 and 2018 ranged from a decrease of 2.2 p.p. in the Republic of the Congo to an increase of 1.1 p.p. in Chad (Figure 1.4). The magnitude of annual changes in corporate income tax (CIT) revenues was more significant in most countries than changes in personal income tax (PIT) changes remained more modest (at less than 0.1% of GDP).

Figure 1.4. **Annual changes in revenue from taxes on income and profits, by sub-category and by country between 2017 and 2018 (percentage points)**

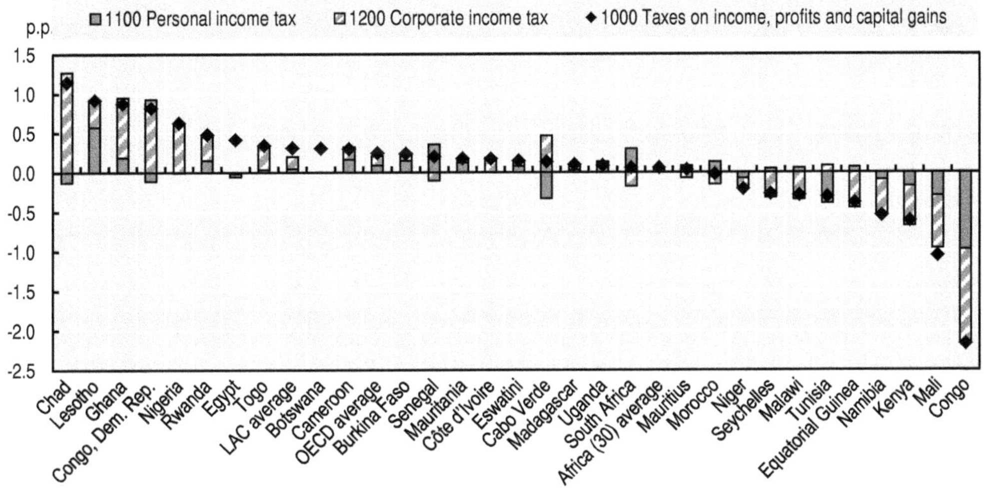

Notes: The Africa (30) average, the averages for LAC (25 countries) and the OECD (36 countries) are unweighted. Some income tax revenues cannot be broken down into personal income tax and corporate income taxes for Botswana and Egypt.

Source: Authors' calculations based on data in (OECD/ATAF/AUC, 2020[3]), "Revenue Statistics in Africa: Comparative tables", *OECD Tax Statistics* (database), *https://doi.org/10.1787/be755711-en.*

StatLink *https://doi.org/10.1787/888934181356*

Evolution of tax-to-GDP ratios since 2010

In 2018, the tax-to-GDP ratio for the Africa (30) average was 1.4 p.p. higher than in 2010. In comparison, the LAC and the OECD averages increased by 1.9 p.p. and 2.0 p.p. respectively between 2010 and 2018. The average tax-to-GDP ratio for the 30 African countries increased steadily between 2010 and 2014 with a strong increase of 0.7 p.p. in 2011, marking a recovery from the global financial crisis. Since 2014, the average has stabilised at between 16.4% and 16.5% of GDP (Figure 1.5).

Many African countries were strongly affected by the global financial crisis. In particular, countries relying on commodities experienced a slowdown in economic activity due to lower commodity prices. A number of countries implemented measures to stimulate the economy. For example, Morocco reduced the CIT rate by 5 percentage points in 2008 with a view to improving companies' competitiveness and to enhance their resilience.

Tax revenues in other regions were also affected by the global crisis. The LAC average tax-to-GDP ratio decreased between 2008 and 2010 by 0.5 p.p., while the OECD average was most affected by the crisis between 2007 and 2009, registering a decrease in the tax-to-GDP ratio of 1.4 p.p. over that period.

VAT receipts contributed most to the increase of the Africa (30) average tax-to-GDP ratio between 2010 and 2018, increasing by 1.0 p.p. to reach 5% of GDP in 2018. The highest annual increase in the average was registered between 2012 and 2013 (0.4% of GDP) following the introduction of VAT in 2012 in the Democratic Republic of the Congo and Eswatini.

Figure 1.5. **Average tax-to-GDP ratios for Africa (30), LAC and OECD, 2000-18**

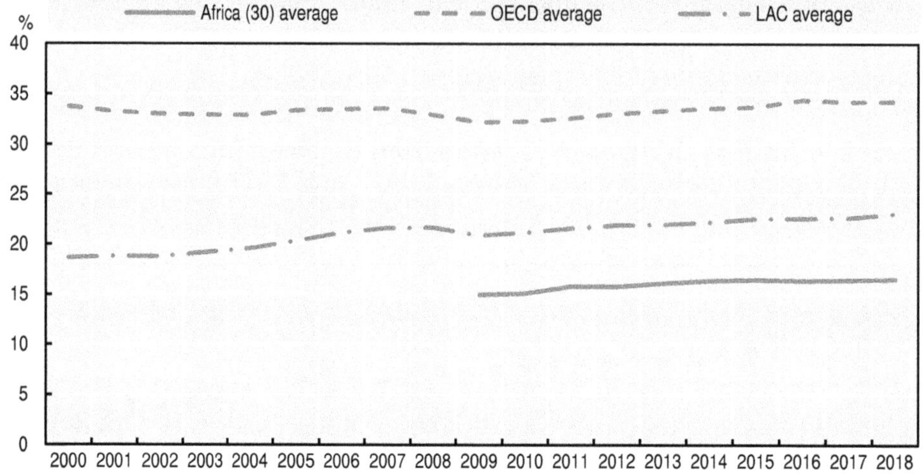

Notes: The Africa (30) should be interpreted with caution as data for social security contributions are not available or are partial in a few countries. See the country tables in Chapter 5 for further information. The figures include sub-national government tax revenues for Eswatini, Mauritius, Mauritania, Morocco, Nigeria (state revenues only) and South Africa for 2002-2018. The Africa (30) average is estimated for 2009 as the data are not available for Chad and Nigeria. No estimation was made prior to 2009 because of the unavailability of data for a few countries.
The Africa (30), the average for LAC (25 countries) and the OECD average (36 countries) are unweighted.
Source: Table 4.1 in Chapter 4 and (OECD/ATAF/AUC, 2020[3]), "Revenue Statistics in Africa: Comparative tables", *OECD Tax Statistics* (database), *https://doi.org/10.1787/be755711-en*.

StatLink *https://doi.org/10.1787/888934181375*

Income taxes were the second driver of the increase in the Africa (30) average tax-to-GDP ratio between 2010 and 2018. Income tax revenues increased by 0.3 p.p. between 2010 and 2018 to reach 6.2% of GDP in 2018. Income tax revenues reached their highest level in 2013 (6.5% of GDP) and have since steadily declined. The decline is entirely driven by CIT revenues, which decreased by 0.5 p.p. over the period. The decline of oil and mineral prices between 2013 and 2016 may have contributed to this decrease.

Average revenues from other taxes on goods and services, equivalent to 3.7% of GDP in 2018, have decreased slightly as a percentage of GDP since 2010 and over a longer time period before then, in part due to declines in revenues from trade taxes. This decline is associated with trade liberalisation across the continent that resulted in the reduction of import tariffs, the narrowing of the base of products and services subject to excises and the elimination of taxes on exports. Tariffs will be further reduced under the African Continental Free Trade Agreement (AfCFTA) (see the special feature "COVID-19 and AfCFTA: Risks and opportunities for domestic revenue mobilisation in Africa").

As with the Africa (30) average, VAT contributed most strongly to the increase in LAC's average tax-to-GDP ratio between 2010 and 2018, rising by 0.8 p.p. over the period. Increases in revenues from social security contributions (SSCs) and income tax (0.5 p.p. for both) also contributed to the overall increase in the average tax-to-GDP ratio of the LAC region. These increases led to a marked difference in the level of SSCs as a percentage of GDP between the regions: in 2018, SSC revenues stood at 4.0% of GDP in the LAC region compared to the Africa (30) average of 1.3%.

Tax-to-GDP ratios rose in 23 countries between 2010 and 2018 and they declined in 7. Mauritania and Tunisia recorded the highest increases, of 6.3 p.p. and 4.9 p.p. respectively, while the largest decline occurred in Chad (7.3 p.p.) (Figure 1.9).

- The increase in Mauritania's tax-to-GDP ratio between 2010 and 2018 was driven principally by revenues from taxes on goods and services; VAT revenues increased by 1.7 p.p. and the other taxes on goods and services increased by 3.0 p.p. (of which customs duties increased by 2.3 p.p.).
- The increase in Tunisia's tax-to-GDP ratio between 2010 and 2018 was mainly attributable to higher revenues from SSCs (2.0 p.p.) and from VAT (1.1 p.p.).

Box 1.2. **Convergence of tax levels in Africa**

The Africa (30) average tax-to-GDP ratio increased from 15.1% in 2010 to 16.5% in 2018. Twenty-three of the 30 countries in the publication have recorded increases in their tax-to-GDP ratios over this period. This raises the question of whether countries' tax-to-GDP ratios have concentrated more around the average over time or whether they have grown more dispersed.

Figure 1.6 shows the dispersion of tax-to-GDP ratios around the Africa (30) average using different measures,[6] including the standard deviation, coefficient of variation, the distance from the median and the Gini coefficient. All these measures show similar trends between 2010 and 2018. The dispersion of tax-to GDP ratios around the Africa (30) average decreased between 2010 and 2013 and has been steadily increasing since 2014, reaching its highest level in 2018.

Figure 1.6. **Dispersion of tax-to-GDP ratios around the Africa (30) average, 2010-2018**

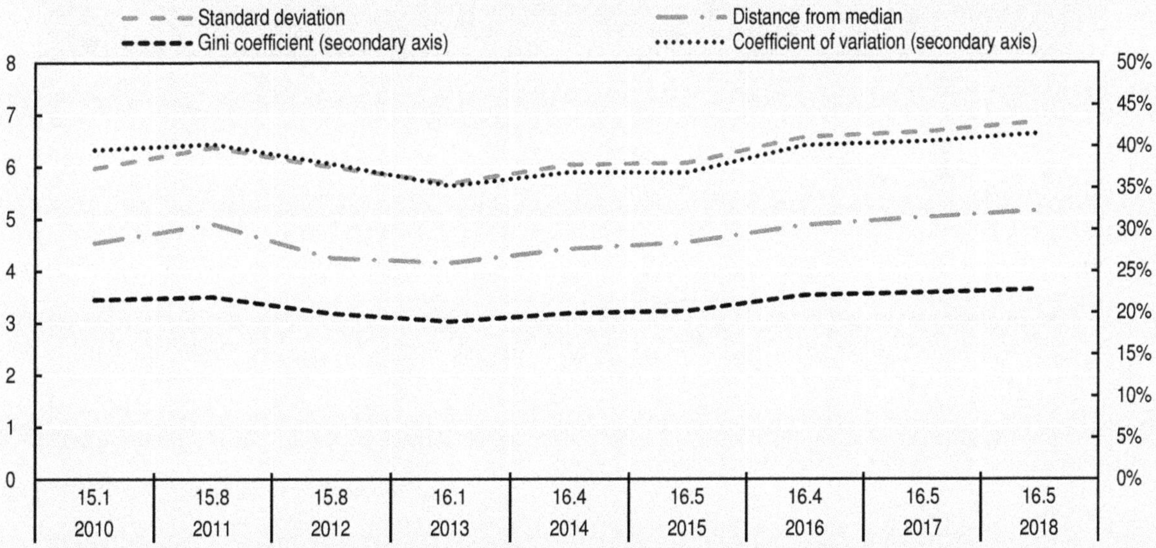

Note: The figures on the horizontal axis (above the years) show the Africa (30) average tax-to-GDP ratio in each year.
Source: Authors' calculations based on (OECD/ATAF/AUC, 2020[3]); "Revenue Statistics in Africa: Comparative tables", *OECD Tax Statistics* (database), *https://doi.org/10.1787/be755711-en.*

StatLink https://doi.org/10.1787/888934181394

Figure 1.7 shows the difference between the tax-to-GDP ratios for each country and that of the Africa (30) average in 2010 and 2018. The group on the left shows the countries whose tax-to-GDP ratios were further away from the Africa (30) average in 2018 compared to 2010. For example Chad's tax-to-GDP ratio was 0.4 percentage points lower than the Africa (30) average in 2010, and 9.4 percentage points lower than the Africa (30) average in 2018, implying a divergence of 9 p.p. over this period. In total, 15 countries (Chad, Botswana, Tunisia, Equatorial Guinea, Togo, Nigeria, the Democratic Republic of the Congo, South

Box 1.2. **Convergence of tax levels in Africa** *(cont.)*

Africa, the Seychelles, Mali, Cabo Verde, Malawi, the Republic of the Congo, Lesotho and Côte d'Ivoire) were further away from the Africa (30) average in 2018 than in 2010.

The group on the right shows countries whose tax-to-GDP ratios were closer to the Africa (30) average in 2018 than in 2010. They are ordered by the increasing degree by which they are closer to the average in 2018 compared to 2010. The highest reduction in differences with the Africa (30) average between 2010 and 2018 is observed in Mauritania. Mauritania's tax-to-GDP ratio was 5.3 p.p. below the Africa (30) average in 2010 and 0.5 p.p. below in 2018. In total, 15 countries (Mauritius, Niger, Namibia, Madagascar, Senegal, Eswatini, Burkina Faso, Egypt, Cameroon, Morocco, Uganda, Rwanda, Ghana, Kenya, Mauritania) were closer to the Africa (30) average in 2018 than in 2010.

Figure 1.7. **Differences between tax-to-GDP ratios and Africa (30) average in 2010 and 2018 (percentage points)**

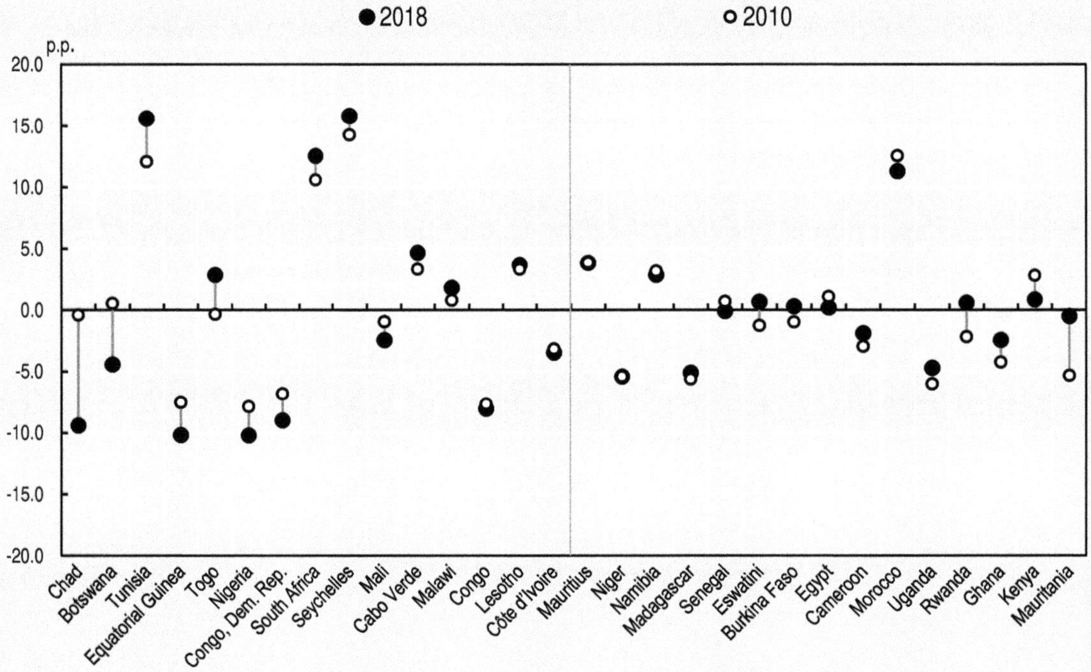

Source: Authors' calculations based on (OECD/ATAF/AUC, 2020[3]); "Revenue Statistics in Africa: Comparative tables", *OECD Tax Statistics* (database), *http://dx.doi.org/10.1787/be755711-en*.

StatLink https://doi.org/10.1787/888934181413

The group of countries in this publication was evenly split between those whose tax-to-GDP ratios were closer to the Africa (30) average in 2018 compared to 2010 and those whose tax-to-GDP ratios were further away. However, the degree to which half of the countries concentrated around the average in 2018 was lower than that by which the other half of the countries dispersed from the average (respectively 1.6 p.p. and 2.2 p.p.). This accounts for the greater dispersion in 2018 seen in Figure 1.6. This suggests that although the Africa (30) average tax-to-GDP ratio has increased between 2010 and 2018, there has been no general trend for countries to concentrate around this higher average, suggesting that domestic resource mobilisation efforts remain fragmented.

Figure 1.8. **Revenue from taxes on income and profits, VAT and other tax headings as a percentage of GDP, 2010-18**

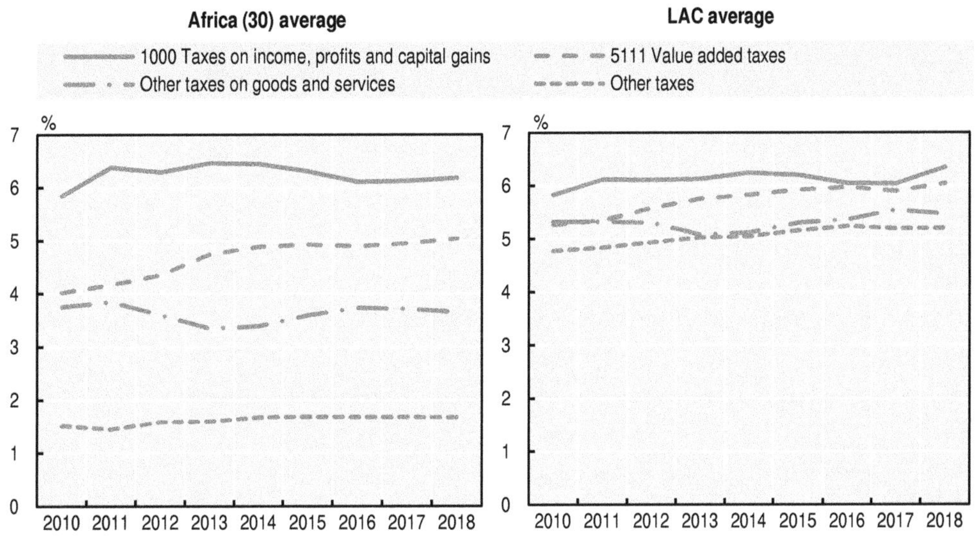

Notes: The figures for the Africa (30) average include sub-national government tax revenues for Eswatini, Mauritania, Mauritius, Morocco, Nigeria (state revenues only) and South Africa for 2002-18 (2018 figures are estimates).
Source: Authors' calculations based on (OECD/ATAF/AUC, 2020[3]), "Revenue Statistics in Africa: Comparative tables", *OECD Tax Statistics* (database), *https://doi.org/10.1787/be755711-en*.

StatLink *https://doi.org/10.1787/888934181432*

Figure 1.9. **Change in tax-to-GDP ratios between 2010 and 2018 (percentage points)**

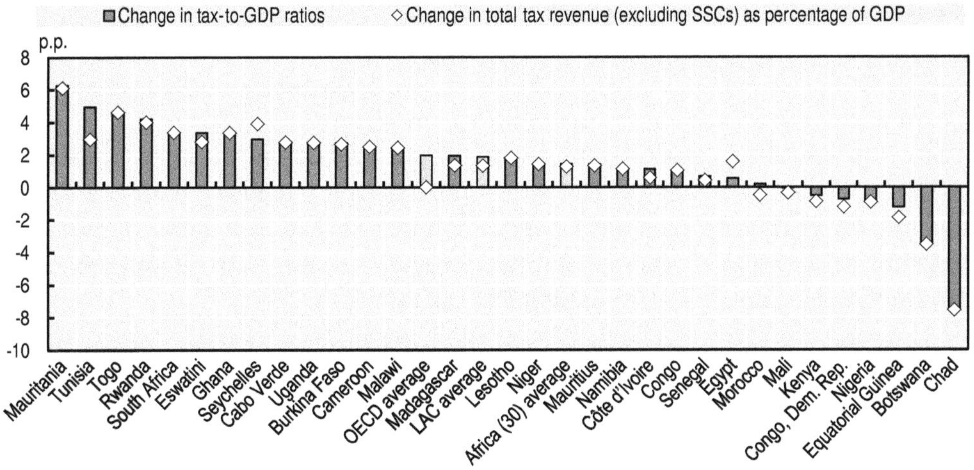

Notes: The figures include sub-national government tax revenues for Eswatini, Mauritius, Mauritania, Morocco, Nigeria (state revenues only) and projected values for South Africa for 2018.
The Africa (30) average, the averages for LAC (25 Latin American and Caribbean countries) and the OECD (36 countries) are unweighted.
Source: Tables 4.1 and 4.2 in Chapter 4 and (OECD/ATAF/AUC, 2020[3]), "Revenue Statistics in Africa: Comparative tables", *OECD Tax Statistics* (database), *https://doi.org/10.1787/be755711-en*.

StatLink *https://doi.org/10.1787/888934181451*

Figure 1.10 shows the differences between countries' tax-to-GDP ratios and the Africa (30) average ratio in 2010 and 2018. Four countries increased from below the average in 2010 to above it in 2018 while two dropped from above the average in 2010 to below it in 2018. The remainder did not change position relative to the average between 2010 and 2018. Box 1.2 examines in more detail the convergence of tax-to-GDP ratios in Africa.

Figure 1.10. **Differences in tax-to-GDP ratios to the Africa (30) average between 2010 and 2018 (percentage points)**

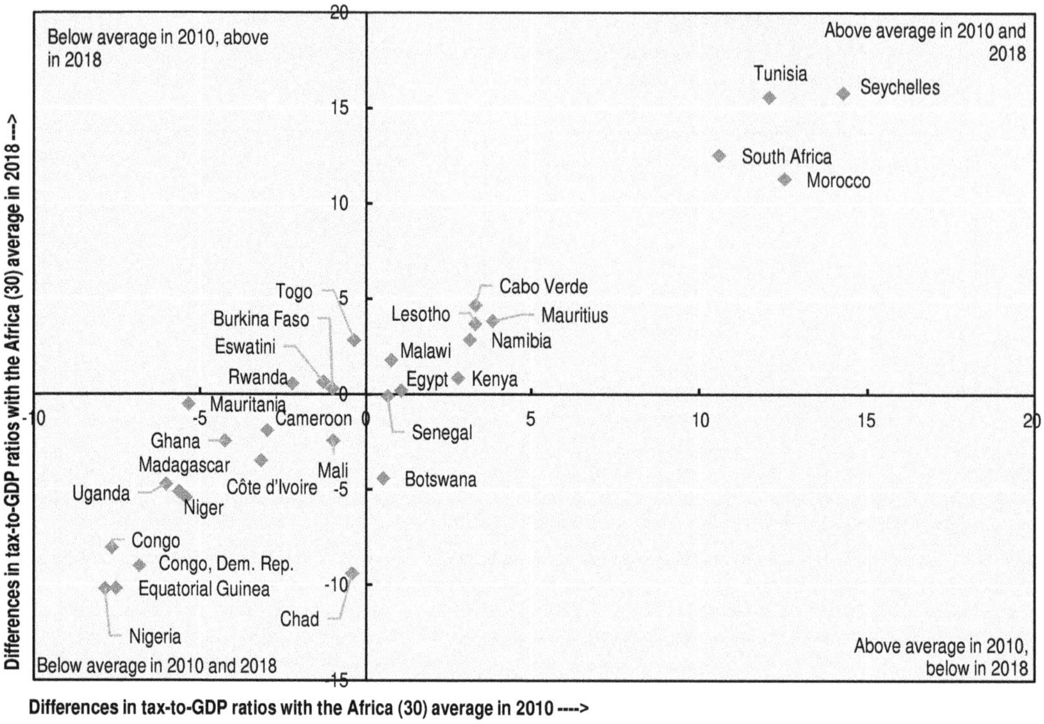

Note: The figures include sub-national government tax revenues for Eswatini, Mauritania, Mauritius, Morocco, Nigeria (state revenues only) and projected values for South Africa for 2018.

Source: Authors' calculations based on (OECD/ATAF/AUC, 2020[3]), "Revenue Statistics in Africa: Comparative tables", *OECD Tax Statistics* (database), *https://doi.org/10.1787/be755711-en.*

StatLink *https://doi.org/10.1787/888934181470*

Five countries (Chad, Equatorial Guinea, the Republic of Congo, the Democratic Republic of the Congo, Nigeria) had tax-to-GDP ratios more than 8 p.p. lower than the Africa (30) average in both years. The economy of these countries relies heavily on mineral and oil exports and the countries receive substantial non-tax revenues from oil and mineral rents and royalties. Such countries often exhibit low tax ratios.

Togo is one of the countries whose ratios increased from below the average in 2010 to above it in 2018. Togo was below the Africa (30) average in 2010 by 0.4 p.p. and was higher than the Africa (30) average in 2018 by 2.8 p.p. Togo has made significant efforts to improve the operations of its three revenue administrations. Measures implemented by Togo between 2010 and 2012 included initiatives such as the monitoring and modernisation of revenue collection and information systems, measures to tackle fraud and tax evasion. Another reform was the establishment of the OTR (Office togolais des recettes), which unified customs and tax services into a single administration in 2014. In 2019, the IMF acknowledged the more recent reforms of the revenue administration to improve revenue collection. The measures included the introduction of tax identification numbers, the reduction of tax exemptions, and controls to combat corruption. Initiatives continue to be implemented to improve taxpayers' compliance, which may contribute to further improve revenue collection (IMF, 2019[15]).

Figure 1.11. **Change in tax-to-GDP ratios by main tax headings between 2010 and 2018 and by country (percentage points)**

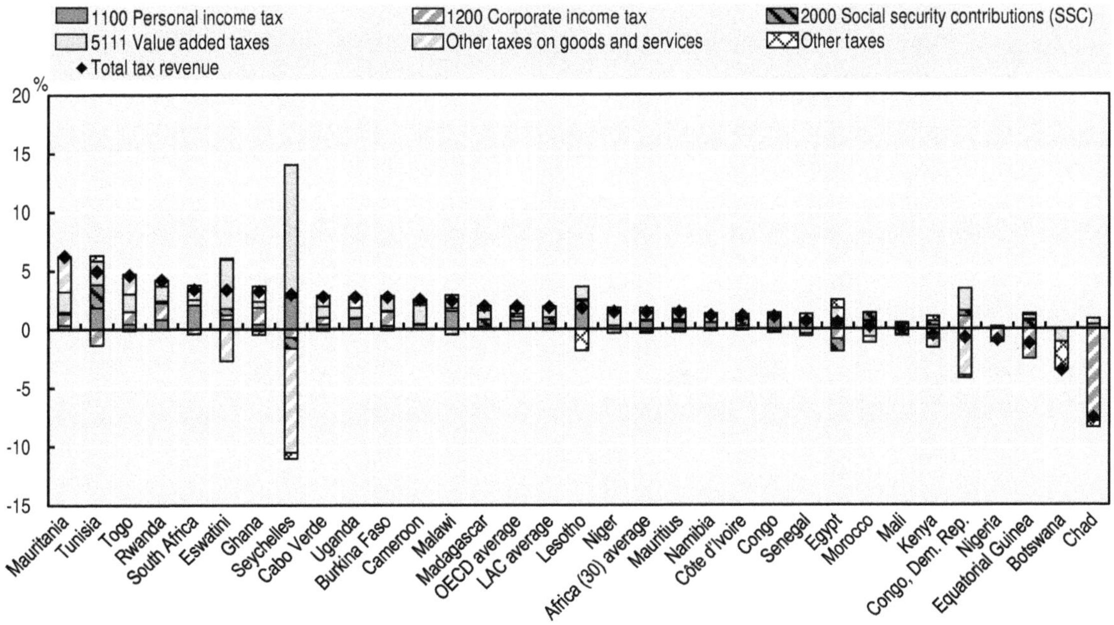

Notes: The figures include sub-national government tax revenues for Eswatini, Mauritania, Mauritius, Morocco, Nigeria (state revenues only) and projected values for South Africa for 2018.

The Africa (30) average, the averages for LAC (25 Latin American and Caribbean countries) and the OECD (36 countries) are unweighted.

Source: Authors' calculations based on (OECD/ATAF/AUC, 2020[3]), "Revenue Statistics in Africa: Comparative tables", *OECD Tax Statistics* (database), *https://doi.org/10.1787/be755711-en.*

StatLink *https://doi.org/10.1787/888934181489*

Box 1.3. **Changes in tax-to-GDP ratios in SACU countries**

Five of the 30 countries included in this publication belong to the Southern African Customs Union (SACU): Botswana, Eswatini, Lesotho, Namibia and South Africa. SACU was founded in 1910, making it the oldest customs union in the world (SACU, 2020[16]).

In 2018, the average of the SACU countries (the SACU average) was around 3 p.p. higher than the Africa (30) average and amounted to 19.6%. The evolution of the tax-to-GDP ratio between 2010 and 2018 in SACU countries was, on average, similar to that of the Africa (30) average over the same period. While the average tax-to-GDP ratio of the Africa (30) rose from 15.1% of GDP in 2010 to 16.5% in 2018, the SACU average rose from 18.4% of GDP in 2010 to 19.6% in 2018.

VAT revenue was the main driver of changes in both averages during this period, increasing by 1.0 p.p. in both cases. Eswatini, Lesotho, Namibia and South Africa increased their tax-to-GDP ratio by between 1.1 p.p. (Namibia) and 3.4 p.p. (South Africa), while Botswana's tax-to-GDP ratio declined by 3.5 p.p. over the period, due to decreases in revenues from income tax (2.4 p.p.) and VAT (1.1 p.p.).

Box 1.3. **Changes in tax-to-GDP ratios in SACU countries** *(cont.)*

Figure 1.12. **Tax-to-GDP ratios in SACU countries, 2010 to 2018**

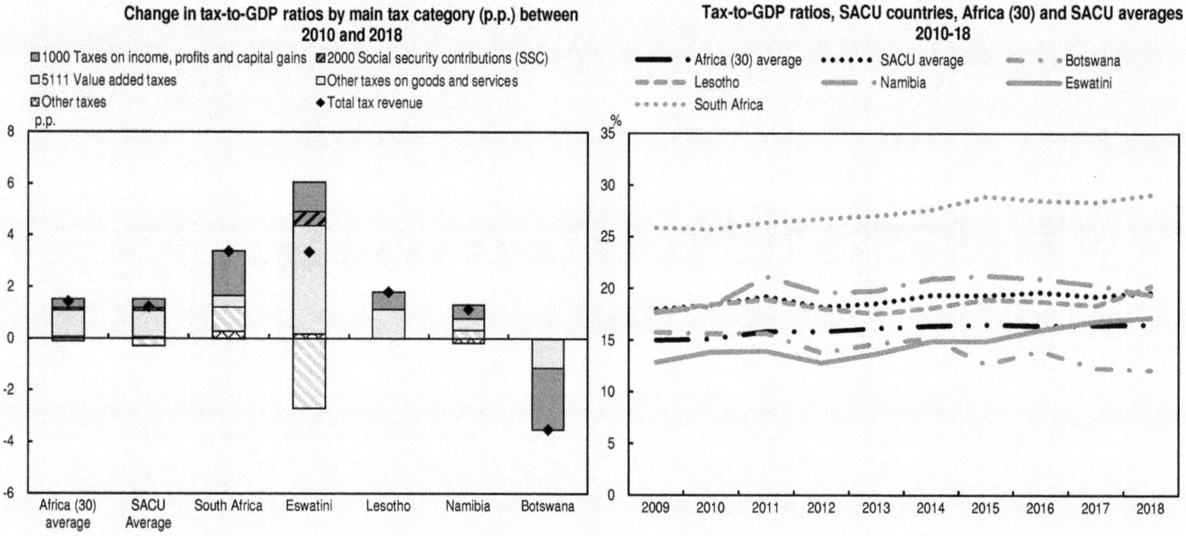

Source: Authors' calculations based on (OECD/ATAF/AUC, 2020[3]), "Revenue Statistics in Africa: Comparative tables", *OECD Tax Statistics* (database), *https://doi.org/10.1787/be755711-en*.

StatLink *https://doi.org/10.1787/888934181508*

Factors influencing tax-to-GDP ratios

Tax-to-GDP ratios are influenced by a variety of domestic and international factors. Domestically, macroeconomic characteristics such as the diversification of an economy, the importance of agriculture in the economy, resource endowments, openness to trade and the size of the informal economy can influence tax-to-GDP ratios. The power of tax administrations, the levels of corruption and tax morale (or willingness of people to pay taxes) are also strongly linked to the level of tax revenues (OECD, 2014[17]) (OECD, 2019[18]). Location is relevant: landlocked countries are less able to impose taxes on goods and services entering the country than island states. In addition, international factors, including the tax policies of other countries, can impact tax-to-GDP ratios.

Tax-to-GDP ratios tend to be higher in high-income countries: in general, OECD countries collect a higher amount of tax revenues than non-OECD countries, measured as a percentage of GDP. Most of the 30 countries included in this publication have lower income per capita and lower tax-to-GDP ratios than OECD and LAC countries (Figure 1.13). Levels of GDP per capita vary more between African countries than between LAC and OECD countries.

By contrast, higher shares of agriculture in GDP are associated with lower tax-to-GDP ratios in many studies (Addison and Levin, 2012[22]) (Profeta and Scabrosetti, 2010[23]). This reflects the fact that agriculture is a challenging sector to tax in many countries:

- There is less taxation of the agricultural sector in Africa due to a high level of informality and a low level of monetisation (AfDB/OECD/ECA, 2010[24]).
- The agriculture sector often benefits from numerous tax exemptions. In Ghana, tax exemptions are dependent on the type of crop and farmers can benefit from a tax holiday for up to 10 years (Grey, 2020[25]) while Nigeria grants a tax holiday of five years for agriculture companies (PWC, 2020[26]) and Uganda exempts income generated by agricultural processing from taxes for a year (KPMG, 2020[27]).

Figure 1.13. **Tax-to-GDP ratios and GDP per capita (in PPP) in African, LAC, OECD and selected Asian and Pacific economies, 2018**

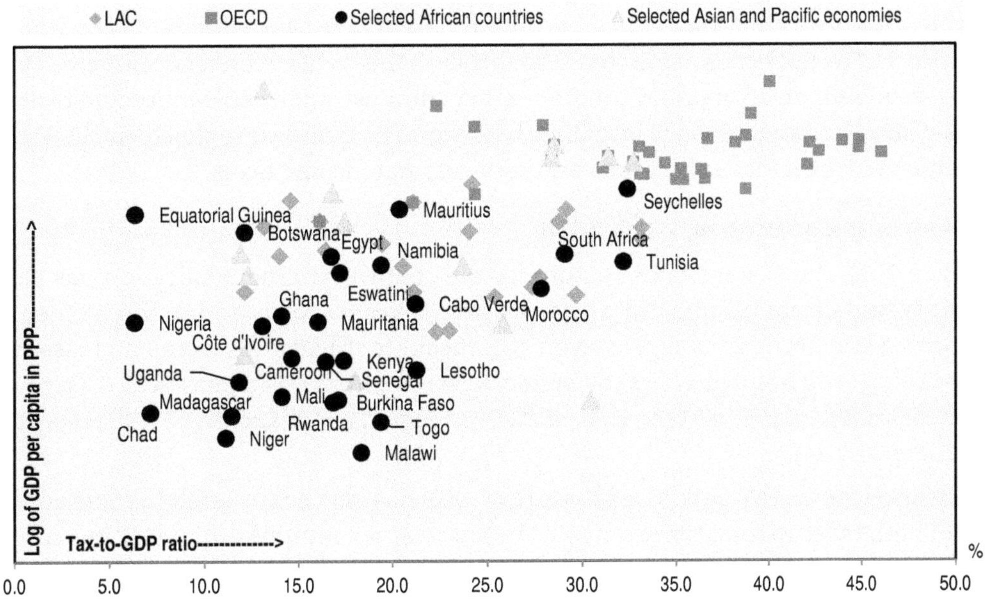

Notes: The y-axis is on a logarithmic scale. The purchasing-power-parity (PPP) between two countries is the rate at which the currency of one country needs to be converted into that of a second country to ensure that a given amount of the first country's currency will purchase the same volume of goods and services in the second country as it does in the first. The implied PPP conversion rate is expressed as national currency per current international dollar. An international dollar has the same purchasing power as the US dollar has in the United States. An international dollar is a hypothetical currency that is used as a means of translating and comparing costs from one country to the other using a common reference point, the US dollar (definitions derived from (IMF, 2019[19]) and (WHO, 2015[20])

Source: (IMF, 2020[21]) for GDP per capita. Tax-to-GDP ratios are sourced from the regional Revenue Statistics publications.

StatLink https://doi.org/10.1787/888934181527

Countries that receive substantial revenues from oil exports often exhibit low tax ratios. Countries with more revenues from natural resources are able to resort to less politically-demanding forms of taxation (AfDB/OECD/ECA, 2010[24]) and often have relatively narrow tax bases. The three countries (the Republic of the Congo, Equatorial Guinea, and Chad) that collected revenues from oil production of over 15% of their GDP, all had low tax-to-GDP ratios (below 9% of GDP). Revenues generated through oil rents and royalties, which are not classified as taxes, are discussed in detail in Chapter 2.

As mentioned previously, tax morale may play a role in tax levels. The OECD has analysed tax morale across regions and examined its drivers (OECD, 2019[18]). With respect to individuals, support for democracy, faith, educational attainment and trust in government were all identified as factors influencing tax morale. Other possible drivers include perceived improvement in the quality of tax administration, making taxes simpler to pay and providing quality public services. Gender can also play a role; while in most regions men have lower tax morale than women, the opposite is the case in Africa. With respect to businesses, the study conducted by the OECD uses data on tax certainty among multinational enterprises (MNEs).[7] In developing countries, including Africa, tax certainty seems to have an impact on business, resulting in modified business structures, increased costs and changes to investment decisions. With some regional variations, both international taxation and the relationship between the authorities and businesses are consistent concerns across developing countries. In Africa, clarity of legislation and tax certainty were the highest concerns (OECD, 2019[18]).

Tax structures

The composition of a country's tax revenues across different tax types is known as its tax structure. This is an important indicator, since different taxes have different economic and social effects. The tax structures in the 30 countries in this publication reflect different policy choices, economic structures and conditions, tax administration capabilities and historical factors. Countries can be divided into three broad groups according to their principal source of revenue: VAT, other taxes on goods and services, and income taxes.

Evolution of tax structures, 2010-2018

Since 2010, the average tax structure for the countries in the publication has shifted toward revenues from PIT and VAT and away from taxes on goods and services other than VAT. Increases in both tax categories were significant in driving the overall increase in the tax-to-GDP ratio on average across the period. Revenues from PIT increased by 0.7 p.p. while VAT increased by 1.0 p.p. between 2010 and 2018, reaching 3.1% and 5% of GDP respectively in 2018 (Figure 1.14).

The increase in VAT and PIT as a share of GDP has also contributed to increasing the share of both taxes in total tax revenues. The share of tax revenues from VAT increased by 2.8 p.p. to 29.7% of total taxation in 2018, continuing the longer-term shift toward VAT from other taxes on goods and services (including sales tax, excises and taxes on specific goods). Similarly, the share of tax revenues from PIT increased by 2.1 p.p. over this period to 17.5% of total tax revenues in 2018 whereas the share of CIT revenues decreased (by 2.3 p.p.) over the same period. The share of PIT revenues remains lower than the share of CIT revenues (19.2% of total taxation in 2018).

Figure 1.14. **Tax structure, Africa (30) average as a percentage of total tax revenue and percentage of GDP, 2010 and 2018**

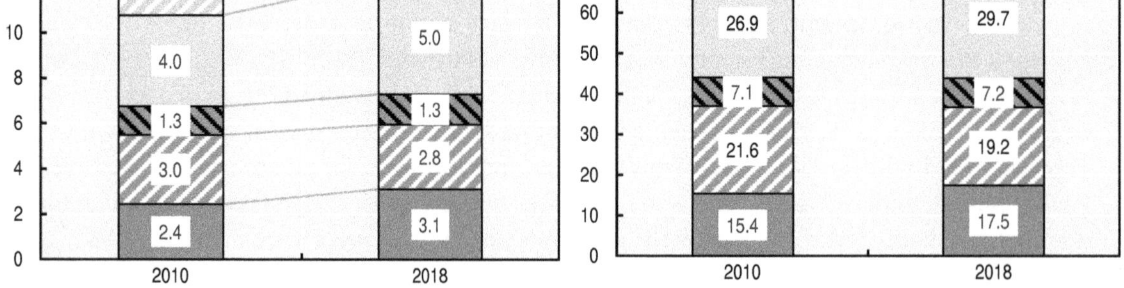

Note: The Africa (30) average, the averages for LAC (25 Latin American and Caribbean countries) and the OECD (36 countries) are unweighted. The Africa (30) average should be interpreted with caution as data for social security contributions are not available or are partial in a few countries. See the country tables in Chapter 5 for further information. The figures include sub-national government tax revenues for Eswatini, Mauritania, Mauritius, Morocco, Nigeria (state revenues only) and projected values for South Africa for 2018.

Source: Authors' calculations based on data on (OECD/ATAF/AUC, 2020[3]), "Revenue Statistics in Africa: Comparative tables", *OECD Tax Statistics* (database), *https://doi.org/10.1787/be755711-en*.

StatLink https://doi.org/10.1787/888934181546

Tax structures in 2018

In 2018, VAT generated the largest share of tax revenues in the countries studied in this publication (Figure 1.15). Revenues from VAT contributed 29.7% of total tax revenues on average, a share similar to the LAC average (27.8%) and approximately 10 percentage points higher than the OECD average (20.2%, 2017 figure). However, given the overall lower average tax-to-GDP ratio, VAT revenues for the Africa (30) average are lower than the LAC and OECD averages when measured as a share of GDP [5% of GDP in Africa, compared to 6% in LAC and 6.8% in the OECD (2017 figure)].

The average share of CIT revenues in total tax revenue in Africa amounted to 19.2% in 2018, above both the LAC and OECD average shares (15.5% and 9.3%, respectively). Reported as a percentage of GDP, the average shares of CIT revenues for the 30 African countries and for the OECD were similar [2.8% and 3.0% of GDP (2017 figure) respectively]; both were lower than the LAC average (3.5% of GDP in 2018) (Figure 1.15).

In contrast, the Africa (30) average share of PIT revenues (17.5% of total tax revenues) was lower than the OECD average of 23.9% (2017 figure) and higher than the LAC average (9.6%). As a percentage of GDP, the average level of PIT revenues across the OECD was more than double the Africa (30) average.

Figure 1.15. **Tax structure for the Africa (30), LAC and OECD averages as a percentage of total tax revenues and as a percentage of GDP, 2018**

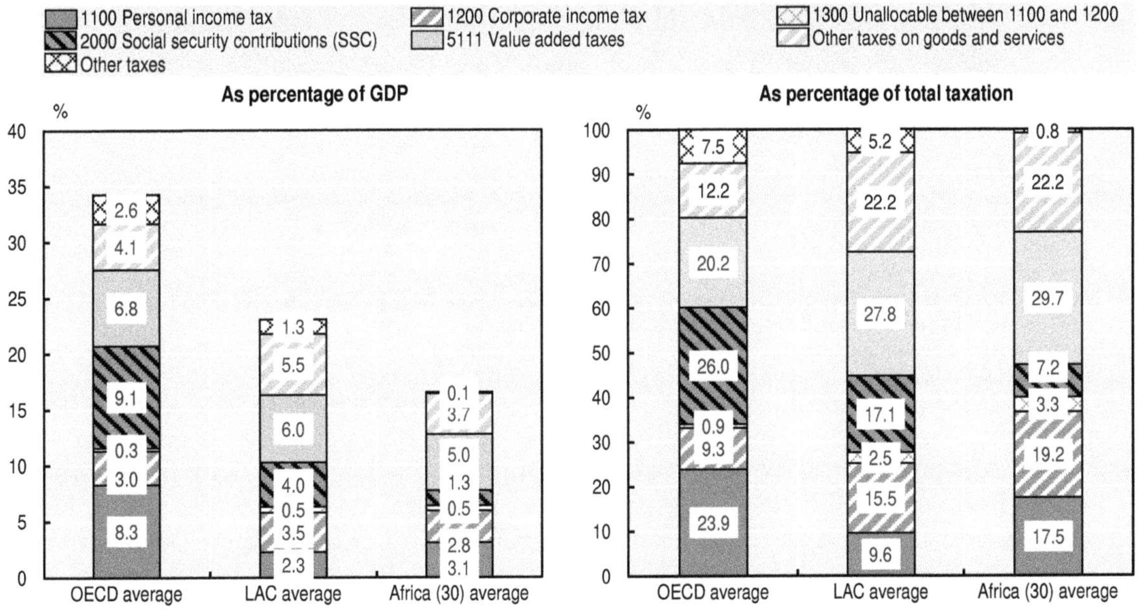

Note: The Africa (30) average, the averages for LAC (25 Latin American and Caribbean countries) and the OECD (36 countries) are unweighted. The Africa (30) average should be interpreted with caution as data for social security contributions are not available or are partial in a few countries. See the country tables in Chapter 5 for further information. The figures for the Africa (30) average include sub-national government tax revenues for Eswatini, Mauritius, Mauritania, Morocco, Nigeria (state revenues only) and projected values for South Africa for 2018.

The data for the OECD are for 2017 as data for 2018 are not available.

Source: Authors' calculations based on data on (OECD/ATAF/AUC, 2020[3]), "Revenue Statistics in Africa: Comparative tables", *OECD Tax Statistics* (database), *https://doi.org/10.1787/be755711-en*.

StatLink *https://doi.org/10.1787/888934181565*

Figure 1.16 shows the decomposition of tax revenues across all countries included in this publication, differentiating between income taxes (both personal and corporate), SSCs, and taxes on goods and services (including VAT and other goods and services taxes).

Taxes on goods and services were the principal source of tax revenues for 21 of the 30 countries included in this publication (the first two groups of countries in Figure 1.16). Among these countries, they generated between 39.7% of tax revenues in Tunisia and 76.3% of tax revenues in Togo. VAT generated the largest share of revenues from taxes on goods and services in these countries, with the exception of Côte d'Ivoire, the Republic of the Congo, Egypt, Ghana, Kenya, Mauritania and Uganda.

Figure 1.16. **Tax structure by country, 2018**

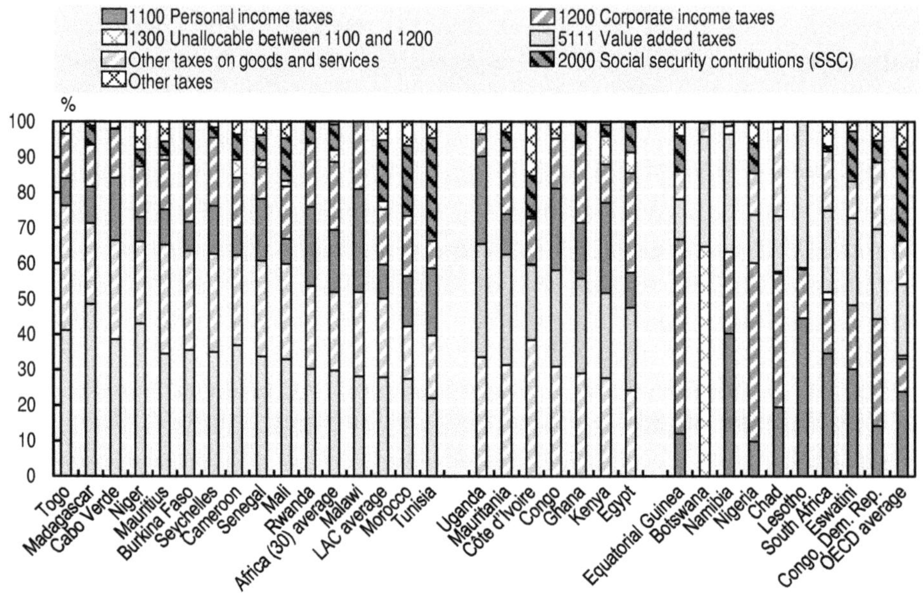

Note: Figures include sub-national government tax revenues for Eswatini, Mauritania, Mauritius, Morocco, Nigeria (state revenues only) and projected values for South Africa for 2018. The Africa (30) average, the averages for LAC (25 Latin American and Caribbean countries) and the OECD (36 countries) are unweighted.

The Africa (30) average should be interpreted with caution as data for social security contributions are not available or are partial in a few countries. See the country tables in Chapter 5 for further information.

Botswana: The breakdown of revenue from income tax by personal income tax and corporate income tax is not available.

OECD average: The data are for 2017 as data for 2018 are not available.

Source: Authors' calculations based on data from (OECD/ATAF/AUC, 2020[3]), "Revenue Statistics in Africa: Comparative tables", *OECD Tax Statistics* (database), *https://doi.org/10.1787/be755711-en*.

StatLink https://doi.org/10.1787/888934181584

For nine countries (Botswana, Chad, the Democratic Republic of the Congo, Equatorial Guinea, Eswatini, Lesotho, Namibia, Nigeria and South Africa), taxes on income and profits accounted for the principal share of total tax revenue. In all of these countries, taxes on income and profits represented a greater share of total tax revenues than for the OECD and LAC averages, ranging from 44.4% of total tax revenue in the Democratic Republic of the Congo to 66.8% in Equatorial Guinea.

The importance of SSCs[8] in total tax revenues varies greatly across the 30 countries in this publication. The share is highest in Morocco and Tunisia at 19.8% of total tax revenues in Morocco and 29.1% of total tax revenues in Tunisia; in the remaining countries; SSCs range from less than 0.2% of total tax revenues in Cabo Verde to around 14.1% in Eswatini.

This variation reflects the diversity of social security systems and contribution rates as many countries make use of a variety of systems to fund social security benefits. For example, SSCs in South Africa finance the Unemployment Insurance Fund while other benefits, such as social assistance programmes covering old age, sickness and maternity, are financed by general revenues. In contrast, social security schemes in Morocco and Tunisia are modelled on the French system and cover a wide range of social security benefits including old-age, disability, sickness and maternity, work injury (Tunisia), unemployment (Morocco) and family benefits (SSA, 2015[28]).

VAT revenue ratio

This section discusses the VAT revenue ratio (VRR) for the countries included in this publication.[9] The VRR "measures the difference between the VAT revenue actually collected and what would theoretically be raised if VAT was applied at the standard rate to the entire potential tax base in a "pure" VAT regime and all revenue was collected" (OECD, 2018[29]). The VRR is the ratio of actual VAT revenues to the product of final consumption (net of VAT revenues) and the standard VAT rate. The calculation is shown below.

$$\frac{\text{VAT revenues}}{\text{(final consumption expenditure-VAT revenues).standard VAT rate}}$$

This indicator provides an insight into VAT revenue loss related to exemptions and reduced rates, fraud, evasion and tax planning as well as weaknesses in tax administrations. However this indicator needs to be interpreted with caution and with reference to the underlying characteristics of the VAT system in each country, as a high VRR could result from cascading effects (for example when exemption occurs early in the supply chain) or a failure to refund VAT input credits. Other factors may also increase the ratio, for example when the place of taxation rules for international trade diverge from the destination principle or when there is a high level of informality. For example, in Africa, many workers operate in the informal sector. Not being registered for tax purposes, they do not benefit from VAT refunds on their inputs, while workers and companies in the formal sector are able to do so (AfDB, OECD, UNDP, 2016[30]).

Figure 1.17. **VAT revenue ratio by country, 2018**

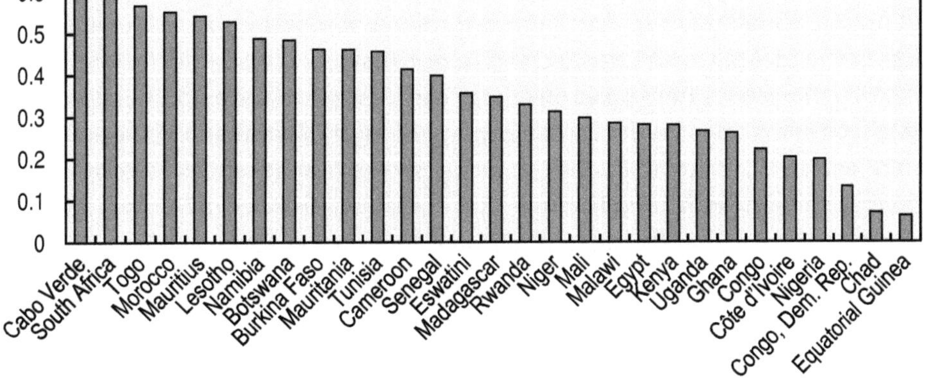

Note: The Seychelles are excluded due to unavailability of some data.

Source: VAT rates are sourced from Consumption Tax Trends (OECD, 2018[29]) Trading Economics and Deloitte websites, the final expenditure consumption figures from IMF WEO (IMF, 2020[4]) and VAT revenues from the country tables in Chapter 5.

StatLink https://doi.org/10.1787/888934181603

Figure 1.17 shows the VRRs for African countries in this publication. In 2018, Cabo Verde, South Africa and Togo had the highest VRRs (0.73, 0.61 and 0.57 respectively) whereas the Democratic Republic of the Congo, Chad and Equatorial Guinea had the lowest (0.13, 0.07 and 0.06 respectively).

- The high VRR in South Africa may be explained by some features of its VAT system. South Africa has limited VAT exemptions and zero-rated products and services compared to many other African countries. In addition, the threshold for VAT registration is high in South Africa thus enabling the South African tax administration to focus on large companies (Cnossen, 2015[31]).
- Cabo Verde has a VAT rate of 15%, and passed several tax reforms between 2013 and 2015 to increase VAT receipts (and corporate taxes). It also automated VAT revenue collection in December 2017 (UNCTAD, 2018[32]).
- Togo applies a single VAT rate of 18% to all activities and all products except those exempt. Thus, Togo does not apply any reduced rates. In addition, its high VRR can be partly explained by improvements in tax administration since 2010, as discussed earlier in this chapter, which contributed to an increase in VAT revenue collection.
- By contrast, the Democratic Republic of the Congo showed a VRR of 0.07. VAT revenues declined sharply since its introduction in 2012, from 4.2% of GDP to 1.9% of GDP in 2018. This decline and the low VRR reflect difficulties in the administration of the VAT by the authorities. For example, VAT on imports of mining companies is no longer collected due to difficulties in reimbursing VAT credits. The IMF has recommended a strengthening of the institutional arrangements to resume collecting these revenues (IMF, 2019[33]).

Environmentally related tax revenues

Through the Paris Agreement of 2016, countries have committed to decarbonise their economies by the middle of this century, implying a shift away from fossil fuels as a source of energy. Environmentally-related taxes, and price-based policy instruments more generally, play an increasingly significant role in many countries. By incorporating a price signal into consumer decisions, these taxes give effect to the polluter-pays principle and encourage businesses and households to consider the environmental costs of their behaviour.

An environmentally related tax is a tax whose base is a physical unit (or a proxy of a physical unit) of something that has a proven, specific harmful impact on the environment regardless of whether the tax is intended to change behaviours or is levied for another purpose (OECD, 2005[34]). Revenues from taxes on energy can increase in the medium term if countries increase effective tax rates on the carbon content of fuels (Marten and Van Dender, 2019[35]). A joint ITF and OECD study (OECD/ITF, 2019[36]) shows how revenues from road transport can be stabilised in the long term through a mix of taxing distance driven, vehicles and fuel.

Although environmentally related tax revenues cannot be identified in the standard OECD classification of tax revenues, they can be identified through the detailed list of specific taxes included for most countries within this overarching classification. It is on this basis that they are included in the OECD Policy Instruments for the Environment (PINE) database (OECD, 2020[37]).

The PINE database classifies environmentally related taxes under four bases:[10]

- *Energy*: This covers taxation of energy products such as fossil fuels and electricity also including fuels for transportation such as petrol and diesel. All CO_2-related taxes are in this category.

- *Motor vehicles and transport services*: This category includes imports or sales taxes on transport equipment, recurrent taxes on ownership, registration or road use of motor vehicles, and other transport-related taxes.
- *Resources*: This category includes taxes on mining and quarrying, forestry, wildlife and fisheries.
- *Pollution*: This category includes taxes on ozone-depleting substances, water and wastewater, waste management.

A detailed examination of country-specific taxes for the 30 African countries in this report for which the breakdown is available demonstrates that, on average, revenue from environmentally related taxes amounted to 1.1% of GDP in 2018, the same level as the LAC average but lower than the OECD unweighted average of 2.3% of GDP. Across countries, environmentally related tax revenue ranged from less than 0.1% of GDP in Senegal and Chad to 3.8% in the Seychelles (Figure 1.18). These figures need to be taken with caution as it is not possible to identify exactly the environmentally related tax revenue for each country; the level of revenues shown in Figure 1.18 depends on the granularity of tax revenue data available for each country.

Figure 1.18. **Environmentally related tax revenue by countries and main tax base, as a percentage of GDP, 2018**

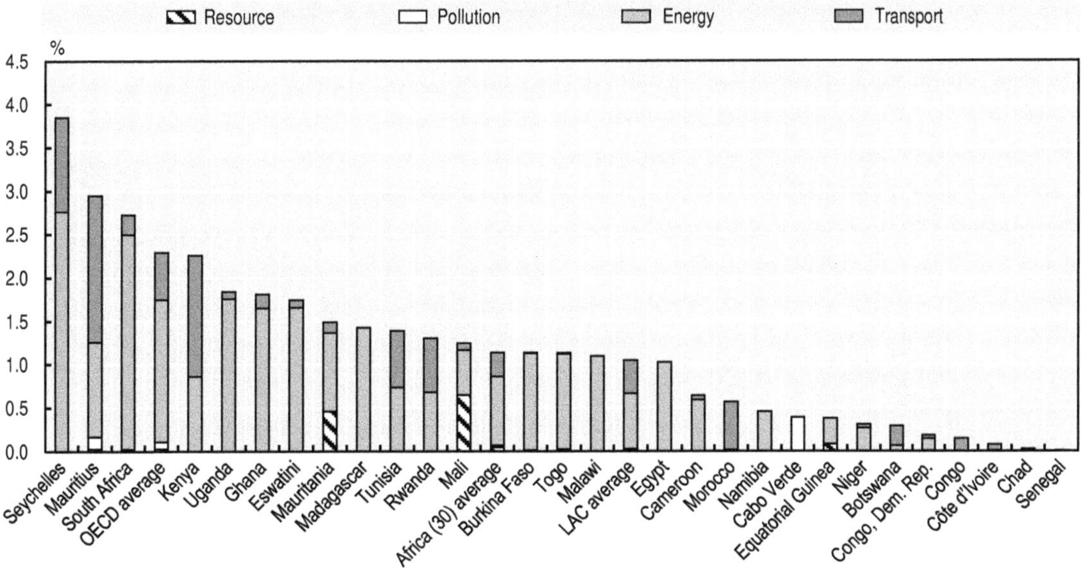

Note: Nigeria and Lesotho are excluded as it has not been possible to identify environmentally related tax revenue.
Source: Authors' calculations based on data on (OECD/ATAF/AUC, 2020[3]), (OECD, 2020[37]) PINE database for the OECD average and (OECD et al., 2020[1]) for the LAC average.

StatLink https://doi.org/10.1787/888934181622

In 2018, tax revenues from energy products generated the highest level of total environmentally related tax revenue for the countries in this publication (0.8% of GDP on average). Revenues from energy products, most commonly from taxes on diesel and gasoline, amounted to about two-thirds of environmentally related tax revenue on average. Revenues from motor vehicle and transport taxes represented most of the remainder and tax revenues from other environmentally related bases were negligible, at 0.07% of environmentally related tax revenues on average. This is very similar to the breakdown of these revenues for OECD and LAC countries.

Taxes on energy products also accounted for the largest share of environmentally related tax revenues in all but nine countries. Taxes on motor vehicles and transport were the main source of environmentally related revenues for Botswana, the Republic of the Congo, Côte d'Ivoire, Kenya, Mauritius, and Morocco. Cabo Verde, Chad and Mali levied the main part of their environmentally related tax revenues either from revenues from resource taxes or pollution taxes.

South Africa has one of the highest levels of revenue from environmentally related taxes, amounting to 2.7% of GDP in 2018, with the fuel levy providing the largest share (1.4% of GDP). Over the past decade, South Africa has introduced the incandescent light bulb levy (2009/10); the electricity levy (2009/10); the CO_2 tax on vehicle emissions (2010/11) and the tyre levy (2016/17). More recently, South Africa also introduced a carbon tax in 2019 with a tax rate of ZAR 120 (USD 8.34) per ton of carbon dioxide equivalent (Reuters, 2019[38]); (OECD, 2020[39])

Figure 1.19. **Environmentally related tax revenue as a percentage of GDP, for the Africa, OECD and LAC averages, 2010-2018**

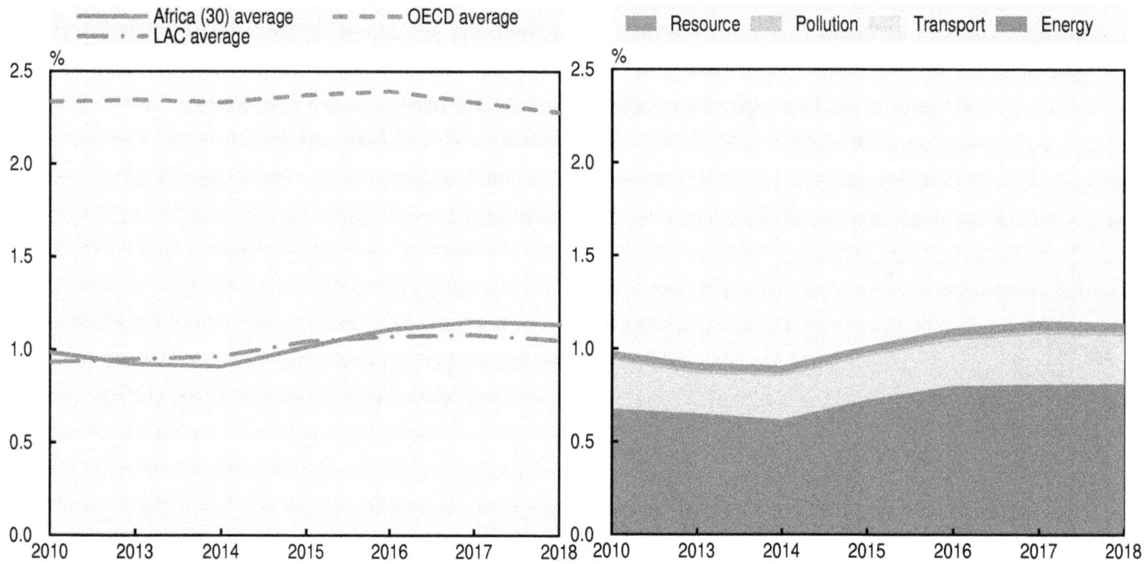

Note: Nigeria and Lesotho are excluded as it has not been possible to identify environmentally related tax revenue.
Source: Authors' calculations based on data on (OECD/ATAF/AUC, 2020[3]) and PINE database for the OECD average and (OECD et al., 2020[1]) for the LAC average.

StatLink https://doi.org/10.1787/888934181641

Revenues from taxes on energy can increase in the medium term, if countries increase effective tax rates on the carbon content of fuels (Marten and Van Dender, 2019[35]). Figure 1.19 shows the evolution of environmentally related tax revenue for the Africa (30), OECD and LAC averages since 2010. The Africa (30) average rose by 0.2 p.p. between 2010 and 2018 whereas the LAC average increased by 0.1 p.p. and the OECD average decreased by 0.1 p.p. over the period. The Africa (30) average of environmentally related tax revenue declined between 2010 and 2014, rebounded for two years and then plateaued at 1.1% of GDP from 2016 onwards. In 2014 and 2015, the Africa (30) average of environmentally related tax revenue showed the highest increase of 0.1 p.p. for both years. This growth was principally driven by energy-related tax revenues.

The countries that showed the highest increases between 2010 and 2018 were Ghana, Eswatini and Mauritania; environmentally related tax revenue increased in those countries by 1.3 p.p., 1.2 p.p. and 1.0 p.p. respectively over the period. These increases were all due to increases in fuel and petroleum taxes. During this period, Ghana enacted the Energy Sector Levies Act, 2015 (Act 899) with a view to stabilising petroleum prices, financing road maintenance and supporting power generation (Ghana Web, 2019[40]). The Act led to the introduction of different levies such as the Road Fund Levy, the Energy Debt Recovery Levy and the Price Stabilisation and Recovery Levy. The increase for all three levies between 2010 and 2018 amounted to 1% of GDP.

In comparison to OECD countries, the use of taxation to address environmental issues is low in the region and there is a significant scope to enhance this form of taxation. The underutilisation of environmental taxes in the Africa region needs also to be understood in the context of the extensive use of fossil fuels subsidies. For example, fossil fuels subsidies in Sub Sahara Africa are estimated to amount to 5% of GDP in 2013 (Coady et al., 2015[41]). Among the countries in this publication, Côte d'Ivoire, Nigeria and South Africa provided fossil fuel subsidies in excess of USD 1 billion in 2015 (Worrall, Whitley and Scott, 2018[42]) Reforming energy subsidies while at the same time implementing environmental taxation has the potential to mobilise significant government revenues and help to meet Agenda 2063 and the SDGs.

As the COVID-19 crisis continues to unfold and governments continue to implement packages to support businesses and taxpayers, some governments are granting tax relief or waiving certain taxes. ATAF encourages African governments to "refrain from suspending environmental taxes during this period as (...) short-term tax relief should not compromise longer-term environmental goals" (ATAF, 2020[43]).

Taxes by level of government

Analysis of taxation by level of government for the countries participating in this publication is limited by the fact that data on sub-national tax revenues were only available for six countries: Eswatini, Mauritania, Mauritius,[11] Morocco, Nigeria[12] and South Africa. Revenues collected at sub-national level are considered to be low in the 30 African countries. (AfDB/OECD/UNDP, 2015[44]) states that "in Africa, on average, the weight of local government revenue is 7% of the total revenue of local, regional and national governments combined". In 2018, sub-national government revenues accounted for less than 1% of total tax revenues in Mauritius, 1.9% in Eswatini, 2.8% in Mauritania, 3.4% in Morocco and 5.6% in South Africa. In contrast, sub-national government tax revenues amounted to 14.3% of total tax revenues in Nigeria.

In general, sub-national governments in Africa tend to have limited tax collection responsibilities. The 2015 *African Economic Outlook* (AfDB/OECD/UNDP, 2015[44]) observed that "Many local governments receive a significant share of their total revenues from central government transfers". Local governments across Africa have limited resources and many local tax administrations are not adequately equipped to collect taxes or to account for them. This results in high collection costs and an extensive number of low-yield taxes. Moreover, processing of data on revenue collections and the exchange of information with other public institutions is poor and there is usually little co-operation with the central government. This can lead to a duplication of taxes or a levying of taxes that are contrary to national objectives (such as local taxes on export crops).

Revenues from property taxes are the most important source of reported tax revenue for sub-national governments in Eswatini, Mauritania, Mauritius, Morocco and South Africa. They accounted for all the reported tax revenue collected locally in Eswatini, Mauritania and Mauritius and for more than 80% in Morocco and South Africa. Most of the remainder derives from taxes on goods and services. In contrast, sub-national government tax revenues in Nigeria are mostly sourced from income taxes.

There are wide differences in local taxation among African countries and many countries do not levy any local taxes on buildings and landholdings, or on economic activities (AfDB/OECD/UNDP, 2015[44]). Apart from South Africa, property registers are lacking or incomplete, which is a major challenge for the collection of property taxes (Fjeldstad; Chambas; Brun, 2014[45]). In Mauritius, for instance, property tax provides a low yield partly due to outdated cadastres and valuations of property (IMF, 2014[46]).

Some countries have been working on improving their property taxes, which has led to improved land registries and better administrative tools. Morocco has been reforming local government tax systems and administrations since 2007 to strengthen local tax revenue (Boisard; de Freitas; Hidouci, 2014[47]). Côte d'Ivoire has introduced GIS software in their land registries. South Africa has successfully decentralised urban property tax collection and has developed a modern system to collect property tax revenue including use of statistical techniques to conduct computer-assisted mass-appraisals, or CAMA (Monkam and Moore, 2015[48]).

Although many countries have undertaken major reforms of their central tax legislation and administrations over the last decades, less focus has been put on the local government level. Central government taxation has been prioritised because of the need to reduce national fiscal deficits.

Notes

1. The Africa (30) average should be interpreted with caution as data on social security contributions are not available for Chad, the Republic of the Congo, the Democratic Republic of the Congo (prior to 2012), Madagascar (prior to 2011), Namibia, Togo and Uganda and are only partially available for Cameroon and Senegal. Social security contributions for Botswana, Lesotho and Malawi are deemed to be null as they do not meet the criteria to be classified as social security contributions set out in the OECD classification of taxes in the Interpretative Guide. See the country tables in Chapter 5 for further information.
2. Burundi, South Sudan, Tanzania, Kenya, Rwanda and Uganda belong to the East Africa Community (EAC).
3. Burkina Faso, Benin, Côte d'Ivoire, Guinea Bissau, Mali, Niger, Senegal and Togo belong to the West African Economic and Monetary Union (WAEMU, also known by its French acronym, UEMOA).
4. Botswana, Eswatini, Lesotho, Namibia and South Africa constitute the Southern African Customs Union (SACU).
5. This information was provided by the Agence Comptable Centrale du Trésor (ACCT) Mali during exchanges with the OECD Secretariat in preparation of this publication.
6. Further discussion on these measures can be found in the special feature: "Convergence of tax levels and tax structures in OECD countries" (OECD, 2018[49]).
7. The analysis is based on a unique data source, the 2016 OECD business survey that gathered views from senior staff from over 500 companies, almost all MNEs, providing views on tax certainty in 82 developing countries.
8. Data on social security contributions are not available for Chad, the Republic of the Congo, the Democratic Republic of the Congo (prior to 2012), Madagascar (prior to 2011), Namibia, Togo and Uganda and are only partially available for Cameroon and Senegal. See the country tables in Chapter 5 for further information.
9. The Seychelles is excluded due to unavailability of some data.
10. The OECD PINE DB (*http://oe.cd/pine*) collects detailed instrument-level information which is aggregated to produce revenue totals. The database supports the monitoring, design and implementation of effective policies. The OECD PINE database hosts, since 2005, a unique set of detailed information on 3 476 policy instruments in 94 countries.

11. Data from Mauritius were derived from financial statements produced by Statistics Mauritius.
12. Sub-national tax revenues figures include state revenues but exclude local government revenues.

References

Addison, T. and J. Levin (2012), *The Determinants of Tax Revenue in Sub-Saharan Africa*, Swedish Business School at Örebro University, Örebro, Sweden, *http://oru.diva-portal.org/smash/record.jsf?pid=diva2%3A570456&dswid=4207.* [22]

AfDB/OECD/ECA (2010), *African Economic Outlook 2010: Domestic Resource Mobilisation and Aid*, OECD Publishing, Paris, *http://dx.doi.org/10.1787/aeo-2010-en.* [24]

AfDB, OECD, UNDP (2016), "Sustainable Cities and Structural Transformation", *African Economic Outlook*, *https://dx.doi.org/10.1787/aeo-2016-en.* [30]

AfDB/OECD/UNDP (2015), *African Economic Outlook 2015: Regional Development and Spatial Inclusion*, OECD Publishing, Paris, *http://dx.doi.org/10.1787/aeo-2015-en.* [44]

ATAF (2020), *Mining Tax Policy Responses to COVID-19: Webinar Q&A*, *www.ataftax.org/mining-tax-policy-responses-to-covid-19-webinar-q-a.* [43]

Boisard; de Freitas; Hidouci (2014), *Renforcer les recettes fiscales locales pour financer le développement urbain en Afrique*, Fonds Mondial pour le Développement des Villes (FMDV), Paris, *http://delog.org/web/wp-content/uploads/2016/03/Etude-FMDV-Fiscalite%CC%81-locale-Villes-Afrique-8-Cas.pdf.* [47]

Cnossen, S. (2015), *Mobilizing VAT revenues in African countries*, *www.researchgate.net/publication/276344974_Mobilizing_VAT_revenues_in_African_countries.* [31]

Coady, D. et al. (2015), "How Large Are Global Energy Subsidies?", *IMF Working Paper*, *www.imf.org/external/pubs/ft/wp/2015/wp15105.pdf.* [41]

Diallo, M. (2018), "UEMOA : L'optimisation de la mobilisation des recettes fiscales propres, au centre d'un séminaire", *LE Faso;net*, *https://lefaso.net/spip.php?article84079.* [5]

Direction générale du Trésor France (2020), *Indicateurs et conjoncture - MAURITANIE | Direction générale du Trésor*, *www.tresor.economie.gouv.fr/Pays/MR/mauritanie-situation-economique-et-financiere* (accessed on 11 September 2020). [11]

Fjeldstad; Chambas; Brun (2014), *Local government taxation in Sub-Saharan Africa: a review and an agenda for research*, 2, Chr. Michelsen Institute, Bergen, *www.cmi.no/publications/file/5098-local-government-taxation-in-sub-saharan-africa.pdf.* [45]

Ghana Web (2019), *Parliament asks Government to address energy sector debts*, *www.ghanaweb.com/GhanaHomePage/business/Parliament-asks-Government-to-address-energy-sector-debts-760166.* [40]

Grey, A. (2020), "Here are Ghana's tax incentives available to business persons & entrepreneurs", *Ghana talks business*, *https://ghanatalksbusiness.com/2020/08/here-are-ghanas-tax-incentives-available-to-business-persons-entrepreneurs/.* [25]

IMF (2020), "2019 Article IV consultation—press release; staff report; and statement by the Executive Director for the Republic of Congo", *IMF Country Report No. 20/26*, *www.imf.org/en/Publications/CR/Issues/2020/01/27/Republic-of-Congo-2019-Article-IV-Consultation-Press-Release-Staff-Report-and-Statement-by-48984.* [13]

IMF (2020), *World Economic Outlook Database April 2020*, *www.imf.org/external/pubs/ft/weo/2020/01/weodata/index.aspx* (accessed on 8 September 2020). [21]

IMF (2020), *World Economic Outlook, April 2020: The Great Lockdown.* [4]

IMF (2019), "2019 Article IV consultation, fourth review under the extended credit facility, and requests for waiver of nonobservance of a performance criterion, modification of performance criteria, and extension and rephasing of the extended credit facility arrangem", *IMF Country Report No. 19/239*, *www.imf.org/en/Publications/CR/Issues/2019/07/22/Niger-2019-Article-IV-Consultation-Fourth-Review-Under-the-Extended-Credit-Facility-and-48514.* [10]

IMF (2019), *Democratic Republic of the Congo : 2019 Article IV Consultation-Press Release; Staff Report; and Statement by the Executive Director for the Democratic Republic of the Congo*, *www.imf.org/en/Publications/CR/Issues/2019/09/04/Democratic-Republic-of-the-Congo-2019-Article-IV-Consultation-Press-Release-Staff-Report-and-48648* (accessed on 8 September 2020). [33]

IMF (2019), "L'équipe du FMI achève une mission de revue au Togo", *Communiqué de presse N° 19/473*, *www.imf.org/fr/News/Articles/2019/12/18/pr19473-togo-imf-staff-completes-review-mission.* [15]

IMF (2019), *World Economic Outlook - Frequently Asked Questions*, *www.imf.org/external/pubs/ft/weo/faq.htm#q4d* (accessed on 6 September 2019). [19]

IMF (2018), "Mali : 2018 Article IV Consultation and Eighth and Ninth Reviews Under the Extended Credit Facility Arrangement-Press Release; Staff Report; and Statement by the Executive Director for Mali", *Country Report No. 18/141*, *www.imf.org/en/Publications/CR/Issues/2018/05/31/Mali-2018-Article-IV-Consultation-and-Eighth-and-Ninth-Reviews-Under-the-Extended-Credit-45921.* [14]

IMF (2014), *Mauritius: 2014 article IV consultation-staff report (2014b)*, IMF, *www.imf.org/external/pubs/ft/scr/2014/cr14107.pdf.* [46]

Jeune Afrique (2019), *En Mauritanie, une vertueuse diversification qui reste à confirmer*, *www.jeuneafrique.com/mag/844828/economie/en-mauritanie-une-vertueuse-diversification-qui-reste-a-confirmer/.* [12]

KPMG (2020), "*https://assets.kpmg/content/dam/kpmg/ng/pdf/tax/ng-incentives-in-africa.pdf*", *Investing in Africa*, *https://assets.kpmg/content/dam/kpmg/ng/pdf/tax/ng-incentives-in-africa.pdf.* [27]

Lesotho Times (2019), *LRA meets revenue target - Lesotho Times*, *http://lestimes.com/lra-meets-revenue-target/* (accessed on 11 September 2020). [8]

Lesotho Times (2019), *LRA ups tax lottery stakes - Lesotho Times*, *http://lestimes.com/lra-ups-tax-lottery-stakes/* (accessed on 11 September 2020). [6]

Lesotho Times (2018), *LRA on course to meet revenue target - Lesotho Times*, *http://lestimes.com/lra-on-course-to-meet-revenue-target/* (accessed on 11 September 2020). [9]

LRA (2018), *Value Added Tax (VAT) Rates Change.* [7]

Marten, M. and K. Van Dender (2019), *The use of revenues from carbon pricing*. *OECD Taxation Working Papers*, OECD, *https://doi.org/10.1787/3cb265e4-en.* [35]

Monkam, N. and M. Moore (2015), *How Property Tax Would Benefit Africa*, Africa Research Institute, *www.africaresearchinstitute.org/publications/property-tax-benefit-africa.* [48]

OECD (2020), "OECD analysis of budgetary support and tax expenditures. 2020 country notes", *Inventory of Support Measures for Fossil Fuels database*, *www.oecd.org/fossil-fuels/data/.* [39]

OECD (2020), *PINE database*, *www.oecd.org/environment/tools-evaluation/environmentaltaxation.htm.* [37]

OECD (2019), *Revenue Statistics: 1965-2018*, OECD Publishing, Paris, *https://doi.org/10.1787/rev_stats-2018-en.* [2]

OECD (2019), *Tax Morale: What Drives People and Businesses to Pay Tax?*, OECD Publishing, *https://doi.org/10.1787/f3d8ea10-en.* [18]

OECD (2018), *Consumption Tax Trends 2018: VAT/GST and Excise Rates, Trends and Policy Issues*, OECD publishing, *https://doi.org/10.1787/ctt-2018-en.* [29]

OECD (2018), *Revenue Statistics: 1965-2017*, OECD Publishing, Paris, *https://doi.org/10.1787/rev_stats-2018-en.* [49]

OECD (2014), *Development Co-operation Report 2014: Mobilising Resources for Sustainable Development*, OECD Publishing, Paris, *https://doi.org/10.1787/dcr-2014-en.* [17]

OECD (2005), *Glossary of statistical terms*, *https://stats.oecd.org/glossary/detail.asp?ID=6437.* [34]

OECD/ATAF/AUC (2020), *Revenue Statistics in Africa: Comparative tables*, OECD Publishing, Paris, *https://doi.org/10.1787/be755711-en.* [3]

OECD/ITF (2019), *Tax revenue implications from the decarbonisation of road transport: scenarios for Slovenia*, OECD, *https://doi.org/10.1787/87b39a2f-en.* [36]

OECD et al. (2020), *Revenue Statistics in Latin America and the Caribbean*, OECD Publishing, Paris, *https://doi.org/10.1787/68739b9b-en-es.* [1]

Profeta, S. and S. Scabrosetti (2010), *The Political Economy of Taxation: Lessons from Developing Countries*, Edward Elgar Publishing, *https://books.google.fr/books?isbn=1849805490.* [23]

PWC (2020), "Worldwide Tax summaries", *Nigeria. Corporate - Tax credits and incentives*, *https://taxsummaries.pwc.com/nigeria/corporate/tax-credits-and-incentives.* [26]

Reuters (2019), *South African carbon tax finally becomes law*, *www.reuters.com/article/us-safrica-carbontax/south-african-carbon-tax-finally-becomes-law-idUSKCN1SW0K6* (accessed on 6 September 2019). [38]

SACU (2020), *What is SACU?*, *www.sacu.int/about/what_is.html* (accessed on 10 September 2020). [16]

SSA (2015), *Social Security Through the World: Africa*, SSA Publication Social Security Administration, Washington, DC, *www.ssa.gov/policy/docs/progdesc/ssptw/2014-2015/africa/ssptw15africa.pdf*. [28]

UNCTAD (2018), *Investment Policy Review of Cabo Verde*, *http://unctad.org/ipr* (accessed on 7 September 2020). [32]

WHO (2015), *Purchasing Power Parity 2005*, World Health Organization, *www.who.int/choice/costs/ppp/en/*. [20]

Worrall, L., S. Whitley and A. Scott (2018), "Reforming Africa's Fossil Fuel Subsidies", *sun-connect-news.org*, *www.sun-connect-news.org/de/articles/business/details/reforming-africas-fossil-fuel-subsidies/*. [42]

Chapitre 1

Tendances des recettes fiscales, 2010-2018

Pour atteindre les Objectifs de développement durable (ODD) des Nations Unies et mettre en œuvre le Programme d'action d'Addis-Abeba et l'Agenda 2063 de l'Union africaine, il est nécessaire de mobiliser des financements supplémentaires, et notamment des ressources intérieures, afin de financer l'offre de biens et de services publics. L'impôt représente une source de recettes publiques prévisible et stable, qui contraste avec la volatilité d'autres sources importantes de recettes publiques, comme l'aide publique au développement et les redevances minières.

Ce rapport contient un ensemble d'indicateurs internationalement comparables sur les recettes fiscales et non fiscales qui peuvent servir à mesurer les progrès en matière de mobilisation des ressources intérieures (comme le prévoient les ODD, le Programme d'action d'Addis-Abeba ainsi que des initiatives connexes telles que l'initiative fiscale d'Addis-Abeba) et à éclairer les politiques et les réformes fiscales. Ce rapport et les données qu'il contient contribuent aussi au Programme statistique panafricain, une initiative conjointe de l'Union européenne et de l'Union africaine visant à renforcer les capacités statistiques en Afrique, en fournissant des données statistiques de qualité sur les recettes publiques. Ces données faciliteront le processus d'élaboration des politiques et leur suivi, de manière à soutenir l'intégration africaine. Ce rapport contient des informations essentielles sur les systèmes fiscaux dans la région et sur leur efficacité en termes de recettes mobilisées au cours des dernières années ; il apporte une contribution importante à la compréhension de la capacité budgétaire des pays de la région à surmonter la crise du COVID-19.

Ce chapitre examine l'évolution du ratio impôts/PIB, de la structure fiscale et de la part des recettes fiscales par niveau d'administration dans 30 pays d'Afrique, de 1990 (si disponible) jusqu'en 2018 : Afrique du Sud, Botswana, Burkina Faso, Cabo Verde, Cameroun, Côte d'Ivoire, Guinée équatoriale, Égypte, Eswatini, Ghana, Kenya, Lesotho, Madagascar, Malawi, Mali, Maroc, Maurice, Mauritanie, Namibie, Niger, Nigéria, Ouganda, République du Congo, République démocratique du Congo, Rwanda, Sénégal, Seychelles, Tchad, Togo et Tunisie. Il compare également les moyennes de ces 30 pays d'Afrique avec celles de 25 pays d'Amérique latine et des Caraïbes (ALC) (OCDE et al., 2020[1]) et celles de 36 pays de l'OCDE (OCDE, 2019[2]). L'analyse proposée vient compléter les informations détaillées par pays relatives aux recettes fiscales figurant au chapitre 5.

Ratios impôts/PIB

Ratios impôts/PIB en 2018

Le ratio moyen impôts/PIB dans les 30 pays d'Afrique couverts par la publication [désigné ci-après « moyenne Afrique (30) »] s'est établi à 16.5 % en 2018 (Graphique 1.1). Le ratio impôts/PIB correspond aux recettes fiscales (y compris les cotisations de sécurité sociale versées à l'administration générale) exprimées en pourcentage du produit intérieur brut (PIB)[1]. À titre de comparaison, les ratios impôts/PIB moyens pour la région ALC et pour la zone OCDE étaient respectivement de 23.1 % et 34.3 % en 2018.

En 2018, les ratios impôts/PIB ont affiché de grandes variations entre les pays couverts par la publication, allant de 6.3 % en Guinée équatoriale et au Nigéria à 32.4 % aux Seychelles. Les pays comptant les revenus par habitant les plus élevés parmi les pays étudiés, l'Afrique du Sud, le Maroc, les Seychelles et la Tunisie obtenaient chacun un ratio impôts/PIB supérieur à 25 %. Vingt-et-un pays affichaient des ratios compris entre 11 % et 22 %, tandis que la République du Congo, la République démocratique du Congo, la Guinée équatoriale, le Nigéria et le Tchad avaient un ratio inférieur à 9 %.

Graphique 1.1. **Ratios impôts/PIB et total des recettes fiscales (hors cotisations de sécurité sociale) en pourcentage du PIB, 2018**

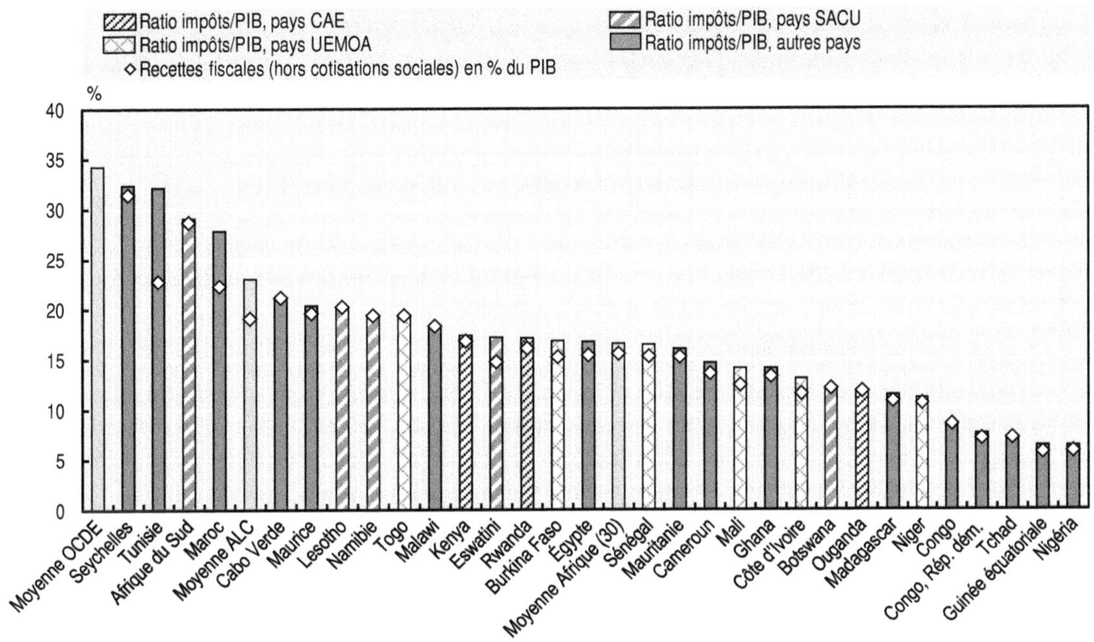

Notes : Les chiffres prennent en compte les recettes fiscales des administrations infranationales pour l'Afrique du Sud (projections pour 2018), l'Eswatini, le Maroc, Maurice, la Mauritanie et le Nigéria (recettes des États uniquement).

La moyenne Afrique (30) et les moyennes ALC (25 pays) et OCDE (36 pays) sont des moyennes non pondérées.

Il convient d'interpréter la moyenne Afrique (30) avec précaution car des données relatives aux cotisations de sécurité sociale sont indisponibles pour la République du Congo, la République démocratique du Congo (avant 2012), Madagascar (avant 2011), la Namibie, l'Ouganda, le Tchad et le Togo et sont incomplètes pour le Cameroun et le Sénégal. Les cotisations de sécurité sociale pour le Botswana, le Lesotho et le Malawi sont égales à zéro dans la mesure où elles ne remplissent pas les critères retenus pour être considérées comme des cotisations de sécurité sociale, selon la classification des impôts de l'OCDE figurant dans le guide d'interprétation. Pour plus de précisions, se reporter aux tableaux par pays présentés dans le chapitre 5.

Le ratio impôts/PIB de l'Afrique du Sud prend en compte les sommes recouvrées par l'Afrique du Sud au profit de l'Union douanière de l'Afrique australe (SACU).

Source : Tableaux 4.1 et 4.2 figurant au chapitre 4 et « Statistiques des recettes publiques en Afrique : Tableaux comparatifs » (OCDE/ATAF/CUA, 2020[3]), *Statistiques fiscales de l'OCDE* (base de données) *https://doi.org/10.1787/7f54581d-fr*.

StatLink *https://doi.org/10.1787/888934182002*

La plupart des pays couverts par cette publication appartiennent à des organisations régionales dont les membres adoptent des règles communes en matière fiscale et douanière et forment une union douanière.

- Le ratio impôts/PIB moyen des trois pays de la Communauté d'Afrique de l'Est (CAE)[2] inclus dans cette publication était de 15.5 % en 2018, soit un niveau inférieur à la moyenne Afrique (30). En 2018, les ratios impôts/PIB au Kenya et au Rwanda dépassaient 17.0 % et atteignaient 11.8 % en Ouganda.

- L'Union économique et monétaire ouest-africaine (UEMOA)[3] a fixé pour objectif à ses pays membres d'atteindre des ratios impôts/PIB d'au moins 20 % (Diallo, 2018[5]). Le ratio impôts/PIB des six pays de l'UEMOA inclus dans cette publication s'établissait en moyenne à 15.2 % en 2018. Les ratios variaient de 11.1 % au Niger à 19.4 % au Togo ; deux des six pays de l'UEMOA de cette publication (Burkina Faso et Togo) affichaient des ratios impôts/PIB supérieurs à la moyenne Afrique (30).
- La moyenne des pays de l'Union douanière d'Afrique australe (SACU)[4] était supérieure à la moyenne Afrique (30) et s'élevait à 19.6 % en 2018. Les ratios impôts/PIB dans les pays de la SACU variaient entre 12.1 % du PIB au Botswana et 29.1 % du PIB en Afrique du Sud. L'Eswatini et la Namibie affichaient des ratios impôts/PIB inférieurs à 20 % du PIB (respectivement 17.2 % et 19.4 %), tandis que le Lesotho enregistrait un ratio de 20.2 % en 2018. L'encadré 1.2 examine l'évolution des ratios impôts/PIB des pays de la SACU depuis 2010 et leurs variations entre 2010 et 2018.

Encadré 1.1. **Méthodologie : le ratio impôts/PIB**

Les ratios impôts/PIB utilisés dans cette publication expriment les recettes fiscales totales en pourcentage du PIB. La valeur de ce ratio dépend de son dénominateur (PIB) et de son numérateur (recettes fiscales).

Le numérateur (recettes fiscales)

Pour le numérateur, cette publication utilise les chiffres des recettes qui sont soumis chaque année par les points de contact au sein des ministères des Finances, des administrations fiscales ou des offices statistiques nationaux. Les données rétrospectives sur les recettes fiscales font l'objet de révisions chaque année, des révisions plus importantes ayant lieu pour les années les plus récentes. Les données historiques peuvent également changer d'une édition à l'autre lorsque de nouvelles données sont obtenues par des points de contact pour améliorer la publication. C'est le cas en Mauritanie, qui a fourni pour la première fois dans cette édition des données sur les recettes des collectivités locales et les cotisations de sécurité sociale versées à la CNAM (Caisse Nationale d'Assurance Maladie), et en Guinée équatoriale, qui a communiqué des données sur les cotisations de sécurité sociale.

Le dénominateur (PIB)

Pour le dénominateur, les chiffres du PIB utilisés pour la série *Statistiques des recettes publiques en Afrique* proviennent des *Perspectives de l'économie mondiale* publiées par le FMI. L'utilisation de ces chiffres du PIB garantit une cohérence maximale entre les pays, ainsi qu'une comparabilité internationale des ratios impôts/PIB. Les chiffres du PIB sont également révisés et actualisés pour tenir compte de l'amélioration des sources de données et des procédures d'estimation, ou pour appliquer de nouvelles lignes directrices convenues à l'échelle internationale pour mesurer la valeur du PIB.

Les chiffres les plus récents provenant des *Perspectives de l'économie mondiale* ont été publiés en avril 2020 (FMI, 2020[4]) et incluent les révisions du PIB effectuées par certains pays pour s'aligner sur l'édition la plus récente du Système de comptabilité nationale (SCN 2008). Dans cette édition, le Burkina Faso, la Côte d'Ivoire, Madagascar, la Mauritanie, le Niger et l'Ouganda ont révisé leurs données sur le PIB, ce qui a entraîné une baisse des ratios impôts/PIB dans ces pays et du ratio moyen des pays d'Afrique, par rapport à l'édition précédente. L'écart entre les ratios impôts/PIB en 2017 entre l'édition de cette année et celle de l'année dernière était compris entre 2.1 points de pourcentage en Ouganda et 4.6 points de pourcentage en Côte d'Ivoire ; et la moyenne pour les pays africains couverts par cette publication est inférieure de 0.6 point de pourcentage en 2017 dans cette édition par rapport à l'édition de l'année dernière.

Variation des ratios impôts/PIB entre 2017 et 2018

Le ratio moyen impôts/PIB pour les pays d'Afrique a augmenté d'un peu moins de 0.1 % du PIB, entre 2017 et 2018. Il a augmenté dans 19 pays, a diminué dans 10 et est resté inchangé dans 1 pays. Dans sept pays, les ratios ont augmenté de plus d'un point de pourcentage, alors qu'ils ont diminué de plus d'un point de pourcentage dans quatre pays. C'est au Lesotho (1.9 point), au Niger (1.6 point) et en Mauritanie (1.5 point) que les augmentations les plus marquées se sont produites entre 2017 et 2018. La République du Congo a enregistré la plus forte baisse du ratio impôts/PIB en 2018 (5.1 points), suivie du Mali (2.6 points) et du Togo (1.6 point).

Graphique 1.2. **Variation des ratios impôts/PIB entre 2017 et 2018 (points de pourcentage)**

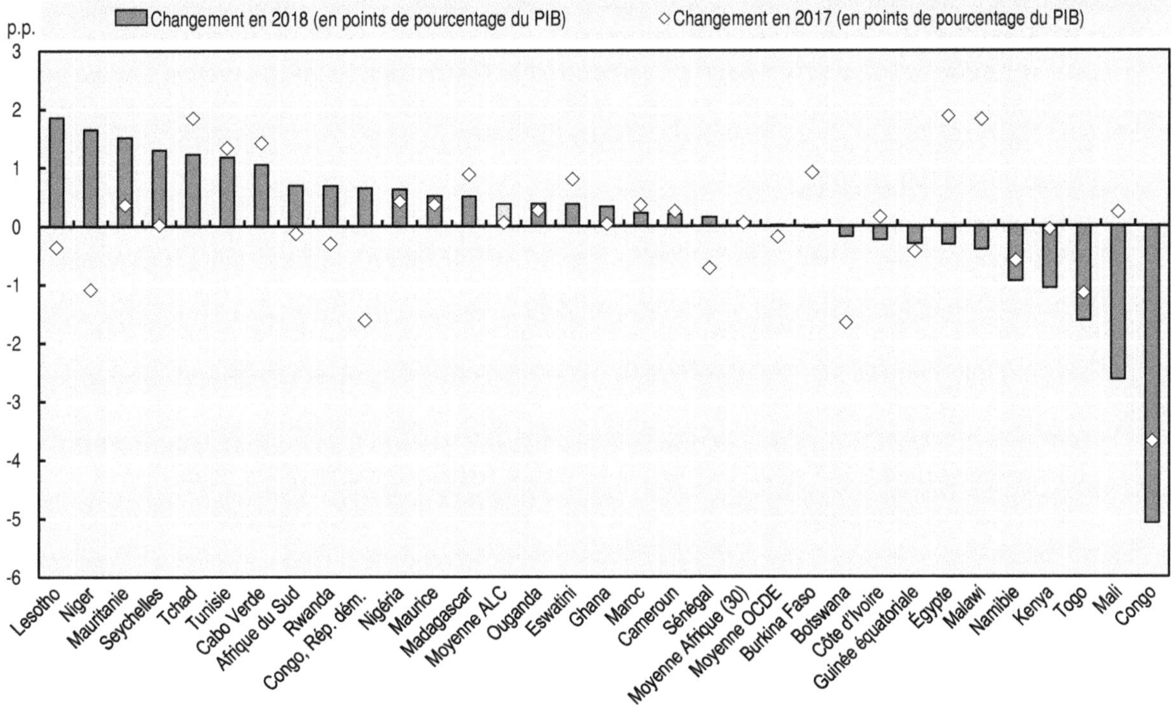

Notes : Les chiffres prennent en compte les recettes fiscales des administrations infranationales pour l'Afrique du Sud (projections pour 2018), l'Eswatini, le Maroc, Maurice, la Mauritanie et le Nigéria (recettes des États uniquement).

La moyenne Afrique (30) et les moyennes ALC (25 pays) et OCDE (36 pays) sont des moyennes non pondérées.

Il convient d'interpréter l'évolution de la moyenne Afrique (30) avec précaution car des données relatives aux cotisations de sécurité sociale sont indisponibles ou incomplètes pour quelques pays. Pour plus de précisions, se reporter aux tableaux par pays présentés dans le chapitre 5.

Source : Calculs des auteurs basés sur des données figurant dans le tableau 4.1 du chapitre 4 et « Statistiques des recettes publiques en Afrique : Tableaux comparatifs » (OCDE/ATAF/CUA, 2020[3]), *Statistiques fiscales de l'OCDE* (base de données) *https://doi.org/10.1787/7f54581d-fr.*

StatLink *https://doi.org/10.1787/888934182021*

Au Lesotho, la hausse du ratio impôts/PIB en 2018 a suivi deux années de baisse des recettes fiscales en pourcentage du PIB. Cette progression entre 2017 et 2018 était alimentée par des augmentations des recettes de TVA ainsi que des recettes de l'impôt sur le revenu (0.9 % du PIB dans les deux cas). Le Lesotho a mis en place une nouvelle stratégie pour remédier aux problèmes de discipline fiscale concernant tous les types d'impôts et de contribuables et mettre un terme à l'érosion des recettes, en améliorant la qualité des services de son administration fiscale et en allégeant les contraintes administratives. Cette stratégie comprend des initiatives telles que le système simplifié d'imposition des sociétés, un programme de discipline fiscale volontaire et une loterie fiscale pour gagner des voitures (Lesotho Times, 2019[6]). En outre, le Lesotho a relevé son taux normal de TVA de 14 % à 15 %, ainsi que d'autres taux de TVA (par exemple, sur l'électricité et les télécommunications) en avril 2018 (LRA, 2018[7]). Outre ces réformes, le Lesotho a bénéficié en 2018 d'une augmentation significative des recettes fiscales provenant de l'industrie minière et extractive, qui ont plus que doublé par rapport à l'année précédente (Lesotho Times, 2019[8]; Lesotho Times, 2018[9]). Ces facteurs ont contribué à la hausse de 1.9 point de pourcentage du ratio impôts/PIB entre 2017 et 2018.

Au Niger, le ratio impôts/PIB a augmenté de 1.6 point entre 2017 et 2018, principalement grâce aux recettes de TVA, qui ont progressé de 1.9 point. Les recettes issues de la TVA intérieure ont plus que doublé au cours de cette période. Dans le cadre de son budget 2018, le Niger a adopté des mesures visant à accroître le recouvrement des recettes intérieures après deux années de baisse des recettes fiscales (respectivement de 2.0 points et 1.1 point en 2016 et 2017). Le budget de 2018 comprenait une réforme de l'administration fiscale visant à renforcer les vérifications et les contrôles, l'introduction de nouvelles taxes et l'élargissement de l'assiette de la TVA pour certains secteurs des transports. Le Niger a aussi connu une croissance économique vigoureuse en 2018 (la croissance du PIB réel a atteint 6.5 % en 2018) (FMI, 2019[10]).

L'augmentation des recettes fiscales en Mauritanie entre 2017 et 2018 était principalement due à la hausse des recettes de la TVA (0.7 % du PIB) et d'autres taxes sur les biens et services (0.6 % du PIB). Bien que fortement tributaire du secteur minier, la Mauritanie a vu son PIB croître de 3.6 % en 2018 dans le secteur non extractif (agriculture, construction et télécommunications) (Direction générale du Trésor France, 2020[11]) (Jeune Afrique, 2019[12]).

Graphique 1.3. **Variations des ratios impôts/PIB (en points de pourcentage du PIB) observées entre 2017 et 2018 par principales rubriques d'impôts et par pays**

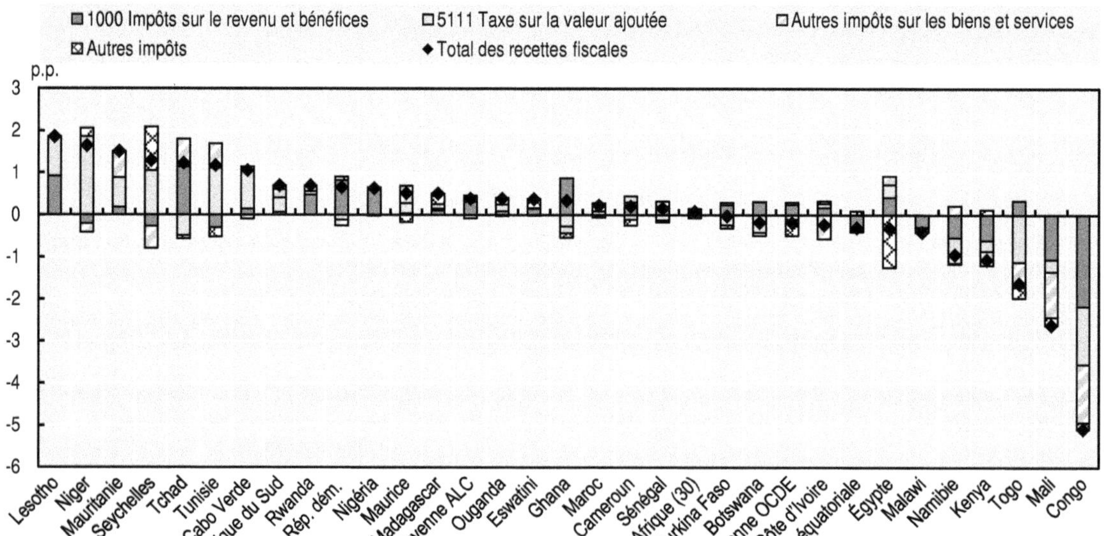

Notes : Les chiffres prennent en compte les recettes fiscales des administrations infranationales pour l'Afrique du Sud (projections pour 2018), l'Eswatini, le Maroc, Maurice, la Mauritanie et le Nigéria (recettes des États uniquement).
La moyenne Afrique (30) et les moyennes ALC (25 pays) et OCDE (36 pays) sont des moyennes non pondérées.
Il convient d'interpréter la moyenne Afrique (30) avec prudence car les données relatives aux cotisations de sécurité sociale ne sont pas disponibles ou ne sont que partielles pour quelques pays. Pour plus de précisions, se reporter aux tableaux par pays présentés dans le chapitre 5.
Source : Calculs des auteurs basés sur des données figurant dans « Statistiques des recettes publiques en Afrique : Tableaux comparatifs » (OCDE/ATAF/CUA, 2020[3]), *Statistiques fiscales de l'OCDE* (base de données) *https://doi.org/10.1787/7f54581d-fr*.
StatLink *https://doi.org/10.1787/888934182040*

Le Mali et la République du Congo sont les deux pays d'Afrique qui ont accusé les plus fortes baisses de leur ratio impôts/PIB entre 2017 et 2018. En République du Congo, le ratio a baissé de 5.1 points de pourcentage en 2018 sous l'effet du recul des recettes tirées de toutes les principales catégories d'impôts (2.2 points pour les impôts sur le revenu et 1.4 point pour la TVA et les autres impôts sur les biens et services). Le PIB nominal du Congo a connu une augmentation de 25 % en 2018 (sous l'effet du rétablissement des prix du pétrole), tandis que les recettes fiscales nominales se sont contractées de 22 % entre 2017 et 2018. Le recul des recettes fiscales en 2018, consécutif à la contraction de l'économie hors pétrole, représentait la troisième baisse annuelle consécutive. Le FMI a noté « qu'il existe un potentiel important d'augmentation des recettes non pétrolières à court terme étant donné l'importance des arriérés d'impôts et les mesures visant à réduire les exonérations fiscales » (FMI, 2020[13]).

Le Mali a connu la deuxième plus forte baisse de son ratio impôts/PIB entre 2017 et 2018, sous l'effet de reculs dans toutes les principales catégories d'impôts (1.1 points pour l'impôt sur le revenu, 0.3 point pour les recettes de TVA et 1.1 point pour les impôts sur les autres biens et services). La diminution des recettes fiscales en 2018 s'est produite après trois années consécutives d'augmentation des recettes fiscales imputable aux réformes de la politique et de l'administration fiscales (notamment à la hausse des taux d'imposition, à l'élargissement des bases d'imposition et au renforcement des administrations fiscales) (FMI, 2018[14]). La baisse des recettes fiscales en 2018 peut s'expliquer par divers facteurs, dont un ralentissement économique, une augmentation de la fraude due à l'insécurité croissante, des attaques terroristes récurrentes et des difficultés administratives[5].

Graphique 1.4. **Variations annuelles, entre 2017 et 2018, des recettes tirées des impôts sur le revenu et les bénéfices, par sous-rubrique et par pays (points de pourcentage du PIB)**

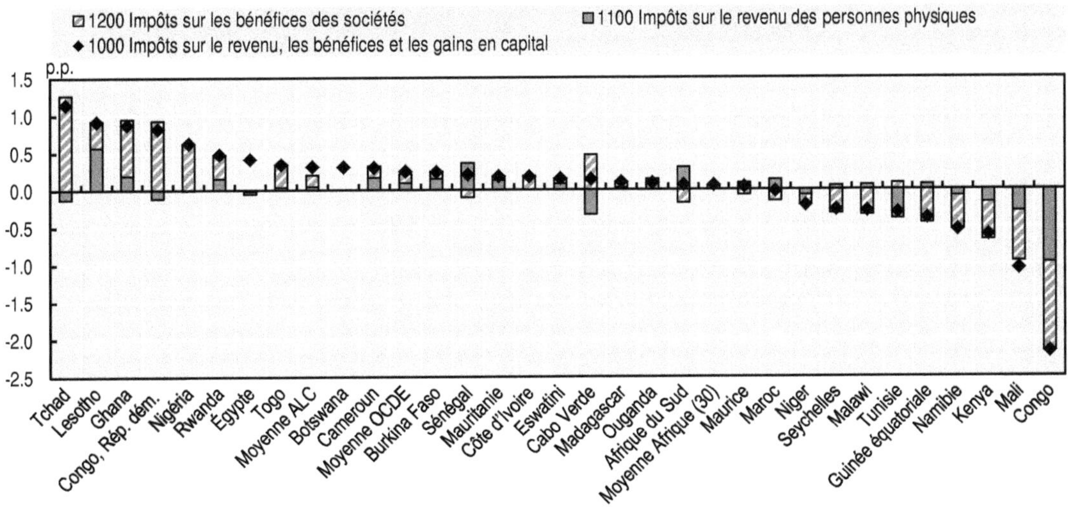

Notes : La moyenne Afrique (30) et les moyennes ALC (25 pays) et OCDE (36 pays) sont des moyennes non pondérées. La ventilation de certaines recettes de l'impôt sur le revenu entre la rubrique « 1100 Impôt sur le revenu des personnes physiques » et la rubrique « 1200 Impôt sur les bénéfices des sociétés » n'est pas disponible pour le Botswana et l'Égypte.
Source : Calculs des auteurs basés sur des données figurant dans « Statistiques des recettes publiques en Afrique : Tableaux comparatifs » (OCDE/ATAF/CUA, 2020[3]), *Statistiques fiscales de l'OCDE* (base de données) *https://doi.org/10.1787/7f54581d-fr*.

StatLink *https://doi.org/10.1787/888934182059*

Dans tous les pays, les variations des ratios impôts/PIB entre 2017 et 2018 ont été principalement dues à l'évolution des recettes de TVA et des impôts sur le revenu

(Graphique 1.3). L'évolution des recettes de TVA s'échelonnait entre une baisse de 1.4 point en République du Congo et une hausse de 1.9 point au Niger sur la même période ; en ce qui concerne l'impôt sur le revenu, les variations entre 2017 et 2018 allaient d'une baisse de 2.2 points en République du Congo et une hausse de 1.1 point au Tchad (Graphique 1.4). Les variations annuelles des recettes de l'impôt sur les sociétés (IS) ont été de moins grande ampleur dans la plupart des pays que celles des recettes de l'impôt sur le revenu des personnes physiques (IRPP) (moins de 0.1 % du PIB).

Évolution des ratios impôts/PIB depuis 2010

En 2018, le ratio impôts/PIB dans les 30 pays d'Afrique était supérieur de 1.4 point à son niveau de 2010. Par comparaison, les moyennes de la région ALC et de l'OCDE ont augmenté de respectivement 1.9 et 2.0 points entre 2010 et 2018. Le ratio moyen impôts/PIB des 30 pays africains a progressé régulièrement entre 2010 et 2014, avec une forte hausse de 0.7 point en 2011, traduisant une reprise après la crise financière mondiale. Depuis 2014, le ratio impôts/PIB dans les 30 pays d'Afrique est resté relativement stable entre 16.4% et 16.5 % du PIB (Graphique 1.5).

De nombreux pays africains ont été fortement touchés par la crise financière mondiale. En particulier, les pays tributaires des produits de base ont vu leur activité économique ralentir en raison de la baisse des prix de ces produits. Un certain nombre de pays ont mis en œuvre des mesures visant à stimuler l'activité économique. Le Maroc, par exemple, a réduit le taux de l'impôt sur les bénéfices des sociétés de 5 points de pourcentage en 2008 en vue d'améliorer la compétitivité de ses entreprises et de les aider à devenir plus résilientes.

Graphique 1.5. **Ratios moyens impôts/PIB pour l'Afrique (30), l'ALC et l'OCDE, 2000-18**

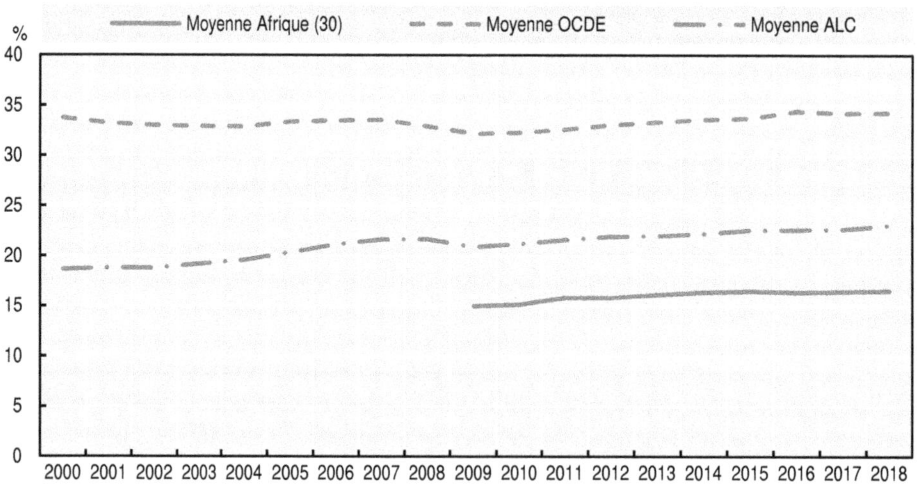

Notes : La moyenne Afrique (30) et les moyennes ALC (25 pays) et OCDE (36 pays) sont des moyennes non pondérées. Il convient d'interpréter la moyenne Afrique (30) avec prudence car les données relatives aux cotisations de sécurité sociale ne sont pas disponibles ou ne sont que partielles pour quelques pays. Pour plus de précisions, se reporter aux tableaux par pays présentés dans le chapitre 5. Les chiffres prennent en compte les recettes fiscales des administrations infranationales pour l'Afrique du Sud (pour la période 2002-18 ; projections pour 2018), l'Eswatini, le Maroc, Maurice, la Mauritanie et le Nigéria (recettes des États uniquement). La moyenne Afrique (30) est une estimation pour 2009 car les données ne sont pas disponibles pour le Nigéria et le Tchad. On ne dispose pas d'estimation antérieure à 2009 faute de données relatives à certains pays.

Source : Tableau 4.1 au chapitre 4 et « Recettes fiscales en Afrique : Tableaux comparatifs » (OCDE/ATAF/CUA, 2020[3]), *Statistiques fiscales de l'OCDE* (base de données)

StatLink https://doi.org/10.1787/888934182078

Encadré 1.2. **Convergence des ratios impôts/PIB en Afrique**

Le ratio moyen impôts/PIB de l'Afrique (30) est passé de 15.1 % en 2010 à 16.5 % en 2018. Vingt-trois des 30 pays couverts par la publication ont enregistré des augmentations de leurs ratios impôts/PIB au cours de cette période. Aussi, la question se pose de savoir si les ratios des pays se sont davantage concentrés autour de la moyenne au fil du temps, ou s'ils ont connu une évolution plus dispersée.

Le Graphique 1.6 illustre la dispersion des ratios impôts/PIB autour du ratio moyen de l'Afrique (30) à l'aide de différentes mesures[6], notamment l'écart-type, le coefficient de variation, la distance par rapport à la médiane et le coefficient de Gini. Toutes ces mesures révèlent des tendances similaires entre 2010 et 2018. La dispersion des ratios impôts/PIB autour de la moyenne Afrique (30) a diminué entre 2010 et 2013 et n'a cessé d'augmenter depuis 2014. Elle a atteint son plus haut niveau en 2018.

Graphique 1.6. **Dispersion des ratios impôts/PIB autour de la moyenne Afrique (30), 2010-2018**

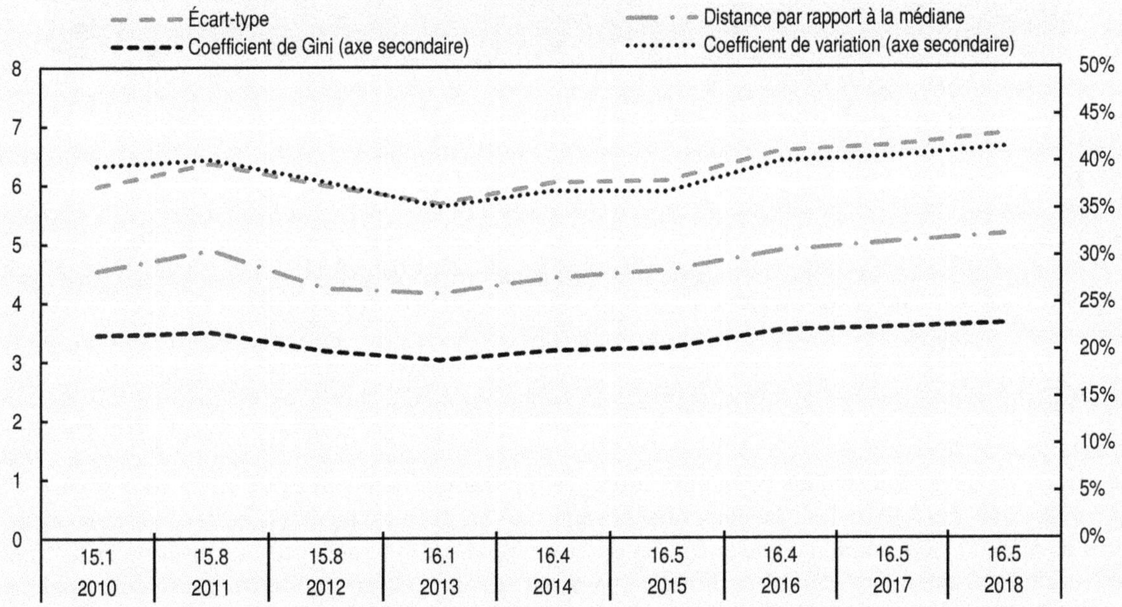

Note : Les chiffres sur l'axe horizontal (au-dessus des années) indiquent le ratio impôts/PIB moyen de l'Afrique (30) pour chaque année.
Source : Calculs des auteurs basés sur « Statistiques des recettes publiques en Afrique : Tableaux comparatifs » (OCDE/ATAF/CUA, 2020[3]), *Statistiques fiscales de l'OCDE* (base de données) *https://doi.org/10.1787/7f54581d-fr*.

StatLink https://doi.org/10.1787/888934182097

Le Graphique 1.7 illustre la différence entre les ratios impôts/PIB de chaque pays et la moyenne Afrique (30) en 2010 et 2018. Le groupe de gauche rassemble les pays dont les ratios impôts/PIB étaient plus éloignés de la moyenne Afrique (30) en 2018 qu'en 2010. Par exemple, le ratio impôts/PIB du Tchad était inférieur de 0.4 point à la moyenne Afrique (30) en 2010, et de 9.4 points en 2018, ce qui correspond à une divergence de 9 points pendant cette période. Au total, 15 pays (Afrique du Sud, Botswana, Cabo Verde, Côte d'Ivoire, Guinée équatoriale, Lesotho, Mali, Malawi, Nigéria, République démocratique du Congo, République du Congo, Seychelles, Tchad, Togo et Tunisie) étaient plus éloignés de la moyenne Afrique (30) en 2018 qu'en 2010.

Le groupe de droite réunit les pays dont les ratios impôts/PIB étaient plus proches de la moyenne Afrique (30) en 2018 qu'en 2010. Ils sont classés en fonction de leur degré croissant de proximité de la moyenne en 2018 par rapport à 2010. C'est en Mauritanie que l'on observe la plus forte réduction des écarts avec la moyenne Afrique (30) entre 2010 et 2018. Le ratio impôts/PIB de la Mauritanie était de 5.3 points inférieur à la moyenne Afrique (30) en 2010 et de 0.5 point inférieur en 2018. Au total, 15 pays (Burkina Faso, Cameroun, Égypte, Eswatini, Ghana, Kenya, Maroc, Maurice, Mauritanie, Niger, Namibie, Madagascar, Ouganda, Rwanda et Sénégal) étaient plus proches de la moyenne Afrique (30) en 2018 qu'en 2010.

Encadré 1.2. **Convergence des ratios impôts/PIB en Afrique** *(suite)*

Graphique 1.7. **Écarts entre les ratios impôts/PIB et le ratio moyen de l'Afrique (30) en 2010 et 2018 (points de pourcentage)**

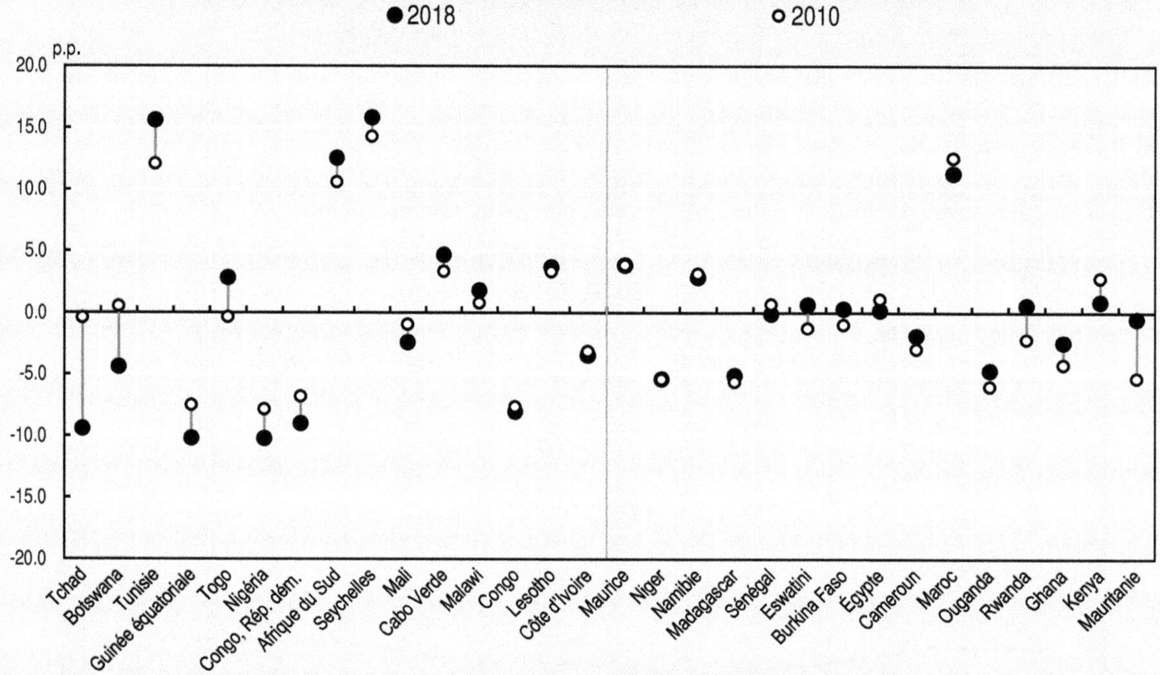

Source : Calculs des auteurs basés sur « Statistiques des recettes publiques en Afrique : Tableaux comparatifs » (OCDE/ATAF/CUA, 2020[3]), *Statistiques fiscales de l'OCDE* (base de données) *https://doi.org/10.1787/7f54581d-fr*.

StatLink *https://doi.org/10.1787/888934182116*

Le groupe de pays étudiés dans cette publication se répartissait de façon égale entre ceux dont le ratio impôts/PIB était plus proche de la moyenne Afrique (30) en 2018 qu'en 2010, et ceux dont le ratio en était plus éloigné. Cependant, la concentration de la moitié des pays autour de la moyenne en 2018 était inférieure à la dispersion de l'autre moitié des pays par rapport à la moyenne (respectivement de 1.6 et 2.2 points). Ce résultat reflète la dispersion plus prononcée en 2018, comme le montre le Graphique 1.6. On pourrait également en déduire que, même si le ratio moyen impôts/PIB de l'Afrique (30) a augmenté entre 2010 et 2018, on ne constate pas de tendance générale à une concentration des pays autour de cette moyenne plus élevée, ce qui donne à penser que les efforts de mobilisation des ressources intérieures restent fragmentés.

Les recettes fiscales d'autres régions ont également été affectées par la crise mondiale. Le ratio moyen impôts/PIB de la région ALC a reculé entre 2008 et 2010 de 0.5 point par an, tandis que la moyenne de l'OCDE a été la plus touchée par la crise entre 2007 et 2009, avec une baisse du ratio impôts/PIB de 1.4 point pendant cette période.

Les recettes de TVA ont le plus contribué à l'accroissement du ratio moyen impôts/PIB des pays d'Afrique (30) entre 2010 et 2018. Pendant cette période, ces recettes ont progressé de 1.0 point pour atteindre 5.0 % du PIB en 2018. La plus forte hausse annuelle s'est produite entre 2012 et 2013 (0.4 % du PIB) après l'introduction de la TVA en 2012 en République démocratique du Congo et en Eswatini.

Les impôts sur le revenu et les bénéfices étaient le deuxième principal moteur de l'augmentation du ratio moyen impôts/PIB des pays d'Afrique (30) entre 2010 et 2018. Au cours de cette période, les recettes tirées de ces impôts ont progressé de 0.3 point pour atteindre 6.2 % du PIB en 2018. Les recettes de l'impôt sur le revenu et les bénéfices ont atteint leur plus haut niveau en 2013 (6.5 % du PIB) et ont régulièrement diminué par la suite. Cette baisse est entièrement due aux recettes de l'IS qui ont diminué de 0,5 p.p. sur la période. La baisse des prix du pétrole et des produits miniers entre 2013 et 2016 pourrait avoir contribué à cette diminution.

Les recettes moyennes provenant des taxes sur les biens et services autres que la TVA, soit l'équivalent de 3.7 % du PIB en 2018, ont légèrement diminué en pourcentage du PIB depuis 2010 et sur une période plus longue avant cette date, en partie en raison de la baisse des recettes provenant des taxes sur les échanges. Ce déclin est associé à la libéralisation des échanges à l'échelle du continent, qui s'est traduite par l'abaissement des droits à l'importation, le rétrécissement de l'assiette des produits et services soumis à des droits d'accise et l'élimination des taxes sur les exportations. Les droits de douane seront de nouveau réduits dans le cadre de la Zone de libre-échange continentale africaine (ZLECAf) (voir le chapitre 3 « COVID-19 et ZLECAf : risques et opportunités pour l'avenir de la mobilisation des recettes intérieures en Afrique »).

Graphique 1.8. **Recettes tirées des impôts sur le revenu et les bénéfices, de la TVA et d'autres catégories d'impôts, en pourcentage du PIB, 2010-18**

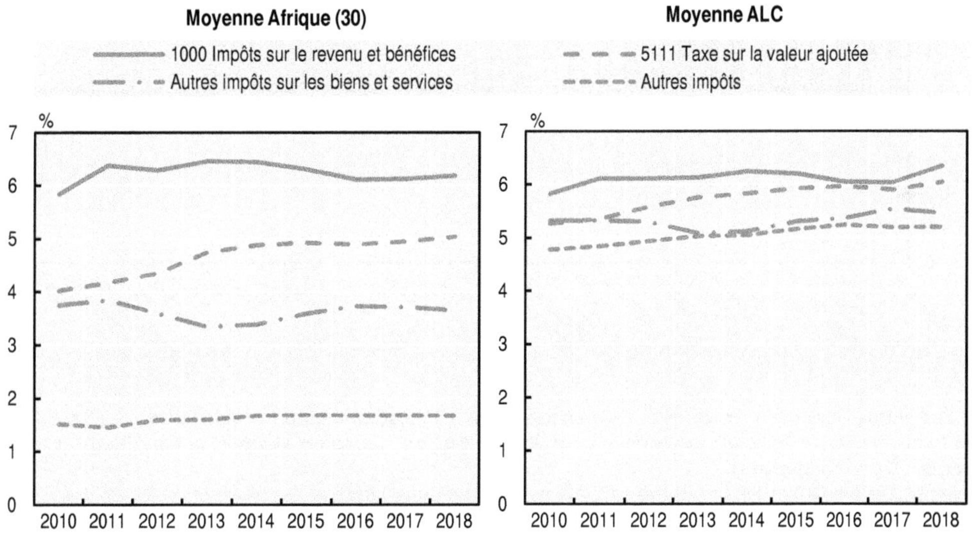

Note : Les chiffres pour la moyenne Afrique (30) prennent en compte les recettes fiscales des administrations infranationales pour l'Afrique du Sud (pour la période 2002-18 ; projections pour 2018), l'Eswatini, le Maroc, Maurice, la Mauritanie et le Nigéria (recettes des États uniquement).

Source : Calculs des auteurs basés sur des données figurant dans « Statistiques des recettes publiques en Afrique : Tableaux comparatifs » (OCDE/ATAF/CUA, 2020[3]), *Statistiques fiscales de l'OCDE* (base de données) *https://doi.org/10.1787/7f54581d-fr*.

StatLink https://doi.org/10.1787/888934182135

À l'instar de la moyenne Afrique (30), les recettes de TVA ont le plus contribué à l'accroissement du ratio moyen impôts/PIB des pays ALC entre 2010 et 2018, puisqu'elles ont progressé de 0.8 point pendant cette période. Les hausses des recettes provenant des cotisations de sécurité sociale (CSS) et de l'impôt sur le revenu (0.5 point dans les deux cas) ont également favorisé l'augmentation globale du ratio moyen impôts/PIB de la région ALC.

Ces hausses ont entraîné un écart marqué du niveau des CSS en pourcentage du PIB entre les deux régions : en 2018, les recettes provenant des CSS s'établissaient à 4.0 % du PIB dans la région ALC, contre 1.3 % en moyenne pour les pays d'Afrique (30).

Les ratios impôts/PIB ont augmenté dans 23 pays entre 2010 et 2018 et ont diminué dans 7 pays. La Mauritanie et la Tunisie ont enregistré les plus fortes hausses, de respectivement 6.3 et 4.9 points, alors que c'est au Tchad que la baisse a été la plus prononcée (7.3 points) (Graphique 1.9).

- L'augmentation du ratio impôts/PIB de la Mauritanie entre 2010 et 2018 est principalement due aux recettes tirées des taxes sur les biens et services ; les recettes de TVA ont augmenté de 1.7 point et celles provenant des autres taxes sur les biens et services ont progressé de 3.0 points (dont 2.3 points pour les droits de douane).
- L'augmentation du ratio impôts/PIB de la Tunisie entre 2010 et 2018 s'explique essentiellement par l'augmentation des recettes provenant des cotisations de sécurité sociale (2.0 points) et de la TVA (1.1 point).

Graphique 1.9. **Variation des ratios impôts/PIB entre 2010 et 2018 (points de pourcentage)**

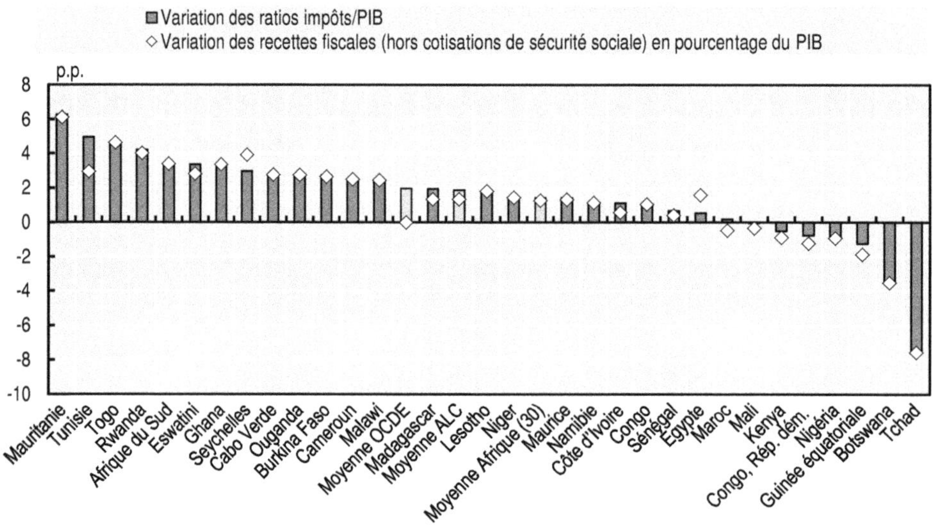

Notes : Les chiffres prennent en compte les recettes fiscales des administrations infranationales pour l'Afrique du Sud (pour la période 2002-18 ; projections pour 2018), l'Eswatini, le Maroc, Maurice, la Mauritanie et le Nigéria (recettes des États uniquement).

La moyenne Afrique (30) et les moyennes ALC (25 pays d'Amérique latine et Caraïbes) et OCDE (36 pays) sont des moyennes non pondérées.

Source : Tableaux 4.1 et 4.2 au chapitre 4 et « Statistiques des recettes publiques en Afrique : Tableaux comparatifs » (OCDE/ATAF/CUA, 2020[3]), *Statistiques fiscales de l'OCDE* (base de données) *https://doi.org/10.1787/7f54581d-fr.*

StatLink *https://doi.org/10.1787/888934182154*

Le Graphique 1.10 illustre les différences entre les ratios impôts/PIB des pays et le ratio moyen de l'Afrique (30) en 2010 et 2018. Quatre pays sont passés d'un niveau inférieur à la moyenne en 2010 à un niveau supérieur à la moyenne en 2018, tandis que deux autres ont connu l'évolution inverse. Les autres pays n'ont pas changé de position par rapport à la moyenne entre 2010 et 2018. L'Encadré 1.2 examine plus en détail la convergence des ratios impôts/PIB en Afrique.

Cinq pays (République du Congo, République démocratique du Congo, Guinée équatoriale, Nigéria, Tchad) affichaient des ratios impôts/PIB inférieurs de plus de 8 points à la moyenne Afrique (30) les deux années. L'économie de ces pays est étroitement dépendante des exportations de minerais et de pétrole, et ces pays peuvent tirer d'importantes recettes non fiscales des rentes et redevances pétrolières et minérales. Ces pays affichent souvent des ratios impôts/PIB faibles.

Le Togo est l'un des pays dont le ratio est passé d'un niveau inférieur à la moyenne en 2010 à un niveau supérieur en 2018. Le Togo se situait à un niveau inférieur de 0.4 point à la moyenne Afrique (30) en 2010, mais supérieur de 2.8 points en 2018. Le Togo a déployé d'importants efforts pour améliorer les procédures de ses trois administrations des finances publiques. Les mesures mises en œuvre entre 2010 et 2012 comprenaient des initiatives visant à suivre et à moderniser les systèmes d'information et de recouvrement de l'impôt, ainsi que des mesures de lutte contre la fraude fiscale. En 2014, le pays a par ailleurs regroupé ses services douaniers et fiscaux au sein d'une même administration, avec la création de l'Office togolais des recettes (OTR). En 2019, le FMI a pris acte des réformes plus récentes de l'administration fiscale visant à améliorer le recouvrement des recettes. Ces mesures ont notamment consisté à introduire des numéros d'identification fiscale, à réduire le nombre d'exonérations fiscales et à établir des contrôles pour combattre la corruption. Des initiatives continuent d'être mises en œuvre en vue d'améliorer la discipline fiscale des contribuables, ce qui pourrait avoir un effet positif sur le recouvrement des recettes (FMI, 2019[15]).

Graphique 1.10. **Écarts des ratios impôts/PIB par rapport à la moyenne Afrique entre 2010 et 2018 (points de pourcentage)**

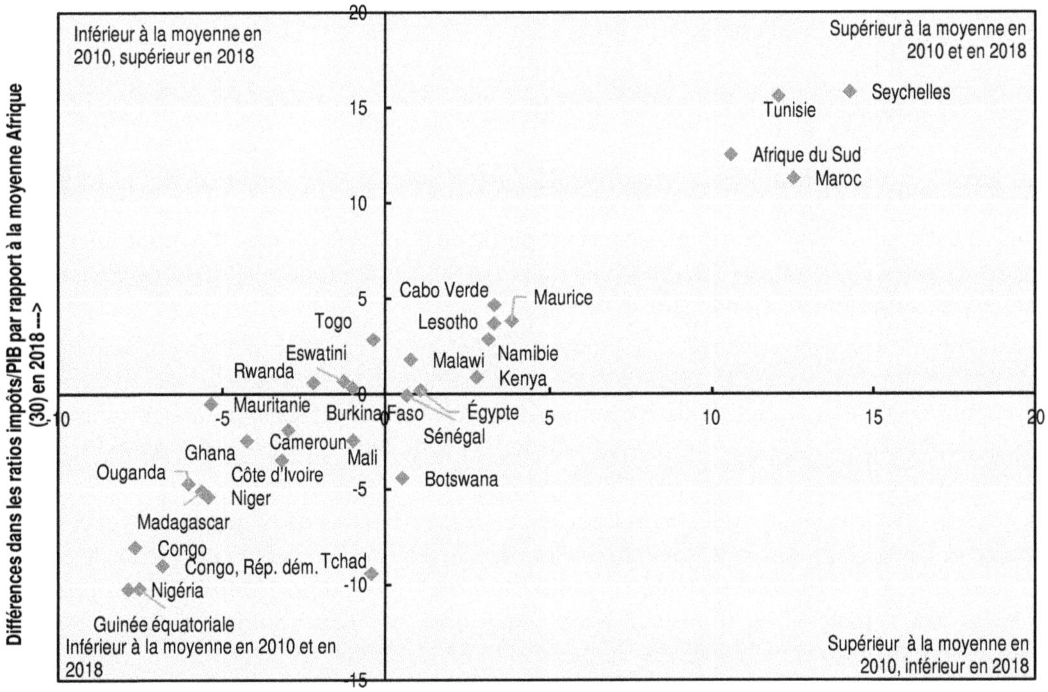

Note : Les chiffres prennent en compte les recettes fiscales des administrations infranationales pour l'Afrique du Sud (projections pour 2018), l'Eswatini, le Maroc, Maurice, la Mauritanie et le Nigéria (recettes des États uniquement).
Source : Calculs des auteurs basés sur « Statistiques des recettes publiques en Afrique : Tableaux comparatifs » (OCDE/ATAF/CUA, 2020[3]), *Statistiques fiscales de l'OCDE* (base de données) *https://doi.org/10.1787/7f54581d-fr*.

StatLink *https://doi.org/10.1787/888934182173*

Graphique 1.11. **Variation des ratios impôts/PIB par principales rubriques d'impôt entre 2010 et 2018 et par pays (points de pourcentage)**

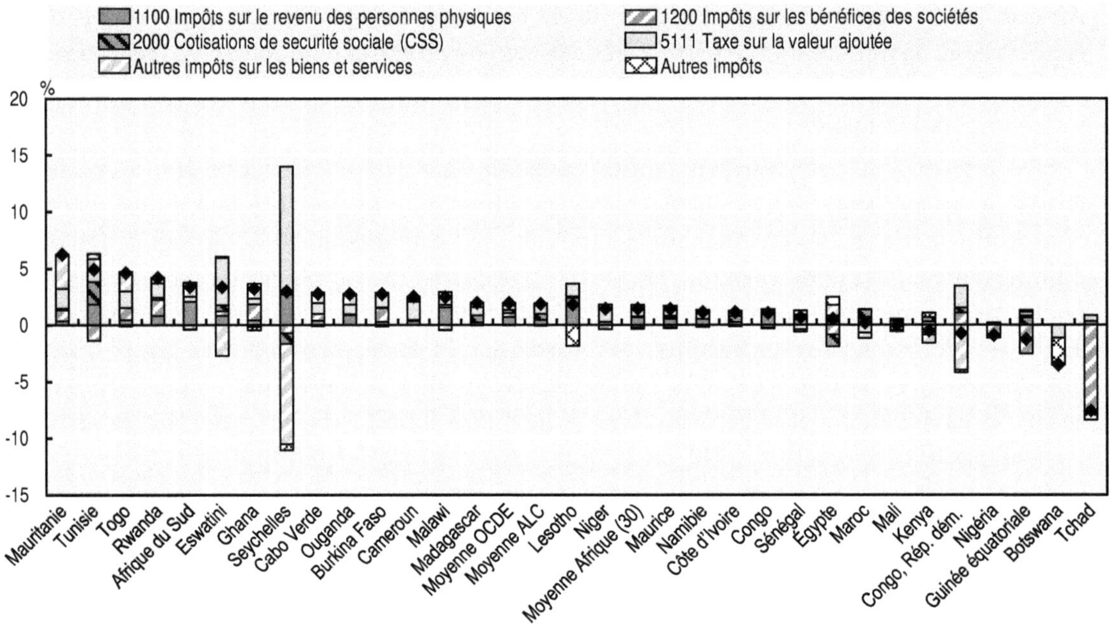

Notes : Les chiffres prennent en compte les recettes fiscales des administrations infranationales pour l'Afrique du Sud (projections pour 2018), l'Eswatini, le Maroc, Maurice, la Mauritanie, et le Nigéria (recettes des États uniquement).

La moyenne Afrique (30) et les moyennes ALC (25 pays d'Amérique latine et Caraïbes) et OCDE (36 pays) sont des moyennes non pondérées.

Source : Calculs des auteurs basés sur « Statistiques des recettes publiques en Afrique : Tableaux comparatifs » (OCDE/ATAF/CUA, 2020[3]), *Statistiques fiscales de l'OCDE* (base de données) *https://doi.org/10.1787/7f54581d-fr*.

StatLink https://doi.org/10.1787/888934182192

Encadré 1.3. **Variations des ratios impôts/PIB dans les pays membres de la SACU**

Cinq des 30 pays inclus dans cette publication font partie de l'Union douanière d'Afrique australe (SACU) : Afrique du Sud, Botswana, Eswatini, Lesotho et Namibie. La SACU a été fondée en 1910, ce qui en fait l'union douanière la plus ancienne au monde (SACU, 2020[16]).

En 2018, la moyenne des pays de la SACU (la moyenne SACU) était supérieure d'environ 3 points à celle de l'Afrique (30) et s'élevait à 19.6%. L'évolution du ratio impôts/PIB entre 2010 et 2018 dans les pays de la SACU a été, en moyenne, similaire à celle de la moyenne Afrique (30) au cours de la même période. Alors que le ratio moyen impôts/PIB de l'Afrique (30) a progressé de 15.1 % du PIB en 2010 à 16.5 % en 2018, la moyenne SACU est passée de 18.4 % du PIB en 2010 à 19.6 % en 2018.

Les recettes de TVA ont été le principal moteur de la progression des deux moyennes au cours de cette période, avec une augmentation de 1.0 point dans les deux cas. L'Afrique du Sud, l'Eswatini, le Lesotho et la Namibie ont accru leur ratio impôts/PIB de 1.1 point (Namibie) à 3.4 points (Afrique du Sud), tandis que le ratio du Botswana a reculé de 3.5 points sur la même période, sous l'effet d'un repli des recettes tirées de l'impôt sur le revenu et les bénéfices (2.4 points) et de la TVA (1.1 point).

Encadré 1.3. **Variations des ratios impôts/PIB dans les pays membres de la SACU** *(suite)*

Graphique 1.12. **Ratios impôts/PIB dans les pays de la SACU, 2010 à 2018**

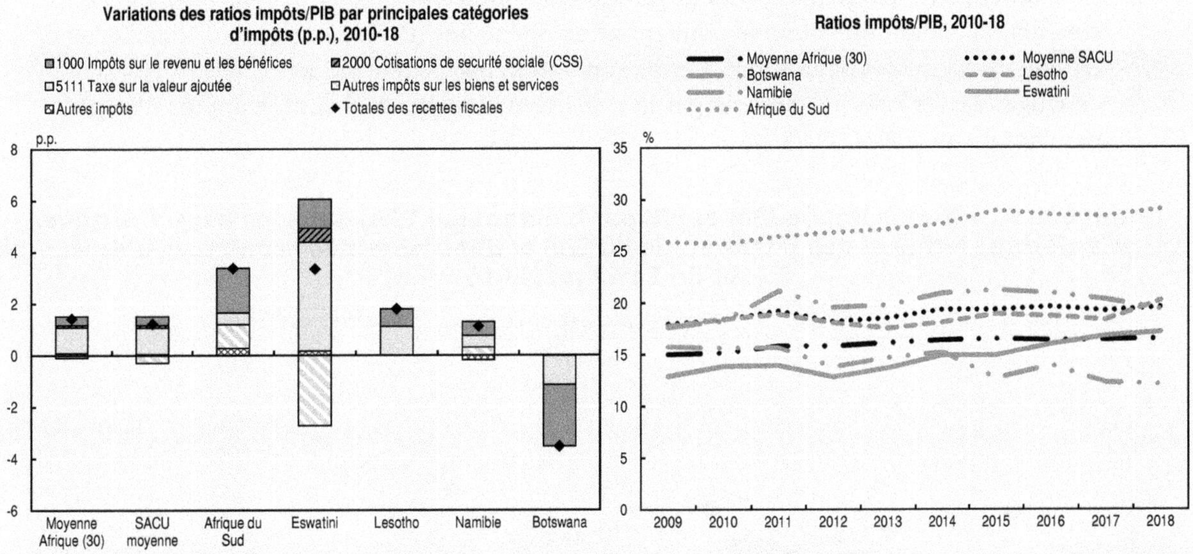

Source : Calculs des auteurs basés sur « Statistiques des recettes publiques en Afrique : Tableaux comparatifs » (OCDE/ATAF/CUA, 2020[3]), *Statistiques fiscales de l'OCDE* (base de données) *https://doi.org/10.1787/7f54581d-fr*.

StatLink *https://doi.org/10.1787/888934182211*

Facteurs ayant un effet sur les ratios impôts/PIB

Les ratios impôts/PIB sont influencés par divers facteurs de portée nationale et internationale. Sur le plan national, des caractéristiques macroéconomiques telles que la diversification d'une économie, l'importance de l'agriculture, les dotations en ressources, l'ouverture aux échanges et la taille de l'économie informelle peuvent agir sur les ratios impôts/PIB. Le pouvoir de l'administration fiscale, le niveau de corruption et le civisme fiscal (le consentement à l'impôt) sont aussi étroitement liés au niveau des recettes fiscales (OCDE, 2015[17]) (OCDE, 2019[18]). L'emplacement géographique peut exercer une influence sur les ratios impôts/PIB: par exemple, les pays enclavés peuvent plus difficilement taxer les biens et services au port d'entrée que les pays ayant un accès à la mer. Enfin, des facteurs internationaux, y compris les politiques fiscales d'autres pays, peuvent se répercuter sur les ratios impôts/PIB.

Les ratios impôts/PIB sont habituellement supérieurs dans les pays à haut revenu : en général, les pays de l'OCDE collectent des recettes fiscales plus importantes que les pays hors OCDE, en pourcentage du PIB. La plupart des 30 pays couverts dans cette publication affichent des niveaux de revenu par habitant et des ratios impôts/PIB plus bas que les pays de l'OCDE et de la région ALC (Graphique 1.13). Les niveaux de PIB par habitant varient davantage entre les pays africains qu'entre les pays ALC et les pays de l'OCDE.

En revanche, dans de nombreuses études, un pourcentage plus élevé du PIB généré par l'agriculture est associé à un ratio impôts/PIB plus faible (Addison; Levin, 2012[22]) (Profeta, S; Scabrosetti, S., 2010[23]). Cela traduit le fait que, dans de nombreux pays, l'agriculture est un secteur difficile à taxer :

- Le secteur agricole en Afrique est moins taxé en raison de l'ampleur de l'activité informelle et du faible degré de monétisation (BAfD/OCDE/CEA, 2010[24]).
- Le secteur agricole bénéficie souvent de nombreuses exemptions d'impôt. Au Ghana, les exonérations fiscales dépendent du type de culture et les agriculteurs peuvent en bénéficier pendant une période pouvant atteindre 10 ans (Grey, 2020[25]) ; au Nigéria, les entreprises agricoles bénéficient d'une exonération fiscale de cinq ans (PWC, 2020[26]) et en Ouganda, les revenus générés par la transformation agricole sont exonérés d'impôt pendant un an (KPMG, 2020[27]).

Graphique 1.13. **Ratios impôts/PIB et PIB par habitant (en PPA) dans les pays d'Afrique, d'Amérique latine et des Caraïbes, de l'OCDE et dans certaines économies d'Asie et du Pacifique, 2018**

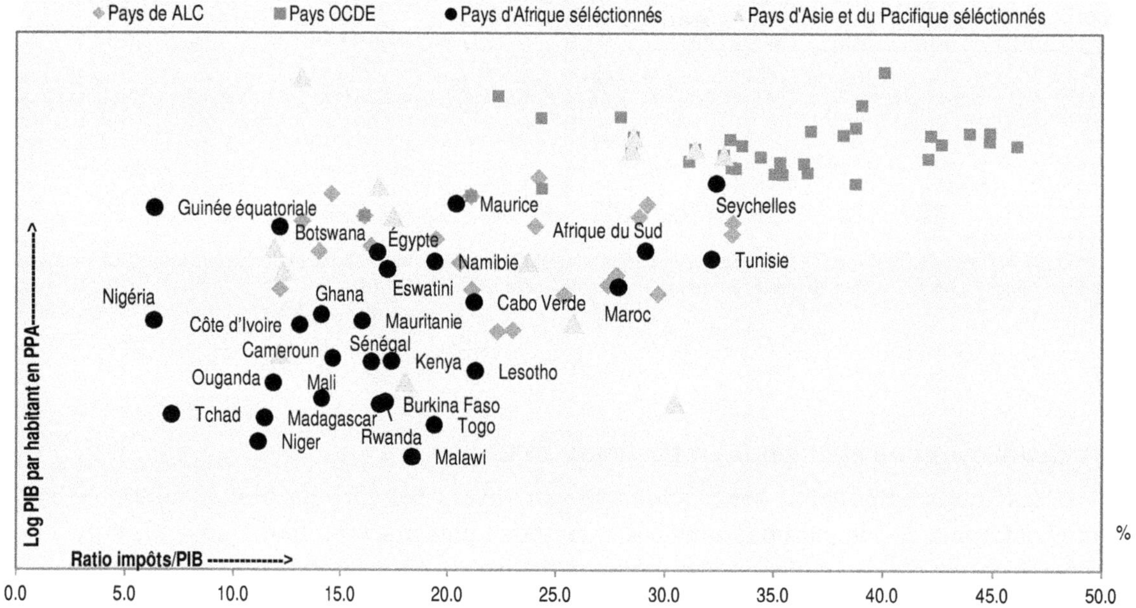

Note : L'axe y est sur une échelle logarithmique. La parité de pouvoir d'achat (PPA) entre deux pays est le taux auquel la monnaie d'un pays doit être convertie dans celle d'un second pays pour qu'un volume donné de monnaie du premier pays permette d'acheter la même quantité de biens et de services dans chaque pays. Le taux de conversion PPA est le taux utilisé pour convertir une monnaie nationale en dollar international courant. Un dollar international a le même pouvoir d'achat que le dollar US aux États-Unis. Un dollar international est une monnaie hypothétique utilisée comme moyen pour convertir et comparer les coûts d'un pays à l'autre grâce à un point de référence commun, le dollar US (définitions issues de (FMI, 2019[19])) et (OMS, 2015[20]).

Source : (FMI, 2020[21]) pour les chiffres du PIB par habitant. Les ratios impôts/PIB proviennent des éditions régionales des Statistiques des recettes publiques.

StatLink https://doi.org/10.1787/888934182230

Les pays qui tirent des recettes substantielles des exportations de pétrole ont souvent un faible ratio impôts/PIB. Les pays qui tirent d'importantes recettes de leurs ressources naturelles ont généralement recours à des formes d'imposition moins contraignantes politiquement (BAfD/OCDE/CEA, 2010[24]), et leurs bases d'imposition sont souvent relativement étroites. Les trois pays (la République du Congo, la Guinée équatoriale et le Tchad) qui ont perçu des recettes de la production pétrolière représentant plus de 15 % de leur PIB, affichaient tous des ratios impôts/PIB faibles (inférieurs à 9% du PIB). Les recettes provenant des rentes et redevances pétrolières, qui ne sont pas considérées comme des recettes fiscales, sont examinées plus en détail au chapitre 2.

Comme indiqué précédemment, le civisme fiscal peut influer sur le niveau des recettes fiscales. L'OCDE a analysé le civisme fiscal dans différentes régions et examiné ses déterminants (OCDE, 2019[18]). S'agissant des particuliers, l'attachement à la démocratie, la foi, le niveau d'études et la confiance dans l'administration sont autant de facteurs qui influent sur le civisme fiscal. L'amélioration perçue de la qualité de l'administration fiscale, la simplification du paiement de l'impôt et l'offre de services publics de qualité semblent tous exercer une influence sur le civisme fiscal. Le genre peut aussi jouer un rôle : alors que dans la plupart des régions le civisme fiscal est plus élevé chez les femmes que chez les hommes, c'est l'inverse en Afrique. S'agissant des entreprises, l'étude menée par l'OCDE a recours à des données relatives à la sécurité juridique en matière fiscale concernant les entreprises multinationales (EMN)[7]. Dans les pays en développement, y compris en Afrique, la sécurité juridique en matière fiscale semble se répercuter sur l'activité économique, entraînant une modification de la structure des activités, une augmentation des coûts et des changements de décision en matière d'investissement. Même s'il existe des variations d'une région à l'autre, la fiscalité internationale et les relations entre les autorités et les entreprises sont des préoccupations communes à tous les pays en développement. En Afrique, la clarté de la législation et la sécurité juridique en matière fiscale représentent les principaux sujets de préoccupation (OCDE, 2019[18]).

Structures fiscales

La structure fiscale d'un pays mesure la composition de ses recettes fiscales en fonction des différents types d'impôts. Il s'agit là d'un indicateur important, car différents impôts ont différents effets économiques et sociaux. La composition des impôts dans les 30 pays étudiés reflète des différences concernant leurs choix politiques, leurs structures et situations économiques, les capacités de leur administration fiscale et d'autres facteurs historiques. Les pays peuvent être divisés en trois grands groupes en fonction de leur principale source de recettes : TVA, autres impôts sur les biens et services et impôts sur le revenu.

Évolution des structures fiscales, 2010-2018

Depuis 2010, la structure fiscale moyenne des pays étudiés a opéré un transfert vers les recettes de l'IRPP et de la TVA, au détriment des impôts sur les biens et services autres que la TVA. Les hausses intervenues dans ces deux catégories d'impôts expliquent également pour beaucoup l'augmentation globale du ratio impôts/PIB moyen au cours de la période. Les recettes tirées de l'IRPP ont progressé de 0.7 point, tandis que celles issues de la TVA ont augmenté de 1.0 point entre 2010 et 2018, atteignant respectivement 3.1 % et 5 % du PIB en 2018 (Graphique 1.14).

L'augmentation de la TVA et de l'IRPP en pourcentage du PIB a également contribué à accroître la part de ces deux impôts dans les recettes fiscales totales. La fraction des recettes fiscales provenant de la TVA a crû de 2.8 point pour s'établir à 29.7 % du total en 2018, ce qui traduit la poursuite d'une tendance durable à l'augmentation des recettes de TVA au détriment de celles d'autres impôts sur des biens et services (y compris de la taxe sur les ventes, des accises et des impôts sur des biens et services spécifiques). De même, la part des recettes issues de l'IRPP a augmenté de 2.1 points au cours de cette période, atteignant 17.5 % des recettes fiscales totales en 2018 alors que la part des recettes provenant de l'IS a diminué (2.3 points). Cependant la part des recettes de l'IRPP reste toujours inférieure à celle des recettes de l'IS (19.2 % des recettes fiscales totales en 2018.

Graphique 1.14. **Structure fiscale, moyenne Afrique (30) en pourcentage du total des recettes fiscales et en pourcentage du PIB, 2010 et 2018**

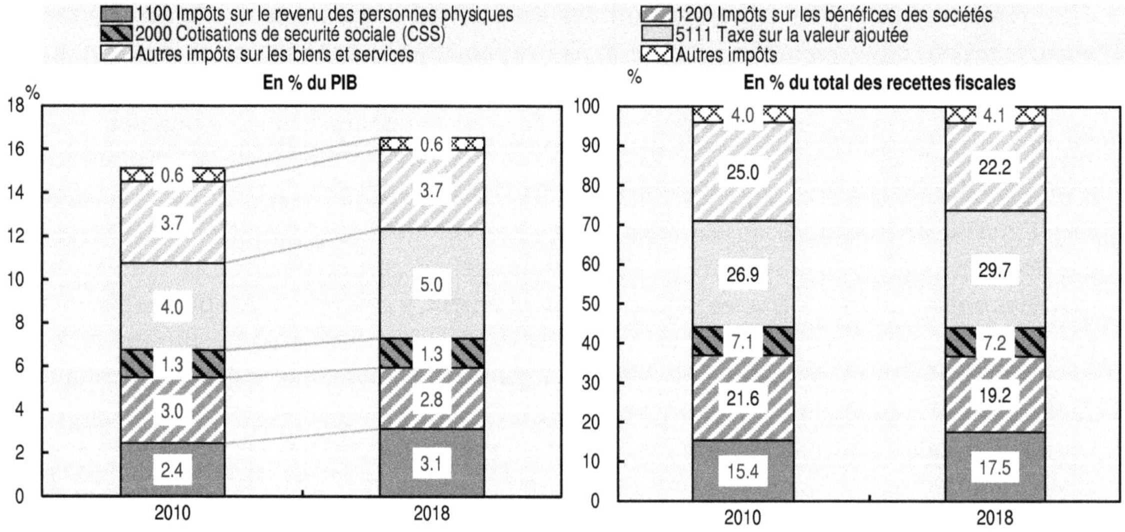

Note : La moyenne Afrique (30) et les moyennes ALC (25 pays d'Amérique latine et Caraïbes) et OCDE (36 pays) sont des moyennes non pondérées.

La moyenne Afrique (30) doit être interprétée avec précaution car des données relatives aux cotisations de sécurité sociale sont indisponibles ou incomplètes pour quelques pays. Pour plus de précisions, se reporter aux tableaux par pays présentés dans le chapitre 5.

Les chiffres prennent en compte les recettes fiscales des administrations infranationales pour l'Afrique du Sud (pour la période 2002-18 ; projections pour 2018), l'Eswatini, le Maroc, Maurice, la Mauritanie et le Nigéria (recettes des États uniquement).

Source : Calculs des auteurs basés sur des données figurant dans « Statistiques des recettes publiques en Afrique : Tableaux comparatifs » (OCDE/ATAF/CUA, 2020[3]), *Statistiques fiscales de l'OCDE* (base de données) *https://doi.org/10.1787/7f54581d-fr*.

StatLink *https://doi.org/10.1787/888934182249*

Structures fiscales en 2018

En 2018, les recettes de TVA ont généré la majeure partie des recettes fiscales dans les pays couverts par cette publication (Graphique 1.15). Elles ont représenté 29.7 % du total des recettes fiscales, soit un pourcentage comparable à la moyenne ALC (27.8 %) et environ 10 points de plus que la moyenne de l'OCDE (20.2 %, chiffre de 2017). Toutefois, compte tenu du fait que le ratio moyen impôts/PIB est plus faible, les recettes de TVA pour la moyenne Afrique (30) sont inférieures aux moyennes ALC et OCDE lorsqu'elles sont mesurées en pourcentage du PIB [5 % du PIB en Afrique contre 6 % dans la région ALC et 6.8 % dans la zone OCDE (chiffre de 2017)].

La part moyenne des recettes de l'IS dans le total des recettes fiscales en Afrique s'élevait à 19.2 % en 2018, soit davantage que dans la région ALC et la zone OCDE (respectivement 15.5 % et 9.3 %). En pourcentage du PIB, les parts moyennes des recettes de l'IS pour les 30 pays d'Afrique et pour l'OCDE étaient similaires [respectivement 2.8 % et 3.0 % du PIB (chiffre de 2017)] ; ces pourcentages sont néanmoins inférieurs à la moyenne ALC de 3.5 % du PIB en 2018 (Graphique 1.15).

En revanche, la part moyenne, dans les 30 pays d'Afrique, des recettes de l'impôt sur le revenu des personnes physiques (17.5 % du total des recettes) était inférieure à la moyenne de l'OCDE de 23.9 % (chiffre de 2017) mais supérieure à la moyenne ALC (9.6 %). En pourcentage du PIB, le niveau moyen des recettes de l'IRPP dans la zone OCDE était plus de deux fois supérieur à la moyenne des 30 pays d'Afrique.

Graphique 1.15. **Structure fiscale pour la moyenne Afrique (30), ALC et OCDE en pourcentage du total des recettes fiscales et du PIB, 2018**

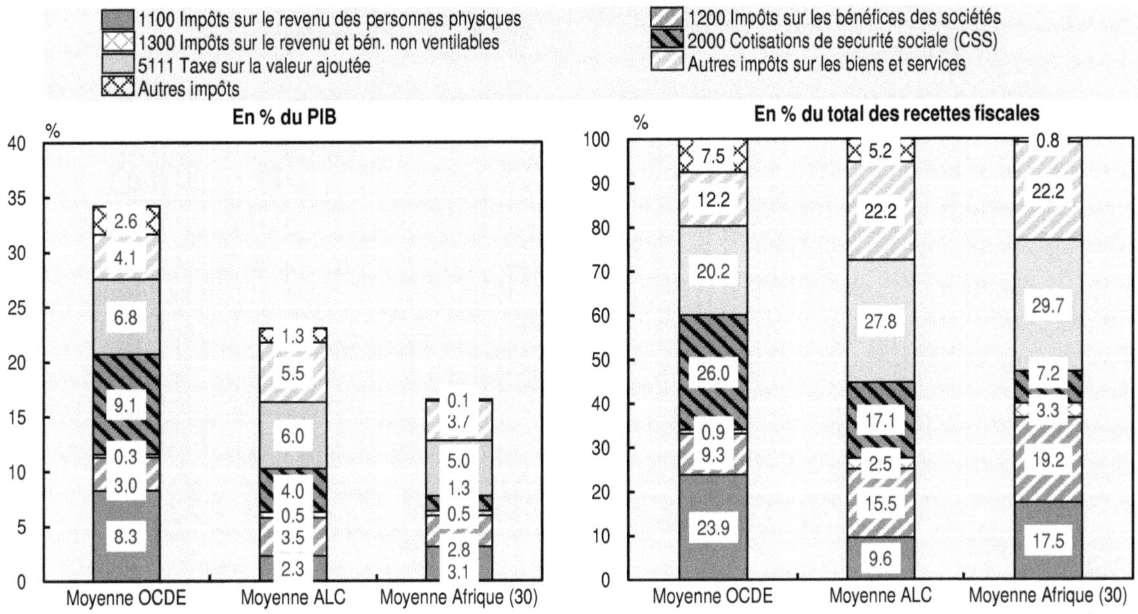

Notes : La moyenne Afrique (30) et les moyennes ALC (25 pays d'Amérique latine et Caraïbes) et OCDE (36 pays) sont des moyennes non pondérées. Il convient d'interpréter la moyenne Afrique (30) avec prudence car les données relatives aux cotisations de sécurité sociale ne sont pas disponibles ou ne sont que partielles pour quelques pays. Pour plus de précisions, se reporter aux tableaux par pays présentés dans le chapitre 5. Les chiffres prennent en compte les recettes fiscales des administrations infranationales pour l'Afrique du Sud (projections pour 2018), l'Eswatini, le Maroc, Maurice, la Mauritanie et le Nigéria (recettes des États uniquement).
Les données concernant l'OCDE portent sur l'année 2017 car les données de 2018 ne sont pas disponibles.
Source : Calculs des auteurs basés sur des données figurant dans « Statistiques des recettes publiques en Afrique : Tableaux comparatifs » (OCDE/ATAF/CUA, 2020[3]), *Statistiques fiscales de l'OCDE* (base de données) *https://doi.org/10.1787/7f54581d-fr*.

StatLink https://doi.org/10.1787/888934182268

Le Graphique 1.16 illustre, pour tous les pays couverts dans cette publication, la ventilation des recettes fiscales entre impôts sur le revenu (personnes physiques et sociétés), cotisations de sécurité sociale et impôts sur les biens et services (y compris la TVA ainsi que d'autres impôts sur les biens et services).

Les impôts sur les biens et services constituaient la principale source de recettes fiscales pour 21 des 30 pays étudiés (les deux premiers groupes de pays représentés dans le Graphique 1.16). Dans ces pays, ils ont généré de 39.7 % des recettes fiscales en Tunisie à 76.3 % des recettes fiscales au Togo. La TVA y représentait le principal poste de recettes tirées des impôts sur les biens et services, sauf en Côte d'Ivoire, en Égypte, au Ghana, au Kenya, en Mauritanie, en Ouganda et en République du Congo.

Dans neuf pays (Afrique du Sud, Botswana, Eswatini, Guinée équatoriale, Lesotho, Namibie, Nigéria, République démocratique du Congo, Tchad), la plus grande partie des recettes fiscales provient des impôts sur le revenu et les bénéfices. En effet, ils représentaient une part plus importante des recettes fiscales totales que les moyennes OCDE et ALC, allant de 44.4 % des recettes totales en République démocratique du Congo à 66.8 % en Guinée équatoriale.

L'importance des cotisations de sécurité sociale[8] dans le total des recettes fiscales varie considérablement entre les 30 pays étudiés. La part des cotisations de sécurité sociale dans le total des recettes fiscales est la plus élevée au Maroc (19.8 %) et en Tunisie (29.1 %) ; dans les autres pays, elle s'échelonne entre moins de 0.2 % au Cabo Verde à environ 14.1 % en Eswatini.

Graphique 1.16. **Structure fiscale, par pays, 2018**

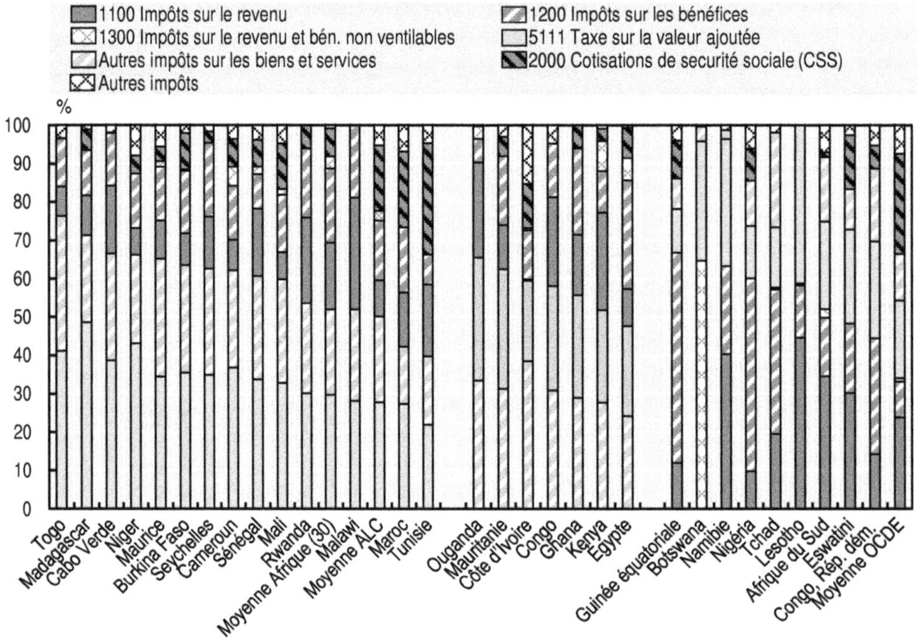

Note : Les chiffres prennent en compte les recettes fiscales des administrations infranationales pour l'Afrique du Sud (pour la période 2002-18 ; projections pour 2018), l'Eswatini, le Maroc, Maurice, la Mauritanie et le Nigéria (recettes des États uniquement). La moyenne Afrique (30) et les moyennes ALC (25 pays d'Amérique latine et Caraïbes) et OCDE (36 pays) sont des moyennes non pondérées.

Il convient d'interpréter la moyenne Afrique (30) avec prudence car les données relatives aux cotisations de sécurité sociale ne sont pas disponibles ou ne sont que partielles pour quelques pays. Pour plus de précisions, se reporter aux tableaux par pays présentés dans le chapitre 5.

Botswana : La ventilation des recettes tirées des impôts sur le revenu et sur les bénéfices entre la rubrique « 1100 Impôt sur le revenu des personnes physiques » et la rubrique « 1200 Impôt sur les bénéfices des sociétés » n'est pas disponible.

Moyenne OCDE : Les données portent sur l'année 2017 car les données de 2018 ne sont pas disponibles.

Source : Calculs des auteurs basés sur des données figurant dans « Statistiques des recettes publiques en Afrique : Tableaux comparatifs » (OCDE/ATAF/CUA, 2020[3]), *Statistiques fiscales de l'OCDE* (base de données) *https://doi.org/10.1787/7f54581d-fr*.

StatLink https://doi.org/10.1787/888934182287

Cette hétérogénéité reflète la diversité des régimes de sécurité sociale et des taux de cotisation, car de nombreux pays utilisent des systèmes différents pour financer les prestations de sécurité sociale. Par exemple, les cotisations de sécurité sociale en Afrique du Sud financent le Fonds d'assurance chômage, tandis que d'autres prestations, telles que les programmes d'aide sociale couvrant la vieillesse, la maladie et la maternité, sont financées par les recettes générales. À l'inverse, les régimes de sécurité sociale marocain et tunisien sont calqués sur le système français et couvrent un large éventail de prestations, y compris la vieillesse, l'incapacité, la maladie, la maternité, les accidents du travail (Tunisie), le chômage (Maroc) et les allocations familiales (SSA, 2015[28]).

Ratio des recettes de TVA

Cette section examine le ratio des recettes de TVA (RRT) dans les pays de cette publication[9]. Le RRT « mesure l'écart entre les recettes de TVA effectivement collectées et celles qui auraient théoriquement pu être obtenues dans l'hypothèse où l'on aurait appliqué le taux normal à la totalité de la base d'imposition potentielle dans le cadre d'un régime de TVA 'pur' et où la totalité de ces recettes aurait été perçue » (OCDE, 2018[29]). Il correspond au rapport entre les recettes de TVA effectives et le produit de la consommation finale (net des recettes de TVA) et du taux normal de TVA. La formule de calcul est la suivante :

$$\frac{\text{Recettes de TVA}}{\text{(dépenses de consommation finale-recettes de TVA).taux normal de TVA}}$$

Cet indicateur donne un aperçu de la part des recettes de TVA non recouvrées sous l'effet des exemptions, des taux réduits, des pratiques de fraude et d'optimisation fiscales, ainsi que des défaillances de l'administration fiscale. Néanmoins, cet indicateur doit être interprété avec prudence en se référant aux caractéristiques fondamentales du système de TVA propre à chaque pays, car un RRT élevé peut résulter d'effets de cascade (lorsque l'exemption intervient très en amont dans la chaîne d'approvisionnement, par exemple) ou du non-remboursement de la TVA acquittée sur les intrants. D'autres facteurs peuvent également gonfler le ratio, par exemple lorsque les règles relatives au lieu d'imposition des ventes internationales dérogent au principe de destination, ou le niveau de développement de l'économie informelle dans un pays. Par exemple, en Afrique, de nombreux travailleurs opèrent dans le secteur informel. N'étant pas déclarés à des fins fiscales, ils ne bénéficient pas de remboursements de TVA sur leurs intrants, tandis que les travailleurs et les entreprises du secteur formel peuvent y prétendre (BAfD/OCDE/PNUD, 2016[30]).

Graphique 1.17. **Ratio des recettes de TVA par pays, 2018**

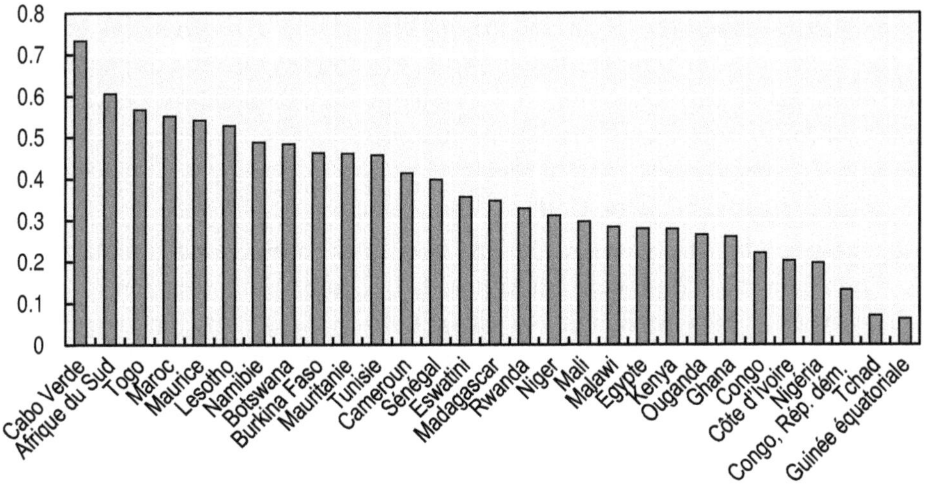

Note : Les Seychelles sont exclues du fait de l'indisponibilité de certaines données.
Source : Les taux de TVA proviennent des *Tendances des impôts sur la consommation* (OCDE, 2018[29]) des sites web de Trading Economics et de Deloitte, les chiffres relatifs aux dépenses de consommation finale de la base de données des *Perspectives de l'économie mondiale* du FMI (FMI, 2020[4]) et les recettes de TVA des tableaux par pays.
StatLink https://doi.org/10.1787/888934182306

Le Graphique 1.17 rend compte des RRT des pays africains couverts par cette publication. En 2018, le Cabo Verde, l'Afrique du Sud et le Togo enregistraient les RRT les plus élevés (respectivement 0.73, 0.61, et 0.57), tandis que la République démocratique du Congo, le Tchad et la Guinée équatoriale affichaient les RRT les plus bas (respectivement 0.13, 0.07 et 0.06).

- Le RRT élevé en Afrique du Sud peut s'expliquer par certaines caractéristiques de son système de TVA. Les exemptions de TVA sont limitées et la gamme des produits et services exonérés de TVA est restreinte, contrairement à de nombreux autres pays d'Afrique. En outre, le seuil d'enregistrement à la TVA y est élevé, ce qui permet à l'administration fiscale sud-africaine d'axer ses efforts sur les grandes entreprises (Cnossen, 2015[31]).

- Le Cabo Verde applique un taux de TVA de 15 %, et a adopté diverses réformes fiscales entre 2013 et 2015 en vue d'augmenter les recettes de la TVA (et des impôts sur les sociétés). Il a également automatisé le recouvrement des recettes de TVA en décembre 2017 (CNUCED, 2018[32]).
- Le Togo applique un taux unique de TVA de 18 % à l'ensemble des activités et des produits, sauf ceux exemptés. Aussi, aucun taux réduit n'y a cours. De plus, son RRT élevé s'explique en partie par les améliorations apportées à son administration fiscale depuis 2010, qui ont permis d'atteindre un haut niveau de recouvrement des recettes de TVA, comme mentionné précédemment dans ce chapitre.
- À l'inverse, la République démocratique du Congo affiche un RRT faible de 0.07. Les recettes de TVA ont fortement baissé après la mise en place de cette taxe en 2012, passant de 4.2 % à 1.9 % du PIB en 2018. Ce déclin et le faible niveau du RRT reflètent les difficultés rencontrées par les autorités pour administrer la TVA. Par exemple, la TVA sur les importations de sociétés minières n'est plus perçue en raison de difficultés à rembourser les crédits de TVA. Le FMI a recommandé de renforcer les mécanismes institutionnels afin de recommencer à recouvrer ces recettes (FMI, 2019[33]).

Recettes fiscales liées à l'environnement

En vertu de l'Accord de Paris de 2016, les pays se sont engagés à décarboner leurs économies d'ici le milieu du siècle, ce qui implique de se détourner des combustibles fossiles comme source d'énergie. Les taxes liées à l'environnement, et plus généralement les instruments fondés sur les prix, jouent un rôle croissant dans de nombreux pays. En intégrant un signal-prix dans les décisions des consommateurs, ces taxes mettent en application le principe du pollueur-payeur et incitent les entreprises et les ménages à prendre en compte le coût environnemental de leurs choix.

Une taxe liée à l'environnement est une taxe dont l'assiette est une unité physique (ou une approximation d'une unité physique) de quelque chose qui a un impact négatif spécifique et avéré sur l'environnement, que la taxe vise à changer les comportements ou soit perçue dans un autre but (OCDE, 2005[34]). Les recettes tirées des taxes sur l'énergie peuvent augmenter à moyen terme si les pays relèvent les taux effectifs de la taxe sur la teneur en carbone des carburants (Marten et van Dender, 2019[35]). Une étude (OCDE/FIT, 2019[36]) montre comment les recettes tirées du transport routier peuvent être stabilisées à long terme en associant des taxes sur les distances parcourues, les véhicules et les carburants.

Bien que les recettes tirées des taxes liées à l'environnement ne ressortent pas de la classification type des recettes fiscales établie par l'OCDE, on peut les identifier en examinant la liste détaillée des taxes spécifiques fournies pour la plupart des pays, qui s'inscrivent dans la classification globale. C'est sur cette base qu'elles ont été intégrées dans la base de données de l'OCDE sur les instruments de la politique de l'environnement (PINE) (OCDE, 2020[37]).

La base de données PINE ventile les taxes liées à l'environnement entre les quatre catégories suivantes[10] :

- *Énergie* : Cette catégorie couvre l'imposition des produits énergétiques tels que les combustibles fossiles et l'électricité, y compris les carburants utilisés pour les transports comme l'essence et le gazole. Toutes les taxes sur les émissions de CO_2 font partie de cette catégorie.

- *Véhicules à moteur et services de transport* : Cette catégorie englobe les taxes sur les importations ou les ventes de matériel de transport, les taxes périodiques sur la propriété, l'immatriculation ou l'usage routier de véhicules à moteur et d'autres taxes liées aux transports.
- *Ressources* : Cette catégorie inclut les taxes sur les industries extractives, l'exploitation forestière, la protection de la vie sauvage et les produits de la pêche.
- *Pollution* : Cette catégorie comprend les taxes sur les substances appauvrissant la couche d'ozone, l'eau et les eaux usées, et la gestion des déchets.

Un examen détaillé des taxes prélevées par les 30 pays africains couverts pour lesquels cette ventilation est disponible montre qu'en moyenne, les recettes tirées des taxes liées à l'environnement s'élevaient à 1.1 % du PIB en 2018, le même niveau que la moyenne ALC mais moins que la moyenne non pondérée de l'OCDE de 2.3 % du PIB. Les recettes générées par les taxes liées à l'environnement s'échelonnaient entre un peu moins de 0.1% du PIB au Sénégal et au Tchad et 3.8 % aux Seychelles (Graphique 1.18). Ces chiffres doivent être interprétés avec prudence car il n'est pas possible d'identifier précisément les recettes issues des taxes liées à l'environnement pour chaque pays ; aussi, le niveau des recettes indiqué dans le Graphique 1.18 dépend de la granularité des données disponibles pour chaque pays.

Graphique 1.18. **Recettes des taxes liées à l'environnement par pays et par principales catégories de taxe, en pourcentage du PIB, 2018**

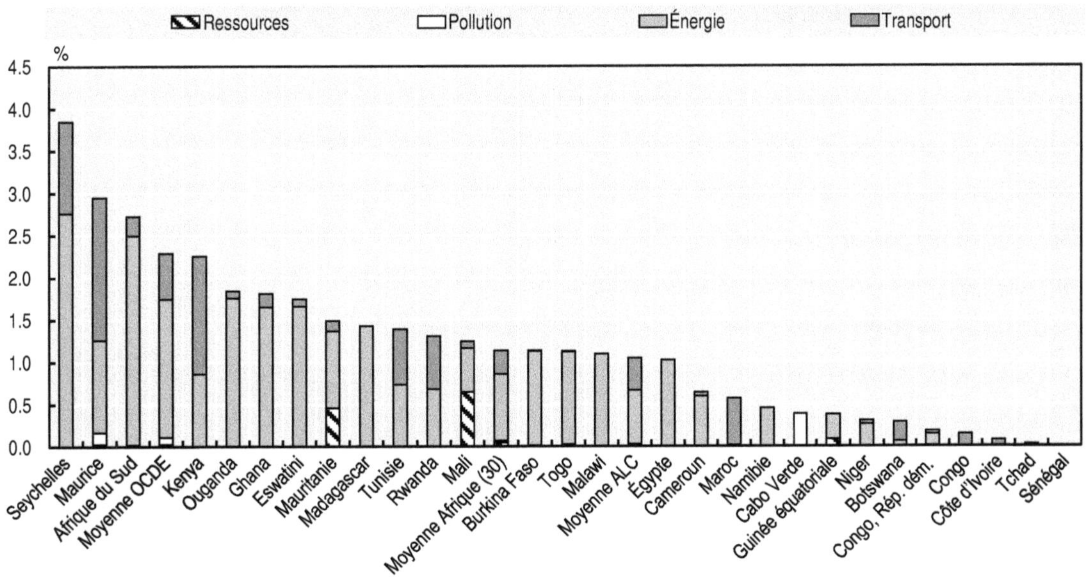

Note : Le Nigéria et le Lesotho sont exclus compte tenu de l'impossibilité d'identifier des recettes tirées de taxes liées à l'environnement.
Source : Calculs des auteurs basés sur des données figurant dans « Statistiques des recettes publiques en Afrique : Tableaux comparatifs » (OCDE/ATAF/CUA, 2020[3]), la base de données PINE (OCDE, 2020[37]) pour la moyenne de l'OCDE et (OCDE et al., 2020[1]) pour la moyenne de la région ALC.

StatLink https://doi.org/10.1787/888934182325

En 2018, les recettes provenant des taxes sur les produits énergétiques constituaient l'essentiel des recettes tirées des taxes liées à l'environnement dans les pays couverts par cette publication (0.8 % du PIB en moyenne). Les recettes issues des produits énergétiques, généralement des taxes sur le gazole et sur l'essence, représentaient environ les deux tiers du total des recettes générées par les taxes liées à l'environnement en moyenne. Les recettes tirées des taxes sur les transports et sur les véhicules à moteur constituaient l'essentiel du solde, tandis que celles générées par d'autres catégories étaient négligeables, de l'ordre de 0.07 % du total en moyenne. Cette structure est très similaire à la ventilation de ces recettes dans les pays de l'OCDE et de la région ALC.

Les taxes sur les produits énergétiques représentaient également la majeure partie des recettes des taxes liées à l'environnement dans tous les pays sauf neuf. Les taxes sur les véhicules à moteur et sur les transports constituaient la principale source de recettes provenant des taxes liées à l'environnement au Botswana, en République du Congo, en Côte d'Ivoire, au Kenya, à Maurice et au Maroc. Les recettes provenant des taxes sur les ressources et sur la pollution arrivaient en tête au Cabo Verde, au Mali et au Tchad.

L'Afrique du Sud affiche l'un des plus hauts niveaux de recettes des taxes liées à l'environnement, soit l'équivalent de 2.7 % du PIB en 2018, la taxe sur les carburants occupant la première place (1.4 % du PIB). Au cours de la dernière décennie, l'Afrique du Sud a mis en place une taxe sur les ampoules incandescentes (2009/10) ; une taxe sur l'électricité (2009/10) ; une taxe sur les émissions de CO_2 des véhicules (2010/11) et une taxe sur les pneus (2016/17). En 2019, l'Afrique du Sud a également instauré une taxe carbone au taux de 120 rands (8.34 USD) par tonne d'équivalent dioxyde de carbone (Reuters, 2019[38]) (OCDE, 2020[39]).

Graphique 1.19. **Recettes tirées des taxes liées à l'environnement en pourcentage du PIB moyennes Afrique (30), OCDE et ALC, 2010-18**

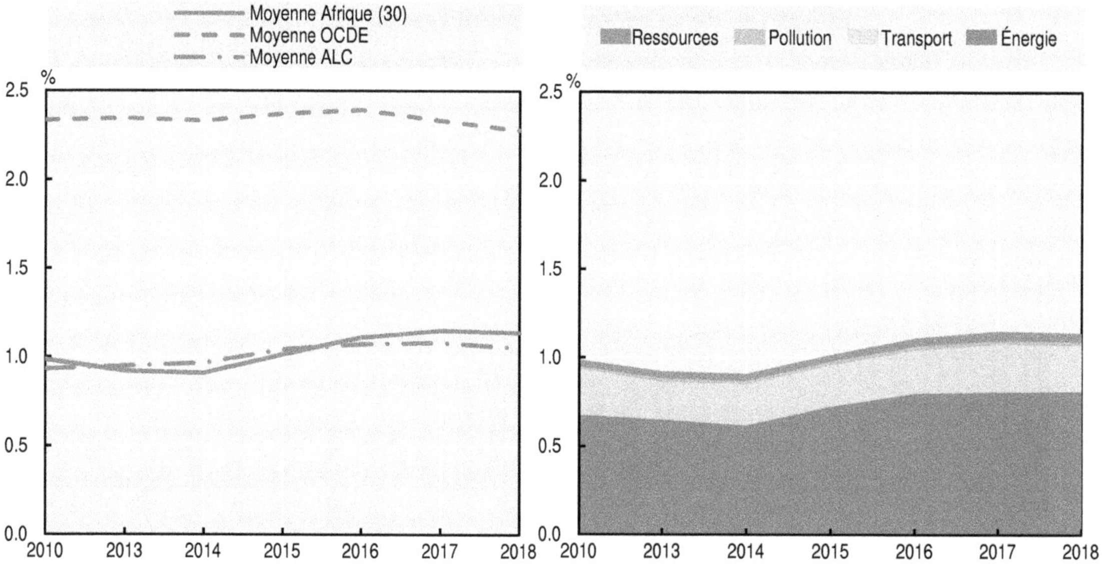

Note : Le Nigéria et le Lesotho sont exclus compte tenu de l'impossibilité d'identifier des recettes tirées des taxes liées à l'environnement.
Source : Calculs des auteurs basés sur des données figurant dans les « Statistiques des recettes publiques en Afrique : Tableaux comparatifs » (OCDE/ATAF/CUA, 2020[3]), sur la base de données PINE pour la moyenne de l'OCDE et *Revenue Statistics in Latin America and the Caribbean* (OCDE et al., 2020[1]) pour la moyenne ALC.

StatLink https://doi.org/10.1787/888934182344

Les recettes tirées des taxes sur l'énergie peuvent augmenter à moyen terme si les pays relèvent les taux effectifs de la taxe sur la teneur en carbone des carburants (Marten et van Dender, 2019[35]). Le Graphique 1.19 illustre l'évolution des recettes des taxes liées à l'environnement pour l'Afrique (30), l'OCDE et la région ALC depuis 2010 (moyennes). La moyenne Afrique (30) a augmenté de 0.2 point entre 2010 et 2018, alors que la moyenne de la région ALC a progressé de 0.1 point et la moyenne de l'OCDE a diminué de 0.1 point sur la période. La moyenne pour l'Afrique (30) des recettes tirées des taxes liées à l'environnement a reculé entre 2010 et 2014, avant de rebondir pendant deux ans et de se stabiliser à 1.1 %

du PIB à partir de 2016. En 2014 et 2015, la moyenne Afrique (30) a enregistré la plus forte hausse (0.1 point sur les deux années). Cette croissance a été principalement tirée par les recettes des taxes sur l'énergie.

Les pays qui ont enregistré les plus fortes augmentations entre 2010 et 2018 sont le Ghana, l'Eswatini et la Mauritanie ; les recettes générées par les taxes liées à l'environnement ont augmenté dans ces pays de respectivement 1.3 point, 1.2 point et 1.0 point au cours de la période. Ces hausses sont toutes dues à des augmentations des taxes sur les carburants et les produits pétroliers. Au cours de cette période, le Ghana a adopté la loi de 2015 sur les prélèvements dans le secteur de l'énergie (loi 899) qui visait à stabiliser les prix du pétrole, financer l'entretien des routes et soutenir la production d'électricité (Ghana Web, 2019$_{[40]}$). Cette loi a conduit à la mise en place de différentes taxes, comme la taxe alimentant les fonds routiers, la taxe de remboursement de la dette du secteur énergétique et la taxe de stabilisation des prix. L'augmentation des trois prélèvements intervenue entre 2010 et 2018 représentait 1 point du PIB.

Par rapport aux pays de l'OCDE, le recours à la fiscalité pour remédier aux problèmes environnementaux est faible dans la région et il est possible de mobiliser bien davantage ces formes de prélèvements. La sous-utilisation des taxes environnementales en Afrique doit également être comprise dans le contexte de l'utilisation généralisée des subventions aux combustibles fossiles. On estime que les subventions aux combustibles fossiles en Afrique subsaharienne représentaient 5 % du PIB en 2013 (Coady et al., 2015$_{[41]}$). Parmi les pays figurant dans cette publication, la Côte d'Ivoire, le Nigéria et l'Afrique du Sud ont accordé des subventions aux combustibles fossiles supérieures à 1 milliard USD en 2015 (Worrall, Whitley et Scott, 2018$_{[42]}$). La réforme des subventions à l'énergie, parallèlement à la mise en œuvre de la fiscalité environnementale, pourrait permettre de mobiliser d'importantes recettes publiques et contribuer à la réalisation des Objectifs de développement durable (ODD).

À l'heure où la crise du COVID-19 continue de sévir et où les pouvoirs publics déploient toujours des programmes d'aide aux entreprises et aux ménages, certains pays accordent des allégements d'impôts ou renoncent à certaines taxes. L'ATAF encourage les gouvernements africains à « s'abstenir de suspendre les taxes environnementales pendant cette période car (...) les allégements fiscaux à court terme ne devraient pas compromettre les objectifs environnementaux à plus long terme » (ATAF, 2020$_{[43]}$).

Impôts par niveaux d'administration

L'analyse de la répartition des impôts par niveaux d'administration dans les pays couverts par cette publication est limitée par le fait que les données sur les recettes fiscales perçues par les administrations infranationales étaient disponibles pour six pays seulement : Afrique du Sud, Eswatini, Maroc, Maurice[11], Mauritanie et Nigéria[12]. Les recettes fiscales des collectivités locales sont considérées comme faibles dans les 30 pays africains. Selon la publication *Perspectives économiques en Afrique 2015* (BAfD/OCDE/PNUD, 2015$_{[44]}$), « en Afrique, en moyenne, le poids des recettes des administrations locales équivaut à 7 % des recettes totales perçues par les collectivités locales et régionales et l'administration centrale combinées ». En 2018, les recettes des administrations infranationales étaient inférieures à 1 % du total des recettes fiscales à Maurice, et représentaient 1.9 % en Eswatini, 2.8 % en Mauritanie, 3.4 % au Maroc et 5.6 % en Afrique du Sud. En revanche, les recettes des administrations infranationales s'élevaient à 14.3 % du total des recettes fiscales au Nigéria.

En général, les compétences fiscales dévolues aux administrations infranationales en Afrique sont limitées. La publication *Perspectives économiques en Afrique 2015* (BAfD/OCDE/PNUD, 2015[44]) observent que « de nombreuses administrations locales perçoivent une fraction importante de leurs recettes totales grâce aux transferts opérés par l'administration centrale ». Les collectivités locales dans la plupart des pays d'Afrique se heurtent à des contraintes de ressources et les outils dont disposent leurs administrations fiscales sont inadaptés pour recouvrer les impôts et les imputer correctement en comptabilité. Cette situation entraîne des coûts de recouvrement élevés et un grand nombre d'impôts peu productifs. En outre, le traitement des données relatives aux recettes collectées et l'échange de renseignements avec d'autres institutions publiques sont peu développés, et les administrations locales coopèrent généralement peu avec l'administration centrale. Cela se traduit par des impôts en double ou qui vont à l'encontre des objectifs nationaux (comme des taxes locales sur les cultures d'exportation).

Les impôts sur le patrimoine constituent la plus importante source de revenu pour les administrations infranationales en Afrique du Sud, en Eswatini, au Maroc, à Maurice et en Mauritanie. Ils représentent la totalité des recettes fiscales locales recouvrées en Eswatini, à Maurice et en Mauritanie, et plus de 80 % en Afrique du Sud et au Maroc. Le solde se compose principalement des impôts sur les biens et services. À l'inverse, les recettes des administrations infranationales au Nigéria proviennent principalement des impôts sur le revenu.

On observe de grandes disparités en ce qui concerne la fiscalité locale, et de nombreux pays africains ne lèvent aucune taxe locale sur le foncier bâti et non bâti, ni même sur les activités économiques (BAfD/OCDE/PNUD, 2015[44]). À l'exception de l'Afrique du Sud, les registres fonciers en bonne et due forme font défaut ou sont incomplets, ce qui entrave la collecte des impôts fonciers (Fjeldstad, Chambas et Brun, 2014[45]). À Maurice, par exemple, la taxe foncière est peu productive en partie à cause de cadastres périmés et de valeurs de biens qui ne sont plus à jour (FMI, 2014[46]).

Certains pays s'emploient à améliorer leur régime des impôts sur le patrimoine, avec une mise à jour des registres fonciers et des outils administratifs plus efficaces. En 2007, le Maroc a lancé une réforme du système fiscal et des administrations fiscales locales en vue d'augmenter les recettes générées par les impôts locaux (Boisard, de Freitas et Hidouci, 2014[47]). La Côte d'Ivoire a déployé un logiciel SIG pour mieux gérer ses registres fonciers. L'Afrique du Sud a décentralisé avec succès le processus de recouvrement de la taxe foncière urbaine et a élaboré un système moderne de collecte de cette taxe en utilisant des techniques statistiques afin de réaliser des évaluations de masse assistées par ordinateur (Monkam et Moore, 2015[48]).

Bien que de nombreux pays africains aient entrepris de vastes réformes de leur administration fiscale centrale et de la législation correspondante au cours des dernières décennies, il n'y a guère eu d'initiatives de ce genre au niveau des administrations locales. On a donné la priorité aux recettes perçues par l'administration centrale parce que c'est à cet échelon que la nécessité de réduire les déficits budgétaires s'est fait sentir le plus.

Notes

1. Il convient d'interpréter la moyenne Afrique (30) avec précaution car des données relatives aux cotisations de sécurité sociale sont indisponibles pour la République du Congo, la République démocratique du Congo (avant 2012), Madagascar (avant 2011), la Namibie, l'Ouganda, le Tchad et le Togo et sont incomplètes pour le Cameroun et le Sénégal. Les cotisations de sécurité sociale pour le Botswana, le Lesotho et le Malawi sont égales à zéro dans la mesure où elles ne remplissent pas les critères retenus pour être considérées comme des cotisations de sécurité sociale, selon la classification des impôts de l'OCDE figurant dans le Guide d'interprétation. Pour plus de précisions, se reporter aux tableaux par pays présentés dans le chapitre 5.
2. Le Burundi, le Kenya, l'Ouganda, le Rwanda, le Sud-Soudan et la Tanzanie font partie de la Communauté de l'Afrique de l'Est (CAE).
3. Le Burkina Faso, le Bénin, la Côte d'Ivoire, la Guinée Bissau, le Mali, le Niger, le Sénégal et le Togo font partie de l'Union économique et monétaire ouest-africaine.
4. L'Afrique du Sud, le Botswana, Eswatini, le Lesotho et la Namibie constituent l'Union douanière d'Afrique australe (SACU).
5. Ces informations ont été fournies par l'Agence Comptable Centrale du Trésor (ACCT) Mali lors d'échanges avec le Secrétariat de l'OCDE au cours de la préparation de cette publication.
6. On trouvera de plus amples informations sur ces mesures dans l'étude spéciale : « Convergence des niveaux d'imposition et des structures fiscales dans les pays de l'OCDE » (OCDE, 2018[49])
7. L'analyse repose sur une source de données unique, en l'occurrence l'enquête auprès des entreprises réalisée en 2016 par l'OCDE pour recueillir l'avis des équipes dirigeantes de 500 entreprises, en majorité multinationales, et recueillir ainsi leurs vues sur la sécurité juridique en matière fiscale dans 82 pays en développement.
8. Les données sur les cotisations de sécurité sociale sont indisponibles pour le Tchad, la République du Congo, la République démocratique du Congo (avant 2012), Madagascar (avant 2011), la Namibie, l'Ouganda et le Togo et sont incomplètes au Cameroun et au Sénégal. Pour plus de précisions, se reporter aux tableaux par pays présentés dans le chapitre 5.
9. Les Seychelles sont exclues du fait de l'indisponibilité de certaines données.
10. La base de données PINE de l'OCDE (*http://oe.cd/pine*) réunit des informations détaillées sur les instruments qui sont agrégées pour aboutir à des recettes totales. Cette base de données facilite le suivi, la conception et la mise en œuvre de politiques efficaces. Depuis 2005, elle rassemble un jeu unique d'informations détaillées sur 3 476 instruments utilisés dans 94 pays.
11. Les données concernant Maurice proviennent des états financiers établis par le Bureau des statistiques de Maurice.
12. Les recettes fiscales infranationales intègrent les recettes des États mais excluent celles des collectivités locales.

Références

Addison, T. et J. Levin (2012), *The Determinants of Tax Revenue in Sub-Saharan Africa*, Swedish Business School at Örebro University, Örebro, Suède, *http://oru.diva-portal.org/smash/record.jsf?pid=diva2%3A570456&dswid=4207*. [22]

ATAF (2020), *Mining Tax Policy Responses to COVID-19: Webinar Q&A*, *www.ataftax.org/mining-tax-policy-responses-to-covid-19-webinar-q-a*. [43]

BAfD/OCDE/CEA (2010), *Perspectives économiques en Afrique 2010*, Éditions OCDE, Paris, *https://doi.org/10.1787/aeo-2010-fr*. [24]

BAfD/OCDE/PNUD (2016), *Perspectives économiques en Afrique 2016 : Villes durables et transformation structurelle*, Éditions OCDE, Paris, *https://dx.doi.org/10.1787/aeo-2016-fr*. [30]

BAfD/OCDE/PNUD (2015), *Perspectives économiques en Afrique 2015 : Développement territorial et inclusion spatiale*, Éditions OCDE, Paris, *https://doi.org/10.1787/aeo-2015-fr*. [44]

Boisard, de Freitas et Hidouci (2014), *Renforcer les recettes fiscales locales pour financer le développement urbain en Afrique*, Fonds mondial pour le développement des villes (FMDV), Paris, *http://delog.org/web/wp-content/uploads/2016/03/Etude-FMDV-Fiscalite%CC%81-locale-Villes-Afrique-8-Cas.pdf*. [47]

Cnossen, S. (2015), *Mobilizing VAT revenues in African countries, www.researchgate.net/publication/276344974_Mobilizing_VAT_revenues_in_African_countries.* [31]

CNUCED (2018), *Investment Policy Review of Cabo Verde, http://unctad.org/ipr* (consulté le 7 septembre 2020). [32]

Coady, D. et al. (2015), "How Large Are Global Energy Subsidies?", *FMI, document de travail, www.imf.org/external/pubs/ft/wp/2015/wp15105.pdf.* [41]

Diallo, M. (2018), "UEMOA : L'optimisation de la mobilisation des recettes fiscales propres, au centre d'un séminaire", *LeFaso.net, https://lefaso.net/spip.php?article84079.* [5]

Direction générale du Trésor France (2020), *Indicateurs et conjoncture - MAURITANIE | Direction générale du Trésor, www.tresor.economie.gouv.fr/Pays/MR/mauritanie-situation-economique-et-financiere* (consulté le 11 septembre 2020). [11]

Fjeldstad, Chambas et Brun (2014), *Local government taxation in Sub-Saharan Africa: a review and an agenda for research*, 2, Chr. Michelsen Institute, Bergen, *www.cmi.no/publications/file/5098-local-government-taxation-in-sub-saharan-africa.pdf.* [45]

FMI (2020), *Base de données des Perspectives de l'économie mondiale, avril 2020, www.imf.org/external/pubs/ft/weo/2020/01/weodata/index.aspx* (consulté le 8 septembre 2020). [21]

FMI (2020), "République du Congo : Consultations de 2019 au titre de l'Article IV — Communiqué de presse ; Rapport des services du FMI ; Analyse de viabilité de la dette ; Annexe d'information ; et Déclaration de l'Administrateur pour la République du Congo", *Rapport du FMI No. 20/26, www.imf.org/~/media/Files/Publications/CR/2020/French/1COGFA2020001.ashx.* [13]

FMI (2020), *World Economic Outlook, April 2020: The Great Lockdown.* [4]

FMI (2019), *Democratic Republic of the Congo : 2019 Article IV Consultation-Press Release; Staff Report; and Statement by the Executive Director for the Democratic Republic of the Congo, www.imf.org/en/Publications/CR/Issues/2019/09/04/Democratic-Republic-of-the-Congo-2019-Article-IV-Consultation-Press-Release-Staff-Report-and-48648* (consulté le 8 septembre 2020). [33]

FMI (2019), "L'équipe du FMI achève une mission de revue au Togo", *Communiqué de presse n° 19/473, www.imf.org/fr/News/Articles/2019/12/18/pr19473-togo-imf-staff-completes-review-mission.* [15]

FMI (2019), "Niger : 2019 Article IV Consultation, Fourth Review Under the Extended Credit Facility, and Requests for Waiver of Nonobservance of a Performance Criterion, Modification of Performance Criteria, and Extension and Rephasing of the Extended Credit Facility Arrangement-Press Release; Staff Report and Statement by the Executive Director for Niger", *IMF Country Report No. 19/239, www.imf.org/en/Publications/CR/Issues/2019/07/22/Niger-2019-Article-IV-Consultation-Fourth-Review-Under-the-Extended-Credit-Facility-and-48514.* [10]

FMI (2019), *World Economic Outlook - Frequently Asked Questions, www.imf.org/external/pubs/ft/weo/faq.htm#q4d.* [19]

FMI (2018), "Mali: 2018 Article IV Consultation and Eighth and Ninth Reviews Under the Extended Credit Facility Arrangement-Press Release; Staff Report; and Statement by the Executive Director for Mali", *Country Report n° 18/141, www.imf.org/en/Publications/CR/Issues/2018/05/31/Mali-2018-Article-IV-Consultation-and-Eighth-and-Ninth-Reviews-Under-the-Extended-Credit-45921.* [14]

FMI (2014), *Mauritius: Staff Report for the 2014 Article IV Consultationv(2014b)*, FMI, *www.imf.org/external/pubs/ft/scr/2014/cr14107.pdf.* [46]

Ghana Web (2019), *Parliament asks Government to address energy sector debts, www.ghanaweb.com/GhanaHomePage/business/Parliament-asks-Government-to-address-energy-sector-debts-760166.* [40]

Grey, A. (2020), "Here are Ghana's tax incentives available to business persons & entrepreneurs", *Ghana talks business, https://ghanatalksbusiness.com/2020/08/here-are-ghanas-tax-incentives-available-to-business-persons-entrepreneurs/.* [25]

Jeune Afrique (2019), *En Mauritanie, une vertueuse diversification qui reste à confirmer, www.jeuneafrique.com/mag/844828/economie/en-mauritanie-une-vertueuse-diversification-qui-reste-a-confirmer/.* [12]

KPMG (2020), "*https://assets.kpmg/content/dam/kpmg/ng/pdf/tax/ng-incentives-in-africa.pdf*", *Investing in Africa, https://assets.kpmg/content/dam/kpmg/ng/pdf/tax/ng-incentives-in-africa.pdf.* [27]

Lesotho Times (2019), *LRA meets revenue target - Lesotho Times, http://lestimes.com/lra-meets-revenue-target/* (consulté le 11 septembre 2020). [8]

Lesotho Times (2019), *LRA ups tax lottery stakes - Lesotho Times, http://lestimes.com/lra-ups-tax-lottery-stakes/* (consulté le 11 septembre 2020). [6]

Lesotho Times (2018), *LRA on course to meet revenue target - Lesotho Times*, *http://lestimes.com/lra-on-course-to-meet-revenue-target/* (consulté le 11 septembre 2020). [9]

LRA (2018), *Value Added Tax (VAT) Rates Change.* [7]

Marten, M. et K. van Dender (2019), *The use of revenues from carbon pricing*, Éditions OCDE, Paris, *https://dx.doi.org/10.1787/3cb265e4-en.* [35]

Monkam, N. et M. Moore (2015), *How Property Tax Would Benefit Africa*, Africa Research Institute, *www.africaresearchinstitute.org/publications/property-tax-benefit-africa.* [48]

OCDE (2020), "OECD analysis of budgetary support and tax expenditures 2020 country notes", *Inventory of Support Measures for Fossil Fuels database*, *www.oecd.org/fossil-fuels/data/.* [39]

OCDE (2020), *Pine Database*, *www.oecd.org/fr/environnement/outils-evaluation/environmentaltaxation.htm.* [37]

OCDE (2019), *Statistiques des recettes publiques 2019*, Éditions OCDE, Paris, *https://doi.org/10.1787/df3c3b17-fr.* [2]

OCDE (2019), *Tax Morale: What Drives People and Businesses to Pay Tax?*, Éditions OCDE, *https://doi.org/10.1787/f3d8ea10-en.* [18]

OCDE (2018), *Statistiques des recettes publiques 2018*, Éditions OCDE, Paris, *https://dx.doi.org/10.1787/rev_stats-2018-fr.* [49]

OCDE (2018), *Tendances des impôts sur la consommation 2018 : TVA/TPS et droits d'accise : taux, tendances et questions stratégiques*, Éditions OCDE, Paris, *https://dx.doi.org/10.1787/g2g9fa9e-fr.* [29]

OCDE (2014), *Coopération pour le développement 2014 : Mobiliser les ressources au service du développement durable*, Éditions OCDE, Paris, *https://dx.doi.org/10.1787/dcr-2014-fr.* [17]

OCDE (2005), *Glossary of statistical terms*, *https://stats.oecd.org/glossary/detail.asp?ID=6437.* [34]

OCDE/ATAF/CUA (2020), *Recettes fiscales en Afrique : Tableaux comparatifs*, Éditions OCDE, Paris, *https://doi.org/10.1787/7f54581d-fr.* [3]

OCDE/FIT (2019), *Tax Revenue Implications of Decarbonising Road Transport: Scenarios for Slovenia*, OCDE, *https://doi.org/10.1787/87b39a2f-en.* [36]

OCDE et al. (2020), *Revenue Statistics in Latin America and the Caribbean*, Éditions OCDE, Paris, *https://doi.org/10.1787/68739b9b-en-es.* [1]

OMS (2015), *Purchasing Power Parity 2005*, Organisation mondiale de la santé, *www.who.int/choice/costs/ppp/en/.* [20]

Profeta, S. et S. Scabrosetti (2010), *The Political Economy of Taxation: Lessons from Developing Countries*, Edward Elgar Publishing, *https://books.google.fr/books?isbn=1849805490.* [23]

PWC (2020), "Worldwide Tax summaries", *Nigeria. Corporate - Tax credits and incentives*, *https://taxsummaries.pwc.com/nigeria/corporate/tax-credits-and-incentives.* [26]

Reuters (2019), *South African carbon tax finally becomes law*, *www.reuters.com/article/us-safrica-carbontax/south-african-carbon-tax-finally-becomes-law-idUSKCN1SW0K6.* [38]

SACU (2020), *What is SACU?*, *www.sacu.int/about/what_is.html* (consulté le 10 septembre 2020). [16]

SSA (2015), *Social Security Through the World: Africa*, SSA Publication Social Security Administration, Washington, DC, *www.ssa.gov/policy/docs/progdesc/ssptw/2014-2015/africa/ssptw15africa.pdf.* [28]

Worrall, L., S. Whitley et A. Scott (2018), "Reforming Africa's Fossil Fuel Subsidies", *sun-connect-news.org*, *www.sun-connect-news.org/de/articles/business/details/reforming-africas-fossil-fuel-subsidies/.* [42]

Chapter 2

Non-tax revenue trends, 2000-2018

Chapitre 2

Tendances des recettes non fiscales, 2000-2018

Revenue Statistics in Africa 1990-2018/Statistiques des recettes publiques en Afrique 1990-2018

Chapter 2

Non-tax revenue trends, 2000-2018

Introduction

A complete picture of public finances requires statistics that go beyond taxation, especially in the case of many African countries that obtain substantial revenues in the form of grants or royalties from oil and minerals. *Revenue Statistics in Africa* collects statistics on both tax and non-tax revenues, non-tax revenues being government revenues that do not meet the OECD definition of taxation. Although data on non-tax revenues might not come from the same sources or have the same reliability as tax statistics (see Box 2.1), they need to be included in any accounting of a country's total financial resources. This chapter provides cross-country comparisons of non-tax revenues for the countries in this publication.[1]

The main categories of non-tax revenues[2] reported as part of this project are (see also Annex B):

- grants from foreign governments or international organisations (budget aid, food aid, capital transfers, current transfers, project grants, programme grants, international debt relief, etc.)
- rents and royalties (such as oil or mining royalties)
- other property income (interest, dividends and other returns on government investment)
- sales of goods and services (which include some administrative fees)
- fines and penalties (including fines and penalties due to tax violations)
- miscellaneous and unidentified revenues (non-tax revenues that cannot be classified according to the other categories).

Box 2.1. **Non-tax revenues and data reliability**

Data on non-tax revenues are often less detailed than tax revenue data. Some countries might have aggregate figures for total non-tax revenues in some years but do not break this information down beyond grants and other non-tax revenue categories. This may be because data on non-tax revenues often comes from several different sources. *Revenue Statistics in Africa* indicates cases where total non-tax revenues are reported but may be incomplete.

Non-tax revenue data are not necessarily subject to the same level of scrutiny as tax revenues. Many types of non-tax revenue are not part of the main budget process, nor are they defined by legislation so they are not subject to the same oversight mechanisms as tax revenues. Non-tax revenues that are not accompanied by legal compulsions do not always require the same documentation.

Non-tax revenues are often under the responsibility of different authorities than tax revenues, so there is not necessarily a separation made between revenues and expenses. Some revenues, such as administrative fees, might be used as cost-recovery mechanisms and subtracted from cost figures rather than reported as revenues. This could be the case for local governments or other public institutions for which data only exists on net transfers of funds to the central government.

Grants, legal settlements and mining and oil contracts also often involve large payments by external entities such as multinational corporations and foreign governments that do not necessarily have incentives to maintain transparency. There could also be incentives to collude with local authorities to conceal costs. In addition, some countries may negotiate large payments from resource extraction payments as a lump sum that bundles together many categories of both tax and non-tax revenue, making detailed breakdowns less feasible.

Non-tax revenues as a percentage of GDP

In 2018, non-tax revenues as a percentage of GDP varied significantly among the 30 countries included in this publication. They ranged from 25.2% of GDP in Lesotho to 0.6% of GDP in South Africa. In every country except Lesotho, the Republic of the Congo, Botswana, and Equatorial Guinea, non-tax revenues were lower than tax revenues (Figure 2.1). On average, the amount of non-tax revenue collected in each country was 49.9% of the amount collected in tax revenues.

Figure 2.1. **Total tax and non-tax revenue by country, 2018**

Percentage of GDP

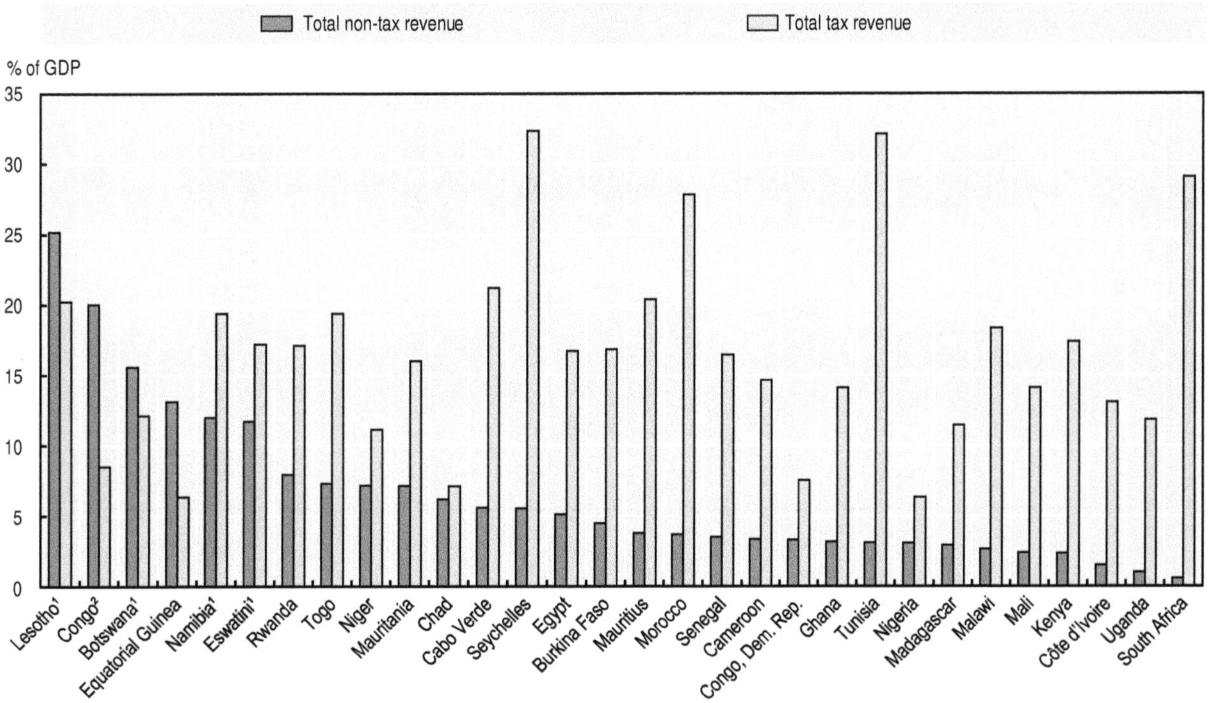

Note: Non-tax revenue includes sub-national non-tax government revenues for Eswatini, Kenya, Mauritius and Morocco, the only countries for which such revenues are reported. In 2018, these represented, respectively, 1%, 16%, 3% and 45% of all non-tax revenue collected for each country. Mauritania, Nigeria and South Africa reported some local and regional taxes, but no local and regional non-tax revenues.

1. Non-tax revenues for Botswana, Eswatini, Lesotho and Namibia include funds from excises and customs duties collected by South Africa and then transferred to them through the Southern African Customs Union (SACU) revenue-sharing agreement.

2. Figures for grant revenues and oil revenues for the Republic of the Congo are those reported by the IMF in its April 2020 *World Economic Outlook*.

The tax-to-GDP ratios and non-tax-to-GDP ratios need to be interpreted with caution for some countries due to incomplete data. See the country tables in Chapters 5 and 6 for further information.

Source: Table 4.1 in Chapter 4 and Table 6.1 in Chapter 6.

StatLink https://doi.org/10.1787/888934181660

Different clusters of countries appear when looking at the relationship between tax revenues and non-tax revenues as a percentage of GDP (Figure 2.2). Countries with exceptionally high oil revenues, such as Chad, the Republic of the Congo and Equatorial Guinea, are among those with the lowest tax-to-GDP ratios. Countries that are net recipients of revenues through the Southern African Customs Union (SACU) also have high non-tax revenues (see further explanation in the section on SACU revenues). Upper middle-income countries that are not major oil producers tend to have less of both grant revenues and resource revenues, which may increase the need to mobilise domestic resources via taxation.

Figure 2.2. **Total tax and non-tax revenue by country, 2018**

Percentage of GDP

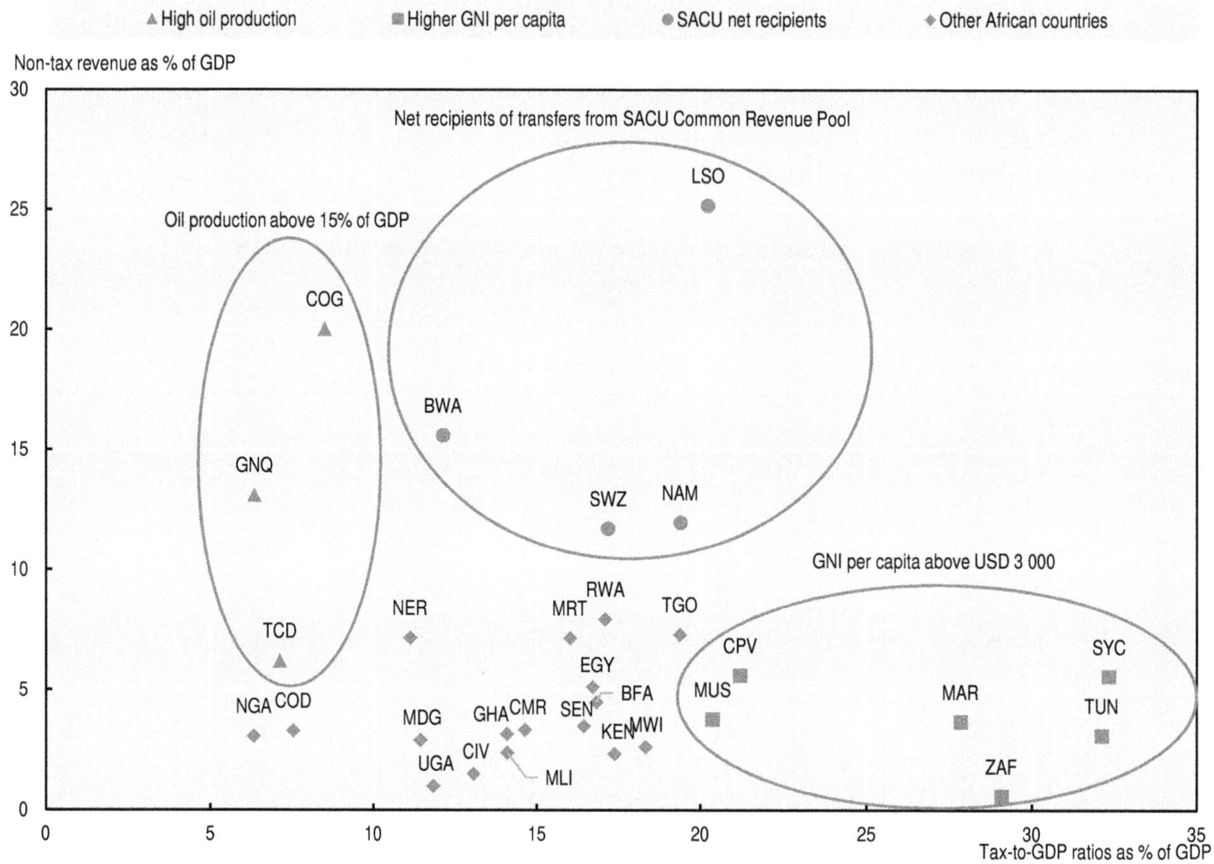

Note: See footnotes to Figure 2.1 and country tables in Chapters 5 and 6 for further information.

Source: Authors' calculations based on data from (OECD/ATAF/AUC, 2020[1]), "Revenue Statistics in Africa: Comparative tables", *OECD Tax Statistics* (database), *https://doi.org/10.1787/be755711-en*.

StatLink *https://doi.org/10.1787/888934181679*

While the Africa (30) average tax-to-GDP ratio rose between 2010 and 2018, average non-tax revenues have gone down substantially (Figure 2.3). After peaking in 2012 at 9.2% of GDP, average non-tax revenues dropped to 6.0% in 2016 before reaching 6.5% in 2018. This decline was driven by declines in rents and royalties and in grant revenues as a percentage of GDP. In 2018, grant revenues were at 1.3% of GDP, their lowest point since 2010. Rents and royalties were at 1.9% of GDP, 1.1 percentage points lower than in 2012, having rebounded only slightly from their 2016 low point. These declines have been enough to cause total revenues to go down over this period, leading to increased deficits and indebtedness (Box 2.2).

Different sources of non-tax revenues are associated with different types of risk, such as susceptibility to sudden changes, or vulnerability to economic shocks and political changes. Figure 2.5 shows the contribution of each sub-category to total non-tax revenues for each country. Four distinct groups are apparent in these data:

- Twelve countries received a majority of their non-tax revenue in the form of grants in 2018 (in descending order, Rwanda, Togo, Niger, Chad, Burkina Faso, Senegal, the Democratic Republic of the Congo, Madagascar, Malawi, Mali, Côte d'Ivoire and Uganda).

Figure 2.3. **Africa (30) average non-tax revenues, 2010-18**

Percentage of GDP

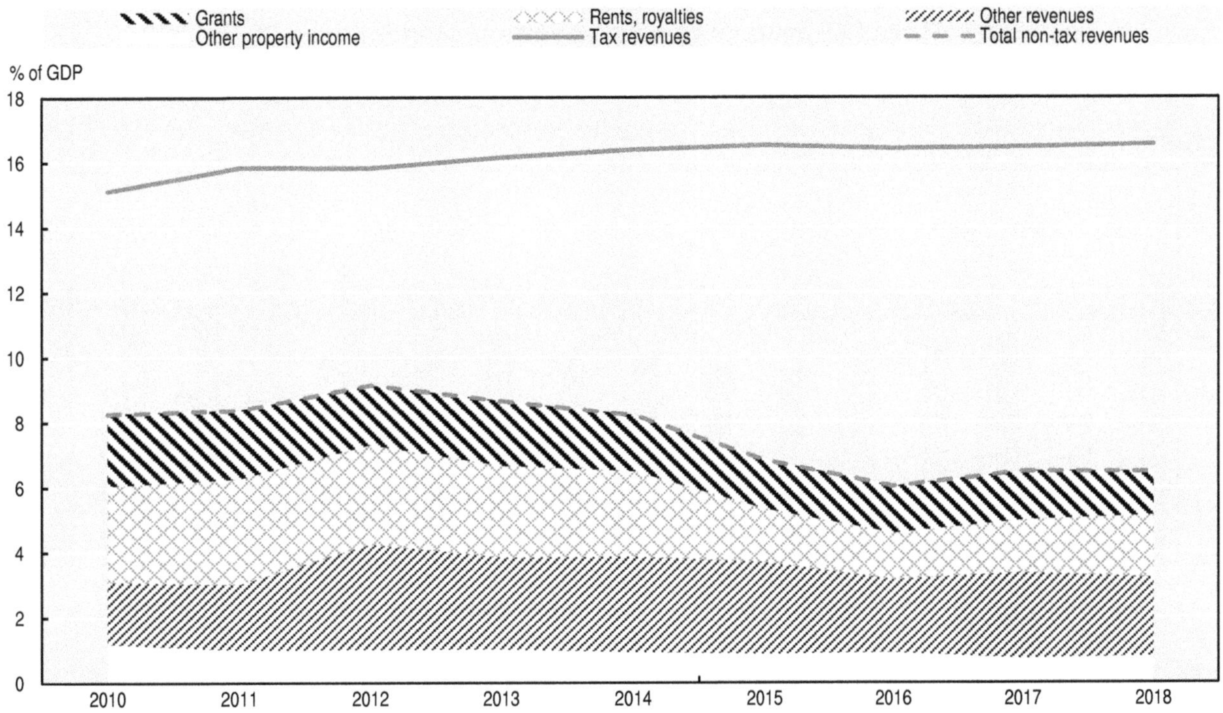

Source: Authors' calculations based on data from (OECD/ATAF/AUC, 2020[1])), "Revenue Statistics in Africa: Comparative tables", *OECD Tax Statistics* (database), *https://doi.org/10.1787/be755711-en*.

StatLink https://doi.org/10.1787/888934181698

Box 2.2. **Revenues and debt**

Since 2010, the public debt levels of the 30 countries in this report have risen substantially after a period of decline resulting from the Heavily Indebted Poor Countries (HIPC) debt-relief programme. The average general government debt for these countries rose from 34.6% of GDP in 2010 to 53.1% in 2018 (Figure 2.4). Of even greater concern, debt in foreign currency rose from 19.7% of GDP to 29.9% over the same period.[3] Before the onset of the COVID-19 pandemic, the International Monetary Fund (IMF) projected that the average debt level for these countries would rise to 61.5% of GDP. By the beginning of October 2020, the IMF projected that between the end of 2019 and 2021, average debt-to-GDP ratios around the world would rise 20% in advanced economies, 10% in emerging market economies and 7% in low-income countries (Georgieva, Pazarbasioglu and Weeks-Brown, 2020[2]).

Until 2014, revenue and expenditure in the 30 African countries were both rising, but average non-tax revenues declined by over 3 percentage points of GDP between 2012 and 2016 as resource revenues dropped due to falling commodity prices and as financial inflows slowed. Average expenditures as a percentage of GDP also declined, but with a lag: they peaked at 28.0% in 2015, before declining to a low of 25.2% of GDP in 2018. As a result, during this period of adjustments, deficits doubled.

Rising debt levels in countries with more difficult access to financing carry the risk that they will avail themselves of sources of financing around which there is less transparency, or for which long-term risks could be hidden. These risks are even more complicated in the cases of Burkina Faso, Côte d'Ivoire, Mali, Niger, Senegal and Togo who use the West African CFA franc, and Chad, the Republic of the Congo, Cameroon and Equatorial Guinea who use the Central African CFA franc, and therefore do not have the option of borrowing in their own currency.

Box 2.2. **Revenues and debt** *(cont.)*

Figure 2.4. **Africa (30) average general government gross debt, 2005-2020**

Percentage of GDP

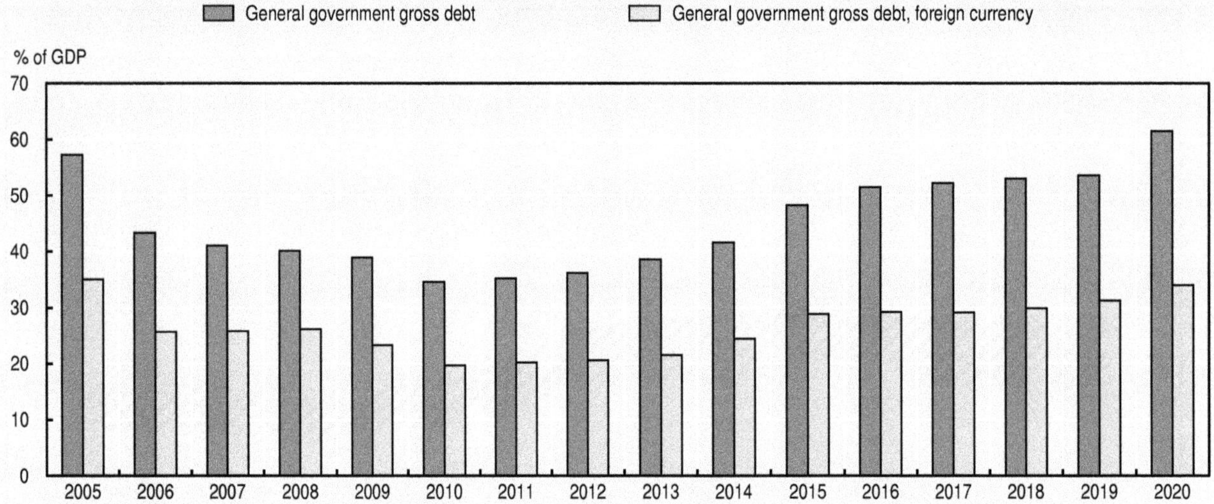

Notes: Averages are unweighted. 2020 figures are projections based upon calculations conducted when the COVID-19 was still in its early stages.

Source: Author's calculations based on figures from April 2020 *World Economic Outlook* (IMF, 2020[3]).

StatLink https://doi.org/10.1787/888934181717

With the onset of the COVID-19 pandemic in 2020, there is now an urgent need for African countries to restructure their debts and reform their finances. The COVID-19 pandemic has created a shock to African economies and public finances at a time when they were already trying to adjust to the commodity price shocks of 2014 (see Chapter 3 for more details). According to the IMF's *Debt Sustainability Framework* (IMF, 2020[4]), the Republic of the Congo is in debt distress and six other African countries in this publication (Cameroon, Cabo Verde, Chad, Ghana, Kenya and Mauritania) are at high risk of debt distress. Although there was an unprecedented series of measures in early 2020 to avoid a debt repayment crisis during the crisis, countries now need to find medium- and long-term solutions to ensure they can continue to finance their development needs.

The *African Development Dynamics* report of 2020 highlights steps African countries can take to improve their fiscal outlooks while maintaining their access to capital (AUC/OECD, n.d.[5]):

- African countries can make use of the exceptional circumstances of a global pandemic to negotiate debt restructurings. Creditors, who normally fear setting unfavourable precedents around debt repayment, may be amenable to accepting more debt relief measures when they are understood to apply only to the present crisis.
- African countries can work to adopt common negotiating positions on debt relief measures in order to increase their leverage in the face of the rising number of their private and non-concessional creditors. Consolidation has already begun on the other side of the negotiating table. In April 2020, the Institute for international Finance (IIF) put forth a list of conditions for private sector involvement in debt restructurings on behalf of 450 leading financial institutions.
- African countries can also make technical improvements to their borrowing strategies and the use of financial instruments to improve their borrowing terms. Improvements to collective action clauses in bond issuances, for example, can reduce risks to borrowers and uncertainty for investors. Developing local currency bond markets could also allow African countries to borrow in their own currency and avoid exchange rate and inflation risks.

- Six countries received more revenues from rents and royalties than other sources of non-tax revenues (in descending order, the Republic of the Congo, Equatorial Guinea, Mauritania, Cameroon, Tunisia and Nigeria). For all these countries except Tunisia, oil royalties provided the majority of non-tax revenues.
- Botswana, Lesotho, Namibia and Eswatini, the four neighbours of South Africa that belong to SACU, received substantial non-tax revenues in terms of transfers from the SACU Common Revenue Pool (Box 2.4).
- For the remaining eight countries, most non-tax revenues were not grants, rents and royalties or SACU revenues. The main alternative sources of non-tax revenues for these countries included: interest and dividends for Kenya, Seychelles and South Africa; fees for goods and services for Cabo Verde, Ghana and Morocco; and miscellaneous and unallocated revenues for Egypt and Mauritius.

Figure 2.5. **Structure of non-tax revenues by country, 2018**

Percentage of GDP

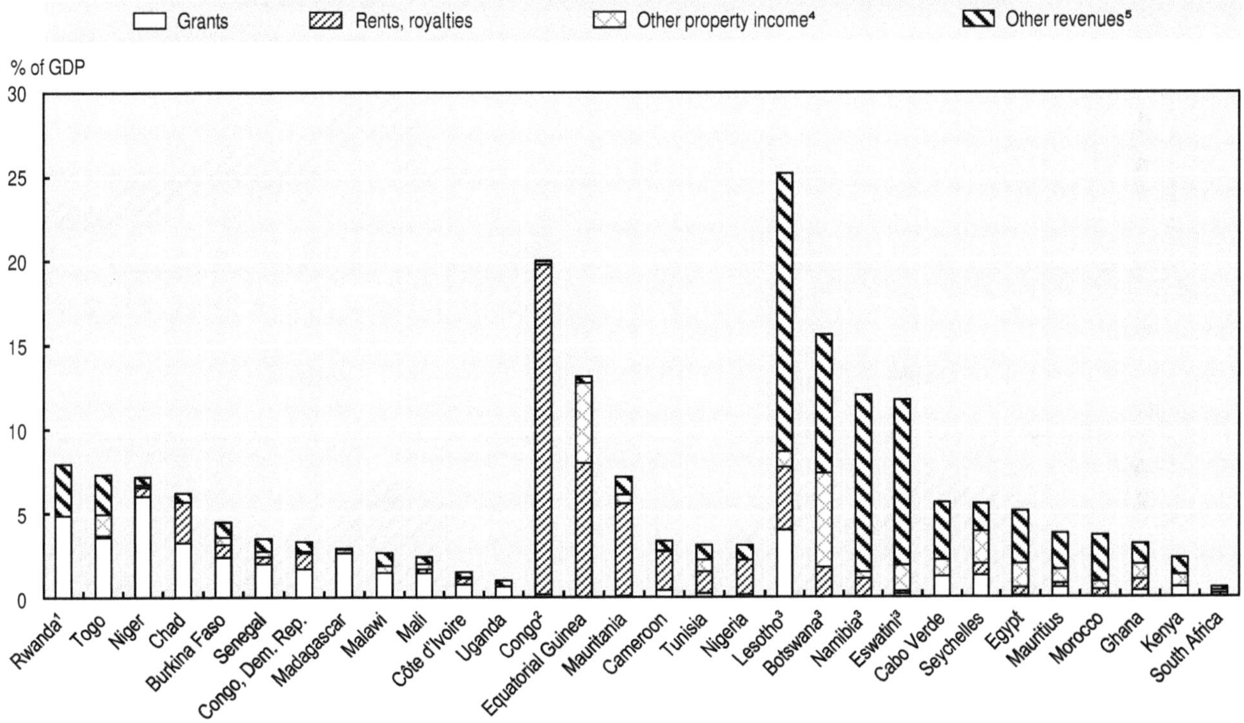

Note: Data include sub-national government non-tax revenues for Eswatini, Kenya, Mauritius and Morocco.

1. For Rwanda, non-tax revenues aside from grants were not disaggregated in the data and are therefore classified as miscellaneous and unidentified revenues.
2. Figures reported here represent mainly grant revenue and oil revenue obtained from the IMF's April 2020 *World Economic Outlook* classified as rents and royalties.
3. For Botswana, Eswatini, Lesotho and Namibia, "Other revenues" include funds from excises and customs duties collected by South Africa and then transferred to these countries through the Southern African Customs Union (SACU) revenue-sharing agreement.
4. Interest, dividends, etc.
5. Sales, fines, SACU revenues, etc.

See the footnotes to Figure 2.1 and country tables in Chapters 5 and 6 for further information.

Source: Table 6.2 in Chapter 6.

StatLink https://doi.org/10.1787/888934181736

Different sources of non-tax revenues behave differently over time (Figure 2.6). Many African countries experienced substantial variation in non-tax revenues, regardless of whether they obtained most of their revenues from grants (Rwanda and Malawi), resource rents (Republic of the Congo and Equatorial Guinea), SACU transfers (Lesotho and Botswana) or other non-tax revenues (Egypt and Seychelles).

Figure 2.6. **Change in the structure of non-tax revenues for selected countries, 2000-18**

Percentage of GDP

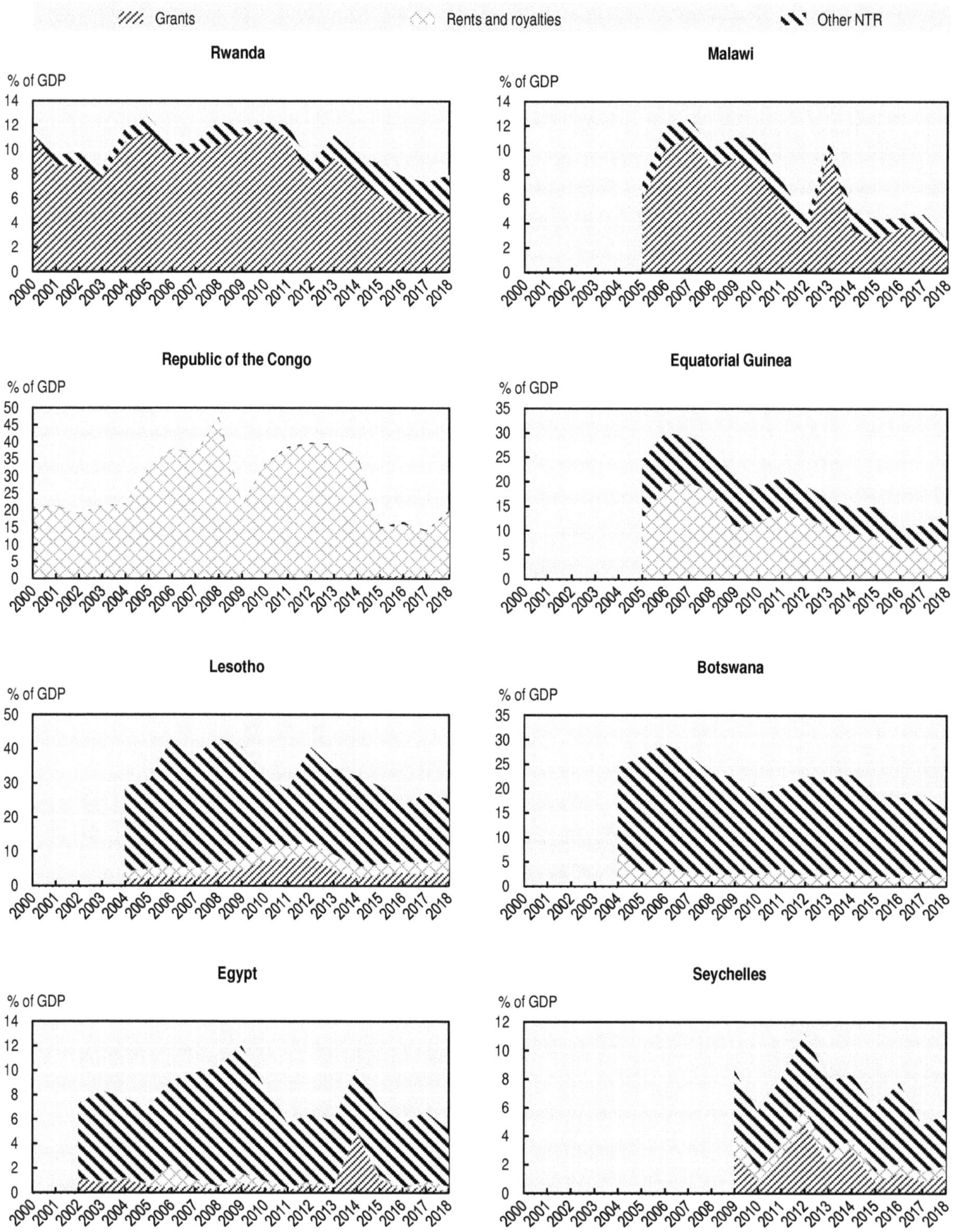

Note: See footnotes to Figure 2.1 and country tables in Chapters 5 and 6 for further information. Charts for all countries in the publication can be found online at the *Statlink* below.

Source: Authors' calculations based on data from (OECD/ATAF/AUC, 2020[1]), "Revenue Statistics in Africa: Comparative tables", *OECD Tax Statistics* (database), *https://doi.org/10.1787/be755711-en*.

StatLink *https://doi.org/10.1787/888934181755*

Although there are long-term trends in non-tax revenues, these revenues tend to vary more from year to year than do tax revenues. Over the past decade, 17 of the 30 countries in this publication showed at least one year-on-year increase in non-tax revenue equivalent to at least 2% of GDP, while 16 countries registered at least one year-on-year decrease of a similar magnitude. Such fluctuations are often driven by resource rents (caused by swings in commodity prices or production) or by grant revenues (reflecting the shorter duration and lower predictability of grant flows in comparison to tax revenues). Other sources of non-tax revenue, such as Eswatini's SACU revenues, have also proven highly variable.

- In the Republic of the Congo, oil royalties jumped from 36.0% of GDP in 2007 to 46.5% of GDP in 2008 before declining by 25.3 percentage points the following year as both oil prices and oil production declined. Between 2014 and 2015, after another fall in oil prices, these revenues dropped from 35.4% of GDP to 14.0% of GDP. In 2015, Congo changed its hydrocarbons code in order to strengthen the national share in oil profits (EIU, 2015[6]).
- Between 2011 and 2012, Mali experienced a sudden drop in grant revenues, from 4.5% of GDP down to 0.1% during a year of multiple political crises.
- Eswatini's non-tax revenues fell from 18.2% of GDP to 8.1% between 2009 and 2010, when its SACU revenues fell by 80% following the collapse in customs and excise taxes in the two years following the global financial crisis.

Grants

This publication contains countries that receive substantial grant revenues alongside some for which grants are negligible. In 2018, 13 countries received grant revenues amounting to less than 0.5% of GDP and 11 received grant revenues which were less than 2% of total tax revenues (Figure 2.7). All of these countries were middle-income countries, according to the World Bank's classification based on gross national incomes (World Bank, 2020[7]). On the other hand, of the ten low-income countries covered by this report, only Uganda received grants amounting to less than 1% of GDP. For five of these countries, grant revenues were equivalent to more than 15% of tax revenues.

Figure 2.7. **Grants by country, 2018**

Percentage of GDP

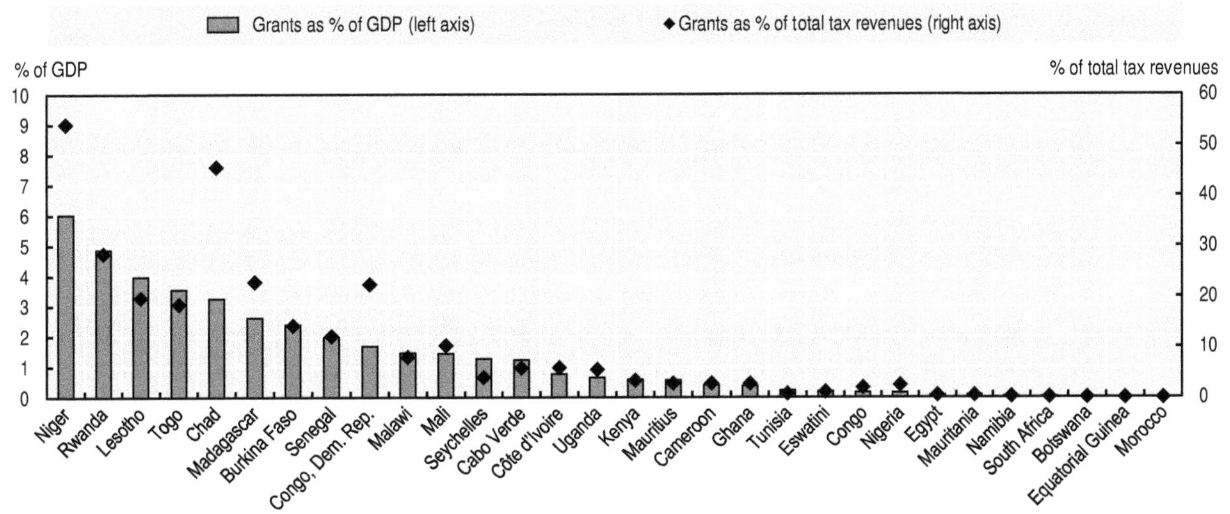

Source: Tables 6.2 and 6.3 in Chapter 6.

StatLink https://doi.org/10.1787/888934181774

Figure 2.8 presents grants as a percentage of GDP received by countries in this publication and their gross national income (GNI) per capita. The figure has an empty upper right-hand quadrant as higher income African countries receive proportionately lower grant revenues. However, many countries occupy the bottom left quadrant of the graph, as there are countries with relatively low levels of grant income despite having lower incomes. For example, Burkina Faso, Rwanda and Uganda had GNI per capita in 2018 between USD 750 and USD 780, but they reported grants as a percentage of GDP in that year ranging from 0.7% (Uganda) and 2.4% (Burkina Faso) to 4.9% (Rwanda). The Seychelles is another outlier, receiving grants equivalent to 1.3% of GDP, the 12th highest out of the 30 countries, despite being the only country in the publication to be classified as high-income.

Figure 2.8. **Grants as a percentage of GDP and GNI per capita by country, 2018**

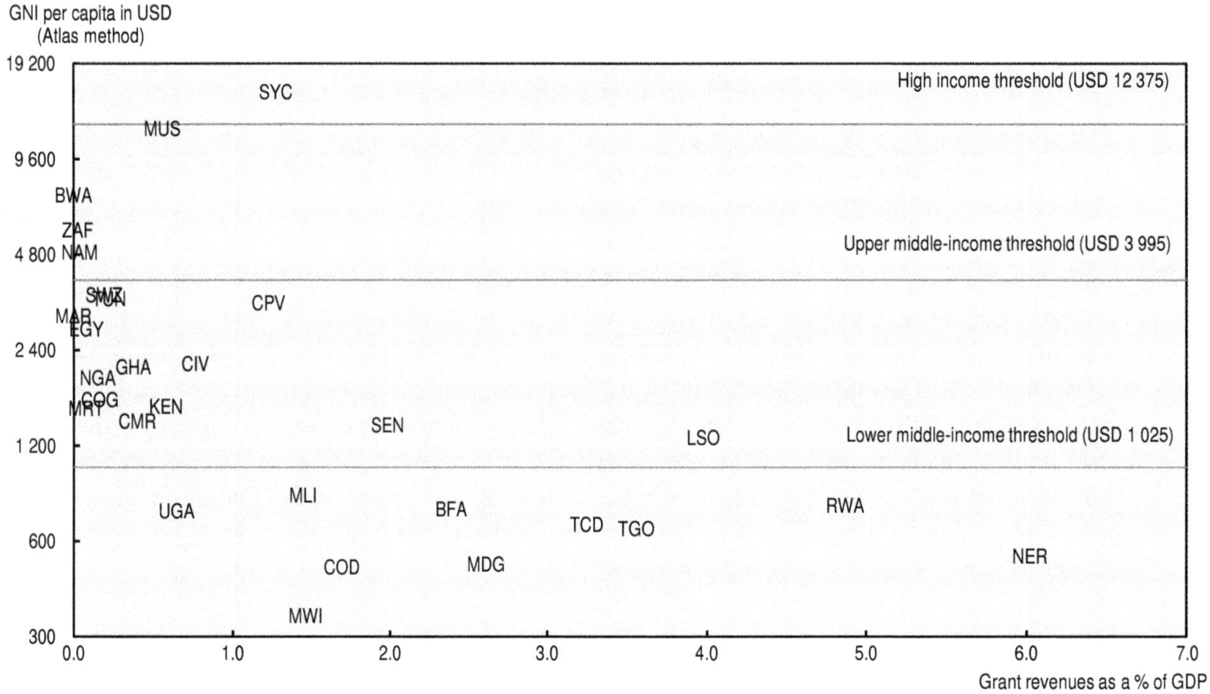

Note: GNI figures are converted to USD using the World Bank Atlas Method.

Source: Table 6.2 in Chapter 6, and World Bank *World Development Indicators* (database).

StatLink https://doi.org/10.1787/888934181793

Grant revenues and foreign aid are similar concepts, although in practice it is difficult to align aid statistics, as reported by donor countries, with the aid revenues reported by recipient countries, due to data, methodological, and conceptual issues.

Grant revenues have some overlap with official development assistance (ODA), as defined by the OECD Development Assistance Committee (DAC).[4] Grants covered by this publication focus on revenues received by countries from foreign governments and international organisations, whereas ODA is a measure of donor countries' efforts to support development in low- and middle-income countries. ODA not only covers flows captured under "grants" in this publication (budget aid, food aid, capital transfers, current transfers, project grants, programme grants, international debt relief, etc.), but also encompasses concessional loans, in-kind technical assistance, in-donor administrative costs, in-donor refugee costs and scholarships, as well as other activities that do not generate a (net) revenue flow to the country. The volume of ODA received by a given country will thus be different from – and usually higher than – the volume of grants reported in *Revenue Statistics*.

Statistics collected by the DAC on ODA flows to African countries include public flows from all members of the DAC and some countries outside the DAC, as well as multilateral organisations such as the World Bank, the IMF and the UN. Statistics on development co-operation provided by some large non-OECD economies, such as Brazil, China and India, are not included (OECD, 2020[8]).

Figure 2.9. **Grants and net official development assistance (ODA) received, 2018**

Percentage of GDP

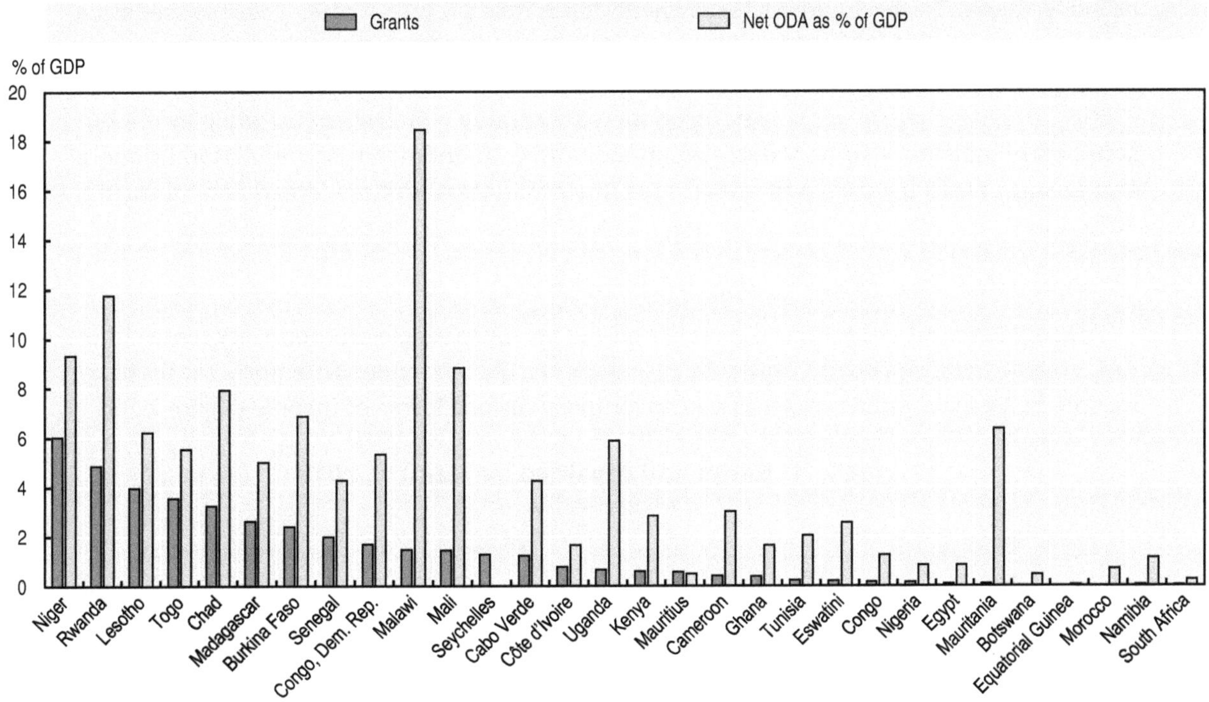

Note: Figures for net ODA include donations from the 30 member countries of the OECD Development Assistance Committee (DAC), the 20 non-DAC countries, as well as multilateral institutions, and private donations. Some major donor countries, such as China are not yet accounted for in these data.

Source: Table 6.2 in Chapter 6 and OECD Development Assistance Committee (DAC) 2020 for the ODA data.

StatLink https://doi.org/10.1787/888934181812

Comparing grant revenues to net ODA (Figure 2.9) shows that the assistance received by African countries is far greater than the amounts that end up going in to their national budgets. Although the countries receiving the most net ODA tend to receive the most grant revenues, the relationship is not linear and there are notable outliers, such as Malawi, whose net ODA as a percentage of GDP of 18.5% far outstrips all other African countries, but whose grant revenues as a percentage of GDP trail behind 9 other African countries.

African countries relying on grant revenues often face sudden drops in grants from one year to the next. Five of the eight countries receiving grants in excess of 5% of GDP in at least one year had at least one single-year drop in grants over this period of at least 2 percentage points of GDP. Malawi received grants amounting to over 10% of GDP in 2013, but they dropped by 65% the following year, the year of the CashGate Scandal (VOANews, 2013[9]). In total, 14 countries among the 30 participating in this publication registered a one-year drop in grant revenues equivalent to at least 1.0% of GDP over the decade.

Average grant revenues as a percentage of GDP for the countries in this publication declined to 1.3% in 2018 from 2.2% in 2010. Between 2010 and 2018, the only years in which average grants as a percentage of GDP for the countries in this publication increased were 2013 and 2017, with 2014 the year in which average grants decreased the most. Changes in grant revenues often depend on circumstances unique to the country. Egypt, for example, saw a spike in grant revenues in 2014 following the normalisation of international relations after its internal political crisis, while Mali saw its grant revenues disappear in 2012 with the outbreak of the Mali War before resuming the following year.

The COVID-19 crisis could be another exogenous event that dramatically impacts aid flows to African countries. Based upon the historic behaviour of ODA over the past several decades, the OECD Development Assessment Committee proposed three possible scenarios for how international aid in 2020 will change as a result of COVID-19, ranging from a possible increase in ODA volumes to a possible decline in ODA flows by up to USD 14 billion in 2020 (OECD, 2020[10]). There is not yet enough data to determine which scenario will play out but some early indicators show a decrease in aid commitments from some bilateral donors and an increase in aid commitments from some multilateral donors (Breed and Sternberg, 2020[11]).

Resource revenues and other property income

One of the most important sources of non-tax revenues for governments originates from their status as property owner, especially as land owner. Such revenues are reported as property income in *Revenue Statistics in Africa* and encompass various forms of income (Figure 2.10).

Figure 2.10. **Rents and royalties by country, 2018**

Percentage of GDP

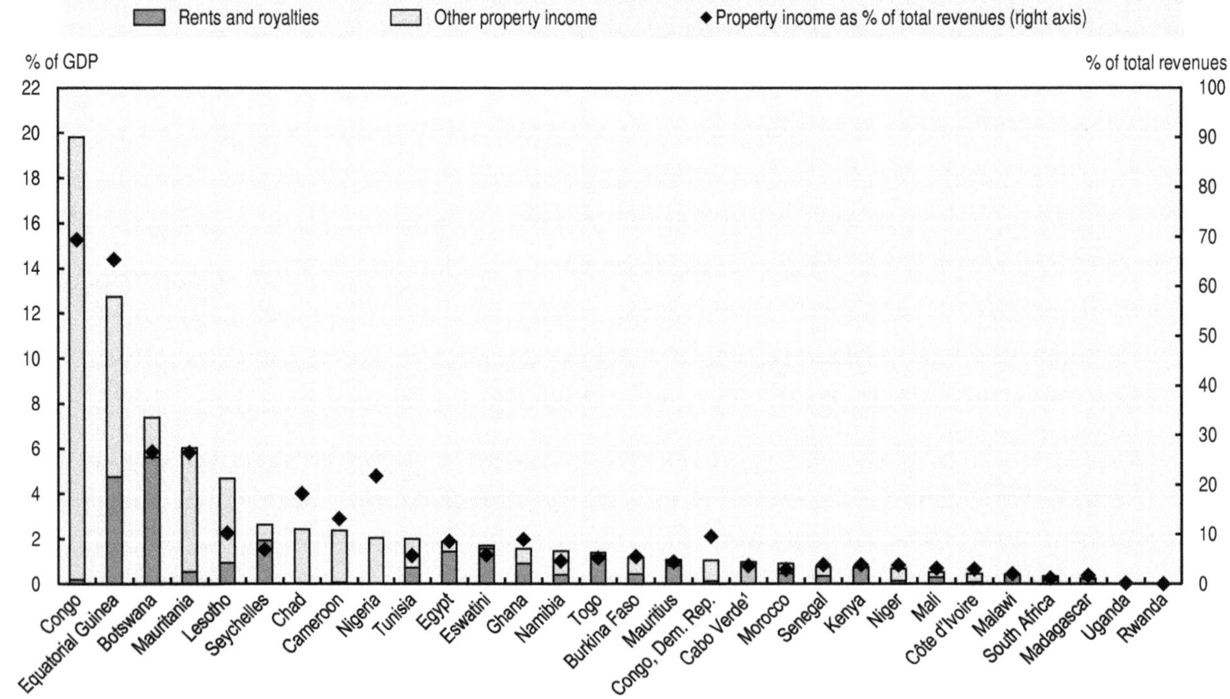

Note: Rwanda is excluded as data are not available.

1. Cabo Verde property income is not disaggregated.

Source: Authors' calculations based on Tables 6.5-6.34 and Table 4.17.

StatLink https://doi.org/10.1787/888934181831

Rents and royalties are revenues generated from property the government owns, usually by prospecting and extracting non-renewable resources from government land or from harvesting government-owned farms and forests. Interest and dividends are returns on government-owned investments in corporations. In general, royalties from oil and minerals are kept distinct from other forms of investment income, but the issue can become complicated. Many African governments create public corporations that manage oil revenues or maintain revenue-sharing agreements with private corporations that exploit these natural resources. The classification of such funds is not always clear. For example, in Botswana, a significant proportion of property income comes from companies investing in diamond extraction (Box 2.3).

Box 2.3. **Natural resources and public finances**[5]

There are various mechanisms by which natural resources can generate revenues or savings for government:

- Rents and royalties are the most direct means of deriving revenue from natural resource wealth. The government charges fees to companies and individuals in exchange for the right to access government lands. It does this in its capacity as landowner and these fees are generally decided through negotiation. These are recorded under property income.
- Payment for services provided by the government is another source of non-tax revenue paid for by businesses in the primary sector. This can include, for example, payments for environmental inspections or for the construction of infrastructure, or, in the case of Mauritius, payment for weather data and maps. These are recorded under sales of goods and services.
- Public ownership (full or partial) of a corporation that exploits natural resources on the government's behalf results in government revenues in the form of profits and dividends. These are recorded under property income. The government of Botswana, for example, collects most of its resource-related revenues from dividends it receives from its 50% stake in Debswana, the company that operates the main diamond mines in Botswana (MiningTechnology, 2020[13]).
- Taxes targeting the activity of natural resource exploitation could be introduced, such as an excise tax on the sale of materials extracted from public lands or a tax on mining that targets the activity, rather than the individual or company exploiting natural resources. These, too, will be recorded as taxes. Such taxes on mining activity exist in Niger and Senegal, who impose taxes on mining activities which are classified under other taxes on goods and services.
- Companies and individuals exploiting natural resources are generally subject to the same taxes (such as income taxes and value-added taxes) as the rest of the population. Revenues from these general taxes will be included in government financial statements, but not necessarily attributed to sectors exploiting natural resources.
- Companies and individuals may use some of the wealth they obtain from natural resource extraction to build infrastructure or provide services. Where this satisfies demand for public investment or services, it could result in savings on government expenditure, but it would not be recorded as revenue. In some cases, as a condition for access to publicly-owned natural resources, governments may demand that companies and individuals provide certain services, for example paying for at least part of the cost of constructing and maintaining roads to mines. An example of this was mining companies participating in a proposed 3 000 km rail link between Benin, Burkina Faso, Niger, Côte d'Ivoire, Ghana, Nigeria and Togo (CNN, 2015[14]).

Revenues from natural resources

Rents and royalties among the 30 countries participating in this publication consist mostly of oil revenues. In 2018, over 77.2% of total rents and royalties in USD were specifically reported as oil revenues (royalties and revenues from revenue-sharing agreements with oil companies), which accounted for a majority of rents and royalties for Cameroon, Chad, the Republic of the Congo, Egypt, Ghana, Equatorial Guinea and Nigeria. Meanwhile, minerals were the source of most rents and royalties for Botswana, Burkina Faso, the Democratic Republic of the Congo, Togo, South Africa and Uganda. Fishing accounted for all revenue recorded as rents and royalties in Seychelles and for 54.2% in Mauritania. In Mauritania, fishing rents were USD 210 million, or 3.0% of GDP. Over 92.5% of total rents and royalties for the 30 countries were resource-related; the remainder included revenues from the construction and operation of airports in Kenya and Togo, for example. Tunisia is only a minor producer of natural gas, but it collects over TND 500 million (Tunisian dinars) each year in rents from the Trans-Mediterranean gas pipeline, which carries Algerian natural gas to Europe (AfricanManager, 2019[12]).

Natural resource revenues tend to be a highly volatile source of financing. Six countries (Chad, Republic of the Congo, Equatorial Guinea, Lesotho, Mauritania and Nigeria) generated rents and royalties equivalent to more than 5% of GDP in at least one of the most recent ten years and they all registered year-over-year decreases in rents and royalties as a percentage of GDP of 25% or more. Chad and Equatorial Guinea both saw at least one year with a decrease of over 60%.

As oil royalties are the dominant form of rents and royalties in Africa, these revenues are highly dependent on actual oil prices (Figure 2.11). With or without Nigerian rents and royalties, which, since 2010, have amounted to between 45% and 70% of total rents and royalties collected by African governments, the evolution of African rents and royalties tracks the international crude oil price.

Figure 2.11. **Total rents and royalties in USD and crude oil price in USD, 2010-18**

Percentage of 2010-18 average

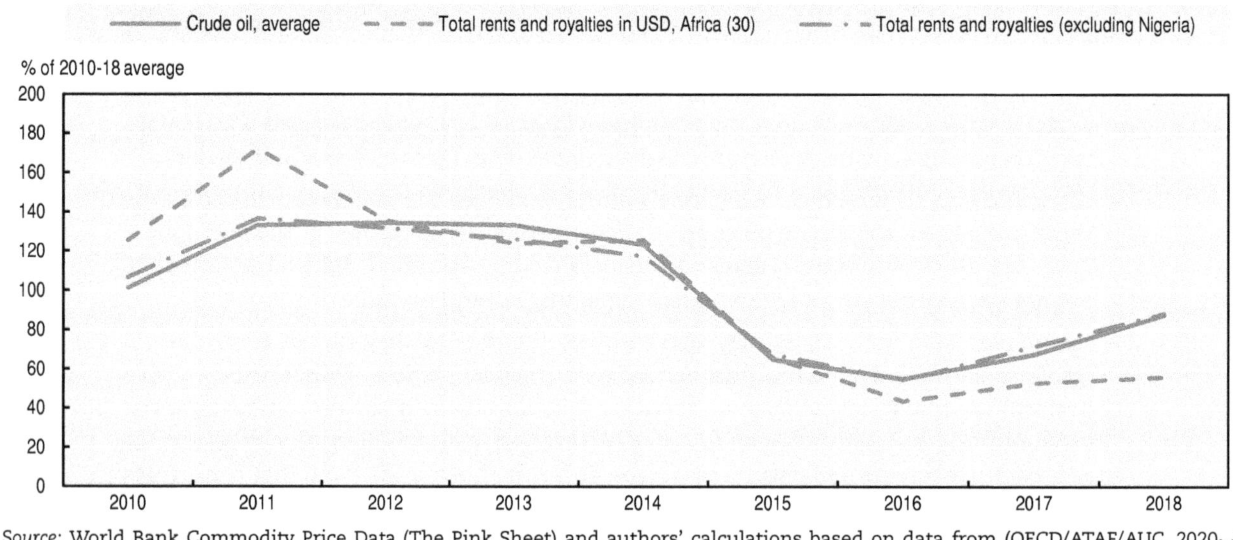

Source: World Bank Commodity Price Data (The Pink Sheet) and authors' calculations based on data from (OECD/ATAF/AUC, 2020[1]), "Revenue Statistics in Africa: Comparative tables", *OECD Tax Statistics* (database), *https://doi.org/10.1787/be755711-en.*

StatLink https://doi.org/10.1787/888934181850

Although resource revenues in African countries are dominated by oil revenues, the countries in this publication have considerable natural resource wealth outside oil, even if, with the exception of Botswana, this generally does not translate into large revenues.

There is a great deal of variation in the size and type of natural resource endowments in African countries. The contribution of this natural wealth to countries' GDP also varies, as does its impact on government budgets. For example, according to World Bank estimates of the contribution of natural resources to economic output (Figure 2.12), Chad, the Republic of the Congo and Equatorial Guinea (mostly oil), the Democratic Republic of the Congo and Mauritania (mostly minerals), and Ghana were the five countries for which natural resources contributed an estimated equivalent of 15% of GDP to economic output in 2018 (World Bank, 2020[15]).[6]

Figure 2.12. **Estimated natural resource extraction, 2018**

Percentage of GDP

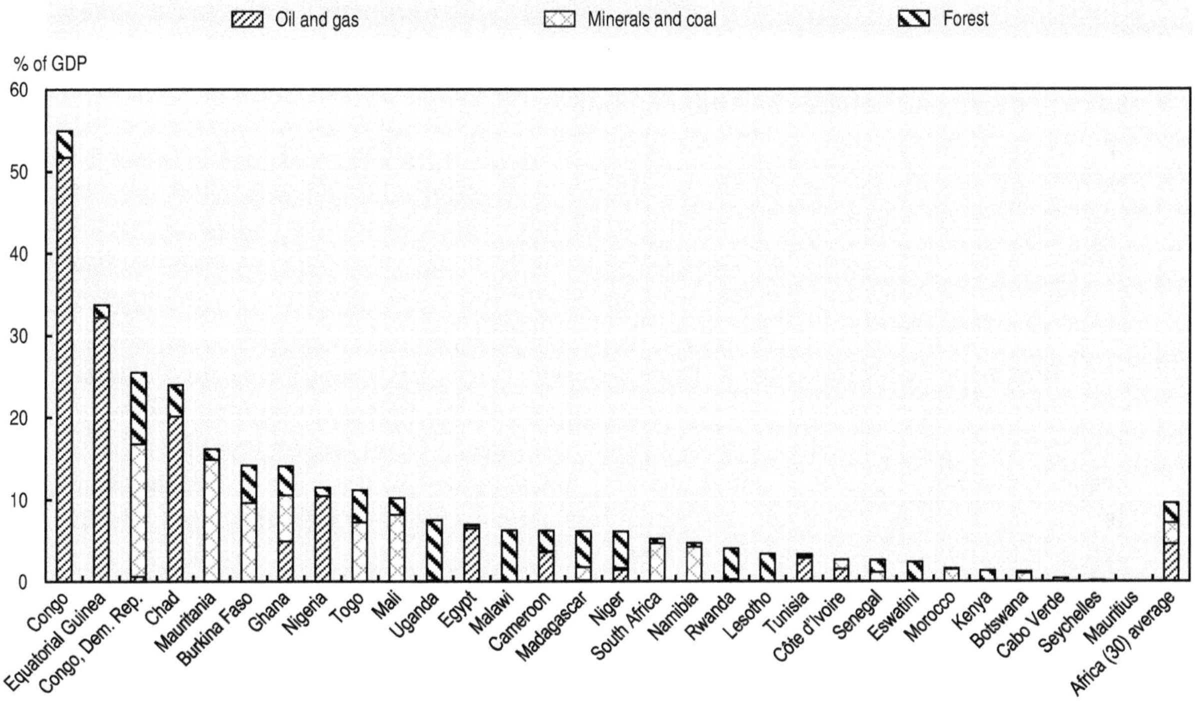

Source: World Bank *World Development Indicators* (database) for estimates of the total value of natural resource production in each country.

StatLink https://doi.org/10.1787/888934181869

The impact of countries' natural resource endowment on public finances also varies greatly. Countries such as Chad, the Republic of the Congo, Mauritania and Equatorial Guinea generate significant public revenues from their natural wealth, while Togo, for example, reported public revenues from natural resource rents equivalent to no more than 0.1% of GDP despite its natural resource wealth production exceeding 10% of GDP.

In three countries (the Democratic Republic of the Congo, Malawi and Uganda), wealth generated by forests exceeded 5% of GDP but did not contribute much to national revenues. Although countries such as Cameroon and Niger did collect some royalties on logging, forest revenues were a small part of the non-tax revenues for the countries in question. Due to the fragility of its Sahel and Saharan ecology, and the importance of wood as an energy source to local communities, Niger has been working with villages on forest management, to establish sustainable forest harvesting practices (Rives, Peltier and Montagne, 2010[16]).

Other non-tax revenues

Certain countries generate substantial non-tax revenues from the normal operations of government. These revenues can be divided into sales of goods and services, fines and penalties, and miscellaneous and unidentified non-tax revenues. The challenges in compiling non-tax revenues outlined in Box 2.3 are often encountered in these kinds of revenues, since they are typically not collected by tax administrations and are often not defined by legislation. They might not even be captured by government budgets.

For all these categories of revenues, there can be arguments about the degree to which they are unrequited or compulsory, and therefore whether they are more properly classified as taxes. The question of which administrative fees are taxes and which are not is discussed in Annexes A and B. However, this is not always clear for the question of fines and penalties.

Institutions and governments that have less authority, and thus less tax collection power, may rely more on these kinds of non-tax revenues. This means that the lack of information in this publication on local government finances might under-estimate the non-tax revenues collected by these institutions.

Sales of goods and services and administrative fees

Governments produce goods and services both as a market- and as a non-market participant. As a market participant, governments sometimes provide goods and services that can also be obtained from private companies (such as selling food or providing transportation). At the same time, they also provide services in the course of administering programmes and executing laws that are unique to the function of government. Fees charged for these non-market services are generally classified as administrative fees.

Administrative fees are often difficult to classify since they occupy a grey area between payments for services (which are non-tax revenues) and compulsory unrequited payments collected during government operations (which are taxes).[7] Court fees and fees for driver's licences, passports, patent registrations and marriage certificates tend to be classified as non-tax revenues. When administrative fees are classified as taxes, they are typically assigned to one of the following categories:

- 4400 Taxes on financial and capital transactions (for example, taxes on sales of land)
- 5200 Taxes on use of goods and performing activities (for example hunting licences, vehicle registrations)
- 6000 Other taxes (for example, sales of fiscal stamps, where stamps are used to pay for taxes and administrative fees).

Six countries generated revenues from sales of goods and services and administrative fees equivalent to at least 1% of GDP in 2018 (Figure 2.13): Cabo Verde (3.4% of GDP), Ghana (1.2% of GDP), Morocco (3.1% of GDP), Seychelles (3.0% of GDP), Mauritius (2.6% of GDP) and Togo (2.4% of GDP). In the cases of Cabo Verde, these revenues were equivalent to 16.0% of total tax revenues, and for Togo, 12.2%.

The composition of these revenues varied by country. In Cabo Verde, 96% of revenues listed under "sales of goods and services" were fees. In Ghana, most revenues listed as sales of goods and services were collected by Municipalities, Departments and Agencies or by Metropolitan, Municipal and District Assemblies. In Morocco, 58% of revenue from government sales of goods and services were collected at the local level.

Figure 2.13. **Sales of goods and services and administrative fees and other revenues related to administration, 2018**

Percentage of GDP

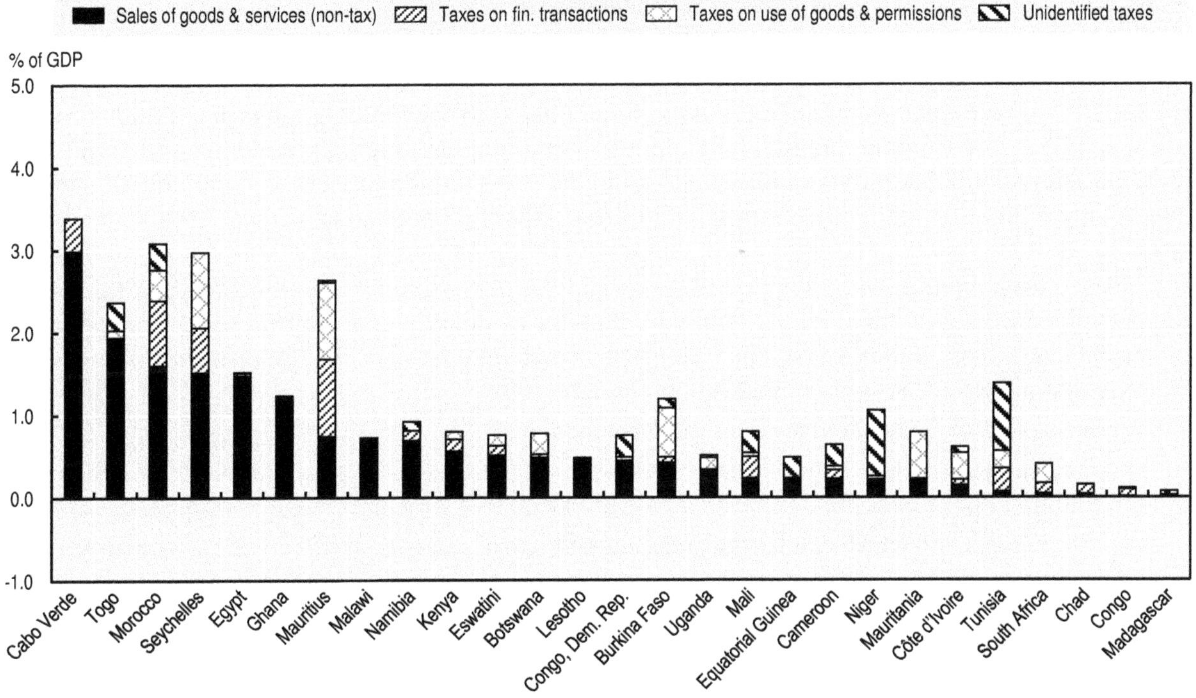

Note: Figures reported here include sub-national tax revenues for Mauritius, Morocco, and South Africa and sub-national non-tax revenues for Eswatini, Kenya, Mauritius, and Morocco, the only countries for which such revenues were reported for 2018. Nigeria, Rwanda, and Senegal are excluded as data are not available.

Source: Authors' calculations based on data from (OECD/ATAF/AUC, 2020[1]), "Revenue Statistics in Africa: Comparative tables", *OECD Tax Statistics* (database), *https://doi.org/10.1787/be755711-en*.

StatLink https://doi.org/10.1787/888934181888

Miscellaneous or unidentified revenue

Some notable categories of non-tax revenue do not fit within any of the categories listed above. These include:

- capital transfers not included elsewhere;
- voluntary donations to government agencies from individuals or private corporations (not including donations from international organisations, which are classified as grants);
- private payments to government made as a result of major court settlements or insurance claims (such as the EUR 100 million payment Arcelor Mittal agreed to pay to the government of Senegal after a court case following the cancelation of an iron mine (RFI, 2014[17]);
- payments covering different categories in the classification list where a breakdown is not available;
- payments whose proper classification is unknown due to a lack of data. Rwanda did not disaggregate non-tax revenue outside of grants, so these were included in this category;
- SACU revenues to Botswana, Eswatini, Lesotho and Namibia (see Box 2.4).

Miscellaneous and unidentified revenues can be a significant component of non-tax revenues in certain countries. These include exceptional voluntary contributions to government in Tunisia, capital transfers from special statutory funds in Mauritius and, in Morocco, payments made to government in exchange for the right to compete with state institutions in the provision of services.

Box 2.4. **SACU revenue**

The Southern African Customs Union (SACU) incorporates Botswana, Eswatini, Lesotho, Namibia and South Africa. It is headquartered in Windhoek, Namibia. Its vision is "an economic community with equitable and sustainable development, dedicated to the welfare of its people for a common future".

SACU is the oldest customs union in the world, having been founded in 1899 between the British colony of Cape of Good Hope and the Orange Free State Boer Republic. Subsequent agreements in 1910 and 1969 included Botswana, Eswatini and Lesotho. Following Namibia's independence in 1990 and the end of apartheid in South Africa in 1994, new negotiations led to the current SACU agreement, which was signed in 2002.

The SACU agreement provides for free movement of SACU manufactured products within the union, without application of tariffs or duties. It also provides for common external tariffs and for the payment of customs and excise duties into a common pool to be shared between the SACU countries under the revenue-sharing formula set out in the Annex to the agreement.

The revenue-sharing agreement includes three components:

- A customs component, which divides the gross amount of customs duties according to the value of goods each country imports from other SACU countries in a given year (as a percentage of intra-SACU imports).
- An excise component, which divides the gross amount of excise duties according to each country's GDP as a percentage of SACU's combined GDP.
- A development component, which is funded from 15% of the excise component and is weighted toward less developed SACU countries using a formula based on GDP per capita.

In this publication, revenue from excises, tariffs and customs duties are included as tax revenues in the SACU country that collected the revenue. They are included under headings 5121 (Excises) and 5123 (Customs and import duties) in the tax revenue tables. Revenues received from the SACU Common Revenue Pool are included as miscellaneous revenue in the non-tax revenue tables, as seen in Table 6.13 for Eswatini. In the case of South Africa, where payments exceed the revenue share received from the Pool, the payments net of the share received are recorded as a memorandum item in the non-tax revenue table (Table 6.22).

Sources: (SACU, 2017[19]), (SACU, 2014[20]).

The volatility of miscellaneous and unidentified revenues may be due to large capital transfers, revenue streams that are short-lived or funds that are reclassified as unidentified due to lack of information. The higher values for this category could reflect uncertainty as to the true amount of revenue within other non-tax revenue classifications.

Southern African Customs Union revenues

For the first time, all five members of SACU are participating in the *Revenue Statistics in Africa* initiative. This permits a full accounting of all revenues going into the SACU Common Revenue Pool and the amount allocated to member countries (Figure 2.14).

All five members of SACU collect customs and excise taxes under a unified tax regime and then transfer those funds to the SACU Common Revenue Pool. The SACU Revenue Pool in turn redistributes the moneys collected under a complex revenue sharing formula. In practice, however, South Africa possesses the main ports of entry into Southern Africa and ends up collecting almost all the customs duties and excises allocated to the SACU Common Revenue Pool. South Africa therefore ends up making net payments into the SACU Revenue Pool, while the other SACU countries are net recipients of funds from the Pool.

Figure 2.14. **Total SACU and other non-tax revenues by country**

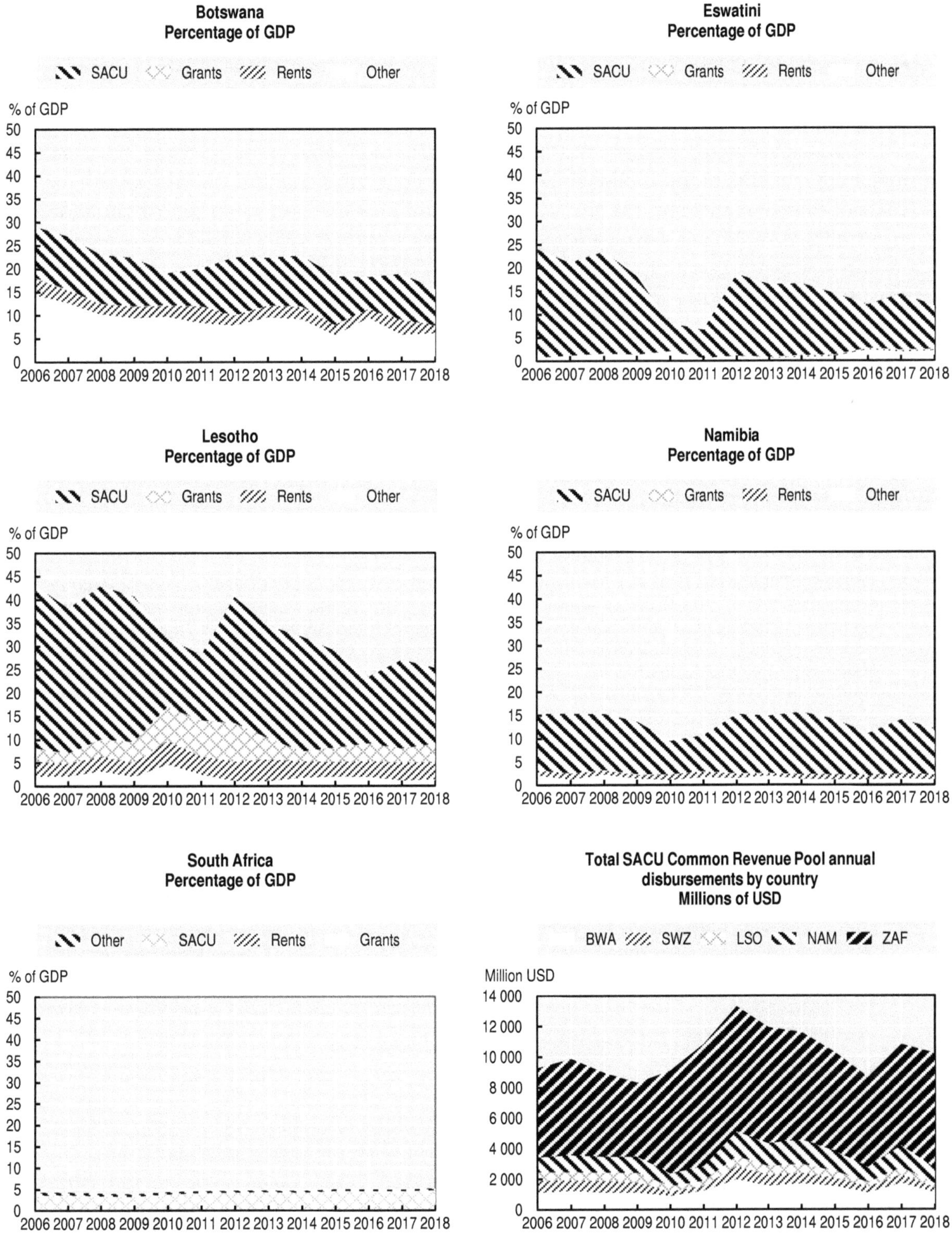

Note: SACU revenues reported here are classified as non-tax revenues for all countries presented here except for South Africa. For South Africa, SACU revenues received by the government of South Africa are classified under customs duties and excise taxes, and not non-tax revenues.

Source: Authors' calculations based on data from (OECD/ATAF/AUC, 2020[1]), "Revenue Statistics in Africa: Comparative tables", *OECD Tax Statistics* (database), *https://doi.org/10.1787/be755711-en*.

StatLink https://doi.org/10.1787/888934181907

SACU revenues to South Africa are negligible but they have a strong impact on the finances of the other members of the customs union. In 2018, these revenues boosted the revenues of Botswana, Eswatini, Lesotho and Namibia by 7.7%, 9.2%, 16.0% and 9.8% of GDP, respectively. Besides exogenous economic shocks, member countries also saw their SACU revenues rise and fall due to changes in the parameters used in the SACU revenue-sharing formula. The economic shock of the global financial crisis rendered many economic forecasts of the time inaccurate; because SACU payments were calculated based on these forecasts, major adjustments to SACU payments were required in 2010 and 2011 to compensate for years of overpayments into the SACU pool (Mongardini et al., 2011[18]). A similar situation occurred in 2014, when a slowdown in South Africa's economy again caused forecasts to be revised downward; Eswatini, Lesotho and Namibia's SACU revenues declined as a percentage of GDP in 2015 and 2016, although this trend was reversed in 2017.

Notes

1 There is no comparison with the averages of the 25 Latin American and Caribbean (LAC) countries (see OECD et al., 2018[22]) and the 36 OECD countries (see OECD, 2017[21]), as these publications do not cover non-tax revenues.

2 Please see the Interpretative Guide to non-tax revenue in Annex B of this report for the definitions of these revenue categories.

3 Not counting Burkina Faso, the Democratic Republic of the Congo, Egypt, Madagascar, Malawi and Nigeria for which data is not available.

4 The official definition of ODA is: "flows to countries and territories on the Development Assistance Committee List of ODA Recipients and to multilateral institutions which are provided by official agencies, including state and local governments, or by their executive agencies. In addition, each transaction must be administered with the promotion of the economic development and welfare of developing countries as its main objective; and be concessional in character and conveys a grant element of at least 25% (calculated at a rate of discount of 10%)". Further information is available at: *www.oecd.org/dac/financing-sustainable-development/index-terms.htm#ODA*.

5 (Mansour and Rota-Graziosi, 2013[23]) note that taxes on oil extraction can include corporate income tax, excise taxes on energy products, un-refunded sales taxes such as VATs and non-tax revenue can include royalties, profit sharing, dividends received from state enterprises, and other investment income received from government direct participation in extractive enterprises.

6 The World Bank refers to "natural resource rents". This is calculated as the difference between the value of natural resource production in the countries according to commodity prices and the estimated cost of resource extraction. It is not to be confused with the definition of resource rent used by the OECD, for which it is defined as a form of government revenue. Please see the documentation of resource rents in the World Bank World Development Indicators dataset (see *https://databank.worldbank.org/metadataglossary/adjusted-net-savings/series/NY.GDP.TOTL.RT.ZS*) and the Interpretative Guide for more details.

7 See paragraphs 9-13 of the OECD Interpretative Guide in Annex A for an explanation of how administrative fees are classified in this publication.

References

AfricanManager (2019), *Gazoduc-ENI: Des royalties de 500 millions de dinars par an pour la Tunisie*, *https://africanmanager.com/la-tunisie-tirera-500-millions-de-dinars-par-an-du-gazoduc-avec-litalie/*. [12]

AUC/OECD (n.d.), *Africa's Development Dynamics 2020: Digital Transformation for Quality Jobs*, OECD Publishing, Paris/African Union Commission, Addis Ababa. [5]

Breed, D. and L. Sternberg (2020), *Tracking aid flows to the Covid-19 response*, Development Initiatives Poverty Research Ltd, *https://devinit.org/data/tracking-aid-flows-in-light-of-the-covid-19-crisis/#downloads* (accessed on 2 October 2020). [11]

CNN (2015), *Mammoth rail network to put West African economies on the right track*, *https://edition.cnn.com/2015/03/05/africa/west-africa-minerals-railway/index.html* (accessed on 21 September 2020). [14]

EIU (2015), *Government approves new hydrocarbons code*, *https://country.eiu.com/article.aspx?articleid=1303035314&Country=Congo%20(Brazzaville)&topic=Eco_9*. [6]

Georgieva, K., C. Pazarbasioglu and R. Weeks-Brown (2020), *Reform of the International Debt Architecture is Urgently Needed*, *https://blogs.imf.org/2020/10/01/reform-of-the-international-debt-architecture-is-urgently-needed/?utm_medium=email&utm_source=govdelivery*. [2]

IMF (2020), *List of LIC DSAs for PRGT-Eligible Countries*, *www.imf.org/external/Pubs/ft/dsa/DSAlist.pdf*. [4]

IMF (2020), *World Economic Outlook Database April 2020*, *www.imf.org/external/pubs/ft/weo/2020/01/weodata/index.aspx* (accessed on 8 September 2020). [3]

Mansour, M. and G. Rota-Graziosi (2013), "Tax Coordination, Tax Competition, and Revenue Mobilization in the West African Economic and Monetary Union", *IMF Working Paper*, Vol. 13/163, *www.imf.org/en/Publications/WP/Issues/2016/12/31/Tax-Coordination-Tax-Competition-and-Revenue-Mobilization-in-the-West-African-Economic-and-40756*. [23]

MiningTechnology (2020), *Debswana diamond mines*, *www.mining-technology.com/projects/debswana/* (accessed on 20 September 2020). [13]

Mongardini, J. et al. (2011), *In the wake of the global economic crisis : adjusting to lower revenue of the Southern African Customs*, International Monetary Fund, *www.imf.org/external/pubs/ft/dp/2011/afr1101.pdf*. [18]

OECD (2020), *DAC Data Submitters*, *www.oecd.org/dac/financing-sustainable-development/development-finance-standards/dacdatasubmitters.htm* (accessed on 18 September 2020). [8]

OECD (2020), *Six decades of ODA: insights and outlook in the COVID-19 crisis*, OECD, *https://doi.org/10.1787/2dcf1367-en*. [10]

OECD (2018), *Global Outlook on Financing for Development*, OECD Publishing, *www.oecd.org/dac/global-outlook-on-financing-for-sustainable-development-2019-9789264307995-en.htm*. [24]

OECD (2017), *Revenue Statistics 2017*, OECD Publishing, Paris, *https://dx.doi.org/10.1787/9789264283183-en*. [21]

OECD/ATAF/AUC (2020), *Revenue Statistics in Africa: Comparative tables*, OECD Publishing, Paris, *http://dx.doi.org/10.1787/be755711-en*. [1]

OECD et al. (2018), *Revenue Statistics in Latin America and the Caribbean 2018*, OECD Publishing, Paris, *https://dx.doi.org/10.1787/rev_lat_car-2018-en-fr*. [22]

RFI (2014), *Le gros chèque d'Arcelor Mittal au Sénégal*, *www.rfi.fr/economie/20140605-le-gros-cheque-arcelor-mittal-senegal*. [17]

Rives, F., R. Peltier and P. Montagne (2010), *Fifteen years of forest community management in Niger: from a technician's dream to social reality*, CIRAD, *https://agritrop.cirad.fr/555467/1/document_555467.pdf*. [16]

SACU (2017), *Southern African Customs Union Agreement 2002 (As amended on 12 April 2013)*, *www.sacu.int/list.php?type=Agreements*. [19]

SACU (2014), *Implementing a Common Agenda Towards Regional Integration: 2014 Annual Report*, *www.sacu.int/docs/reports_annual/2014/annual_report.pdf*. [20]

VOANews (2013), *Malawi: Donors Withhold Aid Over Cashgate Scandal*, *www.voanews.com/africa/malawi-donors-withhold-aid-over-cashgate-scandal* (accessed on 21 September 2020). [9]

World Bank (2020), *World Bank Country and Lending Groups*, *https://datahelpdesk.worldbank.org/knowledgebase/articles/906519* (accessed on June 2020). [7]

World Bank (2020), *World Development Indicators*, *https://data.worldbank.org/* (accessed on 8 September 2020). [15]

Revenue Statistics in Africa 1990-2018/Statistiques des recettes publiques en Afrique 1990-2018

Chapitre 2

Tendances des recettes non fiscales, 2000-2018

Introduction

Les statistiques relatives à la fiscalité ne sauraient suffire pour dresser le panorama complet des finances publiques, en particulier dans le cas de nombreux pays africains, qui perçoivent d'importantes recettes sous la forme de dons ou de redevances pétrolières et minières. Les *Statistiques des recettes publiques en Afrique* présentent des données sur les recettes fiscales et non fiscales, ces dernières étant les recettes des administrations publiques qui ne correspondent pas à la définition des recettes fiscales établie par l'OCDE. Si les données relatives aux recettes non fiscales ne sont pas nécessairement aussi fiables que les statistiques des recettes fiscales ou peuvent provenir de sources différentes (voir encadré 2.1), il n'en convient pas moins de prendre en compte ces recettes dans le total des ressources financières d'un pays. Le présent chapitre livre des comparaisons des recettes non fiscales entre les pays couverts par la présente publication[1].

Encadre 2.1. **Recettes non fiscales et fiabilité des données**

Les données relatives aux recettes non fiscales sont souvent moins détaillées que celles relatives aux recettes fiscales. Il arrive que, pour certaines années, des pays fournissent un total agrégé de leurs recettes non fiscales, sans autre détail que la répartition entre dons et autres catégories. Cela tient probablement au fait que les données relatives aux recettes non fiscales proviennent souvent d'une multiplicité de sources. Les *Statistiques des recettes publiques en Afrique* contiennent des cas où le montant total des recettes non fiscales indiqué peut être incomplet.

Les données sur les recettes non fiscales ne font pas nécessairement l'objet de vérifications aussi strictes que celles relatives aux recettes fiscales. Un grand nombre de catégories ne sont pas prises en compte dans l'élaboration du budget principal et ne sont pas non plus définies par la loi, en conséquence de quoi elles ne sont pas soumises aux mêmes mécanismes de contrôle que les recettes fiscales. En l'absence de dispositions juridiques contraignantes, les recettes non fiscales ne sont pas toujours soumises aux mêmes obligations documentaires.

Les recettes non fiscales relèvent souvent d'autorités différentes que les recettes fiscales, de sorte que la distinction n'est pas nécessairement faite entre les recettes et les dépenses. Il est possible que certaines recettes, comme les frais administratifs, servent de mécanismes d'amortissement et viennent minorer les coûts au lieu d'être comptabilisées comme recettes. Cela peut notamment être le cas pour les collectivités locales et autres institutions publiques pour lesquelles on ne dispose pas de données autres que celles relatives aux transferts nets de fonds à destination de l'administration centrale.

Les dons, les règlements juridiques, les contrats d'exploitation minière ou pétrolière donnent aussi souvent lieu à des versements importants de la part d'entités extérieures telles que des entreprises multinationales ou des administrations étrangères qui ne sont pas toujours incitées à faire preuve de transparence. Il est également possible que ces entités soient tentées de s'entendre avec les autorités locales en vue de masquer les coûts. En outre, il est plus difficile d'établir des ventilations détaillées dès lors qu'un pays négocie en contrepartie de l'extraction de ressources le versement de sommes forfaitaires élevées, qui regroupent plusieurs catégories de recettes, fiscales et non fiscales.

Les principales catégories de recettes non fiscales[2] examinées dans le cadre de ce projet sont les suivantes (voir également annexe B) :

- dons émanant de pays étrangers ou d'organisations internationales (aide budgétaire, aide alimentaire, transferts de capitaux, transferts courants, subventions de projets, bourses de programme, allégement de la dette internationale, etc.)
- loyers et redevances (par exemple, redevances pétrolières ou minières)
- autres revenus de la propriété (intérêts, dividendes et autres rémunérations d'investissements publics)
- produits de la vente de biens et de services (ce qui inclut certains frais administratifs)
- produits des amendes et pénalités (notamment pour infraction à la législation fiscale)
- recettes diverses non identifiées (recettes non fiscales qui ne peuvent être classées dans les autres catégories).

Recettes non fiscales exprimées en pourcentage du PIB

Dans les 30 pays couverts par la présente publication, les recettes non fiscales, exprimées en pourcentage du PIB, allaient de 0.6 % du PIB en Afrique du Sud à 25.2 % au Lesotho. Dans tous les pays, à l'exception du Lesotho, de la République du Congo, du Botswana et de la Guinée équatoriale, les recettes non fiscales ont été inférieures aux recettes fiscales (Graphique 2.1). En moyenne, le montant des recettes non fiscales perçues dans chacun de ces pays a représenté 49.9 % du montant des recettes fiscales recouvrées.

Graphique 2.1. **Recettes fiscales et non fiscales totales par pays, 2018**

En pourcentage du PIB

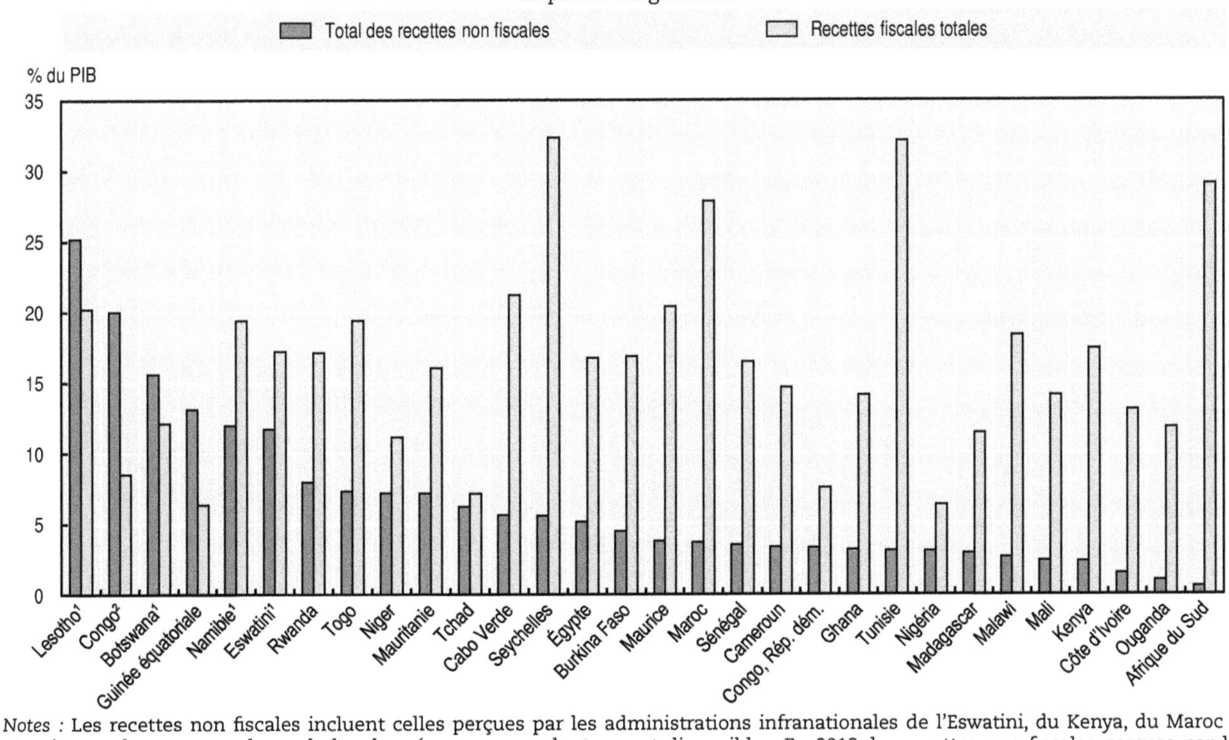

Notes : Les recettes non fiscales incluent celles perçues par les administrations infranationales de l'Eswatini, du Kenya, du Maroc et Maurice, seuls pays pour lesquels les données correspondantes sont disponibles. En 2018, les recettes non fiscales perçues par les administrations infranationales représentaient, pour chacun de ces pays, respectivement 1 %, 16 %, 3 % et 45 % des recettes non fiscales totales. L'Afrique du Sud, la Mauritanie et le Nigéria ont déclaré percevoir des taxes locales et régionales, mais n'ont pas fait état de recettes non fiscales locales ou régionales.

1. Dans les cas du Botswana, de l'Eswatini, du Lesotho et de la Namibie, les recettes non fiscales incluent les fonds qui leur sont transférés en vertu de l'accord de partage des recettes de l'Union douanière d'Afrique australe (SACU) après perception des droits de douane et d'accise par l'Afrique du Sud.

2. Les montants indiqués ici pour les dons et recettes pétrolières de la République du Congo sont ceux publiés en avril 2020 dans les *Perspectives de l'économie mondiale* du FMI.

Pour certains pays, les valeurs des ratios recettes fiscales/PIB et recettes non fiscales/PIB sont à interpréter avec prudence, car elles reposent sur des données incomplètes. Pour de plus amples informations, se reporter aux tableaux par pays des chapitres 5 et 6.

Source : Tableau 4.1 du chapitre 4 et tableau 6.1 du chapitre 6.

StatLink https://doi.org/10.1787/888934182363

L'examen du rapport entre recettes fiscales et non fiscales exprimées en pourcentage du PIB fait apparaître différents groupes de pays (Graphique 2.2). Les pays bénéficiaires de recettes pétrolières exceptionnellement élevées, comme la Guinée équatoriale, la République du Congo et le Tchad, font partie de ceux qui affichent les ratios impôts /PIB les plus faibles. Les pays bénéficiaires nets des recettes redistribuées par l'Union douanière d'Afrique australe (South African Customs Union, SACU) se caractérisent également par un niveau élevé de recettes non fiscales (se reporter à la section sur les recettes issues de la SACU pour de plus amples explications). En général, les pays à revenu intermédiaire supérieur qui ne sont pas de grands producteurs de pétrole perçoivent moins de dons et de recettes tirées des ressources naturelles, ce qui les contraint davantage à recourir à la voie fiscale pour mobiliser des ressources intérieures.

Graphique 2.2. **Recettes fiscales et non fiscales totales par pays, 2018**

En pourcentage du PIB

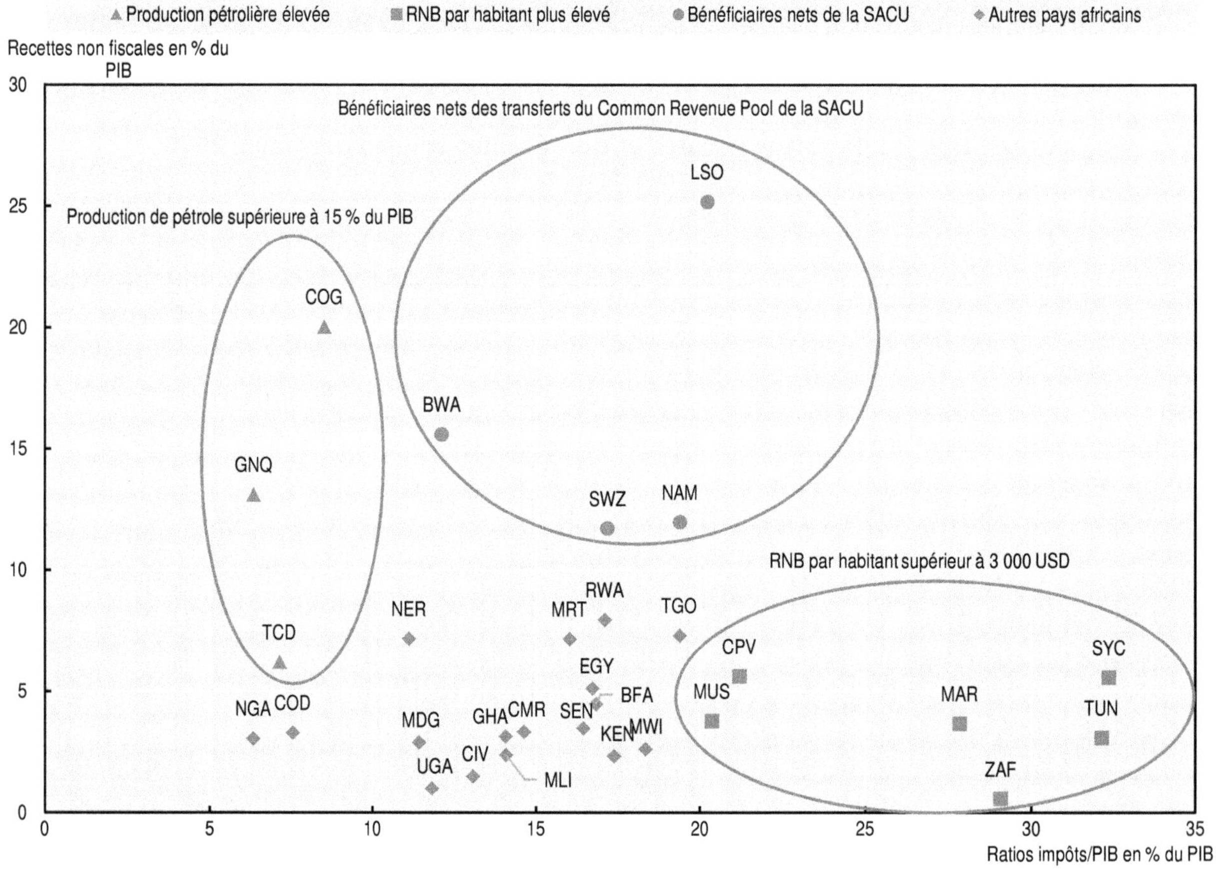

Note : Pour de plus amples informations, se reporter aux notes du graphique 2.1 et aux tableaux par pays présentés dans les chapitres 5 et 6.

Source : Calculs des auteurs basés sur des données figurant dans « Statistiques des recettes publiques en Afrique : Tableaux comparatifs » (OCDE/ATAF/CUA, 2020[1]), *Statistiques fiscales de l'OCDE* (base de données), *https://doi.org/10.1787/7f54581d-fr*.

StatLink *https://doi.org/10.1787/888934182382*

En Afrique (30 pays), le ratio moyen impôts/PIB a progressé entre 2010 et 2018, tandis que celui des recettes non fiscales a chuté (Graphique 2.3). Après avoir culminé en 2012 à 9.2 %, le montant moyen des recettes non fiscales est tombé à 6.0 % du PIB en 2016 avant de remonter à 6.5 % en 2018. Cette diminution tient au recul des recettes tirées des loyers et redevances et des recettes perçues sous forme de dons, exprimées en pourcentage du

PIB. En 2018, les recettes des dons en pourcentage du PIB étaient de 1.3 % du PIB, atteignant leur point le plus bas depuis 2010. Les loyers et les redevances étaient de 1.9 % en 2018, 1.1 point de pourcentage de moins qu'en 2012, après avoir légèrement rebondi depuis le creux de 2016. Ces baisses ont suffi à entraîner une baisse des recettes totales au cours de cette période, entraînant une augmentation des déficits et de l'endettement (encadré 2.2).

Graphique 2.3. **Niveau moyen des recettes non fiscales en Afrique (30), 2010-18**

En pourcentage du PIB

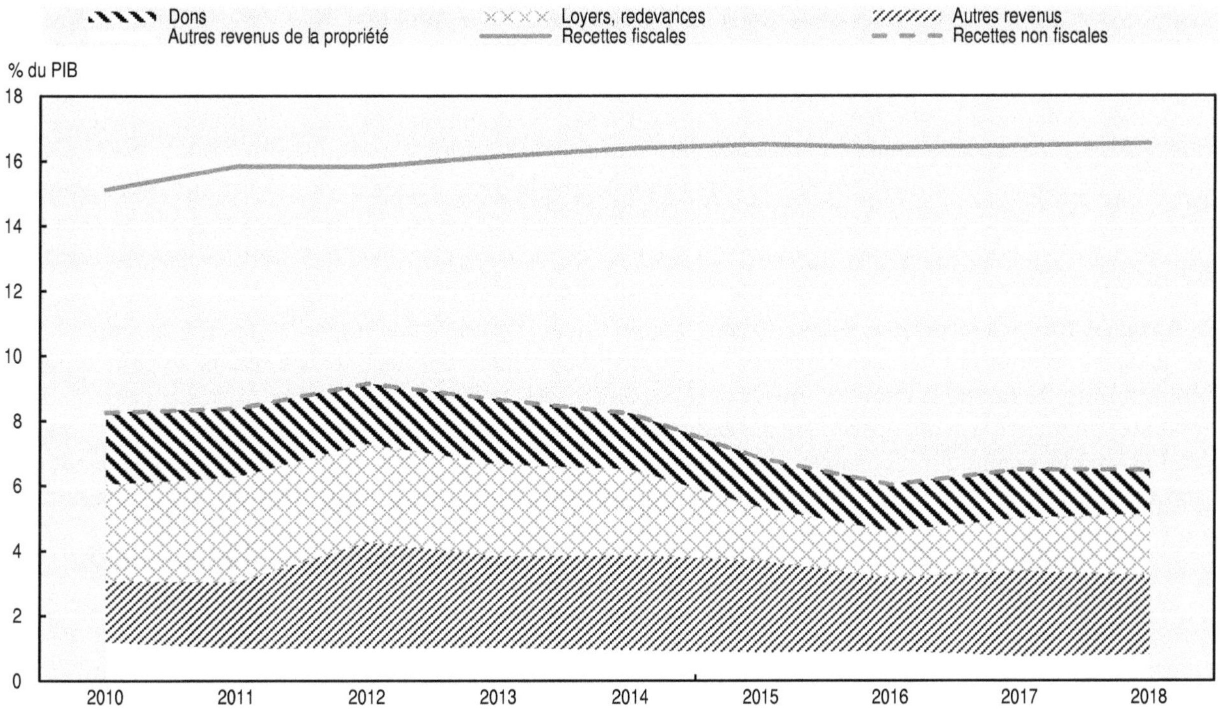

Source : Calculs des auteurs basés sur des données figurant dans « Statistiques des recettes publiques en Afrique : Tableaux comparatifs » (OCDE/ATAF/CUA, 2020[1]), *Statistiques fiscales de l'OCDE* (base de données), *https://doi.org/10.1787/7f54581d-fr*.

StatLink *https://doi.org/10.1787/888934182401*

Selon leur origine, les recettes non fiscales sont sensibles aux changements brusques ou bien vulnérables aux chocs économiques ou aux changements politiques, notamment. Le Graphique 2.5 montre la part de chaque sous-catégorie dans le total des recettes non fiscales des pays. Ces données font apparaître quatre groupes distincts :

- Douze pays ont perçu en 2018 la majeure partie de leurs recettes non fiscales sous la forme de dons (par ordre décroissant : le Rwanda, le Togo, le Niger, le Tchad, le Burkina Faso, le Sénégal, la République démocratique du Congo, Madagascar, le Malawi, le Mali, la Côte d'Ivoire et l'Ouganda).
- Pour six autres, c'est sous la forme de loyers et de redevances (par ordre décroissant : la République du Congo, la Guinée équatoriale, la Mauritanie, le Cameroun, la Tunisie et le Nigéria). Dans tous ces pays à l'exception de la Tunisie, les redevances pétrolières ont représenté l'essentiel des recettes non fiscales.
- Les quatre voisins de l'Afrique du Sud membres de la SACU, à savoir le Botswana, le Lesotho, la Namibie et l'Eswatini, ont perçu une grande partie de leurs recettes non fiscales sous la forme de revenus transférés par la SACU (encadré 2.4).

- Les huit pays restants tirent l'essentiel de leurs recettes non fiscales, non pas des dons, loyers, redevances ou recettes redistribuées par la SACU, mais : des intérêts et dividendes dans les cas de l'Afrique du Sud, du Kenya et des Seychelles; des produits de la vente de biens et services dans les cas du Cabo Verde, du Ghana, et du Maroc; et de recettes diverses et non affectées dans les cas de l'Égypte et de Maurice.

Encadré 2.2. **Recettes et dette**

Depuis 2010, les 30 pays étudiés dans le présent rapport voient leur dette publique augmenter considérablement alors que l'initiative pays pauvres très endettés (PPTE) d'allègement des dettes avait préalablement conduit à leur diminution. Entre 2010 et 2018, la dette moyenne des administrations publiques, exprimée en pourcentage du PIB, est passée de 34.6 % à 53.1 % (Graphique 2.4). Fait plus préoccupant encore, la dette en devises s'est elle aussi creusée au cours de la même période, passant de 19.7 % à 29.9 %[3]. Avant l'arrivée de la pandémie de COVID-19, le FMI a calculé que la dette de ces pays s'alourdirait en passant à 61.5 % du PIB. Début octobre 2020, le FMI prévoyait qu'entre fin 2019 et 2021, les ratios moyens de la dette au PIB dans le monde augmenteraient de 20% dans les économies avancées, 10% dans les pays émergents et 7% dans les pays à faible revenu (Georgieva, Pazarbasioglu et Weeks-Brown, 2020[2]).

Jusqu'en 2014, les recettes et dépenses des 30 pays africains étudiés ont augmenté ; pourtant, entre 2012 et 2016, les recettes non fiscales exprimées en pourcentage du PIB ont decliné de 3 points de pourcentage en moyenne, du fait de la chute des recettes tirées des ressources qu'ont provoquée la baisse des prix des matières premières et le ralentissement des flux financiers. Les dépenses moyennes exprimées en pourcentage du PIB ont également diminué, mais avec un certain décalage : elles ont culminé à 28.0 % en 2015 avant de tomber à 25.2 % du PIB en 2018. En conséquence, les déficits ont doublé durant cette période d'ajustements.

Graphique 2.4. **Dette brut moyenne des administrations publiques en Afrique (30), 2005-2020**

En pourcentage du PIB

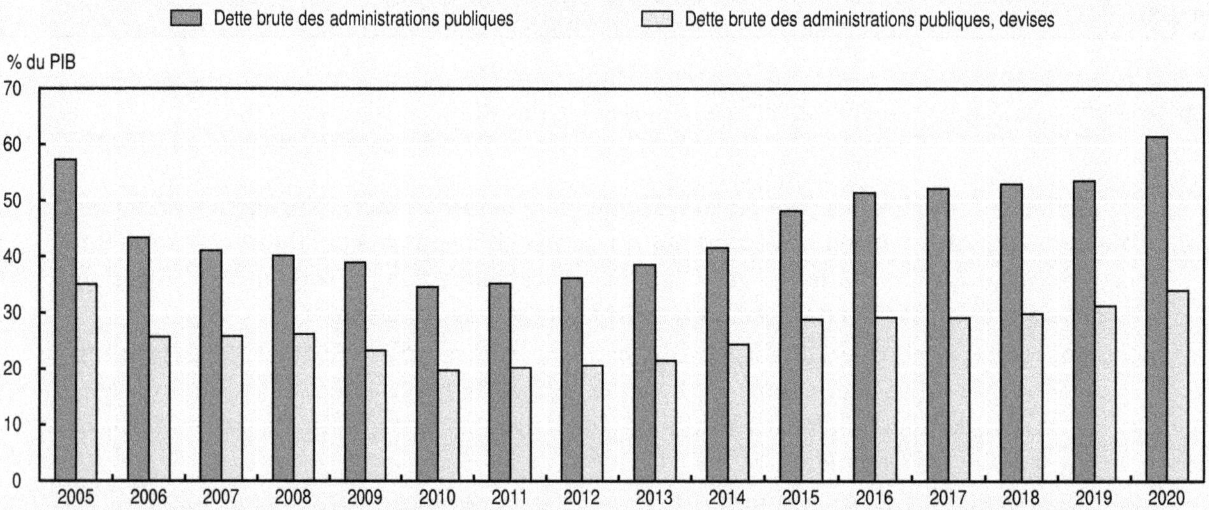

Note : Il s'agit de moyennes non pondérées. Les chiffres indiqués pour 2020 sont des projections résultant de calculs effectués aux tout premiers stades de la pandémie de COVID-19.

Source : Calculs de l'auteur d'après les chiffres de l'édition d'avril 2020 des *Perspectives de l'économie mondiale* (FMI, 2020[3]).

StatLink https://doi.org/10.1787/888934182420

La hausse des niveaux d'endettement dans les pays qui pâtissent déjà d'une plus grande difficulté d'accès au financement risque d'inciter ces pays à se tourner vers des sources de financement plus opaques ou potentiellement porteuses de risque à long terme. Cette situation est encore plus complexe dans les cas du Burkina Faso, de la Côte d'Ivoire, du Mali, du Niger, du Sénégal et du Togo, qui utilisent le franc CFA d'Afrique

Encadré 2.2. **Recettes et dette** *(suite)*

de l'Ouest, ainsi que dans les cas de la République du Congo, du Cameroun, de la Guinée équatoriale, et du Tchad qui utilisent le franc CFA d'Afrique Centrale, car ces pays n'ont pas la possibilité d'emprunter dans leur propre monnaie.

Avec l'arrivée de la pandémie de COVID-19 en 2020, il est désormais impérieux pour les pays Africains de restructurer leur dette et de réformer leurs finances. Cette nouvelle crise est venue ébranler leurs économies et finances publiques au moment même où ils s'efforçaient de s'adapter aux chocs des prix des matières premières survenus en 2014 (voir le chapitre 3 pour de plus amples informations). Au regard du *Cadre de viabilité de la dette* défini par le FMI (FMI, 2020[4]), la République du Congo est surendettée, et six autres pays étudiés (Cameroun, Cabo Verde, Ghana, Kenya, Mauritanie et Tchad) risquent fortement de le devenir. Malgré l'adoption d'une série de mesures sans précédent début 2020 visant à éviter une crise du remboursement de la dette pendant la crise, ces pays ont à présent besoin de trouver des solutions à moyen et long termes pour pouvoir continuer de financer leurs besoins de développement.

L'édition 2020 du rapport *Dynamiques du développement en Afrique* met en relief les dispositions que les pays africains peuvent prendre pour améliorer leurs perspectives budgétaires, tout en conservant leur accès aux capitaux (CUA/OCDE, n.d.[5]) :

- Les pays africains peuvent tirer parti des circonstances exceptionnelles qu'offrent la pandémie mondiale pour négocier la restructuration de leur dette. Les créanciers, habituellement soucieux de ne pas créer de précédent défavorable en matière de remboursement, pourraient être disposés à accepter davantage de mesures d'allégement des dettes dès lors qu'il serait entendu qu'elles ne s'appliqueraient que le temps de la crise.
- Les pays africains peuvent s'employer à adopter des positions de négociation communes sur les mesures d'allègement de la dette afin de peser davantage face au nombre grandissant de leurs créanciers du secteur privé ou opérant aux conditions du marché. Un phénomène de regroupement a également commencé à se manifester à l'autre bout de la table des négociations. En avril, l'Institut de la finance internationale (IIF) a présenté, au nom de 450 grandes institutions financières internationales, la liste des conditions requises pour que le secteur privé participe à la restructuration de la dette.
- De leur côté, les pays africains peuvent améliorer des aspects techniques de leur stratégie d'emprunt et tirer parti des instruments financiers pour modifier leurs conditions d'emprunt à leur avantage. L'aménagement de clauses d'action collective dans les émissions obligataires, par exemple, peut réduire les risques, du côté des emprunteurs, et l'incertitude, du côté des investisseurs. La mise en place de marchés obligataires en monnaie locale permettrait en outre aux pays africains d'emprunter dans leur propre monnaie sans s'exposer aux risques de change et d'inflation.

La composition des recettes non fiscales évolue dans le temps (Graphique 2.6). De nombreux pays africains ont subi de fortes variations de leurs recettes non fiscales, qu'elles proviennent majoritairement de dons (Rwanda et Malawi), de rentes provenant de ressources (République du Congo et Guinée équatoriale), des revenus transférés par la SACU (Lesotho et Botswana) ou d'autres sources (Égypte et Seychelles).

Malgré les tendances à long terme qui se dégagent, les recettes non fiscales semblent fluctuer davantage d'une année sur l'autre que les recettes fiscales. Ces dix dernières années, 17 des 30 pays couverts par la présente publication ont connu au moins une année où leurs recettes non fiscales ont augmenté d'au moins 2 % du PIB par rapport à l'année précédente, et 16 pays ont connu au moins une année où leurs recettes non fiscales ont enregistré un recul d'une ampleur similaire par rapport à l'année précédente. Ces fluctuations sont souvent imputables aux rentes provenant de ressources (qui subissent les effets des variations des prix des matières premières, ou des variations de la production) ou aux recettes provenant de dons (qui s'inscrivent moins dans la durée et sont moins prévisibles que les recettes fiscales). D'autres sources de recettes non fiscales, notamment les revenus de l'Eswatini issus de la SACU, se sont également révélées sujettes à une grande variabilité.

- En République du Congo, les redevances pétrolières ont bondi de 36.0 % à 46.5 % du PIB entre 2007 et 2008, avant un déclin de 25.3 points de pourcentage l'année suivante sous l'effet du recul des prix et de la production dans le secteur pétrolier. Une nouvelle baisse des prix pétroliers les a derechef fait chuter entre 2014 et 2015, où elles sont passées de 35.4 % à 14.0% du PIB. En 2015, le Congo a réformé son code des hydrocarbures de manière à accroître la part des bénéfices pétroliers versés à l'État (EIU, 2015[6]).
- Entre 2011 et 2012, les recettes sous forme de dons ont chuté au Mali, passant de 4.5 % à 0.1 % du PIB, en l'espace d'une année marquée par de multiples crises politiques.
- L'Eswatini a vu ses recettes non fiscales passer de 18.2 % à 8.1 % du PIB entre 2009 et 2010 du fait que ses revenus issus de la SACU avaient chuté de 80 %, comme suite à l'effondrement des droits de douane et d'accise durant les deux années qui ont suivi la crise financière mondiale.

Graphique 2.5. **Structure des recettes non fiscales par pays, 2018**

En pourcentage du PIB

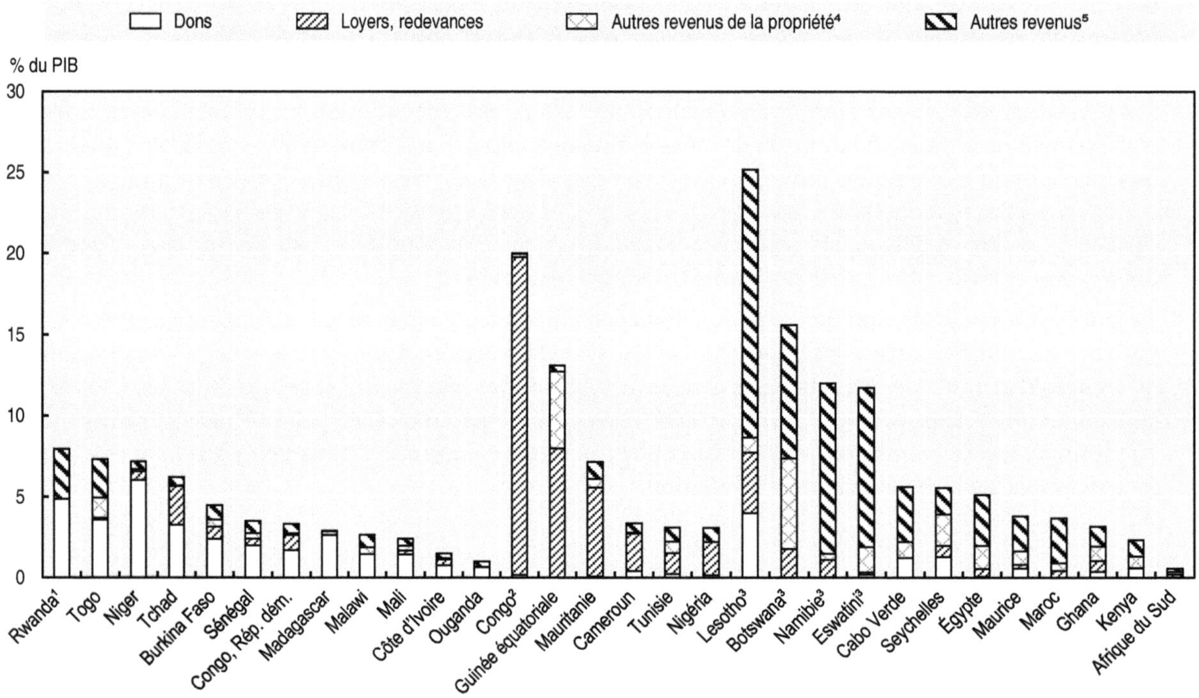

Note : Les données prennent en compte les recettes non fiscales perçues par les administrations infranationales pour l'Eswatini, le Kenya, le Maroc et Maurice.

1. Dans le cas du Rwanda, les recettes non fiscales autres que les dons ne sont pas ventilées par sous-catégorie et sont donc assimilées aux recettes diverses et non identifiées.
2. Les chiffres présentés ici correspondent principalement aux dons et recettes pétrolières recensés dans les *Perspectives de l'économie mondiale* du FMI d'avril 2020 au titre des loyers et redevances.
3. Dans les cas du Botswana, de l'Eswatini, du Lesotho et de la Namibie, les « autres recettes » incluent les fonds qui leur sont transférés en vertu de l'accord de partage des recettes de l'Union douanière d'Afrique australe (SACU) après perception des droits de douane et d'accise par l'Afrique du Sud.
4. Intérêts, dividendes, etc.
5. Ventes, amendes, revenus issus de la SACU, etc.

Pour de plus amples informations, se reporter aux notes du graphique 2.1 et aux tableaux par pays présentés dans les chapitres 5 et 6.

Source : Tableau 6.2 du chapitre 6.

StatLink https://doi.org/10.1787/888934182439

Graphique 2.6. **Évolution de la structure des recettes non fiscales dans certains pays, 2000-18**

En pourcentage du PIB

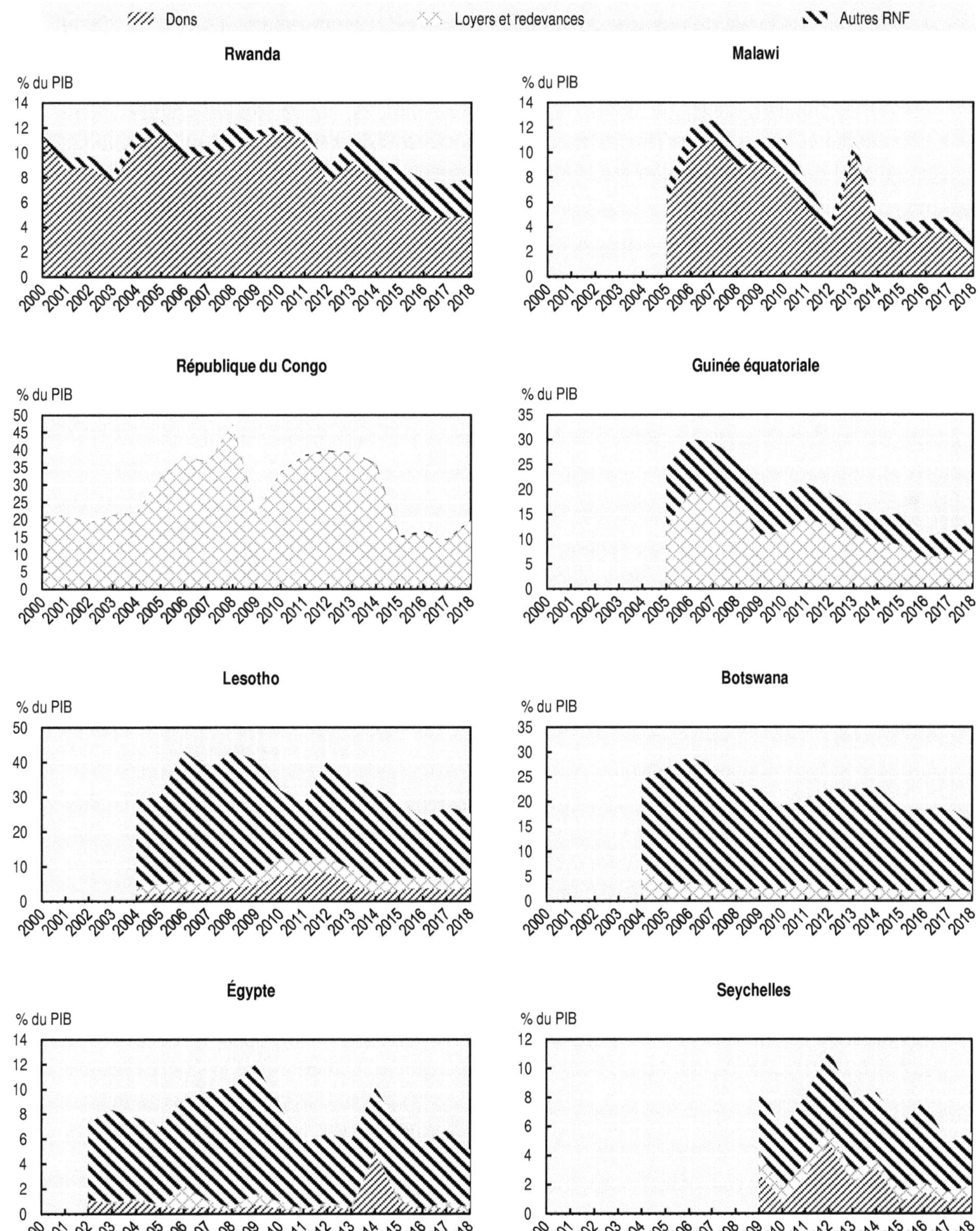

Note : Pour de plus amples informations, se reporter aux notes du graphique 2.1 et aux tableaux par pays présentés dans les chapitres 5 et 6. Les graphiques de tous les pays de la publication sont disponibles en ligne sur le lien Statlink ci-dessous.

Source : Calculs des auteurs basés sur des données figurant dans « Statistiques des recettes publiques en Afrique : Tableaux comparatifs » (OCDE/ATAF/CUA, 2020[1]), *Statistiques fiscales de l'OCDE* (base de données), *https://doi.org/10.1787/7f54581d-fr*.

StatLink https://doi.org/10.1787/888934182458

Dons

Les dons constituent une source de recettes plus ou moins importante selon les pays étudiés dans la présente publication. En 2018, ils ont représenté moins de 0.5 % du PIB de 13 pays et, dans 11 cas, moins de 2 % du total des recettes fiscales (Graphique 2.7). Tous sont des pays à revenu intermédiaire d'après la classification de la Banque mondiale fondée sur le revenu national brut (Banque mondiale, 2020[7]). En revanche, sur les 10 pays à faible revenu considérés, les dons ont représenté moins de 1 % du PIB dans seulement un cas (Ouganda), et plus de 15 % des recettes fiscales dans cinq autres.

Graphique 2.7. **Dons par pays, 2018**

En pourcentage du PIB

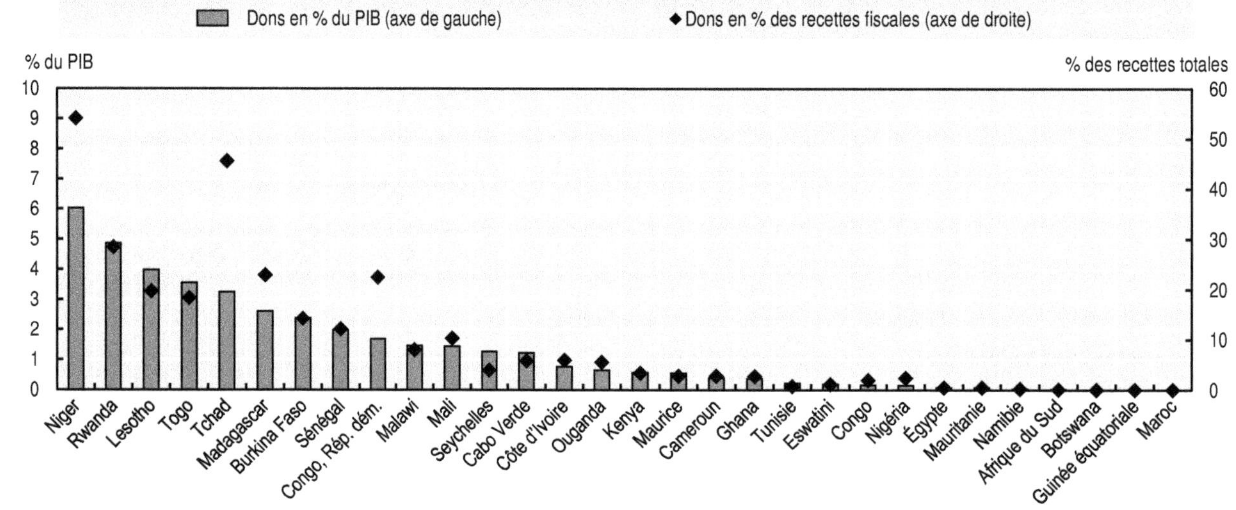

Source : Tableaux 6.2 et 6.3 du chapitre 6.

StatLink https://doi.org/10.1787/888934182477

Le Graphique 2.8 indique le volume des dons perçus par les pays étudiés dans la présente publication (en pourcentage du PIB) ainsi que le montant de leur revenu national brut (RNB) par habitant. Si la partie supérieure droite est vide, c'est parce que les dons constituent, en proportion, une source de recettes moins importante pour les pays africains dont le revenu est plus élevé. Cependant, un grand nombre de pays figurent dans la partie inférieure gauche, car il y a des pays qui, malgré un revenu faible, perçoivent proportionnellement peu de recettes sous forme de dons. Par exemple, le Burkina Faso, l'Ouganda et le Rwanda ont enregistré un RNB par habitant compris entre 750 USD et 780 USD en 2018, alors que les dons qu'ils ont déclaré avoir perçus cette même année ont représenté respectivement 2.4 %, 0.7 % et 4.9 % de leur PIB. Les Seychelles constituent également un cas à part : de par le montant des dons perçus (1.3 % du PIB), ce pays occupe le 12e rang du classement, alors qu'il est le seul des 30 pays étudiés à appartenir à la catégorie des économies à revenu élevé.

Graphique 2.8. **Dons en pourcentage du PIB et du RNB par habitant et par pays, 2018**

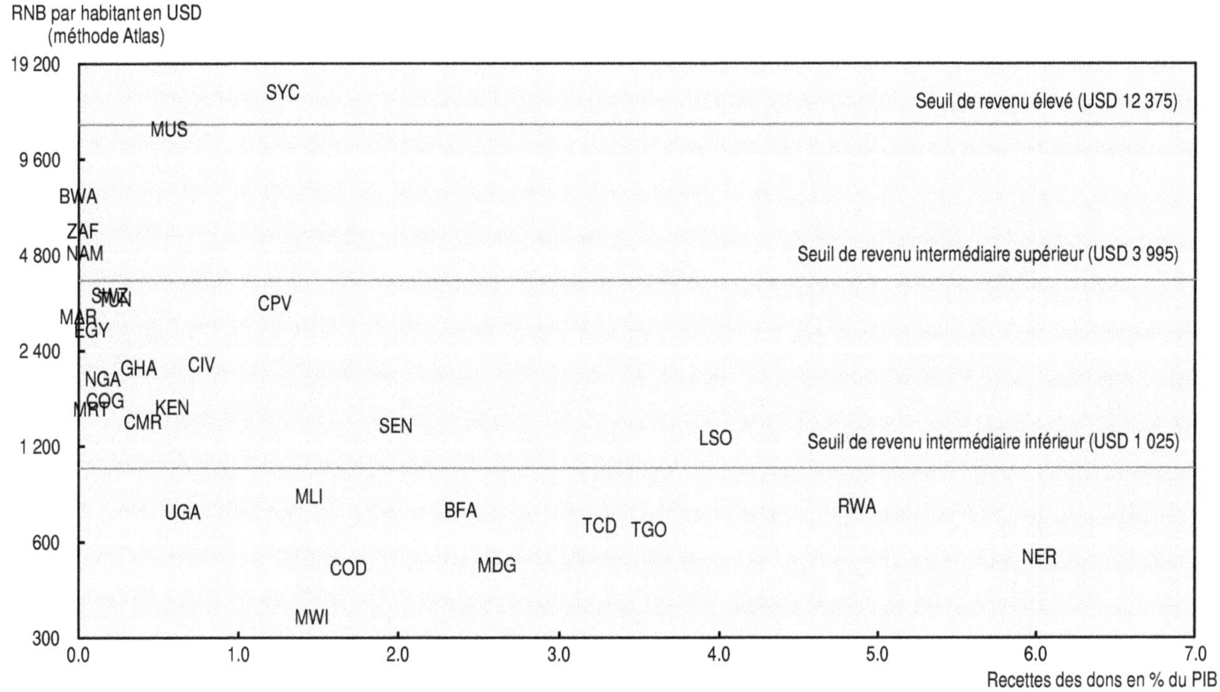

Note : Les chiffres du RNB ont été convertis en USD suivant la méthode Atlas de la Banque mondiale.

Source : Tableau 6.2 du chapitre 6, et Banque mondiale *World Development Indicators* (base de données).

StatLink https://doi.org/10.1787/888934182496

Si les recettes sous forme de dons et l'aide extérieure recouvrent des notions similaires, dans la pratique, la diversité des données, méthodes et concepts employés fait qu'il difficile d'accorder les statistiques de l'aide tirées des déclarations des pays donneurs avec les revenus issus de l'aide dont les pays récipiendaires font état.

Les recettes sous forme de dons présentent des éléments communs avec l'aide publique au développement (APD), telle que définie par le Comité d'aide au développement (CAD) de l'OCDE[4]. Les dons couverts par la présente publication correspondent principalement à des recettes perçues d'autres États et d'organisations internationales, tandis que l'APD mesure essentiellement les efforts déployés par les pays donneurs en faveur du développement dans les pays à faible revenu et à revenu intermédiaire. L'APD recouvre les apports considérés comme des « dons » dans la présente publication (aide budgétaire, aide alimentaire, transferts de capitaux, transferts courants, subventions de projets, bourses de programme, allégement de la dette internationale, etc.), mais elle englobe également les prêts concessionels, l'assistance technique en nature, les dépenses administratives supportées par les donneurs, le coût des réfugiés dans les pays donneurs et les bourses d'étude, ainsi que d'autres activités ne générant pas d'entrées de recettes (nettes) dans le pays. C'est pour cette raison que le volume de l'APD reçue par un pays donné diffère du montant des dons – généralement plus élevé – qui est indiqué dans les *Statistiques des recettes publiques*.

Les statistiques relatives aux apports d'APD à destination de l'Afrique qui sont recueillies par le CAD englobent les apports publics provenant de l'ensemble des membres du CAD et de certains pays non membres du CAD, ainsi que des organisations multilatérales comme la Banque mondiale, le FMI et l'ONU. En sont exclues les statistiques relatives à la coopération pour le développement de grandes économies non membres de l'OCDE, comme la Chine, le Brésil et l'Inde (OCDE, 2020[8]).

Graphique 2.9. **Dons et apports nets d'aide publique au développement (APD) perçus, 2018**

En pourcentage du PIB

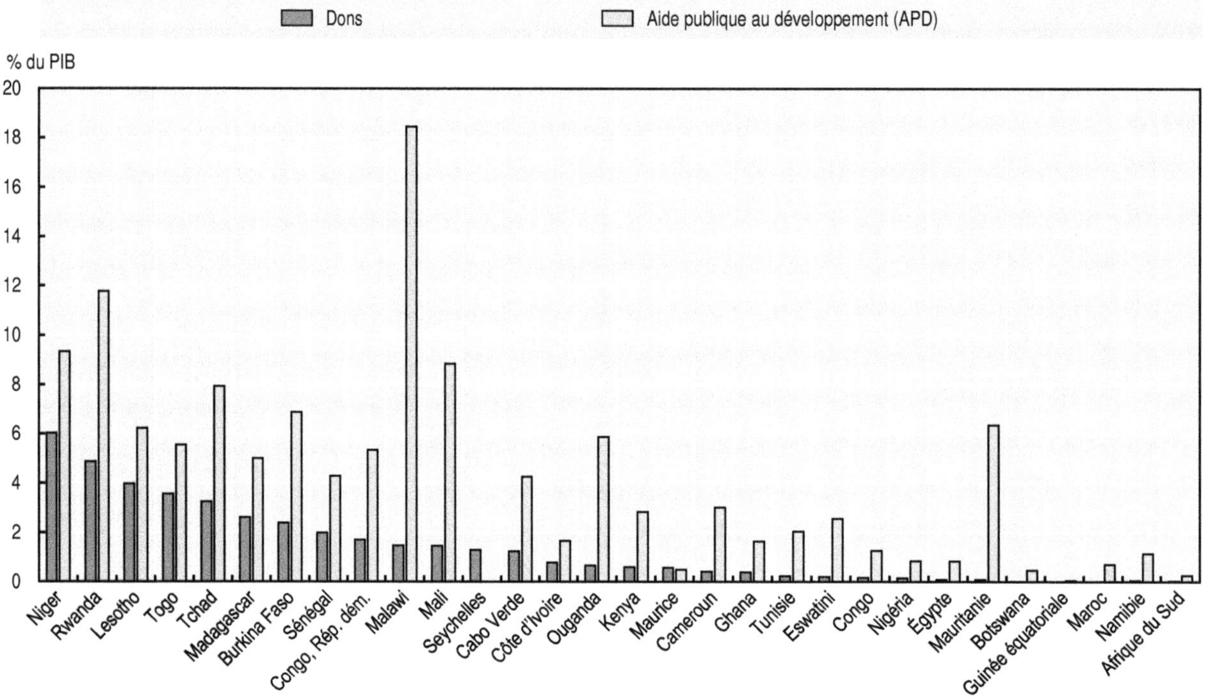

Note : Les valeurs de l'APD nette incluent les dons versés par les 30 pays membres du Comité d'aide au développement (CAD) de l'OCDE, 20 pays non nombres du CAD, ainsi que des organisations multilatérales et des organismes privés. De grands donneurs, comme la Chine, ne sont pas encore pris en compte.

Source : Tableau 6.2 du chapitre 6 et Comité d'aide au développement (CAD) de l'OCDE pour les données relatives à l'APD versée en 2020.

StatLink https://doi.org/10.1787/888934182515

En comparant les valeurs des recettes sous forme de dons et des apports nets d'APD (Graphique 2.9), on constate que le montant de l'assistance perçu par les pays africains dépasse nettement les sommes versées dans leur budget national. Si, en règle générale, les pays qui perçoivent les apports nets d'APD les plus élevés sont aussi ceux dont les recettes sous forme de dons sont les plus importantes, la corrélation n'est pas linéaire et l'on observe des cas atypiques, comme celui du Malawi, dont l'APD nette en pourcentage du PIB (18.5 %) le place loin en tête des pays africains, alors qu'il arrive bon dixième du classement des recettes sous forme de dons exprimées en pourcentage du PIB.

Il n'est pas rare que les pays tributaires des dons se trouvent confrontés à de fortes diminutions annuelles de cette source de recettes. Cinq des huit pays dont les recettes sous forme de dons ont dépassé 5 % du PIB au moins une année ont enregistré au cours de la période considérée une ou plusieurs diminutions annuelles de ces recettes d'au moins 2 points de pourcentage. Au Malawi, les dons, qui représentaient plus de 10 % du PIB en 2013, ont chuté de 65 % l'année suivante, marquée par le scandale du cashgate (VOANews, 2013[9]). Au total, 14 pays parmi les 30 étudiés ont enregistré, au cours de la décennie écoulée, une baisse de leurs recettes annuelles sous forme de dons équivalant à au moins 1.0 % du PIB.

En moyenne, les recettes sous forme de dons perçues par les pays étudiés sont tombées à 1.3 % du PIB en 2018, alors qu'elles se situaient à 2.2 % du PIB en 2010. Entre 2010 et 2018, le niveau moyen des dons, exprimé en pourcentage du PIB, n'a augmenté dans les pays étudiés qu'en 2013 et 2017, et a accusé la plus forte diminution en 2014. Les fluctuations de ces recettes sont souvent liées au contexte national. L'Égypte, par exemple, a vu ses recettes sous forme de dons augmenter brusquement en 2014, dans le contexte de la normalisation des relations internationales qui a suivi sa crise politique interne, tandis que le Mali a vu cette source de recettes se tarir en 2012, avec l'éclatement de la guerre du Mali, avant de réapparaître l'année suivante.

La crise du COVID-19 pourrait avoir un impact dramatique sur les flux d'aide vers les pays africains. Sur la base des tendances passées de l'APD au cours des dernières décennies, le Comité d'évaluation du développement de l'OCDE a proposé trois scénarios possibles sur la manière dont l'aide internationale en 2020 pourrait changer à cause du COVID-19, allant d'une augmentation possible des volumes d'APD dans le monde à une baisse possible des flux d'APD de 14 milliards USD en 2020 (OCDE, 2020[10]). Il n'y a pas encore suffisamment de données pour déterminer quel scénario se déroulera en 2020, mais certains indicateurs précoces montrent une baisse des engagements d'aide de certains pays donneurs bilatéraux et une augmentation des engagements d'aide de certains pays donneurs multilatéraux (Breed et Sternberg, 2020[11]).

Recettes tirées des ressources et autres revenus de la propriété

C'est en leur qualité de propriétaire, et en particulier de propriétaire terrien, que les États tirent une grande partie de leurs recettes non fiscales. Ces recettes sont comptabilisées comme revenus de la propriété dans les *Statistiques des recettes publiques en Afrique* et englobent différents types de revenus (Graphique 2.10).

Graphique 2.10. **Loyers et redevances par pays, 2018**

En pourcentage du PIB

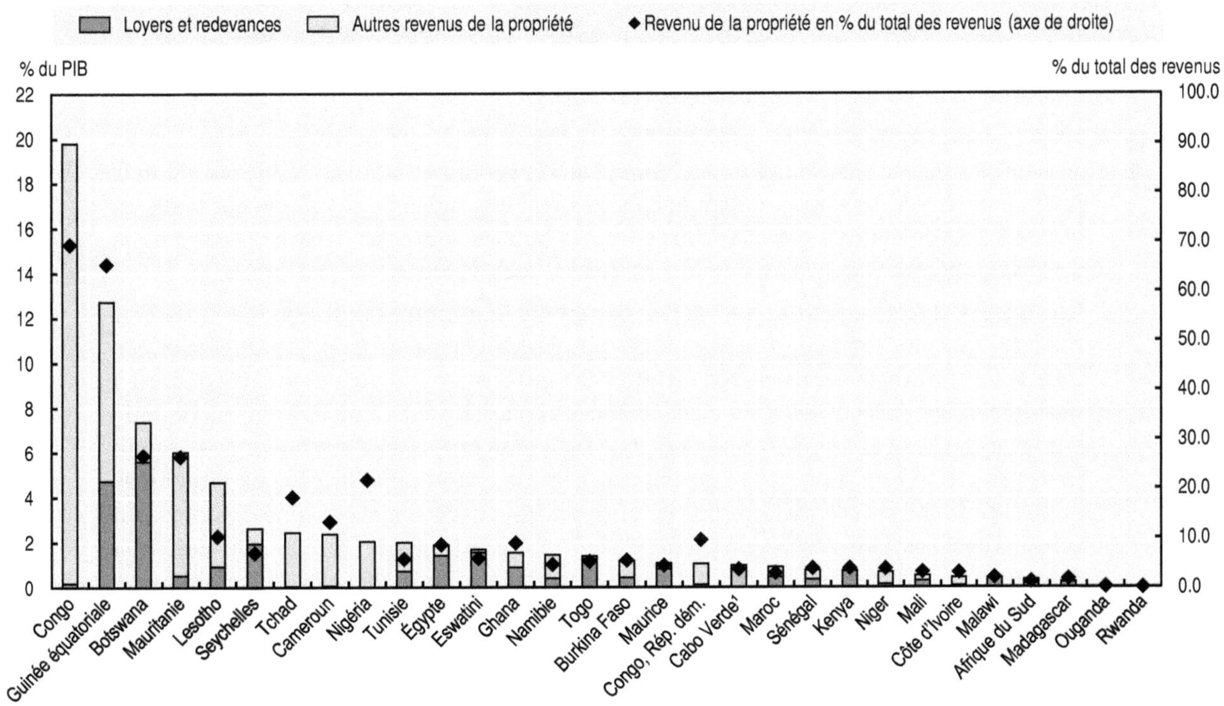

Note : Le Rwanda n'apparaît pas dans ce graphique, faute de données disponibles.

1. Les données relatives aux revenus de la propriété pour le Cabo Verde n'ont pas été ventilées.

Source : Calculs réalisés par les auteurs à partir des données des tableaux 6.5-6.34 et 4.17.

StatLink https://doi.org/10.1787/888934182534

Encadré 2.3. **Ressources naturelles et finances publiques**[5]

Il existe différentes façons pour les États de dégager des recettes ou des économies à partir des ressources naturelles :

- Le moyen le plus direct réside dans les loyers et redevances. L'État exige des entreprises et particuliers qu'ils s'acquittent de redevances en échange du droit d'accéder aux terres appartenant au domaine public. Il agit en sa qualité de propriétaire des terrains concernés et les montants à verser sont généralement fixés par voie de négociations. Ces redevances sont comptabilisées comme revenus de la propriété.
- Le paiement des services fournis par les administrations publiques constitue une autre source de recettes non fiscales, lesquelles sont versées par des entreprises du secteur primaire. Il peut s'agir des contrôles environnementaux, de la construction d'ouvrages ou, dans le cas de Maurice, de la fourniture de données météorologiques et de cartes. Les recettes correspondantes sont comptabilisées comme produits de la vente de biens et de services.
- Le fait, pour l'État, de détenir une partie ou la totalité du capital d'une société exploitant en son nom des ressources naturelles peut lui procurer des recettes sous forme de bénéfices et de dividendes. Ces redevances sont comptabilisées comme revenus de la propriété. Le Botswana, par exemple, tire l'essentiel de ses recettes liées aux ressources naturelles des dividendes que lui rapporte sa participation de 50 % au capital de la société Debswana, qui exploite les principales mines de diamant du pays (MiningTechnology, 2020[13]).
- Il est possible de taxer l'exploitation des ressources naturelles, notamment sous la forme de droits d'accise sur les matières premières extraites de terres appartenant au domaine public ou de taxes minières qui ciblent non pas la personne physique ou morale qui exploite les ressources naturelles, mais l'activité d'exploitation proprement dite. Les revenus correspondants sont alors comptabilisés dans les recettes fiscales. Le Niger et le Sénégal appliquent de telles taxes sur les activités d'extraction, qui relèvent de la catégorie « autres impôts sur les biens et services ».
- Les sociétés et les particuliers qui exploitent des ressources naturelles acquittent le plus souvent les mêmes impôts et taxes (impôts sur le revenu et taxe sur la valeur ajoutée, par exemple) que les autres contribuables. Les recettes tirées de ces impôts et taxes de portée générale figurent bien dans les comptes publics, mais pas nécessairement dans une catégorie spécifique attribuée aux recettes issues de ressources naturelles.
- Par ailleurs, il arrive que des sociétés et des particuliers consacrent une partie de leur richesse issue de l'extraction de ressources naturelles à la construction d'infrastructures ou à la fourniture de services. Dès lors que ces infrastructures ou services répondent à une demande d'investissements ou de services publics, il peut en résulter une économie sur les dépenses publiques, qui toutefois ne sera pas comptabilisée comme une recette pour l'État. Dans certains cas, l'État impose, comme condition à l'accès aux ressources naturelles dont il est propriétaire, que les entreprises et particuliers concernés fournissent certains services, par exemple en prenant à leur charge une partie au moins du coût de la construction et de l'entretien des routes desservant les mines. Des entreprises minières ont ainsi été mises à contribution dans le financement d'un réseau ferroviaire proposé qui reliera sur 3 000 km le Bénin, le Burkina Faso, le Niger, la Côte d'Ivoire, le Ghana, le Nigéria et le Togo (CNN, 2015[14]).

Les loyers et redevances sont des recettes tirées de l'utilisation du domaine de l'État, habituellement dans le cadre d'activités de prospection et d'exploitation de ressources naturelles non renouvelables sur des terres appartenant au domaine de l'État, ou de l'exploitation de fermes et de forêts détenues par l'État. Les intérêts et dividendes sont la rémunération d'investissements réalisés par l'État dans des sociétés. En règle générale, les redevances pétrolières et minières ne sont pas comptabilisés avec les autres catégories de revenus d'investissement, mais la question peut se révéler complexe. De nombreux pays africains créent des entreprises publiques chargées de gérer les recettes pétrolières ou nouent des accords de partage des recettes avec des entreprises privées qui exploitent ces ressources naturelles. La classification de ces fonds n'est pas toujours claire. À titre d'exemple, au Botswana, une part importante des revenus de la propriété provient des entreprises qui investissent dans l'extraction du diamant (encadré 2.3).

Recettes tirées des ressources naturelles

Dans les 30 pays étudiés ici, les loyers et redevances correspondent principalement à des recettes minières et pétrolières. En 2018, plus de 77.2 % du total des loyers et redevances, exprimés en USD, ont été spécifiquement déclarés comme recettes pétrolières (redevances et recettes perçues au titre d'accords de partage des recettes conclus avec des compagnies pétrolières), celles-ci représentant la majeure partie des loyers et redevances perçus par le Cameroun, l'Égypte, le Ghana, la Guinée équatoriale, le Nigéria, la République du Congo et le Tchad. Parallèlement, les ressources minières ont constitué la source principale de loyers et redevances de l'Afrique du Sud, du Botswana, du Burkina Faso, de l'Ouganda, de la République démocratique du Congo et du Togo. La pêche a représenté l'intégralité des recettes comptabilisées en loyers et redevances aux Seychelles, et 54.2 % à Maurice. En Mauritanie, les rentes de la pêche ont rapporté 210 millions USD, soit 3.0 % du PIB. Plus de 92.5 % du total des loyers et redevances perçus par les 30 pays étudiés sont liés aux ressources naturelles ; le reste de ces recettes proviennent de la construction et de l'exploitation d'aéroports, comme dans les cas du Kenya et du Togo. Le gazoduc Transméditerranéen, qui achemine du gaz naturel algérien en Europe, rapporte chaque année plus de 500 millions TND (dinars tunisiens) en loyers à la Tunisie, qui n'est pourtant qu'un modeste producteur de gaz naturel (AfricanManager, 2019[12]).

Les recettes tirées des ressources naturelles constituent une source de financement qui se caractérise souvent par une forte volatilité. Six pays (Guinée équatoriale, Lesotho, Mauritanie, Nigéria, République du Congo et Tchad) ont perçu des loyers et redevances équivalant à plus de 5 % du PIB au moins une année au cours de la décennie écoulée et tous ont enregistré une baisse annuelle de 25 % ou plus de ces recettes en pourcentage du PIB. La Guinée équatoriale et le Tchad ont accusé au moins une fois une diminution annuelle de plus de 60 %.

Comme les redevances pétrolières dominent dans les rentes et redevances perçues en Afrique, les recettes qu'elles procurent sont fortement tributaires de l'évolution des prix pétroliers (Graphique 2.11). Le montant total des rentes et redevances perçues par les États africains – que l'on compte ou non celles du Nigéria, qui représentent entre 45 % et 70 % de ce total depuis 2010 – évolue au même rythme que les cours internationaux du pétrole brut.

Bien que le pétrole soit la ressource naturelle qui apporte le plus aux caisses des États africains, les pays étudiés ici en possèdent bien d'autres encore, en quantités considérables, sans toutefois en tirer d'importants revenus, sauf dans le cas du Botswana.

On observe des différences marquées entre les pays africains, que l'on considère l'ampleur ou la composition de leurs richesses naturelles. La contribution des richesses naturelles au PIB est également variable selon les pays, de même que leur impact sur les budgets publics. Ainsi, d'après les estimations de la Banque mondiale, eu égard à la contribution des ressources naturelles à la production économique (Graphique 2.12), les cinq pays pour lesquels les ressources naturelles ont contribué à la production économique à hauteur de 15 % du PIB en 2018 sont le Tchad, la République du Congo et la Guinée équatoriale (principalement des hydrocarbures), la République démocratique du Congo, la Mauritanie (principalement des minerais) et le Ghana (Banque Mondiale, 2020[15]) [6].

Graphique 2.11. **Total des loyers et redevances en USD et prix du pétrole brut en USD, 2010-18**

En pourcentage de la moyenne calculée pour la période 2010-18

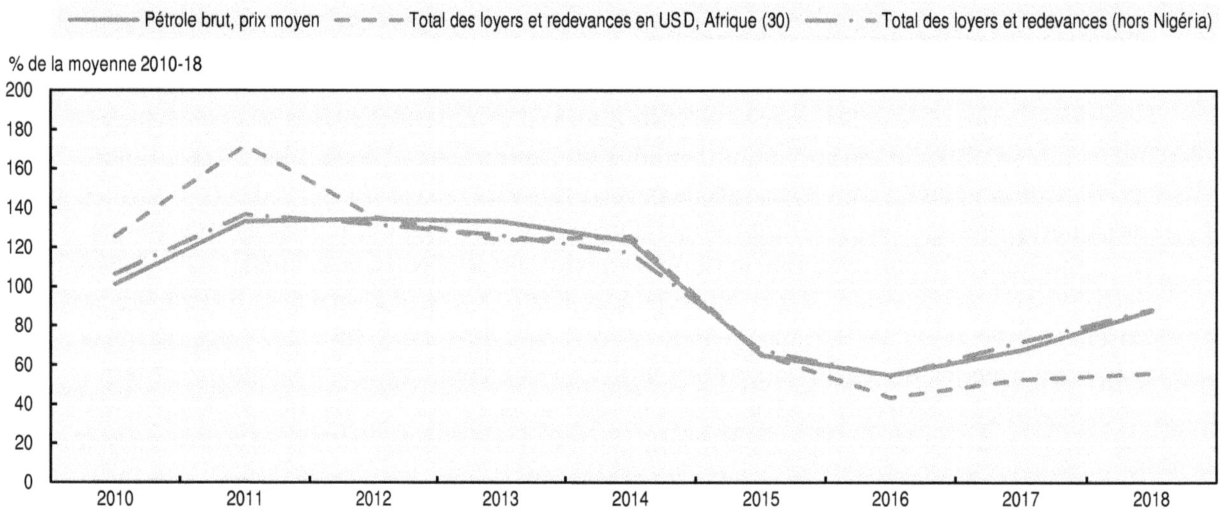

Source : Données de la Banque mondiale sur les prix des matières premières (« The Pink Sheet ») et calculs des auteurs basés sur des données figurant dans « Statistiques des recettes publiques en Afrique : Tableaux comparatifs » (OCDE/ATAF/CUA, 2020[1]), *Statistiques fiscales de l'OCDE* (base de données), *https://doi.org/10.1787/7f54581d-fr*.

StatLink *https://doi.org/10.1787/888934182553*

L'impact des ressources naturelles dont dispose chaque pays sur les finances publiques varie aussi considérablement. Des pays comme la Mauritanie, la Guinée équatoriale, la République du Congo et le Tchad tirent des recettes publiques importantes de leurs ressources naturelles, tandis que d'autres, comme le Togo, dont la richesse issue de l'exploitation des ressources naturelles représente pourtant plus de 10 % du PIB, ont déclaré un montant de recettes publiques au titre des rentes des ressources naturelles inférieur à 0.1 % du PIB.

Dans trois pays (République démocratique du Congo, Malawi, et Ouganda), la richesse produite à partir des forêts équivaut à plus de 5 % du PIB, mais ne contribue guère aux recettes publiques. Bien que certains pays, comme le Cameroun et le Niger, n'aient pas perçu de redevances au titre de l'exploitation de leurs forêts, les recettes forestières ont tout de même représenté une petite part de leurs recettes non fiscales. Au Niger, vu que l'écologie du Sahel et du Sahara est fragile et que le bois constitue une importance source d'énergie pour les communautés locales, le gouvernement étudie la question de la gestion forestière en partenariat avec les villages en vue de mettre en place des pratiques d'exploitation durables (Rives, Peltier et Montagne, 2010[16]).

Graphique 2.12. **Extraction de ressources naturelles, estimations, 2018**

En pourcentage du PIB

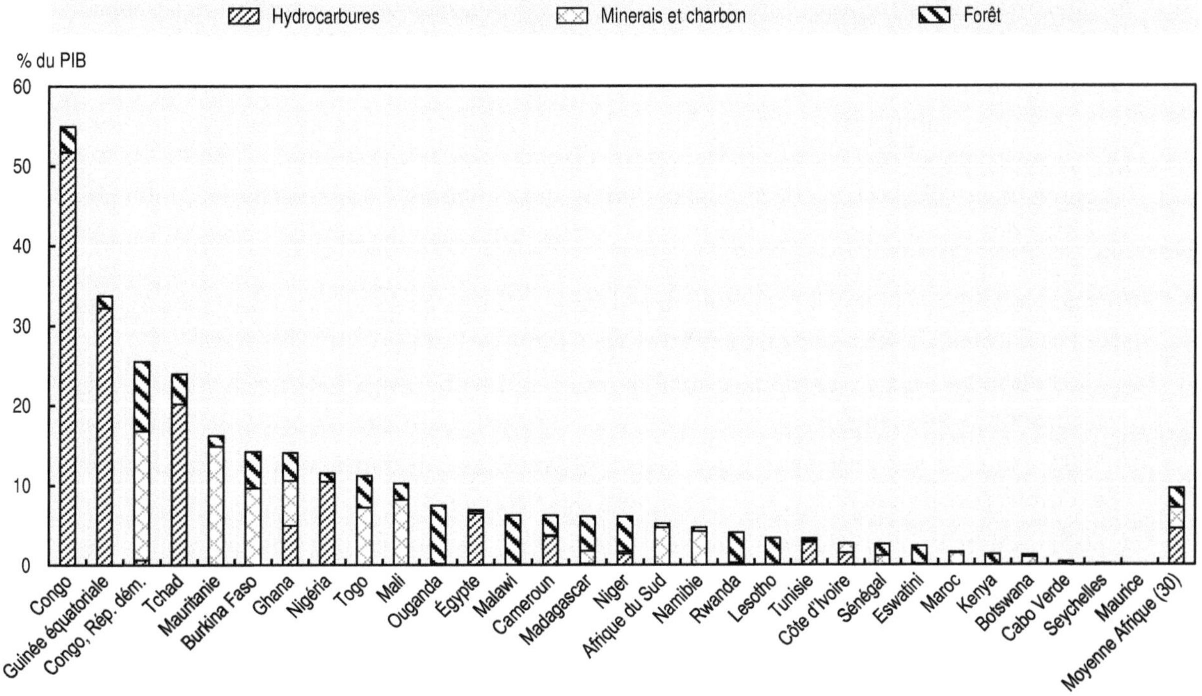

Source : Banque mondiale, *Indicateurs du développement dans le monde* (base de données) pour les estimations de la valeur totale de la production de ressources naturelles de chaque pays.

StatLink https://doi.org/10.1787/888934182572

Autres recettes non fiscales

Certains pays tirent d'importantes recettes non fiscales du fonctionnement habituel des administrations publiques. Ces recettes peuvent être regroupées en trois catégories : produits de la vente de biens et de services, produits des amendes et pénalités, et recettes diverses et non identifiées. Les difficultés posées par le recueil des recettes non fiscales, exposées à l'encadré 2.3, sont fréquemment accentuées avec ce type de recettes, dans la mesure où elles ne sont généralement pas perçues par les administrations fiscales et ne sont, bien souvent, pas définies par la législation. Elles peuvent même ne pas figurer dans les comptes publics.

Pour tous ces types de recettes, on peut se demander s'il s'agit de versements obligatoires effectués sans contrepartie et, par conséquent, dans quelle mesure il ne serait pas plus approprié de les classer dans les recettes fiscales. La question de savoir quels frais administratifs doivent être ou non considérés comme des impôts est examinée dans les annexes A et B. Toutefois, la question de la classification des amendes et des pénalités n'est pas toujours facile à trancher.

Les institutions et administrations publiques qui ont moins de pouvoir, et donc moins d'autorité pour prélever l'impôt, peuvent s'appuyer davantage sur ce type de recettes non fiscales. Autrement dit, le montant de recettes non fiscales perçues par ces collectivités locales peut être sous-estimé dans la présente publication, faute d'informations sur leurs finances.

Produits de la vente de biens et de services et frais administratifs

Les administrations peuvent produire des biens et des services relevant aussi bien du secteur marchand que non marchand. Dans le secteur marchand, les administrations publiques fournissent parfois des biens et services pouvant être aussi fournis auprès d'entreprises privées (tels que la vente d'aliments ou la prestation de services de transport). Parallèlement, elles assurent, lorsqu'elles gèrent des programmes ou garantissent le respect de la loi, différents services qui sont du seul ressort de l'État. Les frais facturés pour ces services non marchands sont le plus souvent considérés comme des frais administratifs.

Les frais administratifs sont souvent difficiles à classer, car ils se situent dans une zone grise, à mi-chemin entre les rémunérations de services (qui sont des recettes non fiscales) et les versements obligatoires effectués sans contrepartie au profit d'administrations publiques (qui sont des recettes fiscales)[7]. Les frais de justice, ainsi que les frais de dossiers pour les permis de conduire, passeports, enregistrements de brevets et certificats de mariage sont très souvent classés dans les recettes non fiscales. Lorsqu'ils sont considérés comme des recettes fiscales, ils sont en principe rattachés à l'une des catégories suivantes :

- 4400 - Impôts sur les transactions mobilières et immobilières (par exemple, taxes sur les transactions foncières)
- 5200 - Impôts sur l'utilisation des biens et l'autorisation d'exercer des activités (par exemple, permis de chasse, enregistrement des véhicules)
- 6000 - Autres impôts (par exemple, vente de timbres fiscaux, dans les cas où ces timbres sont utilisés pour le paiement des taxes et frais administratifs).

Graphique 2.13. **Produits de la vente de biens et de services, frais administratifs et autres recettes liées à l'administration, 2018**

En pourcentage du PIB

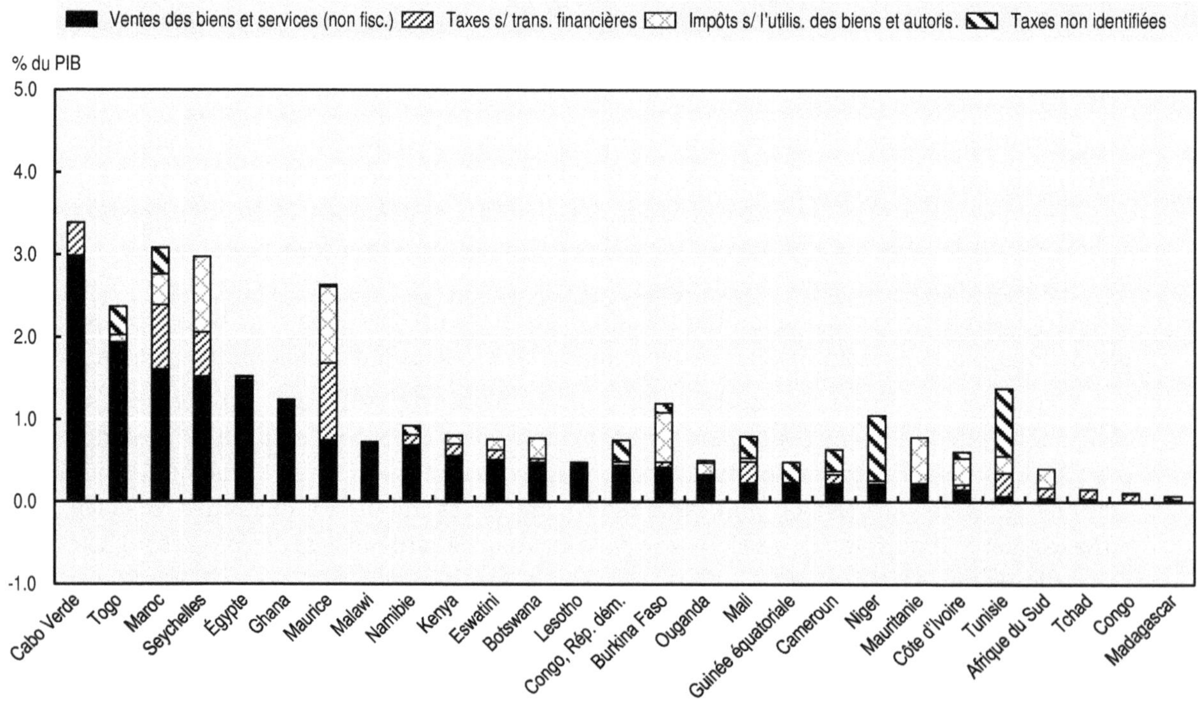

Note : Les montants indiqués ici incluent les recettes fiscales perçues par les administrations infranationales dans les cas de l'Afrique du Sud, le Maroc, et Mauricie, et les recettes non fiscales perçues par les administrations infranationales dans les cas d'Eswatini, du Kenya, du Maroc, et de Maurice, seuls pays pour lesquels les données correspondantes sont disponibles pour 2018. Faute de données, il n'est pas tenu compte du Nigéria, du Rwanda et du Sénégal.

Source : Calculs des auteurs basés sur des données figurant dans « Statistiques des recettes publiques en Afrique : Tableaux comparatifs » (OCDE/ATAF/CUA, 2020[1]), *Statistiques fiscales de l'OCDE* (base de données), *https://doi.org/10.1787/7f54581d-fr*.

StatLink https://doi.org/10.1787/888934182591

Dans six des pays étudiés, les recettes tirées de la vente de biens et de services et de la perception de frais administratifs représentaient au moins 1 % du PIB en 2018 (Graphique 2.13) : Cabo Verde (3.4 % du PIB), Ghana (1.2 % du PIB), Maroc (3.1 % du PIB), Seychelles (3.0 % du PIB), Maurice (2.6 % du PIB) et Togo (2.4 % du PIB). Ces recettes ont représenté 16.0 % du total des recettes fiscales du Cabo Verde, et 12.2 % dans le cas du Togo.

La ventilation de ces recettes a été variable selon les pays. Au Cabo Verde, les frais administratifs représentaient 96 % des recettes enregistrées dans la vente de biens et de services. Au Ghana, l'essentiel des recettes tirées de la vente de biens et de services ont été perçues soit au niveau des communes, départements et agences administratives, soit au niveau des districts, assemblées municipales et métropolitaines. Au Maroc, 58 % des recettes issues de la vente de biens et de services par des administrations publiques sont collectées au niveau local.

Recettes diverses ou non identifiées

Certaines recettes non fiscales représentent des montants significatifs, mais ne relèvent d'aucune des catégories citées ci-dessus. Il s'agit notamment :

- des transferts en capital ne rentrant pas dans les principales catégories de recettes non fiscales
- des dons versés par des particuliers ou sociétés à des organismes publics (à l'exception des dons émanant d'organisations internationales comme le FMI, qui relèvent de la catégorie des dons)
- des sommes versées par des entités privées aux administrations publiques à l'issue d'importantes procédures judiciaires ou au titre d'indemnités d'assurance (comme les 100 millions EUR d'indemnités qu'Arcelor Mittal a dû payer à l'État sénégalais en application de la décision de justice rendue suite à l'annulation d'un projet de mine de fer (RFI, 2014[17])
- des versements qui relèvent de différentes catégories de la classification et pour lesquels aucune ventilation n'est disponible
- des versements inclassables faute de données pertinentes. Le Rwanda n'ayant pas donné le détail de ses recettes non fiscales, sauf en ce qui concerne les dons, elles ont été classées dans la catégorie des recettes diverses et non identifiées
- des revenus transférés par la SACU au Botswana, à l'Eswatini, au Lesotho et à la Namibie (voir encadré 2.4).

Les recettes diverses et non identifiées peuvent représenter une composante non négligeable des recettes non fiscales de certains pays. C'est le cas de la Tunisie (contributions volontaires exceptionnelles versées à l'administration), de Maurice (transferts en capital provenant de fonds statutaires spéciaux) et du Maroc (versements effectués au bénéfice de l'administration en contrepartie du droit à entrer en concurrence avec des institutions publiques pour la fourniture de services).

La variabilité des recettes diverses et non identifiées peut être imputable à des transferts de capitaux importants, à des entrées de recettes éphémères ou à des reclassifications de fonds dans la catégorie des recettes non identifiées en raison de l'absence de données. La présence de montants élevés dans cette rubrique pourrait conduire à s'interroger sur la précision des montants inscrits dans les autres catégories de recettes non fiscales.

Encadré 2.4. **Recettes issues de la SACU**

L'Union douanière d'Afrique australe (*South African Customs Union*, SACU) réunit l'Afrique du Sud, le Botswana, l'Eswatini, le Lesotho et la Namibie. Son siège se trouve à Windhoek (Namibie). Cette union douanière vise à établir « une communauté économique qui favorise un développement équitable et durable, au service du bien-être des peuples, pour construire un avenir commun ».

La SACU, qui est la plus ancienne union douanière au monde, a été créée en 1899 entre la colonie britannique du Cap de Bonne-Espérance et la République boer de l'État libre d'Orange. Des accords conclus par la suite, en 1910 puis en 1969, ont marqué l'adhésion du Botswana, de l'Eswatini et du Lesotho. Après l'accession à l'indépendance de la Namibie, en 1990, et la fin de l'apartheid en Afrique du Sud, en 1994, de nouvelles négociations ont été ouvertes pour aboutir, en 2002, à la conclusion de l'accord en vigueur à ce jour.

Cet accord prévoit la libre circulation entre les pays membres de la SACU de tous les produits manufacturés fabriqués dans ces pays, en franchise de droits. Il définit également des tarifs extérieurs communs et la mise en commun des droits de douane et d'accise, en vue de leur partage entre les pays membres de la SACU suivant la formule de répartition des recettes figurant en annexe à l'Accord.

Les règles de partage des recettes comprennent trois composantes :

- Une composante douanière, qui divise le montant brut des droits de douane en fonction de la valeur des marchandises importées par chaque pays depuis les autres pays membres de la SACU au cours de l'année considérée (en pourcentage des importations totales intra-SACU).
- Une composante portant sur les droits d'accise, qui divise le montant brut de ces droits selon le ratio correspondant au PIB de chaque pays rapporté au PIB total de la SACU.
- Une composante de développement, financée par 15 % de la composante liée aux droits d'accise et pondérée en faveur des pays moins développés de la SACU selon une formule fondée sur le PIB par habitant.

Dans la présente publication, les recettes issues des droits de douane et d'accise sont incluses dans les recettes fiscales du pays de la SACU qui les a collectées. Elles sont rapportées dans les rubriques 5121 (accises) et 5123 (droits de douane et droits à l'importation) des tableaux des recettes fiscales. Les montants redistribués par le fonds commun des recettes de la SACU sont classés dans les tableaux des recettes non fiscales, sous la rubrique des recettes diverses et non identifiées, comme indiqué dans le tableau 6.13 à propos de l'Eswatini. En ce qui concerne l'Afrique du Sud, contributeur net au mécanisme de la SACU, les contributions, nettes des reversements perçus, sont indiquées pour mémoire dans le tableau des recettes non fiscales (tableau 6.22).

Sources : (SACU, 2017[19]), (SACU, 2014[20]).

Recettes issues de l'Union douanière d'Afrique australe

Pour la première fois, les cinq membres de la SACU ont participé à l'élaboration des présentes *Statistiques des recettes publiques en Afrique*. Cela a permis de comptabiliser la totalité des sommes versées au fonds commun des recettes de la SACU ainsi que les montants attribués aux différents pays membres (Graphique 2.14).

Les cinq membres de la SACU prélèvent des droits de douane et d'accise dans le cadre d'un régime fiscal uniforme, puis transfèrent les sommes collectées dans le fonds commun de recettes de la SACU. Ce fonds les redistribue ensuite selon une complexe formule de partage des recettes. Dans les faits, toutefois, comme l'Afrique du Sud détient les principaux ports d'entrée de l'Afrique australe, ce pays collecte la quasi-totalité des droits de douane et d'accise destinés au fonds commun de recettes de la SACU. En conséquence, l'Afrique du Sud en est un contributeur net, et les autres pays membres des bénéficiaires nets.

Si les revenus issus la SACU sont quantité négligeable pour l'Afrique du Sud, ils sont en revanche essentiels pour les finances des autres membres de l'Union douanière. En 2018, ils ont fait grimper les recettes du Botswana, de l'Eswatini, du Lesotho et de la Namibie,

Graphique 2.14. **Total des recettes issues de la SACU et autres recettes non fiscales, par pays**

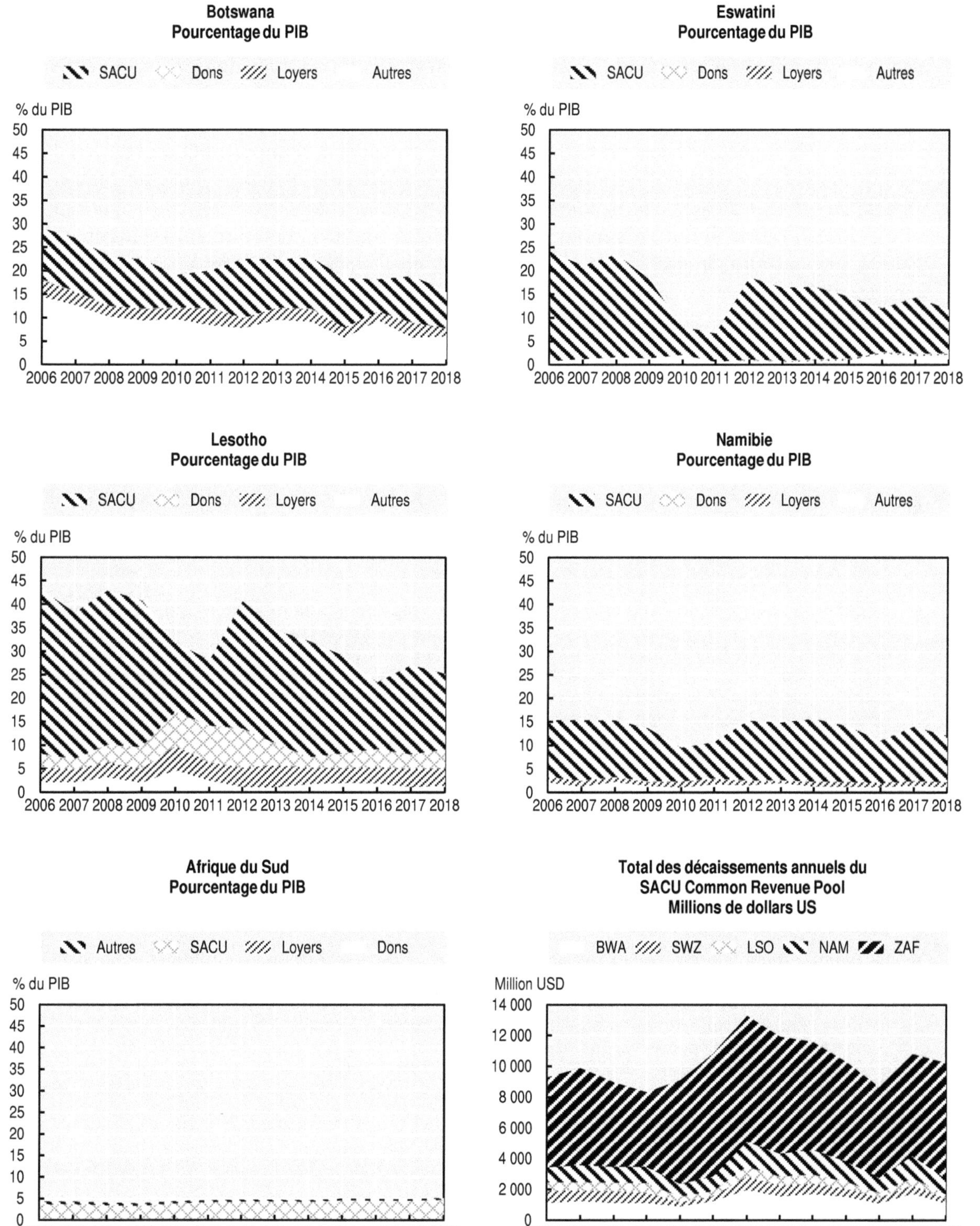

Note : Les recettes issues de la SACU relèvent des recettes non fiscales de tous les pays étudiés, sauf dans le cas de l'Afrique du Sud, où elles sont assimilées aux droits de douane et d'accise.

Source : Calculs des auteurs basés sur des données figurant dans « Statistiques des recettes publiques en Afrique : Tableaux comparatifs » (OCDE/ATAF/CUA, 2020[1]), *Statistiques fiscales de l'OCDE* (base de données), *https://doi.org/10.1787/7f54581d-fr*.

StatLink *https://doi.org/10.1787/888934182610*

exprimées en pourcentage du PIB, de 7.7 %, 9.2 %, 16.0 % et 9.8 %, respectivement. Indépendamment des chocs économiques exogènes, le montant des recettes redistribuées par la SACU a fluctué au gré de l'évolution des paramètres employés dans la formule de partage des recettes. Le choc économique causé par la crise financière mondiale a rendu caduques une grande partie des prévisions économiques d'alors ; les paiements de la SACU étant calculés à partir de ces prévisions, il a fallu procéder à d'importants ajustements en 2010 et 2011 pour compenser les versements excessifs effectués pendant plusieurs années au titre du système de regroupement et de redistribution des recettes de la SACU (Mongardini et al., 2011[18]). Une situation similaire s'est produite en 2014, où le ralentissement de l'économie sud-africaine a de nouveau contraint à corriger les prévisions à la baisse. Les recettes redistribuées par la SACU à l'Eswatini, au Lesotho et à la Namibie, en pourcentage du PIB, ont diminué en 2015 et 2016, mais la tendance s'est inversée en 2017.

Notes

1 Il n'y a pas de comparaison possible avec les moyennes des 25 pays d'Amérique latine et des Caraïbes (ALC) (voir OCDE et al., 2020[23]) et des 36 pays de l'OCDE (voir OCDE, 2018[22]), car les publications correspondantes ne couvrent pas les recettes non fiscales.

2 Voir le Guide d'interprétation sur les recettes non fiscales dans l'annexe B du présent rapport pour la définition de ces catégories de revenus.

3 Le Burkina Faso, l'Égypte, Madagascar, le Malawi, le Nigeria et la République démocratique du Congo ne sont pas pris en compte, faute de données disponibles.

4 La définition officielle de l'APD est la suivante : « Tous les apports de ressources qui sont fournis aux pays et territoires figurant sur la Liste des bénéficiaires d'APD établie par le Comité d'aide au développement ou à des institutions multilatérales et qui émanent d'organismes publics, y compris des États et des collectivités locales, ou d'organismes agissant pour le compte d'organismes publics, sachant que chaque opération doit en outre avoir pour but essentiel de favoriser le développement économique et l'amélioration du niveau de vie des pays en développement, et être assortie de conditions favorables et comporter un élément de libéralité au moins égal à 25 % (sur la base d'un taux d'actualisation de 10 % ». Des informations supplémentaires sont disponibles à l'adresse suivante : *www.oecd.org/dac/financing-sustainable-development/index-terms.htm#ODA*.

5 (Mansour et Rota-Graziosi, 2013[21]) notent que les recettes fiscales tirées de l'extraction pétrolière peuvent englober l'impôt sur les bénéfices des sociétés, les droits indirects sur des produits énergétiques, ainsi que des taxes sur les ventes non remboursables, telles que la TVA, tandis que les recettes non fiscales peuvent inclure les redevances, les transferts de bénéfices, les dividendes versés par les entreprises publiques et d'autres revenus d'investissements perçus au titre de la participation directe de l'État dans le capital d'entreprises du secteur extractif.

6 La Banque mondiale utilise l'expression « bénéfices tirés des ressources naturelles ». Ceux-ci correspondent à la différence entre la valeur des ressources naturelles produites dans les pays, qui est fonction des prix des matières premières, et le coût estimé de l'extraction des ressources. Veuillez consulter la documentation sur les rentes de ressources dans l'ensemble de données des indicateurs de développement mondial de la Banque mondiale (voir *https://databank.worldbank.org/metadataglossary/adjusted-net-savings/series/NY.GDP.TOTL.RT.ZS*) et le guide d'interprétation pour plus de détails.

7 Pour de plus amples informations sur la classification des frais administratifs, consulter, à l'annexe A, les paragraphes 9 à 13 du Guide d'interprétation de l'OCDE.

Références

AfricanManager (2019), *Gazoduc-ENI : Des royalties de 500 millions de dinars par an pour la Tunisie, https://africanmanager.com/la-tunisie-tirera-500-millions-de-dinars-par-an-du-gazoduc-avec-litalie/.* [12]

Banque mondiale (2020), *Indicateurs de développement dans le monde* (base de données), *https://donnees.banquemondiale.org* (consulté le 8 septembre). [15]

Banque mondiale (2020), *World Bank Country and Lending Groups, https://datahelpdesk.worldbank.org/knowledgebase/articles/906519* (consulté le 25 juin 2020). [7]

Breed, D. et L. Sternberg (2020), *Tracking aid flows to the Covid-19 response*, Development Initiatives Poverty Research Ltd, *https://devinit.org/data/tracking-aid-flows-in-light-of-the-covid-19-crisis/#downloads* (consulté le 2 octobre 2020). [11]

CNN (2015), *Mammoth rail network to put West African economies on the right track, https://edition.cnn.com/2015/03/05/africa/west-africa-minerals-railway/index.html* (consulté le 21 septembre 2020). [14]

CUA/OCDE (n.d.), *Dynamiques du développement en Afrique 2020 : Transformation digitale et qualité de l'emploi*, Éditions OCDE, Paris/Commission de l'Union Africaine, Addis-Abeba. [5]

EIU (2015), *Government approves new hydrocarbons code, https://country.eiu.com/article.aspx?articleid=1303035314&Country=Congo%20(Brazzaville)&topic=Eco_9.* [6]

FMI (2020), *Base de données des Perspectives de l'économie mondiale, avril 2020, www.imf.org/external/pubs/ft/weo/2020/01/weodata/index.aspx* (consulté le 8 septembre 2020). [3]

FMI (2020), *List of LIC DSAs for PRGT-Eligible Countries, www.imf.org/external/Pubs/ft/dsa/DSAlist.pdf.* [4]

Georgieva, K., C. Pazarbasioglu et R. Weeks-Brown (2020), *Reform of the International Debt Architecture is Urgently Needed, https://blogs.imf.org/2020/10/01/reform-of-the-international-debt-architecture-is-urgently-needed/?utm_medium=email&utm_source=govdelivery.* [2]

Mansour, M. et G. Rota-Graziosi (2013), "Tax Coordination, Tax Competition, and Revenue Mobilization in the West African Economic and Monetary Union", *IMF Working Paper*, Vol. 13/163, *www.imf.org/en/Publications/WP/Issues/2016/12/31/Tax-Coordination-Tax-Competition-and-Revenue-Mobilization-in-the-West-African-Economic-and-40756.* [21]

MiningTechnology (2020), "Debswana diamond mines", *www.mining-technology.com/projects/debswana/* (consulté le 20 septembre 2020). [13]

Mongardini, J. et al. (2011), *In the wake of the global economic crisis : adjusting to lower revenue of the Southern African Customs Union in Botswana, Lesotho, Namibia, and Swaziland*, Fonds monétaire international, *www.imf.org/external/pubs/ft/dp/2011/afr1101.pdf.* [18]

OCDE (2020), *DAC Data Submitters, www.oecd.org/dac/financing-sustainable-development/development-finance-standards/dacdatasubmitters.htm* (consulté le 18 septembre 2020). [8]

OCDE (2020), *Six decades of ODA: insights and outlook in the COVID-19 crisis*, OCDE, *https://doi.org/10.1787/2dcf1367-en.* [10]

OCDE (2019), *Perspectives mondiales du financement du développement durable*, Éditions OCDE, *https://doi.org/10.1787/eee36eb1-fr.* [24]

OCDE (2018), *Statistiques des recettes publiques 2018*, Éditions OCDE, Paris, *https://dx.doi.org/10.1787/rev_stats-2018-fr.* [22]

OCDE/ATAF/CUA (2020), *Recettes fiscales en Afrique : Tableaux comparatifs*, Éditions OCDE, Paris, *https://doi.org/10.1787/7f54581d-fr.* [1]

OCDE et al. (2020), *Revenue Statistics in Latin America and the Caribbean*, Éditions OCDE, Paris, *https://doi.org/10.1787/68739b9b-en-es.* [23]

RFI (2014), *Le gros chèque d'Arcelor Mittal au Sénégal, www.rfi.fr/economie/20140605-le-gros-cheque-arcelor-mittal-senegal.* [17]

Rives, F., R. Peltier et P. Montagne (2010), *Fifteen years of forest community management in Niger: from a technician's dream to social reality*, CIRAD, *https://agritrop.cirad.fr/555467/1/document_555467.pdf.* [16]

SACU (2017), *Southern African Customs Union Agreement 2002 (tel qu'amendé le 12 avril 2013), www.sacu.int/list.php?type=Agreements.* [19]

SACU (2014), *Implementing a Common Agenda Towards Regional Integration: 2014 Annual Report, www.sacu.int/docs/reports_annual/2014/annual_report.pdf.* [20]

VOANews (2013), *Malawi: Donors Withhold Aid Over Cashgate Scandal, www.voanews.com/africa/malawi-donors-withhold-aid-over-cashgate-scandal* (consulté le 21 septembre 2020). [9]

Chapter 3

COVID-19 and AfCFTA: Risks and opportunities for domestic revenue mobilisation in Africa

Chapitre 3

COVID-19 et ZLECAf : Risques et opportunités liés à la mobilisation des ressources intérieures en Afrique

Revenue Statistics in Africa 1990-2018/Statistiques des recettes publiques en Afrique 1990-2018

Chapter 3

COVID-19 and AfCFTA: Risks and opportunities for domestic revenue mobilisation in Africa

Chapter 3 discusses long-term trends and factors likely to affect the future of domestic revenue mobilisation in Africa in the aftermath of the COVID-19 pandemic.[1]

Introduction

For the past decade, African countries have made good progress in domestic revenue mobilisation (DRM). Between 2010 and 2018, the 30 African countries participating in *Revenue Statistics in Africa* increased their tax revenues, on average, from 15.1% to 16.5% of GDP (see Chapter 1). The increase in the average tax-to-GDP ratio in the continent is of particular importance as tax revenues are a more sustainable source of public revenues over the long term in comparison to non-tax-revenues, which have been declining over the past years largely due to a fall in commodity prices driving down revenues from royalties and continuing decreases in grants (see Chapter 2). However, tax revenues in Africa remain lower than the averages for Latin America and Caribbean countries and for OECD countries (23.1% and 34.3%, respectively in 2018) and have been comparatively flat in recent years.

The overall economic context has worsened in 2020 due to the global COVID-19 pandemic. As of September 2020, the World Health Organisation (WHO) has reported more than one million cases of COVID-19 in 47 African countries (WHO, $2020_{[1]}$) (WHO, $2020_{[2]}$). Africa is experiencing its first recession in decades as a result of this pandemic and millions of people in the continent could potentially face extreme poverty (UNECA, $2020_{[3]}$). Prior to COVID-19, the African economy was expected to grow in 2020 (African Development Bank, $2020_{[4]}$) but it is now projected at a minimum to decelerate and very likely to contract (Table 3.1).

The economic consequences of the pandemic will affect public revenues. The lower demand for commodities and consequent sharp falls in commodity prices will put a strain on countries highly reliant on revenues generated from these resources. African countries dependent on tourism will record decreases in their revenues from this sector due to ongoing travel restrictions and border closures. Lower international trade flows will impact revenues from trade taxes and overall lower levels of economic activity are likely to impact income taxes and social security contributions.

The IMF has estimated that the revenues in Africa, south of the Sahara, will decrease on average by 2.6% of GDP compared to 2019; while expenditure will increase by 0.9% of GDP on average over the same period (IMF, $2020_{[5]}$) as a result of the fiscal packages to mitigate the impact of the crisis on the economy and to support the most vulnerable groups in the population. As fiscal space continues to deteriorate – the IMF estimated fiscal deficits will increase on average by 7.6% of GDP in 2020 – it might be challenging for the continent and for some African countries to finance the health, economic and social measures necessary to achieve a sustainable recovery.

Countries are undertaking a range of measures to respond to the COVID-19 pandemic and to the economic and social crisis it has created. These responses have evolved at different rates in different countries, from emergency response measures designed to protect businesses and individuals from the immediate impact of the pandemic and the lockdowns, towards policies seeking to encourage the economic recovery. Although there is considerable uncertainty about how the health and economic side of the pandemic will evolve, fiscal policies will be an important tool in contributing to both the economic and fiscal recovery. Over the longer term, DRM will be an important part of this discussion, as countries seek to restore public finances in a fair and sustainable way, to boost resources to reduce inequalities and promote development, and to allow a greater degree of fiscal space to respond to future shocks.

The implementation of the African Continental Free Trade Area (AfCFTA) is likely to play an important role in the future of DRM in Africa. Although the COVID-19 pandemic has delayed implementation of the new agreement, it has also underlined the importance of this key pillar of African integration. In the short term, it has the potential to mitigate the effects of COVID-19 by deepening intra-African trade and accelerating post-pandemic economic recovery; over the longer term, it will likely play an important role in insulating the continent against future shocks. While the short-term adjustment costs for fiscal systems might be significant, especially in low-income countries for which trade taxes continue to provide a significant proportion of revenues, these losses could be reversed in the long term.

This special feature discusses the future of DRM in Africa in light of the impact of, and responses to, the COVID-19 pandemic as well as the opportunities brought by the future implementation of the AfCFTA.

Impact of COVID-19 on African economies and revenues

The COVID-19 pandemic has reversed the economic gains made in Africa in recent years. Since the 2014 drop in commodity prices, economic growth in Africa has been lower than in the previous decade, but it remained positive. GDP growth was projected to increase in Africa before the pandemic. Forecasts made prior to the COVID-19 pandemic indicated economic growth of 3.9% in 2020, 4.1% in 2021, up from 3.4% in 2019 for Africa (African Development Bank, 2020[4]). These have been revised since the COVID-19 pandemic started, as shown in Figure 3.1.

Projections indicate that Africa will go into recession for the first time in 25 years as a result of the effects of the COVID-19 pandemic. There is a consensus that there will be a contraction in economic growth (Table 3.1), with associated output losses estimated between USD 37 billion and USD 79 billion (World Bank, 2020[8]). According to (UNECA, 2020[3]) before the pandemic, most African countries were already recording weak macro-fiscal conditions, coupled with high external debt levels and fiscal deficits above 3% of GDP. The rising cost of borrowing also limited the ability of African governments to put in place strong economic responses to mitigate the impact of the pandemic.

Figure 3.1. **GDP growth in Africa and Africa south of Sahara (SSA), forecasts for 2010-21**

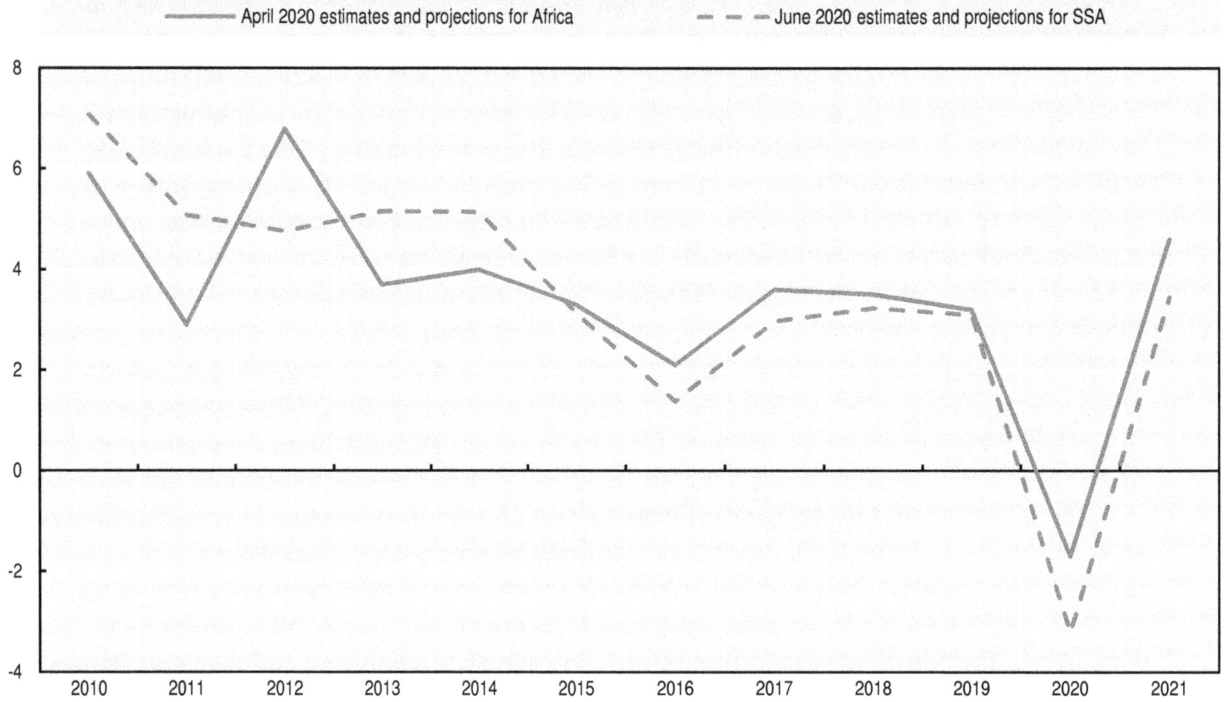

Note: Figures for 2020 and 2021 are projections.

Source: World Economic Outlook April 2020 (IMF, 2020[7]) and *World Economic Outlook Update, June 2020* (IMF, 2020[5]).

StatLink https://doi.org/10.1787/888934181926

Table 3.1. **GDP growth in Africa, 2020 projections**

AUC	-2.1% to -4.9%
AfDB	-1.7% to -3.4%
UNECA	1.8% to -2.6%
IMF	-3.2% (Africa south of the Sahara)
World Bank	-2.5% to -5.1% (Africa south of the Sahara)

Source: AUC compilation based on (AUC, 2020[9]), (African Development Bank, 2020[6]), (IMF, 2020[5]), (UNECA, 2020[3]), (World Bank, 2020[8])

Socio-economic impact

The decline in economic growth is a result of the decline in commodity prices, the negative effect of lockdown measures aimed at containing the spread of the virus on travel and tourism sectors, and a reduction in tax receipts due to businesses shutting down, among other factors. Demand for African exports has dropped as pandemic-containment measures led to economic contraction in traditional trade partners in China and Europe. Tourism and mineral and oil exports were especially vulnerable, due to the sudden disruptions to air travel and the decline in commodity prices. Figure 3.2 shows the trend in commodity prices between 1992 and 2020. The recent decline in commodity prices was driven by the economic shock resulting from the impact of COVID-19 on many economies, resulting in a fall in demand. Oil prices have lost about 54% of their value dropping from USD 67 a barrel to below USD 30 a barrel and non-oil commodity prices with natural gas and metal prices dropping by 30% and 4%, respectively (Coulibaly and Madden, 2020[10]). Aluminum has also fallen by 0.49%, copper 0.47%, lead 1.64% and cocoa 21% (AUC, 2020[9]).

Figure 3.2. **Monthly commodity prices, January 1992-August 2020**

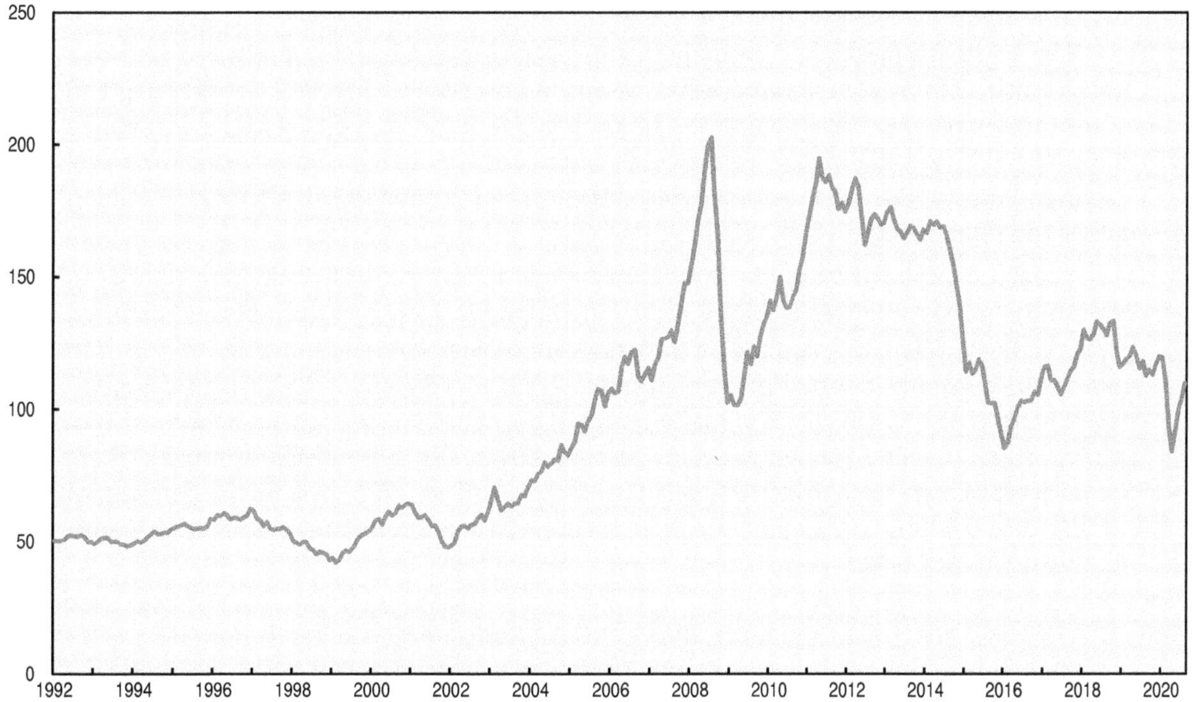

Source: (IMF, 2020[11]), *www.imf.org/en/Research/commodity-prices.*

StatLink https://doi.org/10.1787/888934181945

African countries will continue to be negatively affected as the effects of the pandemic are felt across the world. The resultant social and human impact is set to affect the most vulnerable in society the most. Unemployment and poverty are set to rise as the informal sector is affected by the extreme social distancing measures. UNECA estimated that between 5 million and 29 million people will fall below the poverty line and over 19 million jobs will be lost as a result of the decline in economic growth (UNECA, 2020[3]). Food insecurity and malnutrition are expected to worsen as food imports, transportation and agricultural production have all been hampered by the advent of the COVID-19 pandemic. Recent estimates of food insecurity have suggested that about 73 million people in Africa are food insecure (WHO, 2020[12]).

Channels of impact on revenues

African countries have lost revenues from both domestic and external sources as economies suffered the effects of the mitigation and containment measures aimed at combating the COVID-19 pandemic (African Union, 2020[13]). The decline in the prices and demand for commodities has resulted in decreased government revenues, thereby limiting resources for emergency and long-term financing of public services. The effect was particularly felt when governments were unable to provide for their most vulnerable populations amidst the lockdowns aimed at combating and controlling the spread of COVID-19. Many rural and urban communities were negatively affected, with the impact continuing to throw many into unemployment and poverty. The impact is even worse for the informal sector, which stands at over 60% of employment in many African countries, where state-provisioned social protection and social insurance systems are basically non-existent. Businesses also suffered the effects of the lockdowns, with only a few African countries providing stimulus packages for the survival of the private sector. This will likely result in a drop in corporate and personal income tax revenue.

The negative impact of the pandemic on travel and tourism has also resulted in declining tax revenues from these sectors, both directly and indirectly. In an effort to control the spread of the virus, most countries closed their borders to international travel, with an immediate impact on airlines and the tourism sector. According to (AUC, 2020[9]), the tourism and travel sector in Africa could lose at least USD 50 billion due to the pandemic and at least 2 million direct and indirect jobs.

Rising unemployment in the United States and in Europe is affecting remittances to the continent. Remittances to Africa contribute approximately one third of total external financial flows. The economic crisis that has been induced by the pandemic will result in nearly a 25% decline in remittances to Africa in 2020 (World Bank, 2020[14]). Due to limited regional trade and lack of access to markets within the continent, foreign financial flows into Africa will also decline. Foreign direct investment (FDI) to Africa is mostly resource-seeking and is set to decline further with the fall in commodity prices. With the combined impact of COVID-19 and falling commodity prices, Africa is set to lose FDI flows amounting to 25-40% in 2020 (UNCTAD, 2020[15]).

Africa's tax policy and administration responses to COVID-19

The dire economic impacts of the COVID-19 lockdowns compelled governments worldwide to put in place a raft of tax and non-tax relief measures designed to support businesses and employees in the face of the pandemic. Some of the measures introduced across African countries included deferral of tax payments, tax rebates, exemptions and reliefs, suspension of penalties and interest for late payments and extension of filing periods. Among a total of 23 ATAF member countries, Rwanda, Lesotho and Uganda imposed the highest number of measures. In terms of tax types, Personal Income Tax (PIT), Corporate Income Tax (CIT) and Value Added Tax (VAT) registered the highest number of tax relief measures. Regarding frequency of these measures, tax deferral had the highest (60), followed by measures to enhance business cashflow (53) and measures to support health systems (25). In fourth position were measures to enhance business continuity, with 23 occurrences (ATAF, 2020[16]).

Health crises such as COVID-19 and Ebola bring the twin challenge of granting tax relief to business and individuals while generating expectation that tax administrations will meet or surpass revenue targets (ATAF, 2020[16]). Several African countries granted relief measures without sunset clauses and specific budgetary support. This could eventually have negative effects in relation to perpetuity of supposedly temporary measures and lack of a transparent system, respectively. On business continuity and enterprise risk management, there are gaps that need to be closed, beside the fact that some tax administrations are still not putting in place and implementing these two crucial elements. With respect to customs revenue, the ATAF study (ATAF, 2020[17]) estimated that 18 ATAF member countries lost approximately USD 500 million in three months, from February to April 2020, with the share of the loss in total customs revenue ranging from 5% to 10%.

To support economic recovery, policy makers and African tax administrations could consider measures such as:

- **Revise revenue targets** to account for the negative impact caused by the pandemic. This would be vital easing the pressure on revenue collection agencies.

- **Focus on revenue streams not fully explored**, for instance by increasing focus on wealth taxes, such as taxation of High Net Worth Individuals (HNWI) and property taxes.
- **Modernise information and communications technology (ICT) systems:** the impact of the COVID-19 pandemic has emphasised the need for tax authorities to rethink ICT systems for tax administrations. There is also a need to invest in existing virtual systems of communication that safeguard data security and taxpayer confidentiality. These systems are necessary for continued communications within and across tax administrations, including communicating with taxpayers and other stakeholders.
- **Place caps and sunset clauses on tax relief measures:** it appears from the ATAF survey responses that several countries might have put in place these tax relief measures without stipulating caps and sunset clauses. It is critical for tax administrations to remain watchful and advise policy makers when reviews are necessary. Policy makers could also consider putting in place caps and sunset clauses to these measures where they have not yet been put in place.
- **Put in place teams to monitor the impact of these measures:** it is important for tax administrations to put in place teams that monitor and report on the impact of these tax relief measures. They should quantify revenue forgone due to these measures versus economic benefits derived. However, this will require funding and political support. Development partners may be requested to provide technical support and funding for such initiatives.
- **Adopt non-tax measures:** it would be critical to find ways of automating and tracking expenditures related to some of these measures, especially those on support to businesses. Quantifying revenue forgone through granting these relief measures will assist in future impacts analyses. Since many African countries have high levels of informal economic activity, full lockdown measures could have serious, negative socio-economic effects and should therefore be reviewed, especially in cases of reasonably low mortality rates from the pandemic. African governments should also consider increasing support to the informal sector, a key engine of most economies in Africa but also a sector with the most vulnerable workers, highly susceptible to economic shocks and health and safety risks.
- **Ensure business continuity and minimise tax fraud:** African tax administrations should consider putting in place disaster recovery plans. It is imperative that tax administrations have in place plans for continuity of operations in the event of disaster that destroys part or all resources and assets of the tax administration, due to pandemics and other unforeseen emergencies. It is also imperative to enhance the reporting and tracking of the COVID-19 related tax measures through leveraging on ICT by registering and tracking beneficiaries. Heavy fines should be implemented to deter offenders of tax fraud or would-be offenders. Furthermore, tax authorities should ensure that tax offences are criminalised (OECD, 2017[18]).
- **Safeguard customs revenue:** Countries that rely more on customs revenues may need to undertake action to safeguard revenues, for instance, by intensifying post clearance audits (PCAs) and putting in place systems to curb smuggling activities. During COVID-19, significant increases in smuggling activities around tobacco and alcohol have been reported in some countries. Another consideration amidst PCA is that tax administrations should determine how to safeguard the health and safety of staff and taxpayers due to the contact nature of the audits. Detailed recommendations on customs revenue are presented in an ATAF policy brief (ATAF, 2020[17]).

The opportunity of the African Continental Free Trade Area

Africa's economic future – and thus the future of its public revenues – will be profoundly shaped by the establishment of the African Continental Free Trade Area (AfCFTA). The AfCFTA is one of the flagship projects of Agenda 2063 and an important milestone towards an integrated market that forms an African Economic Community (OECD/ATAF/AUC, 2019[19]). At the time of writing, 54 African countries have signed the agreement and 28 have deposited their instruments of ratification. Several countries have ratified at the national level but have yet to submit their instrument of ratification to the AUC.

The initial implementation of AfCFTA, expected on 1 July 2020, has been delayed by the COVID-19 pandemic. A new implementation date of 1 January 2021 is planned, contingent on the COVID-19 situation. While the pandemic has delayed the launch, work towards effective implementation has been progressing. The legal instrument of the AfCFTA has been concluded, including the protocols on trade in goods and trade in services. A few outstanding issues remain on tariff offers, service offers and rules of origin, which are to be finalised before the launch. On 18 August 2020, the President of Ghana, Nana Addo Dankwa Akufo-Addo, handed over the premises in Accra which will house the AfCFTA Secretariat to the AUC.

The role of trade in the region's COVID-19 response

The pandemic has delayed implementation of AfCFTA but it has not undermined its goals. While total African trade with the rest of the world amounted to around USD 760 billion on average, or 31% of Africa's GDP, between 2015 and 2017 (UNCTAD, 2019[20]), intra-African trade was equivalent to just 2%. Intra-African exports in 2017 stood at 16.6% of total African exports, as compared to 68.4%, 59.4% and 55% for Europe, Asia and America respectively. Since the pandemic, the region's trade with the rest of the world has fallen further, making the case for strengthening intra-African regional value chains and trade; and hence the need to expedite the operationalisation of the AfCFTA.

According to the UNECA, the operationalisation of AfCFTA has the potential to help mitigate the effects of COVID-19, specifically as regards the pharmaceutical and agricultural sectors (Africa Renewal, 2020[21]). The rapid implementation of the AfCFTA will hasten a post-pandemic economic recovery while insulating the continent against future shocks. Considering Africa spends around USD 16 billion to import pharmaceutical products from Europe and Asia annually, in addition to the USD 35 billion spent annually to import food, AfCFTA presents a unique opportunity for the region to build long-term continental resilience and volatility management, by increasing intra-African trade to achieve food security while strengthening the local pharmaceutical industry (Modern Ghana, 2020[22]) (Africa News, 2017[23]).

COVID-19's impact on trade will affect public revenues across Africa

According to *Revenue Statistics in Africa* data, the taxation of trade is a more important source of government revenues in Africa than in other regions. On average, taxes on trade,[2] generated 10.8% of total revenues for the African countries covered by this report in 2018. In comparison, the equivalent figure for Latin America and Caribbean was 6.2% and 0.4% for OECD countries. In four of the 30 countries, trade taxes accounted for over 20% of total tax revenues in 2018. In Africa, 93% of trade taxes were import duties.

The importance of intra-African tariffs and customs duties varies by country; so too, therefore, will the potential cost to public revenues of joining AfCFTA. Figure 3.3 shows trade tax revenues as a percentage of GDP for the 30 countries in this report, alongside the percentage of imports that come from other African countries. Countries like Cabo Verde and Mauritania, for example, have high levels of trade taxes (over 4% of GDP) but revenue losses from integration within an Africa-wide customs union would be low since almost all of their imports originate outside of Africa. Countries such as Burkina Faso and Malawi, on the other hand, generate more than 10% of tax revenues from customs duties while receiving over 30% of imports from other African countries.

Figure 3.3. **Trade tax and intra-African trade levels**

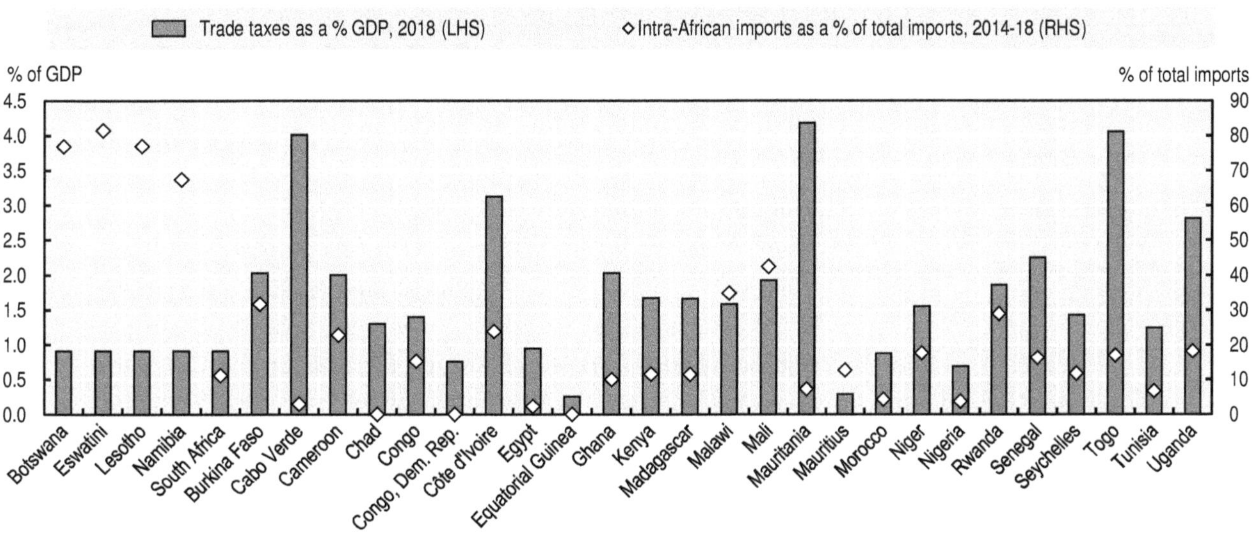

Note: Due to the fact that the SACU countries (Botswana, Eswatini, Lesotho, Namibia, and South Africa) pool their customs revenues, figures for trade taxes as a % of GDP for these countries represent their combined total customs revenues divided by their combined GDP.

Source: ESA/UNSD, *United Nations Comtrade database* (retrieved on 21 August 2020); authors' calculations based on data from (OECD/ATAF/AUC, $2020_{[24]}$), "Revenue Statistics in Africa: Comparative tables", *OECD Tax Statistics* (database), *https://doi.org/10.1787/be755711-en*.

StatLink *https://doi.org/10.1787/888934181964*

The five members of the Southern African Customs Union (SACU), Botswana, Eswatini, Lesotho, Namibia and South Africa, remain the group of African countries with the most highly integrated economies and among those with the lowest overall level of trade taxes. Botswana, Eswatini, Lesotho, and Namibia are the only countries receiving most of their imports from Africa (mostly South Africa). Total trade taxes for these countries amounted to 0.9% of their combined GDP in 2018.

The countries with the highest levels of trade taxes as a percentage of GDP and as a percentage of total taxation are generally lower-income countries. Fourteen of 17 countries with GDP per capita in purchasing power parity (PPP) terms lower than USD 5 000 had trade taxes equivalent to over 1.5% of GDP, while 12 out of the 16 African countries with PPP GDP per capita greater than USD 5 000 had trade taxes amounting to less than 1.5% of GDP.

The importance of trade taxes to African budgets declined between 2008 and 2018. On average, trade taxes for 25 non-SACU[3] African countries declined from 2% of GDP in 2008 to 1.8% in 2018 and from 14.8% of total tax revenues collected to 12.7% (Figure 3.4). The increase in Chad's trade taxes as a percentage of total taxation between 2010 and 2018 was more due to a fall in tax revenues from oil companies, which reduced Chad's total taxes by half, than it was a result of an increase in trade taxes.

Figure 3.4. **Trade tax to total tax ratios, 2008 and 2018**

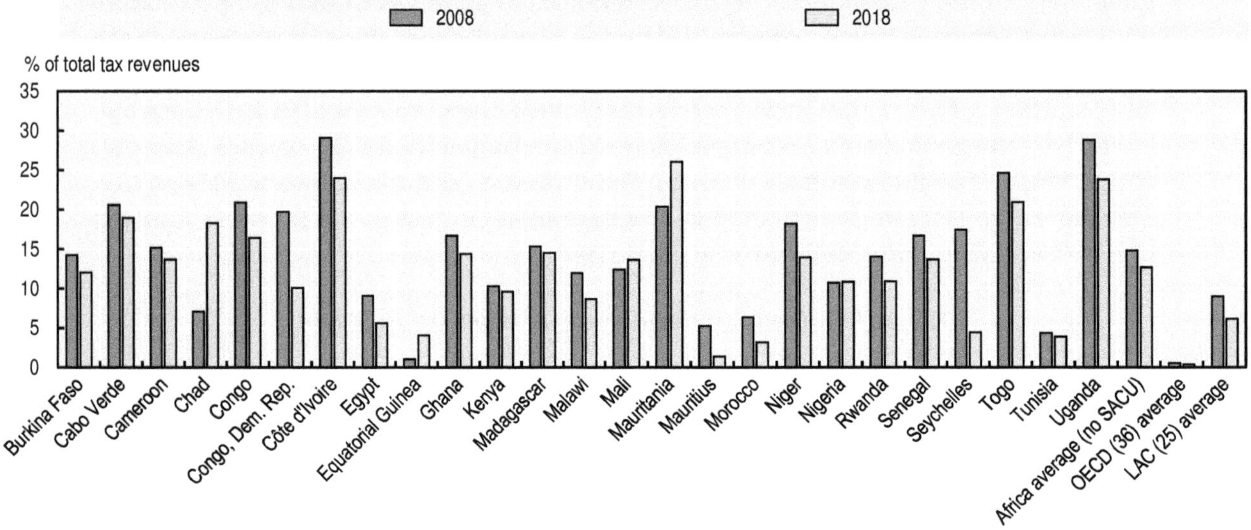

Note: Due to missing figures, 2010 figures are used in place of 2008 figures for Chad and Nigeria.

Source: Authors' calculations based on data from (OECD/ATAF/AUC, 2020[24]), "Revenue Statistics in Africa: Comparative tables", *OECD Tax Statistics* (database), *https://doi.org/10.1787/be755711-en*.

StatLink *https://doi.org/10.1787/888934181983*

In a recent addition to the growing body of research around the impact of AfCFTA, the World Bank (World Bank, 2020[25]) calculated that tariff revenues would decline by less than 1.5% for 49 out of 54 countries and total tax revenues would decline by less than 0.3% in 50 of the 54. The report attributed the small decline to the aforementioned small share of revenues from trade taxes related to intra-African trade and the fact that the majority of revenues related to intra-African trade will be protected by exclusion lists permissible under the AfCFTA. Indeed, the report expects AfCFTA to increase tariff revenues by 3% by 2035 due to the removal of non-tariff barriers to trade and broader trade facilitation measures.

Conclusion

The COVID-19 pandemic has brought the sharpest decline in economic activity worldwide in recent history (OECD, 2020[26]) and, in the case of Africa, might undermine much of the socio-economic progress made over the past ten years (IMF, 2020[5]). In the short term, it is also likely to lead to a fall in fiscal revenues, from tax and non-tax sources, both from the fall in economic activity and from the measures governments are taking to protect businesses and households from the impacts of the crisis. As the pandemic evolves and governments seek to promote economic and fiscal recovery, improving DRM will be an important goal in restoring public finances fairly and sustainably, providing assistance to vulnerable groups and allowing investment in key sectors affected by the pandemic, including the health sector.

Post-pandemic, engagement from both public and private sectors will be crucial in paving the way to economic recovery. On the private sector side, foreign direct investment (FDI), portfolio equity and loans could play an important role in re-igniting economic growth in Africa, as happened in the early 2000s. In the public sector, after the pandemic, governments will need to make renewed efforts to mobilise domestic revenues to restore their fiscal positions and to provide revenues to fund public goods and services and provide social protection to their citizens. The implementation of AfCFTA is likely to play an important role in the economic recovery and has the capacity to transform intra-African trade in the longer run, but its short-term impact on public revenues will need to be monitored, particularly in low-income countries, which might have the most to lose from the elimination of taxes on trade.

Comparable, high-quality data on public revenues will be an important part of these efforts, allowing monitoring and comparisons of DRM across the continent. Supplementing countries' own data sources, *Revenue Statistics in Africa* will continue to provide a clear and comparable picture of the state of domestic revenue mobilisation in the continent before, during and after COVID-19. It will provide a basis for understanding how public revenues are affected and permit analysis of the economic and social impacts of the crisis, the resilience of different revenue types in times of crisis, and the potential for tapping into underutilised sources of revenues. The reliable data on public revenues provided by *Revenue Statistics* can inform evidence-based analysis and policy-making to support the post-COVID-19 economic and fiscal recovery.

Notes

1 This chapter summarises a discussion on long-term trends and factors likely to affect the future of domestic revenue mobilisation in Africa which took place during two ATAF-AUC-OECD technical webinars on 29-30 June 2020. For more information, visit: *www.oecd.org/tax/tax-policy/revenue-statistics-africa-technical-webinar-june-2020.htm*

2 Trade taxes include those taxes classified under the headings "5123 – Customs and Import Duties", "5124 – Taxes on Exports", and "5127 – Other taxes on international trade and transactions".

3 Due to their revenue-sharing agreement, the amount of trade taxes assigned to the five SACU countries is ambiguous. It could refer to funds collected by national taxation agencies or to the funds that are transferred to governments from the SACU Common Revenue Pool.

References

Africa News (2017), *Why is Africa importing $35bn in food annually? - AfDB boss asks*, *www.africanews.com/2017/04/21/why-is-africa-importing-35bn-in-food-annually-afdb-boss-asks/*. [23]

Africa Renewal (2020), *Ways Africa's Free Trade Area could help mitigate effects of COVID-19*, *www.un.org/africarenewal/web-features/coronavirus/ways-africa%E2%80%99s-free-trade-area-could-help-mitigate-effects-covid-19*. [21]

African Development Bank (2020), *African Economic Outlook 2020 - Supplement*, *www.afdb.org/en/documents/african-economic-outlook-2020-supplement*. [6]

African Development Bank (2020), *African Economic Outlook 2020 | Building today, a better Africa tomorrow*, *www.afdb.org/en/documents/african-economic-outlook-2020*. [4]

African Union (2020), *Report of the Teleconference of the Committee of Fifteen (F15) Ministers of Finance and Special Envoys for COVID-19, May 6, 2020*. [13]

ATAF (2020), *Policy Brief: The Erosive Impact of COVID-19 on Customs Revenues in Africa*, *https://events.ataftax.org/includes/preview.php?file_id=73&language=en_US* (accessed on 21 September 2020). [17]

ATAF (2020), *Tax Administration & Policy Developments in Response to the COVID-19 Pandemic in Africa*, *https://events.ataftax.org/index.php?page=documents&func=view&document_id=66&token=f844792f1f76d916358680a52528f976&thankyou*. [16]

AUC (2020), *Impact of the coronavirus COVID-19 on the African economy*, *www.tralac.org/documents/resources/covid-19/3218-impact-of-the-coronavirus-covid-19-on-the-african-economy-african-union-report-april-2020/file.html*. [9]

Coulibaly, B. and P. Madden (2020), *Strategies for coping with the health and economic effects of the COVID-19 pandemic in Africa*, *www.brookings.edu/blog/africa-in-focus/2020/03/18/strategies-for-coping-with-the-health-and-economic-effects-of-the-covid-19-pandemic-in-africa/*. [10]

IMF (2020), *IMF Primary Commodity Prices*, *www.imf.org/en/Research/commodity-prices* (accessed on 16 September 2020). [11]

IMF (2020), *Regional Economic Outlook for Sub-Saharan Africa, June 2020 Update*, *www.imf.org/en/Publications/REO/SSA/Issues/2020/06/29/sreo0629.* [5]

IMF (2020), *World Economic Outlook: The Great Lockdown*, International Monetary Fund, *www.imf.org/~/media/Files/Publications/WEO/2020/April/English/text.ashx?la=en.* [7]

Modern Ghana (2020), *AfCFTA Can Be A Mechanism For Building Long-Term Continental Resilience: Ways Africa's Free Trade Area Could Help Mitigate Effects Of COVID-19*, *www.modernghana.com/news/992564/afcfta-can-be-a-mechanism-for-building-long-term.html.* [22]

OECD (2020), *Tax and Fiscal Policy in Response to the Coronavirus Crisis*, *https://read.oecd-ilibrary.org/view/?ref=128_128575-o6raktc0aa&title=Tax-and-Fiscal-Policy-in-Response-to-the-Coronavirus-Crisis* (accessed on 18 September 2020). [26]

OECD (2017), *Fighting Tax Crime: The Ten Global Principles*, OECD, *www.oecd.org/tax/crime/fighting-tax-crime-the-ten-global-principles.pdf.* [18]

OECD/ATAF/AUC (2020), *Revenue Statistics in Africa: Comparative tables*, OECD Publishing, Paris, *http://dx.doi.org/10.1787/be755711-en.* [24]

OECD/ATAF/AUC (2019), *Revenue Statistics in Africa 2019*, *https://doi.org/10.1787/5daa24c1-en-fr.* [19]

UNCTAD (2020), *Investment flows in Africa set to drop 25% to 40% in 2020*, *https://unctad.org/en/pages/newsdetails.aspx?OriginalVersionID=2400.* [15]

UNCTAD (2019), *Economic Development in Africa Report 2019; Made in Africa: Rules of origin for enhanced intra-African trade*, *https://unctad.org/en/PublicationsLibrary/aldcafrica2019_en.pdf.* [20]

UNECA (2020), *COVID-19 in Africa: Protecting Lives and Economies*, Economic Commission for Africa, *www.uneca.org/sites/default/files/PublicationFiles/eca_covid_report_en_24apr_web1.pdf.* [3]

WHO (2020), *COVID-10 could deepen food insecurity, malnutrition in Africa*, *https://who-africa.africa-newsroom.com/press/coronavirus-africa-covid19-could-deepen-food-insecurity-malnutrition-in-africa.* [12]

WHO (2020), *Health Emergency Information and Risk Assessment*, *https://apps.who.int/iris/bitstream/handle/10665/334127/SITREP_COVID-19_WHOAFRO_20200902-eng.pdf* (accessed on 17 September 2020). [1]

WHO (2020), *WHO African Region numbers at a glance*, *www.afro.who.int/health-topics/coronavirus-covid-19* (accessed on 9 17 2020). [2]

World Bank (2020), "Assessing the Economic Impact of COVID-19 and Policy Responses in Sub-Saharan Africa", *Africa's Pulse*, Vol. 21/April, 2020, *https://openknowledge.worldbank.org/bitstream/handle/10986/33541/9781464815683.pdf?sequence=18&isAllowed=y.* [8]

World Bank (2020), *The African Continental Free Trade Area: Economic and Distributional Effects*, World Bank, *http://dx.doi.org/10.1596/978-1-4648-1559-1.* [25]

World Bank (2020), *World Bank Predicts Sharpest Decline of Remittances in Recent History*, *www.worldbank.org/en/news/press-release/2020/04/22/world-bank-predicts-sharpest-decline-of-remittances-in-recent-history.* [14]

Revenue Statistics in Africa 1990-2018/Statistiques des recettes publiques en Afrique 1990-2018

Chapitre 3

COVID-19 et ZLECAf : Risques et opportunités liés à la mobilisation des ressources intérieures en Afrique

Le chapitre 3 examine les tendances à long terme et les facteurs susceptibles d'influer sur l'avenir de la mobilisation des ressources intérieures en Afrique après la pandémie de COVID-19[1].

Introduction

Ces dix dernières années, les pays africains ont réalisé des progrès en matière de mobilisation des ressources intérieures (MRI). De 2010 à 2018, les 30 pays africains participant aux *Statistiques des recettes publiques en Afrique* ont accru leurs recettes fiscales, qui ont grimpé en moyenne de 15.1 % à 16.5 % du PIB (voir le chapitre 1). L'augmentation du ratio impôts/PIB moyen sur le continent revêt une importance particulière, les recettes fiscales constituant à long terme une source de recettes publiques plus durable que les recettes non fiscales. Celles-ci ont diminué ces dernières années en grande partie en raison d'une diminution continue des dons et parce qu'un recul des prix des matières premières a fait baisser les recettes tirées des redevances (voir le chapitre 2). Quoi qu'il en soit, les recettes fiscales en Afrique restent inférieures aux moyennes enregistrées dans les pays d'Amérique latine et des Caraïbes et dans ceux de l'OCDE (soit 23.1 % et 34.3 % du PIB, respectivement) et ont été relativement stables ces dernières années.

Le contexte économique global s'est détérioré en 2020 du fait de la pandémie mondiale de COVID-19. En septembre 2020, l'Organisation mondiale de la santé (OMS) a fait état de plus d'un million de cas de COVID-19 dans 47 pays d'Afrique (OMS, 2020[1]) (OMS, 2020[2]). L'Afrique subit, en raison de cette pandémie, sa première récession depuis des décennies et des millions de personnes pourraient être confrontées à une pauvreté extrême sur ce continent (CEA, 2020[3]). Avant le COVID-19, les estimations tablaient sur une croissance de l'économie africaine en 2020 (Banque africaine de développement, 2020[4]), mais celle-ci devrait désormais au minimum décélérer et très probablement accuser un recul (tableau 3.1).

Les conséquences économiques de la pandémie pèseront sur les recettes publiques. Le fléchissement de la demande de produits de base et la forte chute des prix de ces produits mettront à rude épreuve les pays qui sont fortement tributaires des recettes générées par ces ressources. Les pays africains dépendants du tourisme enregistreront une baisse des recettes qu'ils tirent de ce secteur en raison des restrictions des voyages et des fermetures des frontières en cours. La diminution des flux commerciaux internationaux influera sur les recettes découlant des taxes sur les échanges commerciaux. La contraction globale de l'activité économique va probablement se répercuter sur les impôts sur le revenu et les bénéfices et sur les cotisations de sécurité sociale.

Le FMI a estimé qu'en Afrique située au sud du Sahara, les recettes vont enregistrer en moyenne un repli équivalent à 2.6 % du PIB en 2020 par rapport à 2019, les dépenses progressant à hauteur de 0.9 % du PIB en moyenne sur la même période (FMI, 2020[5]), en raison de l'ensemble de mesures budgétaires destinées à atténuer l'impact de la crise sur l'économie et à soutenir les catégories de la population les plus vulnérables. La marge de manœuvre budgétaire continuant de se réduire – selon les estimations du FMI, les déficits budgétaires enregistreront une hausse correspondant à 7.6 % du PIB en 2020 – le continent et certains pays africains pourraient éprouver des difficultés à financer les mesures sanitaires, économiques et sociales nécessaires pour parvenir à une reprise durable.

Les pays adoptent actuellement un certain nombre de mesures pour lutter contre la pandémie de COVID-19 et faire face à la crise économique et sociale en résultant. Celles-ci ont évolué, à un rythme différent selon les pays, de mesures d'urgence destinées à protéger entreprises et particuliers contre les effets immédiats de la pandémie et du confinement vers des politiques visant à encourager la reprise économique. Bien qu'il existe des incertitudes considérables quant à l'évolution du volet sanitaire et économique de la pandémie, les politiques budgétaires constitueront un outil important en contribuant au redressement de l'économie et des comptes publics. À plus long terme, la MRI jouera un rôle non négligeable à cet égard, lorsque les pays s'efforceront d'assainir les finances publiques de manière équitable et durable, de stimuler les ressources pour réduire les inégalités et promouvoir le développement et de ménager une marge de manœuvre budgétaire accrue pour faire face aux chocs futurs.

La mise en application de la Zone de libre-échange continentale africaine (ZLECAf) devrait jouer un rôle important dans l'avenir de la MRI en Afrique. Bien qu'ayant retardé la mise en application du nouvel accord, la pandémie de COVID-19 a aussi souligné l'importance de ce pilier essentiel de l'intégration africaine. À court terme, cet accord pourrait permettre d'atténuer les effets du COVID-19 en intensifiant le commerce intra-africain et en accélérant la reprise économique après la pandémie ; à plus long terme, il est probable qu'il contribuera sensiblement à protéger le continent contre des chocs futurs. Si à court terme, les coûts d'ajustement des systèmes budgétaires pourraient être élevés, notamment dans les pays à faible revenu où les taxes sur les échanges commerciaux continuent de représenter une part importante des recettes, ces pertes pourraient être effacées à long terme.

Cette étude spéciale analyse l'avenir de la MRI en Afrique à la lumière de l'impact de la pandémie de COVID-19 et des mesures prises pour y faire face, ainsi que les opportunités découlant de la mise en application future de l'Accord sur la ZLECAf.

Impact du COVID-19 sur les économies et les recettes en Afrique

La pandémie de COVID-19 a effacé les gains économiques acquis en Afrique ces dernières années. Depuis la chute des prix des produits de base observée en 2014, la croissance économique y a été plus faible qu'au cours de la décennie précédente, mais elle est restée positive. Avant la pandémie, il était prévu que le PIB progresse sur le continent. Les prévisions établies avant la pandémie du COVID-19 faisaient état d'une croissance économique de 3.9 % en 2020 et de 4.1 % en 2021, contre 3.4 % en 2019 (Banque africaine de développement, 2020[4]). Elles ont été révisées depuis le début de la pandémie, comme le montre le graphique 3.1.

Les projections indiquent que l'Afrique entrera en récession pour la première fois en 25 ans en raison des effets de la pandémie de COVID-19. On s'accorde à reconnaître que la croissance économique se contractera (tableau 3.1), avec des pertes de production variant, selon les estimations, de 37 milliards USD à 79 milliards USD (Banque mondiale, 2020[8]). Selon (CEA, 2020[3]), avant la pandémie, la plupart des pays africains connaissaient déjà une situation macro-budgétaire défavorable, associée à une dette extérieure élevée et à un déficit budgétaire dépassant 3 % du PIB. La hausse du coût d'emprunt a aussi limité la capacité des gouvernments africains de mettre en place des mesures économiques fortes pour atténuer l'impact de la pandémie.

Graphique 3.1. **Croissance du PIB en Afrique et Afrique au sud du Sahara (ASS), prévisions pour 2010-21**

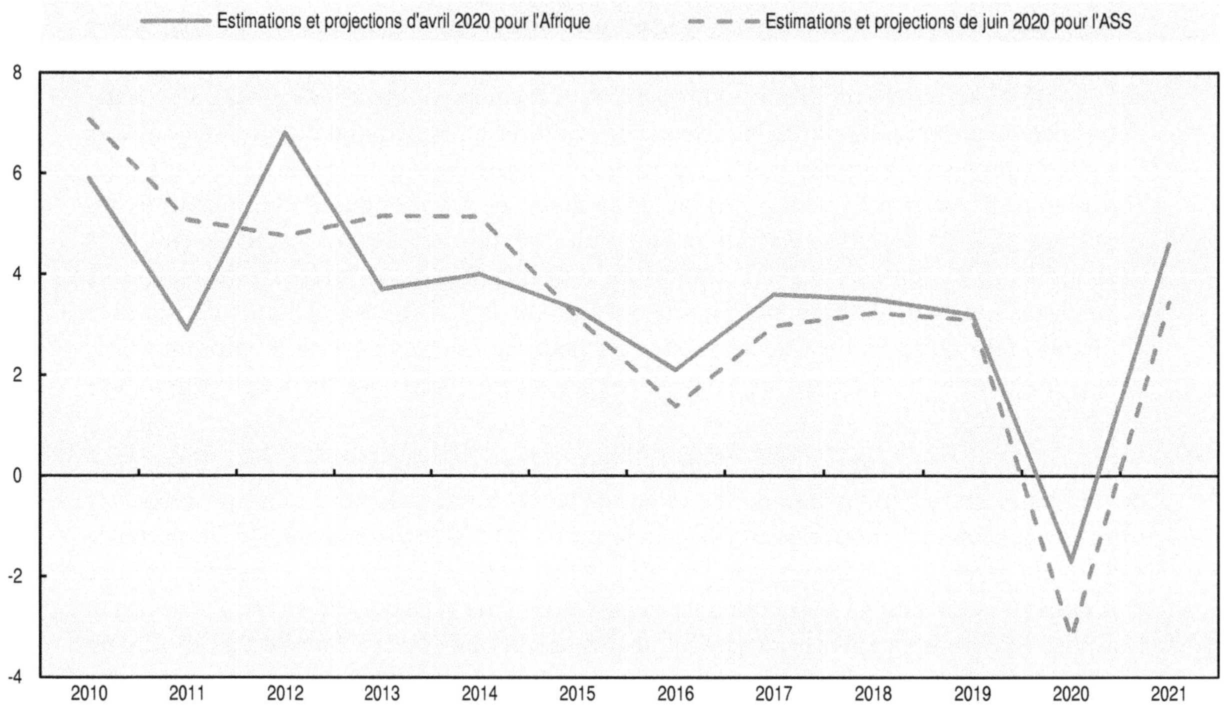

Note : Les chiffres de 2020 et 2021 sont des projections.

Source : Perspectives de l'économie mondiale, avril 2020 (FMI, 2020[7]) et *Mise à jour des Perspectives de l'économie mondiale, juin 2020* (FMI, 2020[5]).

StatLink https://doi.org/10.1787/888934182629

Tableau 3.1. **Croissance du PIB en Afrique, projections pour 2020**

CUA	-2.1 % à -4.9 %
BAfD	-1.7 % à -3.4 %
CEA	1.8 % à -2.6 %
FMI	-3.2 % (Afrique au sud du Sahara)
Banque mondiale	-2.5 % à -5.1% (Afrique au sud du Sahara)

Source : CUA, compilation d'après (CUA, 2020[9]), (Banque africaine de développement, 2020[6]), (FMI, 2020[5]), (CEA, 2020[3]) , (Banque mondiale, 2020[8]).

StatLink

Impact socio-économique

Le fléchissement de la croissance économique résulte, entre autres facteurs, du recul des prix des produits de base, des répercussions négatives des mesures de confinement destinées à contenir la propagation du virus sur les secteurs des voyages et du tourisme et d'une érosion des recettes fiscales due à la fermeture des entreprises. La demande d'exportations africaines a chuté, les mesures d'endiguement de la pandémie ayant entraîné une contraction de l'activité économique des partenaires commerciaux traditionnels en Chine et en Europe. Le tourisme et les exportations de minerais et de pétrole ont été particulièrement touchés, en raison des perturbations brutales du trafic aérien et du repli des prix des produits de base. Le graphique 3.2 montre l'évolution des prix de ces produits entre 1992 et 2020. Leur diminution récente s'explique par le choc économique dû à l'impact du COVID-19 sur de nombreuses économies, qui a conduit à une contraction de la demande. Les cours du pétrole ont perdu environ 54 % de leur valeur, revenant ainsi de 67 USD le baril à moins de 30 USD, et les prix des produits de base non pétroliers ont chuté de 30 % pour le gaz naturel et de 4 % pour les métaux (Coulibaly et Madden, 2020[10]). L'aluminium s'est également replié de 0.49 %, le cuivre de 0.47 %, le plomb de 1.64 % et le cacao de 21 % (CUA, 2020[9]).

Graphique 3.2. **Prix des produits de base mensuels, de janvier 1992 à août 2020**

Source : (FMI, 2020[11]), *www.imf.org/en/Research/commodity-prices.*

StatLink https://doi.org/10.1787/888934182648

Les pays africains continueront d'être touchés, les effets de la pandémie se faisant sentir dans le monde entier. L'impact social et humain en résultant devrait principalement concerner les membres les plus vulnérables de la société. Le chômage et la pauvreté vont s'aggraver en raison de l'impact négatif des mesures strictes de distanciation sociale particulièrement sur le secteur informel. Selon les estimations de la CEA, entre 5 et 29 millions de personnes passeront sous le seuil de pauvreté et plus de 19 millions d'emplois seront perdus du fait du recul de la croissance économique (CEA, 2020[3]). L'insécurité alimentaire et la malnutrition devraient s'accentuer, car les importations et le transport de denrées alimentaires, ainsi que la production agricole ont été entravés par l'apparition de la pandémie de COVID-19. Selon des estimations récentes, quelque 73 millions de personnes souffrent d'insécurité alimentaire en Afrique (OMS, 2020[12]).

Répercussions sur les recettes

Les pays africains ont perdu des recettes provenant à la fois de sources intérieures et extérieures, car les économies ont souffert des mesures d'atténuation et d'endiguement destinées à lutter contre la pandémie de COVID-19 (CUA, 2020[13]). Le recul des prix et de la demande de produits de base a entraîné une érosion des recettes publiques, limitant ainsi les ressources disponibles pour le financement d'urgence et à long terme des services publics. Ces répercussions ont été particulièrement marquées dans les pays où les gouvernements n'ont pas été en mesure de subvenir aux besoins de leurs populations les plus vulnérables pendant le confinement destiné à lutter contre la propagation du COVID-19 et à la contrôler. De nombreuses communautés rurales et urbaines ont été touchées, l'impact de la pandémie continuant de faire sombrer de nombreuses personnes dans le chômage et dans la pauvreté. Cet impact est encore plus sensible dans le secteur informel, qui représente plus de 60 % de l'emploi dans de nombreux pays africains, où les systèmes de protection et d'assurance sociales provisionnés par l'État sont pratiquement inexistants. Les entreprises ont également souffert des effets du confinement, les pays africains n'ayant été qu'une poignée à mettre en place des plans de relance pour assurer la survie du secteur privé. Cela se traduira vraisemblablement par une chute des recettes provenant de l'impôt sur les sociétés et de l'impôt sur le revenu des personnes physiques.

L'impact négatif de la pandémie sur les voyages et le tourisme a également conduit à une diminution des recettes fiscales tirées de ces secteurs, de façon directe et indirecte. Pour maîtriser la propagation du virus, la plupart des pays ont fermé leurs frontières aux voyages internationaux, ce qui a eu des effets immédiats sur les compagnies aériennes et le tourisme. Selon (CUA, 2020[9]), les secteurs du tourisme et des voyages en Afrique pourraient perdre au moins 50 milliards USD à cause de la pandémie et au moins 2 millions d'emplois directs et indirects.

La flambée du chômage aux États-Unis et en Europe restreint les envois de fonds vers le continent. Les envois de fonds vers l'Afrique constituent approximativement un tiers du total des flux financiers extérieurs. La crise économique provoquée par la pandémie entraînera une baisse de ces envois de près de 25 % en 2020 (Banque mondiale, 2020[14]). En raison d'un commerce régional limité et d'un manque d'accès aux marchés au sein du continent, les flux financiers étrangers vers l'Afrique reculeront également. L'investissement direct étranger (IDE) vers l'Afrique est essentiellement motivé par la recherche de ressources et devrait poursuivre son recul avec la chute des prix des produits de base. Sous l'effet conjugué du COVID-19 et du repli des prix des produits de base, l'Afrique devrait perdre des flux d'IDE à hauteur de 25 à 40 % en 2020 (CNUCED, 2020[15]).

Les réponses des politiques et des administrations fiscales face au COVID-19 en Afrique

Les terribles conséquences économiques du confinement dû au COVID-19 ont contraint les pays du monde entier à mettre en place tout un arsenal de mesures d'allégement fiscal et non fiscal pour soutenir les entreprises et les salariés face à la pandémie. Parmi les mesures introduites dans les pays africains figurent des remboursements, exonérations et allègements d'impôt, le report du paiement de l'impôt, la suspension des pénalités et intérêts de retard de paiement ou encore la prolongation des délais de dépôt des déclarations. Parmi les 23 pays membres de l'ATAF, le Rwanda, le Lesotho et l'Ouganda sont ceux qui ont pris le plus grand nombre de mesures. L'impôt sur le revenu des personnes physiques (IRPP), l'impôt sur les sociétés (IS) et la taxe sur la valeur ajoutée (TVA) ont concentré les mesures d'allégement fiscal. En ce qui concerne le nombre de ces mesures, le report d'impôt arrivait en tête (60 mesures), suivi des mesures visant à améliorer la trésorerie des entreprises (53) et à soutenir les systèmes de santé (25). Les mesures destinées à assurer la continuité de l'activité arrivaient en quatrième position, avec 23 cas (ATAF, 2020[16]).

Les crises sanitaires comme celles du COVID-19 ou d'Ebola présentent un double défi : accorder des allégements fiscaux aux entreprises et aux particuliers tout en générant l'espoir que les administrations fiscales atteindront ou dépasseront les objectifs de recettes définis (ATAF, 2020[16]). Plusieurs pays africains ont accordé des mesures d'allégement sans clause d'extinction ni soutien budgétaire spécifique. Cela pourrait, *in fine*, produire des effets négatifs liés au caractère pérenne de mesures censées être temporaires et à l'absence de système transparent. En ce qui concerne la continuité de l'activité et la gestion des risques d'entreprise, certaines lacunes doivent être comblées, outre le fait que certaines administrations fiscales n'ont toujours pas mis en place et appliqué ces deux éléments cruciaux. S'agissant des recettes douanières, l'étude de l'ATAF (ATAF, 2020[17]) estime que 18 pays de l'ATAF ont perdu environ 500 millions USD en trois mois, de février à avril 2020, la part de ces pertes dans les recettes douanières totales allant de 5 % à 10 %.

Pour soutenir la reprise économique, les responsables de politiques fiscale et les administrations fiscales africaines pourraient notamment envisager les mesures suivantes :

- **revoir les objectifs de recettes** pour tenir compte de l'impact négatif de la pandémie. Ce point est primordial allégeant ainsi les pressions pesant sur les organismes de recouvrement des recettes ;
- **donner la priorité aux flux de recettes qui n'ont pas été pleinement exploités**, par exemple en mettant davantage l'accent sur les impôts sur le patrimoine, comme l'imposition des particuliers fortunés et les impôts fonciers ;
- **moderniser les systèmes de technologies de l'information et de la communication (TIC) :** l'impact de la pandémie de COVID-19 a souligné la nécessité, pour les autorités fiscales, de repenser les systèmes TIC des administrations fiscales. Il faut également investir dans les systèmes de communication virtuels existants afin de préserver la sécurité des données et la confidentialité des informations concernant les contribuables. Ces systèmes sont nécessaires pour assurer des communications constantes au sein et entre les administrations fiscales, notamment avec les contribuables et d'autres parties prenantes ;
- **plafonner les mesures d'allégement fiscal et les assortir de clauses d'extinction :** il ressort des réponses à l'enquête de l'ATAF que plusieurs pays pourraient avoir mis en place ces mesures d'allégement fiscal sans définir de plafonds ni de clauses d'extinction. Les administrations fiscales doivent absolument rester vigilantes et informer les responsables de l'action publique lorsque des réexamens s'imposent. Ces responsables pourraient aussi envisager de plafonner ces mesures et de les assortir de clauses d'extinction, lorsque cela n'a pas déjà été fait ;
- **mettre en place des équipes pour suivre l'impact de ces mesures :** il importe que les administrations fiscales mettent en place des équipes chargées de suivre et de rendre compte de l'impact de ces mesures d'allégement fiscal. Ces équipes devraient quantifier les recettes perdues en raison de ces mesures au regard des avantages économiques en découlant. Cela nécessitera toutefois des financements et un soutien politique. Les partenaires du développement pourraient être priés d'apporter un soutien technique et des financements pour ces initiatives ;
- **adopter des mesures non fiscales :** il faut impérativement trouver des moyens d'automatiser et de suivre les dépenses liées à certaines de ces mesures, notamment celles qui concernent l'aide aux entreprises. La quantification des recettes perdues en raison des mesures d'allégement accordées facilitera les analyses d'impact ultérieures. Le niveau d'activité économique informelle étant élevé dans de nombreux pays

africains, les mesures strictes de confinement pourraient avoir de lourdes conséquences socio-économiques et devraient donc être réexaminées, surtout lorsque le taux de mortalité dû à la pandémie est relativement faible. Les gouvernements africains devraient aussi envisager d'accroître le soutien au secteur informel, qui constitue un moteur essentiel de la plupart des économies du continent, mais aussi un secteur où les travailleurs sont les plus vulnérables et très exposés aux chocs économiques et aux risques pour la santé et la sécurité.

- **assurer la continuité de l'activité et minimiser la fraude fiscale :** les administrations fiscales africaines devraient envisager de mettre en place des plans de reprise après sinistres. Elles doivent impérativement se doter de plans leur permettant d'assurer la continuité de leurs opérations lorsqu'un sinistre détruit une partie ou la totalité de leurs ressources et de leurs actifs, en raison d'une pandémie ou autre urgence imprévue. Il est également indispensable de renforcer le reporting et le suivi des mesures fiscales liées au COVID-19 en tirant parti des TIC, c'est-à-dire en enregistrant et en suivant les bénéficiaires. De lourdes amendes devraient être imposées pour dissuader les auteurs de fraude fiscale ou les auteurs d'infractions potentiels. De plus, les autorités fiscales devraient veiller à l'incrimination des infractions fiscales (OCDE, 2017[18]) ;
- **préserver les recettes douanières :** les pays qui sont davantage tributaires des recettes douanières devront peut-être prendre des mesures pour préserver ces recettes, par exemple en intensifiant les contrôles après dédouanement et en mettant en place des mécanismes visant à infléchir les activités de contrebande. Pendant la pandémie de COVID-19, une forte hausse des activités de contrebande concernant le tabac et l'alcool a été signalée dans certains pays. Toujours en ce qui concerne les contrôles après dédouanement, les administrations fiscales devraient déterminer comment préserver la santé et la sécurité de leur personnel et des contribuables en raison des contacts induits par ces contrôles. Des recommandations détaillées sur les recettes douanières sont présentées dans une note stratégique de l'ATAF (ATAF, 2020[17]).

L'opportunité offerte par la Zone de libre-échange continentale africaine

L'avenir économique de l'Afrique – et donc l'avenir de ses recettes publiques – sera entièrement façonné par l'établissement de la Zone de libre-échange continentale africaine (ZLECAf). La ZLECAf est l'un des projets phares de l'Agenda 2063 et marque une étape importante vers un marché intégré formant une Communauté économique africaine (OCDE/ATAF/CUA, 2019[19]). Au moment de la rédaction de cette publication, 54 pays africains ont signé l'Accord sur la ZLECAf et 28 ont déposé leur instrument de ratification. Plusieurs pays ont ratifié l'Accord au niveau national, mais n'ont pas encore soumis leur instrument de ratification à la CUA.

La mise en application initiale de l'Accord sur la ZLECAf, programmée pour le 1er juillet 2020, a été retardée par la pandémie de COVID-19. Une nouvelle date de mise en application, le 1er janvier 2021, est prévue sous réserve de l'évolution de la situation liée au COVID-19. Si la pandémie a différé le lancement, les travaux aux fins de la mise en application effective progressent. L'instrument juridique de la ZLECAf a été finalisé, et notamment les protocoles sur le commerce des biens et le commerce des services. Certaines questions restent en suspens, comme les offres tarifaires, les offres de services et les règles d'origine, et doivent être finalisées avant le lancement. Le 18 août 2020, le Président du Ghana, Nana Addo Dankwa Akufo-Addo, a mis à disposition, à Accra, les locaux qui accueilleront le Secrétariat de la ZLECAf auprès de la CUA.

Le rôle du commerce dans les mesures prises par la région pour lutter contre le COVID-19

La pandémie a retardé la mise en application de l'Accord sur la ZLECAf, mais elle n'a pas ébranlé ses objectifs. Si le commerce total de l'Afrique avec le reste du monde représentait quelque 760 milliards USD en moyenne, ou 31 % du PIB du continent, entre 2015 et 2017 (CNUCED, 2019[20]), le commerce intra-africain n'en constituait que 2 %. Les exportations intra-africaines en 2017 s'établissaient à 16.6 % du total des exportations africaines, contre 68.4 %, 59.4 % et 55 % pour l'Europe, l'Asie et l'Amérique, respectivement. Depuis la pandémie, le commerce de la région avec le reste du monde a continué de se contracter, ce qui plaide en faveur d'un renforcement des chaînes de valeur et du commerce régionaux intra-africains, et donc d'une accélération du lancement opérationnel de la ZLECAf.

Selon la CEA, le lancement opérationnel de la ZLECAf devrait permettre d'atténuer les effets du COVID-19, notamment en ce qui concerne les secteurs pharmaceutique et agricole (Africa Renewal, 2020[21]). La mise en application rapide de l'Accord sur la ZLECAf accélérera une reprise économique post-pandémie tout en protégeant le continent contre des chocs futurs. Sachant que l'Afrique dépense environ 16 milliards USD par an pour importer des produits pharmaceutiques d'Europe et d'Asie, qui viennent s'ajouter aux 35 milliards USD dépensés chaque année pour importer des denrées alimentaires, la ZLECAf offre à la région une occasion unique de garantir la résilience et gérer l'instabilité du continent à long terme, en développant le commerce intra-africain, de manière à assurer la sécurité alimentaire tout en renforçant l'industrie pharmaceutique locale (Modern Ghana, 2020[22]) (Africa News, 2017[23]).

L'impact du COVID-19 sur le commerce pèsera sur les recettes publiques en Afrique

Selon les données des *Statistiques des recettes publiques en Afrique*, les impôts sur les échanges commerciaux sont une source de recettes publiques plus importante en Afrique que dans d'autres régions. En moyenne, les taxes sur les échanges commerciaux[2] généraient en 2018 10.8 % des recettes totales des pays africains pris en compte dans le présent rapport. Par comparaison, le chiffre équivalent était de 6.2 % pour l'Amérique latine et les Caraïbes et de 0.4 % pour les pays de l'OCDE. Dans quatre de ces 30 pays africains, les taxes sur les échanges commerciaux constituaient plus de 20 % des recettes fiscales totales en 2018. En Afrique, 93 % de ces taxes correspondaient à des droits à l'importation.

L'importance des droits de douane intra-africains varie suivant les pays ; et ce sera donc aussi le cas pour le coût potentiel de l'adhésion à la ZLECAf pour les recettes publiques. Le graphique 3.3 fait apparaître les recettes des taxes sur les échanges commerciaux en pourcentage du PIB pour les 30 pays figurant dans le présent rapport, ainsi que le pourcentage des importations provenant d'autres pays africains. Des pays comme Cabo Verde ou la Mauritanie, par exemple, se caractérisent par des recettes élevées provenant des taxes sur les échanges commerciaux (supérieures à 4 % du PIB) mais les pertes de recettes découlant de leur intégration dans une union douanière à l'échelle de l'Afrique seraient modérées, la quasi-totalité de leurs importations ne provenant pas de pays africains. Des pays comme le Burkina Faso ou le Malawi, en revanche, tirent plus de 10 % de leurs recettes fiscales des droits de douane, tandis que plus de 30 % de leurs importations proviennent d'autres pays africains.

Les cinq membres de l'Union douanière d'Afrique australe (SACU), soit l'Afrique du Sud, le Botswana, l'Eswatini, le Lesotho et la Namibie, demeurent le groupe de pays africains dont les économies sont les plus intégrées et comptent parmi ceux dont le niveau global des taxes commerciales est le plus bas. Le Botswana, l'Eswatini, le Lesotho et la Namibie sont les seuls pays dont les importations viennent pour l'essentiel de pays africains (principalement l'Afrique du Sud). Pour ces pays, les taxes sur les échanges commerciaux totales représentaient 0.9 % de leur PIB global en 2018.

Graphique 3.3. **Recettes des taxes sur les échanges commerciaux et commerce intra-africain**

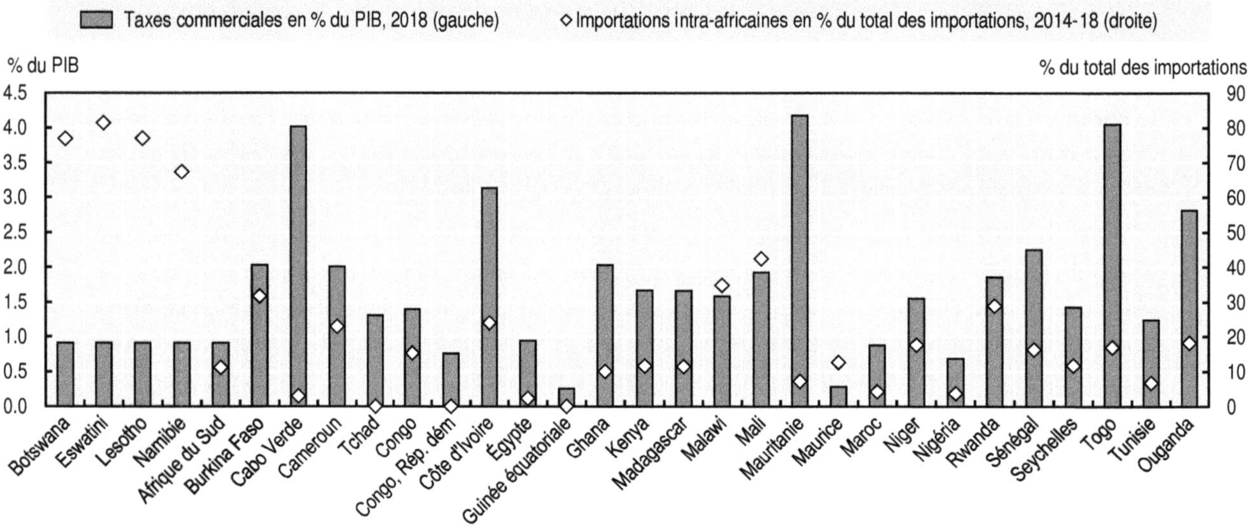

Note : Les pays de la SACU (Afrique du Sud, Botswana, Eswatini, Lesotho et Namibie) mettant en commun leurs recettes douanières, les chiffres des taxes commerciales en % du PIB apparaissant pour ces pays correspondent à leurs recettes douanières totales globales divisées par leur PIB global.

Source : SEC/DSNU, *Base de données statistiques des Nations Unies sur le commerce des marchandises (COMTRADE)* (extraction du 21 août 2020) ; *Statistiques des recettes publiques en Afrique*, données comparatives disponibles sur : *https://doi.org/10.1787/7f54581d-fr*.

StatLink *https://doi.org/10.1787/888934182667*

Les pays où les taxes sur les échanges commerciaux sont les plus élevées en pourcentage du PIB et en pourcentage des taxes totales sont généralement des pays à faible revenu. Dans 14 des 17 pays affichant un PIB par habitant à parité de pouvoir d'achat (PPA) inférieur à 5 000 USD, les taxes commerciales représentaient plus de 1.5 % du PIB, tandis que dans 12 des 16 pays africains où le PIB par habitant à PPA dépassait 5 000 USD, elles s'élevaient à moins de 1.5 % du PIB.

La part des taxes sur les échanges commerciaux dans les budgets africains a diminué entre 2008 et 2018. En moyenne, les taxes sur les échanges commerciaux de 25 pays africains ne faisant pas partie de la SACU[3] sont passées de 2 % du PIB en 2008 à 1.8 % en 2018, et de 14.8 % des recettes fiscales totales perçues à 12.7 % (graphique 3.4). La progression des taxes commerciales en pourcentage des taxes totales observée au Tchad entre 2010 et 2018 tenait davantage à une baisse des recettes fiscales provenant des compagnies pétrolières, qui a amputé les taxes totales du pays de moitié, qu'à une hausse des taxes sur les échanges commerciaux.

Dans un ajout récent au corpus grandissant de recherches sur l'impact de la ZLECAf, la Banque mondiale (Banque mondiale, 2020$_{[24]}$) a calculé que les recettes douanières allaient reculer de moins de 1.5 % dans 49 pays sur 54, et les recettes fiscales totales de moins de 0.3 % dans 50 pays sur 54. Le rapport a attribué ce léger repli à la faible part des recettes tirées des taxes sur les échanges commerciaux liées au commerce intra-africain mentionnée précédemment et au fait que la majorité des recettes liées au commerce intra-africain seront protégées par les listes d'exclusion autorisées par l'accord sur la ZLECAf. Selon le rapport, en effet, la ZLECAf devrait faire progresser les recettes douanières de 3 % d'ici 2035 en raison de la suppression des obstacles non tarifaires aux échanges et des mesures renforcées de facilitation des échanges.

Graphique 3.4. **Recettes des taxes sur les échanges commerciaux en pourcentage des recettes fiscales totales 2008 et 2018**

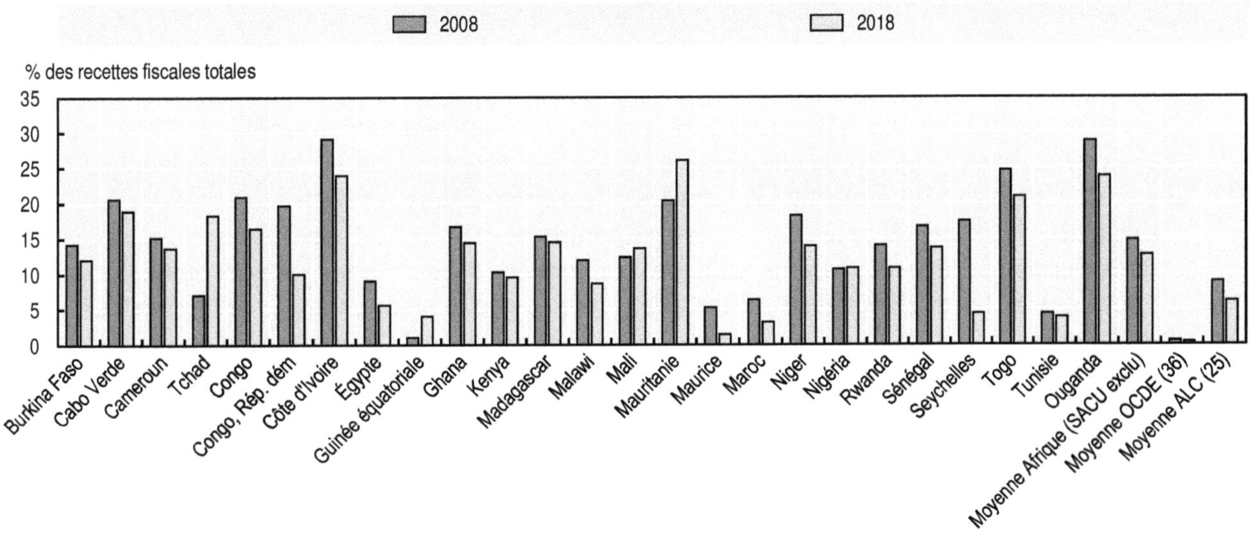

Note : Faute de données disponibles, ce sont les chiffres de 2010, et pas de 2008, qui sont utilisés pour le Tchad et le Nigéria

Source : Calculs des auteurs basés sur des données figurant dans « Statistiques des recettes publiques en Afrique : Tableaux comparatifs » (OCDE/ATAF/CUA, 2020[3]), *Statistiques fiscales de l'OCDE* (base de données), *https://doi.org/10.1787/7f54581d-fr.*

StatLink https://doi.org/10.1787/888934182686

Conclusion

La pandémie de COVID-19 a provoqué la plus forte baisse de l'activité économique observée à l'échelle mondiale dans l'histoire récente (OCDE, 2020[25]) et, en ce qui concerne l'Afrique, elle pourrait ébranler une grande partie des progrès socio-économiques réalisés ces dix dernières années (FMI, 2020[5]). À court terme, elle devrait aussi entraîner une contraction des recettes budgétaires, provenant de sources fiscales et non fiscales, sous l'effet du recul de l'activité économique et des mesures prises par les États pour protéger les entreprises et les ménages contre les répercussions de la crise. À mesure que la pandémie évolue, et que les autorités cherchent à favoriser la reprise économique et le redressement des comptes publics, il faudra améliorer la MRI pour rétablir les finances publiques de manière équitable et durable, apporter une aide aux catégories vulnérables et faciliter les investissements dans les secteurs clés touchés par la pandémie, dont le secteur de la santé.

L'implication des secteurs public et privé après la pandémie sera déterminante pour préparer la reprise économique. En ce qui concerne le secteur privé, l'investissement direct étranger (IDE), les investissements de portefeuille et les prêts pourraient jouer un rôle important afin de relancer la croissance économique en Afrique, comme cela s'est produit au début des années 2000. Dans le secteur public, après la pandémie, les gouvernements devront renouveler leurs efforts en vue de mobiliser les ressources intérieures pour rétablir leur situation budgétaire, et de dégager des recettes pour financer les biens et les services publics et assurer une protection sociale à leurs ressortissants. La mise en application de l'Accord sur la ZLECAf va probablement contribuer de manière significative à la reprise économique et elle a la capacité de transformer le commerce intra-africain à plus long terme, mais son impact à court terme sur les recettes publiques devra faire l'objet d'un suivi, en particulier dans les pays à faible revenu, qui pourraient être les grands perdants de la suppression des taxes sur les échanges commerciaux.

Des données comparables de qualité sur les recettes publiques contribueront notablement à ces efforts, en permettant de suivre et de comparer la MRI sur l'ensemble du continent. Les *Statistiques des recettes publiques en Afrique*, qui viennent compléter les propres sources de données des pays, continueront de dresser un tableau clair et comparable de l'état de la mobilisation des ressources intérieures sur le continent avant, pendant et après le COVID-19. Elles serviront en outre de point de départ pour comprendre comment les recettes publiques sont touchées et permettront d'analyser les effets économiques et sociaux de la crise, la résilience de différents types de recettes en temps de crise et les possibilités de puiser dans ces sources de recettes sous-utilisées. Les données fiables sur les recettes publiques figurant dans les *Statistiques des recettes publiques* peuvent éclairer l'analyse et la prise de décisions fondées sur des observations factuelles afin de soutenir la reprise économique et le redressement des comptes publics post-COVID-19.

Notes

1 Ce chapitre fait la synthèse des débats sur les tendances à long terme et les facteurs susceptibles d'influer sur l'avenir de la mobilisation des ressources intérieures en Afrique ; débats qui se sont tenus les 29 et 30 juin 2020 au cours de deux webinaires techniques ATAF-CUA-OCDE. Pour de plus amples informations, veuillez consulter : *www.oecd.org/fr/fiscalite/politiques-fiscales/statistiques-recettes-publiques-afrique-webinaire-technique-juin-2020.htm*

2 Les taxes sur les échanges commerciaux comprennent les taxes figurant sous les rubriques « 5123 – Droits de douane et droits à l'importation », « 5124 – Taxes à l'exportation » et « 5127 – Autres impôts sur les transactions et les échanges internationaux ».

3 En raison de leur accord de répartition des recettes, le montant des taxes commerciales attribué aux cinq pays de la SACU est ambigu. Il pourrait correspondre aux fonds recueillis par les organismes fiscaux nationaux ou aux fonds transférés aux gouvernements par la Caisse commune de la SACU.

Références

Africa News (2017), *Why is Africa importing $35bn in food annually? - AfDB boss asks*, *www.africanews.com/2017/04/21/why-is-africa-importing-35bn-in-food-annually-afdb-boss-asks/*. [23]

Africa Renewal (2020), *Ways Africa's Free Trade Area could help mitigate effects of COVID-19*, *www.un.org/africarenewal/web-features/coronavirus/ways-africa%E2%80%99s-free-trade-area-could-help-mitigate-effects-covid-19*. [21]

ATAF (2020), *Policy Brief: The Erosive Impact of COVID-19 on Customs Revenues in Africa*, *https://events.ataftax.org/includes/preview.php?file_id=73&language=en_US* (consulté le 21 September 2020). [17]

ATAF (2020), *Tax Administration & Policy Developments in Response to the COVID-19 Pandemic in Africa*, *events.ataftax.org/index.php?page=documents&func=view&document_id=66&token=f844792f1f76d916358680a52528f976&thankyou*. [16]

Banque africaine de développement (2020), *Perspectives économiques en Afrique 2020 - Supplément*, *www.afdb.org/fr/documents/perspectives-economiques-en-afrique-2020-supplement*. [6]

Banque africaine de développement (2020), *Perspectives économiques en Afrique 2020 : Former la main-d'œuvre africaine de demain*, *www.afdb.org/en/documents/african-economic-outlook-2020*. [4]

Banque mondiale (2020), « Africa's Pulse. Évaluation de l'impact économique du COVID-19 et des réponses politiques en Afrique subsaharienne », *Africa's Pulse*, vol. 21/avril, *www.afdb.org/fr/documents/perspectives-economiques-en-afrique-2020*. [8]

Banque mondiale (2020), *Selon la Banque mondiale, les remises migratoires devraient connaître un repli sans précédent dans l'histoire récente*, *www.banquemondiale.org/fr/news/press-release/2020/04/22/world-bank-predicts-sharpest-decline-of-remittances-in-recent-history.* [14]

Banque mondiale (2020), *Zone de libre-échange continentale africaine : effets économiques et redistributifs*, Banque mondiale, *http://dx.doi.org/10.1596/978-1-4648-1559-1.* [24]

CEA (2020), *Le COVID-19 en Afrique : Sauver des vies et l'économie*, Commission économique pour l'Afrique, *www.uneca.org/fr/publications/le-covid-19-en-afrique-sauver-des-vies-et-l%E2%80%99%C3%A9conomie.* [3]

CNUCED (2020), *Investment flows in Africa set to drop 25% to 40% in 2020*, *https://unctad.org/en/pages/newsdetails.aspx?OriginalVersionID=2400.* [15]

CNUCED (2019), *Le développement économique en Afrique - Rapport 2019 : Made in Africa - Les règles d'origine, un tremplin pour le commerce intra-africain*, *https://unctad.org/fr/PublicationsLibrary/aldcafrica2019_fr.pdf.* [20]

Coulibaly, B. et P. Madden (2020), *Strategies for coping with the health and economic effects of the COVID-19 pandemic in Africa*, *www.brookings.edu/blog/africa-in-focus/2020/03/18/strategies-for-coping-with-the-health-and-economic-effects-of-the-covid-19-pandemic-in-africa/.* [10]

CUA (2020), *Impact of the coronavirus COVID-19 on the African economy*, *www.tralac.org/documents/resources/covid-19/3218-impact-of-the-coronavirus-covid-19-on-the-african-economy-african-union-report-april-2020/file.html.* [9]

CUA (2020), *Report of the Teleconference of the Committee of Fifteen (F15) Ministers of Finance and Special Envoys for COVID-19, 6 mai.* [13]

FMI (2020), *IMF Primary Commodity Prices*, *www.imf.org/en/Research/commodity-prices* (consulté le 16 septembre 2020). [11]

FMI (2020), *Regional Economic Outlook for Sub-Saharan Africa, June 2020 Update*, *www.imf.org/en/Publications/REO/SSA/Issues/2020/06/29/sreo0629.* [5]

FMI (2020), *World Economic Outlook: The Great Lockdown*, Fonds monétaire international, *www.imf.org/~/media/Files/Publications/WEO/2020/April/English/text.ashx?la=en.* [7]

Modern Ghana (2020), *AfCFTA Can Be A Mechanism For Building Long-Term Continental Resilience: Ways Africa's Free Trade Area Could Help Mitigate Effects Of COVID-19*, *www.modernghana.com/news/992564/afcfta-can-be-a-mechanism-for-building-long-term.html.* [22]

OCDE (2020), *Tax and Fiscal Policy in Response to the Coronavirus Crisis*, *https://read.oecd-ilibrary.org/view/?ref=128_128575-o6raktc0aa&title=Tax-and-Fiscal-Policy-in-Response-to-the-Coronavirus-Crisis* (consulté le 18 septembre 2020). [25]

OCDE (2017), *Lutte contre la délinquance fiscale : Les dix principes mondiaux*, OCDE, *www.oecd.org/fr/fiscalite/delits/lutte-contre-la-delinquance-fiscale-les-dix-principes-mondiaux.pdf.* [18]

OCDE/ATAF/CUA (2020), *Recettes fiscales en Afrique : Tableaux comparatifs*, Éditions OCDE, Paris, *https://doi.org/10.1787/7f54581d-fr.* [26]

OCDE/ATAF/CUA (2019), *Statistiques des recettes publiques en Afrique 2019*, *https://doi.org/10.1787/5daa24c1-en-fr.* [19]

OMS (2020), *COVID-10 could deepen food insecurity, malnutrition in Africa*, *https://who-africa.africa-newsroom.com/press/coronavirus-africa-covid19-could-deepen-food-insecurity-malnutrition-in-africa.* [12]

OMS (2020), *Health Emergency Information and Risk Assessment*, *https://apps.who.int/iris/bitstream/handle/10665/334127/SITREP_COVID-19_WHOAFRO_20200902-eng.pdf* (consulté le 17 septembre 2020). [1]

OMS (2020), *WHO African Region numbers at a glance*, *www.afro.who.int/fr/node/12206* (consulté le 17 septembre 2020). [2]

Chapter 4

Tax levels and tax structures, 1990-2018

Chapitre 4

Niveaux et structures des impôts, 1990-2018

Chapter 4 / Chapitre 4

Comparative tables, 1990-2018

In all of the following tables a ("..") indicates not available. The main series in this volume cover the years 1990 to 2018.

Figures referring to 1991-99 in Table 4.1 and 4.2 and figures relating to 1990-97, 1999, 2001-07, 2009, and 2011-12 in Tables 4.5 to 4.19 have been omitted because of lack of space. Complete series are, however, available on line at OECD/ATAF/AUC (2020), "Revenue Statistics in Africa: Comparative tables", OECD Tax Statistics (database), *https://doi.org/10.1787/be755711-en*.

The OECD average is taken from Revenue Statistics (2019). Colombia was not an OECD Member at the time of preparation of this publication. Accordingly, Colombia does not appear in the list of OECD Members and is not included in the zone aggregates.

Tableaux comparatifs, 1990-2018

Dans tous les tableaux suivants le symbole («..») signifie que l'information n'est pas disponible. La principale série dans ce volume couvre les années 1990 à 2018.

Les années 1991 à 1999 dans le tableau 4.1 et 4.2 et les années 1990-97, 1999, 2001-07, 2009, et 2011-12 dans les tableaux 4.5 à 4.19 ont été omis en raison du manque d'espace. Les séries complètes ont cependant disponibles en ligne sur OCDE/ATAF/CUA (2020), « Statistiques des recettes publiques en Afrique: Tableaux comparatifs », Statistiques fiscales de l'OCDE (base de données), *http://dx.doi.org/10.1787/7f54581d-fr*.

La moyenne de l'OCDE est tirée des Statistiques des recettes publiques (2019). La Colombie n'était pas membre de l'OCDE au moment de la préparation de cette publication. En conséquence, la Colombie n'apparaît pas dans la liste des Membres de l'OCDE et n'est pas incluse dans les agrégats de la zone OCDE.

Table 4.1. **Total tax revenue as percentage of GDP, 1990-2018**
Tableau 4.1. **Total des recettes fiscales en pourcentage du PIB, 1990-2018**

	1990	2000	2001	2002	2003	2004	2005	2006	2007	2008
Botswana	..	..	..	..	..	15.5	15.2	15.2	13.7	17.1
Burkina Faso	..	10.2	10.3	10.7	11.4	12.4	11.8	12.3	12.8	12.0
Cabo Verde	10.5	15.6	16.9	19.3	17.7	18.7	19.5	20.9	20.8	21.2
Cameroon / Cameroun	..	11.3	12.6	11.8	12.3	11.3	12.0	12.4	12.8	12.5
Chad / Tchad	..	..	..	..	..	..	..	..	..	..
Congo[1]	..	4.3	6.0	7.2	8.7	8.2	6.4	5.8	7.0	6.9
Congo, Dem. Rep. / Congo, Rép. dém.[2]	..	0.6	2.3	3.0	3.4	4.7	5.2	5.8	6.9	8.5
Côte d'Ivoire	15.6	11.1	11.3	11.5	10.6	11.5	11.3	11.7	12.4	12.2
Egypt / Égypte	..	..	..	16.2	16.3	16.8	16.3	18.4	17.9	17.8
Equatorial Guinea / Guinée équatoriale	..	..	..	..	..	..	8.2	9.7	7.5	7.8
Eswatini	..	10.7	10.5	10.8	11.8	11.4	11.6	11.7	11.8	12.9
Ghana	..	7.8	8.3	8.5	9.7	10.7	11.1	10.4	10.8	10.6
Kenya	..	..	16.6	16.1	16.7	17.1	18.4	17.5	18.1	18.9
Lesotho	..	..	..	..	..	17.4	15.9	15.0	15.7	16.9
Madagascar[3]	..	9.6	8.3	6.5	8.8	9.6	8.9	9.4	10.0	11.4
Malawi	..	..	..	..	..	..	12.6	12.6	13.6	14.6
Mali	..	11.4	11.4	12.3	13.9	14.9	14.5	14.1	14.3	13.3
Mauritania / Mauritanie	..	..	..	..	..	..	..	..	10.0	10.1
Mauritius / Maurice[4]	22.3	18.3	16.3	16.0	17.3	17.4	17.9	17.8	17.0	18.7
Morocco / Maroc[3,5]	..	23.5	23.4	23.1	22.8	23.1	24.7	25.4	27.7	30.2
Namibia	..	..	..	..	..	..	..	16.2	17.2	17.7
Niger	..	7.3	7.7	8.1	8.1	8.8	8.2	8.6	9.1	9.1
Nigeria / Nigéria	..	..	..	..	..	..	..	..	..	..
Rwanda[3]	..	10.2	11.3	12.4	12.2	12.1	12.1	11.7	12.1	13.1
Senegal / Sénégal[6]	..	13.2	13.3	13.9	14.0	14.4	15.3	15.5	15.9	15.0
Seychelles	..	..	..	..	..	..	..	..	..	25.6
South Africa / Afrique du Sud[7]	23.9	22.4	23.7	23.1	22.7	23.7	25.5	26.8	28.1	27.8
Togo	..	9.4	10.9	9.6	11.9	13.2	13.3	14.5	15.2	14.4
Tunisia / Tunisie[3]	..	24.4	24.8	24.8	24.2	24.1	24.2	24.4	25.2	26.8
Uganda / Ouganda	..	9.4	9.3	9.6	10.0	10.2	10.5	10.7	10.8	10.6
Africa (30) average / Moyenne Afrique (30)[8]	..	..	..	..	..	..	..	..	..	..
LAC average / Moyenne ALC[9]	**15.9**	**18.7**	**18.8**	**18.8**	**19.2**	**19.6**	**20.4**	**21.2**	**21.6**	**21.7**
OECD average / Moyenne OCDE[10]	**31.9**	**33.8**	**33.2**	**33.0**	**32.9**	**32.9**	**33.4**	**33.5**	**33.6**	**32.9**

	2009	2010	2011	2012	2013	2014	2015	2016	2017	2018
Botswana	15.8	15.6	15.7	13.8	14.7	15.2	12.7	14.0	12.3	12.1
Burkina Faso	12.8	14.1	13.8	15.5	16.5	15.3	15.3	16.0	16.9	16.8
Cabo Verde	18.4	18.4	19.6	17.7	17.8	16.9	18.7	18.7	20.2	21.2
Cameroon / Cameroun	13.1	12.1	13.0	13.5	14.1	14.4	14.7	14.2	14.4	14.6
Chad / Tchad	..	14.7	17.9	14.6	15.3	11.0	5.7	4.1	5.9	7.1
Congo[1]	8.3	7.5	7.9	8.9	11.1	12.3	17.8	17.3	13.6	8.5
Congo, Dem. Rep. / Congo, Rép. dém.[2]	7.9	8.3	8.8	10.6	10.1	9.5	9.7	8.5	6.9	7.5
Côte d'Ivoire	12.2	11.9	11.1	12.8	12.7	12.2	12.6	13.1	13.3	13.1
Egypt / Égypte	17.6	16.2	15.8	15.1	16.2	15.1	15.6	15.2	17.0	16.7
Equatorial Guinea / Guinée équatoriale	12.8	7.6	7.0	8.8	8.9	9.8	12.0	7.1	6.6	6.3
Eswatini	12.9	13.9	13.9	12.8	13.7	14.9	14.9	16.0	16.8	17.2
Ghana	10.5	10.9	11.8	12.1	11.4	12.2	13.1	13.7	13.8	14.1
Kenya	18.2	17.9	18.6	17.9	18.0	19.3	18.6	18.5	18.5	17.4
Lesotho	17.8	18.4	18.9	18.1	17.5	18.1	18.9	18.7	18.4	20.2
Madagascar[3]	9.5	9.5	9.9	9.2	9.3	8.9	9.5	10.0	10.9	11.4
Malawi	15.3	15.9	16.3	14.5	16.2	17.9	16.8	16.9	18.7	18.3
Mali	14.4	14.1	13.7	14.0	14.2	13.9	15.2	16.5	16.7	14.1
Mauritania / Mauritanie	10.4	9.8	10.6	13.5	13.3	15.1	14.5	14.2	14.5	16.0
Mauritius / Maurice[4]	19.2	19.0	19.0	19.5	19.2	19.3	19.3	19.5	19.9	20.4
Morocco / Maroc[3,5]	26.9	27.7	28.5	29.5	27.7	28.3	26.4	27.2	27.6	27.8
Namibia	17.6	18.3	21.1	19.6	19.8	20.9	21.2	20.9	20.3	19.4
Niger	10.4	9.7	10.2	10.7	12.8	12.4	12.6	10.6	9.5	11.1
Nigeria / Nigéria	..	7.3	9.6	9.4	8.3	7.6	6.1	5.3	5.7	6.3
Rwanda[3]	12.6	12.9	13.5	14.1	15.4	15.8	16.7	16.7	16.4	17.1
Senegal / Sénégal[6]	14.8	15.8	16.0	16.0	15.4	16.2	16.4	17.0	16.3	16.5
Seychelles	27.0	29.4	32.0	30.6	28.5	29.5	28.7	31.0	31.1	32.4
South Africa / Afrique du Sud[7]	25.9	25.7	26.4	26.8	27.1	27.6	28.9	28.5	28.4	29.1
Togo	14.6	14.8	16.2	16.8	19.5	20.9	21.6	22.1	21.0	19.4
Tunisia / Tunisie[3]	26.8	27.2	29.1	29.1	29.8	30.9	30.2	29.6	31.0	32.1
Uganda / Ouganda	9.7	9.1	9.3	9.5	9.9	10.0	10.9	11.2	11.4	11.8
Africa (30) average / Moyenne Afrique (30)[8]	**15.0**	**15.1**	**15.8**	**15.8**	**16.1**	**16.4**	**16.5**	**16.4**	**16.5**	**16.5**
LAC average / Moyenne ALC[9]	**20.9**	**21.2**	**21.6**	**21.9**	**22.0**	**22.2**	**22.6**	**22.6**	**22.7**	**23.1**
OECD average / Moyenne OCDE[10]	**32.2**	**32.3**	**32.6**	**33.1**	**33.4**	**33.6**	**33.7**	**34.4**	**34.2**	**34.3**

Table 4.1. **Total tax revenue as percentage of GDP, 1990-2018** *(cont.)*
Tableau 4.1. **Total des recettes fiscales en pourcentage du PIB, 1990-2018** *(suite)*

.. Not available

Note: The figures include sub-national government tax revenues for Eswatini, Mauritania (for 2009-18), Mauritius, Morocco, Nigeria (only state revenues) and South Africa (for 2002-18). Sub-national government tax revenues are not available in other countries.

Data on social security contributions are not available for Chad, the Republic of the Congo, the Democratic Republic of the Congo (prior to 2012), Madagascar (prior to 2011), Namibia, Togo and Uganda; and are only partially available in Cameroon and Senegal. Social security contributions for Botswana, Lesotho and Malawi are deemed to be null as they do not meet the criteria to be classified as social security contributions set out in the OECD classification of taxes in the Interpretative Guide.

In Ghana, Nigeria and Uganda, revenues from property taxes are mainly levied by local governments for which data on revenue are not available. In the Democratic Republic of the Congo only data for property taxes levied by the Direction Générale des Recettes Administratives, Judiciaires, Domaniales et de Participation (DGRAD) are available for 2010-18.

See the country tables in Chapter 5 for further information on data issues for individual countries.

1. Revenues from customs duties for 2018 are estimated
2. The figures should be interpreted with caution as they are affected by macroeconomic instability in the early 2000s. For the years prior to 2010, the figures exclude some revenues collected by the Direction Générale des Recettes Administratives, Judiciaires, Domaniales et de Participation DGRAD), which are estimated to be less than 1% of total tax revenue. See Table 5.6 in Chapter 5 for further information.
3. Madagascar, Morocco, Rwanda and Tunisia do not include social security contributions in the tax-to-GDP ratio in their official publications as these countries do not consider them to be taxes. They are included as tax revenue in this publication, following the classification set out in the OECD Interpretative Guide.
4. The fiscal year for Mauritius changed in 2010 and in 2015. Figures for 2015 needed to be estimated as a result.
5. Social security contributions in Morocco are estimated for years prior to 2002.
6. These figures include contributions to the Senegalese Pension Institute (IPRES) (estimated prior to 2006) and contributions to the social security fund (CSS) from 2012. Data for previous years are not available.Social security contributions in Senegal are estimated for 2018.
7. Includes payments made by South Africa to the Southern African Customs Union (SACU) pool.
8. Represents an unweighted average of the 30 African countries in this publication. In 2009, the Africa (30) average is calculated based on estimated tax-to-GDP ratios for Chad and Nigeria in that year, as data were not available prior to 2010 in these countries. The estimations in 2009 for these two countries are based on data for later years and on IMF figures from the World Economic Outlook April 2020. The Africa (30) should be interpreted with caution as data for social security contributions (category 2000) and property taxes (category 4000) are not available or are partial in a few countries. See the country tables in Chapter 5 for further information.
9. Represents an unweighted average for 25 Latin American and Caribbean (LAC) countries included in the publication *Revenue Statistics in Latin America and the Caribbean 2020.*
10. Represents an unweighted average for 36 OECD countries.

.. Non disponible

Note : Les chiffres incluent les recettes fiscales collectées par les administrations infranationales pour l'Afrique du Sud (pour les années 2002 à 2018), Eswatini, le Maroc, Maurice, la Mauritanie (pour les années 2009 à 2018) et le Nigéria (recettes des administrations régionales). Les données des recettes fiscales collectées par les administrations infranationales ne sont pas disponibles pour les autres pays.

Les données des cotisations de sécurité sociale ne sont pas disponibles pour la République du Congo, la République démocratique du Congo (avant 2012), Madagacascar (avant 2011), la Namibie, l'Ouganda, le Tchad et le Togo et ne sont que partiellement disponibles au Cameroun et au Sénégal. Les cotisations de sécurité sociale pour le Botswana, le Lesotho et le Malawi sont nulles car elles ne répondent pas aux critères de classification des cotisations de sécurité sociale de la classification des impôts de l'OCDE du Guide d'interprétation.

Au Ghana, au Nigéria et en Ouganda, les recettes provenant des impôts sur le patrimoine sont principalement perçues par les administrations locales pour lesquelles les données ne sont pas disponibles. En République démocratique du Congo, seules les données des impôts sur le patrimoine qui sont prélevées par la Direction Générale des Recettes Administratives, Judiciaires, Domaniales et de Participation (DGRAD) sont disponibles pour 2010-18.

Voir les tableaux des pays au chapitre 5 pour plus d'informations sur les problèmes de données pour chaque pays.

1. Les recettes provenant des droits d'importation sont estimées pour 2018
2. Les chiffres doivent être interprétés avec prudence car ils sont affectés par une instabilité macroéconomique au début des années 2000. Pour les années antérieures à 2010, les chiffres excluent certaines recettes perçues par la Direction Générale des Recettes Administratives, Judiciaires, Domaniales et de Participation (DGRAD) estimées inférieures à 1 % du total des recettes fiscales. Voir le tableau 5.6 du chapitre 5 pour plus d'informations.
3. Madagascar, le Maroc, le Rwanda et la Tunisie n'incluent pas les cotisations de sécurité sociale dans le ratio impôts/PIB dans leurs publications officielles car ces pays ne les considèrent pas comme des impôts. Elles sont incluses dans les recettes fiscales de cette publication en accordance avec la classification des impôts établie dans le Guide d'interprétation de l'OCDE.
4. L'année fiscale pour Maurice a changé en 2010 et en 2015. Les chiffres pour 2015 ont dû être estimés en conséquence.
5. Les cotisations de sécurité sociale au Maroc antérieures à 2002 sont estimées.
6. Les chiffres comprennent les cotisations de sécurité sociale de l'Institution de prévoyance retraite du Sénégal (IPRES) (estimées pour les années antérieures à 2006) et les cotisations de sécurité sociale de la Caisse de Sécurité Sociale (CSS) (à partir de 2012 car les données pour les années précédentes ne sont pas disponibles). Les cotisations de sécurité sociale de 2018 sont estimées.
7. Comprend les paiements effectués par l'Afrique du Sud au fond collectif de l'Union douanière d'Afrique australe (SACU).
8. Représente une moyenne non pondérée des 30 pays africains inclus dans cette publication. En 2009, la moyenne de l'Afrique (30) est calculée sur la base des ratios impôts/PIB estimés pour le Tchad et le Nigeria,, car les données n'étaient pas disponibles avant 2010 dans ces pays. Les estimations en 2009 pour ces deux pays sont basées sur des données des années ultérieures et sur les chiffres du FMI tirés des Perspectives de l'économie mondiale d'avril 2020. Les détails des estimations sont disponibles dans les métadonnées.. Il convient d'interpréter cette moyenne avec prudence à cause de valeurs manquantes ou incomplètes pour la rubrique 2000 (cotisations de sécurité sociale) et la rubrique 4000 (taxes sur le patrimoine). Veuillez voir les tableaux de pays au chapitre 5 pour plus d'informations.
9. Représente la moyenne non pondérée pour 25 pays d'Amérique latine et des Caraïbes (ALC) inclus dans la publication *Revenue Statistics in Latin America and the Caribbean 2020.*
10. Représente la moyenne non pondérée pour 36 pays de l'OCDE.

StatLink https://doi.org/10.1787/888934182705

Table 4.2. **Total tax revenue (excluding social security) as percentage of GDP**
Tableau 4.2. **Total des recettes fiscales (sécurité sociale non comprise) en pourcentage du PIB**

	1990	2000	2001	2002	2003	2004	2005	2006	2007	2008
Botswana	..	..	..	..	..	15.5	15.2	15.2	13.7	17.1
Burkina Faso	..	8.6	8.7	9.2	9.8	10.7	10.2	10.7	11.2	10.5
Cabo Verde	10.5	14.8	16.5	18.9	17.2	18.2	18.9	20.4	20.7	21.2
Cameroon / Cameroun	..	10.4	11.6	10.8	11.3	10.3	11.1	11.6	12.0	11.7
Chad / Tchad	..	..	..	..	..	..	..	..	..	..
Congo	..	4.3	6.0	7.2	8.7	8.2	6.4	5.8	7.0	6.9
Congo, Dem. Rep. / Congo, Rép. dém.[1]	..	0.6	2.3	3.0	3.4	4.7	5.2	5.8	6.9	8.5
Côte d'Ivoire	14.6	10.1	10.3	10.5	9.7	10.5	10.4	10.8	11.4	11.3
Egypt / Égypte	..	..	..	12.6	12.7	13.5	13.3	15.4	15.1	15.2
Equatorial Guinea / Guinée équatoriale	..	..	..	..	..	..	8.2	9.7	7.5	7.8
Eswatini	..	9.5	9.3	9.6	10.6	10.1	10.2	10.2	10.2	11.4
Ghana	..	7.1	7.5	7.6	8.8	9.8	10.3	9.3	9.7	9.6
Kenya	..	..	16.4	15.9	16.5	16.9	18.1	17.2	17.9	18.7
Lesotho	..	..	..	..	..	17.4	15.9	15.0	15.7	16.9
Madagascar	..	9.6	8.3	6.5	8.8	9.6	8.9	9.4	10.0	11.4
Malawi	..	..	..	..	..	..	12.6	12.6	13.6	14.6
Mali	..	10.5	10.5	11.3	12.8	13.6	13.1	12.7	12.8	11.9
Mauritania / Mauritanie	..	..	..	..	..	..	..	..	9.4	9.5
Mauritius / Maurice[2]	21.4	17.5	15.5	15.2	16.6	16.7	17.2	17.2	16.4	18.1
Morocco / Maroc	..	19.6	19.5	19.5	19.0	19.2	20.7	21.5	23.8	26.5
Namibia	..	..	..	..	..	..	..	16.2	17.2	17.7
Niger	..	6.9	7.4	7.8	7.8	8.4	7.9	8.3	8.7	8.6
Nigeria / Nigéria	..	..	..	..	..	..	..	..	..	..
Rwanda	..	9.7	10.7	11.9	11.6	11.2	11.3	11.1	11.3	12.2
Senegal / Sénégal	..	12.7	12.7	13.4	13.4	13.7	14.6	14.9	15.2	14.3
Seychelles	..	..	..	..	..	..	..	..	..	22.6
South Africa / Afrique du Sud[3]	23.9	22.4	23.7	22.9	22.3	23.3	25.2	26.4	27.7	27.4
Togo	..	9.4	10.9	9.6	11.9	13.2	13.3	14.5	15.2	14.4
Tunisia / Tunisie	..	19.2	19.5	19.3	18.6	18.6	18.7	18.4	19.0	20.4
Uganda / Ouganda	..	9.4	9.3	9.6	10.0	10.2	10.5	10.7	10.8	10.6
Africa (30) average / Moyenne Afrique (30)[4]	**..**	**..**	**..**	**..**	**..**	**..**	**..**	**..**	**..**	**..**
LAC average / Moyenne ALC[5]	**13.7**	**15.8**	**15.9**	**15.9**	**16.3**	**16.7**	**17.4**	**18.2**	**18.6**	**18.6**
OECD average / Moyenne OCDE[6]	**24.6**	**25.2**	**24.6**	**24.3**	**24.2**	**24.3**	**24.9**	**25.1**	**25.1**	**24.4**

	2009	2010	2011	2012	2013	2014	2015	2016	2017	2018
Botswana	15.8	15.6	15.7	13.8	14.7	15.2	12.7	14.0	12.3	12.1
Burkina Faso	11.2	12.6	12.4	14.0	14.9	13.8	13.6	14.3	15.2	15.2
Cabo Verde	18.4	18.4	19.5	17.7	17.7	16.9	18.7	18.7	20.1	21.2
Cameroon / Cameroun	12.2	11.1	12.0	12.5	13.1	13.5	13.8	13.1	13.4	13.6
Chad / Tchad	..	14.7	17.9	14.6	15.3	11.0	5.7	4.1	5.9	7.1
Congo	8.3	7.5	7.9	8.9	11.1	12.3	17.8	17.3	13.6	8.5
Congo, Dem. Rep. / Congo, Rép. dém.[1]	7.9	8.3	8.8	10.2	9.5	8.9	9.2	8.0	6.4	7.1
Côte d'Ivoire	11.2	11.0	10.3	11.6	11.3	10.8	11.2	11.6	11.8	11.6
Egypt / Égypte	15.4	13.8	13.7	12.8	13.7	12.6	12.9	13.3	14.5	15.4
Equatorial Guinea / Guinée équatoriale	12.8	7.6	7.0	8.8	8.4	9.2	11.3	6.3	5.9	5.7
Eswatini	11.1	12.0	12.2	11.3	12.2	13.1	13.0	14.0	14.6	14.8
Ghana	9.2	9.9	10.8	11.1	10.4	11.0	11.9	12.5	12.8	13.3
Kenya	18.0	17.7	18.4	17.7	17.8	19.0	18.3	18.0	18.0	16.8
Lesotho	17.8	18.4	18.9	18.1	17.5	18.1	18.9	18.7	18.4	20.2
Madagascar	9.5	9.5	9.6	8.9	8.9	8.6	9.1	9.7	10.5	10.8
Malawi	15.3	15.9	16.3	14.5	16.2	17.9	16.8	16.9	18.7	18.3
Mali	12.9	12.8	12.3	12.5	12.8	12.4	13.7	14.6	15.0	12.4
Mauritania / Mauritanie	9.8	9.1	10.0	12.8	12.7	14.2	13.6	13.4	13.8	15.2
Mauritius / Maurice[2]	18.6	18.3	18.3	18.8	18.5	18.6	18.5	18.7	19.0	19.6
Morocco / Maroc	23.0	22.8	23.2	24.1	22.8	22.4	21.5	22.0	22.3	22.3
Namibia	17.6	18.3	21.1	19.6	19.8	20.9	21.2	20.9	20.3	19.4
Niger	9.9	9.2	9.7	10.2	12.2	11.8	12.0	10.0	8.9	10.6
Nigeria / Nigéria	..	6.7	9.0	8.7	7.6	6.9	5.5	4.7	5.1	5.8
Rwanda	11.8	12.1	12.6	13.2	14.3	14.8	15.7	15.6	15.4	16.1
Senegal / Sénégal	14.1	14.9	15.3	14.9	14.3	15.2	15.3	15.9	15.1	15.3
Seychelles	23.9	27.5	32.0	30.6	28.5	29.5	28.7	31.0	31.1	31.4
South Africa / Afrique du Sud[3]	25.4	25.3	26.0	26.3	26.7	27.2	28.5	28.1	28.0	28.7
Togo	14.6	14.8	16.2	16.8	19.5	20.9	21.6	22.1	21.0	19.4
Tunisia / Tunisie	19.8	19.8	21.1	20.8	21.2	22.4	21.3	20.2	21.3	22.8
Uganda / Ouganda	9.7	9.1	9.3	9.5	9.9	10.0	10.9	11.2	11.4	11.8
Africa (30) average / Moyenne Afrique (30)[4]	**..**	**14.5**	**15.3**	**15.2**	**15.5**	**15.7**	**15.8**	**15.7**	**15.7**	**15.5**
LAC average / Moyenne ALC[5]	**17.5**	**17.8**	**18.1**	**18.3**	**18.3**	**18.5**	**18.7**	**18.7**	**18.7**	**19.1**
OECD average / Moyenne OCDE[6]	**23.3**	**23.5**	**23.7**	**24.1**	**24.3**	**24.6**	**24.7**	**25.3**	**25.1**	**..**

Table 4.2. **Total tax revenue (excluding social security) as percentage of GDP** *(cont.)*
Tableau 4.2. **Total des recettes fiscales (sécurité sociale non comprise) en pourcentage du PIB** *(suite)*

.. Not available

Note: The figures include sub-national government tax revenues for Eswatini, Mauritania (for 2009-18), Mauritius, Morocco, Nigeria (only state revenues) and South Africa (for 2002-18). Sub-national government tax revenues are not available in other countries.

In Ghana, Nigeria and Uganda, revenues from property taxes are mainly levied by local governments for which data on revenue are not available.

In the Democratic Republic of the Congo only data for property taxes levied by the Direction Générale des Recettes Administratives, Judiciaires, Domaniales et de Participation (DGRAD) are available for 2010-18.

1. The figures should be interpreted with caution as they are affected by macroeconomic instability in the early 2000s. For the years prior to 2010, the figures exclude some revenues collected by the Direction Générale des Recettes Administratives, Judiciaires, Domaniales et de Participation DGRAD), which are estimated to be less than 1% of total tax revenue. See Table 5.6 in Chapter 5 for further information.
2. The fiscal year for Mauritius changed in 2010 and in 2015. Figures for 2015 needed to be estimated as a result.
3. Includes payments made by South Africa to the Southern African Customs Union (SACU) pool.
4. Represents an unweighted average of the 30 African countries in this publication. In 2009, the Africa (30) average is calculated based on estimated tax-to-GDP ratios for Chad and Nigeria in that year, as data were not available prior to 2010 in these countries. The estimations in 2009 for these two countries are based on data for later years and on IMF figures from the World Economic Outlook April 2020. The Africa (30) should be interpreted with caution as data for social security contributions (category 2000) and property taxes (category 4000) are not available or are partial in a few countries. See the country tables in Chapter 5 for further information.
5. Represents an unweighted average for 25 Latin American and Caribbean (LAC) countries included in the publication *Revenue Statistics in Latin America and the Caribbean 2020*.
6. Represents an unweighted average for 36 OECD countries.

.. Non disponible

Note : Les chiffres incluent les recettes fiscales collectées par les administrations infranationales pour l'Afrique du Sud (pour les années 2002 à 2018), Eswatini, le Maroc, Maurice, la Mauritanie (pour les années 2009 à 2018) et le Nigéria (recettes des administrations régionales). Les données des recettes fiscales collectées par les administrations infranationales ne sont pas disponibles pour les autres pays.

Au Ghana, au Nigéria et en Ouganda, les recettes provenant des impôts sur le patrimoine sont principalement perçues par les administrations locales pour lesquelles les données ne sont pas disponibles. En République démocratique du Congo, seules les données des impôts sur le patrimoine qui sont prélevées par la Direction Générale des Recettes Administratives, Judiciaires, Domaniales et de Participation (DGRAD) sont disponibles pour 2010-18.

1. Les chiffres doivent être interprétés avec prudence car ils sont affectés par une instabilité macroéconomique au début des années 2000. Pour les années antérieures à 2010, les chiffres excluent certaines recettes perçues par la Direction Générale des Recettes Administratives, Judiciaires, Domaniales et de Participation (DGRAD) estimées inférieures à 1 % du total des recettes fiscales. Voir le tableau 5.6 du chapitre 5 pour plus d'informations.
2. L'année fiscale pour Maurice a changé en 2010 et en 2015. Les chiffres pour 2015 ont dû être estimés en conséquence.
3. Comprend les paiements effectués par l'Afrique du Sud au fond collectif de l'Union douanière d'Afrique australe (SACU).
4. Représente une moyenne non pondérée des 30 pays africains inclus dans cette publication. En 2009, la moyenne de l'Afrique (30) est calculée sur la base des ratios impôts/PIB estimés pour le Tchad et le Nigeria,, car les données n'étaient pas disponibles avant 2010 dans ces pays. Les estimations en 2009 pour ces deux pays sont basées sur des données des années ultérieures et sur les chiffres du FMI tirés des Perspectives de l'économie mondiale d'avril 2020. Les détails des estimations sont disponibles dans les métadonnées.. Il convient d'interpréter cette moyenne avec prudence à cause de valeurs manquantes ou incomplètes pour la rubrique 2000 (cotisations de sécurité sociale) et la rubrique 4000 (taxes sur le patrimoine). Veuillez voir les tableaux de pays au chapitre 5 pour plus d'informations.
5. Représente la moyenne non pondérée pour 25 pays d'Amérique latine et des Caraïbes (ALC) inclus dans la publication *Revenue Statistics in Latin America and the Caribbean 2020*.
6. Représente la moyenne non pondérée pour 36 pays de l'OCDE.

StatLink https://doi.org/10.1787/888934182724

Table 4.3. **Tax revenue of the main headings as percentage of GDP, 2018**
Tableau 4.3. **Recettes fiscales sous les principales rubriques en pourcentage du PIB, 2018**

	1000 Income & profits / Impôts & profits	2000 Social security / Sécurité sociale	3000 Payroll / Salaires	4000 Property / Patrimoine	5000 Goods and services / Biens et services	6000 Other taxes / Autres impôts
Botswana	7.8	0.0	0.0	0.0	4.2	0.0
Burkina Faso	4.2	1.6	0.1	0.1	10.7	0.1
Cabo Verde	6.7	0.0	0.0	0.4	14.1	0.0
Cameroon / Cameroun	3.9	1.1	0.1	0.1	9.1	0.3
Chad / Tchad	4.1	..	0.0	0.1	2.9	0.0
Congo[1]	3.2	..	0.3	0.1	4.9	0.0
Congo, Dem. Rep. / Congo, Rép. dém.	3.4	0.5	0.1	0.0	3.3	0.3
Côte d'Ivoire	1.8	1.5	1.6	0.4	7.8	0.1
Egypt / Égypte	7.3	1.3	0.0	0.1	8.0	0.0
Equatorial Guinea / Guinée équatoriale	4.2	0.6	0.0	0.0	1.2	0.3
Eswatini	8.3	2.4	0.0	0.4	6.0	0.0
Ghana	5.4	0.8	0.0	..	7.9	0.0
Kenya	7.7	0.6	0.0	0.2	9.0	0.0
Lesotho	11.9	0.0	0.0	0.0	8.3	0.0
Madagascar[2]	2.5	0.6	0.0	0.1	8.2	0.0
Malawi	8.8	0.0	0.0	0.0	9.5	0.0
Mali	3.3	1.7	0.1	0.3	8.4	0.3
Mauritania / Mauritanie	4.7	0.8	0.0	0.5	10.0	0.0
Mauritius / Maurice	5.2	0.8	0.1	1.0	13.3	0.0
Morocco / Maroc[2]	8.7	5.5	0.0	1.6	11.8	0.3
Namibia	12.3	..	0.0	0.1	6.9	0.1
Niger	2.4	0.5	0.1	0.0	7.4	0.8
Nigeria / Nigéria	3.8	0.5	0.0	..	1.6	0.3
Rwanda[2]	6.9	1.0	0.0	0.0	9.2	0.0
Senegal / Sénégal[3]	4.7	1.2	0.1	0.4	10.0	0.2
Seychelles	10.6	0.9	0.0	0.5	20.3	0.0
South Africa / Afrique du Sud[4]	15.1	0.4	0.4	1.7	11.5	0.0
Togo	3.9	..	0.2	0.2	14.8	0.3
Tunisia / Tunisie[2]	8.5	9.3	0.4	0.3	12.8	0.8
Uganda / Ouganda	4.1	..	0.0	..	7.7	0.0
Africa (30) average / Moyenne Afrique (30)[5]	**6.2**	**1.3**	**0.1**	**0.3**	**8.7**	**0.1**
LAC average / Moyenne ALC[6]	**6.3**	**4.0**	**0.2**	**0.8**	**11.5**	**0.4**
OECD average / Moyenne OCDE[7]	**11.6**	**9.1**	**0.4**	**1.9**	**10.9**	**0.1**

Table 4.3. **Tax revenue of the main headings as percentage of GDP, 2018** *(cont.)*
Tableau 4.3. **Recettes fiscales sous les principales rubriques en pourcentage du PIB, 2018** *(suite)*

.. Not available

Note: The figures include sub-national government tax revenues for Eswatini, Mauritania (for 2009-18), Mauritius, Morocco, Nigeria (only state revenues) and South Africa (for 2002-18). Sub-national government tax revenues are not available in other countries.

Heading 2000: Data on social security contributions are not available for Chad, the Republic of the Congo, the Democratic Republic of the Congo (prior to 2012), Madagascar (prior to 2011), Namibia, Togo and Uganda; and are only partially available in Cameroon and Senegal. Social security contributions for Botswana, Lesotho and Malawi are deemed to be null as they do not meet the criteria to be classified as social security contributions set out in the OECD classification of taxes in the Interpretative Guide.

Heading 4000: In Ghana, Nigeria and Uganda, revenues from property taxes are mainly levied by local governments for which data on revenue are not available. In the Democratic Republic of the Congo only data for property taxes levied by the Direction Générale des Recettes Administratives, Judiciaires, Domaniales et de Participation (DGRAD) are available for 2010-18.

1. Revenues from customs duties for 2018 are estimated
2. Madagascar, Morocco, Rwanda and Tunisia do not include social security contributions in the tax-to-GDP ratio in their official publications as neither country considers them as taxes. They are included as tax revenue in this publication, following the classification set out in the OECD Interpretative Guide.
3. Social security contributions are estimated for 2018.
4. The figures for heading 5000 goods and services should be interpreted with caution as they include payments made by South Africa to the Southern African Customs Union (SACU) pool.
5. Represents an unweighted average of the 30 African countries in this publication. The Africa (30) should be interpreted with caution as data for social security contributions (category 2000) and property taxes (category 4000) are not available or are partial in a few countries. See the country tables in Chapter 5 for further information.
6. Represents an unweighted average for 25 Latin American and Caribbean (LAC) countries included in the publication *Revenue Statistics in Latin America and the Caribbean 2020.*
7. Represents an unweighted average for 36 OECD countries. Data are for 2017 as data for 2018 were not available at the date of publication.

.. Non disponible

Note : Les chiffres incluent les recettes fiscales collectées par les administrations infranationales pour l'Afrique du Sud (pour les années 2002 à 2018), Eswatini, le Maroc, Maurice, la Mauritanie (pour les années 2009 à 2018) et le Nigéria (recettes des administrations régionales). Les données des recettes fiscales collectées par les administrations infranationales ne sont pas disponibles pour les autres pays.

Rubrique 2000: Les données des cotisations de sécurité sociale ne sont pas disponibles pour la République du Congo, la République démocratique du Congo (avant 2012), Madagacascar (avant 2011), la Namibie, l'Ouganda, le Tchad et le Togo et ne sont que partiellement disponibles au Cameroun et au Sénégal. Les cotisations de sécurité sociale pour le Botswana, le Lesotho et le Malawi sont nulles car elles ne répondent pas aux critères de classification des cotisations de sécurité sociale de la classification des impôts de l'OCDE du Guide d'interprétation.

Rubrique 4000: Au Ghana, au Nigéria et en Ouganda, les recettes provenant des impôts sur le patrimoine sont principalement perçues par les administrations locales pour lesquelles les données ne sont pas disponibles. En République démocratique du Congo, seules les données des impôts sur le patrimoine qui sont prélevées par la Direction Générale des Recettes Administratives, Judiciaires, Domaniales et de Participation (DGRAD) sont disponibles pour 2010-18.

1. Les recettes provenant des droits d'importation sont estimées pour 2018.
2. Madagascar, le Maroc, le Rwanda et la Tunisie n'incluent pas les cotisations de sécurité sociale dans le ratio impôts/PIB dans leurs publications officielles car ces pays ne les considèrent pas comme des impôts. Elles sont incluses dans les recettes fiscales de cette publication en accordance avec la classification des impôts établie dans le Guide d'interprétation de l'OCDE.
3. Les cotisations de sécurité sociale sont estimées pour 2018
4. Les chiffres relatifs à la rubrique 5000 produits et services doivent être interprétés avec prudence car ils incluent les paiements effectués par l'Afrique du Sud à l'Union douanière d'Afrique australe (SACU).
5. Représente une moyenne non pondérée des 30 pays africains inclus dans cette publication. Il convient d'interpréter cette moyenne avec prudence à cause de valeurs manquantes ou incomplètes pour la rubrique 2000 (cotisations de sécurité sociale) et la rubrique 4000 (taxes sur le patrimoine). Veuillez voir les tableaux des pays au chapitre 5 pour plus d'informations.
6. Représente la moyenne non pondérée pour 25 pays d'Amérique latine et des Caraïbes (ALC) inclus dans la publication *Revenue Statistics in Latin America and the Caribbean 2020.*
7. Représente la moyenne non pondérée pour 36 pays de l'OCDE. Les données sont pour 2017 car les données pour 2018 n'étaient pas disponibles à la date de la publication.

StatLink https://doi.org/10.1787/888934182743

Table 4.4. Tax revenue of the main headings as percentage of total taxation, 2018
Tableau 4.4. Recettes fiscales sous les principales rubriques en pourcentage du total des recettes fiscales, 2018

	1000 Income & profits / Impôts & profits	2000 Social security / Sécurité sociale	3000 Payroll / Salaires	4000 Property / Patrimoine	5000 Goods and services / Biens et services	6000 Other taxes / Autres impôts
Botswana	64.7	0.0	0.0	0.3	35.0	0.0
Burkina Faso	24.9	9.5	0.8	0.7	63.5	0.6
Cabo Verde	31.4	0.2	0.0	1.9	66.5	0.0
Cameroon / Cameroun	27.0	7.2	1.0	0.8	62.2	1.8
Chad / Tchad	57.7	..	0.3	1.6	40.4	0.0
Congo[1]	37.2	..	3.7	1.0	58.1	0.0
Congo, Dem. Rep. / Congo, Rép. dém.	44.4	6.1	1.6	0.2	44.2	3.5
Côte d'Ivoire	13.7	11.4	11.9	2.9	59.5	0.6
Egypt / Égypte	43.8	7.9	0.0	0.6	47.6	0.0
Equatorial Guinea / Guinée équatoriale	66.8	9.9	0.0	0.1	19.2	4.0
Eswatini	48.3	14.1	0.0	2.6	35.0	0.0
Ghana	38.6	5.7	0.0	..	55.7	0.0
Kenya	44.2	3.2	0.0	0.9	51.7	0.0
Lesotho	58.8	0.0	0.0	0.0	41.2	0.0
Madagascar[2]	22.2	5.3	0.0	0.8	71.3	0.4
Malawi	48.0	0.0	0.0	0.0	51.9	0.0
Mali	23.5	11.9	0.9	2.0	59.9	1.8
Mauritania / Mauritanie	29.4	5.0	0.1	2.9	62.6	0.0
Mauritius / Maurice	25.4	3.8	0.5	4.9	65.2	0.1
Morocco / Maroc[2]	31.1	19.8	0.0	5.7	42.2	1.1
Namibia	63.3	..	0.0	0.6	35.5	0.6
Niger	21.2	4.8	0.5	0.3	66.2	7.1
Nigeria / Nigéria	60.1	8.4	0.6	..	25.4	5.5
Rwanda[2]	40.3	5.9	0.0	0.1	53.6	0.0
Senegal / Sénégal[3]	28.4	7.1	0.3	2.5	60.7	1.0
Seychelles	32.8	2.9	0.0	1.7	62.6	0.0
South Africa / Afrique du Sud[4]	52.0	1.4	1.2	5.8	39.7	0.0
Togo	20.3	..	0.8	0.8	76.3	1.8
Tunisia / Tunisie[2]	26.5	29.1	1.2	0.9	39.7	2.5
Uganda / Ouganda	34.3	..	0.0	..	65.5	0.2
Africa (30) average / Moyenne Afrique (30)[5]	**38.7**	**7.2**	**0.9**	**1.6**	**51.9**	**1.1**
LAC average / Moyenne ALC[6]	**27.8**	**17.1**	**0.7**	**3.6**	**50.1**	**1.5**
OECD average / Moyenne OCDE[7]	**34.0**	**26.0**	**1.1**	**5.8**	**32.4**	**0.4**

Table 4.4. **Tax revenue of the main headings as percentage of total taxation, 2018** *(cont.)*
Tableau 4.4. **Recettes fiscales sous les principales rubriques en pourcentage du total des recettes fiscales, 2018** *(suite)*

.. Not available

Note: The figures include sub-national government tax revenues for Eswatini, Mauritania (for 2009-18), Mauritius, Morocco, Nigeria (only state revenues) and South Africa (for 2002-18). Sub-national government tax revenues are not available in other countries.

Heading 2000: Data on social security contributions are not available for Chad, the Republic of the Congo, the Democratic Republic of the Congo (prior to 2012), Madagascar (prior to 2011), Namibia, Togo and Uganda; and are only partially available in Cameroon and Senegal. Social security contributions for Botswana, Lesotho and Malawi are deemed to be null as they do not meet the criteria to be classified as social security contributions set out in the OECD classification of taxes in the Interpretative Guide.

Heading 4000: In Ghana, Nigeria and Uganda, revenues from property taxes are mainly levied by local governments for which data on revenue are not available. In the Democratic Republic of the Congo only data for property taxes levied by the Direction Générale des Recettes Administratives, Judiciaires, Domaniales et de Participation (DGRAD) are available for 2010-18.

1. Revenues from customs duties for 2018 are estimated
2. Madagascar, Morocco, Rwanda and Tunisia do not include social security contributions in the tax-to-GDP ratio in their official publications as neither country considers them as taxes. They are included as tax revenue in this publication, following the classification set out in the OECD Interpretative Guide.
3. Social security contributions are estimated for 2018
4. The figures for heading 5000 goods and services should be interpreted with caution as they include payments made by South Africa to the Southern African Customs Union (SACU) pool.
5. Represents an unweighted average of the 30 African countries in this publication. The Africa (30) should be interpreted with caution as data for social security contributions (category 2000) and property taxes (category 4000) are not available or are partial in a few countries. See the country tables in Chapter 5 for further information.
6. Represents an unweighted average for 25 Latin American and Caribbean (LAC) countries included in the publication *Revenue Statistics in Latin America and the Caribbean 2020.*
7. Represents an unweighted average for 36 OECD countries. Data are for 2017 as data for 2018 were not available at the date of publication.

.. Non disponible

Note : Les chiffres incluent les recettes fiscales collectées par les administrations infranationales pour l'Afrique du Sud (pour les années 2002 à 2018), Eswatini, le Maroc, Maurice, la Mauritanie (pour les années 2009 à 2018) et le Nigéria (recettes des administrations régionales). Les données des recettes fiscales collectées par les administrations infranationales ne sont pas disponibles pour les autres pays.

Rubrique 2000: Les données des cotisations de sécurité sociale ne sont pas disponibles pour la République du Congo, la République démocratique du Congo (avant 2012), Madagacascar (avant 2011), la Namibie, l'Ouganda, le Tchad et le Togo et ne sont que partiellement disponibles au Cameroun et au Sénégal. Les cotisations de sécurité sociale pour le Botswana, le Lesotho et le Malawi sont nulles car elles ne répondent pas aux critères de classification des cotisations de sécurité sociale de la classification des impôts de l'OCDE du Guide d'interprétation.

Rubrique 4000: Au Ghana, au Nigéria et en Ouganda, les recettes provenant des impôts sur le patrimoine sont principalement perçues par les administrations locales pour lesquelles les données ne sont pas disponibles. En République démocratique du Congo, seules les données des impôts sur le patrimoine qui sont prélevées par la Direction Générale des Recettes Administratives, Judiciaires, Domaniales et de Participation (DGRAD) sont disponibles pour 2010-18.

1. Les recettes provenant des droits d'importation sont estimées pour 2018
2. Madagascar, le Maroc, le Rwanda et la Tunisie n'incluent pas les cotisations de sécurité sociale dans le ratio impôts/PIB dans leurs publications officielles car ces pays ne les considèrent pas comme des impôts. Elles sont incluses dans les recettes fiscales de cette publication en accordance avec la classification des impôts établie dans le Guide d'interprétation de l'OCDE.
3. Les cotisations de sécurité sociale sont estimées pour 2018
4. Les chiffres relatifs à la rubrique 5000 produits et services doivent être interprétés avec prudence car ils incluent les paiements effectués par l'Afrique du Sud à l'Union douanière d'Afrique australe (SACU).
5. Représente une moyenne non pondérée des 30 pays africains inclus dans cette publication. Il convient d'interpréter cette moyenne avec prudence à cause de valeurs manquantes ou incomplètes pour la rubrique 2000 (cotisations de sécurité sociale) et la rubrique 4000 (taxes sur le patrimoine). Veuillez voir les tableaux des pays au chapitre 5 pour plus d'informations.
6. Représente la moyenne non pondérée pour 25 pays d'Amérique latine et des Caraïbes (ALC) inclus dans la publication *Revenue Statistics in Latin America and the Caribbean 2020.*
7. Représente la moyenne non pondérée pour 36 pays de l'OCDE. Les données sont pour 2017 car les données pour 2018 n'étaient pas disponibles à la date de la publication.

StatLink https://doi.org/10.1787/888934182762

Table 4.5. **Taxes on income and profits (1000) as percentage of GDP**
Tableau 4.5. **Impôts sur le revenu et les bénéfices (1000) en pourcentage du PIB**

	1998	2000	2008	2010	2013	2014	2015	2016	2017	2018
Botswana	..	..	10.8	10.2	10.5	10.9	8.6	9.7	7.5	7.8
Burkina Faso	..	2.5	2.5	2.7	4.2	3.8	3.4	3.8	4.0	4.2
Cabo Verde	5.1	5.5	6.3	5.7	5.6	5.0	6.1	6.1	6.5	6.7
Cameroon / Cameroun	3.1	3.2	3.8	3.3	4.3	4.5	4.7	4.0	3.6	3.9
Chad / Tchad	..	..	..	11.3	11.4	7.3	3.3	2.1	3.0	4.1
Congo	3.3	2.1	2.4	2.5	3.8	4.2	6.8	6.7	5.3	3.2
Congo, Dem. Rep. / Congo, Rép. dém.	..	0.2	2.2	2.3	2.6	3.0	3.5	2.6	2.5	3.4
Côte d'Ivoire	2.3	1.8	2.3	1.5	2.0	1.7	1.5	1.5	1.6	1.8
Egypt / Égypte	..	..	8.3	7.3	7.8	7.4	6.9	7.0	6.9	7.3
Equatorial Guinea / Guinée équatoriale	..	..	7.3	6.8	7.6	8.3	9.9	4.8	4.6	4.2
Eswatini	5.7	5.5	7.0	7.2	6.8	7.6	7.3	8.0	8.2	8.3
Ghana	..	2.3	3.1	3.9	4.4	4.7	4.2	3.8	4.6	5.4
Kenya	..	..	7.8	7.3	8.7	8.9	8.6	8.4	8.3	7.7
Lesotho	..	..	10.3	11.2	10.7	10.7	11.8	11.7	11.0	11.9
Madagascar	1.6	1.6	2.9	2.4	2.1	2.0	2.1	2.3	2.4	2.5
Malawi	..	..	5.9	7.0	7.5	8.0	8.2	8.2	9.1	8.8
Mali	2.2	1.6	3.0	3.5	3.5	4.2	3.8	3.9	4.4	3.3
Mauritania / Mauritanie	..	..	3.4	3.4	5.1	5.7	4.9	4.4	4.5	4.7
Mauritius / Maurice[1]	2.5	2.4	4.0	4.9	4.6	4.7	4.8	4.8	5.1	5.2
Morocco / Maroc	..	5.7	11.2	8.0	8.4	8.2	8.0	8.3	8.7	8.7
Namibia	..	..	11.3	11.7	11.6	13.0	12.8	12.9	12.8	12.3
Niger	..	1.3	2.5	2.5	5.0	3.9	3.1	2.8	2.6	2.4
Nigeria / Nigéria	..	..	..	4.6	5.5	4.8	3.6	2.9	3.2	3.8
Rwanda	3.0	2.7	4.6	4.7	6.3	5.9	6.4	6.5	6.4	6.9
Senegal / Sénégal	2.7	2.9	3.5	4.1	4.0	4.1	4.1	4.6	4.5	4.7
Seychelles	..	..	5.7	8.6	9.8	9.7	9.3	10.4	10.9	10.6
South Africa / Afrique du Sud	13.7	12.7	15.7	13.4	13.9	14.3	15.0	14.8	15.1	15.1
Togo	..	2.0	2.7	2.4	3.5	3.5	3.6	4.3	3.6	3.9
Tunisia / Tunisie	..	5.5	8.3	8.1	9.2	9.8	9.1	8.2	8.8	8.5
Uganda / Ouganda	1.5	1.7	3.0	2.9	3.5	3.4	3.8	3.9	4.0	4.1
Africa (30) average / Moyenne Afrique (30)[2]	**..**	**..**	**..**	**5.8**	**6.5**	**6.4**	**6.3**	**6.1**	**6.1**	**6.2**
LAC average / Moyenne ALC[3]	**3.8**	**4.4**	**6.2**	**5.8**	**6.1**	**6.2**	**6.2**	**6.0**	**6.0**	**6.3**
OECD average / Moyenne OCDE[4]	**11.6**	**11.9**	**11.7**	**10.6**	**11.1**	**11.2**	**11.3**	**11.3**	**11.6**	**..**

.. Not available

Note: The figures include sub-national government tax revenues for Eswatini, Mauritania (for 2009-18), Mauritius, Morocco, Nigeria (only state revenues) and South Africa (for 2002-18). Sub-national government tax revenues are not available in other countries.

Data on social security contributions are not available for Chad, the Republic of the Congo, the Democratic Republic of the Congo (prior to 2012), Madagascar (prior to 2011), Namibia, Togo and Uganda; and are only partially available in Cameroon and Senegal. Social security contributions for Botswana, Lesotho and Malawi are deemed to be null as they do not meet the criteria to be classified as social security contributions set out in the OECD classification of taxes in the Interpretative Guide.

In Ghana, Nigeria and Uganda, revenues from property taxes are mainly levied by local governments for which data on revenue are not available. In the Democratic Republic of the Congo only data for property taxes levied by the Direction Générale des Recettes Administratives, Judiciaires, Domaniales et de Participation (DGRAD) are available for 2010-18.

1. The fiscal year for Mauritius changed in 2010 and in 2015. Figures for 2015 needed to be estimated as a result.
2. Represents an unweighted average of the 30 African countries in this publication.
3. Represents an unweighted average for 25 Latin American and Caribbean (LAC) countries included in the publication *Revenue Statistics in Latin America and the Caribbean 2020.*
4. Represents an unweighted average for 36 OECD countries.

.. Non disponible

Note : Les chiffres incluent les recettes fiscales collectées par les administrations infranationales pour l'Afrique du Sud (pour les années 2002 à 2018), Eswatini, le Maroc, Maurice, la Mauritanie (pour les années 2009 à 2018) et le Nigéria (recettes des administrations régionales). Les données des recettes fiscales collectées par les administrations infranationales ne sont pas disponibles pour les autres pays.

Les données des cotisations de sécurité sociale ne sont pas disponibles pour la République du Congo, la République démocratique du Congo (avant 2012), Madagascar (avant 2011), la Namibie, l'Ouganda, le Tchad et le Togo et ne sont que partiellement disponibles au Cameroun et au Sénégal. Les cotisations de sécurité sociale pour le Botswana, le Lesotho et le Malawi sont nulles car elles ne répondent pas aux critères de classification des cotisations de sécurité sociale de la classification des impôts de l'OCDE du Guide d'interprétation.

Au Ghana, au Nigéria et en Ouganda, les recettes provenant des impôts sur le patrimoine sont principalement perçues par les administrations locales pour lesquelles les données ne sont pas disponibles. En République démocratique du Congo, seules les données des impôts sur le patrimoine qui sont prélevées par la Direction Générale des Recettes Administratives, Judiciaires, Domaniales et de Participation (DGRAD) sont disponibles pour 2010-18.

1. L'année fiscale pour Maurice a changé en 2010 et en 2015. Les chiffres pour 2015 ont dû être estimés en conséquence.
2. Représente une moyenne non pondérée des 30 pays africains inclus dans cette publication.
3. Représente la moyenne non pondérée pour 25 pays d'Amérique latine et des Caraïbes (ALC) inclus dans la publication *Revenue Statistics in Latin America and the Caribbean 2020.*
4. Représente la moyenne non pondérée pour 36 pays de l'OCDE.

StatLink https://doi.org/10.1787/888934182781

Table 4.6. **Taxes on income and profits (1000) as percentage of total taxation**
Tableau 4.6. **Impôts sur le revenu et les bénéfices (1000) en pourcentage du total des recettes fiscales**

	1998	2000	2008	2010	2013	2014	2015	2016	2017	2018
Botswana	..	..	63.4	65.3	71.4	71.7	67.9	69.5	61.3	64.7
Burkina Faso	..	24.6	20.8	19.1	25.5	25.0	22.1	23.7	23.4	24.9
Cabo Verde	34.3	35.7	29.8	30.9	31.5	29.7	32.6	32.4	32.4	31.4
Cameroon / Cameroun	28.5	28.1	30.0	27.1	30.7	31.5	32.3	28.1	25.3	27.0
Chad / Tchad	..	..	..	77.2	74.6	66.2	57.0	51.0	50.3	57.7
Congo	47.2	48.2	34.4	33.2	34.1	34.0	38.1	38.7	39.2	37.2
Congo, Dem. Rep. / Congo, Rép. dém.	..	34.0	26.1	27.6	25.6	32.1	35.8	30.6	36.8	44.4
Côte d'Ivoire	20.0	16.4	19.0	12.8	16.0	13.6	12.0	11.2	12.2	13.7
Egypt / Égypte	..	..	46.5	44.8	48.4	48.6	44.1	45.9	40.6	43.8
Equatorial Guinea / Guinée équatoriale	..	..	94.0	89.1	85.7	84.7	82.5	67.1	69.4	66.8
Eswatini	53.1	51.0	54.8	51.7	49.4	50.7	48.7	50.1	48.5	48.3
Ghana	..	28.9	28.8	36.1	39.0	38.9	32.1	27.4	33.2	38.6
Kenya	..	..	41.0	40.6	48.3	46.2	46.4	45.6	44.9	44.2
Lesotho	..	..	61.0	60.9	60.8	59.2	62.3	62.4	59.7	58.8
Madagascar	18.8	17.0	25.6	24.8	22.4	22.6	22.5	23.3	22.3	22.2
Malawi	..	..	40.2	44.2	46.4	44.8	48.7	48.4	48.5	48.0
Mali	18.6	14.3	22.6	24.5	24.7	29.9	25.1	23.7	26.1	23.5
Mauritania / Mauritanie	..	..	33.8	34.8	38.4	37.9	33.4	31.3	31.2	29.4
Mauritius / Maurice[1]	14.0	13.0	21.2	25.7	23.7	24.3	25.0	24.8	25.9	25.4
Morocco / Maroc	..	24.3	37.0	28.9	30.4	29.2	30.3	30.5	31.5	31.1
Namibia	..	..	64.0	64.2	58.4	62.1	60.5	61.5	63.0	63.3
Niger	..	18.0	27.7	25.4	38.9	31.4	24.7	26.4	27.0	21.2
Nigeria / Nigéria	..	..	..	63.5	66.3	63.4	59.9	55.8	55.7	60.1
Rwanda	27.7	26.0	34.9	36.2	40.5	37.3	38.1	38.6	39.1	40.3
Senegal / Sénégal	21.9	22.1	23.1	25.9	26.0	25.1	25.3	26.9	27.4	28.4
Seychelles	..	..	22.3	29.3	34.5	32.8	32.4	33.5	35.0	32.8
South Africa / Afrique du Sud	58.3	56.7	56.2	52.1	51.2	51.7	51.9	51.8	53.0	52.0
Togo	..	20.9	18.8	16.5	17.7	16.7	16.6	19.2	17.1	20.3
Tunisia / Tunisie	..	22.6	31.1	29.7	30.7	31.8	30.0	27.8	28.5	26.5
Uganda / Ouganda	15.5	18.2	28.7	31.5	35.7	34.0	34.7	34.9	34.7	34.3
Africa (30) average / Moyenne Afrique (30)[2]	**..**	**..**	**..**	**39.1**	**40.9**	**40.2**	**39.1**	**38.1**	**38.1**	**38.7**
LAC average / Moyenne ALC[3]	**21.5**	**22.7**	**27.9**	**26.9**	**27.9**	**28.0**	**27.4**	**27.2**	**27.2**	**27.8**
OECD average / Moyenne OCDE[4]	**34.4**	**34.8**	**35.5**	**32.8**	**33.4**	**33.3**	**33.6**	**33.2**	**34.0**	**33.3**

.. Not available

Note: The figures include sub-national government tax revenues for Eswatini, Mauritania (for 2009-18), Mauritius, Morocco, Nigeria (only state revenues) and South Africa (for 2002-18). Sub-national government tax revenues are not available in other countries.

Data on social security contributions are not available for Chad, the Republic of the Congo, the Democratic Republic of the Congo (prior to 2012), Madagascar (prior to 2011), Namibia, Togo and Uganda; and are only partially available in Cameroon and Senegal. Social security contributions for Botswana, Lesotho and Malawi are deemed to be null as they do not meet the criteria to be classified as social security contributions set out in the OECD classification of taxes in the Interpretative Guide.

In Ghana, Nigeria and Uganda, revenues from property taxes are mainly levied by local governments for which data on revenue are not available. In the Democratic Republic of the Congo only data for property taxes levied by the Direction Générale des Recettes Administratives, Judiciaires, Domaniales et de Participation (DGRAD) are available for 2010-18.

1. The fiscal year for Mauritius changed in 2010 and in 2015. Figures for 2015 needed to be estimated as a result.
2. Represents an unweighted average of the 30 African countries in this publication.
3. Represents an unweighted average for 25 Latin American and Caribbean (LAC) countries included in the publication *Revenue Statistics in Latin America and the Caribbean 2020.*
4. Represents an unweighted average for 36 OECD countries.

.. Non disponible

Note : Les chiffres incluent les recettes fiscales collectées par les administrations infranationales pour l'Afrique du Sud (pour les années 2002 à 2018), Eswatini, le Maroc, Maurice, la Mauritanie (pour les années 2009 à 2018) et le Nigéria (recettes des administrations régionales). Les données des recettes fiscales collectées par les administrations infranationales ne sont pas disponibles pour les autres pays.

Les données des cotisations de sécurité sociale ne sont pas disponibles pour la République du Congo, la République démocratique du Congo (avant 2012), Madagascar (avant 2011), la Namibie, l'Ouganda, le Tchad et le Togo et ne sont que partiellement disponibles au Cameroun et au Sénégal. Les cotisations de sécurité sociale pour le Botswana, le Lesotho et le Malawi sont nulles car elles ne répondent pas aux critères de classification des cotisations de sécurité sociale de la classification des impôts de l'OCDE du Guide d'interprétation.

Au Ghana, au Nigéria et en Ouganda, les recettes provenant des impôts sur le patrimoine sont principalement perçues par les administrations locales pour lesquelles les données ne sont pas disponibles. En République démocratique du Congo, seules les données des impôts sur le patrimoine qui sont prélevées par la Direction Générale des Recettes Administratives, Judiciaires, Domaniales et de Participation (DGRAD) sont disponibles pour 2010-18.

1. L'année fiscale pour Maurice a changé en 2010 et en 2015. Les chiffres pour 2015 ont dû être estimés en conséquence.
2. Représente une moyenne non pondérée des 30 pays africains inclus dans cette publication.
3. Représente la moyenne non pondérée pour 25 pays d'Amérique latine et des Caraïbes (ALC) inclus dans la publication *Revenue Statistics in Latin America and the Caribbean 2020.*
4. Représente la moyenne non pondérée pour 36 pays de l'OCDE.

StatLink https://doi.org/10.1787/888934182800

Table 4.7. **Social security contributions (2000) as percentage of GDP**
Tableau 4.7. **Cotisations de sécurité sociale (2000) en pourcentage du PIB**

	1998	2000	2008	2010	2013	2014	2015	2016	2017	2018
Botswana	..	..	0.0	0.0	0.0	0.0	0.0	0.0	0.0	0.0
Burkina Faso	..	1.6	1.5	1.5	1.6	1.5	1.7	1.6	1.7	1.6
Cabo Verde	0.0	0.8	0.0	0.0	0.0	0.0	0.0	0.0	0.0	0.0
Cameroon / Cameroun	0.8	0.9	0.8	1.0	1.0	0.9	0.9	1.0	1.1	1.1
Chad / Tchad	..	..	..	..	..	..	..	..	..	..
Congo	..	..	..	..	..	..	..	..	..	..
Congo, Dem. Rep. / Congo, Rép. dém.	..	..	..	..	0.6	0.6	0.6	0.5	0.5	0.5
Côte d'Ivoire	0.8	1.0	0.9	1.0	1.4	1.4	1.4	1.6	1.5	1.5
Egypt / Égypte	..	..	2.6	2.4	2.4	2.6	2.7	1.9	2.6	1.3
Equatorial Guinea / Guinée équatoriale	..	..	..	..	0.6	0.6	0.8	0.7	0.7	0.6
Eswatini	1.3	1.2	1.5	1.9	1.4	1.8	1.9	2.0	2.3	2.4
Ghana	..	0.7	1.0	0.9	0.9	1.1	1.2	1.2	0.9	0.8
Kenya	..	..	0.2	0.2	0.3	0.3	0.3	0.5	0.5	0.6
Lesotho	..	..	0.0	0.0	0.0	0.0	0.0	0.0	0.0	0.0
Madagascar[1]	0.0	0.0	0.0	0.0	0.4	0.4	0.4	0.4	0.4	0.6
Malawi	..	..	0.0	0.0	0.0	0.0	0.0	0.0	0.0	0.0
Mali	0.7	0.9	1.5	1.4	1.4	1.6	1.5	1.8	1.8	1.7
Mauritania / Mauritanie	..	..	0.7	0.7	0.6	0.9	0.9	0.8	0.8	0.8
Mauritius / Maurice[2]	0.9	0.8	0.6	0.7	0.7	0.8	0.8	0.8	0.8	0.8
Morocco / Maroc[1,3]	..	3.9	3.7	4.9	4.9	5.9	4.9	5.3	5.3	5.5
Namibia	..	..	..	..	..	..	..	..	..	..
Niger	..	0.4	0.5	0.5	0.6	0.6	0.6	0.6	0.6	0.5
Nigeria / Nigéria	..	..	..	0.6	0.7	0.7	0.6	0.5	0.6	0.5
Rwanda[1]	0.4	0.5	0.9	0.8	1.1	1.0	1.0	1.1	1.0	1.0
Senegal / Sénégal[4]	0.5	0.5	0.7	0.9	1.0	1.1	1.1	1.1	1.2	1.2
Seychelles	..	..	3.0	1.9	0.0	0.0	0.0	0.0	0.0	0.9
South Africa / Afrique du Sud	0.0	0.0	0.4	0.4	0.4	0.4	0.4	0.4	0.4	0.4
Togo	..	..	..	..	..	..	..	..	..	..
Tunisia / Tunisie[1]	..	5.3	6.5	7.3	8.7	8.5	8.9	9.4	9.6	9.3
Uganda / Ouganda	..	..	..	..	..	..	..	..	..	..
Africa (30) average / Moyenne Afrique (30)[5]	**..**	**..**	**..**	**1.3**	**1.2**	**1.3**	**1.3**	**1.3**	**1.4**	**1.3**
LAC average / Moyenne ALC[6]	**2.6**	**2.9**	**3.1**	**3.4**	**3.7**	**3.7**	**3.9**	**3.9**	**4.0**	**4.0**
OECD average / Moyenne OCDE[7]	**8.6**	**8.6**	**8.6**	**8.8**	**9.0**	**9.0**	**9.0**	**9.1**	**9.1**	**..**

Table 4.7. **Social security contributions (2000) as percentage of GDP** *(cont.)*
Tableau 4.7. **Cotisations de sécurité sociale (2000) en pourcentage du PIB** *(suite)*

.. Not available

Note: The figures include sub-national government tax revenues for Eswatini, Mauritania (for 2009-18), Mauritius, Morocco, Nigeria (only state revenues) and South Africa (for 2002-18). Sub-national government tax revenues are not available in other countries.

Data on social security contributions are not available for Chad, the Republic of the Congo, the Democratic Republic of the Congo (prior to 2012), Madagascar (prior to 2011), Namibia, Togo and Uganda; and are only partially available in Cameroon and Senegal. Social security contributions for Botswana, Lesotho and Malawi are deemed to be null as they do not meet the criteria to be classified as social security contributions set out in the OECD classification of taxes in the Interpretative Guide.

In Ghana, Nigeria and Uganda, revenues from property taxes are mainly levied by local governments for which data on revenue are not available. In the Democratic Republic of the Congo only data for property taxes levied by the Direction Générale des Recettes Administratives, Judiciaires, Domaniales et de Participation (DGRAD) are available for 2010-18.

1. Madagascar, Morocco, Rwanda and Tunisia do not include social security contributions in the tax-to-GDP ratio in their official publications as neither country considers them as taxes. They are included as tax revenue in this publication, following the classification set out in the OECD Interpretative Guide.
2. The fiscal year for Mauritius changed in 2010 and in 2015. Figures for 2015 needed to be estimated as a result.
3. Estimated figures for years prior to 2002.
4. These figures include contributions to the Senegalese Pension Institute (IPRES) (estimated prior to 2006) and contributions to the social security fund (CSS) from 2012. Data for previous years are not available.Social security contributions in Senegal are estimated for 2018.
5. Represents an unweighted average of the 30 African countries in this publication. The Africa (30) should be interpreted with caution as data for social security contributions (category 2000) and property taxes (category 4000) are not available or are partial in a few countries. See the country tables in Chapter 5 for further information.
6. Represents an unweighted average for 25 Latin American and Caribbean (LAC) countries included in the publication *Revenue Statistics in Latin America and the Caribbean 2020.*
7. Represents an unweighted average for 36 OECD countries.

.. Non disponible

Note : Les chiffres incluent les recettes fiscales collectées par les administrations infranationales pour l'Afrique du Sud (pour les années 2002 à 2018), Eswatini, le Maroc, Maurice, la Mauritanie (pour les années 2009 à 2018) et le Nigéria (recettes des administrations régionales). Les données des recettes fiscales collectées par les administrations infranationales ne sont pas disponibles pour les autres pays.

Les données des cotisations de sécurité sociale ne sont pas disponibles pour la République du Congo, la République démocratique du Congo (avant 2012), Madagascar (avant 2011), la Namibie, l'Ouganda, le Tchad et le Togo et ne sont que partiellement disponibles au Cameroun et au Sénégal. Les cotisations de sécurité sociale pour le Botswana, le Lesotho et le Malawi sont nulles car elles ne répondent pas aux critères de classification des cotisations de sécurité sociale de la classification des impôts de l'OCDE du Guide d'interprétation.

Au Ghana, au Nigéria et en Ouganda, les recettes provenant des impôts sur le patrimoine sont principalement perçues par les administrations locales pour lesquelles les données ne sont pas disponibles. En République démocratique du Congo, seules les données des impôts sur le patrimoine qui sont prélevées par la Direction Générale des Recettes Administratives, Judiciaires, Domaniales et de Participation (DGRAD) sont disponibles pour 2010-18.

1. Madagascar, le Maroc, le Rwanda et la Tunisie n'incluent pas les cotisations de sécurité sociale dans le ratio impôts/PIB dans leurs publications officielles car ces pays ne les considèrent pas comme des impôts. Elles sont incluses dans les recettes fiscales de cette publication en accordance avec la classification des impôts établie dans le Guide d'interprétation de l'OCDE.
2. L'année fiscale pour Maurice a changé en 2010 et en 2015. Les chiffres pour 2015 ont dû être estimés en conséquence.
3. Les chiffres sont estimés pour les années antérieures à 2002.
4. Les chiffres comprennent les cotisations de sécurité sociale de l'Institution de prévoyance retraite du Sénégal (IPRES) (estimées pour les années antérieures à 2006) et les cotisations de sécurité sociale de la Caisse de Sécurité Sociale (CSS) (à partir de 2012 car les données pour les années précédentes ne sont pas disponibles). Les cotisations de sécurité sociale de 2018 sont estimées.
5. Représente une moyenne non pondérée des 30 pays africains inclus dans cette publication. Il convient d'interpréter cette moyenne avec prudence à cause de valeurs manquantes ou incomplètes pour la rubrique 2000 (cotisations de sécurité sociale) et la rubrique 4000 (taxes sur le patrimoine). Veuillez voir les tableaux de pays au chapitre 5 pour plus d'informations.
6. Représente la moyenne non pondérée pour 25 pays d'Amérique latine et des Caraïbes (ALC) inclus dans la publication *Revenue Statistics in Latin America and the Caribbean 2020.*
7. Représente la moyenne non pondérée pour 36 pays de l'OCDE.

StatLink https://doi.org/10.1787/888934182819

Table 4.8. **Social security contributions (2000) as percentage of total taxation**
Tableau 4.8. **Cotisations de sécurité sociale (2000) en pourcentage du total des recettes fiscales**

	1998	2000	2008	2010	2013	2014	2015	2016	2017	2018
Botswana	..	..	0.0	0.0	0.0	0.0	0.0	0.0	0.0	0.0
Burkina Faso	..	15.8	12.6	10.8	9.5	10.0	11.2	10.3	9.9	9.5
Cabo Verde	0.0	5.2	0.2	0.2	0.2	0.2	0.2	0.2	0.2	0.2
Cameroon / Cameroun	7.3	8.1	6.7	8.6	7.1	6.2	6.0	7.3	7.3	7.2
Chad / Tchad	..	..	..	..	..	..	..	..	..	..
Congo	..	..	..	..	..	..	..	..	..	..
Congo, Dem. Rep. / Congo, Rép. dém.	..	..	..	..	5.6	6.3	5.9	6.0	7.5	6.1
Côte d'Ivoire	6.7	8.8	7.7	8.0	11.3	11.6	11.2	11.9	11.4	11.4
Egypt / Égypte	..	..	14.6	14.6	15.0	16.9	17.0	12.6	15.1	7.9
Equatorial Guinea / Guinée équatoriale	..	..	..	..	6.2	5.7	6.3	10.5	10.8	9.9
Eswatini	12.5	11.6	11.7	13.6	10.6	12.2	13.0	12.3	13.4	14.1
Ghana	..	9.4	9.7	8.6	8.3	9.4	9.0	8.8	6.6	5.7
Kenya	..	..	1.2	1.1	1.5	1.4	1.5	2.6	2.5	3.2
Lesotho	..	..	0.0	0.0	0.0	0.0	0.0	0.0	0.0	0.0
Madagascar[1]	0.0	0.0	0.0	0.0	3.8	4.2	4.2	3.5	3.6	5.3
Malawi	..	..	0.0	0.0	0.0	0.0	0.0	0.0	0.0	0.0
Mali	6.1	7.7	11.1	9.8	9.9	11.2	9.9	11.2	10.5	11.9
Mauritania / Mauritanie	..	..	6.6	6.7	4.8	5.8	6.2	5.4	5.3	5.0
Mauritius / Maurice[2]	4.9	4.5	3.4	3.6	3.8	4.0	4.1	4.1	4.1	3.8
Morocco / Maroc[1,3]	..	16.8	12.3	17.6	17.9	20.9	18.5	19.4	19.3	19.8
Namibia	..	..	..	..	..	..	..	..	..	..
Niger	..	5.4	5.1	5.3	4.7	5.1	4.7	5.5	6.1	4.8
Nigeria / Nigéria	..	..	..	7.6	8.5	9.3	9.9	10.2	10.9	8.4
Rwanda[1]	3.8	5.0	6.6	6.4	7.0	6.4	6.0	6.7	6.0	5.9
Senegal / Sénégal[4]	4.0	4.0	4.6	5.8	6.7	6.6	6.7	6.7	7.1	7.1
Seychelles	..	..	11.8	6.4	0.0	0.0	0.0	0.0	0.0	2.9
South Africa / Afrique du Sud	0.0	0.0	1.5	1.6	1.5	1.5	1.5	1.4	1.4	1.4
Togo	..	..	..	..	..	..	..	..	..	..
Tunisia / Tunisie[1]	..	21.6	24.1	27.0	29.0	27.5	29.5	31.6	31.1	29.1
Uganda / Ouganda	..	..	..	..	..	..	..	..	..	..
Africa (30) average / Moyenne Afrique (30)[5]	**..**	**..**	**..**	**7.1**	**6.9**	**7.3**	**7.3**	**7.5**	**7.6**	**7.2**
LAC average / Moyenne ALC[6]	**14.5**	**15.4**	**14.7**	**16.1**	**16.8**	**16.7**	**16.9**	**17.0**	**17.3**	**17.1**
OECD average / Moyenne OCDE[7]	**24.8**	**25.0**	**25.5**	**26.8**	**26.5**	**26.3**	**26.2**	**26.1**	**26.0**	**27.0**

Table 4.8. **Social security contributions (2000) as percentage of total taxation** *(cont.)*
Tableau 4.8. **Cotisations de sécurité sociale (2000) en pourcentage du total des recettes fiscales** *(suite)*

.. Not available

Note: The figures include sub-national government tax revenues for Eswatini, Mauritania (for 2009-18), Mauritius, Morocco, Nigeria (only state revenues) and South Africa (for 2002-18). Sub-national government tax revenues are not available in other countries.

Data on social security contributions are not available for Chad, the Republic of the Congo, the Democratic Republic of the Congo (prior to 2012), Madagascar (prior to 2011), Namibia, Togo and Uganda; and are only partially available in Cameroon and Senegal. Social security contributions for Botswana, Lesotho and Malawi are deemed to be null as they do not meet the criteria to be classified as social security contributions set out in the OECD classification of taxes in the Interpretative Guide.

In Ghana, Nigeria and Uganda, revenues from property taxes are mainly levied by local governments for which data on revenue are not available. In the Democratic Republic of the Congo only data for property taxes levied by the Direction Générale des Recettes Administratives, Judiciaires, Domaniales et de Participation (DGRAD) are available for 2010-18.

1. Madagascar, Morocco, Rwanda and Tunisia do not include social security contributions in the tax-to-GDP ratio in their official publications as neither country considers them as taxes. They are included as tax revenue in this publication, following the classification set out in the OECD Interpretative Guide.
2. The fiscal year for Mauritius changed in 2010 and in 2015. Figures for 2015 needed to be estimated as a result.
3. Estimated figures for years prior to 2002.
4. These figures include contributions to the Senegalese Pension Institute (IPRES) (estimated prior to 2006) and contributions to the social security fund (CSS) from 2012. Data for previous years are not available.Social security contributions in Senegal are estimated for 2018.
5. Represents an unweighted average of the 30 African countries in this publication. The Africa (30) should be interpreted with caution as data for social security contributions (category 2000) and property taxes (category 4000) are not available or are partial in a few countries. See the country tables in Chapter 5 for further information.
6. Represents an unweighted average for 25 Latin American and Caribbean (LAC) countries included in the publication *Revenue Statistics in Latin America and the Caribbean 2020.*
7. Represents an unweighted average for 36 OECD countries.

.. Non disponible

Note : Les chiffres incluent les recettes fiscales collectées par les administrations infranationales pour l'Afrique du Sud (pour les années 2002 à 2018), Eswatini, le Maroc, Maurice, la Mauritanie (pour les années 2009 à 2018) et le Nigéria (recettes des administrations régionales). Les données des recettes fiscales collectées par les administrations infranationales ne sont pas disponibles pour les autres pays.

Les données des cotisations de sécurité sociale ne sont pas disponibles pour la République du Congo, la République démocratique du Congo (avant 2012), Madagascar (avant 2011), la Namibie, l'Ouganda, le Tchad et le Togo et ne sont que partiellement disponibles au Cameroun et au Sénégal. Les cotisations de sécurité sociale pour le Botswana, le Lesotho et le Malawi sont nulles car elles ne répondent pas aux critères de classification des cotisations de sécurité sociale de la classification des impôts de l'OCDE du Guide d'interprétation.

Au Ghana, au Nigéria et en Ouganda, les recettes provenant des impôts sur le patrimoine sont principalement perçues par les administrations locales pour lesquelles les données ne sont pas disponibles. En République démocratique du Congo, seules les données des impôts sur le patrimoine qui sont prélevées par la Direction Générale des Recettes Administratives, Judiciaires, Domaniales et de Participation (DGRAD) sont disponibles pour 2010-18.

1. Madagascar, le Maroc, le Rwanda et la Tunisie n'incluent pas les cotisations de sécurité sociale dans le ratio impôts/PIB dans leurs publications officielles car ces pays ne les considèrent pas comme des impôts. Elles sont incluses dans les recettes fiscales de cette publication en accordance avec la classification des impôts établie dans le Guide d'interprétation de l'OCDE.
2. L'année fiscale pour Maurice a changé en 2010 et en 2015. Les chiffres pour 2015 ont dû être estimés en conséquence.
3. Les chiffres sont estimés pour les années antérieures à 2002.
4. Les chiffres comprennent les cotisations de sécurité sociale de l'Institution de prévoyance retraite du Sénégal (IPRES) (estimées pour les années antérieures à 2006) et les cotisations de sécurité sociale de la Caisse de Sécurité Sociale (CSS) (à partir de 2012 car les données pour les années précédentes ne sont pas disponibles). Les cotisations de sécurité sociale de 2018 sont estimées.
5. Représente une moyenne non pondérée des 30 pays africains inclus dans cette publication. Il convient d'interpréter cette moyenne avec prudence à cause de valeurs manquantes ou incomplètes pour la rubrique 2000 (cotisations de sécurité sociale) et la rubrique 4000 (taxes sur le patrimoine). Veuillez voir les tableaux de pays au chapitre 5 pour plus d'informations.
6. Représente la moyenne non pondérée pour 25 pays d'Amérique latine et des Caraïbes (ALC) inclus dans la publication *Revenue Statistics in Latin America and the Caribbean 2020.*
7. Représente la moyenne non pondérée pour 36 pays de l'OCDE.

StatLink https://doi.org/10.1787/888934182838

Table 4.9. **Taxes on property (4000) as percentage of GDP**
Tableau 4.9. **Impôts sur le patrimoine (4000) en pourcentage du PIB**

	1998	2000	2008	2010	2013	2014	2015	2016	2017	2018
Botswana	..	..	0.0	0.1	0.0	0.0	0.0	0.0	0.0	0.0
Burkina Faso	..	0.0	0.1	0.1	0.1	0.2	0.1	0.2	0.1	0.1
Cabo Verde	0.6	0.8	1.1	0.5	0.4	0.4	0.4	0.3	0.3	0.4
Cameroon / Cameroun	0.1	0.2	0.2	0.1	0.1	0.1	0.1	0.2	0.2	0.1
Chad / Tchad	..	..	..	0.5	0.6	0.4	0.2	0.1	0.1	0.1
Congo	0.1	0.1	0.1	0.1	0.1	0.1	0.3	0.1	0.1	0.1
Congo, Dem. Rep. / Congo, Rép. dém.[1]	..	..	..	0.0	0.0	0.0	0.0	0.0	0.0	0.0
Côte d'Ivoire	0.2	0.3	0.3	0.3	0.4	0.3	0.3	0.4	0.3	0.4
Egypt / Égypte	..	..	0.1	0.1	0.1	0.1	0.1	0.1	0.1	0.1
Equatorial Guinea / Guinée équatoriale	..	..	0.0	0.0	0.0	0.0	0.0	0.0	0.0	0.0
Eswatini	0.2	0.3	0.3	0.3	0.3	0.3	0.3	0.3	0.4	0.4
Ghana[1]	..	..	..	..	..	..	..	..	..	..
Kenya	..	..	0.3	0.2	0.2	0.2	0.2	0.2	0.1	0.2
Lesotho	..	..	0.0	0.0	0.0	0.0	0.0	0.0	0.0	0.0
Madagascar	0.1	0.1	0.2	0.1	0.1	0.1	0.1	0.1	0.1	0.1
Malawi	..	..	0.0	0.0	0.0	0.0	0.0	0.0	0.0	0.0
Mali	0.2	0.1	0.2	0.2	0.2	0.2	0.2	0.3	0.4	0.3
Mauritania / Mauritanie	..	..	0.0	0.4	0.4	0.5	0.7	0.6	0.5	0.5
Mauritius / Maurice[2]	1.3	1.2	1.3	1.1	1.0	1.1	1.0	1.1	1.1	1.0
Morocco / Maroc	..	1.3	1.7	1.6	1.9	1.9	2.0	2.0	1.6	1.6
Namibia	..	..	0.2	0.2	0.2	0.2	0.2	0.2	0.2	0.1
Niger	..	0.1	0.0	0.1	0.0	0.0	0.0	0.0	0.0	0.0
Nigeria / Nigéria[1]	..	..	..	..	..	..	..	..	..	..
Rwanda	0.0	0.0	0.0	0.0	0.0	0.0	0.0	0.0	0.0	0.0
Senegal / Sénégal	0.2	0.3	0.4	0.5	0.4	0.4	0.4	0.5	0.4	0.4
Seychelles	..	..	0.8	1.1	0.6	0.5	0.8	0.5	0.4	0.5
South Africa / Afrique du Sud	0.3	0.4	1.4	1.5	1.5	1.5	1.5	1.5	1.6	1.7
Togo	..	0.0	0.1	0.1	0.1	0.2	0.2	0.2	0.2	0.2
Tunisia / Tunisie	..	0.3	0.3	0.3	0.3	0.3	0.3	0.3	0.3	0.3
Uganda / Ouganda[1]	..	..	..	..	..	..	..	..	..	..
Africa (30) average / Moyenne Afrique (30)[3]	**..**	**..**	**..**	**0.4**	**0.3**	**0.4**	**0.4**	**0.4**	**0.3**	**0.3**
LAC average / Moyenne ALC[4]	**0.6**	**0.7**	**0.9**	**0.8**	**0.8**	**0.9**	**0.9**	**0.8**	**0.8**	**0.8**
OECD average / Moyenne OCDE[5]	**1.7**	**1.8**	**1.7**	**1.7**	**1.8**	**1.9**	**1.9**	**2.3**	**1.9**	**..**

.. Not available

Note: The figures include sub-national government tax revenues for Eswatini, Mauritania (for 2009-18), Mauritius, Morocco, Nigeria (only state revenues) and South Africa (for 2002-18). Sub-national government tax revenues are not available in other countries.

1. In Ghana, Nigeria and Uganda, revenues from property taxes are mainly levied by local governments whose data are not available. In the Democratic Republic of the Congo, only data for property tax revenues levied by the Direction Générale des Recettes Administratives, Judiciaires, Domaniales et de Participation (DGRAD) are available for 2010-18. See the country tables in Chapter 5 for further information.
2. The fiscal year for Mauritius changed in 2010 and in 2015. Figures for 2015 needed to be estimated as a result.
3. Represents an unweighted average of the 30 African countries in this publication. The Africa (30) should be interpreted with caution as data for social security contributions (category 2000) and property taxes (category 4000) are not available or are partial in a few countries. See the country tables in Chapter 5 for further information.
4. Represents an unweighted average for 25 Latin American and Caribbean (LAC) countries included in the publication *Revenue Statistics in Latin America and the Caribbean 2020.*
5. Represents an unweighted average for 36 OECD countries.

.. Non disponible

Note : Les chiffres incluent les recettes fiscales collectées par les administrations infranationales pour l'Afrique du Sud (pour les années 2002 à 2018), Eswatini, le Maroc, Maurice, la Mauritanie (pour les années 2009 à 2018) et le Nigéria (recettes des administrations régionales). Les données des recettes fiscales collectées par les administrations infranationales ne sont pas disponibles pour les autres pays.

1. Au Ghana, au Nigéria et en Ouganda, les recettes provenant des impôts sur le patrimoine sont principalement perçues par les administrations locales pour lesquelles les données ne sont pas disponibles. En République démocratique du Congo, seules les données des recettes relatives aux impôts sur le patrimoine qui sont prélevées par la Direction Générale des Recettes Administratives, Judiciaires, Domaniales et de Participation (DGRAD) sont disponibles pour la période 2010-18. Voir les tableaux des pays au chapitre 5 pour plus d'informations.
2. L'année fiscale pour Maurice a changé en 2010 et en 2015. Les chiffres pour 2015 ont dû être estimés en conséquence.
3. Représente une moyenne non pondérée des 30 pays africains inclus dans cette publication. Il convient d'interpréter cette moyenne avec prudence à cause de valeurs manquantes ou incomplètes pour la rubrique 2000 (cotisations de sécurité sociale) et la rubrique 4000 (taxes sur le patrimoine). Veuillez voir les tableaux de pays au chapitre 5 pour plus d'informations.
4. Représente la moyenne non pondérée pour 25 pays d'Amérique latine et des Caraïbes (ALC) inclus dans la publication *Revenue Statistics in Latin America and the Caribbean 2020.*
5. Représente la moyenne non pondérée pour 36 pays de l'OCDE.

StatLink https://doi.org/10.1787/888934182857

Table 4.10. **Taxes on property (4000) as percentage of total taxation**
Tableau 4.10. **Impôts sur le patrimoine (4000) en pourcentage du total des recettes fiscales**

	1998	2000	2008	2010	2013	2014	2015	2016	2017	2018
Botswana	..	..	0.3	0.4	0.3	0.2	0.3	0.3	0.3	0.3
Burkina Faso	..	0.4	0.7	0.7	0.8	1.0	0.8	1.0	0.7	0.7
Cabo Verde	4.1	5.3	5.1	2.7	2.4	2.6	2.0	1.5	1.5	1.9
Cameroon / Cameroun	0.8	1.6	1.2	1.1	0.9	0.8	0.9	1.1	1.1	0.8
Chad / Tchad	..	..	..	3.1	3.9	3.2	3.2	3.2	1.7	1.6
Congo	0.9	1.3	0.8	1.2	1.0	0.9	1.8	0.8	0.9	1.0
Congo, Dem. Rep. / Congo, Rép. dém.[1]	..	..	..	0.4	0.1	0.1	0.1	0.2	0.2	0.2
Côte d'Ivoire	2.2	2.8	2.5	2.4	3.0	2.7	2.6	2.9	2.6	2.9
Egypt / Égypte	..	..	0.6	0.6	0.4	0.4	0.6	0.6	0.6	0.6
Equatorial Guinea / Guinée équatoriale	..	..	0.0	0.0	0.0	0.0	0.0	0.1	0.0	0.1
Eswatini	2.1	2.6	2.0	2.0	2.1	1.9	1.9	1.8	2.3	2.6
Ghana[1]	..	..	..	..	..	..	..	..	..	..
Kenya	..	..	1.3	1.2	1.2	1.1	1.2	0.9	0.7	0.9
Lesotho	..	..	0.0	0.0	0.0	0.0	0.0	0.0	0.0	0.0
Madagascar	0.8	0.7	1.4	0.5	0.6	0.7	0.8	0.7	0.6	0.8
Malawi	..	..	0.0	0.0	0.0	0.0	0.0	0.0	0.0	0.0
Mali	1.4	1.3	1.5	1.6	1.3	1.7	1.5	2.1	2.2	2.0
Mauritania / Mauritanie	..	..	0.0	4.3	2.6	3.2	4.8	4.1	3.3	2.9
Mauritius / Maurice[2]	7.5	6.4	6.7	5.7	5.0	5.7	5.2	5.7	5.5	4.9
Morocco / Maroc	..	5.6	5.5	5.9	6.8	6.8	7.5	7.3	5.7	5.7
Namibia	..	..	1.4	0.9	1.1	1.0	1.0	0.8	0.8	0.6
Niger	..	1.1	0.5	0.8	0.3	0.2	0.4	0.3	0.4	0.3
Nigeria / Nigéria[1]	..	..	..	..	..	..	..	..	..	..
Rwanda	0.2	0.2	0.0	0.0	0.0	0.0	0.1	0.1	0.1	0.1
Senegal / Sénégal	1.9	2.0	2.8	3.1	2.5	2.5	2.4	2.7	2.5	2.5
Seychelles	..	..	3.2	3.6	2.0	1.8	2.7	1.6	1.4	1.7
South Africa / Afrique du Sud	1.5	1.8	5.1	5.7	5.4	5.5	5.0	5.4	5.6	5.8
Togo	..	0.4	0.8	0.8	0.7	0.8	0.8	0.8	0.7	0.8
Tunisia / Tunisie	..	1.1	1.1	1.0	1.1	1.0	1.1	1.1	1.0	0.9
Uganda / Ouganda[1]	..	..	..	..	..	..	..	..	..	..
Africa (30) average / Moyenne Afrique (30)[3]	**..**	**..**	**..**	**1.9**	**1.8**	**1.8**	**1.9**	**1.8**	**1.6**	**1.6**
LAC average / Moyenne ALC[4]	**3.7**	**3.7**	**4.7**	**3.9**	**4.0**	**3.9**	**3.9**	**3.7**	**3.6**	**3.6**
OECD average / Moyenne OCDE[5]	**5.3**	**5.4**	**5.3**	**5.4**	**5.5**	**5.6**	**5.7**	**6.5**	**5.8**	**5.5**

.. Not available

Note: The figures include sub-national government tax revenues for Eswatini, Mauritania (for 2009-18), Mauritius, Morocco, Nigeria (only state revenues) and South Africa (for 2002-18). Sub-national government tax revenues are not available in other countries.

1. In Ghana, Nigeria and Uganda, revenues from property taxes are mainly levied by local governments whose data are not available. In the Democratic Republic of the Congo, only data for property tax revenues levied by the Direction Générale des Recettes Administratives, Judiciaires, Domaniales et de Participation (DGRAD) are available for 2010-18. See the country tables in Chapter 5 for further information.
2. The fiscal year for Mauritius changed in 2010 and in 2015. Figures for 2015 needed to be estimated as a result.
3. Represents an unweighted average of the 30 African countries in this publication. The Africa (30) should be interpreted with caution as data for social security contributions (category 2000) and property taxes (category 4000) are not available or are partial in a few countries. See the country tables in Chapter 5 for further information.
4. Represents an unweighted average for 25 Latin American and Caribbean (LAC) countries included in the publication *Revenue Statistics in Latin America and the Caribbean 2020*.
5. Represents an unweighted average for 36 OECD countries.

.. Non disponible

Note : Les chiffres incluent les recettes fiscales collectées par les administrations infranationales pour l'Afrique du Sud (pour les années 2002 à 2018), Eswatini, le Maroc, Maurice, la Mauritanie (pour les années 2009 à 2018) et le Nigéria (recettes des administrations régionales). Les données des recettes fiscales collectées par les administrations infranationales ne sont pas disponibles pour les autres pays.

1. Au Ghana, au Nigéria et en Ouganda, les recettes provenant des impôts sur le patrimoine sont principalement perçues par les administrations locales pour lesquelles les données ne sont pas disponibles. En République démocratique du Congo, seules les données des recettes relatives aux impôts sur le patrimoine qui sont prélevées par la Direction Générale des Recettes Administratives, Judiciaires, Domaniales et de Participation (DGRAD) sont disponibles pour la période 2010-18. Voir les tableaux des pays au chapitre 5 pour plus d'informations.
2. L'année fiscale pour Maurice a changé en 2010 et en 2015. Les chiffres pour 2015 ont dû être estimés en conséquence.
3. Représente une moyenne non pondérée des 30 pays africains inclus dans cette publication. Il convient d'interpréter cette moyenne avec prudence à cause de valeurs manquantes ou incomplètes pour la rubrique 2000 (cotisations de sécurité sociale) et la rubrique 4000 (taxes sur le patrimoine). Veuillez voir les tableaux de pays au chapitre 5 pour plus d'informations.
4. Représente la moyenne non pondérée pour 25 pays d'Amérique latine et des Caraïbes (ALC) inclus dans la publication *Revenue Statistics in Latin America and the Caribbean 2020*.
5. Représente la moyenne non pondérée pour 36 pays de l'OCDE.

StatLink https://doi.org/10.1787/888934182876

Table 4.11. **Taxes on goods and services (5000) as percentage of GDP**
Tableau 4.11. **Impôts sur les biens et services (5000) en pourcentage du PIB**

	1998	2000	2008	2010	2013	2014	2015	2016	2017	2018
Botswana	..	..	6.2	5.4	4.1	4.3	4.0	4.2	4.7	4.2
Burkina Faso	..	5.8	7.7	9.6	10.4	9.6	9.9	10.2	10.9	10.7
Cabo Verde	9.1	8.4	13.8	12.2	11.7	11.4	12.2	12.4	13.3	14.1
Cameroon / Cameroun	6.9	7.0	7.4	7.3	8.1	8.4	8.4	8.5	9.1	9.1
Chad / Tchad	..	..	..	2.7	3.1	3.2	2.1	1.7	2.7	2.9
Congo[1]	3.3	2.0	4.2	4.6	6.9	7.7	10.2	10.0	7.7	4.9
Congo, Dem. Rep. / Congo, Rép. dém.	..	0.4	5.4	5.4	6.2	5.3	5.3	5.2	3.6	3.3
Côte d'Ivoire	7.1	6.6	7.5	7.9	7.3	7.4	7.9	8.2	8.2	7.8
Egypt / Égypte	..	..	6.8	6.5	5.8	5.1	6.0	6.2	7.5	8.0
Equatorial Guinea / Guinée équatoriale	..	..	0.4	0.7	0.7	0.8	1.2	1.4	1.2	1.2
Eswatini	3.5	3.7	4.0	4.5	5.2	5.2	5.4	5.7	6.0	6.0
Ghana	..	4.8	6.5	6.0	6.0	6.3	7.7	8.7	8.3	7.9
Kenya	..	..	10.7	10.2	8.8	9.9	9.5	9.4	9.6	9.0
Lesotho	..	..	6.6	7.2	6.9	7.4	7.1	7.1	7.4	8.3
Madagascar	6.7	7.8	8.2	7.1	6.8	6.5	6.9	7.2	8.0	8.2
Malawi	..	..	8.7	8.8	8.6	9.9	8.6	8.7	9.6	9.5
Mali	8.1	8.2	8.0	8.6	8.5	7.4	8.9	9.8	9.8	8.4
Mauritania / Mauritanie	..	..	6.0	5.3	7.2	8.0	8.1	8.4	8.7	10.0
Mauritius / Maurice[2]	12.8	13.6	12.7	12.2	12.9	12.6	12.5	12.6	12.6	13.3
Morocco / Maroc	..	12.3	13.4	12.9	12.2	11.9	11.3	11.3	11.7	11.8
Namibia	..	..	5.9	6.1	7.8	7.5	8.0	7.7	7.3	6.9
Niger	..	5.2	5.7	6.1	6.3	6.9	7.5	6.4	5.7	7.4
Nigeria / Nigéria	..	..	..	1.9	1.8	1.8	1.6	1.5	1.6	1.6
Rwanda	7.4	7.0	7.7	7.4	8.1	8.9	9.3	9.1	9.0	9.2
Senegal / Sénégal	8.4	9.1	10.1	10.0	9.6	10.3	10.3	10.5	10.0	10.0
Seychelles	..	..	16.1	17.8	18.1	19.3	18.6	20.1	19.7	20.3
South Africa / Afrique du Sud	9.2	8.9	10.0	10.2	11.0	11.0	11.6	11.4	11.0	11.5
Togo	..	7.1	11.1	11.6	15.3	16.4	17.3	17.2	16.5	14.8
Tunisia / Tunisie	..	12.7	11.0	10.7	10.8	11.3	10.8	10.6	11.1	12.8
Uganda / Ouganda	8.0	7.7	7.6	6.1	6.3	6.6	7.1	7.3	7.4	7.7
Africa (30) average / Moyenne Afrique (30)[3]	**..**	**..**	**..**	**7.8**	**8.1**	**8.3**	**8.5**	**8.6**	**8.7**	**8.7**
LAC average / Moyenne ALC[4]	**10.1**	**10.3**	**10.9**	**10.6**	**10.8**	**10.9**	**11.2**	**11.3**	**11.4**	**11.5**
OECD average / Moyenne OCDE[5]	**10.9**	**10.9**	**10.3**	**10.6**	**10.8**	**10.8**	**10.9**	**11.0**	**10.9**	**..**

.. Not available

Note: The figures include sub-national government tax revenues for Eswatini, Mauritania (for 2009-18), Mauritius, Morocco, Nigeria (only state revenues) and South Africa (for 2002-18). Sub-national government tax revenues are not available in other countries.

1. Revenues from customs duties for 2018 are estimated
2. The fiscal year for Mauritius changed in 2010 and in 2015. Figures for 2015 needed to be estimated as a result.
3. Represents an unweighted average of the 30 African countries in this publication.
4. Represents an unweighted average for 25 Latin American and Caribbean (LAC) countries included in the publication *Revenue Statistics in Latin America and the Caribbean 2020.*
5. Represents an unweighted average for 36 OECD countries.

.. Non disponible

Note : Les chiffres incluent les recettes fiscales collectées par les administrations infranationales pour l'Afrique du Sud (pour les années 2002 à 2018), Eswatini, le Maroc, Maurice, la Mauritanie (pour les années 2009 à 2018) et le Nigéria (recettes des administrations régionales). Les données des recettes fiscales collectées par les administrations infranationales ne sont pas disponibles pour les autres pays.

1. Les recettes provenant des droits d'importation sont estimées pour 2018
2. L'année fiscale pour Maurice a changé en 2010 et en 2015. Les chiffres pour 2015 ont dû être estimés en conséquence.
3. Représente une moyenne non pondérée des 30 pays africains inclus dans cette publication.
4. Représente la moyenne non pondérée pour 25 pays d'Amérique latine et des Caraïbes (ALC) inclus dans la publication *Revenue Statistics in Latin America and the Caribbean 2020.*
5. Représente la moyenne non pondérée pour 36 pays de l'OCDE.

StatLink https://doi.org/10.1787/888934182895

Table 4.12. **Taxes on goods and services (5000) as percentage of total taxation**

Tableau 4.12. **Impôts sur les biens et services (5000) en pourcentage du total des recettes fiscales**

	1998	2000	2008	2010	2013	2014	2015	2016	2017	2018
Botswana	..	..	36.4	34.3	28.3	28.1	31.7	30.2	38.4	35.0
Burkina Faso	..	57.2	64.3	67.7	63.1	62.6	64.5	63.6	64.5	63.5
Cabo Verde	61.6	53.8	64.9	66.2	65.9	67.5	65.3	65.9	66.0	66.5
Cameroon / Cameroun	63.5	62.2	59.4	60.1	57.4	58.3	57.0	59.9	62.8	62.2
Chad / Tchad	..	..	..	18.7	20.5	29.2	36.8	43.1	46.1	40.4
Congo[1]	47.6	45.5	61.8	62.0	62.4	62.5	57.3	57.7	56.7	58.1
Congo, Dem. Rep. / Congo, Rép. dém.	..	65.3	63.3	65.0	61.8	55.3	54.5	60.7	52.0	44.2
Côte d'Ivoire	61.5	59.8	61.1	66.0	57.6	60.6	62.7	62.1	62.0	59.5
Egypt / Égypte	..	..	38.2	40.0	36.1	34.0	38.2	40.8	43.7	47.6
Equatorial Guinea / Guinée équatoriale	..	..	5.5	9.4	7.6	8.1	10.3	20.0	18.7	19.2
Eswatini	32.3	34.8	31.5	32.6	37.9	35.1	36.5	35.8	35.7	35.0
Ghana	..	61.7	61.5	55.3	52.8	51.7	58.9	63.8	60.2	55.7
Kenya	..	..	56.4	57.1	49.0	51.2	50.9	50.8	51.9	51.7
Lesotho	..	..	39.0	39.1	39.2	40.8	37.7	37.6	40.3	41.2
Madagascar	79.0	81.3	71.6	74.3	73.1	72.4	72.4	72.1	73.2	71.3
Malawi	..	..	59.7	55.6	53.4	55.1	51.2	51.5	51.3	51.9
Mali	68.6	72.2	59.6	60.6	59.8	53.0	58.8	59.3	58.7	59.9
Mauritania / Mauritanie	..	..	59.4	54.0	54.0	53.0	55.4	59.2	60.1	62.6
Mauritius / Maurice[2]	71.9	74.6	67.8	64.4	67.0	65.2	64.9	64.6	63.6	65.2
Morocco / Maroc	..	52.1	44.3	46.7	43.9	42.0	42.8	41.6	42.4	42.2
Namibia	..	..	33.5	33.5	39.5	35.9	37.9	37.0	35.8	35.5
Niger	..	72.0	62.4	62.9	49.4	55.9	59.8	60.9	60.2	66.2
Nigeria / Nigéria	..	..	..	25.8	22.0	23.3	26.4	29.0	27.8	25.4
Rwanda	68.4	68.8	58.6	57.4	52.5	56.3	55.9	54.7	54.8	53.6
Senegal / Sénégal	69.0	69.2	67.5	63.4	62.6	63.7	63.1	61.9	61.3	60.7
Seychelles	..	..	62.6	60.6	63.5	65.3	64.9	64.9	63.6	62.6
South Africa / Afrique du Sud	39.3	39.9	35.9	39.5	40.7	40.0	40.3	40.1	38.7	39.7
Togo	..	74.8	76.7	78.4	78.2	78.5	80.1	77.5	78.5	76.3
Tunisia / Tunisie	..	51.8	41.0	39.5	36.2	36.4	35.8	35.8	35.8	39.7
Uganda / Ouganda	84.2	81.6	71.6	67.3	64.0	65.7	65.1	65.1	64.9	65.5
Africa (30) average / Moyenne Afrique (30)[3]	**..**	**..**	**..**	**51.9**	**50.0**	**50.2**	**51.2**	**52.2**	**52.3**	**51.9**
LAC average / Moyenne ALC[4]	**57.9**	**56.0**	**50.8**	**51.0**	**49.7**	**49.7**	**50.2**	**50.4**	**50.5**	**50.1**
OECD average / Moyenne OCDE[5]	**33.3**	**33.0**	**31.8**	**33.2**	**32.7**	**32.7**	**32.7**	**32.5**	**32.4**	**32.5**

.. Not available

Note: The figures include sub-national government tax revenues for Eswatini, Mauritania (for 2009-18), Mauritius, Morocco, Nigeria (only state revenues) and South Africa (for 2002-18). Sub-national government tax revenues are not available in other countries.

1. Revenues from customs duties for 2018 are estimated
2. The fiscal year for Mauritius changed in 2010 and in 2015. Figures for 2015 needed to be estimated as a result.
3. Represents an unweighted average of the 30 African countries in this publication.
4. Represents an unweighted average for 25 Latin American and Caribbean (LAC) countries included in the publication *Revenue Statistics in Latin America and the Caribbean 2020*.
5. Represents an unweighted average for 36 OECD countries.

.. Non disponible

Note : Les chiffres incluent les recettes fiscales collectées par les administrations infranationales pour l'Afrique du Sud (pour les années 2002 à 2018), Eswatini, le Maroc, Maurice, la Mauritanie (pour les années 2009 à 2018) et le Nigéria (recettes des administrations régionales). Les données des recettes fiscales collectées par les administrations infranationales ne sont pas disponibles pour les autres pays.

1. Les recettes provenant des droits d'importation sont estimées pour 2018
2. L'année fiscale pour Maurice a changé en 2010 et en 2015. Les chiffres pour 2015 ont dû être estimés en conséquence.
3. Représente une moyenne non pondérée des 30 pays africains inclus dans cette publication.
4. Représente la moyenne non pondérée pour 25 pays d'Amérique latine et des Caraïbes (ALC) inclus dans la publication *Revenue Statistics in Latin America and the Caribbean 2020*.
5. Représente la moyenne non pondérée pour 36 pays de l'OCDE.

StatLink https://doi.org/10.1787/888934182914

Table 4.13. **Taxes on general consumption (5110) as percentage of GDP**
Tableau 4.13. **Impôts généraux sur la consommation (5110) en pourcentage du PIB**

	1998	2000	2008	2010	2013	2014	2015	2016	2017	2018
Botswana	..	..	5.7	4.9	3.6	3.8	3.6	3.8	4.2	3.8
Burkina Faso	..	3.0	4.3	4.7	6.4	5.7	5.6	5.8	6.2	6.0
Cabo Verde	0.0	0.0	8.2	7.2	6.5	6.1	6.8	6.6	7.3	8.2
Cameroon / Cameroun	3.4	3.6	4.1	3.8	4.6	4.8	4.8	4.8	5.2	5.4
Chad / Tchad	..	..	..	1.5	1.8	2.0	1.0	1.2	1.6	1.1
Congo	2.9	1.7	2.2	2.6	3.8	4.3	5.6	5.4	4.3	2.7
Congo, Dem. Rep. / Congo, Rép. dém.	..	0.1	3.2	3.0	3.3	2.4	2.5	2.8	2.0	1.9
Côte d'Ivoire	2.5	2.4	2.8	2.9	2.7	2.6	2.6	2.5	2.7	2.8
Egypt / Égypte	..	..	3.7	3.3	2.8	2.6	2.8	2.8	3.6	3.9
Equatorial Guinea / Guinée équatoriale	..	..	0.3	0.6	0.4	0.5	0.8	0.8	0.7	0.7
Eswatini	2.7	3.0	3.5	3.8	3.7	3.9	4.0	4.2	4.2	4.2
Ghana	..	2.0	3.5	3.3	3.3	3.6	4.2	4.0	4.0	3.8
Kenya	..	..	4.8	4.7	4.1	4.6	4.5	4.4	4.4	4.2
Lesotho	..	..	6.6	7.2	6.9	7.4	7.1	7.1	7.4	8.3
Madagascar	3.3	4.5	5.7	4.8	4.8	4.5	4.7	4.9	5.5	5.6
Malawi	..	..	4.5	4.0	4.3	5.3	4.8	4.7	5.2	5.2
Mali	3.0	3.9	4.6	5.0	5.1	4.0	4.3	4.8	4.9	4.6
Mauritania / Mauritanie	..	..	3.7	3.3	4.6	5.0	4.7	4.3	4.3	5.0
Mauritius / Maurice[1]	2.8	4.6	6.9	6.8	7.0	6.7	6.8	6.8	6.8	7.0
Morocco / Maroc	..	5.2	8.5	8.3	8.4	8.1	7.6	7.5	7.7	7.6
Namibia	..	..	5.7	6.0	7.7	7.5	7.9	7.5	7.0	6.4
Niger	..	2.0	3.3	3.6	3.6	4.2	4.5	3.7	3.2	5.0
Nigeria / Nigéria	..	..	..	1.0	1.0	0.9	0.8	0.8	0.8	0.9
Rwanda	2.0	2.0	4.3	3.9	4.5	5.1	5.1	4.9	5.1	5.2
Senegal / Sénégal	4.2	5.2	5.7	6.0	5.5	5.7	5.9	5.8	5.7	5.5
Seychelles	..	..	6.5	3.9	9.5	11.0	10.3	11.0	10.8	11.8
South Africa / Afrique du Sud	5.6	5.5	6.4	6.2	6.5	6.7	6.9	6.8	6.3	6.7
Togo	..	3.5	6.2	6.8	8.8	10.0	10.1	10.2	9.7	8.6
Tunisia / Tunisie	..	6.2	6.1	6.1	6.1	6.5	6.2	5.9	6.1	7.3
Uganda / Ouganda	3.0	3.1	3.6	2.9	3.3	3.2	3.5	3.6	3.6	3.8
Africa (30) average / Moyenne Afrique (30)[2]	**..**	**..**	**..**	**4.4**	**4.8**	**5.0**	**5.0**	**5.0**	**5.0**	**5.1**
LAC average / Moyenne ALC[3]	**5.7**	**5.8**	**6.9**	**6.5**	**7.0**	**7.1**	**7.2**	**7.3**	**7.2**	**7.3**
OECD average / Moyenne OCDE[4]	**6.6**	**6.7**	**6.6**	**6.7**	**6.8**	**6.9**	**6.9**	**7.0**	**7.0**	**..**

.. Not available

Note: The figures include sub-national government tax revenues for Eswatini, Mauritania (for 2009-18), Mauritius, Morocco, Nigeria (only state revenues) and South Africa (for 2002-18). Sub-national government tax revenues are not available in other countries.

1. The fiscal year for Mauritius changed in 2010 and in 2015. Figures for 2015 needed to be estimated as a result.
2. Represents an unweighted average of the 30 African countries in this publication.
3. Represents an unweighted average for 25 Latin American and Caribbean (LAC) countries included in the publication *Revenue Statistics in Latin America and the Caribbean 2020.*
4. Represents an unweighted average for 36 OECD countries.

.. Non disponible

Note : Les chiffres incluent les recettes fiscales collectées par les administrations infranationales pour l'Afrique du Sud (pour les années 2002 à 2018), Eswatini, le Maroc, Maurice, la Mauritanie (pour les années 2009 à 2018) et le Nigéria (recettes des administrations régionales). Les données des recettes fiscales collectées par les administrations infranationales ne sont pas disponibles pour les autres pays.

1. L'année fiscale pour Maurice a changé en 2010 et en 2015. Les chiffres pour 2015 ont dû être estimés en conséquence.
2. Représente une moyenne non pondérée des 30 pays africains inclus dans cette publication.
3. Représente la moyenne non pondérée pour 25 pays d'Amérique latine et des Caraïbes (ALC) inclus dans la publication *Revenue Statistics in Latin America and the Caribbean 2020.*
4. Représente la moyenne non pondérée pour 36 pays de l'OCDE.

StatLink https://doi.org/10.1787/888934182933

Table 4.14. **Taxes on general consumption (5110) as percentage of total taxation**
Tableau 4.14. **Impôts généraux sur la consommation (5110) en pourcentage du total des recettes**

	1998	2000	2008	2010	2013	2014	2015	2016	2017	2018
Botswana	..	..	33.5	31.3	24.6	25.3	28.2	27.1	34.0	31.1
Burkina Faso	..	29.0	36.1	33.5	38.7	37.0	36.8	36.4	36.9	35.6
Cabo Verde	0.0	0.0	38.8	39.3	36.6	36.3	36.5	35.5	36.2	38.7
Cameroon / Cameroun	31.0	32.2	33.0	31.2	32.9	33.2	32.9	33.8	36.3	36.8
Chad / Tchad	..	..	..	10.1	11.7	18.0	18.0	30.0	27.3	15.7
Congo	41.6	40.2	31.9	34.9	34.0	35.3	31.7	31.5	31.6	32.1
Congo, Dem. Rep. / Congo, Rép. dém.	..	18.4	37.6	36.4	32.9	25.5	26.1	33.1	29.4	25.3
Côte d'Ivoire	21.7	21.8	23.1	24.1	21.3	21.0	20.3	19.2	20.3	21.4
Egypt / Égypte	..	..	21.0	20.6	17.1	17.2	18.3	18.2	21.2	23.4
Equatorial Guinea / Guinée équatoriale	..	..	4.4	7.4	4.5	4.8	6.3	11.1	11.0	11.3
Eswatini	25.2	28.0	27.3	27.4	27.2	25.9	26.6	26.3	25.0	24.5
Ghana	..	26.1	32.6	30.0	29.4	29.9	32.1	28.9	29.4	26.7
Kenya	..	..	25.3	26.1	22.6	23.9	24.5	23.6	24.1	24.1
Lesotho	..	..	39.0	39.1	39.2	40.8	37.7	37.6	40.3	41.2
Madagascar	39.2	46.5	49.6	50.7	51.3	50.4	49.1	48.6	50.4	48.6
Malawi	..	..	30.6	25.4	26.4	29.5	28.3	27.6	27.7	28.1
Mali	25.9	33.9	34.2	35.0	35.7	28.4	28.1	28.9	29.5	33.0
Mauritania / Mauritanie	..	..	36.5	33.4	34.7	33.2	32.5	30.4	29.7	31.3
Mauritius / Maurice[1]	15.8	25.3	36.8	36.1	36.6	34.6	35.4	35.0	34.1	34.5
Morocco / Maroc	..	22.1	28.3	30.1	30.2	28.6	28.8	27.4	27.8	27.4
Namibia	..	..	32.5	32.8	38.9	35.7	37.1	35.8	34.6	33.2
Niger	..	27.4	35.9	36.7	28.4	34.1	35.6	35.2	34.2	45.3
Nigeria / Nigéria	..	..	..	14.0	11.9	11.7	13.3	15.3	14.9	13.6
Rwanda	18.3	20.0	33.1	29.9	28.9	32.3	30.6	29.5	31.0	30.2
Senegal / Sénégal	34.6	39.6	38.2	37.7	35.6	35.4	35.8	33.9	34.8	33.7
Seychelles	..	..	25.5	13.3	33.3	37.3	35.8	35.3	34.8	36.4
South Africa / Afrique du Sud	23.8	24.6	23.0	24.1	24.2	24.4	23.7	23.7	22.2	22.9
Togo	..	36.9	42.6	45.9	45.1	47.8	46.9	46.2	46.0	44.6
Tunisia / Tunisie	..	25.2	22.7	22.3	20.4	21.1	20.3	19.9	19.9	22.8
Uganda / Ouganda	31.4	33.0	34.3	32.3	33.4	32.4	32.3	32.4	31.6	32.0
Africa (30) average / Moyenne Afrique (30)[2]	**..**	**..**	**..**	**29.7**	**29.6**	**29.7**	**29.7**	**29.9**	**30.2**	**30.2**
LAC average / Moyenne ALC[3]	**30.8**	**30.0**	**31.1**	**30.4**	**31.1**	**31.1**	**31.3**	**31.8**	**31.5**	**31.5**
OECD average / Moyenne OCDE[4]	**20.1**	**20.1**	**20.3**	**21.0**	**20.8**	**21.0**	**20.9**	**20.7**	**20.8**	**21.3**

.. Not available

Note: The figures include sub-national government tax revenues for Eswatini, Mauritania (for 2009-18), Mauritius, Morocco, Nigeria (only state revenues) and South Africa (for 2002-18). Sub-national government tax revenues are not available in other countries.

1. The fiscal year for Mauritius changed in 2010 and in 2015. Figures for 2015 needed to be estimated as a result.
2. Represents an unweighted average of the 30 African countries in this publication.
3. Represents an unweighted average for 25 Latin American and Caribbean (LAC) countries included in the publication *Revenue Statistics in Latin America and the Caribbean 2020*.
4. Represents an unweighted average for 36 OECD countries.

.. Non disponible

Note : Les chiffres incluent les recettes fiscales collectées par les administrations infranationales pour l'Afrique du Sud (pour les années 2002 à 2018), Eswatini, le Maroc, Maurice, la Mauritanie (pour les années 2009 à 2018) et le Nigéria (recettes des administrations régionales). Les données des recettes fiscales collectées par les administrations infranationales ne sont pas disponibles pour les autres pays.

1. L'année fiscale pour Maurice a changé en 2010 et en 2015. Les chiffres pour 2015 ont dû être estimés en conséquence.
2. Représente une moyenne non pondérée des 30 pays africains inclus dans cette publication.
3. Représente la moyenne non pondérée pour 25 pays d'Amérique latine et des Caraïbes (ALC) inclus dans la publication *Revenue Statistics in Latin America and the Caribbean 2020*.
4. Représente la moyenne non pondérée pour 36 pays de l'OCDE.

StatLink https://doi.org/10.1787/888934182952

Table 4.15. **Taxes on specific goods and services (5120) as percentage of GDP**
Tableau 4.15. **Impôts sur les biens et services déterminés (5120) en pourcentage du PIB**

	1998	2000	2008	2010	2013	2014	2015	2016	2017	2018
Botswana	..	..	0.2	0.2	0.3	0.2	0.3	0.3	0.3	0.2
Burkina Faso	..	2.2	2.8	2.8	3.4	3.3	3.6	3.7	4.0	4.1
Cabo Verde	9.1	8.4	5.5	5.0	5.2	5.3	5.4	5.7	6.0	5.9
Cameroon / Cameroun	3.5	3.3	3.2	3.4	3.4	3.5	3.5	3.6	3.8	3.7
Chad / Tchad	..	..	..	1.2	1.3	1.2	1.0	0.5	1.1	1.8
Congo[1]	0.4	0.2	2.0	2.0	3.1	3.3	4.5	4.5	3.4	2.2
Congo, Dem. Rep. / Congo, Rép. dém.	..	0.3	2.2	2.4	2.9	2.8	2.8	2.3	1.5	1.4
Côte d'Ivoire	4.4	4.0	4.4	4.7	4.3	4.5	5.0	5.3	5.2	4.7
Egypt / Égypte	..	..	3.0	3.1	3.1	2.5	3.1	3.4	3.8	4.0
Equatorial Guinea / Guinée équatoriale	..	..	0.1	0.2	0.3	0.3	0.5	0.6	0.5	0.5
Eswatini	0.7	0.6	0.4	0.6	1.3	1.2	1.3	1.4	1.7	1.7
Ghana	..	2.8	3.0	2.8	2.7	2.7	3.5	4.8	4.2	4.1
Kenya	..	..	5.7	5.4	4.6	5.1	4.8	4.9	5.1	4.7
Lesotho	..	..	0.0	0.0	0.0	0.0	0.0	0.0	0.0	0.0
Madagascar	3.3	3.3	2.5	2.2	2.0	1.9	2.2	2.3	2.5	2.6
Malawi	..	..	4.2	4.8	4.4	4.6	3.9	4.0	4.4	4.4
Mali	5.0	4.3	3.4	3.6	3.4	3.4	4.6	5.0	4.8	3.7
Mauritania / Mauritanie	..	..	2.2	1.9	2.4	2.8	3.2	3.6	3.9	4.5
Mauritius / Maurice[2]	9.8	8.8	4.8	4.4	4.9	4.9	4.7	4.8	4.9	5.3
Morocco / Maroc	..	6.8	4.6	4.3	3.5	3.5	3.4	3.5	3.7	3.8
Namibia	..	..	0.2	0.1	0.1	0.0	0.2	0.3	0.2	0.5
Niger	..	3.1	2.4	2.5	2.6	2.7	3.0	2.7	2.4	2.3
Nigeria / Nigéria	..	..	..	0.8	0.8	0.9	0.8	0.7	0.7	0.7
Rwanda	5.3	4.9	3.3	3.5	3.6	3.8	4.1	4.1	3.8	3.9
Senegal / Sénégal	4.1	3.9	4.3	4.0	4.1	4.5	4.4	4.6	4.2	4.4
Seychelles	..	..	8.3	12.8	7.7	7.4	7.3	8.1	8.0	7.5
South Africa / Afrique du Sud	3.6	3.4	3.4	3.8	4.3	4.1	4.6	4.5	4.4	4.6
Togo	..	3.6	4.9	4.8	6.4	6.3	7.1	6.8	6.7	6.1
Tunisia / Tunisie	..	6.3	4.7	4.4	4.5	4.5	4.4	4.5	4.7	5.2
Uganda / Ouganda	4.7	4.4	3.7	3.0	2.9	3.2	3.4	3.5	3.7	3.8
Africa (30) average / Moyenne Afrique (30)[3]	**..**	**..**	**..**	**3.2**	**3.1**	**3.2**	**3.4**	**3.5**	**3.5**	**3.4**
LAC average / Moyenne ALC[4]	**4.1**	**4.1**	**3.6**	**3.7**	**3.4**	**3.5**	**3.6**	**3.7**	**3.8**	**3.8**
OECD average / Moyenne OCDE[5]	**3.7**	**3.6**	**3.1**	**3.3**	**3.3**	**3.2**	**3.2**	**3.3**	**3.2**	**..**

.. Not available

Note: The figures include sub-national government tax revenues for Eswatini, Mauritania (for 2009-18), Mauritius, Morocco, Nigeria (only state revenues) and South Africa (for 2002-18). Sub-national government tax revenues are not available in other countries.

1. Revenues from customs duties for 2018 are estimated
2. The fiscal year for Mauritius changed in 2010 and in 2015. Figures for 2015 needed to be estimated as a result.
3. Represents an unweighted average of the 30 African countries in this publication.
4. Represents an unweighted average for 25 Latin American and Caribbean (LAC) countries included in the publication *Revenue Statistics in Latin America and the Caribbean 2020.*
5. Represents an unweighted average for 36 OECD countries.

.. Non disponible

Note : Les chiffres incluent les recettes fiscales collectées par les administrations infranationales pour l'Afrique du Sud (pour les années 2002 à 2018), Eswatini, le Maroc, Maurice, la Mauritanie (pour les années 2009 à 2018) et le Nigéria (recettes des administrations régionales). Les données des recettes fiscales collectées par les administrations infranationales ne sont pas disponibles pour les autres pays.

1. Les recettes provenant des droits d'importation sont estimées pour 2018
2. L'année fiscale pour Maurice a changé en 2010 et en 2015. Les chiffres pour 2015 ont dû être estimés en conséquence.
3. Représente une moyenne non pondérée des 30 pays africains inclus dans cette publication.
4. Représente la moyenne non pondérée pour 25 pays d'Amérique latine et des Caraïbes (ALC) inclus dans la publication *Revenue Statistics in Latin America and the Caribbean 2020.*
5. Représente la moyenne non pondérée pour 36 pays de l'OCDE.

StatLink https://doi.org/10.1787/888934182971

Table 4.16. **Taxes on specific goods and services (5120) as percentage of total taxation**
Tableau 4.16. **Impôts sur les biens et services déterminés (5120) en pourcentage du total des recettes fiscales**

	1998	2000	2008	2010	2013	2014	2015	2016	2017	2018
Botswana	..	..	1.3	1.3	2.3	1.6	2.2	1.8	2.5	1.8
Burkina Faso	..	21.6	23.2	20.1	20.4	21.4	23.8	23.2	23.6	24.1
Cabo Verde	61.6	53.8	26.1	26.9	29.3	31.3	28.8	30.5	29.7	27.8
Cameroon / Cameroun	32.2	29.6	25.9	28.4	24.1	24.6	23.8	25.7	26.2	25.1
Chad / Tchad	..	..	..	8.4	8.7	11.0	18.2	13.1	18.4	24.6
Congo[1]	6.0	5.1	29.8	27.0	28.3	27.1	25.5	26.0	24.9	25.8
Congo, Dem. Rep. / Congo, Rép. dém.	..	45.6	25.5	28.5	28.7	29.8	28.4	27.1	22.0	18.4
Côte d'Ivoire	38.2	35.8	35.6	39.5	33.9	37.0	40.0	40.5	39.3	35.7
Egypt / Égypte	..	..	16.9	19.2	18.9	16.7	19.9	22.5	22.5	24.1
Equatorial Guinea / Guinée équatoriale	..	..	1.1	2.0	3.1	3.3	4.0	8.8	7.7	7.9
Eswatini	6.1	5.9	2.7	4.1	9.7	8.3	9.0	8.7	10.0	9.7
Ghana	..	35.6	27.9	25.3	23.4	21.8	26.9	34.9	30.8	29.0
Kenya	..	..	30.3	30.2	25.8	26.7	25.9	26.6	27.4	27.1
Lesotho	..	..	0.0	0.0	0.0	0.0	0.0	0.0	0.0	0.0
Madagascar	39.6	34.4	21.8	23.4	21.5	21.8	23.1	23.3	22.6	22.5
Malawi	..	..	29.1	30.2	27.0	25.6	22.9	23.9	23.6	23.8
Mali	42.4	37.9	25.2	25.3	23.9	24.4	30.6	30.1	29.0	26.6
Mauritania / Mauritanie	..	..	21.8	19.2	18.2	18.7	21.8	25.8	26.7	27.8
Mauritius / Maurice[2]	55.1	48.3	25.8	23.4	25.6	25.2	24.3	24.5	24.8	26.2
Morocco / Maroc	..	28.9	15.1	15.6	12.5	12.3	12.9	12.9	13.5	13.5
Namibia	..	..	1.0	0.7	0.6	0.2	0.7	1.2	1.2	2.4
Niger	..	42.9	26.2	25.8	20.7	21.5	23.9	25.3	25.5	20.4
Nigeria / Nigéria	..	..	..	11.6	9.8	11.5	12.7	13.3	12.6	11.5
Rwanda	49.3	47.9	25.1	26.9	23.4	23.9	24.4	24.4	23.3	22.9
Senegal / Sénégal	33.9	29.2	28.9	25.4	26.6	27.8	26.8	27.3	26.0	26.5
Seychelles	..	..	32.5	43.6	27.0	25.2	25.4	26.2	25.6	23.3
South Africa / Afrique du Sud	15.5	15.3	12.2	14.6	15.8	14.9	15.9	15.7	15.7	16.0
Togo	..	37.7	33.9	32.2	32.9	30.4	32.8	30.9	32.1	31.2
Tunisia / Tunisie	..	25.7	17.4	16.3	15.0	14.5	14.7	15.1	15.2	16.3
Uganda / Ouganda	50.0	46.4	35.5	32.9	29.0	31.6	31.2	31.4	32.1	32.3
Africa (30) average / Moyenne Afrique (30)[3]	**..**	**..**	**..**	**20.9**	**19.5**	**19.7**	**20.7**	**21.4**	**21.2**	**20.8**
LAC average / Moyenne ALC[4]	**25.6**	**24.4**	**18.0**	**18.7**	**16.7**	**16.6**	**16.9**	**16.7**	**17.1**	**16.7**
OECD average / Moyenne OCDE[5]	**11.3**	**11.1**	**9.7**	**10.3**	**9.9**	**9.7**	**9.8**	**9.8**	**9.6**	**9.2**

.. Not available

Note: The figures include sub-national government tax revenues for Eswatini, Mauritania (for 2009-18), Mauritius, Morocco, Nigeria (only state revenues) and South Africa (for 2002-18). Sub-national government tax revenues are not available in other countries.

1. Revenues from customs duties for 2018 are estimated
2. The fiscal year for Mauritius changed in 2010 and in 2015. Figures for 2015 needed to be estimated as a result.
3. Represents an unweighted average of the 30 African countries in this publication.
4. Represents an unweighted average for 25 Latin American and Caribbean (LAC) countries included in the publication *Revenue Statistics in Latin America and the Caribbean 2020*.
5. Represents an unweighted average for 36 OECD countries.

.. Non disponible

Note : Les chiffres incluent les recettes fiscales collectées par les administrations infranationales pour l'Afrique du Sud (pour les années 2002 à 2018), Eswatini, le Maroc, Maurice, la Mauritanie (pour les années 2009 à 2018) et le Nigéria (recettes des administrations régionales). Les données des recettes fiscales collectées par les administrations infranationales ne sont pas disponibles pour les autres pays.

1. Les recettes provenant des droits d'importation sont estimées pour 2018
2. L'année fiscale pour Maurice a changé en 2010 et en 2015. Les chiffres pour 2015 ont dû être estimés en conséquence.
3. Représente une moyenne non pondérée des 30 pays africains inclus dans cette publication.
4. Représente la moyenne non pondérée pour 25 pays d'Amérique latine et des Caraïbes (ALC) inclus dans la publication *Revenue Statistics in Latin America and the Caribbean 2020*.
5. Représente la moyenne non pondérée pour 36 pays de l'OCDE.

StatLink https://doi.org/10.1787/888934182990

Table 4.17. **Gross domestic product for tax reporting years at current prices, in national currency units**

Tableau 4.17. **Produit intérieur brut pour les années de déclaration fiscale à prix courants, en monnaie nationale**

	1998	2000	2008	2010	2013	2014	2015	2016	2017	2018
Botswana[1]	21 523	30 165	74 406	91 395	130 336	145 918	152 191	172 949	182 669	192 091
Burkina Faso	1 861 089	2 108 160	4 215 341	5 002 182	6 640 135	6 884 466	6 995 311	7 598 720	8 227 851	8 997 919
Cabo Verde	56 397	70 536	134 698	138 569	153 723	154 436	158 699	165 782	173 097	184 661
Cameroon / Cameroun	6 191 546	7 179 525	11 826 440	12 948 432	15 981 280	17 276 469	18 285 382	19 344 838	20 328 363	21 492 534
Chad / Tchad	1 164 875	1 115 969	4 652 386	5 290 608	6 417 738	6 912 490	6 474 073	6 047 146	5 854 572	6 127 318
Congo	1 150 100	2 292 500	4 556 900	6 082 520	6 927 242	6 959 940	5 056 482	4 615 600	5 188 276	6 475 853
Congo, Dem. Rep. / Congo, Rép. dém.	44 287	1 317 075	11 067 569	19 536 677	30 051 179	33 223 988	35 111 226	37 517 392	55 676 093	76 495 500
Côte d'Ivoire	10 284 785	10 547 104	14 994 944	17 036 122	21 350 243	24 135 859	27 086 150	28 423 874	29 955 010	32 063 000
Egypt / Égypte[2]	286 317	340 520	862 368	1 182 279	1 767 550	1 995 200	2 286 950	2 576 650	3 089 700	3 953 700
Equatorial Guinea / Guinée équatoriale	259 843	822 850	8 844 107	8 072 293	10 840 521	10 746 852	7 795 420	6 661 365	7 084 543	7 564 567
Eswatini[1]	10 150	12 366	27 995	33 123	45 292	48 988	53 103	57 194	60 057	63 334
Ghana	3 965	6 248	40 636	61 596	123 650	155 433	180 399	215 077	256 671	300 596
Kenya[2]	908 299	1 043 127	2 317 204	3 016 495	4 503 229	5 073 867	5 843 416	6 653 575	7 583 668	8 524 678
Lesotho[1]	5 071	6 151	14 955	17 780	25 208	28 602	30 973	31 959	32 600	34 521
Madagascar	4 790 572	6 265 668	18 322 512	20 863 367	27 417 726	30 240 588	33 216 184	37 637 590	41 058 841	46 188 508
Malawi[2]	85 134	157 897	684 072	960 659	1 756 426	2 290 405	2 884 126	3 570 894	4 246 474	4 804 999
Mali	1 959 380	2 103 270	4 387 928	5 288 939	6 540 560	7 093 033	7 747 730	8 317 726	8 921 906	9 425 956
Mauritania / Mauritanie	38 305	42 517	124 019	155 297	217 185	199 573	200 221	225 473	241 913	251 497
Mauritius / Maurice	96 309	121 023	269 733	307 957	372 397	392 062	409 893	422 329	445 983	469 706
Morocco / Maroc	401 524	412 897	716 959	784 624	897 923	925 376	987 950	1 013 229	1 063 351	1 106 822
Namibia[1]	18 511	27 979	71 386	84 476	121 328	136 787	148 125	160 028	171 362	178 131
Niger	1 548 653	1 593 588	3 233 156	3 852 516	5 016 417	5 338 789	5 715 039	6 096 438	6 485 969	7 121 376
Nigeria / Nigéria	4 588 990	6 897 482	39 157 884	55 469 351	81 009 965	90 136 985	95 177 736	102 575 419	114 899 251	129 086 908
Rwanda	605 639	676 000	2 693 000	3 411 000	4 929 000	5 466 000	5 968 000	6 672 000	7 600 000	8 189 000
Senegal / Sénégal	3 756 970	4 235 185	7 590 206	8 030 951	9 367 088	9 775 039	10 508 650	11 283 396	12 191 796	12 907 359
Seychelles	3 201	3 513	9 147	11 705	16 015	17 119	18 340	19 002	20 806	22 064
South Africa / Afrique du Sud	761 658	946 324	2 369 063	2 748 008	3 539 977	3 805 349	4 049 883	4 359 060	4 653 578	4 873 899
Togo	1 032 576	1 059 553	1 482 360	1 696 830	2 134 464	2 259 047	2 471 777	2 649 374	2 788 608	2 974 979
Tunisia / Tunisie	24 828	29 433	55 273	63 055	75 144	80 866	84 689	89 789	96 298	105 268
Uganda / Ouganda[2]	8 515 711	10 641 952	30 314 827	46 761 803	73 279 239	80 374 678	89 456 487	98 757 649	108 586 303	118 915 360

1. The GDP for Botswana, Eswatini, Lesotho and Namibia are adjusted using the following formula: GDP(n)*3/4+GDP(n+1)/4 in order to make them correspond more closely to an April(n)-to-March(n+1) fiscal year.
2. The GDP for Egypt, Kenya, Malawi and Uganda in all years and for Mauritius in the years preceding 2010 and for Mauritius in 2016 are adjusted using the formula GDP(n)/2+GDP(n-1)/2. This is done in order to make the value of the GDP correspond more closely to a July(n-1)-to-June(n) fiscal year. The GDP for Mauritius is not adjusted from 2010 to 2015 because public finance data are reported on a calendar year for those years.

Source: IMF, *World Economic Outlook*, April 2020.

1. Le PIB pour Botswana. Eswatini, Lesotho et la Namibie est ajusté selon la formule PIB(n)*3/4+PIB(n+1)/4 afin de le faire correspondre le mieux possible à une année fiscale de avril (n) à mars (n+1).
2. Le PIB pour l'Egypte, le Kenya, le Malawi et l'Ouganda, pour toutes les années et pour Maurice dans les années antérieures à 2010 et pour lánnee 2016, est ajusté selon la formule suivante : PIB(n)/2+PIB(n-1)/2 afin de le faire correspondre le mieux possible à une année fiscale de juillet (n-1) à juin (n). Le PIB de Maurice n'est pas ajusté de 2010 à 2015 car les données de finances publiques sont reportées sur une année civile pour ces années.

Source : FMI, *Perspectives de l'économie mondiale*, avril 2020.

StatLink https://doi.org/10.1787/888934183009

Table 4.18. **Gross domestic product for tax reporting years at current prices, in millions of US dollars at market exchange rates**

Tableau 4.18. **Produit intérieur brut pour les années de déclaration fiscale à prix courants, en monnaie millions de dollars US aux taux de change du marché**

	1998	2000	2008	2010	2013	2014	2015	2016	2017	2018
Botswana[1]	4 985	5 731	10 839	13 444	15 251	15 806	14 748	16 089	17 732	13 998
Burkina Faso	3 155	2 961	9 450	10 118	13 444	13 947	11 833	12 819	14 165	16 207
Cabo Verde	575	609	1 788	1 664	1 850	1 860	1 597	1 663	1 770	1 977
Cameroon / Cameroun	10 495	9 802	26 514	26 191	32 358	34 999	30 932	32 635	34 997	38 712
Chad / Tchad	1 975	1 572	10 430	10 701	12 994	14 003	10 952	10 202	10 079	11 036
Congo	1 949	3 220	10 216	12 303	14 026	14 100	8 554	7 787	8 932	11 664
Congo, Dem. Rep. / Congo, Rép. dém.	21 089	19 077	19 709	21 566	32 676	35 911	37 915	36 640	37 615	47 099
Côte d'Ivoire	17 433	14 851	33 621	34 431	43 228	48 882	45 815	47 964	51 588	57 725
Egypt / Égypte[2]	84 479	99 896	153 926	214 170	283 388	296 787	318 821	332 279	284 506	243 390
Equatorial Guinea / Guinée équatoriale	440	1 159	19 830	16 314	21 949	21 765	13 185	11 241	12 201	13 619
Eswatini[1]	1 788	1 690	3 372	4 535	4 556	4 338	4 017	3 993	4 484	3 533
Ghana	17 153	11 467	38 413	43 043	63 279	53 173	48 595	54 989	58 978	65 518
Kenya[2]	14 741	14 245	33 927	38 511	52 774	58 336	62 891	66 713	73 940	83 309
Lesotho[1]	894	820	1 745	2 449	2 430	2 449	2 236	2 320	2 488	1 854
Madagascar	4 402	4 629	10 725	9 983	12 424	12 523	11 323	11 849	13 176	13 851
Malawi[2]	3 426	3 647	8 613	10 098	12 576	12 245	11 871	11 025	11 694	13 048
Mali	3 328	2 963	9 837	10 698	13 243	14 369	13 106	14 032	15 360	16 978
Mauritania / Mauritanie	2 027	1 780	5 098	5 618	7 331	6 615	6 182	6 414	6 784	7 048
Mauritius / Maurice	4 274	4 702	9 070	10 004	12 130	12 803	11 692	11 962	12 746	13 735
Morocco / Maroc	41 806	38 859	92 507	93 217	106 826	110 081	101 179	103 312	109 714	117 921
Namibia[1]	3 257	3 821	8 601	11 566	12 190	12 113	11 206	11 178	12 683	10 028
Niger	2 629	2 245	7 248	7 792	10 157	10 815	9 668	10 285	11 166	12 827
Nigeria / Nigéria	209 677	67 824	330 260	369 062	514 966	568 499	492 437	404 649	375 745	398 160
Rwanda	1 931	1 718	4 927	5 850	7 623	8 010	8 294	8 475	9 140	9 510
Senegal / Sénégal	6 404	5 966	17 017	16 244	18 966	19 802	17 777	19 035	20 989	23 248
Seychelles	608	615	998	970	1 328	1 343	1 377	1 427	1 525	1 579
South Africa / Afrique du Sud	137 686	136 453	287 095	375 304	366 821	350 901	317 578	296 273	349 433	368 135
Togo	1 750	1 493	3 323	3 432	4 322	4 576	4 181	4 469	4 801	5 358
Tunisia / Tunisie	21 803	21 474	44 844	44 054	46 248	47 634	43 172	41 801	39 806	39 771
Uganda / Ouganda[2]	7 336	6 869	17 607	22 192	28 775	30 225	29 076	28 178	30 296	32 225

1. The GDP for Botswana, Eswatini, Lesotho and Namibia are adjusted using the following formula: GDP(n)*3/4+GDP(n+1)/4 in order to make them correspond more closely to an April(n)-to-March(n+1) fiscal year.
2. The GDP for Egypt, Kenya, Malawi and Uganda in all years and for Mauritius in the years preceding 2010 and for Mauritius in 2016 are adjusted using the formula GDP(n)/2+GDP(n-1)/2. This is done in order to make the value of the GDP correspond more closely to a July(n-1)-to-June(n) fiscal year. The GDP for Mauritius is not adjusted from 2010 to 2015 because public finance data are reported on a calendar year for those years.

Source: IMF, *World Economic Outlook*, April 2020.

1. Le PIB pour Botswana. Eswatini, Lesotho et la Namibie est ajusté selon la formule PIB(n)*3/4+PIB(n+1)/4 afin de le faire correspondre le mieux possible à une année fiscale de avril (n) à mars (n+1).
2. Le PIB pour l'Egypte, le Kenya, le Malawi et l'Ouganda, pour toutes les années et pour Maurice dans les années antérieures à 2010 et pour lánnee 2016, est ajusté selon la formule suivante : PIB(n)/2+PIB(n-1)/2 afin de le faire correspondre le mieux possible à une année fiscale de juillet (n-1) à juin (n). Le PIB de Maurice n'est pas ajusté de 2010 à 2015 car les données de finances publiques sont reportées sur une année civile pour ces années.

Source : FMI, *Perspectives de l'économie mondiale*, avril 2020.

StatLink https://doi.org/10.1787/888934183028

Table 4.19. **Exchange rates used, national currency per US dollar**
Tableau 4.19. **Taux de change utilisés, unités de monnaie nationale par dollar US**

	1998	2000	2008	2010	2013	2014	2015	2016	2017	2018
Botswana	4.32	5.26	6.86	6.80	8.55	9.23	10.32	10.75	10.30	13.72
Burkina Faso	589.95	711.98	446.05	494.39	493.89	493.63	591.15	592.77	580.86	555.19
Cabo Verde	98.16	115.88	75.34	83.28	83.07	83.03	99.39	99.69	97.81	93.41
Cameroon / Cameroun	589.94	732.49	446.05	494.39	493.89	493.63	591.15	592.77	580.86	555.19
Chad / Tchad	589.95	709.89	446.05	494.39	493.89	493.63	591.15	592.77	580.86	555.19
Congo	589.95	711.98	446.05	494.39	493.89	493.63	591.15	592.77	580.86	555.19
Congo, Dem. Rep. / Congo, Rép. dém.	2.10	69.04	561.54	905.91	919.66	925.17	926.06	1 023.96	1 480.15	1 624.13
Côte d'Ivoire	589.95	710.21	446.00	494.79	493.90	493.76	591.21	592.61	580.66	555.45
Egypt / Égypte	3.39	3.41	5.60	5.52	6.24	6.72	7.17	7.75	10.86	16.24
Equatorial Guinea / Guinée équatoriale	589.95	710.21	446.00	494.79	493.90	493.76	591.21	592.61	580.66	555.45
Eswatini	5.68	7.32	8.30	7.30	9.94	11.29	13.22	14.32	13.39	17.92
Ghana	0.23	0.54	1.06	1.43	1.95	2.92	3.71	3.91	4.35	4.59
Kenya	61.62	73.23	68.30	78.33	85.33	86.98	92.91	99.73	102.57	102.33
Lesotho	5.67	7.50	8.57	7.26	10.37	11.68	13.85	13.77	13.10	18.62
Madagascar	1 088.28	1 353.50	1 708.37	2 089.95	2 206.91	2 414.81	2 933.51	3 176.54	3 116.11	3 334.75
Malawi	24.85	43.29	79.42	95.14	139.67	187.05	242.96	323.90	363.13	368.25
Mali	588.83	709.89	446.05	494.39	493.89	493.63	591.15	592.77	580.86	555.19
Mauritania / Mauritanie	18.90	23.89	24.33	27.64	29.62	30.17	32.39	35.15	35.66	35.68
Mauritius / Maurice	22.53	25.74	29.74	30.78	30.70	30.62	35.06	35.30	34.99	34.20
Morocco / Maroc	9.60	10.63	7.75	8.42	8.41	8.41	9.76	9.81	9.69	9.39
Namibia	5.68	7.32	8.30	7.30	9.95	11.29	13.22	14.32	13.51	17.76
Niger	589.15	709.89	446.05	494.39	493.89	493.63	591.15	592.77	580.86	555.20
Nigeria / Nigéria	21.89	101.70	118.57	150.30	157.31	158.55	193.28	253.49	305.79	324.21
Rwanda	313.72	393.44	546.60	583.12	646.62	682.43	719.60	787.25	831.53	861.08
Senegal / Sénégal	586.70	709.89	446.05	494.39	493.89	493.63	591.15	592.77	580.86	555.19
Seychelles	5.26	5.71	9.16	12.07	12.06	12.75	13.32	13.32	13.65	13.97
South Africa / Afrique du Sud	5.53	6.94	8.25	7.32	9.65	10.84	12.75	14.71	13.32	13.24
Togo	589.95	709.60	446.05	494.39	493.89	493.63	591.15	592.77	580.86	555.19
Tunisia / Tunisie	1.14	1.37	1.23	1.43	1.62	1.70	1.96	2.15	2.42	2.65
Uganda / Ouganda	1 160.82	1 549.25	1 721.78	2 107.12	2 546.64	2 659.25	3 076.67	3 504.74	3 584.22	3 690.15

Note: The exchange rate is calculated by taking the ratio of the estimated fiscal year GDP in national currency for Table 4.17 to the estimated fiscal year GDP in US dollars in Table 4.18.

Note : Le taux de change est calculé en faisant le ratio du PIB de l'année budgétaire estimée en monnaie nationale du tableau 4.17 par rapport à l'année budgétaire estimée en dollars US du tableau 4.18.

StatLink https://doi.org/10.1787/888934183047

Chapter 5

Country tables, tax revenues, 1998-2018

Chapitre 5

Tableaux pays, recettes fiscales, 1998-2018

Chapter 5 / Chapitre 5

Country tables, 1990-2018

In all of the following tables a ("..") indicates not available or not applicable. The main series in this volume cover the years 1990 to 2018.

Figures referring to 1990-97, 1999, 2001-07, 2009 and 2011-12 in Tables 5.1 to 5.30 have been omitted because of lack of space. Complete series are, however, available on line at http://dx.doi.org/10.1787/93add7a4-en.

Tableaux pays, 1990-2018

Dans tous les tableaux suivants le symbole («..») signifie que l'information n'est pas disponible ou qu'elle n'est pas applicable. La principale série dans ce volume couvre les années 1990 à 2018.

Les années 1990-97, 1999, 2001-07, 2009 et 2011-12 dans les tableaux 5.1 à 5.30 ont été omis en raison du manque d'espace. Les séries complètes sont cependant disponibles en ligne sur http://dx.doi.org/10.1787/ef1bbbc4-fr.

Table 5.1. **Botswana**

Details of tax revenue / Recettes fiscales détaillées

Million BWP

	1998	2000	2008	2010	2013	2014	2015	2016	2017	2018
Total tax revenue	..	..	**12 707**	**14 300**	**19 122**	**22 160**	**19 332**	**24 139**	**22 470**	**23 287**
1000 Taxes on income, profits and capital gains	..	..	**8 052**	**9 345**	**13 659**	**15 882**	**13 134**	**16 777**	**13 772**	**15 069**
1100 Of individuals	..	..	..	..	..	..	..	..	..	..
1110 On income and profits	..	..	..	..	..	..	..	..	..	..
1120 On capital gains	..	..	..	..	..	..	..	..	..	..
1200 Corporate	..	..	..	..	..	..	..	..	..	..
1210 On profits	..	..	..	..	..	..	..	..	..	..
1220 On capital gains	..	..	..	..	..	..	..	..	..	..
1300 Unallocable between 1100 and 1200	..	..	8 052	9 345	13 659	15 882	13 134	16 777	13 772	15 069
Assessed income tax	..	..	4 911	5 168	8 157	9 365	6 825	9 454	6 894	7 661
Income tax arrears and deductions	..	..	2 142	3 114	4 508	5 185	5 259	5 172	4 948	5 349
Withholding tax	..	..	1 000	1 062	993	1 332	1 050	2 152	1 930	2 059
PAYE taxes	..	..	0	0	0	0	0	0	0	0
2000 Social security contributions	..	..	**0**	**0**	**0**	**0**	**0**	**0**	**0**	**0**
2100 Employees	..	..	..	..	..	..	..	..	..	..
2110 On a payroll basis	..	..	..	..	..	..	..	..	..	..
2120 On an income tax basis	..	..	..	..	..	..	..	..	..	..
2200 Employers	..	..	..	..	..	..	..	..	..	..
2210 On a payroll basis	..	..	..	..	..	..	..	..	..	..
2220 On an income tax basis	..	..	..	..	..	..	..	..	..	..
2300 Self-employed or non-employed	..	..	..	..	..	..	..	..	..	..
2310 On a payroll basis	..	..	..	..	..	..	..	..	..	..
2320 On an income tax basis	..	..	..	..	..	..	..	..	..	..
2400 Unallocable between 2100, 2200 and 2300	..	..	..	..	..	..	..	..	..	..
2410 On a payroll basis	..	..	..	..	..	..	..	..	..	..
2420 On an income tax basis	..	..	..	..	..	..	..	..	..	..
3000 Taxes on payroll and workforce	..	..	**0**	**0**	**0**	**0**	**0**	**0**	**0**	**0**
4000 Taxes on property	..	..	**33**	**52**	**57**	**54**	**66**	**62**	**63**	**78**
4100 Recurrent taxes on immovable property	..	..	0	0	0	0	0	0	0	0
4110 Households	..	..	..	..	..	..	..	..	..	..
4120 Others	..	..	..	..	..	..	..	..	..	..
4200 Recurrent taxes on net wealth	..	..	0	0	0	0	0	0	0	0
4210 Individual	..	..	..	..	..	..	..	..	..	..
4220 Corporate	..	..	..	..	..	..	..	..	..	..
4300 Estate, inheritance and gift taxes	..	..	0	0	0	0	0	0	0	0
4310 Estate and inheritance taxes	..	..	..	..	..	..	..	..	..	..
4320 Gift taxes	..	..	..	..	..	..	..	..	..	..
4400 Taxes on financial and capital transactions	..	..	33	52	57	54	66	62	63	78
4500 Non-recurrent taxes	..	..	0	0	0	0	0	0	0	0
4510 On net wealth	..	..	..	..	..	..	..	..	..	..
4520 Other non-recurrent taxes	..	..	..	..	..	..	..	..	..	..
4600 Other recurrent taxes on property	..	..	0	0	0	0	0	0	0	0
5000 Taxes on goods and services	..	..	**4 621**	**4 903**	**5 407**	**6 223**	**6 132**	**7 300**	**8 635**	**8 140**
5100 Taxes on production, sale, transfer, etc.	..	..	4 418	4 669	5 136	5 955	5 870	6 981	8 207	7 661
5110 General taxes	..	..	4 251	4 481	4 704	5 606	5 448	6 535	7 650	7 253
5111 Value added taxes	..	..	4 251	4 481	4 704	5 606	5 448	6 535	7 650	7 253
VAT revenues (gross)	..	..	4 251	4 481	4 704	5 606	5 448	6 535	7 650	7 253
VAT accrued interest	..	..	0	0	0	0	0	0	0	0
VAT refunds	..	..	0	0	0	0	0	0	0	0
5112 Sales tax	..	..	0	0	0	0	0	0	0	0
5113 Other	..	..	0	0	0	0	0	0	0	0
5120 Taxes on specific goods and services	..	..	168	188	433	349	422	446	557	408
5121 Excises	..	..	126	157	400	318	393	435	553	405
Alcohol levy	..	..	0	0	218	214	284	327	427	284
Fuel levy	..	..	126	157	182	104	109	107	126	121
5122 Profits of fiscal monopolies	..	..	0	0	0	0	0	0	0	0
5123 Customs and import duties	..	..	2	9	6	2	4	6	2	1
5124 Taxes on exports	..	..	2	2	2	2	2	3	2	2
5125 Taxes on investment goods	..	..	0	0	0	0	0	0	0	0
5126 Taxes on specific services	..	..	38	20	24	28	23	2	0	0
5127 Other taxes on internat. trade and transactions	..	..	0	0	0	0	0	0	0	0
5128 Other taxes	..	..	0	0	0	0	0	0	0	0
5130 Unallocable between 5110 and 5120	..	..	0	0	0	0	0	0	0	0
5200 Taxes on use of goods and perform activities	..	..	203	234	271	268	262	319	428	479

Table 5.1. **Botswana** *(cont.)*

Details of tax revenue / Recettes fiscales détaillées

Million BWP

	1998	2000	2008	2010	2013	2014	2015	2016	2017	2018
5210 Recurrent taxes	..	..	203	234	271	268	262	319	428	479
5211 Paid by households: motor vehicles	..	..	55	62	73	73	77	85	110	115
5212 Paid by others: motor vehicles	..	..	125	144	159	161	180	193	270	317
5213 Paid in respect of other goods	..	..	24	29	38	34	5	40	48	46
5220 Non-recurrent taxes	..	..	0	0	0	0	0	0	0	0
5300 Unallocable between 5100 and 5200	..	..	0	0	0	0	0	0	0	0
6000 Other taxes	**..**	**..**	**0**	**0**	**0**	**0**	**0**	**0**	**0**	**0**
6100 Paid solely by business	..	..	..	..	..	..	..	..	..	..
6200 Other	..	..	..	..	..	..	..	..	..	..

.. Not available

Note: Data are on a fiscal year basis beginning 1st April. For example, the data for 2018 represent April 2018 to March 2019.

Figures exclude tax revenues collected by sub-national governments as the data are not available.

Heading 2000: Social security contributions for Botswana are deemed to be null as they do not meet the criteria to be classified as social security contributions set out in the OECD classification of taxes in the Interpretative Guide.

Source: Botswana Ministry of Finance and Economic Development, and Statistics Botswana.

StatLink https://doi.org/10.1787/888934183370

Table 5.2. **Burkina Faso**

Details of tax revenue / Recettes fiscales détaillées

Million XOF

	1998	2000	2008	2010	2013	2014	2015	2016	2017	2018
Recettes fiscales totales	..	**215 670**	**505 124**	**706 553**	**1 094 753**	**1 056 093**	**1 069 259**	**1 212 469**	**1 387 868**	**1 515 581**
1000 Impôts sur revenu, bénéfices et gains en capital	..	**53 109**	**105 037**	**135 056**	**278 906**	**264 278**	**236 193**	**287 770**	**325 403**	**377 120**
1100 Des personnes physiques	..	15 371	41 456	56 429	82 354	71 703	75 300	88 707	102 422	125 405
1110 Sur le revenu et les bénéfices	..	15 371	41 456	56 429	82 354	71 703	75 300	88 707	102 422	125 405
Impôt sur les revenus	..	0	71	84	35	19	18	14	49	1
Impôt sur les bénéfices industriels, commerciaux et agricoles (pers. phys.)	..	1 235	2 293	3 133	4 775	4 242	4 828	4 884	6 888	16 128
Impôt sur les bénéfices non commerciaux (pers. phys.)	..	754	2 523	2 404	3 884	3 959	4 809	5 492	5 821	8 008
Impôt unique sur les traitements et salaires	..	13 382	36 568	50 809	73 660	63 483	65 646	78 317	89 665	101 268
1120 Sur les gains en capital	..	..	..	..	..	..	..	..	..	..
1200 Des sociétés	..	36 190	60 815	76 008	193 264	189 457	157 319	194 665	217 472	246 558
1210 Sur les bénéfices	..	36 190	60 815	76 008	193 264	189 457	157 319	194 665	217 472	246 558
Impôt sur les sociétés	..	0	0	67 027	169 842	162 667	132 050	163 454	186 641	209 595
Contribution du secteur informel et des micro-entreprises	..	0	1 434	1 475	1 711	1 664	1 638	1 938	1 926	2 244
Impôt sur les bénéfices industriels, commerciaux et agricoles (pers. mor.)	..	32 221	54 495	0	0	0	0	0	0	0
Impôts sur le revenu des créances	..	548	1 427	1 622	4 231	3 746	4 698	5 463	6 155	0
Impôts sur le revenu des valeurs mobilières	..	3 420	3 459	5 884	17 479	21 380	18 932	23 810	22 750	0
Impôts sur le revenu des capitaux mobiliers	..	..	..	..	..	..	..	..	..	..
1220 Sur les gains en capital	..	..	..	..	..	..	..	..	..	..
1300 Non ventilables entre 1100 et 1200	..	1 549	2 767	2 619	3 289	3 118	3 574	4 399	5 509	5 157
Impôts sur les revenus fonciers	..	1 402	2 281	2 337	2 890	2 925	3 206	3 668	4 175	4 813
Reversement des honoraires	..	91	90	19	0	0	0	0	0	0
Taxes sur les plus-values	..	56	396	263	399	193	367	731	1 334	345
2000 Cotisations de sécurité sociale	..	**34 142**	**63 669**	**76 584**	**103 570**	**105 729**	**120 046**	**124 308**	**136 913**	**144 066**
2100 A la charge des salariés	..	10 332	19 785	23 424	30 883	31 521	35 064	36 340	40 508	43 153
2110 Sur la base du salaire	..	10 332	19 785	23 424	30 883	31 521	35 064	36 340	40 508	43 153
2120 Sur la base de l'impôt sur le revenu	..	0	0	0	0	0	0	0	0	0
2200 A la charge des employeurs	..	23 810	43 884	53 160	72 687	74 208	84 983	87 969	96 405	100 914
2210 Sur la base du salaire	..	23 810	43 884	53 160	72 687	74 208	84 983	87 969	96 405	100 914
2220 Sur la base de l'impôt sur le revenu	..	0	0	0	0	0	0	0	0	0
2300 A charge des travailleurs indép. ou sans emploi	..	0	0	0	0	0	0	0	0	0
2310 Sur la base du salaire	..	..	..	..	..	..	..	..	..	..
2320 Sur la base de l'impôt sur le revenu	..	..	..	..	..	..	..	..	..	..
2400 Non ventilables entre 2100, 2200 et 2300	..	0	0	0	0	0	0	0	0	0
2410 Sur la base du salaire	..	..	..	..	..	..	..	..	..	..
2420 Sur la base de l'impôt sur le revenu	..	..	..	..	..	..	..	..	..	..
3000 Sur salaires ou main d'oeuvre	..	**2 678**	**4 996**	**5 479**	**7 293**	**7 407**	**7 889**	**8 762**	**10 813**	**12 331**
4000 Impôts sur le patrimoine	..	**938**	**3 466**	**4 778**	**8 323**	**10 516**	**8 529**	**12 061**	**9 784**	**9 982**
4100 Impôts périodiques sur la propriété immobilière	..	54	463	615	1 169	1 092	1 011	1 366	1 359	2 013
Contribution foncière	..	0	0	0	0	0	0	0	75	169
Taxe de résidence	..	8	296	460	531	558	469	749	624	681
Taxe sur les biens de mainmorte	..	45	167	155	638	534	542	617	659	1 163
4110 Ménages	..	0	0	0	0	0	0	0	0	0
4120 Autres agents	..	0	0	0	0	0	0	0	0	0
4200 Impôts périodiques sur l'actif net	..	0	0	0	0	0	0	0	0	0
4210 Personnes physiques	..	..	..	..	..	..	..	..	..	..
4220 Sociétés	..	..	..	..	..	..	..	..	..	..
4300 Impôts sur mut. par décès, succ. et donations	..	73	65	41	138	148	200	188	101	170
4310 Impôts sur mut. par décès et successions	..	66	56	28	121	132	179	169	95	156
4320 Impôts sur les donations	..	7	9	13	18	15	21	19	5	13
4400 Impôts sur transact. mobilières et immob.	..	646	1 761	2 803	5 568	7 673	6 160	8 836	6 702	5 818
4500 Impôts non-périodiques	..	165	1 178	1 318	1 448	1 604	1 158	1 671	1 621	1 981
4510 Sur l'actif net	..	0	0	0	0	0	0	0	0	0
4520 Autres non-périodiques	..	165	1 178	1 318	1 448	1 604	1 158	1 671	1 621	1 981
4600 Autres impôts périodiques sur patrimoine	..	0	0	0	0	0	0	0	0	0
5000 Impôts sur les biens et services	..	**123 301**	**324 890**	**478 204**	**691 107**	**661 176**	**690 024**	**771 478**	**894 693**	**962 272**
5100 Impôts sur production, vente, transfert, etc.	..	109 072	299 225	378 627	647 248	617 132	648 602	722 883	839 589	903 904
5110 Impôts généraux	..	62 566	182 231	236 876	423 986	390 697	393 878	441 164	512 316	538 824
5111 Taxes sur la valeur ajoutée	..	62 566	181 772	236 198	423 265	389 950	393 160	440 486	511 508	537 954
Recettes TVA (brute)	..	63 634	184 378	243 898	464 265	463 300	443 660	500 986	582 033	588 978
Remboursements de la TVA	..	-1 068	-2 606	-7 700	-41 000	-73 350	-50 500	-60 500	-70 525	-51 025
5112 Impôts sur les ventes	..	0	0	0	0	0	0	0	0	0

Table 5.2. **Burkina Faso** *(cont.)*

Details of tax revenue / Recettes fiscales détaillées

Million XOF

	1998	2000	2008	2010	2013	2014	2015	2016	2017	2018
5113 Autres impôts	..	0	459	678	721	746	719	678	808	870
Taxe sur chiffre d'affaires	..	0	0	0	0	0	0	0	0	0
Taxe de développement touristique	..	0	459	678	721	746	719	678	808	870
5120 Impôts sur biens et services déterminés	..	46 506	116 994	141 750	223 262	226 435	254 723	281 719	327 273	365 080
5121 Accises	..	16 129	38 831	46 912	57 378	77 469	94 105	105 434	129 214	140 930
Boissons	..	4 954	11 036	13 887	22 143	24 434	26 202	30 596	35 726	36 685
Taxes sur le café, le thé et les noix de cola	..	549	511	938	1 187	1 098	1 603	1 417	1 380	1 500
Taxe sur les produits pétroliers	..	10 515	27 057	31 710	33 021	50 988	65 266	71 818	90 167	100 432
Taxe sur les tabacs et allumettes	..	111	226	139	783	691	789	1 187	1 279	1 839
Autres accises	..	0	0	239	245	257	246	415	662	474
5122 Bénéfices des monopoles fiscaux	..	2 912	4 634	7 234	10 915	11 831	15 212	17 668	18 360	22 259
Monopole des tabacs	..	2 912	4 634	7 234	10 915	11 831	15 212	17 668	18 360	22 259
5123 Droits de douane et droits à l'importation	..	25 242	71 440	85 075	150 486	130 085	128 465	140 632	161 095	182 180
Redevance informatique et statistique	..	3 574	8 207	10 030	18 457	15 435	16 218	17 484	20 852	22 277
Droits de douanes	..	21 589	63 233	75 045	132 029	114 649	112 247	123 148	140 243	159 903
Taxe dégressive de protection	..	79	0	0	0	0	0	0	0	0
5124 Taxes à l'exportation	..	572	563	434	632	685	601	416	455	454
Contribution du secteur élevage	..	572	563	434	632	685	601	416	455	454
5125 Impôts sur biens d'équipement	..	0	0	0	0	0	0	0	0	0
5126 Impôts sur services déterminés	..	1 651	1 527	2 096	3 851	6 366	16 339	17 570	18 149	19 139
Taxe sur billets avions	..	3	335	349	709	608	563	671	697	645
Taxe spécifique sur les entreprises de télécommunication	..	0	0	0	0	1 980	11 970	11 965	12 268	13 152
Taxe sur les contrats d'assurance	..	1 648	1 192	1 748	3 141	3 777	3 806	4 373	4 338	4 007
Taxe sur les jeux de hasard	..	0	0	0	0	0	0	561	847	1 335
5127 Autres impôts sur commerce et transact. internat.	..	0	0	0	0	0	0	0	0	0
5128 Autres impôts	..	0	0	0	0	0	0	0	0	119
5130 Non ventilables entre 5110 et 5120	..	0	0	0	0	0	0	0	0	0
5200 Impôts sur utilisation des biens et exerc. activites	..	10 503	24 432	98 077	40 146	43 335	38 970	45 082	52 634	53 794
5210 Impôts périodiques	..	3 837	6 346	70 529	10 144	11 136	12 022	14 361	16 270	19 339
5211 A la charge des ménages: véhicules à moteur	..	0	0	0	0	0	0	0	0	0
5212 A la charge autres agents: véhicules à moteur	..	0	0	0	0	0	0	0	0	0
5213 Autres impôts périodiques	..	3 837	6 346	70 529	10 144	11 136	12 022	14 361	16 270	19 339
Taxe sur les armes	..	0	33	32	34	31	30	34	36	38
Contribution des patentes	..	3 347	5 361	7 218	8 715	9 802	10 736	13 087	13 557	18 186
Taxe de visionnnement et de vérification	..	9	60	82	99	93	0	0	0	0
Matière forestière, faune sauvage et pêche	..	461	859	1 215	1 067	1 190	1 239	1 183	1 159	1 093
Recettes en matière d'hydraulique	..	0	12	0	10	0	0	0	0	0
Autorisation d'exploiter les hôtels et les restaurants	..	0	0	0	0	0	0	0	1	4
Licence de téléphonie mobile	..	0	0	61 793	0	0	0	0	1 500	0
Licence - vente à la consommation	..	20	20	190	219	20	18	56	16	17
5220 Impôts non-périodiques	..	6 666	18 086	27 547	30 002	32 199	26 948	30 721	36 365	34 456
Autres droits d'enregistrement	..	4 418	14 645	22 202	22 251	24 689	21 309	24 410	31 001	29 372
Taxe de jouissance	..	2 241	3 425	5 327	7 748	7 505	5 637	6 302	5 339	5 066
Licences d'agences et de guides touristiques	..	0	4	3	0	0	0	3	17	17
Agrément armes à feu	..	0	0	0	0	1	0	2	0	1
Agréments au code des investissements	..	7	12	14	2	4	2	3	8	0
5300 Non ventilables entre 5100 et 5200	..	3 726	1 234	1 501	3 713	709	2 452	3 514	2 470	4 573
Autres impôts non ventilables	..	74	147	169	436	253	264	668	641	734
Taxe préférentielle communautaire	..	3 154	0	0	0	0	0	0	0	0
Taxe pour le développement de la télévision	..	498	1 087	1 332	3 277	456	2 188	2 846	1 829	3 839
6000 Autres impôts	**..**	**1 502**	**3 066**	**6 452**	**5 553**	**6 988**	**6 579**	**8 089**	**10 262**	**9 810**
Droits de timbre	..	1 436	3 025	5 678	5 524	6 885	6 538	7 995	10 191	9 770
Autres recettes fiscales	..	66	41	774	29	102	41	94	71	39
6100 A la charge exclusive des entreprises	..	..	..	..	..	..	..	..	..	..
6200 A la charge d'autres agents	..	..	..	..	..	..	..	..	..	..

.. Non disponible

Note : Année civile se terminant le 31 décembre.

Les chiffres n'incluent pas les recettes fiscales collectées par les collectivités locales car elles ne sont pas disponibles. Cependant, ils incluent des recettes collectées par l'administration centrale au profit des collectivités locales.

Les recettes provenant de la taxe de location de biens, des droits sur les titres miniers, des redevances minières et des frais administratifs sont incluses dans les recettes non fiscales comme le préconise la classification OCDE (voir le guide d'interprétation en Annexe A). La classification nationale du Burkina Faso les comptabilise comme des recettes fiscales.

À partir de 2018, les impôts sur le revenu des créances et les impôts sur le revenu des valeurs mobilières sont rapportés ensemble sous la rubrique des impôts sur le revenu des capitaux mobiliers.

Source : Ministère de l'Économie, des Finances et du Développement du Burkina Faso.

StatLink https://doi.org/10.1787/888934183142

Table 5.3. **Cabo Verde**

Details of tax revenue / Recettes fiscales détaillées

Million CVE

	1998	2000	2008	2010	2013	2014	2015	2016	2017	2018
Recettes fiscales totales	**8 376**	**10 974**	**28 578**	**25 552**	**27 301**	**26 088**	**29 667**	**31 056**	**34 885**	**39 159**
1000 Impôts sur revenu, bénéfices et gains en capital	**2 874**	**3 913**	**8 526**	**7 892**	**8 596**	**7 747**	**9 669**	**10 050**	**11 292**	**12 300**
1100 Des personnes physiques	2 156	2 958	4 825	4 645	4 793	4 998	5 327	6 317	7 062	6 927
1110 Sur le revenu et les bénéfices	..	..	..	..	..	..	..	..	..	..
1120 Sur les gains en capital	..	..	..	..	..	..	..	..	..	..
1200 Des sociétés	719	955	3 701	3 247	3 802	2 749	4 342	3 733	4 230	5 374
1210 Sur les bénéfices	..	..	..	..	..	..	..	..	..	..
1220 Sur les gains en capital	..	..	..	..	..	..	..	..	..	..
1300 Non ventilables entre 1100 et 1200	0	0	0	0	0	0	0	0	0	0
2000 Cotisations de sécurité sociale	**0**	**569**	**51**	**42**	**43**	**56**	**46**	**56**	**60**	**77**
2100 A la charge des salariés	..	..	..	..	..	..	..	..	..	..
2110 Sur la base du salaire	..	..	..	..	..	..	..	..	..	..
2120 Sur la base de l'impôt sur le revenu	..	..	..	..	..	..	..	..	..	..
2200 A la charge des employeurs	..	..	..	..	..	..	..	..	..	..
2210 Sur la base du salaire	..	..	..	..	..	..	..	..	..	..
2220 Sur la base de l'impôt sur le revenu	..	..	..	..	..	..	..	..	..	..
2300 A charge des travailleurs indép. ou sans emploi	..	..	..	..	..	..	..	..	..	..
2310 Sur la base du salaire	..	..	..	..	..	..	..	..	..	..
2320 Sur la base de l'impôt sur le revenu	..	..	..	..	..	..	..	..	..	..
2400 Non ventilables entre 2100, 2200 et 2300	..	569	51	42	43	56	46	56	60	77
2410 Sur la base du salaire	..	569	51	42	43	56	46	56	60	77
Contributions pour la sécurité sociale	..	11	30	28	38	49	40	56	60	77
Taxe sociale unique	..	558	21	14	5	7	5	0	0	0
2420 Sur la base de l'impôt sur le revenu	..	0	0	0	0	0	0	0	0	0
3000 Sur salaires ou main d'oeuvre	**0**	**0**	**0**	**0**	**0**	**0**	**0**	**0**	**0**	**0**
4000 Impôts sur le patrimoine	**345**	**584**	**1 466**	**701**	**668**	**668**	**582**	**472**	**509**	**742**
4100 Impôts périodiques sur la propriété immobilière	0	0	0	0	0	0	0	0	0	0
4110 Ménages	..	..	..	..	..	..	..	..	..	..
4120 Autres agents	..	..	..	..	..	..	..	..	..	..
4200 Impôts périodiques sur l'actif net	0	0	0	0	0	0	0	0	0	0
4210 Personnes physiques	..	..	..	..	..	..	..	..	..	..
4220 Sociétés	..	..	..	..	..	..	..	..	..	..
4300 Impôts sur mut. par décès, succ. et donations	0	0	0	0	0	0	0	0	0	0
4310 Impôts sur mut. par décès et successions	..	..	..	..	..	..	..	..	..	..
4320 Impôts sur les donations	..	..	..	..	..	..	..	..	..	..
4400 Impôts sur transact. mobilières et immob.	345	584	1 466	701	668	668	582	472	509	742
4500 Impôts non-périodiques	0	0	0	0	0	0	0	0	0	0
4510 Sur l'actif net	..	..	..	..	..	..	..	..	..	..
4520 Autres non-périodiques	..	..	..	..	..	..	..	..	..	..
4600 Autres impôts périodiques sur patrimoine	0	0	0	0	0	0	0	0	0	0
5000 Impôts sur les biens et services	**5 157**	**5 908**	**18 536**	**16 917**	**17 995**	**17 618**	**19 370**	**20 479**	**23 023**	**26 039**
5100 Impôts sur production, vente, transfert, etc.	5 157	5 908	18 536	16 917	17 995	17 618	19 370	20 479	23 023	26 039
5110 Impôts généraux	0	0	11 086	10 035	9 996	9 458	10 824	11 017	12 646	15 139
5111 Taxes sur la valeur ajoutée	..	..	11 086	10 035	9 996	9 458	10 824	11 017	12 646	15 139
TVA à l'importation (brute) - DGA	..	..	6 912	6 180	6 602	6 253	6 358	6 601	7 260	7 801
TVA intérieure (brute) - DGCI	..	..	4 811	4 341	3 921	3 917	4 935	5 385	6 046	8 412
Remboursements de la TVA	..	..	-638	-486	-526	-712	-469	-969	-661	-1 074
5112 Impôts sur les ventes	..	..	0	0	0	0	0	0	0	0
5113 Autres impôts	..	..	0	0	0	0	0	0	0	0
5120 Impôts sur biens et services déterminés	5 157	5 908	7 450	6 882	7 998	8 160	8 546	9 462	10 377	10 900
5121 Accises	1 706	1 938	1 562	1 494	2 235	2 065	2 073	2 228	2 621	2 680
Taxe spéciale sur la consommation	1 706	1 812	1 340	1 227	1 664	1 507	1 478	1 550	1 937	1 963
Taxe écologique	0	126	222	267	571	558	595	678	684	717
5122 Bénéfices des monopoles fiscaux	0	0	0	0	0	0	0	0	0	0
5123 Droits de douane et droits à l'importation	3 451	3 971	5 888	5 388	5 434	5 497	5 827	6 523	6 906	7 409
5124 Taxes à l'exportation	0	0	0	0	0	0	0	0	0	0
5125 Impôts sur biens d'équipement	0	0	0	0	0	0	0	0	0	0
5126 Impôts sur services déterminés	0	0	0	0	329	598	645	711	849	811
Contribution touristique	..	..	..	..	329	598	645	711	849	811
Autres (taxe incendie, taxe touristique)	..	..	..	..	0	0	0	0	0	0
5127 Autres impôts sur commerce et transact. internat.	0	0	0	0	0	0	0	0	0	0
5128 Autres impôts	0	0	0	0	0	0	0	0	0	0
5130 Non ventilables entre 5110 et 5120	0	0	0	0	0	0	0	0	0	0
5200 Impôts sur utilisation des biens et exerc. activites	0	0	0	0	0	0	0	0	0	0

Table 5.3. **Cabo Verde** *(cont.)*

Details of tax revenue / Recettes fiscales détaillées

Million CVE

	1998	2000	2008	2010	2013	2014	2015	2016	2017	2018
5210 Impôts périodiques	..	..	..	..	..	..	..	..	..	..
5211 A la charge des ménages: véhicules à moteur	..	..	..	..	..	..	..	..	..	..
5212 A la charge autres agents: véhicules à moteur	..	..	..	..	..	..	..	..	..	..
5213 Autres impôts périodiques	..	..	..	..	..	..	..	..	..	..
5220 Impôts non-périodiques	..	..	..	..	..	..	..	..	..	..
5300 Non ventilables entre 5100 et 5200	0	0	0	0	0	0	0	0	0	0
6000 Autres impôts	**0**	**0**	**0**	**0**	**0**	**0**	**0**	**0**	**0**	**0**
6100 A la charge exclusive des entreprises	..	..	..	..	..	..	..	..	..	..
6200 A la charge d'autres agents	..	..	..	..	..	..	..	..	..	..

.. Non disponible

Note : Année civile se terminant le 31 décembre.

Les données sont sur la base des encaissements.

Les chiffres n'incluent pas les données recettes fiscales collectées par les collectivités locales car elles ne sont pas disponibles.

Le prélèvement communautaire de la CEDEAO (Communauté économique des États de l'Afrique de l'Ouest) n'est pas compris parmi les impôts selon le guide d'interprétation de l'OCDE (voir § 4). La classification nationale du Cabo Verde le compte comme une recette fiscale. Cette recette qui n'est pas comprise dans le total des recettes fiscales ou des recettes non fiscales est présentée à titre de rubrique « Pour mémoire » dans le tableau 6.7 du chapitre 6.

Rubrique 4400: Cette rubrique comprend les droits de timbre, classifiés au Cabo Verde dans la rubrique « autres impôts ».

Rubrique 5126 : La taxe incendie et le taxe touristique sont classifiés dans la rubrique « autres impôts » au Cabo Verde.

Source : Ministère des Finances et du Plan du Cabo Verde.

StatLink https://doi.org/10.1787/888934183427

Table 5.4. **Cameroon / Cameroun**

Details of tax revenue / Recettes fiscales détaillées

Million XAF

	1998	2000	2008	2010	2013	2014	2015	2016	2017	2018
Recettes fiscales totales	**677 617**	**810 500**	**1 481 859**	**1 571 695**	**2 258 738**	**2 486 045**	**2 687 926**	**2 743 908**	**2 935 179**	**3 146 494**
1000 Impôts sur revenu, bénéfices et gains en capital	**193 000**	**228 100**	**444 902**	**425 741**	**693 317**	**784 122**	**867 834**	**771 155**	**741 551**	**848 398**
1100 Des personnes physiques	77 400	87 100	86 602	102 793	158 622	175 021	185 512	179 475	200 845	247 546
1110 Sur le revenu et les bénéfices	77 400	87 100	86 592	102 728	158 338	174 190	184 213	177 669	199 386	246 321
Traitements, salaires, pensions et rentes viagères	50 000	60 800	74 082	86 440	120 908	127 331	135 738	131 524	139 280	165 187
Revenus fonciers	0	0	2 231	2 402	6 135	13 247	12 405	12 716	13 058	14 401
Bénéfices artisanaux, industriels et commerciaux	0	0	4 722	5 342	16 267	13 648	21 010	15 689	26 107	29 610
Bénéfices agricoles	0	0	52	47	22	27	56	31	30	161
Bénéfices des professions non commerciales	0	0	263	295	612	592	2 875	5 687	9 750	24 643
Autres impôts sur le revenu	27 400	26 300	5 243	8 202	14 394	19 345	12 130	12 022	11 162	12 319
1120 Sur les gains en capital	..	..	10	65	284	831	1 299	1 806	1 459	1 225
Impôts sur plus-values sur cession immobilière	..	..	6	46	263	830	1 297	1 803	1 440	1 223
Impôts sur les autres gains en capital	..	..	4	19	21	1	2	3	19	2
1200 Des sociétés	97 100	119 400	292 488	256 404	428 360	460 571	538 969	460 785	385 971	441 882
1210 Sur les bénéfices	97 100	119 400	292 488	256 404	428 360	460 571	538 969	460 785	385 971	441 882
Bénéfices des sociétés pétrolières	37 700	39 000	124 379	83 764	169 689	161 724	171 891	108 966	66 471	86 948
Bénéfices des sociétés non pétrolières	59 400	80 400	168 109	172 639	258 671	298 847	367 078	351 818	319 500	354 934
1220 Sur les gains en capital	..	..	..	..	..	..	..	..	..	..
1300 Non ventilables entre 1100 et 1200	18 500	21 600	65 812	66 544	106 335	148 530	143 352	130 896	154 735	158 970
Taxe spéciale sur les revenus payés à l'étranger	11 900	12 400	37 301	38 877	61 708	97 511	84 412	68 691	62 806	67 809
Impôts sur les revenus des capitaux mobiliers	6 600	9 200	27 780	27 629	40 177	44 489	48 774	39 350	42 155	42 715
Centimes communaux sur l'impôt sur le revenu	0	0	731	39	4 450	6 530	10 166	22 855	49 774	48 446
2000 Cotisations de sécurité sociale	**49 217**	**65 500**	**99 828**	**135 747**	**160 134**	**153 707**	**160 992**	**200 960**	**213 796**	**226 610**
2100 A la charge des salariés	16 232	19 747	28 944	33 297	42 212	40 917	44 669	44 655	45 763	48 105
2110 Sur la base du salaire	16 232	19 747	28 944	33 297	42 212	40 917	44 669	44 655	45 763	48 105
2120 Sur la base de l'impôt sur le revenu	0	0	0	0	0	0	0	0	0	0
2200 A la charge des employeurs	..	..	..	..	..	..	..	..	..	..
2210 Sur la base du salaire	..	..	..	..	..	..	..	..	..	..
2220 Sur la base de l'impôt sur le revenu	..	..	..	..	..	..	..	..	..	..
2300 A charge des travailleurs indép. ou sans emploi	..	..	..	..	..	..	..	..	..	..
2310 Sur la base du salaire	..	..	..	..	..	..	..	..	..	..
2320 Sur la base de l'impôt sur le revenu	..	..	..	..	..	..	..	..	..	..
2400 Non ventilables entre 2100, 2200 et 2300	32 985	45 753	70 884	102 450	117 922	112 790	116 323	156 305	168 033	178 505
2410 Sur la base du salaire	32 985	45 753	70 884	102 450	117 922	112 790	116 323	156 305	168 033	178 505
2420 Sur la base de l'impôt sur le revenu	0	0	0	0	0	0	0	0	0	0
3000 Sur salaires ou main d'oeuvre	**0**	**0**	**12 656**	**17 860**	**39 817**	**46 902**	**53 572**	**52 826**	**54 350**	**32 131**
4000 Impôts sur le patrimoine	**5 300**	**13 100**	**18 379**	**18 003**	**20 816**	**21 024**	**25 437**	**30 471**	**33 393**	**25 311**
4100 Impôts périodiques sur la propriété immobilière	0	500	1 728	1 552	1 714	1 692	1 743	3 905	3 652	2 443
4110 Ménages	..	..	..	..	..	..	..	..	..	..
4120 Autres agents	..	..	..	..	..	..	..	..	..	..
4200 Impôts périodiques sur l'actif net	0	0	0	0	0	0	0	0	0	0
4210 Personnes physiques	..	..	..	..	..	..	..	..	..	..
4220 Sociétés	..	..	..	..	..	..	..	..	..	..
4300 Impôts sur mut. par décès, succ. et donations	0	0	10	39	157	214	62	160	60	86
4310 Impôts sur mut. par décès et successions	..	..	10	39	157	214	62	160	60	86
4320 Impôts sur les donations	..	..	0	0	0	0	0	0	0	0
4400 Impôts sur transact. mobilières et immob.	5 300	12 600	16 641	16 412	18 945	19 117	23 632	26 406	29 681	22 782
Droits d'enregistrement sur les mutations entre vifs	..	..	32	32	287	586	391	376	577	76
Droits d'enrgmnt. sur les mutations immob.	..	..	1 704	2 747	3 343	3 250	3 080	2 921	3 107	3 924
Droits de bail	..	..	5 223	4 602	2 337	2 725	2 364	2 425	2 452	2 395
Droits autres mutations et transactions	..	..	9 680	9 031	12 978	12 556	17 797	20 685	23 545	16 388
4500 Impôts non-périodiques	0	0	0	0	0	0	0	0	0	0
4510 Sur l'actif net	..	..	..	..	..	..	..	..	..	..
4520 Autres non-périodiques	..	..	..	..	..	..	..	..	..	..
4600 Autres impôts périodiques sur patrimoine	0	0	0	0	0	0	0	0	0	0
5000 Impôts sur les biens et services	**430 100**	**503 800**	**880 141**	**944 412**	**1 296 237**	**1 448 405**	**1 532 668**	**1 642 804**	**1 844 728**	**1 958 026**
5100 Impôts sur production, vente, transfert, etc.	428 400	501 100	873 676	936 564	1 287 824	1 438 522	1 522 834	1 632 420	1 834 787	1 948 068
5110 Impôts généraux	210 000	260 900	489 593	490 521	743 099	826 250	883 618	928 368	1 066 216	1 158 458
5111 Taxes sur la valeur ajoutée	0	260 900	489 592	490 513	743 078	826 225	883 580	928 368	1 066 216	1 158 458
TVA intérieure (brute)	..	186 500	329 785	299 504	472 885	532 980	604 046	629 355	803 903	846 136
TVA à la porte (brute)	..	107 300	224 207	259 343	315 945	358 184	354 701	355 033	344 389	384 310
Remboursements de la TVA	..	-32 900	-64 399	-68 333	-45 752	-64 938	-75 167	-56 020	-82 076	-71 988
5112 Impôts sur les ventes	0	0	0	0	0	0	0	0	0	0
5113 Autres impôts	210 000	0	1	8	20	25	39	0	0	0

Table 5.4. **Cameroon / Cameroun** *(cont.)*

Details of tax revenue / Recettes fiscales détaillées

Million XAF

	1998	2000	2008	2010	2013	2014	2015	2016	2017	2018
5120 Impôts sur biens et services déterminés	218 400	240 200	384 083	446 043	544 726	612 272	639 216	704 052	768 571	789 609
5121 Accises	84 200	84 000	147 182	164 943	220 643	240 269	289 280	323 562	334 313	337 533
Droits d'accises intérieure	21 500	26 500	65 410	68 414	95 553	98 327	170 164	204 785	193 857	192 954
Droits d'accises à la porte	1 600	1 900	10 320	12 936	14 817	14 762	14 608	12 662	17 872	16 655
Taxe spéciale sur les produits pétroliers	61 100	55 600	71 451	82 962	109 598	118 515	103 773	105 579	122 036	127 456
Vignette sur tabac et produits manufacturés	0	0	2	632	675	8 665	736	537	548	469
5122 Bénéfices des monopoles fiscaux	0	0	0	0	0	0	0	0	0	0
5123 Droits de douane et droits à l'importation	97 700	119 900	219 745	261 731	299 976	345 511	320 314	350 705	397 478	394 169
5124 Taxes à l'exportation	25 400	24 300	5 289	8 793	13 054	15 089	17 133	16 330	22 654	36 581
5125 Impôts sur biens d'équipement	0	0	0	0	0	0	0	0	0	0
5126 Impôts sur services déterminés	1 700	1 100	3 223	3 600	4 930	5 238	5 035	6 387	6 059	12 271
5127 Autres impôts sur commerce et transact. internat.	0	0	0	0	0	0	0	0	0	0
5128 Autres impôts	9 400	10 900	8 644	6 977	6 123	6 165	7 454	7 068	8 068	9 054
5130 Non ventilables entre 5110 et 5120	0	0	0	0	0	0	0	0	0	0
5200 Impôts sur utilisation des biens et exerc. activités	1 700	2 700	6 465	7 848	8 413	9 883	9 835	10 385	9 940	9 959
5210 Impôts périodiques	1 700	2 700	6 465	7 848	8 413	9 883	9 835	10 385	9 940	9 959
5211 A la charge des ménages: véhicules à moteur	1 200	1 600	4 734	6 111	6 640	7 819	7 539	8 050	7 386	7 000
5212 A la charge autres agents: véhicules à moteur	500	1 100	1 652	1 663	1 707	1 985	2 213	2 205	2 451	2 710
5213 Autres impôts périodiques	0	0	78	74	67	79	83	130	103	248
5220 Impôts non-périodiques	0	0	0	0	0	0	0	0	0	0
5300 Non ventilables entre 5100 et 5200	0	0	0	0	0	0	0	0	0	0
6000 Autres impôts	**0**	**0**	**25 953**	**29 932**	**48 416**	**31 885**	**47 424**	**45 692**	**47 360**	**56 018**
6100 A la charge exclusive des entreprises	..	..	..	..	..	..	..	..	..	..
6200 A la charge d'autres agents	..	..	..	..	..	..	..	..	..	..

.. Non disponible

Note : Année civile se terminant le 31 décembre.

Les données sont sur la base des encaissements.

Les chiffres n'incluent pas les recettes fiscales collectées par les administrations infranationales car elles ne sont pas disponibles.

Rubrique 2000 : Les cotisations de sécurité sociale du secteur public (APU) incluent uniquement les cotisations pour les retraites et ne couvrent pas les prestations familiales et d'invalidité.

Rubrique 5111 : Les données antérieures à 1999 correspondent aux recettes de la taxe sur le chiffre d'affaire (TCA) et ont été reclassées dans la rubrique « 5113 Autres impôts généraux sur les biens et services ». La TVA a été introduite au Cameroun en 1999. Dans cette édition, les données de recettes TVA sont présentées nettes de remboursements TVA comme le préconise la classification OCDE (voir le guide d'interprétation en Annexe A).

Source : Ministère des Finances du Cameroun.

StatLink https://doi.org/10.1787/888934183389

Table 5.5. **Chad / Tchad**

Details of tax revenue / Recettes fiscales détaillées

Million XAF

	1998	2000	2008	2010	2013	2014	2015	2016	2017	2018
Recettes fiscales totales	..	..	..	**777 726**	**982 340**	**762 016**	**369 818**	**245 465**	**345 712**	**437 105**
1000 Impôts sur revenu, bénéfices et gains en capital	..	..	..	**600 156**	**732 691**	**504 189**	**210 813**	**125 078**	**173 818**	**252 080**
1100 Des personnes physiques	..	..	..	55 327	92 272	97 997	94 216	86 497	88 590	85 027
1110 Sur le revenu et les bénéfices	..	..	..	55 327	92 272	97 997	94 216	86 497	88 590	85 027
Salariés, Bénéficiaires des pensions et rentes viagères	..	..	..	45 127	69 021	67 134	62 041	61 862	62 232	44 714
Bénéfice des proféssions libérales (non commerciales)	..	..	..	4 877	12 157	18 395	21 221	14 983	13 095	15 520
Bénéfice industriel et commercial	..	..	..	307	113	123	82	1 093	1 644	1 056
Propriétaires fonciers	..	..	..	1 470	2 044	1 817	2 434	281	1 094	7 063
Revenus des capitaux et valeurs mobilières	..	..	..	3 546	8 937	10 528	8 438	8 278	10 526	16 674
1120 Sur les gains en capital	..	..	..	0	0	0	0	0	0	0
1200 Des sociétés	..	..	..	539 410	638 233	404 027	114 480	36 730	83 464	165 042
1210 Sur les bénéfices	..	..	..	539 410	638 233	404 027	114 480	36 730	83 464	165 042
Impots sur les bénéfices des sociétés pétrolières	..	..	..	464 428	568 274	314 448	41 797	0	32 339	115 930
Impots sur les bénéfices des sociétés non-pétrolières	..	..	..	53 381	36 379	58 520	60 901	29 937	43 741	39 784
Autres impôts sur les sociétés	..	..	..	21 601	33 580	31 059	11 782	6 794	7 384	9 329
1220 Sur les gains en capital	..	..	..	0	0	0	0	0	0	0
1300 Non ventilables entre 1100 et 1200	..	..	..	5 418	2 186	2 165	2 118	1 850	1 763	2 011
2000 Cotisations de sécurité sociale	..	..	..	..	..	..	..	..	..	..
2100 A la charge des salariés	..	..	..	..	..	..	..	..	..	..
2110 Sur la base du salaire	..	..	..	..	..	..	..	..	..	..
2120 Sur la base de l'impôt sur les revenus	..	..	..	..	..	..	..	..	..	..
2200 A la charge des employeurs	..	..	..	..	..	..	..	..	..	..
2210 Sur la base du salaire	..	..	..	..	..	..	..	..	..	..
2220 Sur la base de l'impôt sur le revenu	..	..	..	..	..	..	..	..	..	..
2300 A charge des travailleurs indép. ou sans emploi	..	..	..	..	..	..	..	..	..	..
2310 Sur la base du salaire	..	..	..	..	..	..	..	..	..	..
2320 Sur la base de l'impôt sur le revenu	..	..	..	..	..	..	..	..	..	..
2400 Non ventilables entre 2100, 2200 et 2300	..	..	..	..	..	..	..	..	..	..
2410 Sur la base du salaire	..	..	..	..	..	..	..	..	..	..
2420 Sur la base de l'impôt sur le revenu	..	..	..	..	..	..	..	..	..	..
3000 Sur salaires ou main d'oeuvre	..	..	..	**8 304**	**10 238**	**11 322**	**10 856**	**6 703**	**6 860**	**1 514**
4000 Impôts sur le patrimoine	..	..	..	**23 875**	**38 254**	**24 268**	**11 922**	**7 909**	**5 740**	**7 013**
4100 Impôts périodiques sur la propriété immobilière	..	..	..	0	0	0	0	0	0	0
4110 Ménages	..	..	..	..	..	..	..	..	..	..
4120 Autres agents	..	..	..	..	..	..	..	..	..	..
4200 Impôts périodiques sur l'actif net	..	..	..	0	0	0	0	0	0	0
4210 Personnes physiques	..	..	..	..	..	..	..	..	..	..
4220 Sociétés	..	..	..	..	..	..	..	..	..	..
4300 Impôts sur mut. par décès, succ. et donations	..	..	..	71	1	0	0	0	1	12
4310 Impôts sur mut. par décès et successions	..	..	..	8	1	0	0	0	0	1
4320 Impôts sur les donations	..	..	..	63	0	0	0	0	1	12
4400 Impôts sur transact. mobilières et immob.	..	..	..	23 651	37 942	24 055	11 473	7 713	5 630	6 883
4500 Impôts non-périodiques	..	..	..	153	311	213	449	197	109	118
4510 Sur l'actif net	..	..	..	0	0	0	0	0	0	0
4520 Autres non-périodiques	..	..	..	153	311	213	449	197	109	118
4600 Autres impôts périodiques sur patrimoine	..	..	..	0	0	0	0	0	0	0
5000 Impôts sur les biens et services	..	..	..	**145 324**	**201 048**	**222 153**	**136 165**	**105 775**	**159 234**	**176 498**
5100 Impôts sur production, vente, transfert, etc.	..	..	..	143 179	199 951	220 860	134 015	105 772	158 034	176 351
5110 Impôts généraux	..	..	..	78 219	114 593	137 290	66 730	73 539	94 375	68 621
5111 Taxes sur la valeur ajoutée	..	..	..	78 219	114 593	137 290	66 730	73 539	94 375	68 621
Taxe sur la valeur ajoutée intérieure	..	..	..	46 148	63 038	65 085	45 476	56 619	69 912	36 401
TVA a l'importation	..	..	..	32 071	51 555	72 205	21 254	16 920	24 463	32 219
5112 Impôts sur les ventes	..	..	..	0	0	0	0	0	0	0
5113 Autres impôts	..	..	..	0	0	0	0	0	0	0
5120 Impôts sur biens et services déterminés	..	..	..	64 960	85 358	83 569	67 285	32 233	63 659	107 730
5121 Accises	..	..	..	9 387	6 916	7 370	10 161	9 290	19 724	27 020
Droit d'accises intérieurs	..	..	..	2 356	4 266	6 369	7 045	7 921	13 728	24 242
Droit d'accises importation	..	..	..	243	415	246	125	126	1 738	1 260
Carburants et lubrifiants	..	..	..	6 168	1 540	0	1 814	0	2 544	0
Taxe sur vente de bétail	..	..	..	621	695	755	1 177	1 243	1 714	1 517
5122 Bénéfices de monopoles fiscaux	..	..	..	0	0	0	0	0	0	0

Table 5.5. **Chad / Tchad** *(cont.)*

Details of tax revenue / Recettes fiscales détaillées

Million XAF

	1998	2000	2008	2010	2013	2014	2015	2016	2017	2018
5123 Droits de douane et droits à l'importation	..	..	..	35 634	61 619	57 285	48 642	19 540	35 988	61 982
Droits de douane	..	..	..	28 548	53 078	49 339	44 056	17 153	25 729	46 428
Redevance statistique	..	..	..	7 086	8 541	7 947	4 586	2 386	10 258	15 554
5124 Taxes à l'exportation	..	..	..	19 078	16 137	18 461	8 016	2 868	4 668	18 008
Redevance statistique consortium	..	..	..	16 821	14 670	15 935	5 419	1 088	1 860	13 893
Droits de sortie	..	..	..	2 257	1 467	2 526	2 597	1 780	2 808	4 116
5125 Impôts sur biens d'équipement	..	..	..	0	0	0	0	0	0	0
5126 Impôts sur services déterminés	..	..	..	775	666	420	431	535	3 253	720
5127 Autres impôts sur commerce et transact. internat.	..	..	..	0	0	0	0	0	0	0
5128 Autres impôts	..	..	..	86	20	33	35	0	27	0
5130 Non ventilables entre 5110 et 5120	..	..	..	0	0	0	0	0	0	0
5200 Impôts sur utilisation des biens et exerc. activites	..	..	..	2 145	1 097	1 293	2 150	4	1 200	147
5210 Impôts périodiques	..	..	..	2 145	1 097	1 293	2 150	4	1 200	147
5211 A la charge des ménages: véhicules à moteur	..	..	..	1 567	846	792	1 929	0	678	0
5212 A la charge autres agents: véhicules à moteur	..	..	..	204	144	427	144	0	395	0
5213 Autres impôts périodiques	..	..	..	374	107	74	77	4	127	147
5220 Impôts non-périodiques	..	..	..	0	0	0	0	0	0	0
5300 Non ventilables entre 5100 et 5200	..	..	..	0	0	0	0	0	0	0
6000 Autres impôts	**..**	**..**	**..**	**67**	**108**	**85**	**62**	**0**	**60**	**0**
6100 A la charge exclusive des entreprises	..	..	..	..	..	..	..	..	..	..
6200 A la charge d'autres agents	..	..	..	..	..	..	..	..	..	..

.. Non disponible

Note : Année civile se terminant le 31 décembre.

Les données sont sur la base des encaissements dans cette édition.

Les chiffres n'incluent pas les recettes fiscales collectées par les collectivités locales car elles ne sont pas disponibles.

Les recettes provenant des amendes fiscales, des recettes des valeurs mobilières de l'Etat et de la redevance audiovisuelle sont incluses dans les recettes non fiscales comme le préconise la classification OCDE (voir le guide d'interprétation en Annexe A). La classification nationale du Tchad les comptabilise comme des recettes fiscales.

Source : Ministère des Finances et du Budget du Tchad.

StatLink https://doi.org/10.1787/888934183693

Table 5.6. **Congo**

Details of tax revenue / Recettes fiscales détaillées

Million XAF

	1998	2000	2008	2010	2013	2014	2015	2016	2017	2018
Recettes fiscales totales	**80 742**	**98 684**	**313 313**	**453 910**	**768 340**	**854 078**	**898 961**	**797 124**	**704 835**	**550 547**
1000 Impôts sur revenu, bénéfices et gains en capital	**38 077**	**47 544**	**107 774**	**150 792**	**261 715**	**290 481**	**342 763**	**308 607**	**276 438**	**204 797**
1100 Des personnes physiques	20 542	22 850	52 094	64 364	120 317	150 696	145 622	148 853	152 790	127 387
1110 Sur le revenu et les bénéfices	20 542	22 850	52 094	64 364	120 317	150 696	145 622	148 853	152 790	127 387
Traitements et salaires	19 896	21 836	46 970	54 763	87 555	107 791	103 818	99 671	113 244	103 858
Revenus fonciers	394	549	1 463	2 259	4 043	4 752	5 531	6 020	3 534	3 658
Bénéfices non commerciaux (BNC)	0	0	274	112	469	50	50	19	37	1 377
Bénéfices industriels et commerciaux (BIC)	0	0	140	25	63	67	152	307	143	175
Revenu des valeurs mobilières (IRVM)	252	466	3 247	7 176	27 306	37 120	35 441	41 625	35 517	18 092
Retenue à la source sur marchés publics et sous-traitant BTP	0	0	0	0	880	858	471	407	313	221
Autres recettes sur le revenu des personnes physiques	0	0	0	29	2	58	159	806	2	6
1120 Sur les gains en capital	0	0	0	0	0	0	0	0	0	0
1200 Des sociétés	17 535	24 694	55 680	86 428	141 398	139 786	197 141	159 753	123 648	77 411
1210 Sur les bénéfices	17 535	24 694	55 680	86 428	141 398	139 786	197 141	159 753	123 648	77 411
1220 Sur les gains en capital	0	0	0	0	0	0	0	0	0	0
1300 Non ventilables entre 1100 et 1200	0	0	0	0	0	0	0	0	0	0
2000 Cotisations de sécurité sociale	**..**	**..**	**..**	**..**	**..**	**..**	**..**	**..**	**..**	**..**
2100 A la charge des salariés	..	..	..	..	..	..	..	..	..	..
2110 Sur la base du salaire	..	..	..	..	..	..	..	..	..	..
2120 Sur la base de l'impôt sur le revenu	..	..	..	..	..	..	..	..	..	..
2200 A la charge des employeurs	..	..	..	..	..	..	..	..	..	..
2210 Sur la base du salaire	..	..	..	..	..	..	..	..	..	..
2220 Sur la base de l'impôt sur le revenu	..	..	..	..	..	..	..	..	..	..
2300 A charge des travailleurs indép. ou sans emploi	..	..	..	..	..	..	..	..	..	..
2310 Sur la base du salaire	..	..	..	..	..	..	..	..	..	..
2320 Sur la base de l'impôt sur le revenu	..	..	..	..	..	..	..	..	..	..
2400 Non ventilables entre 2100, 2200 et 2300	..	..	..	..	..	..	..	..	..	..
2410 Sur la base du salaire	..	..	..	..	..	..	..	..	..	..
2420 Sur la base de l'impôt sur le revenu	..	..	..	..	..	..	..	..	..	..
3000 Sur salaires ou main d'oeuvre	**3 452**	**4 965**	**9 281**	**16 585**	**19 476**	**22 650**	**24 528**	**22 754**	**22 962**	**20 436**
4000 Impôts sur le patrimoine	**748**	**1 299**	**2 638**	**5 311**	**7 627**	**7 289**	**16 410**	**5 979**	**6 036**	**5 547**
4100 Impôts périodiques sur la propriété immobilière	0	0	0	0	0	0	0	0	0	0
4110 Ménages	..	..	..	..	..	..	..	..	..	..
4120 Autres agents	..	..	..	..	..	..	..	..	..	..
4200 Impôts périodiques sur l'actif net	0	0	0	0	0	0	0	0	0	0
4210 Personnes physiques	..	..	..	..	..	..	..	..	..	..
4220 Sociétés	..	..	..	..	..	..	..	..	..	..
4300 Impôts sur mut. par décès, succ. et donations	0	0	0	0	0	0	0	0	0	0
4310 Impôts sur mut. par décès et successions	..	..	..	..	..	..	..	..	..	..
4320 Impôts sur les donations	..	..	..	..	..	..	..	..	..	..
4400 Impôts sur transact. mobilières et immob.	748	1 299	2 638	5 311	7 627	7 289	16 410	5 979	6 036	5 547
4500 Impôts non-périodiques	0	0	0	0	0	0	0	0	0	0
4510 Sur l'actif net	..	..	..	..	..	..	..	..	..	..
4520 Autres non-périodiques	..	..	..	..	..	..	..	..	..	..
4600 Autres impôts périodiques sur patrimoine	0	0	0	0	0	0	0	0	0	0
5000 Impôts sur les biens et services	**38 465**	**44 876**	**193 619**	**281 222**	**479 523**	**533 657**	**515 259**	**459 785**	**399 399**	**319 767**
5100 Impôts sur production, vente, transfert, etc.	38 465	44 809	193 434	280 869	478 898	532 874	513 854	458 170	398 512	318 758
5110 Impôts généraux	33 585	39 641	99 907	158 512	261 471	301 410	284 586	251 308	222 924	176 801
5111 Taxes sur la valeur ajoutée	32 368	36 889	94 796	147 032	239 267	273 943	253 875	221 768	191 438	149 645
TVA Intérieure (brute)	32 368	38 962	48 588	92 054	146 920	177 038	163 875	140 255	125 630	95 165
TVA Douane (brute)	0	0	50 226	57 110	92 347	96 905	90 000	81 512	67 756	54 480
Remboursements de la TVA	0	-2 073	-4 017	-2 132	0	0	0	0	-1 948	0
5112 Impôts sur les ventes	0	0	0	1 742	2 448	2 352	2 214	2 175	2 145	2 568
ASDI (Acompte sur divers impôts)	0	0	0	1 742	2 448	2 352	2 214	2 175	2 145	2 568
5113 Autres impôts	1 217	2 753	5 110	9 738	19 756	25 114	28 497	27 366	29 340	24 588
Taxe spéciale sur les societés (TSS)	1 217	2 753	5 110	9 738	18 633	22 830	26 248	25 999	28 288	23 758
Impôt global forfaitaire	0	0	0	0	1 122	2 285	2 250	1 366	1 052	830
5120 Impôts sur biens et services déterminés	4 824	5 059	93 289	122 357	217 427	231 464	229 268	206 862	175 588	141 956
5121 Accises	4 801	4 966	13 031	17 603	20 276	23 896	24 337	24 112	21 721	20 484
5122 Bénéfices des monopoles fiscaux	0	0	0	0	0	0	0	0	0	0
5123 Droits de douane et droits à l'importation	0	0	65 487	85 775	164 469	172 774	166 613	139 716	119 357	90 600
Recettes import/export	..	0	58 900	77 852	147 620	155 030	148 444	125 944	107 687	82 900
Recettes douanes hors budget	..	0	6 587	7 923	16 849	17 745	18 169	13 771	11 670	7 700

Table 5.6. **Congo** *(cont.)*

Details of tax revenue / Recettes fiscales détaillées

Million XAF

	1998	2000	2008	2010	2013	2014	2015	2016	2017	2018
5124 Taxes à l'exportation	0	0	0	0	0	0	0	0	0	0
5125 Impôts sur biens d'équipement	0	0	0	0	0	0	0	0	0	0
5126 Impôts sur services déterminés	23	93	14 771	18 979	32 683	34 793	38 318	43 034	34 509	30 873
Taxe sur les billets d'avion	0	0	0	597	731	780	849	791	721	634
Taxe sur les télécommunications électroniques	0	0	0	0	0	0	0	3 596	4 306	5 564
Taxe sur les assurances	23	93	826	1 526	2 251	2 009	2 703	2 250	2 418	2 741
Taxe sur le transfert de fonds	0	0	13 946	16 856	29 701	32 004	34 766	36 394	27 049	21 906
Taxe sur les jeux de hasard	0	0	0	0	0	0	0	3	14	27
5127 Autres impôts sur commerce et transact. internat.	0	0	0	0	0	0	0	0	0	0
5128 Autres impôts	0	0	0	0	0	0	0	0	0	0
5130 Non ventilables entre 5110 et 5120	56	109	238	0	0	0	0	0	0	0
5200 Impôts sur utilisation des biens et exerc. activites	0	67	185	353	625	783	1 405	1 615	887	1 009
5210 Impôts périodiques	..	67	185	353	625	783	1 405	1 615	887	834
5211 A la charge des ménages: véhicules à moteur	..	0	0	0	0	0	0	0	0	0
5212 A la charge autres agents: véhicules à moteur	..	67	185	343	625	736	1 405	1 006	887	814
5213 Autres impôts périodiques	..	0	0	10	0	47	0	608	0	20
5220 Impôts non-périodiques	..	0	0	0	0	0	0	0	0	176
Timbres sur les véhicules automobiles	..	0	0	0	0	0	0	0	0	176
5300 Non ventilables entre 5100 et 5200	0	0	0	0	0	0	0	0	0	0
6000 Autres impôts	**0**	**0**	**0**	**0**	**0**	**0**	**0**	**0**	**0**	**0**
6100 A la charge exclusive des entreprises	..	..	..	..	..	..	..	..	..	..
6200 A la charge d'autres agents	..	..	..	..	..	..	..	..	..	..

.. Non disponible

Note : Année civile se terminant le 31 décembre.

Les données sont sur la base des encaissements

Les chiffres n'incluent pas les recettes fiscales collectées par les collectivités locales car elles ne sont pas disponibles.

Les données de 2010-2018 ont été revisées et de nouvelles données ont été integrées notamment dans les rubriques 1110 impôts sur le revenu des personnes physiques, 5112 impôts sur les ventes, 5121 accises et 5126 impôts sur services déterminés.

Rubrique 1110 : les recettes des impôts sur le revenu des valeurs mobilières (IRVM) étaient classifiées dans la rubrique impôts sur les gains des personnes physiques dans l'édition précédente.

Rubrique 5123 : les données pour 2018 sont estimées.

Rubrique 5212 : les recettes de la taxe sur les vehicules de tourisme des societés (TVTS) étaient classifiées dans 5126 impôts sur services déterminés.dans l'édition précédente.

Source : Ministère des Finances de la République du Congo.

StatLink https://doi.org/10.1787/888934183408

Table 5.7. **Congo, Dem. Rep. / Congo, Rép. dém.**

Details of tax revenue / Recettes fiscales détaillées

Million CDF

	1998	2000	2008	2010	2013	2014	2015	2016	2017	2018
Recettes fiscales totales	..	**7 551**	**941 657**	**1 619 224**	**3 033 288**	**3 156 270**	**3 421 942**	**3 189 940**	**3 836 810**	**5 769 782**
1000 Impôts sur revenu, bénéfices et gains en capital	..	**2 565**	**246 095**	**446 534**	**777 735**	**1 011 772**	**1 224 168**	**976 160**	**1 410 469**	**2 563 679**
1100 Des personnes physiques	..	996	108 416	208 596	480 066	515 988	515 073	508 929	659 395	820 826
1110 Sur le revenu et les bénéfices	..	996	108 416	208 596	480 066	515 988	515 073	508 929	659 395	820 826
Impôt sur les revenus des nationaux	..	899	77 129	162 931	394 400	421 427	417 442	409 977	507 845	589 377
Impôt sur les revenus - Institutions politiques	..	0	0	1 842	16 089	20 027	16 698	18 828	17 190	21 901
Impôt sur les revenus - Fonctionnaires et agents publics	..	0	0	0	4 900	9 298	12 825	12 789	9 632	10 968
Impôt sur les revenus - Régies financières	..	0	0	0	7 237	9 727	8 186	5 094	5 022	27 654
Impôt sur les revenus - Expatriés	..	81	31 284	43 779	55 787	55 507	59 921	62 241	119 707	170 926
Impôt sur les revenus - Proféssions libérales	..	15	3	44	1 653	0	0	0	0	0
Taxe ad valorem sur les gains des parieurs (DGRAD)	..	0	0	0	0	0	0	0	0	0
1120 Sur les gains en capital	..	..	..	..	..	..	..	..	..	..
1200 Des sociétés	..	1 569	137 679	237 937	297 669	495 784	709 095	467 230	751 074	1 742 853
Impôts sur les revenus des capitaux mobiliers	..	30	12 950	23 356	45 672	49 931	53 212	53 445	65 017	164 586
1210 Sur les bénéfices	..	1 539	124 730	214 582	251 997	445 853	655 884	413 785	686 057	1 578 267
Impôt sur les bénéfices - Sociétés non pétrolières	..	1 061	106 883	194 758	220 318	390 544	607 004	365 466	604 456	1 466 176
Impôt sur les bénéfices - Non résidents	..	0	0	0	23 360	42 882	46 124	45 450	75 010	102 597
Impôt sur les bénéfices - Entreprises individuelles	..	410	9 587	19 823	8 320	12 426	2 756	2 869	6 590	9 494
Impôts sur les revenus locatifs	..	69	8 260	0	0	0	0	0	0	0
1220 Sur les gains en capital	..	..	..	..	..	..	..	..	..	..
1300 Non ventilables entre 1100 et 1200	..	0	0	0	0	0	0	0	0	0
2000 Cotisations de sécurité sociale	..	..	..	..	**169 836**	**199 653**	**201 805**	**192 372**	**286 973**	**353 019**
2100 A la charge des salariés	..	..	..	..	47 534	55 885	56 493	77 021	114 904	117 412
2110 Sur la base du salaire	..	..	..	..	47 534	55 885	56 493	77 021	114 904	117 412
2120 Sur la base de l'impôt sur le revenu	..	..	..	..	0	0	0	0	0	0
2200 A la charge des employeurs	..	..	..	..	122 231	143 705	145 268	115 287	171 915	235 521
2210 Sur la base du salaire	..	..	..	..	122 231	143 705	145 268	115 287	171 915	235 521
2220 Sur la base de l'impôt sur le revenu	..	..	..	..	0	0	0	0	0	0
2300 A charge des travailleurs indép. ou sans emploi	..	..	..	..	0	0	0	0	0	0
2310 Sur la base du salaire	..	..	..	..	..	..	..	..	..	..
2320 Sur la base de l'impôt sur le revenu	..	..	..	..	..	..	..	..	..	..
2400 Non ventilables entre 2100, 2200 et 2300	..	..	..	..	71	63	44	64	154	86
2410 Sur la base du salaire	..	..	..	..	..	..	..	..	..	..
2420 Sur la base de l'impôt sur le revenu	..	..	..	..	..	..	..	..	..	..
3000 Sur salaires ou main d'oeuvre	..	**56**	**11 856**	**15 370**	**49 092**	**49 047**	**48 503**	**43 343**	**59 173**	**91 777**
Impôt sur les rémunérations des expatriés (IERE)	..	56	11 856	15 370	49 092	49 047	48 503	43 343	59 173	91 777
4000 Impôts sur le patrimoine	..	..	..	**5 949**	**1 804**	**3 988**	**4 166**	**5 601**	**9 066**	**10 121**
4100 Impôts périodiques sur la propriété immobilière	..	0	0	0	0	0	0	0	0	0
4110 Ménages	..	..	..	..	..	..	..	..	..	..
4120 Autres agents	..	..	..	..	..	..	..	..	..	..
4200 Impôts périodiques sur l'actif net	..	0	0	0	0	0	0	0	0	0
4210 Personnes physiques	..	..	..	..	..	..	..	..	..	..
4220 Sociétés	..	..	..	..	..	..	..	..	..	..
4300 Impôts sur mut. par décès, succ. et donations	..	0	0	0	0	0	0	0	0	0
4310 Impôts sur mut. par décès et successions	..	..	..	..	..	..	..	..	..	..
4320 Impôts sur les donations	..	..	..	..	..	..	..	..	..	..
4400 Impôts sur transact. mobilières et immob.	..	..	..	5 949	1 804	3 988	4 166	5 601	9 066	10 121
4500 Impôts non-périodiques	..	0	0	0	0	0	0	0	0	0
4510 Sur l'actif net	..	..	..	..	..	..	..	..	..	..
4520 Autres non-périodiques	..	..	..	..	..	..	..	..	..	..
4600 Autres impôts périodiques sur patrimoine	..	..	..	..	..	..	..	..	..	..
5000 Impôts sur les biens et services	..	**4 931**	**595 916**	**1 052 940**	**1 873 599**	**1 746 900**	**1 864 884**	**1 935 123**	**1 996 741**	**2 550 676**
5100 Impôts sur production, vente, transfert, etc.	..	4 833	593 698	1 050 260	1 871 245	1 744 394	1 863 518	1 920 047	1 972 154	2 517 881
5110 Impôts généraux	..	1 390	353 812	588 868	999 343	804 137	891 546	1 056 002	1 127 381	1 456 884
5111 Taxes sur la valeur ajoutée	..	0	0	0	971 594	802 236	891 404	1 055 955	1 127 186	1 456 766
TVA intérieure (brute)	..	..	..	..	583 798	585 321	639 995	619 212	705 628	939 202
TVA à l'importation (brute)	..	..	..	..	864 543	873 055	879 549	561 978	538 173	766 232
Remboursements TVA	..	..	..	..	-476 747	-656 140	-628 140	-125 234	-116 616	-248 668
5112 Impôts sur les ventes	..	..	..	..	0	0	0	0	0	0

Table 5.7. **Congo, Dem. Rep. / Congo, Rép. dém.** *(cont.)*

Details of tax revenue / Recettes fiscales détaillées

Million CDF

	1998	2000	2008	2010	2013	2014	2015	2016	2017	2018
5113 Autres impôts	..	1 390	353 812	588 868	27 749	1 901	143	47	196	118
Impôt sur le chiffre d'affaires (ICA) - ventes locales	..	194	55 750	110 004	7 912	405	143	47	196	118
Impôt sur le chiffre d'affaires (ICA) - Prestations de services	..	409	112 440	181 338	16 411	1 310	0	0	0	0
Impôt sur le chiffre d'affaires (ICA) - Travaux immobiliers	..	14	1 855	5 969	3 426	186	0	0	0	0
Impôt sur le chiffre d'affaires (ICA) - Exportation produits miniers	..	0	0	0	0	0	0	0	0	0
Impôt sur le chiffre d'affaires (ICA) - Exportation hors produits miniers	..	6	0	0	0	0	0	0	0	0
ICA/ Importation	..	768	183 768	291 557	0	0	0	0	0	0
Autres impôts géneraux sur les biens et services (DGRAD)	..	0	0	0	0	0	0	0	0	0
5120 Impôts sur biens et services déterminés	..	3 442	239 886	461 392	871 902	940 257	971 972	864 044	844 773	1 060 997
5121 Accises	..	1 417	54 572	183 578	331 520	352 267	406 186	439 083	414 019	481 741
Redevances sur produits spécifiques (DGRAD)	..	0	0	0	0	0	0	0	0	0
Droits d'accises perçus en régime intérieur	..	1 380	46 959	153 005	259 580	249 131	241 476	236 188	301 406	352 244
Accises (intérieur) - Boissons	..	..	..	62 785	139 922	145 392	148 179	133 236	178 344	198 758
Accises (intérieur) - Tabacs et allumettes	..	..	..	40 034	39 465	14 316	2 643	9 149	3 875	4 901
Accises (intérieur) - Télécommunication	..	..	..	49 338	74 521	78 063	86 315	88 198	116 686	145 710
Accises (intérieur) - Autres produits	..	..	..	848	5 672	11 360	4 339	5 605	2 501	2 875
Droits d'accises perçus à l'importation	..	37	7 613	30 573	71 940	103 135	164 710	202 895	112 613	129 497
Accises (importation) - Boissons	..	..	..	2 431	12 475	10 474	13 556	13 847	11 696	20 712
Accises (importation) - Tabacs et allumettes	..	..	..	4 739	18 368	35 609	59 422	46 449	60 476	54 475
Accises (importation) - Produits pétroliers	..	..	..	9 257	9 504	12 671	53 350	102 829	0	0
Accises (importation) - Véhicules	..	..	..	9 901	12 757	11 961	15 878	12 022	15 444	23 427
Accises (importation) - Autres produits	..	..	..	4 246	18 836	32 421	22 504	27 749	24 997	30 883
5122 Bénéfices des monopoles fiscaux	..	0	0	0	0	0	0	0	0	0
5123 Droits de douane et droits à l'importation	..	1 942	176 634	270 089	533 071	580 820	560 340	420 432	423 341	569 751
5124 Taxes à l'exportation	..	83	8 680	7 725	7 311	7 171	5 446	4 529	7 413	9 505
Droits de sortie sur les minerais	..	82	7 296	3 850	2 551	2 791	3 238	2 774	5 391	4 780
Droits de sortie sur les produits agricoles	..	1	1 300	3 046	4 760	4 379	2 208	1 755	2 022	4 725
Droits de sortie sur les autres produits	..	0	84	829	0	0	0	0	0	0
5125 Impôts sur biens d'équipement	..	0	0	0	0	0	0	0	0	0
5126 Impôts sur services déterminés	..	0	0	0	0	0	0	0	0	0
5127 Autres impôts sur commerce et transact. internat.	..	0	0	0	0	0	0	0	0	0
5128 Autres impôts	..	0	0	0	0	0	0	0	0	0
5130 Non ventilables entre 5110 et 5120	..	0	0	0	0	0	0	0	0	0
5200 Impôts sur utilisation des biens et exerc. activites	..	98	2 218	2 681	2 354	2 507	1 366	15 076	24 587	32 795
5210 Impôts périodiques	..	0	0	0	0	0	0	0	0	0
5211 A la charge des ménages: véhicules à moteur	..	..	..	..	..	..	..	..	..	..
5212 A la charge autres agents: véhicules à moteur	..	..	..	..	..	..	..	..	..	..
5213 Autres impôts périodiques	..	..	..	..	..	..	..	..	..	..
5220 Impôts non-périodiques	..	98	2 218	2 681	2 354	2 507	1 366	15 076	24 587	32 795
Immatriculation des véhicules routiers (plaques)	..	98	2 218	2 681	2 353	2 507	1 366	1 373	2 425	3 734
Autorisations d'exportation et d'importation	..	0	0	0	0	0	0	2 642	4 013	4 561
Taxe d'implantation établisssements dangeureux, insalubres et incommodes	..	0	0	0	0	0	0	3 184	3 148	12 102
Autres autorisations (DGRAD)	..	0	0	0	1	0	0	7 877	15 001	12 397
5300 Non ventilables entre 5100 et 5200	..	0	0	0	0	0	0	0	0	0
6000 Autres impôts	..	**0**	**87 789**	**98 431**	**161 220**	**144 910**	**78 417**	**37 342**	**74 389**	**200 509**
Recettes des produits pétroliers	..	..	87 789	98 431	161 220	144 910	78 417	35 540	74 389	106 245
Droits proportionnels sur les S.A.R.L. (DGRAD)	..	..	0	0	0	0	0	1 803	0	94 264
6100 A la charge exclusive des entreprises	..	..	..	..	..	..	..	..	..	..
6200 A la charge d'autres agents	..	..	..	..	..	..	..	..	..	..

Table 5.7. **Congo, Dem. Rep. / Congo, Rép. dém.** *(cont.)*

Details of tax revenue / Recettes fiscales détaillées

.. Non disponible

Note : Année civile se terminant le 31 décembre.

Les données sont sur la base des encaissements.

Les chiffres n'incluent pas les données des recettes fiscales collectées par les collectivités locales car elles ne sont pas disponibles.

Les données entre 2000 à 2003 doivent être interprétées avec prudence car elles sont largement affectées par des taux d'inflation élevés.

Les recettes provenant de la vente des imprimés sont incluses dans les recettes non fiscales (Ventes de biens et services) comme le préconise la classification OCDE (voir le guide d'interprétation en Annexe A). Elles sont considérées comme des recettes fiscales en République Démocratique du Congo.

Rubriques 1110, 5113, 5121, 5220, 6000 : Pour la période 2010-18, ces rubriques contiennent des recettes provenant de la Direction Générale des Recettes Administratives, Judiciaires, Domaniales et de Participation (DGRAD) et sont annotées comme telles. Elles sont incluses dans les recettes fiscales comme le préconise la classification OCDE (voir le guide d'interprétation en Annexe A) mais considérées comme des recettes non fiscales en République Démocratique du Congo.

Rubriques 1300, 4100, 4400, 5112, 5126, 5128, 5212, 5213: Pour la période 2010-18, ces rubriques contiennent des recettes provenant exclusivement de la DGRAD. Elles sont incluses dans les recettes fiscales comme le préconise la classification OCDE (voir le guide d'interprétation en Annexe A) mais considérées comme des recettes non fiscales en République Démocratique du Congo. Le total des recettes provenant de la DGRAD considérées comme recettes fiscales représentent en moyenne 1 % du total des recettes fiscales.

Source : Ministère des Finances de la République démocratique du Congo.

StatLink https://doi.org/10.1787/888934183180

Table 5.8. **Côte d'Ivoire**

Details of tax revenue / Recettes fiscales détaillées

Million XOF

	1998	2000	2008	2010	2013	2014	2015	2016	2017	2018
Recettes fiscales totales	**1 185 560**	**1 169 607**	**1 834 334**	**2 035 467**	**2 721 780**	**2 946 103**	**3 414 417**	**3 736 454**	**3 983 682**	**4 189 129**
1000 Impôts sur revenu, bénéfices et gains en capital	**236 607**	**192 282**	**347 938**	**260 799**	**436 606**	**401 740**	**408 880**	**419 405**	**484 103**	**574 179**
1100 Des personnes physiques	5 973	5 108	5 879	6 970	9 202	9 430	10 054	10 762	12 199	13 894
1110 Sur le revenu et les bénéfices	5 958	5 093	5 850	6 937	9 166	9 388	10 011	10 711	12 147	13 822
Impôt général sur le revenu	0	0	203	1 420	995	635	817	663	283	114
Impôt BIC hors pétrole-gaz (personnes physiques)	5 917	5 045	5 558	5 431	8 017	8 610	9 008	9 859	11 660	13 457
IR des valeurs mobilières (pers. physiques)	40	48	89	86	154	143	186	189	204	252
1120 Sur les gains en capital	15	16	29	33	36	42	42	51	52	72
IR des capitaux (pers. physiques)	15	16	29	33	36	42	42	51	52	72
1200 Des sociétés	168 295	148 900	330 502	240 768	407 968	371 821	375 893	384 251	444 595	534 279
1210 Sur les bénéfices	163 230	143 602	320 769	229 732	395 918	357 867	361 782	367 300	427 439	510 483
Impôt BIC pétrole-gaz	0	0	150 351	63 649	141 732	92 389	71 985	54 962	64 392	86 071
Impôt BIC hors pétrole-gaz (personnes morales)	149 801	127 710	140 694	137 500	202 948	217 980	228 043	249 588	295 180	340 667
IR des valeurs mobilieres (pers. morales)	13 428	15 892	29 725	28 583	51 237	47 499	61 753	62 750	67 868	83 745
1220 Sur les gains en capital	5 065	5 297	9 733	11 036	12 050	13 954	14 111	16 951	17 155	23 796
Impôt sur le revenu des capitaux (personnes morales)	5 065	5 297	9 733	11 036	12 050	13 954	14 111	16 951	17 155	23 796
1300 Non ventilables entre 1100 et 1200	62 339	38 274	11 557	13 061	19 436	20 489	22 934	24 392	27 310	26 006
L'acompte d'impôt sur le revenu du secteur informel (ex ASDI)	58 460	33 983	6 464	7 624	12 286	12 509	14 637	16 380	18 567	15 845
Impôt synthétique	3 878	4 291	5 093	5 437	7 150	7 980	8 296	8 011	8 744	10 162
2000 Cotisations de sécurité sociale	**79 200**	**102 700**	**141 400**	**162 754**	**307 259**	**340 667**	**383 540**	**443 310**	**455 744**	**479 197**
2100 A la charge des salariés	..	..	..	64 364	121 401	135 406	151 728	177 045	180 368	189 616
CNPS	..	..	..	39 044	73 287	84 360	92 206	113 016	109 856	115 381
CGRAE	..	..	..	25 320	48 114	51 046	59 522	64 029	70 512	74 235
2110 Sur la base du salaire	..	..	..	..	..	..	..	..	..	..
2120 Sur la base de l'impôt sur le revenu	..	..	..	..	..	..	..	..	..	..
2200 A la charge des employeurs	..	..	..	98 390	185 858	205 261	231 812	266 265	275 376	289 581
CNPS	..	..	..	47 721	89 572	103 107	112 697	138 130	134 268	141 022
CGRAE	..	..	..	50 669	96 286	102 154	119 115	128 135	141 108	148 559
2210 Sur la base du salaire	..	..	..	..	..	..	..	..	..	..
2220 Sur la base de l'impôt sur le revenu	..	..	..	..	..	..	..	..	..	..
2300 A charge des travailleurs indép. ou sans emploi	..	..	..	0	0	0	0	0	0	0
2310 Sur la base du salaire	..	..	..	..	..	..	..	..	..	..
2320 Sur la base de l'impôt sur le revenu	..	..	..	..	..	..	..	..	..	..
2400 Non ventilables entre 2100, 2200 et 2300	79 200	102 700	141 400	0	0	0	0	0	0	0
2410 Sur la base du salaire	..	..	..	..	..	..	..	..	..	..
2420 Sur la base de l'impôt sur le revenu	..	..	..	..	..	..	..	..	..	..
3000 Sur salaires ou main d'oeuvre	**111 114**	**138 023**	**167 904**	**207 243**	**313 695**	**322 884**	**372 524**	**424 516**	**448 740**	**497 124**
Fonds de formation professionnelle	6 742	6 990	8 460	9 776	12 783	12 483	11 805	13 336	18 439	22 674
Impôt sur traitements et salaires (ITS), solde	104 372	131 033	159 445	197 467	300 912	310 400	360 719	411 180	430 301	474 449
4000 Impôts sur le patrimoine	**25 618**	**32 732**	**45 753**	**49 706**	**82 326**	**79 839**	**89 040**	**106 691**	**102 450**	**120 153**
4100 Impôts périodiques sur la propriété immobilière	16 765	24 664	32 471	38 009	61 322	64 645	72 299	79 627	83 394	99 417
4110 Ménages	..	..	..	..	..	..	..	..	..	..
4120 Autres agents	..	..	..	..	..	..	..	..	..	..
4200 Impôts périodiques sur l'actif net	0	0	0	0	0	0	0	0	0	0
4210 Personnes physiques	..	..	..	..	..	..	..	..	..	..
4220 Sociétés	..	..	..	..	..	..	..	..	..	..
4300 Impôts sur mut. par décès, succ. et donations	0	0	0	0	0	0	0	0	0	0
4310 Impôts sur mut. par décès et successions	..	..	..	..	..	..	..	..	..	..
4320 Impôts sur les donations	..	..	..	..	..	..	..	..	..	..
4400 Impôts sur transact. mobilières et immob.	8 853	8 068	13 282	11 697	21 004	15 194	16 741	27 064	19 055	20 735
4500 Impôts non-périodiques	0	0	0	0	0	0	0	0	0	0
4510 Sur l'actif net	..	..	..	..	..	..	..	..	..	..
4520 Autres non-périodiques	..	..	..	..	..	..	..	..	..	..
4600 Autres impôts périodiques sur patrimoine	0	0	0	0	0	0	0	0	0	0
5000 Impôts sur les biens et services	**729 316**	**699 518**	**1 121 317**	**1 344 200**	**1 568 130**	**1 783 891**	**2 139 378**	**2 319 980**	**2 470 068**	**2 494 279**
5100 Impôts sur production, vente, transfert, etc.	710 337	674 206	1 076 911	1 294 834	1 502 963	1 710 241	2 057 990	2 229 494	2 375 613	2 390 766
5110 Impôts généraux	257 406	255 297	423 172	490 520	579 050	619 100	692 416	717 606	809 710	897 333

Table 5.8. **Côte d'Ivoire** *(cont.)*

Details of tax revenue / Recettes fiscales détaillées

Million XOF

	1998	2000	2008	2010	2013	2014	2015	2016	2017	2018
5111 Taxes sur la valeur ajoutée	257 406	255 297	393 439	473 711	570 444	610 020	680 080	703 825	795 365	883 174
Taxes sur la valeur ajoutée (DGI)	86 506	106 797	140 639	178 761	228 450	255 464	286 170	316 361	379 572	428 728
Recettes TVA (brute) - DGI	..	..	159 269	194 241	247 890	280 819	327 995	354 521	422 679	471 327
Remboursements credits de TVA (DGI)	..	..	-18 630	-15 480	-19 440	-25 355	-41 825	-38 159	-43 107	-42 599
Recettes TVA (DGD)	170 900	148 500	252 800	294 950	341 994	354 556	393 909	387 463	415 793	454 446
Recettes TVA (brute) - DGD	..	..	275 570	313 870	365 754	385 546	445 028	446 235	469 599	504 893
Remboursements credits de TVA (DGD)	..	..	-22 770	-18 920	-23 760	-30 989	-51 119	-58 772	-53 806	-50 447
5112 Impôts sur les ventes	0	0	0	0	0	0	0	0	0	0
5113 Autres impôts	0	0	29 733	16 809	8 606	9 080	12 336	13 782	14 345	14 159
Taxe ad-valorem (taxe domaniale)	..	..	0	0	7 972	8 760	12 185	13 679	14 293	13 932
Contribution à la reconstitution nationale	..	..	29 733	1 567	123	63	71	68	42	98
Taxe de solidarité pour la sortie de crise	..	..	0	15 243	511	257	80	35	10	128
5120 Impôts sur biens et services déterminés	452 932	418 909	653 739	804 314	923 913	1 091 140	1 365 574	1 511 888	1 565 903	1 493 432
5121 Accises	79 451	74 908	72 172	128 698	122 689	130 450	243 151	307 895	310 893	308 095
Taxe SIDA	0	0	0	740	832	908	821	621	781	1 048
Taxe sur le caoutchouc	0	0	0	0	17 780	3 124	78	168	5 075	5
Taxe sur le tabac pour le dévelopment du sport	0	0	1 385	1 708	1 946	2 158	2 029	1 529	1 955	2 621
Taxe sur les sacs et sachets en matière plastique	0	0	0	0	179	172	113	37	71	107
Taxe sur les boissons	2 043	3 642	3 043	5 050	7 609	14 563	18 213	19 084	21 695	24 536
Taxes sur le carburant	249	290	90	81	81	95	105	123	130	173
Taxes sur le tabac	14 659	15 518	11 461	12 040	13 191	19 817	14 771	10 731	13 554	18 786
Diverses taxes spécifiques à la DGD	62 500	50 300	47 501	96 560	64 166	72 567	183 719	242 824	232 598	224 397
Diverses accises spécifiques à la DGD	0	5 158	8 692	12 520	16 904	17 046	23 302	32 777	35 034	36 420
5122 Bénéfices des monopoles fiscaux	0	0	0	0	0	0	0	0	0	0
5123 Droits de douane et droits à l'importation	183 000	126 512	223 447	288 039	383 583	459 675	486 873	500 772	540 928	586 583
5124 Taxes à l'exportation	158 000	185 114	310 685	331 261	326 539	363 222	473 333	520 798	535 512	417 137
Droits d'enregistrement du café et cacao	0	21 114	79 773	103 669	27 389	38 033	86 244	128 522	80 719	12 901
Taxe sur le cacao et café (DGD)	150 200	156 700	220 807	221 180	291 819	316 371	377 418	383 637	436 999	343 058
Taxe sur le bois et autres produits (DGD)	7 800	7 300	10 105	6 412	7 331	8 819	9 671	8 639	8 574	2 103
Droits d'enregistrement pour le cola, le coton, l'anacarde ou le karité (DGD)	0	0	0	0	0	0	0	0	9 220	59 076
5125 Impôts sur biens d'équipement	0	0	0	0	0	0	0	0	0	0
5126 Impôts sur services déterminés	32 480	32 375	47 435	56 315	91 102	137 792	162 218	182 423	178 570	181 618
Contribution de solidarité sur les billets d'avion	0	0	211	216	709	1 273	3 088	488	100	47
Taxe sur le transport aérien	0	0	178	799	1 680	2 054	2 569	2 434	1 651	2 101
Taxe pour la promotion de la culture	0	0	1 089	1 598	1 874	2 279	1 884	1 855	1 881	1 849
Taxe développement des NTICs en zone rurale	0	0	9 194	11 486	14 938	16 528	16 977	17 318	20 424	20 318
Taxe sur les télécommunications	0	0	0	0	22 176	43 080	50 618	62 459	47 238	46 893
Taxes sur les transports urbains	0	0	23	1 019	394	174	3	7	0	0
Prélèvement aux jeux de casino	405	168	323	378	245	273	163	7	444	1 080
Taxe d'abattage	2 362	2 434	1 573	1 125	1 335	1 280	1 299	1 354	1 315	659
Taxe sur la publicité	156	137	175	300	508	411	437	258	510	1 051
Taxe pour le développement touristique	0	0	0	0	972	1 001	1 298	1 420	1 569	1 609
Communications téléphoniques	0	0	0	0	0	16 667	20 425	23 395	23 694	20 659
Taxe sur les assurances	7 912	6 942	6 727	7 739	11 466	12 214	14 435	15 076	17 295	19 228
Taxe sur les encours bancaires	1 954	2 002	2 813	3 627	2	3	0	581	0	0
Taxe sur les opérations bancaires	19 692	20 692	25 128	28 028	34 805	40 554	49 023	55 770	62 449	66 122
5127 Autres impôts sur commerce et transact. internat.	0	0	0	0	0	0	0	0	0	0
5128 Autres impôts	0	0	0	0	0	0	0	0	0	0
5130 Non ventilables entre 5110 et 5120	0	0	0	0	0	0	0	0	0	0
5200 Impôts sur utilisation des biens et exerc. activites	18 979	25 312	44 406	49 366	65 167	73 651	81 388	90 486	94 456	103 513
5210 Impôts périodiques	18 979	25 312	44 406	49 366	65 167	73 651	81 388	90 486	94 456	103 513
5211 A la charge des ménages: véhicules à moteur	2 794	4 176	7 361	9 171	12 183	13 403	14 926	16 103	17 206	18 423
5212 A la charge autres agents: véhicules à moteur	0	0	0	0	0	0	0	0	0	0
5213 Autres impôts périodiques	16 185	21 136	37 044	40 195	52 984	60 248	66 462	74 383	77 250	85 091
5220 Impôts non-périodiques	0	0	0	0	0	0	0	0	0	0
5300 Non ventilables entre 5100 et 5200	0	0	0	0	0	0	0	0	0	0
6000 Autres impôts	**3 705**	**4 352**	**10 021**	**10 765**	**13 764**	**17 082**	**21 055**	**22 551**	**22 577**	**24 197**
6100 A la charge exclusive des entreprises	0	0	3 374	3 732	5 428	5 622	6 979	7 719	9 414	10 275
Fonds de soutien à l'habitat	..	..	307	45	0	0	0	0	0	0
Fonds interprofessionnel	..	..	3 067	3 687	5 428	5 622	6 979	7 719	9 414	10 275
6200 A la charge d'autres agents	3 705	4 352	6 647	7 033	8 336	11 460	14 076	14 833	13 163	13 922

Table 5.8. **Côte d'Ivoire** *(cont.)*

Details of tax revenue / Recettes fiscales détaillées

.. Non disponible

Note : Année civile se terminant le 31 décembre.

Les données sont sur la base des encaissements.

Les chiffres n'incluent pas les recettes fiscales collectées par les collectivités locales.

Rubrique 2000 : Des données plus détaillées sont disponibles pour la première fois pour cette édition.

La rubrique 5113 comprend la taxe ad-valorem, une taxe domaniale. Les recettes autres que celles de la taxe ad-valorem sont considérées comme des recettes non fiscales selon la classification OCDE (voir le guide d'interprétation en Annexe A). La classification nationale de la Côte d'Ivoire les comptabilise comme des recettes fiscales.

La rubrique 5113 comprend la Contribution à la reconstruction nationale (CRN) instituée en 2004 pour cinq ans et arrivée à expiration en 2009. Elle a été remplacée par la Contribution pour la sortie de crise. Celle-ci était basée sur les charges d'exploitation des entreprises réalisant un chiffre d'affaire annuel supérieur ou égal à 1 milliard de francs, au titre de l'exercice clos au 31 décembre 2009.

La rubrique 6100 comprend le Fonds de soutien à l'habitat (FSH) alimenté par des recettes fiscales affectées (contribution patronale sur la masse salariale, taxes sur services déterminés et taxe sur le carburant). Il n'est pas possible de distinguer ces différents éléments, d'où sa classification dans la rubrique 6100. Cette taxe a été supprimée en 2010.

Les recettes de la taxe audiovisuelle et la redevance radiodiffusion télévision ivoirienne (RTI) sont considérées comme des recettes non fiscales selon la classification OCDE (voir le guide d'interprétation en Annexe A) et ont été classifiées dans la rubrique « vente de biens et services». La classification nationale de la Côte d'Ivoire les comptabilise comme des recettes fiscales.

Source : Ministère de l'Économie et des Finances.

StatLink https://doi.org/10.1787/888934183161

Table 5.9. **Egypt / Égypte**

Details of tax revenue / Recettes fiscales détaillées

Million EGP

	1998	2000	2008	2010	2013	2014	2015	2016	2017	2018
Total tax revenue	..	..	**153 351**	**191 492**	**285 821**	**302 070**	**356 096**	**391 033**	**526 741**	**661 608**
1000 Taxes on income, profits and capital gains	..	..	**71 317**	**85 767**	**138 327**	**146 954**	**157 032**	**179 538**	**213 744**	**289 901**
1100 Of individuals	..	..	11 469	16 368	26 228	31 411	38 213	42 352	51 011	64 575
1110 On income and profits	..	..	11 426	16 285	26 141	31 193	37 934	42 009	50 627	64 125
Tax on domestic salaries	..	..	6 761	9 623	16 912	19 336	23 803	28 098	34 189	40 976
Taxes on industrial & commercial profits	..	..	3 779	4 570	6 100	8 431	10 589	9 247	11 508	16 815
Stamp duty on salaries	..	..	590	1 778	2 796	2 916	2 998	3 933	3 776	4 683
Tax on professionals income	..	..	296	314	333	509	544	731	1 154	1 650
1120 On capital gains	..	..	43	84	87	218	279	343	384	450
1200 Corporate	..	..	55 563	66 022	104 700	104 768	108 285	125 457	146 747	186 374
1210 On profits	..	..	55 563	66 022	104 700	104 768	108 285	125 457	146 747	186 374
EGPC & foreign partner	..	..	29 268	32 181	45 816	46 060	36 000	37 313	42 464	51 976
Suez Canal Authority	..	..	10 268	9 443	12 150	14 312	13 400	14 903	22 300	29 900
Central Bank of Egypt	..	..	0	0	8 290	4 042	3 691	13 245	3 860	0
Other companies	..	..	16 027	18 591	25 275	25 099	38 512	36 926	47 259	60 776
Interest income from T-Bills and Bonds	..	..	0	5 808	13 168	15 256	16 682	23 069	30 864	43 722
1220 On capital gains	..	..	..	..	..	..	..	..	..	..
1300 Unallocable between 1100 and 1200	..	..	4 285	3 377	7 400	10 775	10 534	11 729	15 987	38 952
Tax on movable capital revenues from C.B.E	..	..	4 285	3 243	7 204	10 604	10 228	10 965	15 691	38 497
Delayed tax income	..	..	0	134	196	171	306	765	296	455
2000 Social security contributions	..	..	**22 450**	**28 032**	**42 990**	**51 139**	**60 693**	**49 331**	**79 454**	**52 500**
2100 Employees	..	..	0	0	0	0	0	0	0	0
2110 On a payroll basis	..	..	..	..	..	..	..	..	..	..
2120 On an income tax basis	..	..	..	..	..	..	..	..	..	..
2200 Employers	..	..	0	0	0	0	0	0	0	0
2210 On a payroll basis	..	..	..	..	..	..	..	..	..	..
2220 On an income tax basis	..	..	..	..	..	..	..	..	..	..
2300 Self-employed or non-employed	..	..	0	0	0	0	0	0	0	0
2310 On a payroll basis	..	..	..	..	..	..	..	..	..	..
2320 On an income tax basis	..	..	..	..	..	..	..	..	..	..
2400 Unallocable between 2100, 2200 and 2300	..	..	22 450	28 032	42 990	51 139	60 693	49 331	79 454	52 500
2410 On a payroll basis	..	..	..	..	..	..	..	..	..	..
2420 On an income tax basis	..	..	..	..	..	..	..	..	..	..
3000 Taxes on payroll and workforce	..	..	**0**	**0**	**0**	**0**	**0**	**0**	**0**	**0**
4000 Taxes on property	..	..	**994**	**1 128**	**1 275**	**1 237**	**2 224**	**2 484**	**3 237**	**4 214**
4100 Recurrent taxes on immovable property	..	..	407	518	531	428	637	1 172	2 055	2 976
4110 Households	..	..	..	..	..	..	..	..	..	..
4120 Others	..	..	..	..	..	..	..	..	..	..
4200 Recurrent taxes on net wealth	..	..	0	0	0	0	0	0	0	0
4210 Individual	..	..	..	..	..	..	..	..	..	..
4220 Corporate	..	..	..	..	..	..	..	..	..	..
4300 Estate, inheritance and gift taxes	..	..	0	0	0	0	0	0	0	0
4310 Estate and inheritance taxes	..	..	..	..	..	..	..	..	..	..
4320 Gift taxes	..	..	..	..	..	..	..	..	..	..
4400 Taxes on financial and capital transactions	..	..	586	610	744	809	1 588	1 312	1 182	1 238
Property transferring fees	..	..	534	607	737	799	948	1 002	1 134	1 235
Stamps taxes	..	..	52	3	7	10	640	310	49	3
4500 Non-recurrent taxes	..	..	0	0	0	0	0	0	0	0
4510 On net wealth	..	..	..	..	..	..	..	..	..	..
4520 Other non-recurrent taxes	..	..	..	..	..	..	..	..	..	..
4600 Other recurrent taxes on property	..	..	0	0	0	0	0	0	0	0
5000 Taxes on goods and services	..	..	**58 591**	**76 564**	**103 229**	**102 741**	**136 146**	**159 680**	**230 306**	**314 993**
5100 Taxes on production, sale, transfer, etc.	..	..	58 213	76 232	102 897	102 459	135 761	159 187	229 874	314 484
5110 General taxes	..	..	32 220	39 519	48 854	51 997	64 996	71 015	111 607	154 816
5111 Value added taxes	..	..	32 220	39 519	48 854	51 997	64 996	71 015	111 607	154 816
Local commodities	..	..	8 927	11 735	14 038	14 577	18 415	21 102	32 690	43 100
Imported goods	..	..	16 521	18 977	25 458	28 398	35 010	36 352	61 694	83 939
Hotel and restaurant services for tourists	..	..	1 908	2 172	1 997	1 704	2 334	2 157	3 061	5 894
Operating services for others	..	..	2 121	2 936	3 409	3 442	4 844	6 845	9 563	15 819
International and local communication services	..	..	2 743	3 700	3 952	3 877	4 393	4 559	4 599	6 065
5112 Sales tax	..	..	0	0	0	0	0	0	0	0
5113 Other	..	..	0	0	0	0	0	0	0	0
5120 Taxes on specific goods and services	..	..	25 992	36 713	54 043	50 462	70 765	88 172	118 267	159 667

Table 5.9. **Egypt / Égypte** *(cont.)*

Details of tax revenue / Recettes fiscales détaillées

Million EGP

	1998	2000	2008	2010	2013	2014	2015	2016	2017	2018
5121 Excises	..	..	8 431	17 170	31 864	25 822	41 207	49 468	72 730	106 447
Tobacco & cigarettes	..	..	4 931	6 997	17 251	19 588	26 463	33 584	35 412	51 654
Petroleum products	..	..	1 487	7 563	12 328	3 934	12 004	13 181	33 072	40 470
Stamp taxes on specific goods	..	..	1 240	1 603	1 334	1 258	1 198	948	1 782	1 214
Other excises	..	..	773	1 006	951	1 042	1 543	1 755	2 465	13 109
5122 Profits of fiscal monopolies	..	..	0	0	0	0	0	0	0	0
5123 Customs and import duties	..	..	13 361	13 733	16 054	17 352	21 460	27 534	33 411	36 848
5124 Taxes on exports	..	..	518	819	597	183	180	216	258	429
5125 Taxes on investment goods	..	..	0	0	0	0	0	0	0	0
5126 Taxes on specific services	..	..	2 149	3 074	3 603	5 030	4 226	5 377	5 655	8 873
Stamp taxes on specific services	..	..	1 228	1 950	2 336	3 685	2 700	3 361	3 286	5 487
Other taxes on specific services	..	..	921	1 123	1 267	1 345	1 526	2 017	2 369	3 386
5127 Other taxes on internat. trade and transactions	..	..	0	0	0	0	0	0	0	0
5128 Other taxes	..	..	1 533	1 919	1 925	2 075	3 690	5 576	6 213	7 070
5130 Unallocable between 5110 and 5120	..	..	0	0	0	0	0	0	0	0
5200 Taxes on use of goods and perform activities	..	..	378	332	332	281	386	494	432	509
5210 Recurrent taxes	..	..	378	332	332	281	386	494	432	509
5211 Paid by households: motor vehicles	..	..	0	0	0	0	0	0	0	0
5212 Paid by others: motor vehicles	..	..	0	0	0	0	0	0	0	0
5213 Paid in respect of other goods	..	..	378	332	332	281	386	494	432	509
5220 Non-recurrent taxes	..	..	0	0	0	0	0	0	0	0
5300 Unallocable between 5100 and 5200	..	..	0	0	0	0	0	0	0	0
6000 Other taxes	**..**	**..**	**0**	**0**	**0**	**0**	**0**	**0**	**0**	**0**
6100 Paid solely by business	..	..	..	..	..	..	..	..	..	..
6200 Other	..	..	..	..	..	..	..	..	..	..
Memo items:										
VAT revenues	..	..	32 220	39 519	48 854	51 997	64 996	71 015	111 607	154 816
VAT revenues (gross)	..	..	32 835	40 142	49 368	52 537	65 708	71 785	112 323	155 565
VAT refunds	..	..	-615	-623	-515	-540	-712	-770	-716	-749

.. Not available

Note: Fiscal year ends on 30 June. For example, the data for 2018 represent July 2017 to June 2018.

The data are on a cash basis.

Figures exclude tax revenues collected by sub-national governments as the data are not available.

Heading 2000: Egypt does not include social security contributions in its tax revenue data as the Egyptian authorities do not consider them as taxes.

Royalties on the Suez Canal as well as other royalties and administrative fees are reported as taxes in Egypt. These revenues are considered as non-tax revenues according to the OECD classification, described in the Interpretative Guide in Annex A.

Source: Ministry of Finance

StatLink https://doi.org/10.1787/888934183446

Table 5.10. **Equatorial Guinea / Guinée équatoriale**

Details of tax revenue / Recettes fiscales détaillées

Million XAF

	1998	2000	2008	2010	2013	2014	2015	2016	2017	2018
Total tax revenue	..	..	**688 635**	**612 377**	**966 495**	**1 050 252**	**935 907**	**472 214**	**471 096**	**480 100**
1000 Taxes on income, profits and capital gains	..	..	**647 333**	**545 376**	**828 243**	**889 915**	**772 421**	**316 872**	**326 993**	**320 639**
1100 Of individuals	..	..	39 182	59 938	80 605	80 236	85 021	67 146	48 799	57 188
1110 On income and profits	..	..	39 182	59 938	80 605	80 236	85 021	67 146	48 799	57 188
Petroleum tax on physical persons	..	..	27 191	44 339	58 640	57 583	64 217	48 186	33 101	39 652
Personal income tax	..	..	11 658	15 325	21 587	22 175	20 421	18 581	15 456	17 201
Taxes on urban farms	..	..	293	129	354	400	379	369	235	305
Taxes on rural farms	..	..	40	145	24	77	4	10	7	30
1120 On capital gains	..	..	0	0	0	0	0	0	0	0
1200 Corporate	..	..	608 151	485 438	747 638	809 679	687 400	249 726	278 194	263 451
1210 On profits	..	..	608 151	485 438	747 638	809 679	687 400	249 726	278 194	263 451
Contractors	..	..	497 783	406 163	544 811	660 251	546 181	175 230	167 822	184 343
Subcontractors	..	..	58 988	29 619	80 309	81 686	51 317	31 498	13 841	36 969
Taxes on companies	..	..	21 248	38 659	48 706	56 508	86 658	38 744	34 795	36 571
Year end (PNT)	..	..	29 791	9 765	72 659	9 402	573	1 180	58 081	609
OCIPEF Tax on wood exporters	..	..	342	1 233	1 153	1 830	2 671	3 074	3 655	4 958
1220 On capital gains	..	..	0	0	0	0	0	0	0	0
1300 Unallocable between 1100 and 1200	..	..	0	0	0	0	0	0	0	0
2000 Social security contributions	..	..	..	..	**60 128**	**60 033**	**58 868**	**49 766**	**51 009**	**47 725**
2100 Employees	..	..	..	..	8 104	8 091	7 935	6 481	6 575	7 054
2110 On a payroll basis	..	..	..	..	0	0	0	0	0	0
2120 On an income tax basis	..	..	..	..	8 104	8 091	7 935	6 481	6 575	7 054
2200 Employers	..	..	..	..	42 813	42 700	41 793	33 954	34 339	36 711
2210 On a payroll basis	..	..	..	..	0	0	0	0	0	0
2220 On an income tax basis	..	..	..	..	42 813	42 700	41 793	33 954	34 339	36 711
2300 Self-employed or non-employed	..	..	..	..	0	0	0	0	0	0
2310 On a payroll basis	..	..	..	..	..	..	..	..	..	..
2320 On an income tax basis	..	..	..	..	..	..	..	..	..	..
2400 Unallocable between 2100, 2200 and 2300	..	..	..	..	9 211	9 241	9 140	9 331	10 094	3 960
2410 On a payroll basis	..	..	..	..	0	0	0	0	0	0
2420 On an income tax basis	..	..	..	..	9 211	9 241	9 140	9 331	10 094	3 960
3000 Taxes on payroll and workforce	..	..	**0**	**0**	**0**	**0**	**0**	**0**	**0**	**0**
4000 Taxes on property	..	..	**178**	**160**	**461**	**367**	**211**	**352**	**192**	**278**
4100 Recurrent taxes on immovable property	..	..	0	0	0	0	0	0	0	0
4110 Households	..	..	..	..	..	..	..	..	..	..
4120 Others	..	..	..	..	..	..	..	..	..	..
4200 Recurrent taxes on net wealth	..	..	0	0	0	0	0	0	0	0
4210 Individual	..	..	..	..	..	..	..	..	..	..
4220 Corporate	..	..	..	..	..	..	..	..	..	..
4300 Estate, inheritance and gift taxes	..	..	0	0	0	0	0	0	0	0
4310 Estate and inheritance taxes	..	..	..	..	..	..	..	..	..	..
4320 Gift taxes	..	..	..	..	..	..	..	..	..	..
4400 Taxes on financial and capital transactions	..	..	178	160	461	367	211	352	192	278
4500 Non-recurrent taxes	..	..	0	0	0	0	0	0	0	0
4510 On net wealth	..	..	..	..	..	..	..	..	..	..
4520 Other non-recurrent taxes	..	..	..	..	..	..	..	..	..	..
4600 Other recurrent taxes on property	..	..	0	0	0	0	0	0	0	0
5000 Taxes on goods and services	..	..	**37 537**	**57 852**	**73 481**	**84 881**	**96 353**	**94 252**	**88 168**	**92 399**
5100 Taxes on production, sale, transfer, etc.	..	..	37 537	57 852	73 481	84 881	96 353	94 252	88 168	92 399
5110 General taxes	..	..	30 251	45 607	43 104	50 409	58 761	52 501	51 978	54 466
5111 Value added taxes	..	..	30 251	45 607	43 104	50 409	58 761	52 501	51 978	54 466
VAT revenues on petroleum products	..	..	7 584	15 066	1 594	2 672	6 799	4 705	3 826	2 355
VAT revenues other products and services	..	..	22 667	30 541	41 510	47 738	51 962	47 796	48 152	52 111
5112 Sales tax	..	..	0	0	0	0	0	0	0	0
5113 Other	..	..	0	0	0	0	0	0	0	0
5120 Taxes on specific goods and services	..	..	7 286	12 245	30 377	34 471	37 592	41 751	36 190	37 933
5121 Excises	..	..	0	0	13 526	14 653	19 961	21 041	15 824	18 570
Taxes on petroleum products	..	..	0	0	13 526	12 749	19 961	21 041	15 824	18 570
Special excise taxes	..	..	0	0	0	1 904	0	0	0	0
5122 Profits of fiscal monopolies	..	..	0	0	0	0	0	0	0	0
5123 Customs and import duties	..	..	6 145	9 667	14 552	14 699	13 434	15 854	12 292	13 015
Imports of petroleum products	..	..	870	1 446	970	1 318	2 009	1 865	1 309	1 448
Imports of other products	..	..	5 274	8 221	13 582	13 381	11 425	13 989	10 983	11 567

Table 5.10. **Equatorial Guinea / Guinée équatoriale** *(cont.)*

Details of tax revenue / Recettes fiscales détaillées

Million XAF

	1998	2000	2008	2010	2013	2014	2015	2016	2017	2018
5124 Taxes on exports	..	..	1 141	2 578	2 299	3 290	4 197	4 856	8 074	6 348
Wood exports	..	..	942	2 517	2 197	3 152	4 088	4 772	7 956	6 253
Exports of other products	..	..	23	21	58	107	91	84	116	89
Re-exports	..	..	175	40	44	31	18	0	3	6
5125 Taxes on investment goods	..	..	0	0	0	0	0	0	0	0
5126 Taxes on specific services	..	..	0	0	0	1 830	0	0	0	0
5127 Other taxes on internat. trade and transactions	..	..	0	0	0	0	0	0	0	0
5128 Other taxes	..	..	0	0	0	0	0	0	0	0
5130 Unallocable between 5110 and 5120	..	..	0	0	0	0	0	0	0	0
5200 Taxes on use of goods and perform activities	..	..	0	0	0	0	0	0	0	0
5210 Recurrent taxes	..	..	..	..	..	..	..	..	..	..
5211 Paid by households: motor vehicles	..	..	..	..	..	..	..	..	..	..
5212 Paid by others: motor vehicles	..	..	..	..	..	..	..	..	..	..
5213 Paid in respect of other goods	..	..	..	..	..	..	..	..	..	..
5220 Non-recurrent taxes	..	..	..	..	..	..	..	..	..	..
5300 Unallocable between 5100 and 5200	..	..	0	0	0	0	0	0	0	0
6000 Other taxes	**..**	**..**	**3 586**	**8 989**	**4 182**	**15 058**	**8 054**	**10 972**	**4 733**	**19 060**
6100 Paid solely by business	..	..	..	..	..	..	..	..	..	..
6200 Other	..	..	..	..	..	..	..	..	..	..

.. Not available

Note: Year ending 31st December.

The data are on a cash basis

Heading 2000: For the first time, social security contributions to the Instituto Nacional de Seguridad Social de Guinea Ecuatorial (INSESO) are reported under this heading for the years 2013-18.

Source: Ministry of Finance, Economy and Planning.

StatLink https://doi.org/10.1787/888934183484

Table 5.11. **Eswatini**

Details of tax revenue / Recettes fiscales détaillées

Million SZL

	1998	2000	2008	2010	2013	2014	2015	2016	2017	2018
Total tax revenue	**1 094**	**1 327**	**3 601**	**4 588**	**6 196**	**7 305**	**7 921**	**9 160**	**10 101**	**10 891**
1000 Taxes on income, profits and capital gains	**581**	**677**	**1 972**	**2 373**	**3 062**	**3 707**	**3 854**	**4 590**	**4 897**	**5 259**
1100 Of individuals	296	428	1 277	1 449	1 773	2 093	2 278	2 766	3 071	3 289
1110 On income and profits	296	428	1 277	1 449	1 773	2 093	2 278	2 766	3 071	3 289
Pay-as-you-earn tax (PAYE)	289	421	1 166	1 321	1 752	2 049	2 176	2 662	2 976	3 181
Provisional income tax	2	2	79	75	1	31	24	31	32	44
Taxes on interest, dividends and trust income	0	0	18	35	1	0	1	1	0	0
Personal income tax on non-residents	0	0	3	3	1	1	1	2	0	0
Tax on benefits	0	0	10	11	17	10	15	15	17	18
Withholding tax on resident suppliers	0	0	0	0	0	0	0	0	0	0
Personal income tax on the self employed	4	4	1	1	0	0	59	52	43	43
Lottery levy	1	1	1	2	2	2	2	3	4	3
1120 On capital gains	0	0	0	0	0	0	0	0	0	0
1200 Corporate	263	236	673	905	1 216	1 570	1 507	1 730	1 825	1 969
1210 On profits	263	236	673	905	1 216	1 570	1 507	1 730	1 825	1 969
Corporate income tax on resident companies	262	233	598	739	1 060	1 468	1 358	1 527	1 388	1 479
Taxes on royalties	0	0	59	144	45	27	42	58	0	0
Corporate income tax on non-resident companies	1	3	16	22	111	75	107	145	438	490
1220 On capital gains	0	0	0	0	0	0	0	0	0	0
1300 Unallocable between 1100 and 1200	22	14	22	20	74	44	68	95	1	1
Income taxes on non-residents	19	11	18	15	72	43	67	93	0	0
Other taxes on income	2	3	3	4	2	1	2	2	1	1
2000 Social security contributions	**136**	**154**	**422**	**626**	**654**	**893**	**1 028**	**1 126**	**1 357**	**1 536**
2100 Employees	32	38	106	157	164	269	309	342	407	472
2110 On a payroll basis	..	..	..	..	..	..	..	..	..	..
2120 On an income tax basis	..	..	..	..	..	..	..	..	..	..
2200 Employers	104	115	317	469	490	624	719	785	950	1 065
2210 On a payroll basis	..	..	..	..	..	..	..	..	..	..
2220 On an income tax basis	..	..	..	..	..	..	..	..	..	..
2300 Self-employed or non-employed	0	0	0	0	0	0	0	0	0	0
2310 On a payroll basis	..	..	..	..	..	..	..	..	..	..
2320 On an income tax basis	..	..	..	..	..	..	..	..	..	..
2400 Unallocable between 2100, 2200 and 2300	0	0	0	0	0	0	0	0	0	0
2410 On a payroll basis	..	..	..	..	..	..	..	..	..	..
2420 On an income tax basis	..	..	..	..	..	..	..	..	..	..
3000 Taxes on payroll and workforce	**0**	**0**	**0**	**0**	**0**	**0**	**0**	**0**	**0**	**0**
4000 Taxes on property	**23**	**34**	**73**	**92**	**131**	**137**	**148**	**168**	**237**	**285**
4100 Recurrent taxes on immovable property	13	24	40	54	64	71	78	77	165	212
Local property taxes	13	24	40	54	64	71	78	77	165	212
4110 Households	0	0	0	0	0	0	0	0	0	0
4120 Others	0	0	0	0	0	0	0	0	0	0
4200 Recurrent taxes on net wealth	0	0	0	0	0	0	0	0	0	0
4210 Individual	..	..	..	..	..	..	..	..	..	..
4220 Corporate	..	..	..	..	..	..	..	..	..	..
4300 Estate, inheritance and gift taxes	0	0	0	0	16	9	15	21	0	0
4310 Estate and inheritance taxes	..	..	..	..	16	9	15	21	..	..
Tax on trust beneficiaries	..	..	..	..	16	9	15	21	..	..
4320 Gift taxes	..	..	..	..	0	0	0	0	..	..
4400 Taxes on financial and capital transactions	10	10	33	39	51	57	56	70	72	73
Transfer duties	4	5	21	26	34	33	30	46	42	49
Stamp duties	5	5	12	12	17	23	25	24	30	23
4500 Non-recurrent taxes	0	0	0	0	0	0	0	0	0	0
4510 On net wealth	..	..	..	..	..	..	..	..	..	..
4520 Other non-recurrent taxes	..	..	..	..	..	..	..	..	..	..
4600 Other recurrent taxes on property	0	0	0	0	0	0	0	0	0	0
5000 Taxes on goods and services	**354**	**462**	**1 134**	**1 496**	**2 348**	**2 567**	**2 892**	**3 276**	**3 609**	**3 811**
5100 Taxes on production, sale, transfer, etc.	342	449	1 083	1 442	2 283	2 499	2 823	3 202	3 532	3 729
5110 General taxes	275	372	984	1 255	1 684	1 895	2 109	2 409	2 521	2 668
5111 Value added taxes	0	0	0	0	1 648	1 883	2 107	2 407	2 520	2 668
VAT revenues (gross)	..	..	..	..	2 390	2 787	3 048	3 337	3 584	3 753
VAT refunds	..	..	..	..	-742	-904	-941	-929	-1 063	-1 085
5112 Sales tax	275	372	984	1 255	36	12	2	1	1	0
5113 Other	0	0	0	0	0	0	0	0	0	0
5120 Taxes on specific goods and services	67	78	99	186	599	604	714	793	1 011	1 061

Table 5.11. **Eswatini** *(cont.)*

Details of tax revenue / Recettes fiscales détaillées

Million SZL

	1998	2000	2008	2010	2013	2014	2015	2016	2017	2018
5121 Excises	65	75	74	148	549	573	667	732	1 005	1 050
Fuel taxes	65	75	74	148	549	573	667	732	1 005	1 050
Levy on alcohol and tobacco	0	0	0	0	0	0	0	0	0	0
5122 Profits of fiscal monopolies	0	0	0	0	0	0	0	0	0	0
5123 Customs and import duties	0	0	0	0	0	0	0	0	0	5
5124 Taxes on exports	0	0	0	0	0	0	0	0	0	0
Cattle export tax	0	0	0	0	0	0	0	0	0	0
5125 Taxes on investment goods	0	0	0	0	0	0	0	0	0	0
5126 Taxes on specific services	2	2	25	39	50	31	47	61	6	5
Tax on management fees	0	0	24	37	45	27	42	58	0	0
Taxes on lotteries, gaming and betting	2	2	1	2	5	4	5	3	6	5
Other taxes on services and hospitality	0	0	0	0	0	0	0	0	0	0
5127 Other taxes on internat. trade and transactions	0	0	0	0	0	0	0	0	0	0
5128 Other taxes	0	0	0	0	0	0	0	0	0	0
5130 Unallocable between 5110 and 5120	0	0	0	0	0	0	0	0	0	0
5200 Taxes on use of goods and perform activities	11	12	51	54	65	68	68	74	77	82
5210 Recurrent taxes	7	8	26	30	35	38	38	43	45	48
5211 Paid by households: motor vehicles	4	4	11	11	14	15	16	18	19	20
5212 Paid by others: motor vehicles	0	0	0	0	0	0	0	0	0	0
5213 Paid in respect of other goods	3	3	15	19	22	23	22	25	26	28
Trading licences	1	1	9	11	13	14	14	16	16	18
Company licences	1	1	5	7	7	8	7	8	8	9
Special licences	1	1	1	1	1	1	1	1	1	1
5220 Non-recurrent taxes	4	5	25	25	29	31	31	31	32	34
Road tolls	4	4	24	24	29	30	30	30	32	33
Firearm registration fees	0	0	1	1	1	1	1	1	1	1
5300 Unallocable between 5100 and 5200	0	0	0	0	0	0	0	0	0	0
6000 Other taxes	**0**	**0**	**0**	**0**	**0**	**0**	**0**	**0**	**0**	**0**
6100 Paid solely by business	..	..	..	..	..	..	..	..	..	..
6200 Other	..	..	..	..	..	..	..	..	..	..

.. Not available

Note: Data are reported on a fiscal year basis beginning 1st April. For example, the data for 2018 represent April 2018 to March 2019.

The data are on a cash basis.

Heading 5211: This heading includes revenue from motor vehicle licences, the change of ownership fees and the registration of new motor vehicles. These revenues are considered as tax revenue according to the OECD classification, described in the interpretative guide in Annex A. The national classification of Eswatini classifies these revenues as non-tax revenues.

Heading 5213: This heading includes revenue from business and sundry licences. These revenues are considered as tax revenues according to the OECD classification, described in the interpretative guide in Annex A. The national classification of Eswatini classifies them as nontax revenues.

Heading 5220: This heading includes revenue from the registrations of specific goods (e.g. firearms). These revenues are considered as tax revenues under the OECD classification, as set out in the Interpretative Guide in Annex A. The national classification of Eswatini classifies these revenues as non-tax revenues.

Revenue from PAYE Penalties, tax interest and penalties on taxes are considered as non-tax revenue under the OECD classification, as set out in the Interpretative Guide in Annex A. The national classification of Eswatini classifies these revenues as tax revenues.

Source: Eswatini Revenue Authority

StatLink https://doi.org/10.1787/888934183674

Table 5.12. **Ghana**

Details of tax revenue / Recettes fiscales détaillées

Million GHS

	1998	2000	2008	2010	2013	2014	2015	2016	2017	2018
Total tax revenue	..	**487**	**4 312**	**6 695**	**14 038**	**18 944**	**23 592**	**29 495**	**35 300**	**42 349**
1000 Taxes on income, profits and capital gains	..	**141**	**1 242**	**2 417**	**5 470**	**7 360**	**7 570**	**8 084**	**11 712**	**16 344**
1100 Of individuals	..	56	595	1 115	2 549	3 219	3 570	3 702	5 191	6 649
1110 On income and profits	..	56	595	1 115	2 549	3 219	3 570	3 702	5 191	6 649
Employees income tax	..	48	527	1 015	2 367	3 000	3 310	3 466	4 859	6 270
Self employers income/profit tax	..	8	68	100	182	219	260	237	332	379
1120 On capital gains	..	..	..	..	..	..	..	..	..	..
1200 Corporate	..	70	540	1 080	2 785	3 992	3 837	4 233	6 214	9 563
1210 On profits	..	70	540	1 080	2 785	3 992	3 837	4 233	6 214	9 563
Income/profit tax on companies (excl. oil)	..	70	539	988	2 316	3 034	3 620	4 052	5 793	8 528
Income/profit tax on oil companies	..	0	0	0	419	797	45	42	225	736
National Fiscal Stabilisation Levy (NFSL)	..	0	0	85	50	162	172	139	196	299
National Reconstruction Levy (NRL)	..	0	1	7	0	0	0	0	0	0
1220 On capital gains	..	..	..	..	..	..	..	..	..	..
1300 Unallocable between 1100 and 1200	..	15	107	222	136	149	163	148	307	132
Other direct taxes aside from oil and mineral royalties	..	15	107	222	136	149	163	148	307	132
2000 Social security contributions	..	**46**	**419**	**577**	**1 160**	**1 784**	**2 122**	**2 593**	**2 331**	**2 399**
2100 Employees	..	..	..	..	..	..	..	..	..	..
2110 On a payroll basis	..	..	..	..	..	..	..	..	..	..
2120 On an income tax basis	..	..	..	..	..	..	..	..	..	..
2200 Employers	..	..	..	..	..	..	..	..	..	..
2210 On a payroll basis	..	..	..	..	..	..	..	..	..	..
2220 On an income tax basis	..	..	..	..	..	..	..	..	..	..
2300 Self-employed or non-employed	..	..	..	..	..	..	..	..	..	..
2310 On a payroll basis	..	..	..	..	..	..	..	..	..	..
2320 On an income tax basis	..	..	..	..	..	..	..	..	..	..
2400 Unallocable between 2100, 2200 and 2300	..	46	419	577	1 160	1 784	2 122	2 593	2 331	2 399
2410 On a payroll basis	..	..	..	..	..	..	..	..	..	..
2420 On an income tax basis	..	..	..	..	..	..	..	..	..	..
3000 Taxes on payroll and workforce	..	**0**	**0**	**0**	**0**	**0**	**0**	**0**	**0**	**0**
4000 Taxes on property	..	..	..	..	..	..	..	..	..	..
4100 Recurrent taxes on immovable property	..	..	..	..	..	..	..	..	..	..
4110 Households	..	..	..	..	..	..	..	..	..	..
4120 Others	..	..	..	..	..	..	..	..	..	..
4200 Recurrent taxes on net wealth	..	..	..	..	..	..	..	..	..	..
4210 Individual	..	..	..	..	..	..	..	..	..	..
4220 Corporate	..	..	..	..	..	..	..	..	..	..
4300 Estate, inheritance and gift taxes	..	..	..	..	..	..	..	..	..	..
4310 Estate and inheritance taxes	..	..	..	..	..	..	..	..	..	..
4320 Gift taxes	..	..	..	..	..	..	..	..	..	..
4400 Taxes on financial and capital transactions	..	..	..	..	..	..	..	..	..	..
4500 Non-recurrent taxes	..	..	..	..	..	..	..	..	..	..
4510 On net wealth	..	..	..	..	..	..	..	..	..	..
4520 Other non-recurrent taxes	..	..	..	..	..	..	..	..	..	..
4600 Other recurrent taxes on property	..	..	..	..	..	..	..	..	..	..
5000 Taxes on goods and services	..	**301**	**2 651**	**3 701**	**7 409**	**9 799**	**13 900**	**18 817**	**21 256**	**23 606**
5100 Taxes on production, sale, transfer, etc.	..	301	2 609	3 701	7 409	9 799	13 900	18 817	21 256	23 606
5110 General taxes	..	127	1 406	2 006	4 124	5 672	7 562	8 530	10 366	11 326
5111 Value added taxes	..	127	1 406	2 006	4 124	5 672	7 562	8 530	10 366	11 326
VAT revenues	..	127	1 088	1 618	3 317	4 672	6 254	7 130	8 549	8 893
VAT revenues (external collection)	..	89	671	970	1 983	2 757	3 489	4 108	4 992	4 912
VAT revenues (domestic)	..	39	417	649	1 334	1 915	2 766	3 022	3 557	3 980
National Health Insurance Levy (NHIL)	..	0	214	316	648	782	1 019	1 119	1 376	1 501
National Health Insurance Levy (customs collection)	..	..	142	183	405	463	558	613	778	810
National Health Insurance Levy (domestic)	..	..	72	133	243	319	461	506	598	691
Social Security and National Insurance Trust (SSNIT)contributions to the National Health Insurance Scheme (NHIS)	..	..	104	72	159	218	289	280	440	377
GETFund Levy	..	0	0	0	0	0	0	0	0	555
GETFund Levy (external collection)	..	..	..	..	..	..	..	..	..	289
GETFund Levy (domestic)	..	..	..	..	..	..	..	..	..	267
5112 Sales tax	..	0	0	0	0	0	0	0	0	0
5113 Other	..	0	0	0	0	0	0	0	0	0

Table 5.12. **Ghana** *(cont.)*

Details of tax revenue / Recettes fiscales détaillées

Million GHS

	1998	2000	2008	2010	2013	2014	2015	2016	2017	2018
5120 Taxes on specific goods and services	..	173	1 203	1 695	3 285	4 127	6 337	10 287	10 890	12 279
5121 Excises	..	75	445	374	694	764	2 402	5 289	4 729	5 282
Petroleum taxes aside from EFL and RFL	..	53	305	221	525	617	2 163	2 319	1 665	1 975
Energy Fund Levy (EFL)	..	0	81	36	0	0	0	25	28	35
Road Fund Levy (RFL)	..	0	0	0	0	0	0	1 002	1 058	1 331
Energy Debt Recovery Levy	..	0	0	0	0	0	0	1 320	1 293	1 072
Price Stabilisation and Recovery Levy	..	0	0	0	0	0	0	326	346	548
Other excise duties	..	21	59	118	169	147	239	297	339	319
5122 Profits of fiscal monopolies	..	0	0	0	0	0	0	0	0	0
5123 Customs and import duties	..	81	679	1 051	2 231	2 773	3 078	4 122	5 485	6 102
5124 Taxes on exports	..	18	40	95	100	319	371	269	0	0
Levies on cocoa exports	..	18	40	95	100	319	371	269	..	..
5125 Taxes on investment goods	..	0	0	0	0	0	0	0	0	0
5126 Taxes on specific services	..	0	39	174	260	272	486	608	676	896
Communication service tax	..	..	28	137	174	217	252	339	329	420
Airport tax	..	..	11	37	86	55	235	269	347	476
5127 Other taxes on internat. trade and transactions	..	0	0	0	0	0	0	0	0	0
5128 Other taxes	..	0	0	0	0	0	0	0	0	0
5130 Unallocable between 5110 and 5120	..	0	0	0	0	0	0	0	0	0
5200 Taxes on use of goods and perform activities	..	0	42	0	0	0	0	0	0	0
5210 Recurrent taxes	..	..	42	..	..	..	..	..	..	..
5211 Paid by households: motor vehicles	..	..	0	..	..	..	..	..	..	..
5212 Paid by others: motor vehicles	..	..	0	..	..	..	..	..	..	..
5213 Paid in respect of other goods	..	..	42	..	..	..	..	..	..	..
5220 Non-recurrent taxes	..	..	0	..	..	..	..	..	..	..
5300 Unallocable between 5100 and 5200	..	0	0	0	0	0	0	0	0	0
6000 Other taxes	..	**0**	**0**	**0**	**0**	**0**	**0**	**0**	**0**	**0**
6100 Paid solely by business	..	..	..	..	..	..	..	..	..	..
6200 Other	..	..	..	..	..	..	..	..	..	..
VAT refunds	..	0	26	45	182	157	627	1 445	1 803	2 125

.. Not available

Note: Year ending 31st December.

The data are on a cash basis.

Figures exclude tax revenues collected by sub-national governments as the data are not available

Heading 2000: The data are not available from 2000 to 2007.

Heading 4000: Property tax is levied annually by local authorities and is not available for this report.

Heading 5111: The national health insurance levy is a tax on goods and services whose funds are allocated to the National Health Insurance Scheme (NHIS).

Royalties from oil and mineral royalties are reported as taxes on income and property in Ghana's budget documents. These revenues are classified as non-tax revenue (Heading "Rents and royalties") in accordance with the OECD classification, as set out in the Interpretative Guide in Annex A.

Source: Ghana Statistical Service.

StatLink https://doi.org/10.1787/888934183465

Table 5.13. **Kenya**

Details of tax revenue / Recettes fiscales détaillées

Million KES

	1998	2000	2008	2010	2013	2014	2015	2016	2017	2018
Total tax revenue	..	..	**438 370**	**540 164**	**811 896**	**976 914**	**1 085 219**	**1 231 771**	**1 399 658**	**1 482 687**
1000 Taxes on income, profits and capital gains	..	..	**179 803**	**219 227**	**392 395**	**451 793**	**504 077**	**561 792**	**628 373**	**654 675**
1100 Of individuals	..	..	88 543	124 392	216 416	259 007	284 222	322 885	348 783	377 353
1110 On income and profits	..	..	88 543	124 392	216 416	259 007	284 222	322 885	348 783	377 353
Paye As You Earn (PAYE)	..	..	85 315	120 593	211 061	252 974	277 068	312 032	336 596	364 104
Individual income tax	..	..	3 228	3 799	5 355	6 033	7 154	8 821	8 179	7 191
Tax on rental income	..	..	0	0	0	0	0	2 033	4 007	6 058
1120 On capital gains	..	..	..	..	..	..	..	..	..	..
1200 Corporate	..	..	72 434	67 661	110 626	135 971	126 541	152 407	180 162	160 059
1210 On profits	..	..	72 434	67 661	110 626	135 971	126 541	152 407	180 162	160 059
Corporation tax	..	..	72 434	67 661	110 626	135 971	126 541	152 407	180 162	160 059
1220 On capital gains	..	..	..	..	..	..	..	..	..	..
1300 Unallocable between 1100 and 1200	..	..	18 826	27 174	65 354	56 816	93 313	86 500	99 427	117 263
Withholding tax	..	..	18 826	27 174	65 354	56 816	92 678	82 690	97 009	100 623
Capital gains tax	..	..	0	0	0	0	636	3 811	2 419	16 640
2000 Social security contributions	..	..	**5 371**	**6 026**	**12 055**	**13 629**	**15 826**	**31 996**	**34 979**	**47 891**
2100 Employees	..	..	825	0	0	0	0	0	0	0
Women and children's pension	..	..	825	0	0	0	0	0	0	0
2110 On a payroll basis	..	..	..	..	..	..	..	..	..	..
2120 On an income tax basis	..	..	..	..	..	..	..	..	..	..
2200 Employers	..	..	..	..	..	..	..	..	..	..
2210 On a payroll basis	..	..	..	..	..	..	..	..	..	..
2220 On an income tax basis	..	..	..	..	..	..	..	..	..	..
2300 Self-employed or non-employed	..	..	..	..	..	..	..	..	..	..
2310 On a payroll basis	..	..	..	..	..	..	..	..	..	..
2320 On an income tax basis	..	..	..	..	..	..	..	..	..	..
2400 Unallocable between 2100, 2200 and 2300	..	..	4 546	6 026	12 055	13 629	15 826	31 996	34 979	47 891
2410 On a payroll basis	..	..	..	..	..	..	..	..	..	..
2420 On an income tax basis	..	..	..	..	..	..	..	..	..	..
3000 Taxes on payroll and workforce	..	..	**0**	**0**	**0**	**0**	**0**	**0**	**0**	**0**
4000 Taxes on property	..	..	**5 852**	**6 465**	**9 670**	**11 203**	**12 630**	**11 654**	**9 492**	**12 857**
4100 Recurrent taxes on immovable property	..	..	1 319	1 133	1 076	1 133	1 051	1 237	940	714
Immovable property (Stand premia on town plots)	..	..	62	86	0	63	6	36	79	113
Land rates	..	..	0	0	0	0	0	0	0	0
Land rent	..	..	1 257	1 047	1 076	1 071	1 045	1 201	861	601
4110 Households	..	..	..	..	..	..	..	..	..	..
4120 Others	..	..	..	..	..	..	..	..	..	..
4200 Recurrent taxes on net wealth	..	..	0	0	0	0	0	0	0	0
4210 Individual	..	..	..	..	..	..	..	..	..	..
4220 Corporate	..	..	..	..	..	..	..	..	..	..
4300 Estate, inheritance and gift taxes	..	..	0	0	0	0	0	0	0	0
4310 Estate and inheritance taxes	..	..	..	..	..	..	..	..	..	..
4320 Gift taxes	..	..	..	..	..	..	..	..	..	..
4400 Taxes on financial and capital transactions	..	..	4 533	5 332	8 594	10 069	11 579	10 417	8 553	12 143
Stamp duty - Domestic taxes	..	..	4 533	5 332	8 594	10 069	11 579	10 417	8 553	12 143
Stamp duty - Other taxes	..	..	0	0	0	0	0	0	0	0
Stamp duty - Customs services	..	..	0	0	0	0	0	0	0	0
4500 Non-recurrent taxes	..	..	0	0	0	0	0	0	0	0
4510 On net wealth	..	..	..	..	..	..	..	..	..	..
4520 Other non-recurrent taxes	..	..	..	..	..	..	..	..	..	..
4600 Other recurrent taxes on property	..	..	0	0	0	0	0	0	0	0
5000 Taxes on goods and services	..	..	**247 122**	**308 283**	**397 570**	**500 039**	**552 536**	**626 168**	**726 730**	**767 178**
5100 Taxes on production, sale, transfer, etc.	..	..	243 915	304 497	392 618	494 128	546 051	619 129	720 044	759 010
5110 General taxes	..	..	111 036	141 152	183 404	233 724	265 501	291 229	336 674	356 881
5111 Value added taxes	..	..	111 008	141 041	183 219	233 558	264 872	290 843	336 572	356 777
VAT - Ordinary imports	..	..	48 702	57 594	88 023	114 556	127 744	125 105	137 232	144 035
VAT - Oil imports	..	..	4 932	5 352	6 661	10 621	7 894	6 368	6 260	7 643
VAT - Net	..	..	57 374	78 095	88 534	108 380	129 234	159 370	193 081	205 099
VAT - Gross	..	..	69 543	92 255	101 446	123 068	143 922	174 051	206 545	219 499
VAT - Refunds	..	..	-12 169	-14 160	-12 912	-14 688	-14 688	-14 681	-13 464	-14 400
5112 Sales tax	..	..	0	0	0	0	0	0	0	0
5113 Other	..	..	28	111	185	166	630	385	102	103
Turnover tax	..	..	28	111	185	166	630	385	102	103
5120 Taxes on specific goods and services	..	..	132 879	163 345	209 215	260 404	280 550	327 900	383 370	402 129

Table 5.13. **Kenya** *(cont.)*

Details of tax revenue / Recettes fiscales détaillées

Million KES

	1998	2000	2008	2010	2013	2014	2015	2016	2017	2018
5121 Excises	..	..	77 896	93 803	105 288	119 122	130 910	168 286	207 200	213 178
Excise duty - Oil	..	..	27 572	35 780	33 148	38 416	42 687	51 611	59 502	61 216
Excise duty - Domestic	..	..	22 070	23 755	33 260	35 855	38 246	48 986	55 499	53 011
Road maintenance levy	..	..	18 896	23 780	25 002	28 163	30 890	45 407	69 557	73 668
Excise duty - Imports	..	..	6 478	6 994	10 307	13 151	15 175	18 096	19 696	22 311
Sugar levy	..	..	1 293	1 590	1 726	1 585	1 329	1 357	115	16
Petroleum development levy	..	..	1 318	1 585	1 702	1 794	1 817	1 974	2 168	2 262
Petroleum regulatory levy	..	..	0	134	143	158	301	485	498	521
Second hand motor vehicles purchase tax	..	..	270	183	0	0	466	369	166	173
5122 Profits of fiscal monopolies	..	..	0	0	0	0	0	0	0	0
5123 Customs and import duties	..	..	44 970	57 047	82 743	113 701	120 612	125 025	131 577	142 194
Import duty - Ordinary	..	..	31 967	40 382	56 734	65 580	72 346	79 372	85 532	92 076
Import declaration fees	..	..	12 431	15 836	24 270	26 627	27 119	25 851	24 486	26 189
Railway development levy	..	..	0	0	0	19 721	18 940	17 273	18 903	20 780
Import duty - Oil	..	..	573	797	1 163	1 016	1 387	1 595	1 329	1 638
Merchant superintendent shipping levy	..	..	0	32	576	757	820	934	1 328	1 512
5124 Taxes on exports	..	..	0	0	0	0	0	0	0	0
5125 Taxes on investment goods	..	..	0	0	0	0	0	0	0	0
5126 Taxes on specific services	..	..	10 013	12 495	21 184	27 580	29 028	34 589	44 592	46 756
Excise on air time	..	..	6 397	7 893	11 315	12 302	13 122	14 884	15 964	15 626
Airport revenue	..	..	1 921	2 464	6 281	6 837	6 619	6 570	11 199	10 414
Aviation revenue	..	..	1 694	2 138	3 589	3 468	3 565	4 122	4 854	4 819
Excise on financial services	..	..	0	0	0	4 973	5 722	9 013	12 575	15 898
5127 Other taxes on internat. trade and transactions	..	..	0	0	0	0	0	0	0	0
5128 Other taxes	..	..	0	0	0	0	0	0	0	0
5130 Unallocable between 5110 and 5120	..	..	0	0	0	0	0	0	0	0
5200 Taxes on use of goods and perform activities	..	..	3 207	3 786	4 952	5 911	6 485	7 039	6 687	8 169
5210 Recurrent taxes	..	..	3 207	3 786	4 952	5 911	6 485	7 039	6 687	8 169
5211 Paid by households: motor vehicles	..	..	2 872	3 367	4 488	5 415	6 010	6 564	6 185	7 678
Road transport fees	..	..	2 348	2 499	3 027	3 691	3 947	3 911	4 100	3 366
Foreign motor vehicles tax	..	..	0	0	0	0	0	0	93	69
Advance and other taxes	..	..	525	868	1 461	1 725	2 064	2 653	1 993	4 243
5212 Paid by others: motor vehicles	..	..	0	0	0	0	0	0	0	0
5213 Paid in respect of other goods	..	..	335	419	464	496	475	475	501	491
Kenya Bureau of Standards (KEBS) tax	..	..	335	419	464	496	475	475	501	491
5220 Non-recurrent taxes	..	..	0	0	0	0	0	0	0	0
5300 Unallocable between 5100 and 5200	..	..	0	0	0	0	0	0	0	0
6000 Other taxes	..	..	**222**	**164**	**206**	**250**	**150**	**161**	**83**	**86**
Other taxes	..	..	222	164	206	250	150	161	83	86
6100 Paid solely by business	..	..	..	..	..	..	..	..	..	..
6200 Other	..	..	..	..	..	..	..	..	..	..

.. Not available

Note: Data are reported on a fiscal year basis beginning 1st July. For example, the data for 2018 represent July 2017 to June 2018

The data are on a cash basis.

Figures exclude tax revenues collected by sub-national governments as the data are not available.

Heading 2000: Data on social security contributions are not readily available but are deemed to be minimal.

Heading 4100: The data for the immovable property (Stand premia on town plots) tax are not readily available for the years 2001-04 and 2006. No estimation was undertaken given the magnitude of the figures.

Heading 5121: Data for the second hand motor vehicles purchase tax are not readily available for the years 2001-04, 2006, 2013 and 2014. No estimation was undertaken given the magnitude of the figures.

Kenya Bureau of Standards (KEBS) tax: These revenues are collected by the Kenya Revenue Authority (KRA) on behalf of other agencies. The national classification of Kenya classifies all agency revenues as non-tax revenues.

Source: Kenya Revenue Authority (KRA).

StatLink https://doi.org/10.1787/888934183199

Table 5.14. **Lesotho**

Details of tax revenue / Recettes fiscales détaillées

Million LSL

	1998	2000	2008	2010	2013	2014	2015	2016	2017	2018
Total tax revenue	..	..	**2 530**	**3 277**	**4 422**	**5 182**	**5 861**	**5 988**	**5 990**	**6 984**
1000 Taxes on income, profits and capital gains	..	..	**1 543**	**1 996**	**2 690**	**3 066**	**3 651**	**3 734**	**3 576**	**4 103**
1100 Of individuals	..	..	851	1 180	2 072	2 159	2 484	2 695	2 751	3 112
1110 On income and profits	..	..	851	1 180	2 072	2 159	2 484	2 695	2 751	3 112
Personal income tax	..	..	851	1 180	1 645	1 651	1 737	1 965	1 977	2 212
Withholding tax	..	..	0	0	427	507	748	730	774	900
1120 On capital gains	..	..	0	0	0	0	0	0	0	0
1200 Corporate	..	..	383	472	602	884	1 133	991	791	959
1210 On profits	..	..	383	472	602	884	1 133	991	791	959
Corporate income tax	..	..	383	472	595	877	1 126	983	784	955
Gambling levy	..	..	0	0	7	7	8	8	7	4
1220 On capital gains of corporates	..	..	0	0	0	0	0	0	0	0
1300 Unallocable between 1100 and 1200	..	..	309	344	15	23	34	48	33	33
2000 Social security contributions	..	..	**0**	**0**	**0**	**0**	**0**	**0**	**0**	**0**
2100 Employees	..	..	..	..	..	..	..	..	..	..
2110 On a payroll basis	..	..	..	..	..	..	..	..	..	..
2120 On an income tax basis	..	..	..	..	..	..	..	..	..	..
2200 Employers	..	..	..	..	..	..	..	..	..	..
2210 On a payroll basis	..	..	..	..	..	..	..	..	..	..
2220 On an income tax basis	..	..	..	..	..	..	..	..	..	..
2300 Self-employed or non-employed	..	..	..	..	..	..	..	..	..	..
2310 On a payroll basis	..	..	..	..	..	..	..	..	..	..
2320 On an income tax basis	..	..	..	..	..	..	..	..	..	..
2400 Unallocable between 2100, 2200 and 2300	..	..	..	..	..	..	..	..	..	..
2410 On a payroll basis	..	..	..	..	..	..	..	..	..	..
2420 On an income tax basis	..	..	..	..	..	..	..	..	..	..
3000 Taxes on payroll and workforce	..	..	**0**	**0**	**0**	**0**	**0**	**0**	**0**	**0**
4000 Taxes on property	..	..	**0**	**0**	**0**	**0**	**0**	**0**	**0**	**0**
4100 Recurrent taxes on immovable property	..	..	..	..	..	..	..	..	..	..
4110 Households	..	..	..	..	..	..	..	..	..	..
4120 Others	..	..	..	..	..	..	..	..	..	..
4200 Recurrent taxes on net wealth	..	..	..	..	..	..	..	..	..	..
4210 Individual	..	..	..	..	..	..	..	..	..	..
4220 Corporate	..	..	..	..	..	..	..	..	..	..
4300 Estate, inheritance and gift taxes	..	..	..	..	..	..	..	..	..	..
4310 Estate and inheritance taxes	..	..	..	..	..	..	..	..	..	..
4320 Gift taxes	..	..	..	..	..	..	..	..	..	..
4400 Taxes on financial and capital transactions	..	..	..	..	..	..	..	..	..	..
4500 Other non-reccurrent taxes on property	..	..	..	..	..	..	..	..	..	..
4510 On net wealth	..	..	..	..	..	..	..	..	..	..
4520 Other non-recurrent taxes	..	..	..	..	..	..	..	..	..	..
4600 Other recurrent taxes on property	..	..	..	..	..	..	..	..	..	..
5000 Taxes on goods and services	..	..	**988**	**1 281**	**1 732**	**2 117**	**2 210**	**2 254**	**2 414**	**2 880**
5100 Taxes on production, sale, transfer, etc	..	..	988	1 281	1 732	2 117	2 210	2 254	2 414	2 880
5110 General taxes on goods and services	..	..	988	1 281	1 732	2 117	2 210	2 254	2 414	2 880
5111 Value added taxes	..	..	988	1 281	1 732	2 117	2 210	2 254	2 414	2 880
VAT on imports	..	..	369	473	552	705	780	798	795	880
Domestic VAT	..	..	619	808	1 180	1 412	1 430	1 456	1 619	2 000
5112 Sales tax	..	..	0	0	0	0	0	0	0	0
5113 Other	..	..	0	0	0	0	0	0	0	0
5120 Taxes on specific goods and services	..	..	0	0	0	0	0	0	0	0
5121 Excises	..	..	..	..	..	..	..	..	..	..
5122 Profits of fiscal monopolies	..	..	..	..	..	..	..	..	..	..
5123 Customs and import duties	..	..	..	..	..	..	..	..	..	..
5124 Taxes on exports	..	..	..	..	..	..	..	..	..	..
5125 Taxes on investment goods	..	..	..	..	..	..	..	..	..	..
5126 Taxes on specific services	..	..	..	..	..	..	..	..	..	..
5127 Other taxes on internat. trade and transactions	..	..	..	..	..	..	..	..	..	..
5128 Other taxes	..	..	..	..	..	..	..	..	..	..
5130 Unallocable between 5110 and 5120	..	..	0	0	0	0	0	0	0	0
5200 Taxes on use of goods and to perform activities	..	..	0	0	0	0	0	0	0	0
5210 Recurrent taxes	..	..	..	..	..	..	..	..	..	..
5211 Paid by households: motor vehicles	..	..	..	..	..	..	..	..	..	..
5212 Paid by others: motor vehicles	..	..	..	..	..	..	..	..	..	..

Table 5.14. **Lesotho** *(cont.)*

Details of tax revenue / Recettes fiscales détaillées

Million LSL

	1998	2000	2008	2010	2013	2014	2015	2016	2017	2018
5213 Paid in respect of other goods	..	..	..	..	..	..	..	..	..	..
5220 Non-recurrent taxes	..	..	..	..	..	..	..	..	..	..
5300 Unallocable between 5100 and 5200	..	..	0	0	0	0	0	0	0	0
6000 Other taxes	**..**	**..**	**0**	**0**	**0**	**0**	**0**	**0**	**0**	**0**
6100 Paid solely by business	..	..	..	..	..	..	..	..	..	..
6200 Other	..	..	..	..	..	..	..	..	..	..
Memo items:										
Excise taxes collected on behalf of the SACU Common Revenue Pool	..	..	75	110	121	108	102	128	191	212
Import duties collected on behalf of the SACU Common Revenue Pool	..	..	32	32	72	94	145	108	121	145

.. Not available

Note: Data are on a fiscal year basis beginning 1st April. For example, the data for 2018 represent April 2018 to March 2019.

Data are reported on a cash basis.

Heading 2000: Social security contributions for Lesotho are deemed to be null as they do not meet the criteria to be classified as social security contributions set out in the OECD classification of taxes in the Interpretative Guide.

Source: Lesotho Revenue Authority for all revenues except for transfers from the SACU Common Revenue Pool. Lesotho Ministry of Finance budget reports for SACU revenues.

StatLink https://doi.org/10.1787/888934183503

Table 5.15. **Madagascar**

Details of tax revenue / Recettes fiscales détaillées

Million MGA

	1998	2000	2008	2010	2013	2014	2015	2016	2017	2018
Recettes fiscales totales	**403 760**	**603 200**	**2 088 414**	**1 980 849**	**2 547 517**	**2 701 917**	**3 146 042**	**3 780 986**	**4 487 041**	**5 283 054**
1000 Impôts sur revenu, bénéfices et gains en capital	**75 760**	**102 580**	**533 978**	**490 294**	**570 480**	**611 375**	**706 750**	**882 598**	**1 002 793**	**1 174 764**
1100 Des personnes physiques	25 220	36 080	247 011	253 868	293 980	306 645	366 600	429 165	474 685	547 816
1110 Sur le revenu et les bénéfices	17 940	25 800	166 145	216 415	266 060	280 558	338 560	387 703	430 830	492 008
Traitements et salaires	17 220	25 260	148 091	201 077	249 470	260 818	315 570	359 334	398 027	446 571
Bénéfices non commerciaux (BNC)	720	540	3 430	1 841	1 750	2 420	3 850	5 994	6 874	6 094
Bénéfices industriels et commerciaux (BIC)	0	0	14 624	13 497	14 840	17 320	19 140	22 376	25 930	39 344
1120 Sur les gains en capital	7 280	10 280	80 866	37 453	27 920	26 087	28 040	41 461	43 855	55 807
1200 Des sociétés	48 340	62 240	285 750	236 426	276 500	304 730	340 150	453 433	528 108	626 948
1210 Sur les bénéfices	43 600	56 880	285 750	236 426	276 500	304 730	340 150	453 433	528 108	626 948
1220 Sur les gains en capital	4 740	5 360	0	0	0	0	0	0	0	0
1300 Non ventilables entre 1100 et 1200	2 200	4 260	1 217	0	0	0	0	0	0	0
2000 Cotisations de sécurité sociale	**0**	**0**	**0**	**0**	**96 913**	**113 099**	**133 072**	**132 033**	**159 300**	**280 098**
2100 A la charge des salariés	..	..	..	..	0	0	0	0	0	0
2110 Sur la base du salaire	..	..	..	..	..	..	..	..	..	..
2120 Sur la base de l'impôt sur le revenu	..	..	..	..	..	..	..	..	..	..
2200 A la charge des employeurs	..	..	..	..	0	0	0	0	0	0
2210 Sur la base du salaire	..	..	..	..	..	..	..	..	..	..
2220 Sur la base de l'impôt sur le revenu	..	..	..	..	..	..	..	..	..	..
2300 A charge des travailleurs indép. ou sans emploi	..	..	..	..	0	0	0	0	0	0
2310 Sur la base du salaire	..	..	..	..	..	..	..	..	..	..
2320 Sur la base de l'impôt sur le revenu	..	..	..	..	..	..	..	..	..	..
2400 Non ventilables entre 2100, 2200 et 2300	..	..	..	..	96 913	113 099	133 072	132 033	159 300	280 098
2410 Sur la base du salaire	..	..	..	..	..	..	..	..	..	..
2420 Sur la base de l'impôt sur le revenu	..	..	..	..	..	..	..	..	..	..
3000 Sur salaires ou main d'oeuvre	**0**	**0**	**0**	**0**	**0**	**0**	**0**	**0**	**0**	**0**
4000 Impôts sur le patrimoine	**3 060**	**4 340**	**29 094**	**10 560**	**15 310**	**18 577**	**24 150**	**25 056**	**25 784**	**41 045**
4100 Impôts périodiques sur la propriété immobilière	0	0	0	0	0	0	0	0	0	0
4110 Ménages	..	..	..	..	..	..	..	..	..	..
4120 Autres agents	..	..	..	..	..	..	..	..	..	..
4200 Impôts périodiques sur l'actif net	0	0	0	0	0	0	0	0	0	0
4210 Personnes physiques	..	..	..	..	..	..	..	..	..	..
4220 Sociétés	..	..	..	..	..	..	..	..	..	..
4300 Impôts sur mut. par décès, succ. et donations	0	0	0	0	0	0	0	0	0	0
4310 Impôts sur mut. par décès et successions	..	..	..	..	..	..	..	..	..	..
4320 Impôts sur les donations	..	..	..	..	..	..	..	..	..	..
4400 Impôts sur transact. mobilières et immob.	0	0	0	0	0	0	0	0	0	0
4500 Impôts non-périodiques	0	0	0	0	0	0	0	0	0	0
4510 Sur l'actif net	..	..	..	..	..	..	..	..	..	..
4520 Autres non-périodiques	..	..	..	..	..	..	..	..	..	..
4600 Autres impôts périodiques sur patrimoine	3 060	4 340	29 094	10 560	15 310	18 577	24 150	25 056	25 784	41 045
5000 Impôts sur les biens et services	**319 000**	**490 160**	**1 494 950**	**1 472 696**	**1 861 820**	**1 955 776**	**2 278 920**	**2 726 608**	**3 283 931**	**3 765 695**
5100 Impôts sur production, vente, transfert, etc.	317 960	488 480	1 491 550	1 468 130	1 855 430	1 949 239	2 271 820	2 718 859	3 276 204	3 757 003
5110 Impôts généraux	158 200	280 700	1 036 711	1 004 032	1 307 760	1 360 458	1 545 130	1 837 385	2 262 049	2 566 967
5111 Taxes sur la valeur ajoutée	136 000	244 860	1 036 663	1 004 032	1 307 760	1 360 458	1 545 130	1 837 385	2 262 049	2 566 967
TVA Intérieure	45 140	102 560	350 101	437 348	435 010	457 308	544 130	693 241	843 911	906 711
TVA Douane import	90 860	142 300	482 514	387 092	515 130	611 850	728 300	881 624	1 088 765	1 232 623
TVA Douane sur les produits pétroliers	0	0	204 048	179 592	357 620	291 300	272 700	262 520	329 373	427 632
5112 Impôts sur les ventes	0	0	0	0	0	0	0	0	0	0
5113 Autres impôts	22 200	35 840	48	0	0	0	0	0	0	0
5120 Impôts sur biens et services déterminés	159 760	207 780	454 839	464 098	547 670	588 781	726 690	881 474	1 014 155	1 190 036
5121 Accises	20 700	43 700	134 520	201 039	248 110	236 881	268 490	342 945	385 177	422 353
Accises domestiques	15 300	31 920	134 042	201 039	248 110	236 881	268 490	342 945	385 177	422 353
Accises à la douane	5 400	11 780	478	0	0	0	0	0	0	0
5122 Bénéfices des monopoles fiscaux	0	0	0	0	0	0	0	0	0	0
5123 Droits de douane et droits à l'importation	139 060	152 380	320 271	262 726	299 530	351 860	458 100	538 485	628 505	767 173
Droit de douanes	29 140	24 700	219 516	172 369	219 880	264 310	331 400	412 085	493 156	535 458
Taxe d'importation	54 000	48 140	0	0	0	0	0	0	0	0
Taxes s/ prod. Pétroliers (total)	55 920	79 540	100 755	90 357	79 650	87 550	126 700	126 400	135 349	231 715
5124 Taxes à l'exportation	0	0	0	0	0	0	0	0	0	0
5125 Impôts sur biens d'équipement	0	0	0	0	0	0	0	0	0	0
5126 Impôts sur services déterminés	0	0	0	0	0	0	0	0	0	0

Table 5.15. **Madagascar** *(cont.)*

Details of tax revenue / Recettes fiscales détaillées

Million MGA

	1998	2000	2008	2010	2013	2014	2015	2016	2017	2018
5127 Autres impôts sur commerce et transact. internat.	0	11 700	48	333	30	40	100	44	473	510
Taxe statistique s/ import	..	8 040	0	0	0	0	0	0	0	0
Autres	..	3 660	48	333	30	40	100	44	473	510
5128 Autres impôts	0	0	0	0	0	0	0	0	0	0
5130 Non ventilables entre 5110 et 5120	0	0	0	0	0	0	0	0	0	0
5200 Impôts sur utilisation des biens et exerc. activités	1 040	1 680	3 400	4 566	6 390	6 537	7 100	7 750	7 727	8 692
5210 Impôts périodiques	1 040	1 680	3 400	4 566	6 390	6 537	7 100	7 750	7 727	8 692
5211 A la charge des ménages: véhicules à moteur	0	0	0	0	0	0	0	0	0	0
5212 A la charge autres agents: véhicules à moteur	0	0	0	0	0	0	0	0	0	0
5213 Autres impôts périodiques	1 040	1 680	3 400	4 566	6 390	6 537	7 100	7 750	7 727	8 692
5220 Impôts non-périodiques	0	0	0	0	0	0	0	0	0	0
5300 Non ventilables entre 5100 et 5200	0	0	0	0	0	0	0	0	0	0
6000 Autres impôts	**5 940**	**6 120**	**30 392**	**7 299**	**2 994**	**3 090**	**3 150**	**14 690**	**15 233**	**21 453**
6100 A la charge exclusive des entreprises	3 240	2 540	6 940	3 739	314	470	650	1 004	944	687
6200 A la charge d'autres agents	2 700	3 580	23 452	3 560	2 680	2 620	2 500	13 686	14 289	20 766

.. Non disponible

Note : Année civile se terminant le 31 décembre.

Les données sont sur la base des encaissements.

Les chiffres n'incluent pas les recettes fiscales collectées par les collectivités locales car elles ne sont pas disponibles.

Les cotisations de sécurité sociale sous la rubrique 2000 ne sont pas considérées comme des recettes fiscales au Madagascar

Source : Ministère de l'Économie et des Finances de Madagascar.

StatLink https://doi.org/10.1787/888934183541

Table 5.16. **Malawi**

Details of tax revenue / Recettes fiscales détaillées

Million MWK

	1998	2000	2008	2010	2013	2014	2015	2016	2017	2018
Total tax revenue	..	..	**99 629**	**152 744**	**284 170**	**409 458**	**485 326**	**604 221**	**795 784**	**880 895**
1000 Taxes on income, profits and capital gains	..	..	**40 069**	**67 576**	**131 759**	**183 316**	**236 126**	**292 729**	**386 078**	**423 259**
1100 Of individuals	..	..	23 241	36 525	72 270	101 902	139 074	186 751	224 334	256 576
1110 On income and profits	..	..	23 241	36 525	72 270	101 902	139 074	186 751	224 334	256 576
Pay as you earn tax (PAYE)	..	..	21 354	32 849	65 117	91 442	126 367	166 855	199 315	228 697
Fringe benefits	..	..	1 138	1 675	2 908	4 495	5 350	7 506	8 981	10 749
Non-resident tax	..	..	506	835	1 737	3 320	4 585	8 488	13 153	13 116
Dividends	..	..	243	1 165	2 508	2 645	2 772	3 901	2 885	4 013
1120 On capital gains	..	..	0	0	0	0	0	0	0	0
1200 Corporate	..	..	16 828	31 051	59 490	81 414	97 052	105 978	161 744	166 683
1210 On profits	..	..	16 828	31 051	59 490	81 414	97 052	105 978	161 744	166 683
Company assessments	..	..	2 990	6 981	6 279	8 092	14 186	14 753	21 125	28 858
Provisional corporate income tax	..	..	8 574	16 253	30 486	39 606	43 723	42 897	64 656	64 987
Withholding tax on corporations	..	..	5 264	7 817	22 725	33 715	39 143	48 328	64 041	72 839
Capital gains tax	..	..	0	0	0	0	0	0	11 923	0
1220 On capital gains of corporates	..	..	0	0	0	0	0	0	0	0
1300 Unallocable between 1100 and 1200	..	..	0	0	0	0	0	0	0	0
2000 Social security contributions	..	..	**0**	**0**	**0**	**0**	**0**	**0**	**0**	**0**
2100 Employees	..	..	..	..	..	..	..	..	..	..
2110 On a payroll basis	..	..	..	..	..	..	..	..	..	..
2120 On an income tax basis	..	..	..	..	..	..	..	..	..	..
2200 Employers	..	..	..	..	..	..	..	..	..	..
2210 On a payroll basis	..	..	..	..	..	..	..	..	..	..
2220 On an income tax basis	..	..	..	..	..	..	..	..	..	..
2300 Self-employed or non-employed	..	..	..	..	..	..	..	..	..	..
2310 On a payroll basis	..	..	..	..	..	..	..	..	..	..
2320 On an income tax basis	..	..	..	..	..	..	..	..	..	..
2400 Unallocable between 2100, 2200 and 2300	..	..	..	..	..	..	..	..	..	..
2410 On a payroll basis	..	..	..	..	..	..	..	..	..	..
2420 On an income tax basis	..	..	..	..	..	..	..	..	..	..
3000 Taxes on payroll and workforce	..	..	**0**	**0**	**0**	**0**	**0**	**0**	**0**	**0**
4000 Taxes on property	..	..	**0**	**0**	**0**	**0**	**0**	**0**	**0**	**0**
4100 Recurrent taxes on immovable property	..	..	0	0	0	0	0	0	0	0
4110 Households	..	..	..	..	..	..	..	..	..	..
4120 Others	..	..	..	..	..	..	..	..	..	..
4200 Recurrent taxes on net wealth	..	..	0	0	0	0	0	0	0	0
4210 Individual	..	..	..	..	..	..	..	..	..	..
4220 Corporate	..	..	..	..	..	..	..	..	..	..
4300 Estate, inheritance and gift taxes	..	..	0	0	0	0	0	0	0	0
4310 Estate and inheritance taxes	..	..	..	..	..	..	..	..	..	..
4320 Gift taxes	..	..	..	..	..	..	..	..	..	..
4400 Taxes on financial and capital transactions	..	..	0	0	0	0	0	0	0	0
4500 Other non-reccurrent taxes on property	..	..	0	0	0	0	0	0	0	0
4510 On net wealth	..	..	..	..	..	..	..	..	..	..
4520 Other non-recurrent taxes	..	..	..	..	..	..	..	..	..	..
4600 Other recurrent taxes on property	..	..	0	0	0	0	0	0	0	0
5000 Taxes on goods and services	..	..	**59 471**	**84 865**	**151 871**	**225 687**	**248 646**	**310 922**	**408 050**	**457 223**
5100 Taxes on production, sale, transfer, etc	..	..	59 471	84 865	151 871	225 687	248 646	310 922	408 050	457 223
5110 General taxes on goods and services	..	..	30 509	38 751	75 131	120 888	137 551	166 781	220 278	247 658
5111 Value added taxes	..	..	30 509	38 751	75 125	120 878	137 539	166 761	220 266	247 632
VAT revenues (domestic)	..	..	14 481	21 932	40 805	56 454	67 149	75 727	108 064	132 750
VAT on imports	..	..	18 628	22 482	41 387	69 595	80 007	99 900	129 668	139 080
VAT refunds	..	..	-2 600	-5 663	-7 067	-5 171	-9 618	-8 866	-17 466	-24 199
5112 Sales tax	..	..	0	0	0	0	0	0	0	0
5113 Other	..	..	0	0	6	9	12	20	13	26
Turnover tax	..	..	0	0	6	9	12	20	13	26
5120 Taxes on specific goods and services	..	..	28 962	46 115	76 739	104 799	111 094	144 141	187 771	209 565
5121 Excises	..	..	17 041	31 122	43 970	63 738	64 856	91 580	117 941	133 326
Local excise taxes	..	..	2 469	5 805	8 909	13 746	15 368	19 860	28 389	32 208
Excise taxes on imports	..	..	11 315	14 233	19 630	28 511	26 419	29 981	41 714	48 544
Road Levy (fuel tax)	..	..	3 257	7 507	7 276	8 281	9 312	19 619	24 002	26 277
Road tax (fuel tax)	..	..	0	0	1 147	3 617	3 837	4 425	4 717	5 580
Rural Electrification Levy (fuel tax)	..	..	0	3 577	5 816	8 368	8 681	16 255	17 530	18 950
Storage Levy (fuel tax)	..	..	0	0	1 191	1 214	1 240	1 441	1 590	1 768

Table 5.16. Malawi *(cont.)*

Details of tax revenue / Recettes fiscales détaillées

Million MWK

	1998	2000	2008	2010	2013	2014	2015	2016	2017	2018
5122 Profits of fiscal monopolies	..	..	0	0	0	0	0	0	0	0
5123 Customs and import duties	..	..	11 921	14 993	32 769	41 061	46 238	52 562	69 830	76 239
Import duty	..	..	11 544	15 775	32 865	41 115	46 121	52 197	69 773	76 179
Prepayments collected on import duties	..	..	376	-783	-96	-53	117	365	57	60
5124 Taxes on exports	..	..	0	0	0	0	0	0	0	0
5125 Taxes on investment goods	..	..	0	0	0	0	0	0	0	0
5126 Taxes on specific services	..	..	0	0	0	0	0	0	0	0
5127 Other taxes on internat. trade and transactions	..	..	0	0	0	0	0	0	0	0
5128 Other taxes	..	..	0	0	0	0	0	0	0	0
5130 Unallocable between 5110 and 5120	..	..	0	0	0	0	0	0	0	0
5200 Taxes on use of goods and to perform activities	..	..	0	0	0	0	0	0	0	0
5210 Recurrent taxes	..	..	0	0	0	0	0	0	0	0
5211 Paid by households: motor vehicles	..	..	..	..	0	0	0	0	0	0
5212 Paid by others: motor vehicles	..	..	..	..	0	0	0	0	0	0
5213 Paid in respect of other goods	..	..	..	..	0	0	0	0	0	0
5220 Non-recurrent taxes	..	..	0	0	0	0	0	0	0	0
5300 Unallocable between 5100 and 5200	..	..	0	0	0	0	0	0	0	0
6000 Other taxes	**..**	**..**	**88**	**303**	**540**	**455**	**554**	**570**	**1 656**	**413**
6100 Paid solely by business	..	..	88	303	540	455	554	570	1 656	413
6200 Other	..	..	0	0	0	0	0	0	0	0

.. Not available

Note: Data are on a fiscal year basis beginning 1st July. For example, the data for 2018 represent July 1, 2017 to June 30, 2018.

Figures exclude tax revenues collected by sub-national governments as the data are not available.

Heading 2000: Social security contributions for Malawi are deemed to be null as they do not meet the criteria to be classified as social security contributions set out in the OECD classification of taxes in the Interpretative Guide.

Source: Ministry of Finance, Economic Planning and Development of Malawi.

StatLink https://doi.org/10.1787/888934183579

Table 5.17. **Mali**

Details of tax revenue / Recettes fiscales détaillées

Million XOF

	1998	2000	2008	2010	2013	2014	2015	2016	2017	2018
Recettes fiscales totales	**230 200**	**239 362**	**585 641**	**748 245**	**930 886**	**988 961**	**1 174 860**	**1 371 149**	**1 491 790**	**1 328 988**
1000 Impôts sur revenu, bénéfices et gains en capital	**42 887**	**34 218**	**132 226**	**183 548**	**229 742**	**295 236**	**294 843**	**325 600**	**389 604**	**312 283**
1100 Des personnes physiques	40 889	32 095	51 613	61 018	69 954	88 538	92 395	101 312	114 724	93 611
1110 Sur le revenu et les bénéfices	40 889	32 095	51 613	61 018	69 954	88 538	92 395	101 312	114 724	93 611
ITS retenue, secteur privé	11 258	12 374	30 731	39 859	56 021	63 658	71 153	76 734	91 859	74 395
ITS retenue, secteur public	3 336	3 311	8 244	8 624	9 425	8 797	13 904	13 882	15 677	12 004
BIC secteur privé	24 375	15 996	9 193	10 643	2 695	14 171	5 024	7 643	4 163	4 107
BIC secteur état	642	38	2 193	0	0	0	0	0	0	0
Impôts sur les revenus fonciers	1 278	376	1 252	1 892	1 813	1 912	2 314	3 053	3 025	3 105
1120 Sur les gains en capital	..	..	..	..	..	..	..	..	..	..
1200 Des sociétés	..	..	66 910	107 703	141 576	182 280	174 434	199 055	246 449	197 655
1210 Sur les bénéfices	..	..	66 910	107 703	141 576	182 280	174 434	199 055	246 449	197 655
Impôt sur les societés (IS privé)	..	..	66 910	107 582	141 574	182 231	174 433	199 055	246 446	197 499
Impôt sur les societés (IS état)	..	..	0	121	2	49	1	0	3	157
1220 Sur les gains en capital	..	..	..	..	..	..	..	..	..	..
1300 Non ventilables entre 1100 et 1200	1 998	2 123	13 703	14 827	18 212	24 418	28 014	25 233	28 431	21 017
2000 Cotisations de sécurité sociale	**14 083**	**18 442**	**65 185**	**73 600**	**91 693**	**110 925**	**116 702**	**153 398**	**156 268**	**158 559**
2100 A la charge des salariés	..	..	..	..	..	..	..	..	..	..
2110 Sur la base du salaire	..	..	..	..	..	..	..	..	..	..
2120 Sur la base de l'impôt sur le revenu	..	..	..	..	..	..	..	..	..	..
2200 A la charge des employeurs	..	..	..	..	..	..	..	..	..	..
2210 Sur la base du salaire	..	..	..	..	..	..	..	..	..	..
2220 Sur la base de l'impôt sur le revenu	..	..	..	..	..	..	..	..	..	..
2300 A charge des travailleurs indép. ou sans emploi	..	..	..	..	..	..	..	..	..	..
2310 Sur la base du salaire	..	..	..	..	..	..	..	..	..	..
2320 Sur la base de l'impôt sur le revenu	..	..	..	..	..	..	..	..	..	..
2400 Non ventilables entre 2100, 2200 et 2300	14 083	18 442	65 185	73 600	91 693	110 925	116 702	153 398	156 268	158 559
Social security contributions (CMSS)	..	..	11 341	12 834	22 570	24 444	26 550	45 311	41 985	34 758
Social security contributions (INPS)	14 083	18 442	53 843	60 766	69 123	86 481	90 152	108 086	114 283	123 801
2410 Sur la base du salaire	..	..	..	..	..	..	..	..	..	..
2420 Sur la base de l'impôt sur le revenu	..	..	..	..	..	..	..	..	..	..
3000 Sur salaires ou main d'oeuvre	**4 575**	**4 671**	**7 843**	**6 278**	**8 451**	**9 881**	**11 567**	**13 192**	**13 685**	**11 938**
4000 Impôts sur le patrimoine	**3 201**	**3 149**	**9 063**	**12 062**	**12 450**	**16 512**	**17 933**	**28 489**	**32 171**	**26 353**
4100 Impôts périodiques sur la propriété immobilière	123	119	771	979	923	1 380	1 561	1 590	2 156	1 779
Droits de conservation de la propriété	123	119	771	979	913	1 341	1 549	1 572	2 139	1 764
Taxe sur les locations des particuliers	0	0	0	0	10	39	12	18	17	15
4110 Ménages	..	..	..	..	..	..	..	..	..	..
4120 Autres agents	..	..	..	..	..	..	..	..	..	..
4200 Impôts périodiques sur l'actif net	0	0	0	0	0	0	0	0	0	0
4210 Personnes physiques	..	..	..	..	..	..	..	..	..	..
4220 Sociétés	..	..	..	..	..	..	..	..	..	..
4300 Impôts sur mut. par décès, succ. et donations	0	0	0	0	0	0	0	0	0	0
4310 Impôts sur mut. par décès et successions	..	..	..	..	..	..	..	..	..	..
4320 Impôts sur les donations	..	..	..	..	..	..	..	..	..	..
4400 Impôts sur transact. mobilières et immob.	3 078	3 030	8 292	11 083	11 527	15 132	16 372	26 899	30 015	24 573
Droits d'enregistrements (DGI)	3 003	2 934	4 175	6 928	6 677	8 726	11 023	18 390	19 941	16 754
Droits d'enregistrements (DND)	0	0	4 117	4 107	4 584	6 150	5 321	8 436	9 815	7 499
Transfert lettre et permis OCC en TF	75	96	0	0	0	0	0	0	0	0
Taxe sur les frais d'édilité	0	0	0	48	266	256	28	73	259	320
4500 Impôts non-périodiques	0	0	0	0	0	0	0	0	0	0
4510 Sur l'actif net	..	..	..	..	..	..	..	..	..	..
4520 Autres non-périodiques	..	..	..	..	..	..	..	..	..	..
4600 Autres impôts périodiques sur patrimoine	0	0	0	0	0	0	0	0	0	0
5000 Impôts sur les biens et services	**157 903**	**172 751**	**348 931**	**453 154**	**556 400**	**523 879**	**691 372**	**812 621**	**875 751**	**795 470**
5100 Impôts sur production, vente, transfert, etc.	157 254	171 923	347 502	451 425	554 301	521 526	688 714	809 335	872 544	791 158
5110 Impôts généraux	59 623	81 113	200 194	261 811	331 998	280 616	329 598	396 055	440 417	438 078
5111 Taxes sur la valeur ajoutée	59 623	80 633	198 385	260 599	330 695	279 167	328 157	394 552	438 914	436 609
TVA à l'importation	35 279	46 622	110 254	161 656	203 494	176 270	210 431	232 434	282 199	268 881
Recettes TVA (privé)	19 967	31 218	77 834	95 383	120 244	99 994	113 512	150 102	153 442	100 982
Recettes TVA (gouvernement)	4 377	2 793	10 297	3 560	6 957	2 903	4 214	12 016	3 273	1 677
Crédits TVA (DGD) - extrabudgétaires	..	..	..	..	..	..	..	..	..	11 501
Crédits TVA (DGI) - extrabudgétaires	..	..	..	..	..	..	..	..	..	53 569
5112 Impôts sur les ventes	0	0	0	0	0	0	0	0	0	0

Table 5.17. **Mali** *(cont.)*

Details of tax revenue / Recettes fiscales détaillées

Million XOF

	1998	2000	2008	2010	2013	2014	2015	2016	2017	2018
5113 Autres impôts	0	480	1 809	1 212	1 303	1 449	1 441	1 503	1 503	1 469
Contribution Générale de Solidarité (FDD) - extrabudgétaire	0	480	1 809	1 212	1 303	1 449	1 441	1 503	1 503	1 469
5120 Impôts sur biens et services déterminés	97 631	90 810	147 308	189 614	222 303	240 910	359 116	413 280	432 127	353 080
5121 Accises	59 322	45 791	54 212	56 909	62 716	68 459	136 898	159 013	148 200	103 676
Taxes intérieures sur produits petroliers (TIPP)	33 400	33 694	34 927	25 660	22 286	27 793	93 264	100 648	87 789	48 611
Taxe Ad Valorem (entreprises minières) (DNDC)	3 612	4 233	11 329	20 479	28 889	25 474	25 253	30 605	30 681	27 246
Taxes locales sur les tabacs	1 566	816	4 746	5 385	3 650	6 445	8 264	12 787	14 725	14 405
Taxes sur les boissons alcoolisés	1 190	1 169	2 648	1 777	1 912	2 880	3 611	3 672	4 806	4 750
Impôt spécial sur les boissons	596	1 519	388	2 088	3 240	3 473	4 237	5 431	6 755	5 459
Taxe sur autres produits	18 958	4 360	174	1 520	2 739	2 394	2 269	5 870	3 444	3 205
5122 Bénéfices des monopoles fiscaux	0	0	0	0	0	0	0	0	0	0
5123 Droits de douane et droits à l'importation	31 140	30 734	58 749	86 853	104 534	105 683	124 049	139 263	161 928	147 355
Droits de douanes	30 352	29 328	52 554	76 287	93 269	93 480	111 062	124 320	144 024	129 869
Redevance Statistique	0	315	5 638	9 702	10 634	11 125	12 940	14 803	17 804	16 939
Taxe degréssive de protection (TDP)	66	6	534	831	542	969	0	0	0	0
Taxe conjoncturelle à l'importation	722	1 085	23	33	89	109	47	140	100	547
5124 Taxes à l'exportation	3 396	4 046	13 924	20 503	26 383	26 407	30 243	29 288	37 421	33 887
CPS sur l'or	3 396	4 046	13 924	20 503	26 383	26 407	30 243	29 288	37 421	33 887
5125 Impôts sur biens d'équipement	0	0	0	0	0	0	0	0	0	0
5126 Impôts sur services déterminés	3 773	10 239	20 423	25 349	28 670	40 361	67 926	85 716	84 578	68 162
Taxes sur les Activités Financières	0	5 785	12 687	17 828	18 378	23 112	39 608	41 562	43 886	32 993
Ristournes sur PMU et CASINO	1 677	1 515	3 172	3 061	4 173	5 173	5 966	6 821	6 832	7 069
Taxes sur les transporteurs routiers	1 240	1 676	2 595	2 659	2 962	3 243	3 499	4 890	4 072	4 212
Taxes sur les contrats d'assurances	826	1 261	1 959	1 787	3 155	3 465	3 321	4 783	4 454	4 066
Autres taxes sur les services déterminés	30	2	10	14	2	3	2	10	1	1
Taxe sur Accès au Reseau de Télécom Ouvert au Public (TARTOP)	0	0	0	0	0	5 365	15 530	27 650	25 333	19 822
5127 Autres impôts sur commerce et transact. internat.	0	0	0	0	0	0	0	0	0	0
5128 Autres impôts	0	0	0	0	0	0	0	0	0	0
5130 Non ventilables entre 5110 et 5120	0	0	0	0	0	0	0	0	0	0
5200 Impôts sur utilisation des biens et exerc. activites	649	828	1 429	1 729	2 099	2 353	2 658	3 286	3 207	4 313
5210 Impôts périodiques	649	828	1 429	1 729	2 099	2 353	2 658	3 286	3 207	4 313
5211 A la charge des ménages: véhicules à moteur	557	716	1 414	1 715	2 083	2 336	2 658	3 286	3 207	3 389
5212 A la charge autres agents: véhicules à moteur	0	0	0	0	0	0	0	0	0	0
5213 Autres impôts périodiques	92	112	15	14	16	17	0	0	0	924
5220 Impôts non-périodiques	0	0	0	0	0	0	0	0	0	0
5300 Non ventilables entre 5100 et 5200	0	0	0	0	0	0	0	0	0	0
6000 Autres impôts	**7 551**	**6 131**	**22 393**	**19 603**	**32 150**	**32 528**	**42 443**	**37 849**	**24 311**	**24 385**
Droits de Timbres (DGI)	5 795	4 188	8 977	10 797	14 719	15 000	16 840	18 821	16 502	17 702
Droits de timbres (DND)	0	0	155	143	390	500	235	277	455	406
Recettes sur exercices antérieurs	1 756	1 943	13 261	8 663	17 041	17 028	25 368	18 751	7 354	6 277
6100 A la charge exclusive des entreprises	..	..	..	..	..	..	..	..	..	..
6200 A la charge d'autres agents	..	..	..	..	..	..	..	..	..	..

.. Non disponible

Note : Année civile se terminant le 31 décembre.

Les données sont sur la base des encaissements.

Les chiffres n'incluent pas les recettes fiscales collectées par les collectivités locales car elles ne sont pas disponibles.

Les données pour 2018 incluent des recettes extrabudgétaires qui n'étaient pas présents dans les années antérieurs. Les recettes extrabudgétaires incluent les recettes des budgets annexes et les recettes des comptes spéciaux du trésor. Ceci affectes les rubriques 5111 et 5113 dans les recette fiscales.

Les données sur les cotisations de la Caisse Malienne de Sécurité Sociale (CMSS) et les données de l'Institut National de Prévoyance Sociale (INPS) ne sont disponibles qu'à partir de 2004 et 2006 respectivement. Ces recettes ne sont pas incluses dans les recettes de l'État du Mali.

Rubrique 5123 : Les recettes de la CEDEAO (Communauté économique des États de l'Afrique de l'Ouest), y compris les redevances statistiques, le prélèvement communautaire, et la taxe dégressive de protection, ne sont pas considérées comme des recettes fiscales ou des recettes non fiscales selon le guide d'interprétation de l'OCDE (voir § 4).

Rubrique 5126 : Les recettes de TARTOP étaient incluses dans les recettes non fiscales (Ventes de biens et services) dans les éditions précédentes.

Source : Ministère de l'Économie et des Finances et la Direction Nationale du Trésor et de la Comptabilité Publique du Mali.

StatLink https://doi.org/10.1787/888934183218

Table 5.18. **Mauritania / Mauritanie**

Details of tax revenue / Recettes fiscales détaillées

Million MRU

	1998	2000	2008	2010	2013	2014	2015	2016	2017	2018
Recettes fiscales totales	..	..	**12 587**	**15 175**	**28 962**	**30 165**	**29 070**	**31 922**	**35 128**	**40 318**
1000 Impôts sur revenu, bénéfices et gains en capital	..	..	**4 251**	**5 282**	**11 116**	**11 442**	**9 722**	**9 980**	**10 971**	**11 853**
1100 Des personnes physiques	..	..	1 496	2 266	4 365	4 847	4 324	4 088	4 110	4 586
1110 Sur le revenu et les bénéfices	..	..	1 496	2 266	4 365	4 847	4 324	4 088	4 110	4 586
Impôt sur le traitement de salaires	..	..	1 150	1 396	3 607	3 901	3 819	3 588	3 635	3 936
Dont: ITS Pétrole	..	..	0	94	1 195	229	129	196	258	342
impot sur le revenu des capitaux mobiliers	..	..	280	777	640	724	400	379	352	526
Impôt sur les revenus fonciers	..	..	25	45	79	142	101	121	119	124
Impôt général sur le revenu	..	..	41	48	39	80	4	0	4	0
1120 Sur les gains en capital	..	..	0	0	0	0	0	0	0	0
1200 Des sociétés	..	..	2 755	3 015	6 751	6 595	5 398	5 892	6 861	7 267
1210 Sur les bénéfices	..	..	2 755	3 015	6 751	6 595	5 398	5 892	6 861	7 267
Bénéfices industriels et commerciaux (BIC), non commerciaux (BNC) et impôt minimum forfaitaire (IMF)	..	..	802	1 400	2 800	3 195	3 400	3 324	3 025	3 398
Dont: BIC Pétrole	..	..	0	144	166	72	43	103	238	296
Taxe unique de la SNIM (Société Nationale Industrielle et Minière de Mauritanie)	..	..	1 070	921	1 896	1 583	223	430	1 249	408
IMF Douanes	..	..	884	695	1 569	1 466	1 452	1 378	1 590	1 850
Régime simplifié d'imposition	..	..	0	0	486	351	323	760	998	1 610
1220 Sur les gains en capital	..	..	0	0	0	0	0	0	0	0
1300 Non ventilables entre 1100 et 1200	..	..	0	0	0	0	0	0	0	0
2000 Cotisations de sécurité sociale	..	..	**828**	**1 019**	**1 403**	**1 753**	**1 796**	**1 721**	**1 865**	**2 025**
2100 A la charge des salariés	..	..	..	..	..	..	..	..	..	..
2110 Sur la base du salaire	..	..	..	..	..	..	..	..	..	..
2120 Sur la base de l'impôt sur le revenu	..	..	..	..	..	..	..	..	..	..
2200 A la charge des employeurs	..	..	..	..	..	..	..	..	..	..
2210 Sur la base du salaire	..	..	..	..	..	..	..	..	..	..
2220 Sur la base de l'impôt sur le revenu	..	..	..	..	..	..	..	..	..	..
2300 A charge des travailleurs indép. ou sans emploi	..	..	..	..	..	..	..	..	..	..
2310 Sur la base du salaire	..	..	..	..	..	..	..	..	..	..
2320 Sur la base de l'impôt sur le revenu	..	..	..	..	..	..	..	..	..	..
2400 Non ventilables entre 2100, 2200 et 2300	..	..	828	1 019	1 403	1 753	1 796	1 721	1 865	2 025
Cotisations CNSS	..	..	368	424	572	587	592	622	646	650
Cotisations CNAM	..	..	460	595	831	1 166	1 204	1 099	1 219	1 376
2410 Sur la base du salaire	..	..	..	..	..	..	..	..	..	..
2420 Sur la base de l'impôt sur le revenu	..	..	..	..	..	..	..	..	..	..
3000 Sur salaires ou main-d'oeuvre	..	..	**25**	**32**	**39**	**32**	**48**	**40**	**42**	**41**
4000 Impôts sur le patrimoine	..	..	**0**	**646**	**763**	**953**	**1 387**	**1 294**	**1 155**	**1 172**
4100 Impôts périodiques sur la propriété immobilière	..	..	0	622	715	902	1 346	1 251	1 097	1 113
4110 Ménages	..	..	..	..	..	..	..	..	..	..
4120 Autres agents	..	..	..	..	..	..	..	..	..	..
4200 Impôts périodiques sur l'actif net	..	..	0	0	0	0	0	0	0	0
4210 Personnes physiques	..	..	..	..	..	..	..	..	..	..
4220 Sociétés	..	..	..	..	..	..	..	..	..	..
4300 Impôts sur mut. par décès, succ. et donations	..	..	0	0	0	0	0	0	0	0
4310 Impôts sur mut. par décès et successions	..	..	..	..	..	..	..	..	..	..
4320 Impôts sur les donations	..	..	..	..	..	..	..	..	..	..
4400 Impôts sur transact. mobilières et immob.	..	..	0	25	48	51	41	43	58	59
Droits de conservation foncière	..	..	0	25	48	51	41	43	58	59
4500 Impôts non-périodiques	..	..	0	0	0	0	0	0	0	0
4510 Sur l'actif net	..	..	..	..	..	..	..	..	..	..
4520 Autres non-périodiques	..	..	..	..	..	..	..	..	..	..
4600 Autres impôts périodiques sur patrimoine	..	..	0	0	0	0	0	0	0	0
5000 Impôts sur les biens et services	..	..	**7 483**	**8 196**	**15 641**	**15 985**	**16 118**	**18 888**	**21 096**	**25 226**
5100 Impôts sur production, vente, transfert, etc.	..	..	7 344	7 983	15 344	15 652	15 785	17 916	19 822	23 812
5110 Impôts généraux	..	..	4 597	5 069	10 064	10 007	9 454	9 691	10 428	12 605
5111 Taxes sur la valeur ajoutée	..	..	4 597	5 069	10 064	10 007	9 454	9 691	10 428	12 605
Recettes TVA intérieur	..	..	950	1 290	3 946	3 284	3 500	3 481	3 264	3 643
Recettes TVA à l'importation	..	..	3 647	3 779	6 118	6 723	5 954	6 210	7 164	8 963
5112 Impôts sur les ventes	..	..	0	0	0	0	0	0	0	0
5113 Autres impôts	..	..	0	0	0	0	0	0	0	0
5120 Impôts sur biens et services déterminés	..	..	2 747	2 915	5 280	5 646	6 330	8 224	9 394	11 207
5121 Accises	..	..	0	0	0	0	0	0	0	0
5122 Bénéfices des monopoles fiscaux	..	..	0	0	0	0	0	0	0	0

Table 5.18. **Mauritania / Mauritanie** *(cont.)*

Details of tax revenue / Recettes fiscales détaillées

Million MRU

	1998	2000	2008	2010	2013	2014	2015	2016	2017	2018
5123 Droits de douane et droits à l'importation	..	..	2 553	2 631	4 662	5 092	5 692	7 502	8 358	10 111
Droit Fiscal à l'importation	..	..	1 635	1 631	2 907	3 143	3 313	4 143	4 716	5 502
Taxe sur les prod. pétroliers	..	..	430	494	654	664	1 042	1 653	1 735	2 277
Taxes de consommation	..	..	149	188	370	471	586	982	1 047	1 256
Taxe statistique	..	..	339	319	508	561	553	539	657	810
Taxe pour la promotion de la culture et du sport	..	..	0	0	223	253	199	186	203	266
5124 Taxes à l'exportation	..	..	11	20	71	61	39	45	410	395
5125 Impôts sur biens d'équipement	..	..	0	0	0	0	0	0	0	0
5126 Impôts sur services déterminés	..	..	183	264	547	492	599	677	626	701
Taxe sur les les operations financieres	..	..	127	208	500	430	538	611	561	628
Taxe d'aéroport et destination à létranger	..	..	56	56	47	62	61	66	65	72
5127 Autres impôts sur commerce et transact. internat.	..	..	0	0	0	0	0	0	0	0
5128 Autres impôts	..	..	0	0	0	0	0	0	0	0
5130 Non ventilables entre 5110 et 5120	..	..	0	0	0	0	0	0	0	0
5200 Impôts sur utilisation des biens et exerc. activités	..	..	139	213	298	333	333	972	1 274	1 414
5210 Impôts périodiques	..	..	139	213	298	333	333	972	1 274	1 414
5211 A la charge des ménages: véhicules à moteur	..	..	72	153	225	234	236	245	247	235
5212 A la charge autres agents: véhicules à moteur	..	..	0	0	0	0	0	0	0	0
5213 Autres impôts périodiques	..	..	67	60	73	99	97	727	1 028	1 179
Patente	..	..	0	0	62	78	76	77	77	80
Droit de pêche	..	..	67	60	11	21	21	650	951	1 098
5220 Impôts non-périodiques	..	..	0	0	0	0	0	0	0	0
5300 Non ventilables entre 5100 et 5200	..	..	0	0	0	0	0	0	0	0
6000 Autres impôts	..	..	**0**	**0**	**0**	**0**	**0**	**0**	**0**	**0**
6100 A la charge exclusive des entreprises	..	..	..	..	..	..	..	..	..	..
6200 A la charge d'autres agents	..	..	..	..	..	..	..	..	..	..

.. Non disponible

Note : Année civile se terminant le 31 décembre.

Les données sont sur la base des encaissements

Les données de cette édition sont en monnaie MRU, devise officielle de la Mauritanie depuis le 1er janvier 2018. Elle remplace la monnaie MRO, devise utilisée dans les éditions précédentes.

Rubrique 4100 : cette rubrique inclut les recettes communales. Ces recettes proviennent des différents impôts communaux et taxes municipales qui comprennent notamment la contribution foncière sur les propriétés bâties, la contribution foncière sur les terrains agricoles affectés à des cultures, la taxe d'habitation, la contribution communale, la patente, la taxe communale et les redevances et les droits domaniaux sur l'occupation du domaine public. Il n'a pas été possible de distinguer chacune de ces recettes ainsi la totalité de ces recettes sont classifiées dans la présente rubrique compte tenu que la majorité proviennent des impôts sur la propriété immobilière

Rubrique 4400 : cette rubrique inclut les recettes des droits de conservation foncière. Elles sont incluses dans les recettes fiscales comme le préconise la classification OCDE (voir le guide d'interprétation en Annexe A) mais considérées comme des recettes non fiscales en Mauritanie.

Source : Ministère des Finances de la Mauritanie.

StatLink https://doi.org/10.1787/888934183560

Table 5.19. **Mauritius / Maurice**

Details of tax revenue / Recettes fiscales détaillées

Million MUR

	1998	2000	2008	2010	2013	2014	2015	2016	2017	2018
Total tax revenue	**17 193**	**22 146**	**50 439**	**58 404**	**71 491**	**75 777**	**79 225**	**82 339**	**88 584**	**95 710**
1000 Taxes on income, profits and capital gains	**2 409**	**2 881**	**10 669**	**15 005**	**16 956**	**18 385**	**19 793**	**20 403**	**22 938**	**24 325**
1100 Of individuals	1 238	1 540	3 524	4 583	6 214	7 049	7 614	7 621	8 661	9 527
1110 On income and profits	..	..	..	..	..	..	..	..	..	..
1120 On capital gains	..	..	..	..	..	..	..	..	..	..
1200 Corporate	1 171	1 341	6 347	9 457	9 763	10 268	10 993	11 686	13 040	13 407
1210 On profits	1 171	1 341	6 347	9 457	9 763	10 268	10 993	11 686	13 040	13 407
Income tax - companies & corporate bodies	..	..	6 236	8 428	8 727	8 972	9 788	10 459	11 881	12 403
Special levy on banks	..	..	67	455	473	772	748	771	846	846
Solidarity levy on telecommunication companies	..	..	0	424	438	358	331	308	313	158
Corporate social responsibility	..	..	0	150	125	166	126	147	0	0
Special contribution from hotels	..	..	43	0	0	0	0	0	0	0
1220 On capital gains	..	..	..	..	..	..	..	..	..	..
1300 Unallocable between 1100 and 1200	..	..	797	965	978	1 068	1 186	1 096	1 236	1 392
Tax deduction at source	..	..	797	965	978	1 068	1 186	1 096	1 236	1 392
2000 Social security contributions	**850**	**986**	**1 713**	**2 113**	**2 702**	**3 019**	**3 252**	**3 380**	**3 648**	**3 630**
2100 Employees	283	329	571	704	901	1 006	1 084	1 127	1 216	1 210
2110 On a payroll basis	..	..	..	..	..	..	..	..	..	..
2120 On an income tax basis	..	..	..	..	..	..	..	..	..	..
2200 Employers	566	657	1 142	1 408	1 801	2 012	2 168	2 253	2 432	2 420
2210 On a payroll basis	..	..	..	..	..	..	..	..	..	..
2220 On an income tax basis	..	..	..	..	..	..	..	..	..	..
2300 Self-employed or non-employed	0	0	0	0	0	0	0	0	0	0
2310 On a payroll basis	..	..	..	..	..	..	..	..	..	..
2320 On an income tax basis	..	..	..	..	..	..	..	..	..	..
2400 Unallocable between 2100, 2200 and 2300	0	0	0	0	0	0	0	0	0	0
2410 On a payroll basis	..	..	..	..	..	..	..	..	..	..
2420 On an income tax basis	..	..	..	..	..	..	..	..	..	..
3000 Taxes on payroll and workforce	**114**	**140**	**272**	**176**	**235**	**507**	**474**	**592**	**638**	**507**
Extra-budgetary taxes on payroll and workforce	114	140	272	176	235	507	474	592	638	507
4000 Taxes on property	**1 282**	**1 411**	**3 402**	**3 328**	**3 568**	**4 299**	**4 095**	**4 680**	**4 894**	**4 711**
4100 Recurrent taxes on immovable property	181	205	357	417	267	279	146	296	318	306
4110 Households	0	0	0	0	0	0	0	0	0	0
4120 Others	181	205	357	417	267	279	146	296	318	306
Local taxes on immovable property	181	205	306	410	261	275	143	292	314	299
Campement taxes	0	0	52	6	6	4	3	4	4	7
4200 Recurrent taxes on net wealth	0	0	0	0	0	0	0	0	0	0
4210 Individual	..	..	..	..	..	..	..	..	..	..
4220 Corporate	..	..	..	..	..	..	..	..	..	..
4300 Estate, inheritance and gift taxes	0	0	0	0	0	0	0	0	0	0
4310 Estate and inheritance taxes	..	..	..	..	..	..	..	..	..	..
4320 Gift taxes	..	..	..	..	..	..	..	..	..	..
4400 Taxes on financial and capital transactions	1 102	1 206	3 045	2 902	3 277	4 000	3 907	4 337	4 543	4 385
Land transfer tax	..	..	1 349	1 190	1 496	1 652	1 650	1 831	2 016	1 971
Registration duty on transfer of immovable property	..	..	1 212	1 180	1 239	1 522	1 708	1 943	1 951	1 884
Tax on transfer of leasehold rights in state lands	..	..	105	175	272	374	157	119	258	168
Registration duty on transfer of shares	..	..	142	84	24	182	122	174	44	50
Registration duty on fixed and floating charges	..	..	126	180	169	162	157	164	162	204
Stamp duties	..	..	79	75	78	109	112	105	113	109
Registration duty on loans	..	..	13	9	0	0	0	0	0	0
Mortgages, inscriptions and transcriptions	..	..	20	11	0	0	0	0	0	0
Other taxes on financial and capital transactions	..	..	0	0	0	0	0	0	0	0
4500 Non-recurrent taxes	0	0	0	10	24	20	42	47	33	20
4510 On net wealth	..	..	..	0	0	0	0	0	0	0
4520 Other non-recurrent taxes	..	..	..	10	24	20	42	47	33	20
4600 Other recurrent taxes on property	0	0	0	0	0	0	0	0	0	0
5000 Taxes on goods and services	**12 364**	**16 514**	**34 214**	**37 618**	**47 864**	**49 379**	**51 422**	**53 173**	**56 355**	**62 410**
5100 Taxes on production, sale, transfer, etc.	12 201	16 312	31 573	34 755	44 450	45 300	47 254	48 943	52 228	58 041
5110 General taxes	2 724	5 604	18 542	21 094	26 158	26 225	28 036	28 805	30 231	32 989
5111 Value added taxes	0	5 604	18 540	21 094	26 000	26 060	28 036	28 805	30 231	32 989
VAT revenues (gross)	..	..	23 534	26 590	31 800	32 853	33 302	34 142	36 555	39 176
VAT refunds	..	..	-4 994	-5 495	-5 800	-6 794	-5 267	-5 337	-6 324	-6 187
5112 Sales tax	2 724	0	2	0	0	0	0	0	0	0

Table 5.19. **Mauritius / Maurice** *(cont.)*

Details of tax revenue / Recettes fiscales détaillées

Million MUR

	1998	2000	2008	2010	2013	2014	2015	2016	2017	2018
5113 Other	0	0	0	0	158	165	0	0	0	0
Extra-budgetary taxes on goods and services	..	..	..	..	158	165	0	0	0	0
Local taxes on goods and services	..	..	..	..	0	0	0	0	0	0
5120 Taxes on specific goods and services	9 478	10 707	13 031	13 660	18 293	19 075	19 218	20 138	21 996	25 052
Unallocated budgetary taxes on goods and services	..	..	0	0	0	0	0	0	0	0
5121 Excises	..	..	8 198	9 331	13 569	14 423	14 834	15 633	17 277	20 109
Spirits, liquors and alcoholic beverages	..	..	2 117	2 351	4 122	4 170	4 448	4 603	4 900	5 349
Tobacco products	..	..	2 479	2 371	3 697	3 823	3 851	4 196	4 735	5 333
Motor vehicles and motor cycles	..	..	1 527	1 928	2 054	2 400	2 471	2 582	3 126	3 384
Petro. products (incl. MIDL)	..	..	1 962	2 421	3 069	3 219	3 292	3 438	3 642	5 141
PET bottles and other plastic products	..	..	112	159	223	242	250	235	232	252
Sugar content of soft drinks	..	..	0	0	177	330	344	345	374	404
Energy inefficient products	..	..	0	0	1	5	3	2	12	4
Sugar brokerage	..	..	0	0	0	0	0	0	0	0
Extra-budgetary excise taxes	..	..	0	0	13	0	0	0	0	0
Other excises	..	..	0	101	214	233	175	231	255	241
5122 Profits of fiscal monopolies	..	..	0	0	0	0	0	0	0	0
5123 Customs and import duties	..	..	2 646	1 525	1 389	1 239	1 302	1 343	1 177	1 344
5124 Taxes on exports	..	..	0	0	0	0	0	0	0	0
5125 Taxes on investment goods	..	..	0	0	0	0	0	0	0	0
5126 Taxes on specific services	..	..	1 985	2 731	3 334	3 413	3 083	3 163	3 543	3 599
Taxes on the national lottery and other lotteries	..	..	14	693	682	652	436	387	242	221
Betting taxes on horse racing, football, etc.	..	..	445	658	793	934	837	887	944	971
Gaming taxes on casinos and gaming houses	..	..	982	818	541	529	591	652	706	778
Passenger fee on air tickets	..	..	543	561	1 219	1 213	1 173	1 230	1 652	1 630
Levy on messaging services	..	..	0	0	99	85	46	7	0	0
Hotel and restaurant tax	..	..	1	0	0	0	0	0	0	0
5127 Other taxes on internat. trade and transactions	..	..	0	0	0	0	0	0	0	0
5128 Other taxes	..	..	201	73	0	0	0	0	0	0
Temporary solidarity tax on hotels	..	..	201	0	0	0	0	0	0	0
Local government taxes on goods and services	..	..	0	73	0	0	0	0	0	0
5130 Unallocable between 5110 and 5120	..	..	0	0	0	0	0	0	0	0
5200 Taxes on use of goods and perform activities	163	203	2 515	2 765	3 414	4 080	4 168	4 230	4 128	4 369
5210 Recurrent taxes	163	203	1 709	1 934	2 343	2 363	2 702	2 795	2 762	2 922
5211 Paid by households: motor vehicles	0	0	810	1 117	1 291	1 345	1 362	1 430	1 463	1 526
5212 Paid by others: motor vehicles	0	0	0	0	0	0	0	0	0	0
5213 Paid in respect of other goods	163	203	899	816	1 052	1 018	1 341	1 366	1 299	1 396
Company licences	..	..	136	148	235	235	306	196	198	200
Incorporation & lodging fees, search duty, etc.	..	..	11	9	17	18	18	16	12	14
Tourist enterprise licences	..	..	61	74	85	85	91	110	99	104
Gambling licences	..	..	69	100	352	317	368	438	411	465
Liquor licences	..	..	9	10	24	23	25	23	23	23
Freeport licences	..	..	5	0	8	7	6	7	7	7
Pharmacy licences	..	..	1	1	1	1	2	1	1	1
Fishing vessel licences	..	..	30	52	64	54	43	53	59	63
Registration of factories	..	..	2	2	3	3	3	3	3	3
Registration of associations	..	..	2	2	1	0	1	1	1	1
Recruitment licences	..	..	0	2	0	0	0	1	0	0
Environment protection fee	..	..	209	141	130	159	391	403	383	400
Advertising structure fee	..	..	0	0	68	67	63	64	58	52
Regional taxes on permission to use goods	0	0	3	2	2	3	2	2	3	3
Local taxes on permission to use goods	163	203	346	255	0	0	0	0	0	21
Other recurrent taxes on goods and activities	..	..	16	20	62	45	23	48	42	39
5220 Non-recurrent taxes	0	0	806	832	1 071	1 716	1 466	1 434	1 366	1 447
Processing fee on acquisitions schemes	..	..	0	0	2	3	4	5	4	5
Registration duty on transfer of motor vehicles	..	..	764	794	972	1 195	1 277	1 266	1 335	1 378
Land conversion tax	..	..	43	38	96	518	185	163	26	64
5300 Unallocable between 5100 and 5200	0	0	127	98	0	0	0	0	0	0
Extra-budgetary taxes on goods and services	0	0	127	98	0	0	0	0	0	0
6000 Other taxes	**175**	**215**	**169**	**164**	**165**	**189**	**188**	**111**	**110**	**126**
Mauritius Revenue Authority penalties	0	0	0	0	34	59	74	22	24	24
Unidentified local government taxes	0	0	0	0	0	0	0	0	0	0
Unidentified taxes	175	215	169	164	131	130	114	89	86	102
6100 Paid solely by business	..	..	..	..	..	..	..	..	..	..

Table 5.19. **Mauritius / Maurice** *(cont.)*

Details of tax revenue / Recettes fiscales détaillées

Million MUR

	1998	2000	2008	2010	2013	2014	2015	2016	2017	2018
6200 Other	..	..	..	..	..	..	..	..	..	..

.. Not available

Note: Data for years prior to 2010 and subsequent to 2015 are on a fiscal year basis beginning 1st July. For example, the data for 2009 represent July 2008 to June 2009 and 2018 represents July 2017 to June 2018. The data for years 2010-15 are on a calendar year (January-December) basis.

Mauritius budget statements cover January-June 2015 and July 2015 to June 2016, but neither the fiscal nor the calendar year for 2015. Figures for 2015 are therefore estimated using quarterly revenue figures at the aggregate level and fiscal year revenue data.

Data for the central government budgetary tax prior to 2007 and all extra-budgetary, regional and local data were classified according to the IMF Government Finance Statistics Manual. The 1986 manual was used for data up to 2009 and the 2001 manual for data up to 2009 onwards. Data from 2007 onwards are classified under the OECD classification, as set out in the Interpretative Guide in Annex A.

The Ministry of Social Services (MSS) collects National Pension Fund (NPF) contributions, National Savings Fund (NSF) contributions, the Training Levy and the Recycling Fee. The NPF revenues are reported here as social security contributions, while revenues collected under the Training Levy and the Recycling Fees are reported as extra-budgetary taxes on payroll and workforce. The contributions to the NSF are part of a compulsory savings scheme, and are not classified as revenue in the Revenue Statistics in Africa project. In the calendar year 2018, there were a total of 7.1 billion rupees collected under these four MSS funds, of which 4.1 billion were collected for the NPF, 1.9 for the NSF, 1.0 for the Training Levy, and 0.7 billion for the Recycling Fee.

Heading 2000: revenues under this heading refer only to contributions to the National Pension Fund (NPF). Employer contributions and employee contributions are calculated by taking respectively one third and two thirds of total NPF contributions since employer contributions rates are set at twice those of employees. Other funds labelled as social security contributions in Mauritius financial statements were reported under heading 2000 in previous editions, but these have been removed in this edition since there was not enough information in order to ensure that they conformed to the definition of social security used in this publication.

Heading 3000: revenues under this heading include revenues collected by the Ministry of Social Services under the Training Levy.

Heading 1210: the solidarity levy on telecommunications companies, the corporate social responsibility tax and the special contribution from hotels are classified as "other taxes" by the Mauritius Revenue Authority.

Heading 5213: the Environment protection fee and advertising structure fee are classified as other taxes by the Mauritius Revenue Authority.

Heading 5220: includes the registration duty on transfer of motor vehicles and the land conversion tax that are classified as taxes on property by the Mauritius Revenue Authority.

Source: Mauritius Revenue Authority for the central government budgetary tax data from 2007 to 2017; Statistics Mauritius for extra-budgetary, local government, regional government and social security revenues from 1990 to 2018, as well as for budgetary central government tax revenues up to 2006; Ministry of Finance budget estimates for detailed revenue figures for the periods July 2005-June 2008, for 2016-18, and for the figures used to estimate calendar year 2015 revenues.

StatLink https://doi.org/10.1787/888934183237

Table 5.20. **Morocco / Maroc**

Details of tax revenue / Recettes fiscales détaillées

Million MAD

	1998	2000	2008	2010	2013	2014	2015	2016	2017	2018
Recettes fiscales totales	..	**97 226**	**216 509**	**216 987**	**248 953**	**261 769**	**260 969**	**276 083**	**293 615**	**308 123**
1000 Impôts sur revenu, bénéfices et gains en capital	..	**23 656**	**80 204**	**62 646**	**75 636**	**76 342**	**78 952**	**84 111**	**92 372**	**95 924**
1100 Des personnes physiques	..	14 540	33 614	26 598	34 846	34 573	37 214	39 792	40 686	43 804
1110 Sur le revenu et les bénéfices	..	12 473	26 118	22 391	30 046	30 651	32 797	35 082	40 135	43 377
Salaires	..	10 829	22 421	19 409	25 815	26 452	28 277	30 833	31 440	32 551
Revenus professionnels	..	1 645	3 698	2 982	4 232	4 199	4 519	4 249	3 296	4 452
Autres types d'impôts sur le revenu	..	0	0	0	0	0	0	0	5 398	6 374
1120 Sur les gains en capital	..	2 067	7 496	4 207	4 799	3 922	4 417	4 710	552	427
1200 Des sociétés	..	9 116	46 590	36 049	40 790	41 769	41 738	44 319	51 686	52 120
1210 Sur les bénéfices	..	8 330	41 606	31 164	33 579	34 327	32 693	44 319	51 607	52 113
Bénéfices	..	8 084	40 253	29 381	31 580	31 017	30 553	42 303	49 410	49 512
Produits bruts versés aux sociétés étrangères	..	246	1 353	1 783	1 999	3 310	2 140	2 016	2 197	2 601
1220 Sur les gains en capital	..	786	4 984	4 884	7 211	7 442	9 045	0	78	7
1300 Non ventilables entre 1100 et 1200	..	0	0	0	0	0	0	0	0	0
2000 Cotisations de sécurité sociale	..	**16 309**	**26 617**	**38 142**	**44 442**	**54 823**	**48 317**	**53 658**	**56 546**	**61 116**
2100 A la charge des salariés	..	..	..	..	..	..	..	..	..	..
2110 Sur la base du salaire	..	..	..	..	..	..	..	..	..	..
2120 Sur la base de l'impôt sur le revenu	..	..	..	..	..	..	..	..	..	..
2200 A la charge des employeurs	..	..	..	..	..	..	..	..	..	..
2210 Sur la base du salaire	..	..	..	..	..	..	..	..	..	..
2220 Sur la base de l'impôt sur le revenu	..	..	..	..	..	..	..	..	..	..
2300 A charge des travailleurs indép. ou sans emploi	..	..	..	..	..	..	..	..	..	..
2310 Sur la base du salaire	..	..	..	..	..	..	..	..	..	..
2320 Sur la base de l'impôt sur le revenu	..	..	..	..	..	..	..	..	..	..
2400 Non ventilables entre 2100, 2200 et 2300	..	16 309	26 617	38 142	44 442	54 823	48 317	53 658	56 546	61 116
2410 Sur la base du salaire	..	..	..	..	..	..	..	..	..	..
2420 Sur la base de l'impôt sur le revenu	..	..	..	..	..	..	..	..	..	..
3000 Sur salaires ou main d'oeuvre	..	**0**	**0**	**0**	**0**	**0**	**0**	**0**	**0**	**0**
4000 Impôts sur le patrimoine	..	**5 405**	**11 930**	**12 702**	**17 002**	**17 926**	**19 536**	**20 182**	**16 693**	**17 412**
4100 Impôts périodiques sur la propriété immobilière	..	3 340	4 592	5 740	7 397	6 101	6 859	7 477	7 712	8 680
4110 Ménages	..	1 989	2 977	3 898	4 878	3 888	4 414	4 781	4 962	5 663
Taxe d'habitation	..	517	317	382	430	301	364	320	361	432
Taxe sur les terrains non bâtis	..	135	602	839	1 121	901	1 113	1 163	1 301	1 350
Taxe de services communaux	..	1 337	2 058	2 677	3 327	2 685	2 937	3 298	3 300	3 881
4120 Autres agents	..	1 351	1 615	1 842	2 519	2 213	2 445	2 696	2 750	3 017
4200 Impôts périodiques sur l'actif net	..	0	0	0	0	0	0	0	0	0
4210 Personnes physiques	..	..	..	..	..	..	..	..	..	..
4220 Sociétés	..	..	..	..	..	..	..	..	..	..
4300 Impôts sur mut. par décès, succ. et donations	..	0	0	0	0	0	0	0	0	0
4310 Impôts sur mut. par décès et successions	..	..	..	..	..	..	..	..	..	..
4320 Impôts sur les donations	..	..	..	..	..	..	..	..	..	..
4400 Impôts sur transact. mobilières et immob.	..	2 065	7 338	6 962	9 605	11 825	12 677	12 705	8 981	8 732
4500 Impôts non-périodiques	..	0	0	0	0	0	0	0	0	0
4510 Sur l'actif net	..	..	..	..	..	..	..	..	..	..
4520 Autres non-périodiques	..	..	..	..	..	..	..	..	..	..
4600 Autres impôts périodiques sur patrimoine	..	0	0	0	0	0	0	0	0	0
5000 Impôts sur les biens et services	..	**50 655**	**95 959**	**101 384**	**109 215**	**110 024**	**111 766**	**114 743**	**124 441**	**130 130**
5100 Impôts sur production, vente, transfert, etc.	..	49 539	93 911	99 056	106 303	107 068	108 848	111 457	121 108	126 012
5110 Impôts généraux	..	21 476	61 228	65 247	75 260	74 995	75 271	75 735	81 479	84 440
5111 Taxes sur la valeur ajoutée	..	21 476	61 228	65 247	75 260	74 995	75 271	75 735	81 479	84 440
5112 Impôts sur les ventes	..	0	0	0	0	0	0	0	0	0
5113 Autres impôts	..	0	0	0	0	0	0	0	0	0
5120 Impôts sur biens et services déterminés	..	28 063	32 683	33 809	31 043	32 073	33 577	35 722	39 629	41 572
5121 Accises	..	15 223	18 872	21 382	23 150	24 119	25 661	26 451	27 720	28 683
Taxes intérieures de consommation	..	15 183	18 693	21 132	22 873	23 849	25 366	26 134	27 383	28 318
Taxe sur la vente de produits forestiers	..	4	19	26	31	20	29	29	18	18
Taxe sur les débits de boissons	..	23	102	143	161	156	162	167	185	219
Taxe sur les eaux minerales et de table	..	13	58	81	85	94	104	121	133	128
5122 Bénéfices des monopoles fiscaux	..	0	0	0	0	0	0	0	0	0
5123 Droits de douane et droits à l'importation	..	12 810	13 679	12 242	7 681	7 738	7 715	9 074	8 610	9 693
5124 Taxes à l'exportation	..	0	0	0	0	0	0	0	0	0
5125 Impôts sur biens d'équipement	..	0	0	0	0	0	0	0	0	0

Table 5.20. **Morocco / Maroc** *(cont.)*

Details of tax revenue / Recettes fiscales détaillées

Million MAD

	1998	2000	2008	2010	2013	2014	2015	2016	2017	2018
5126 Impôts sur services déterminés	..	30	132	184	212	216	201	197	3 299	3 196
Taxe de séjour	..	26	115	160	178	191	173	168	198	229
Taxe sur le transport public de voyageurs	..	4	17	24	34	25	28	29	3 101	2 967
5127 Autres impôts sur commerce et transact. internat.	..	0	0	0	0	0	0	0	0	0
5128 Autres impôts	..	0	0	0	0	0	0	0	0	0
5130 Non ventilables entre 5110 et 5120	..	0	0	0	0	0	0	0	0	0
5200 Impôts sur utilisation des biens et exerc. activites	..	1 116	2 048	2 328	2 913	2 956	2 918	3 286	3 333	4 117
5210 Impôts périodiques	..	964	1 372	1 385	1 933	1 973	1 955	2 348	2 360	3 167
5211 A la charge des ménages: véhicules à moteur	..	959	1 348	1 351	1 898	1 937	1 920	2 310	2 325	3 129
5212 A la charge autres agents: véhicules à moteur	..	0	0	0	0	0	0	0	0	0
5213 Autres impôts périodiques	..	5	24	33	35	36	35	38	35	38
Taxe sur les permis de chasse	..	5	24	33	35	36	35	38	35	38
5220 Impôts non-périodiques	..	152	676	943	980	983	963	938	973	950
Taxe sur les opérations de construction	..	113	504	703	720	718	709	709	716	743
Taxe sur les opérations de lotissement	..	39	172	240	260	265	254	229	257	207
5300 Non ventilables entre 5100 et 5200	..	0	0	0	0	0	0	0	0	0
6000 Autres impôts	..	**1 201**	**1 799**	**2 112**	**2 657**	**2 654**	**2 398**	**3 390**	**3 562**	**3 541**
Droits de timbres	..	1 132	1 492	1 683	2 061	2 010	2 092	3 090	3 305	3 268
Taxes locales	..	69	307	429	596	644	306	300	257	273
6100 A la charge exclusive des entreprises	..	..	..	..	..	..	..	..	..	..
6200 A la charge d'autres agents	..	..	..	..	..	..	..	..	..	..

.. Non disponible

Note : Année civile se terminant le 31 décembre.

Les données sont sur la base des encaissements.

Les impôts affectés aux Fonds Spéciaux du Trésor sont compris dans les données.

Rubrique 2000 : Les données de cotisations de sécurité sociales sont estimées pour les années 2000 et 2001. Les recettes des majorations et pénalités relatives aux impôts sont désormais considérées comme des recettes non fiscales. La classification nationale du Maroc les compte comme des recettes fiscales.

Source : Ministère de l'Économie et des Finances.

StatLink https://doi.org/10.1787/888934183522

Table 5.21. **Namibia**

Details of tax revenue / Recettes fiscales détaillées

Million NAD

	1998	2000	2008	2010	2013	2014	2015	2016	2017	2018
Total tax revenue	..	..	**12 604**	**15 429**	**24 001**	**28 615**	**31 437**	**33 496**	**34 845**	**34 547**
1000 Taxes on income, profits and capital gains	..	..	**8 070**	**9 912**	**14 026**	**17 780**	**19 006**	**20 607**	**21 946**	**21 855**
1100 Of individuals	..	..	4 787	6 156	10 360	10 476	10 982	12 355	13 546	13 923
1110 On income and profits	..	..	4 787	6 156	10 360	10 476	10 982	12 355	13 546	13 923
Income tax on individuals	..	..	4 606	5 945	9 537	10 197	10 794	12 002	13 267	13 588
Non-resident shareholders tax	..	..	155	189	131	77	147	266	183	265
Tax on royalty	..	..	26	21	692	202	41	87	96	70
1120 On capital gains	..	..	0	0	0	0	0	0	0	0
1200 Corporate	..	..	3 282	3 756	3 666	7 304	8 024	8 252	8 400	7 932
1210 On profits	..	..	3 282	3 756	3 666	7 304	8 024	8 252	8 400	7 932
Diamond mining companies	..	..	499	354	655	1 980	2 199	1 611	1 654	1 496
Other mining companies	..	..	731	213	7	94	99	92	256	445
Non-mining companies	..	..	2 039	3 018	2 771	4 945	5 425	6 006	5 950	5 384
Withholding taxes	..	..	0	156	212	264	280	522	510	607
Annual levy on gambling income	..	..	13	15	21	21	21	21	30	..
1220 On capital gains	..	..	0	0	0	0	0	0	0	0
1300 Unallocable between 1100 and 1200	..	..	0	0	0	0	0	0	0	0
2000 Social security contributions	..	..	..	..	..	..	..	..	..	..
2100 Employees	..	..	..	..	..	..	..	..	..	..
2110 On a payroll basis	..	..	..	..	..	..	..	..	..	..
2120 On an income tax basis	..	..	..	..	..	..	..	..	..	..
2200 Employers	..	..	..	..	..	..	..	..	..	..
2210 On a payroll basis	..	..	..	..	..	..	..	..	..	..
2220 On an income tax basis	..	..	..	..	..	..	..	..	..	..
2300 Self-employed or non-employed	..	..	..	..	..	..	..	..	..	..
2310 On a payroll basis	..	..	..	..	..	..	..	..	..	..
2320 On an income tax basis	..	..	..	..	..	..	..	..	..	..
2400 Unallocable between 2100, 2200 and 2300	..	..	..	..	..	..	..	..	..	..
2410 On a payroll basis	..	..	..	..	..	..	..	..	..	..
2420 On an income tax basis	..	..	..	..	..	..	..	..	..	..
3000 Taxes on payroll and workforce	..	..	**0**	**0**	**0**	**0**	**0**	**0**	**0**	**0**
4000 Taxes on property	..	..	**171**	**139**	**261**	**289**	**313**	**284**	**270**	**221**
4100 Recurrent taxes on immovable property	..	..	0	0	0	0	0	0	0	0
4110 Households	..	..	..	..	..	..	..	..	..	..
4120 Others	..	..	..	..	..	..	..	..	..	..
4200 Recurrent taxes on net wealth	..	..	0	0	0	0	0	0	0	0
4210 Individual	..	..	..	..	..	..	..	..	..	..
4220 Corporate	..	..	..	..	..	..	..	..	..	..
4300 Estate, inheritance and gift taxes	..	..	0	0	0	0	0	0	0	0
4310 Estate and inheritance taxes	..	..	..	..	..	..	..	..	..	..
4320 Gift taxes	..	..	..	..	..	..	..	..	..	..
4400 Taxes on financial and capital transactions	..	..	171	139	261	289	313	284	270	221
4500 Non-recurrent taxes	..	..	0	0	0	0	0	0	0	0
4510 On net wealth	..	..	..	..	..	..	..	..	..	..
4520 Other non-recurrent taxes	..	..	..	..	..	..	..	..	..	..
4600 Other recurrent taxes on property	..	..	0	0	0	0	0	0	0	0
5000 Taxes on goods and services	..	..	**4 221**	**5 169**	**9 473**	**10 272**	**11 902**	**12 389**	**12 458**	**12 274**
5100 Taxes on production, sale, transfer, etc.	..	..	4 221	5 169	9 471	10 271	11 901	12 387	12 454	12 274
5110 General taxes	..	..	4 096	5 057	9 327	10 208	11 678	11 978	12 049	11 461
5111 Value added taxes	..	..	4 096	5 057	9 327	10 208	11 678	11 978	12 049	11 461
5112 Sales tax	..	..	0	0	0	0	0	0	0	0
5113 Other	..	..	0	0	0	0	0	0	0	0
5120 Taxes on specific goods and services	..	..	125	113	144	63	223	409	405	813
5121 Excises	..	..	0	0	0	0	0	0	0	0
5122 Profits of fiscal monopolies	..	..	0	0	0	0	0	0	0	0
5123 Customs and import duties	..	..	106	102	131	44	209	382	342	813
Levy on fuel	..	..	106	102	131	44	209	315	342	730
Environmental levies and carbon emission taxes	..	..	0	0	0	0	0	67	0	83
5124 Taxes on exports	..	..	0	0	0	0	0	0	0	0
5125 Taxes on investment goods	..	..	0	0	0	0	0	0	0	0
5126 Taxes on specific services	..	..	0	0	0	0	0	0	0	0
5127 Other taxes on internat. trade and transactions	..	..	0	0	0	0	0	0	0	0
5128 Other taxes	..	..	20	11	13	19	14	27	63	..
5130 Unallocable between 5110 and 5120	..	..	0	0	0	0	0	0	0	0

Table 5.21. **Namibia** *(cont.)*

Details of tax revenue / Recettes fiscales détaillées

Million NAD

	1998	2000	2008	2010	2013	2014	2015	2016	2017	2018
5200 Taxes on use of goods and perform activities	..	..	0	0	2	1	1	2	4	0
5210 Recurrent taxes	..	..	0	0	2	1	1	2	4	0
5211 Paid by households: motor vehicles	..	..	0	0	0	0	0	0	0	0
5212 Paid by others: motor vehicles	..	..	0	0	0	0	0	0	0	0
5213 Paid in respect of other goods	..	..	0	0	2	1	1	2	4	0
5220 Non-recurrent taxes	..	..	0	0	0	0	0	0	0	0
5300 Unallocable between 5100 and 5200	..	..	0	0	0	0	0	0	0	0
6000 Other taxes	**..**	**..**	**142**	**208**	**241**	**274**	**216**	**216**	**171**	**197**
6100 Paid solely by business	..	..	..	..	..	..	..	..	..	..
6200 Other	..	..	..	..	..	..	..	..	..	..

.. Not available

Note: Data are on a cash basis.

Data are on a fiscal year basis beginning 1st April. For example, the data for 2018 represent April 2018 to March 2019.

Figures exclude tax revenues collected by sub-national governments as the data are not available.

Heading 2000: Precise figures for social security contributions were not available for Namibia. In 2018, estimated social security contibutions amounted to less than 2% of total tax revenues.

Heading 5111: This category includes revenue from VAT, additional sales tax and the general sales tax

Source: Ministry of Finance of Namibia.

StatLink https://doi.org/10.1787/888934183598

Table 5.22. Niger

Details of tax revenue / Recettes fiscales détaillées

Million XOF

	1998	2000	2008	2010	2013	2014	2015	2016	2017	2018
Recettes fiscales totales	..	**115 819**	**293 517**	**373 461**	**641 408**	**663 171**	**720 540**	**644 899**	**615 444**	**793 035**
1000 Impôts sur revenu, bénéfices et gains en capital	..	**20 891**	**81 322**	**94 839**	**249 555**	**208 402**	**177 695**	**170 506**	**166 432**	**167 981**
1100 Des personnes physiques	..	9 634	17 252	19 756	43 022	45 697	45 501	50 942	55 054	55 069
1110 Sur le revenu et les bénéfices	..	9 634	17 239	19 623	42 693	45 468	45 294	50 508	54 667	54 567
Impôt sur les traitements et salaires	..	8 000	16 336	18 575	41 663	44 638	44 198	49 415	53 542	51 539
Impôt synthétique	..	1 530	822	974	881	762	1 030	1 047	1 079	2 775
Impôt général sur le revenu (IGR)	..	103	80	74	150	68	66	47	46	253
1120 Sur les gains en capital	..	0	13	133	328	229	208	434	387	502
Plus-values de cessions. immob. (IPVCI)	..	0	13	133	328	229	208	434	387	502
1200 Des sociétés	..	11 257	64 070	75 083	206 534	162 705	132 194	119 564	111 379	112 913
1210 Sur les bénéfices	..	11 257	64 070	75 083	206 534	162 705	132 194	119 564	111 379	112 913
Impôt sur les bénéfices (ISB)	..	10 933	55 873	67 863	192 631	146 385	121 448	109 509	101 156	102 484
Bénéfices non commerciaux (BNC) (arriérés)	..	126	0	0	0	0	0	0	0	140
Impôt sur le revenu des valeurs mobilières (IRVM)	..	198	5 086	5 695	10 428	11 484	7 900	7 966	8 357	8 665
Recettes portuaires	..	0	3 112	1 525	3 475	4 836	2 846	2 089	1 866	1 623
1220 Sur les gains en capital	..	0	0	0	0	0	0	0	0	0
1300 Non ventilables entre 1100 et 1200	..	0	0	0	0	0	0	0	0	0
2000 Cotisations de sécurité sociale	..	**6 216**	**14 934**	**19 950**	**29 972**	**33 610**	**34 117**	**35 453**	**37 261**	**37 840**
2100 A la charge des salariés	..	..	..	..	..	..	..	..	..	..
2110 Sur la base du salaire	..	..	..	..	..	..	..	..	..	..
2120 Sur la base de l'impôt sur le revenu	..	..	..	..	..	..	..	..	..	..
2200 A la charge des employeurs	..	..	..	..	..	..	..	..	..	..
2210 Sur la base du salaire	..	..	..	..	..	..	..	..	..	..
2220 Sur la base de l'impôt sur le revenu	..	..	..	..	..	..	..	..	..	..
2300 A charge des travailleurs indép. ou sans emploi	..	..	..	..	..	..	..	..	..	..
2310 Sur la base du salaire	..	..	..	..	..	..	..	..	..	..
2320 Sur la base de l'impôt sur le revenu	..	..	..	..	..	..	..	..	..	..
2400 Non ventilables entre 2100, 2200 et 2300	..	6 216	14 934	19 950	29 972	33 610	34 117	35 453	37 261	37 840
2410 Sur la base du salaire	..	..	..	..	..	..	..	..	..	..
2420 Sur la base de l'impôt sur le revenu	..	..	..	..	..	..	..	..	..	..
3000 Sur salaires ou main d'oeuvre	..	**401**	**729**	**1 121**	**2 816**	**3 478**	**3 978**	**3 472**	**3 223**	**3 726**
Taxe d'apprentissage (TAP)	..	401	729	1 121	2 816	3 478	3 978	3 472	3 223	3 726
4000 Impôts sur le patrimoine	..	**1 252**	**1 399**	**2 906**	**1 729**	**1 612**	**2 742**	**2 117**	**2 318**	**2 393**
4100 Impôts périodiques sur la propriété immobilière	..	1 252	1 399	2 906	1 729	1 612	2 742	2 117	2 318	2 393
Taxe immobilière	..	1 015	1 383	2 904	1 728	1 612	2 742	2 117	2 318	2 366
Taxe foncière	..	238	0	0	0	0	0	0	0	2
Impôt forfaitaire de droit de propriétés	..	0	15	2	0	0	0	0	0	25
4110 Ménages	..	..	..	..	..	..	..	..	..	..
4120 Autres agents	..	..	..	..	..	..	..	..	..	..
4200 Impôts périodiques sur l'actif net	..	0	0	0	0	0	0	0	0	0
4210 Personnes physiques	..	..	..	..	..	..	..	..	..	..
4220 Sociétés	..	..	..	..	..	..	..	..	..	..
4300 Impôts sur mut. par décès, succ. et donations	..	0	0	0	0	0	0	0	0	0
4310 Impôts sur mut. par décès et successions	..	..	..	..	..	..	..	..	..	..
4320 Impôts sur les donations	..	..	..	..	..	..	..	..	..	..
4400 Impôts sur transact. mobilières et immob.	..	0	0	0	0	0	0	0	0	0
4500 Impôts non-périodiques	..	0	0	0	0	0	0	0	0	0
4510 Sur l'actif net	..	..	..	..	..	..	..	..	..	..
4520 Autres non-périodiques	..	..	..	..	..	..	..	..	..	..
4600 Autres impôts périodiques sur patrimoine	..	0	0	0	0	0	0	0	0	0
5000 Impôts sur les biens et services	..	**83 383**	**183 232**	**234 839**	**316 593**	**370 745**	**431 233**	**392 894**	**370 521**	**524 707**
5100 Impôts sur production, vente, transfert, etc.	..	81 489	182 231	233 477	314 669	368 641	428 892	390 385	367 939	521 777
5110 Impôts généraux	..	31 766	105 367	136 966	181 930	225 855	256 546	227 121	210 787	359 611
5111 Taxes sur la valeur ajoutée	..	31 766	105 367	136 966	154 469	197 683	237 621	204 248	190 420	341 450
TVA intérieure	..	12 375	55 317	76 999	91 790	130 060	145 529	123 186	127 968	259 228
Recettes TVA (douanes) - DGD	..	19 391	50 050	59 967	62 679	67 623	92 092	81 062	62 453	82 222
5112 Impôts sur les ventes	..	..	..	..	0	0	0	0	0	0
5113 Autres impôts	..	0	0	0	27 461	28 171	18 925	22 873	20 367	18 161
Redevance ad valorem	..	0	0	0	27 461	28 171	18 925	22 873	20 367	18 161
5120 Impôts sur biens et services déterminés	..	49 722	76 864	96 511	132 739	142 787	172 345	163 263	157 152	162 166

Table 5.22. **Niger** *(cont.)*

Details of tax revenue / Recettes fiscales détaillées

Million XOF

	1998	2000	2008	2010	2013	2014	2015	2016	2017	2018
5121 Accises	..	13 754	20 685	28 505	43 727	39 124	51 081	46 307	29 660	41 203
Taxe intérieure sur les produits pétroliers (TIPP) (y compris DGD)	..	4 313	6 991	11 694	14 195	11 913	19 375	12 703	10 691	18 804
Taxe sur les tabacs et les cigarettes	..	4 600	7 944	11 279	17 084	14 001	17 926	20 295	10 177	11 451
Taxe sur les boissons alcoolisés (TBA)	..	882	1 170	1 263	2 619	1 817	2 684	2 345	1 097	1 074
Taxe d'exploitation artisanale (TEA)	..	0	0	0	0	2	22	44	29	182
Autres droits d'accises	..	3 959	4 579	4 269	9 829	11 391	11 074	10 919	7 665	9 693
5122 Bénéfices des monopoles fiscaux	..	0	0	0	0	0	0	0	0	0
5123 Droits de douane et droits à l'importation	..	22 930	25 597	36 286	45 430	46 536	59 517	53 482	51 104	62 450
Droits de douane	..	14 722	22 675	28 141	40 170	40 976	53 226	48 392	45 933	56 383
Redevance statistique à l'importation	..	1 652	2 921	8 144	5 260	5 558	6 283	5 087	5 167	6 026
Droits Divers (y compris T.C.I)	..	6 556	2	0	0	1	8	3	5	41
5124 Taxes à l'exportation	..	11 671	27 936	27 567	36 352	37 377	31 025	27 590	43 958	48 130
Taxes sur les réexportations	..	9 997	26 607	25 405	28 647	30 923	25 657	23 056	36 838	41 097
Redevance statistique à l'exportation	..	1 673	1 221	1 465	7 682	6 340	5 342	4 524	7 117	6 671
Taxe forfaitaire sur la réexportation et/ou transit de tabacs et cigarettes (TFEAR)	..	0	107	696	23	113	25	10	3	363
5125 Impôts sur biens d'équipement	..	0	0	0	0	0	0	0	0	0
5126 Impôts sur services déterminés	..	1 238	2 264	3 080	6 614	19 074	30 399	35 691	32 096	10 224
Taxe sur la terminaison du trafic international entrant (TATTIE)	..	0	0	0	0	12 184	18 666	25 706	22 101	1 452
Taxe sur l'utilisation du réseau de télécommunication (TURTEL)	..	0	0	0	2 133	2 332	5 349	4 973	5 417	4 220
Taxe sur les recettes des loteries	..	877	1 072	1 303	2 040	2 238	3 377	2 474	2 292	1 778
Taxe unique sur les assurances (TUA)	..	361	1 162	1 490	2 114	2 007	2 310	2 291	2 275	2 338
Impôt sur les gains des loteries	..	0	0	0	29	25	550	7	1	0
Taxe sur les jeux de hasard (TJH)	..	0	0	246	294	284	140	240	11	435
Taxe sur la publicité commerciale extérieure (TPCE)	..	0	30	41	4	3	8	0	0	1
5127 Autres impôts sur commerce et transact. internat.	..	0	0	0	0	0	0	0	0	0
5128 Autres impôts	..	130	382	1 074	616	677	324	193	333	158
Droits miniers	..	130	382	1 074	616	667	295	120	25	3
Droit fixe mine	..	0	0	0	0	9	28	67	307	155
Droit fixe pétrole	..	0	0	0	0	0	1	6	0	0
5130 Non ventilables entre 5110 et 5120	..	0	0	0	0	0	0	0	0	0
5200 Impôts sur utilisation des biens et exerc. activites	..	894	1 001	1 362	1 925	2 104	2 341	2 509	2 582	2 930
5210 Impôts périodiques	..	529	1 001	1 362	1 914	2 073	2 316	2 474	2 562	2 925
Vignette	..	520	986	1 354	1 903	2 054	2 310	2 471	2 558	2 918
5211 A la charge des ménages: véhicules à moteur	..	0	0	0	0	0	0	0	0	0
5212 A la charge autres agents: véhicules à moteur	..	0	0	0	0	0	0	0	0	0
5213 Autres impôts périodiques	..	9	16	8	11	18	6	3	4	7
Permis de chasse et visite	..	0	0	0	2	9	2	0	0	3
Taxe sur les armes à feu (TAF)	..	9	15	8	8	9	4	3	4	4
5220 Impôts non-périodiques	..	365	0	0	11	31	25	35	20	5
Péage routier	..	365	..	..	0	0	0	0	0	0
Redevance plaque d'immatriculation	..	0	..	..	11	31	25	35	20	5
5300 Non ventilables entre 5100 et 5200	..	1 000	0	0	0	0	0	0	0	0
6000 Autres impôts	**..**	**3 676**	**11 902**	**19 807**	**40 743**	**45 324**	**70 775**	**40 457**	**35 690**	**56 389**
Droits d'enregistrement	..	2 166	8 677	8 048	27 711	29 642	51 113	24 353	18 750	34 344
Prélèvement pour cpte des collectivités locales	..	0	0	6 512	6 463	8 161	11 727	8 577	9 283	12 312
Taxe sur certains frais généraux des entreprises (TCFGE)	..	310	1 264	1 963	3 211	4 060	4 132	4 045	4 314	4 729
Droits de timbre	..	1 201	1 961	3 283	3 358	3 460	3 803	3 481	3 343	5 003
6100 A la charge exclusive des entreprises	..	..	..	..	..	..	..	..	..	..
6200 A la charge d'autres agents	..	..	..	..	..	..	..	..	..	..

Table 5.22. **Niger** *(cont.)*

Details of tax revenue / Recettes fiscales détaillées

.. Non disponible

Note : Année civile se terminant le 31 décembre.

Les données sont sur la base des encaissements.

Les chiffres n'incluent pas les données des recettes fiscales collectées par les collectivités locales car elles ne sont pas disponibles.

Les recettes provenant du domaine public, des redevances minières, des redevances superficiaires des mines et du pétrole et des amendes et pénalités relatives aux impôts sont incluses dans les recettes non fiscales dans cette publication comme le préconise la classification OCDE (voir le guide d'interprétation en Annexe A). La classification du Niger compte ces recettes comme des recettes fiscales.

Rubriques 5111 et 5121 : Ces rubriques contiennent des recettes provenant de la Direction Générale des Douanes (DGD) et sont annotées comme telles.

Rubrique 5220 : Cette rubrique comprend les recettes de la redevance plaques d'immatriculation collectées par la Direction Générale du Trésor et de la Comptabilité Publique (DGTCP) entre 2005 et 2018 comme le préconise la classification OCDE (voir le guide d'interprétation en Annexe A). La classification du Niger compte ces recettes comme des recettes non fiscales.

Source : Ministère des Finances

StatLink https://doi.org/10.1787/888934183256

Table 5.23. **Nigeria / Nigéria**

Details of tax revenue / Recettes fiscales détaillées

Million NGN

	1998	2000	2008	2010	2013	2014	2015	2016	2017	2018
Total tax revenue	..	..	..	**4 023 597**	**6 727 821**	**6 886 137**	**5 761 425**	**5 413 912**	**6 547 014**	**8 167 037**
1000 Taxes on income, profits and capital gains	..	..	..	**2 555 738**	**4 459 437**	**4 367 593**	**3 453 159**	**3 018 256**	**3 649 715**	**4 910 261**
1100 Of individuals	..	..	..	320 771	513 021	520 233	543 561	604 759	711 067	798 630
1110 On income and profits	..	..	..	320 771	513 021	520 233	543 561	604 759	711 067	798 630
State PAYE ("Pay as You Earn") Tax	..	..	..	268 821	434 626	434 006	456 595	511 911	566 212	669 218
Personal Income Tax (Federal)	..	..	..	32 564	48 460	52 846	57 377	59 469	107 682	85 146
Personal Income Tax (State)	..	..	..	19 386	29 936	33 382	29 589	33 379	37 172	44 266
1120 On capital gains	..	..	..	0	0	0	0	0	0	0
1200 Corporate	..	..	..	2 234 967	3 946 416	3 847 360	2 909 598	2 413 498	2 938 649	4 111 631
1210 On profits	..	..	..	2 233 931	3 926 760	3 844 710	2 892 796	2 314 094	2 935 469	4 099 036
Petroleum Profits Tax	..	..	..	1 480 364	2 666 367	2 453 947	1 289 961	1 157 808	1 520 482	2 467 581
Companies Income Tax	..	..	..	658 503	963 451	1 173 491	1 268 977	933 537	1 215 057	1 340 329
Education Tax	..	..	..	89 178	279 359	189 614	206 040	130 123	154 957	203 285
Income tax on gas exploration companies	..	..	..	0	7 727	17 750	115 569	85 878	34 839	75 988
National Information Technology Development Fund	..	..	..	5 886	9 857	9 908	12 249	6 748	10 134	11 853
1220 On capital gains	..	..	..	1 037	19 656	2 650	16 802	99 403	3 180	12 595
1300 Unallocable between 1100 and 1200	..	..	..	0	0	0	0	0	0	0
2000 Social security contributions	..	..	..	**305 163**	**574 063**	**643 447**	**569 879**	**550 052**	**714 218**	**687 080**
2100 Employees	..	..	..	172 418	305 528	333 268	269 328	261 414	332 914	324 012
2110 On a payroll basis	..	..	..	172 418	305 528	333 268	269 328	261 414	332 914	324 012
National Pension Commission (employee-side)	..	..	..	132 745	251 960	290 690	226 596	216 978	291 111	270 022
National Health Insurance Scheme	..	..	..	39 673	53 568	42 578	42 732	44 437	41 803	53 990
2120 On an income tax basis	..	..	..	0	0	0	0	0	0	0
2200 Employers	..	..	..	132 745	268 536	310 178	300 551	288 637	381 304	363 068
2210 On a payroll basis	..	..	..	132 745	268 536	310 178	300 551	288 637	381 304	363 068
National Pension Commission (employer-side)	..	..	..	132 745	251 960	290 690	283 244	271 222	363 889	337 528
Nigerian Social Insurance Trust Fund	..	..	..	0	16 576	19 488	17 307	17 415	17 415	25 540
2220 On an income tax basis	..	..	..	0	0	0	0	0	0	0
2300 Self-employed or non-employed	..	..	..	0	0	0	0	0	0	0
2310 On a payroll basis	..	..	..	..	..	..	..	..	..	..
2320 On an income tax basis	..	..	..	..	..	..	..	..	..	..
2400 Unallocable between 2100, 2200 and 2300	..	..	..	0	0	0	0	0	0	0
2410 On a payroll basis	..	..	..	..	..	..	..	..	..	..
2420 On an income tax basis	..	..	..	..	..	..	..	..	..	..
3000 Taxes on payroll and workforce	..	..	..	**12 610**	**25 274**	**29 980**	**32 766**	**31 704**	**40 890**	**50 310**
4000 Taxes on property	..	..	..	..	..	..	..	..	..	..
4100 Recurrent taxes on immovable property	..	..	..	..	..	..	..	..	..	..
4110 Households	..	..	..	..	..	..	..	..	..	..
4120 Others	..	..	..	..	..	..	..	..	..	..
4200 Recurrent taxes on net wealth	..	..	..	..	..	..	..	..	..	..
4210 Individual	..	..	..	..	..	..	..	..	..	..
4220 Corporate	..	..	..	..	..	..	..	..	..	..
4300 Estate, inheritance and gift taxes	..	..	..	..	..	..	..	..	..	..
4310 Estate and inheritance taxes	..	..	..	..	..	..	..	..	..	..
4320 Gift taxes	..	..	..	..	..	..	..	..	..	..
4400 Taxes on financial and capital transactions	..	..	..	..	..	..	..	..	..	..
4500 Non-recurrent taxes	..	..	..	..	..	..	..	..	..	..
4510 On net wealth	..	..	..	..	..	..	..	..	..	..
4520 Other non-recurrent taxes	..	..	..	..	..	..	..	..	..	..
4600 Other recurrent taxes on property	..	..	..	..	..	..	..	..	..	..
5000 Taxes on goods and services	..	..	..	**1 036 386**	**1 479 363**	**1 606 272**	**1 520 489**	**1 569 281**	**1 821 381**	**2 072 094**
5100 Taxes on production, sale, transfer, etc.	..	..	..	1 029 896	1 463 479	1 593 257	1 501 713	1 548 943	1 799 838	2 047 860
5110 General taxes	..	..	..	564 892	802 684	802 965	767 334	828 199	972 348	1 108 040
5111 Value added taxes	..	..	..	564 892	802 684	802 965	767 334	828 199	972 348	1 108 040
VAT revenues (domestic)	..	..	..	436 610	629 664	616 885	597 412	650 344	770 348	859 018
VAT revenues (imports)	..	..	..	128 281	173 019	186 080	169 921	177 855	202 001	249 022
5112 Sales tax	..	..	..	0	0	0	0	0	0	0
5113 Other	..	..	..	0	0	0	0	0	0	0
5120 Taxes on specific goods and services	..	..	..	465 005	660 795	790 292	734 380	720 743	827 490	939 820
5121 Excises	..	..	..	35 449	24 411	39 763	39 784	41 258	41 600	55 060
5122 Profits of fiscal monopolies	..	..	..	0	0	0	0	0	0	0
5123 Customs and import duties	..	..	..	429 555	636 385	750 530	694 596	679 485	785 890	884 760
Import duties	..	..	..	272 248	387 777	511 548	468 382	462 058	533 560	604 990
Other customs taxes	..	..	..	157 307	248 607	238 982	226 214	217 428	252 330	279 770

Table 5.23. **Nigeria** *(cont.)*

Details of tax revenue / Recettes fiscales détaillées

Million NGN

	1998	2000	2008	2010	2013	2014	2015	2016	2017	2018
5124 Taxes on exports	..	..	..	0	0	0	0	0	0	0
5125 Taxes on investment goods	..	..	..	0	0	0	0	0	0	0
5126 Taxes on specific services	..	..	..	0	0	0	0	0	0	0
5127 Other taxes on internat. trade and transactions	..	..	..	0	0	0	0	0	0	0
5128 Other taxes	..	..	..	0	0	0	0	0	0	0
5130 Unallocable between 5110 and 5120	..	..	..	0	0	0	0	0	0	0
5200 Taxes on use of goods and perform activities	..	..	..	6 490	15 884	13 015	18 775	20 339	21 542	24 234
5210 Recurrent taxes	..	..	..	6 490	15 884	13 015	18 775	20 339	21 542	24 234
5211 Paid by households: motor vehicles	..	..	..	6 121	15 407	12 568	18 412	19 948	21 214	23 957
5212 Paid by others: motor vehicles	..	..	..	0	0	0	0	0	0	0
5213 Paid in respect of other goods	..	..	..	368	477	447	364	391	328	277
5220 Non-recurrent taxes	..	..	..	0	0	0	0	0	0	0
5300 Unallocable between 5100 and 5200	..	..	..	0	0	0	0	0	0	0
6000 Other taxes	**..**	**..**	**..**	**113 700**	**189 683**	**238 846**	**185 133**	**244 619**	**320 811**	**447 292**
6100 Paid solely by business	..	..	..	0	0	0	0	0	0	0
6200 Other	..	..	..	113 700	189 683	238 846	185 133	244 619	320 811	447 292
Other tax revenue from states	..	..	..	107 106	182 077	227 902	178 048	238 714	311 873	431 493
Stamp duties	..	..	..	6 593	7 606	10 944	7 085	5 905	8 938	15 798

.. Not available

Note: Year ending 31st December.

The data are on a cash basis.

Some personal income taxes, capital gains taxes, road taxes, and other taxes are collected at the state level.

Data has been estimated for the categories "State PAYE", "Personal Income Tax (State)" and "Other tax revenue from states" for 2017 and 2018 as disaggregated figures for state revenues was not available.

Heading 1110: State level income taxes on individuals in paid employment is collected on a PAYE ("Pay as you earn") basis, while those who are self-employed or receive business income on a non-salary basis are charged under direct assessment. These are reported separately in this table, but the tax basis is the same for both cases.

Heading 1210: The Petroleum Profits Tax includes all tax revenue payments by oil exploration companies irrespective of the type of exploration arrangement (production sharing, joint ventures, etc) despite the fact that different types of arrangements could give rise to different tax rates. This heading does not include the government's share of company revenue arising from the revenue-sharing component of the exploration arrangements. These latter funds are reported as oil revenues in the non-tax revenue table.

Heading 1220: Capital gains tax for resident companies and non-residents are collected at the federal level while capital gains tax for individuals is collected at the state level.

Heading 2000: The Pension Reform Act was passed in 2004 and mandated both employees and employers to contribute 7.5% each to the pension retirement savings account. However, in 2014 there was an amendment after which the employee was mandated to contribute 8% while the employer contributed a minimum of 10% thereby bringing the total contribution to at leat 18%. For the years up to and including 2014, therefore, 50% of social security contributions are reported under heading 2110 and the other half under heading 2210. Starting in 2015, 4/9 of total pension contributions are reported under heading 2110 and 5/9 of total pension contributions are reported under heading 2210.

Heading 3000: This heading consists of a 2.5% payroll tax that is used to finance the National Housing Fund.

Heading 5211: Road Taxes, or taxes charged on the issuance of motor vehicle licenses, are collected at the state level.

Heading 5213: This heading contains taxes collected under the Pre-Operational Levy. This is a tax charged each year to companies that, more than 18 months after being registered, still have not commenced operations.

Heading 6000: Other state taxes include stamp duties, capital gains taxes, business premise registration, Land Use Charge, market taxes, and levies that are collected by state governments.

Source: Federal Inland Revenue Service.

StatLink https://doi.org/10.1787/888934183617

Table 5.24. **Rwanda**

Details of tax revenue / Recettes fiscales détaillées

Million RWF

	1998	2000	2008	2010	2013	2014	2015	2016	2017	2018
Total tax revenue	**65 263**	**68 909**	**352 997**	**440 724**	**760 158**	**865 554**	**997 232**	**1 115 636**	**1 248 017**	**1 401 503**
1000 Taxes on income, profits and capital gains	**18 058**	**17 943**	**123 024**	**159 567**	**308 107**	**322 827**	**379 676**	**430 431**	**488 184**	**565 235**
1100 Of individuals	4 014	6 621	63 400	102 037	182 996	193 212	224 553	253 893	278 076	312 070
1110 On income and profits	4 014	6 621	63 400	102 037	182 996	193 212	224 553	253 893	278 076	312 070
Pay As You Earn	..	..	..	..	..	..	216 750	245 138	267 311	300 751
Rental income tax	..	..	..	..	..	..	7 803	8 754	10 765	11 319
1120 On capital gains	0	0	0	0	0	0	0	0	0	0
1200 Corporate	14 044	11 322	59 624	57 530	125 111	129 615	155 123	176 538	210 108	253 165
1210 On profits	14 044	11 322	59 624	57 530	125 111	129 615	155 123	176 538	210 108	253 165
Corporation income tax	12 150	3 603	27 788	26 459	48 962	39 157	49 571	58 645	70 053	94 656
Withholding tax	48	59	5 294	10 764	42 363	49 948	58 422	71 929	84 786	71 474
Personal income tax	476	868	5 569	7 316	7 828	6 950	7 358	8 752	10 012	10 991
Other taxes on profits	1 371	6 792	20 973	12 991	25 958	33 561	39 772	37 212	45 257	76 044
1220 On capital gains	0	0	0	0	0	0	0	0	0	0
1300 Unallocable between 1100 and 1200	0	0	0	0	0	0	0	0	0	0
2000 Social security contributions	**2 473**	**3 423**	**23 248**	**28 235**	**53 123**	**55 530**	**59 687**	**74 717**	**74 897**	**83 344**
2100 Employees	927	1 283	8 717	10 586	19 918	20 820	22 379	28 014	28 082	31 249
2110 On a payroll basis	927	1 283	8 717	10 586	19 918	20 820	22 379	28 014	28 082	31 249
2120 On an income tax basis	0	0	0	0	0	0	0	0	0	0
2200 Employers	1 544	2 138	14 528	17 644	33 197	34 701	37 299	46 691	46 803	52 082
2210 On a payroll basis	1 544	2 138	14 528	17 644	33 197	34 701	37 299	46 691	46 803	52 082
2220 On an income tax basis	0	0	0	0	0	0	0	0	0	0
2300 Self-employed or non-employed	3	3	4	4	8	9	9	11	11	13
2310 On a payroll basis	3	3	4	4	8	9	9	11	11	13
2320 On an income tax basis	0	0	0	0	0	0	0	0	0	0
2400 Unallocable between 2100, 2200 and 2300	0	0	0	0	0	0	0	0	0	0
2410 On a payroll basis	..	..	..	..	..	..	..	..	..	..
2420 On an income tax basis	..	..	..	..	..	..	..	..	..	..
3000 Taxes on payroll and workforce	**0**	**0**	**0**	**0**	**0**	**0**	**0**	**0**	**0**	**0**
4000 Taxes on property	**117**	**130**	**26**	**97**	**18**	**19**	**632**	**779**	**1 156**	**1 293**
4100 Recurrent taxes on immovable property	117	130	24	96	18	19	632	779	1 156	1 293
4110 Households	117	130	24	96	18	19	632	779	1 156	1 293
4120 Others	0	0	0	0	0	0	0	0	0	0
4200 Recurrent taxes on net wealth	0	0	0	0	0	0	0	0	0	0
4210 Individual	..	..	..	..	..	..	..	..	..	..
4220 Corporate	..	..	..	..	..	..	..	..	..	..
4300 Estate, inheritance and gift taxes	0	0	0	0	0	0	0	0	0	0
4310 Estate and inheritance taxes	..	..	..	..	..	..	..	..	..	..
4320 Gift taxes	..	..	..	..	..	..	..	..	..	..
4400 Taxes on financial and capital transactions	0	0	0	0	0	0	0	0	0	0
4500 Non-recurrent taxes	0	0	0	0	0	0	0	0	0	0
4510 On net wealth	..	..	..	..	..	..	..	..	..	..
4520 Other non-recurrent taxes	..	..	..	..	..	..	..	..	..	..
4600 Other recurrent taxes on property	0	0	2	0	0	0	0	0	0	0
5000 Taxes on goods and services	**44 615**	**47 413**	**206 698**	**252 826**	**398 910**	**487 178**	**557 238**	**609 709**	**683 780**	**751 631**
5100 Taxes on production, sale, transfer, etc.	44 132	46 777	205 614	250 214	397 084	485 735	549 277	601 651	676 883	744 296
5110 General taxes	11 974	13 777	116 862	131 665	219 501	279 275	305 544	329 331	386 484	422 903
5111 Value added taxes	11 974	13 777	116 862	131 665	219 501	279 275	305 544	329 331	386 484	422 903
VAT revenues (gross)	..	..	129 847	146 295	243 890	310 305	339 493	365 923	429 748	476 671
VAT Refunds	..	..	-12 985	-14 629	-24 389	-31 031	-33 949	-36 592	-43 264	-53 768
5112 Sales tax	0	0	0	0	0	0	0	0	0	0
5113 Other	0	0	0	0	0	0	0	0	0	0
5120 Taxes on specific goods and services	32 157	32 999	88 752	118 548	177 583	206 461	243 733	272 320	290 399	321 393
5121 Excises	13 805	18 849	39 184	75 236	105 304	121 220	138 261	143 701	148 561	169 237
Excise tax on beers	7 697	7 146	17 937	22 548	34 318	36 872	45 950	42 510	47 862	54 801
Excise tax on petroleum	3 093	7 857	6 558	30 941	35 982	37 283	47 043	49 761	50 013	55 791
Strategic reserves levy	0	0	0	0	0	0	4 185	9 485	10 355	10 502
Other excises taxes	3 015	3 846	14 689	21 746	35 003	47 065	41 084	41 946	40 331	48 143
5122 Profits of fiscal monopolies	0	0	0	0	0	0	0	0	0	0
5123 Customs and import duties	16 871	14 151	49 568	43 313	72 280	85 241	105 472	128 620	141 838	152 155
Import duties	12 048	9 260	40 054	26 215	46 448	55 106	69 731	72 062	80 738	83 601
Rwanda road maintenance fund	2 537	2 531	7 378	14 843	23 865	25 167	29 620	43 062	45 768	48 805
Infrastructure development levy	0	0	0	0	0	0	3 837	10 069	11 164	12 228
Other customs and import duties	2 286	2 360	2 137	2 254	1 967	4 968	2 284	3 426	4 168	7 522

Table 5.24. **Rwanda** *(cont.)*

Details of tax revenue / Recettes fiscales détaillées

Million RWF

	1998	2000	2008	2010	2013	2014	2015	2016	2017	2018
5124 Taxes on exports	1 482	0	0	0	0	0	0	0	0	0
5125 Taxes on investment goods	0	0	0	0	0	0	0	0	0	0
5126 Taxes on specific services	0	0	0	0	0	0	0	0	0	0
5127 Other taxes on internat. trade and transactions	0	0	0	0	0	0	0	0	0	0
5128 Other taxes	0	0	0	0	0	0	0	0	0	0
5130 Unallocable between 5110 and 5120	0	0	0	0	0	0	0	0	0	0
5200 Taxes on use of goods and perform activities	483	636	1 084	2 612	1 825	1 442	7 961	8 058	6 897	7 335
5210 Recurrent taxes	483	636	1 084	2 612	1 825	1 442	7 961	8 058	6 897	7 335
5211 Paid by households: motor vehicles	483	636	1 084	2 612	1 825	1 442	3 252	2 947	2 691	2 269
5212 Paid by others: motor vehicles	0	0	0	0	0	0	0	0	0	0
5213 Paid in respect of other goods	0	0	0	0	0	0	4 709	5 111	4 206	5 066
5220 Non-recurrent taxes	0	0	0	0	0	0	0	0	0	0
5300 Unallocable between 5100 and 5200	0	0	0	0	0	0	0	0	0	0
6000 Other taxes	**0**	**0**	**0**	**0**	**0**	**0**	**0**	**0**	**0**	**0**
6100 Paid solely by business	..	..	..	..	..	..	..	..	..	..
6200 Other	..	..	..	..	..	..	..	..	..	..

.. Not available

Note: Year ending 31st December. From 2008, the figures for social security contributions are on a fiscal year basis beginning 1st July. For example, data for 2018 represent July 2017 to June 2018.

The data are on a cash basis.

Figures exclude tax revenues collected by sub-national governments as the data are not available.

Figures include fines related to tax revenues as it is not possible to split these out from tax revenues. These revenues are now classified as non-tax revenues following a change in the OECD classification. Rwanda considers these revenues as tax revenues.

Heading 2000: Rwanda does not include social security contributions in their tax revenue data as the Rwandan authorities do not consider them as taxes.

Source: Rwanda Revenue Authority.

StatLink https://doi.org/10.1787/888934183636

Table 5.25. **Senegal / Sénégal**

Details of tax revenue / Recettes fiscales détaillées

Million XOF

	1998	2000	2008	2010	2013	2014	2015	2016	2017	2018
Recettes fiscales totales	**457 080**	**559 295**	**1 139 131**	**1 267 799**	**1 439 409**	**1 586 865**	**1 723 131**	**1 920 344**	**1 987 098**	**2 123 504**
1000 Impôts sur revenu, bénéfices et gains en capital	**100 300**	**123 771**	**262 980**	**328 200**	**373 800**	**398 500**	**435 600**	**516 600**	**544 800**	**603 022**
1100 Des personnes physiques	56 900	64 021	152 880	192 900	217 300	238 200	261 000	314 500	307 700	371 635
1110 Sur le revenu et les bénéfices	56 500	63 370	151 300	191 000	214 400	234 700	257 900	310 800	304 000	366 904
1120 Sur les gains en capital	400	651	1 580	1 900	2 900	3 500	3 100	3 700	3 700	4 731
1200 Des sociétés	37 100	49 418	86 700	106 100	135 700	133 800	147 300	165 500	191 700	189 986
1210 Sur les bénéfices	37 100	49 418	86 700	106 100	135 700	133 800	147 300	165 500	191 700	189 986
1220 Sur les gains en capital	..	..	..	..	..	..	..	..	..	..
1300 Non ventilables entre 1100 et 1200	6 300	10 332	23 400	29 200	20 800	26 500	27 300	36 600	45 400	41 400
2000 Cotisations de sécurité sociale	**18 200**	**22 215**	**51 943**	**72 999**	**96 689**	**104 381**	**116 260**	**128 210**	**142 070**	**150 000**
2100 A la charge des salariés	..	..	..	..	..	..	..	..	..	..
2110 Sur la base du salaire	..	..	..	..	..	..	..	..	..	..
2120 Sur la base de l'impôt sur le revenu	..	..	..	..	..	..	..	..	..	..
2200 A la charge des employeurs	..	..	..	..	..	..	..	..	..	..
2210 Sur la base du salaire	..	..	..	..	..	..	..	..	..	..
2220 Sur la base de l'impôt sur le revenu	..	..	..	..	..	..	..	..	..	..
2300 A charge des travailleurs indép. ou sans emploi	..	..	..	..	..	..	..	..	..	..
2310 Sur la base du salaire	..	..	..	..	..	..	..	..	..	..
2320 Sur la base de l'impôt sur le revenu	..	..	..	..	..	..	..	..	..	..
2400 Non ventilables entre 2100, 2200 et 2300	18 200	22 215	51 943	72 999	96 689	104 381	116 260	128 210	142 070	150 000
Institution de Prévoyance Retraite du Sénégal (IPRES)	18 200	22 215	51 943	72 999	73 400	77 930	93 400	103 510	115 670	..
Caisse de Sécurité Sociale (CSS)	0	0	0	0	23 289	26 451	22 860	24 700	26 400	..
2410 Sur la base du salaire	..	..	..	..	..	..	..	..	..	..
2420 Sur la base de l'impôt sur le revenu	..	..	..	..	..	..	..	..	..	..
3000 Sur salaires ou main d'oeuvre	**6 200**	**6 668**	**9 600**	**10 800**	**16 100**	**16 900**	**20 200**	**17 310**	**13 900**	**7 007**
4000 Impôts sur le patrimoine	**8 640**	**11 200**	**32 200**	**39 100**	**36 600**	**39 606**	**41 500**	**51 984**	**48 730**	**52 291**
4100 Impôts périodiques sur la propriété immobilière	0	0	0	0	0	0	0	0	0	0
4110 Ménages	..	..	..	..	..	..	..	..	..	..
4120 Autres agents	..	..	..	..	..	..	..	..	..	..
4200 Impôts périodiques sur l'actif net	0	0	0	0	0	0	0	0	0	0
4210 Personnes physiques	..	..	..	..	..	..	..	..	..	..
4220 Sociétés	..	..	..	..	..	..	..	..	..	..
4300 Impôts sur mut. par décès, succ. et donations	1 901	2 464	6 620	12 445	7 809	8 086	8 465	11 564	9 699	3 594
4310 Impôts sur mut. par décès et successions	..	..	..	..	..	..	..	..	..	..
4320 Impôts sur les donations	..	..	..	..	..	..	..	..	..	..
4400 Impôts sur transact. mobilières et immob.	6 739	8 736	25 580	26 655	28 791	31 520	33 035	40 419	39 031	48 697
Droits de mutation (immeubles)	..	..	13 939	15 418	15 713	18 352	15 863	14 995	15 916	23 636
Droits d'enregistrement autre que patrimoine	..	..	11 640	11 237	13 078	13 167	17 172	25 424	23 115	25 061
4500 Impôts non-périodiques	0	0	0	0	0	0	0	0	0	0
4510 Sur l'actif net	..	..	..	..	..	..	..	..	..	..
4520 Autres non-périodiques	..	..	..	..	..	..	..	..	..	..
4600 Autres impôts périodiques sur patrimoine	0	0	0	0	0	0	0	0	0	0
5000 Impôts sur les biens et services	**315 340**	**386 940**	**769 408**	**804 400**	**900 820**	**1 010 678**	**1 086 871**	**1 187 941**	**1 218 798**	**1 289 460**
5100 Impôts sur production, vente, transfert, etc.	313 340	384 590	764 508	799 400	894 420	1 002 678	1 078 171	1 175 841	1 207 498	1 278 189
5110 Impôts généraux	158 240	221 410	435 001	478 000	512 200	561 400	617 000	651 300	691 700	715 700
5111 Taxes sur la valeur ajoutée	158 240	221 410	435 001	478 000	512 200	561 400	617 000	651 300	691 700	715 700
5112 Impôts sur les ventes	0	0	0	0	0	0	0	0	0	0
5113 Autres impôts	0	0	0	0	0	0	0	0	0	0
5120 Impôts sur biens et services déterminés	155 100	163 180	329 507	321 400	382 220	441 278	461 171	524 541	515 798	562 489
5121 Accises	24 200	61 100	78 940	82 600	76 095	84 078	88 821	107 441	125 998	148 561
Taxe spécifique sur les produits pétroliers	..	..	64 040	63 900	53 740	59 579	61 520	74 600	83 600	91 039
Taxes sur les tabacs	..	..	7 661	9 647	13 205	13 289	14 565	15 252	13 660	16 403
Taxes sur les corps gras	..	..	962	978	2 648	1 447	1 964	4 712	4 330	6 413
Taxes sur les alcools	..	..	4 224	5 297	5 498	5 382	5 516	6 824	6 609	7 854
Taxe sur la cola	..	..	247	273	48	25	19	8	4	19
Taxe sur les thés	..	..	162	154	125	124	153	228	118	70
Taxe sur le café	..	..	160	175	285	367	428	441	335	442
Taxe sur les produits comestiques	..	..	0	0	500	1 400	1 465	1 604	1 795	2 544
Taxe spéciale sur le ciment	..	..	0	0	0	0	0	0	10 700	14 087
Accises non classées ailleurs	..	..	1 485	2 176	45	2 466	3 189	3 771	4 848	9 690
5122 Bénéfices des monopoles fiscaux	0	0	0	0	0	0	0	0	0	0
5123 Droits de douane et droits à l'importation	122 100	90 340	190 067	181 600	218 000	221 100	227 600	234 600	263 500	290 400
5124 Taxes à l'exportation	0	0	0	0	0	0	0	0	2 900	0
5125 Impôts sur biens d'équipement	0	0	0	0	0	0	0	0	0	0

Table 5.25. **Senegal / Sénégal** *(cont.)*

Details of tax revenue / Recettes fiscales détaillées

Million XOF

	1998	2000	2008	2010	2013	2014	2015	2016	2017	2018
5126 Impôts sur services déterminés	8 800	11 740	27 100	45 000	63 825	69 500	71 200	76 100	95 500	105 378
Taxe sur les activités financières (TAF)	7 000	9 340	23 100	30 600	40 340	45 800	47 700	51 600	55 400	62 534
Redevance d'utilisation des télécommunications	0	0	0	10 000	18 645	18 700	19 500	18 600	19 600	22 289
Taxe sur les contrats d'assurances	1 800	2 400	4 000	4 400	4 840	5 000	4 000	5 900	6 300	6 905
Contribution au développement économique (CODEC)	0	0	0	0	0	0	0	0	14 200	13 649
5127 Autres impôts sur commerce et transact. internat.	0	0	0	0	0	0	0	0	0	0
5128 Autres impôts	0	0	33 400	12 200	24 300	66 600	73 551	106 400	27 900	18 150
Fonds de sécurisation des importations de produits pétroliers	..	..	33 400	12 200	19 400	62 600	69 451	104 600	26 400	17 266
Contributions spéciales (mines et carrières)	..	..	0	0	4 900	4 000	4 100	1 800	1 500	884
5130 Non ventilables entre 5110 et 5120	0	0	0	0	0	0	0	0	0	0
5200 Impôts sur utilisation des biens et exerc. activites	2 000	2 350	4 900	5 000	6 400	8 000	8 700	12 100	11 300	11 271
5210 Impôts périodiques	2 000	2 350	4 900	5 000	6 400	8 000	8 700	12 100	11 300	11 271
5211 A la charge des ménages: véhicules à moteur	..	..	..	..	..	..	..	..	..	..
5212 A la charge autres agents: véhicules à moteur	..	..	..	..	..	..	..	..	..	..
5213 Autres impôts périodiques	..	..	..	..	..	..	..	..	..	..
5220 Impôts non-périodiques	0	0	0	0	0	0	0	0	0	0
5300 Non ventilables entre 5100 et 5200	0	0	0	0	0	0	0	0	0	0
6000 Autres impôts	**8 400**	**8 500**	**13 000**	**12 300**	**15 400**	**16 800**	**22 700**	**18 300**	**18 800**	**21 725**
6100 A la charge exclusive des entreprises	..	..	..	..	..	..	..	..	..	..
6200 A la charge d'autres agents	..	..	..	..	..	..	..	..	..	..

.. Non disponible

Note : Année civile se terminant le 31 décembre.

Les données sont sur la base des encaissements.

Les chiffres n'incluent pas les recettes fiscales collectées par les administrations infranationales car elles ne sont pas disponibles.

Les chiffres ne comprennent pas les taxes parafiscales car elles ne sont pas disponibles.

La rubrique 2000 comprend les cotisations de sécurité sociale de l'Institution de prévoyance retraite du Sénégal (IPRES) à partir de 2006 et les cotisations de sécurité sociale de la Caisse de Sécurité Sociale (CSS) à partir de 2012. Les cotisations de sécurité sociale au Sénégal antérieures à 2006 sont estimées. Les chiffres de 2017 restent à titre indicatif.

La rubrique 5126 comprend la redevance sur l'accès ou l'utilisation du réseau des télécommunications publiques (RUTEL) classifiée comme accise au Sénégal.

Les recettes fiscales incluent les amendes et pénalités sur impôts et taxes considérées comme des recettes non fiscales. Il n'a pas été possible pour cette édition de séparer le versement des amendes et pénalités des recettes correspondant aux impôts auxquels ces amendes et pénalités se rattachent. La classification nationale du Sénégal les compte comme des recettes fiscales.

Source : Ministère de l'Économie, des Finances et du Plan.

StatLink https://doi.org/10.1787/888934183655

Table 5.26. **Seychelles**

Details of tax revenue / Recettes fiscales détaillées

Million SCR

	1998	2000	2008	2010	2013	2014	2015	2016	2017	2018
Total tax revenue	..	..	**2 346**	**3 440**	**4 559**	**5 053**	**5 258**	**5 897**	**6 462**	**7 138**
1000 Taxes on income, profits and capital gains	..	..	**524**	**1 009**	**1 572**	**1 660**	**1 705**	**1 977**	**2 264**	**2 342**
1100 Of individuals	..	..	0	195	754	878	948	939	900	965
1110 On income and profits	..	..	..	195	754	878	948	939	900	965
1120 On capital gains	..	..	..	0	0	0	0	0	0	0
1200 Corporate	..	..	524	814	818	782	757	1 039	1 364	1 376
1210 On profits	..	..	524	814	818	782	757	1 039	1 364	1 376
Companies	..	..	434	704	699	640	565	854	1 111	1 157
Sole traders	..	..	14	18	17	28	49	39	55	46
Partnerships	..	..	3	9	4	10	13	15	16	18
Witholding tax	..	..	72	59	68	67	87	83	127	96
Residential dwellings	..	..	0	0	27	37	43	47	54	59
Others	..	..	0	0	0	0	0	0	0	0
G&S Tax on rental income	..	..	0	24	2	0	0	0	0	0
1220 On capital gains	..	..	0	0	0	0	0	0	0	0
1300 Unallocable between 1100 and 1200	..	..	0	0	0	0	0	0	0	0
2000 Social security contributions	..	..	**278**	**220**	**0**	**0**	**0**	**0**	**0**	**208**
2100 Employees	..	..	..	..	..	..	..	..	..	..
2110 On a payroll basis	..	..	..	..	..	..	..	..	..	..
2120 On an income tax basis	..	..	..	..	..	..	..	..	..	..
2200 Employers	..	..	..	..	..	..	..	..	..	..
2210 On a payroll basis	..	..	..	..	..	..	..	..	..	..
2220 On an income tax basis	..	..	..	..	..	..	..	..	..	..
2300 Self-employed or non-employed	..	..	..	..	..	..	..	..	..	..
2210 On a payroll basis	..	..	..	..	..	..	..	..	..	..
2220 On an income tax basis	..	..	..	..	..	..	..	..	..	..
2400 Unallocable between 2100, 2200 and 2300	..	..	..	..	..	..	..	..	..	..
2410 On a payroll basis	..	..	..	..	..	..	..	..	..	..
2420 On an income tax basis	..	..	..	..	..	..	..	..	..	..
3000 Taxes on payroll and workforce	..	..	**0**	**0**	**0**	**0**	**0**	**0**	**0**	**0**
4000 Taxes on property	..	..	**75**	**126**	**90**	**91**	**140**	**92**	**91**	**120**
4100 Recurrent taxes on immovable property	..	..	0	0	0	0	0	0	0	0
4110 Households	..	..	..	..	..	..	..	..	..	..
4120 Others	..	..	..	..	..	..	..	..	..	..
4200 Recurrent taxes on net wealth	..	..	0	0	0	0	0	0	0	0
4210 Individual	..	..	..	..	..	..	..	..	..	..
4220 Corporate	..	..	..	..	..	..	..	..	..	..
4300 Estate, inheritance and gift taxes	..	..	0	0	0	0	0	0	0	0
4310 Estate and inheritance taxes	..	..	..	..	..	..	..	..	..	..
4320 Gift taxes	..	..	..	..	..	..	..	..	..	..
4400 Taxes on financial and capital transactions	..	..	75	126	90	91	140	92	91	120
4500 Non-recurrent taxes	..	..	0	0	0	0	0	0	0	0
4510 On net wealth	..	..	..	..	..	..	..	..	..	..
4520 Other non-recurrent taxes	..	..	..	..	..	..	..	..	..	..
4600 Other recurrent taxes on property	..	..	0	0	0	0	0	0	0	0
5000 Taxes on goods and services	..	..	**1 470**	**2 086**	**2 897**	**3 302**	**3 413**	**3 828**	**4 107**	**4 469**
5100 Taxes on production, sale, transfer, etc.	..	..	1 360	1 959	2 750	3 162	3 216	3 630	3 902	4 267
5110 General taxes	..	..	598	458	1 519	1 887	1 883	2 082	2 246	2 602
5111 Value added taxes	..	..	0	0	1 446	1 797	1 799	1 995	2 134	2 493
VAT - Domestic	..	..	..	..	828	1 011	990	1 069	1 294	1 550
VAT - Imported goods	..	..	..	..	618	808	833	949	911	968
VAT - Exemptions	..	..	..	..	0	-22	-24	-24	-71	-25
5112 Sales tax	..	..	598	458	29	6	4	1	17	3
G&S Tax on locally manufactured goods (Alcohol)	..	..	136	27	3	..	..	..	..	..
G&S Tax on locally manufactured goods (tobacco)	..	..	43	12	0	..	..	..	..	..
G&S Tax on locally manufactured goods (other)	..	..	37	42	4	..	..	..	..	..
G&S Tax - Fuel/petroleum products	..	..	70	0	0	..	..	..	..	..
G&S Tax - Imported goods	..	..	313	377	22	..	..	..	..	..
G&S Tax - Arrears	..	..	0	0	0	6	4	1	17	3
5113 Other	..	..	0	0	44	84	79	87	95	106
Corporate Social Responsibility Tax (CSR)	..	..	0	0	44	84	79	87	95	106
5120 Taxes on specific goods and services	..	..	762	1 501	1 231	1 274	1 334	1 547	1 656	1 666

Table 5.26. **Seychelles** *(cont.)*

Details of tax revenue / Recettes fiscales détaillées

Million SCR

	1998	2000	2008	2010	2013	2014	2015	2016	2017	2018
5121 Excises	..	..	0	580	652	858	962	1 144	1 312	1 281
Alcohol (beverages spirits and vinegar)	..	..	..	180	210	224	278	356	366	382
Petroleum (mineral products)	..	..	..	252	289	460	493	531	655	609
Motor Vehicles (vehicles, aircraft, vessels)	..	..	..	47	43	61	44	99	136	123
Tobacco	..	..	..	101	110	114	146	157	155	166
5122 Profits of fiscal monopolies	..	..	0	0	0	0	0	0	0	0
5123 Customs and import duties	..	..	410	356	411	376	326	359	285	315
Alcohol (beverages spirits and vinegar)	..	..	60	29	65	108	97	146	129	128
Petroleum (mineral products)	..	..	175	151	153	14	0	0	0	0
Textiles and textile articles	..	..	10	11	21	27	26	22	20	15
Motor Vehicles (vehicles, aircraft, vessels)	..	..	91	63	48	72	57	40	0	1
Tobacco (tobacco and manufactured tobacco)	..	..	4	2	3	1	2	2	2	2
Prepared Food (prepared foodstuffs)	..	..	14	19	20	20	19	18	11	11
Other customs duties	..	..	56	82	121	139	130	136	133	162
Custom duties exemptions	..	..	0	-3	-19	-5	-5	-6	-10	-4
5124 Taxes on exports	..	..	0	0	0	0	0	0	0	0
5125 Taxes on investment goods	..	..	0	0	0	0	0	0	0	0
5126 Taxes on specific services	..	..	352	565	168	40	45	45	60	70
Gaming Tax (casino)	..	..	0	6	2	0	0	0	0	0
Tourism Marketing Tax (TMT)	..	..	0	0	22	40	45	45	60	70
G&S Tax - Professional services	..	..	16	27	6	..	..	..	..	..
G&S Tax - Tourism	..	..	231	412	97	..	..	..	..	..
G&S Tax - Telecom and utilities	..	..	83	120	38	..	..	..	..	..
G&S Tax - Insurance	..	..	22	0	3	..	..	..	..	..
5127 Other taxes on internat. trade and transactions	..	..	0	0	0	0	0	0	0	0
5128 Other taxes	..	..	0	0	0	0	0	0	0	0
5130 Unallocable between 5110 and 5120	..	..	0	0	0	0	0	0	0	0
5200 Taxes on use of goods and perform activities	..	..	109	127	147	140	197	198	205	202
5210 Recurrent taxes	..	..	109	127	147	140	197	198	205	202
5211 Paid by households: motor vehicles	..	..	44	45	57	63	95	102	115	117
Road tax and other licences	..	..	41	45	54	59	88	95	108	108
Vehicle testing	..	..	2	0	3	3	7	7	8	8
5212 Paid by others: motor vehicles	..	..	0	0	0	0	0	0	0	0
5213 Paid in respect of other goods	..	..	66	81	90	78	102	96	90	85
Trade/industry licences	..	..	7	9	7	7	8	9	11	10
Licences and other licence registration	..	..	5	6	3	2	3	3	6	4
Telecommunications and radio broadcasting licences	..	..	50	63	75	64	88	83	72	71
Casino and hotel licences	..	..	4	4	4	3	3	1	1	1
Liquor and toddy licences	..	..	0	0	0	0	0	0	0	0
5220 Non-recurrent taxes	..	..	0	0	0	0	0	0	0	0
5300 Unallocable between 5100 and 5200	..	..	0	0	0	0	0	0	0	0
6000 Other taxes	..	..	**0**	**0**	**0**	**0**	**0**	**0**	**0**	**0**
6100 Paid solely by business	..	..	..	..	..	..	..	..	..	..
6200 Other	..	..	..	..	..	..	..	..	..	..

.. Not available

Note: Year ending 31st December.

The data are on a cash basis.

Heading 1210: The Goods and Services Tax in Seychelles was also applied to rental payments, which according to Revenue Statistics in Africa definitions are properly classified as business taxes. These revenues are reported under the Goods and Services Tax heading in budget documents for the Seychelles.

Heading 2000: Collection of social security contributions were phased out in 2010. In 2018, there was a collection of arrears of social security contributions.

Heading 5112: The Goods and Services Tax in Seychelles existed until it was replaced by a VAT in 2013. This tax imposed a 15% tax rate on sales of products and services in a long list of items enumerated in the Goods and Services Tax Act. Arrears on the Goods and Services Tax includes arrears on goods and services taxes professional services, tourism, telecom and utilities and insurance, which are reported under Heading 5126.

Heading 5126: Goods and services taxes on professional services, tourism, telecom and utilities, and insurance are now classified as taxes on services. These were reported under Heading 5112 in previous editions.

Figures exclude tax revenues collected by sub-national governments as the data are not available.

The various fishing licences fees are not included in tax revenues (about 0.7% of GDP in 2018) . These revenues are considered as non-tax revenues in accordance with the OECD classication, as set out in the Interpretative Guide in Annex A.

Source: Ministry of Finance.

StatLink https://doi.org/10.1787/888934183275

Table 5.27. **South Africa / Afrique du Sud**

Details of tax revenue / Recettes fiscales détaillées

Million ZAR

	1998	2000	2008	2010	2013	2014	2015	2016	2017	2018
Total tax revenue	**179 107**	**211 561**	**659 774**	**706 387**	**958 022**	**1 050 810**	**1 170 870**	**1 242 774**	**1 320 981**	**1 417 359**
1000 Taxes on income, profits and capital gains	**104 445**	**119 979**	**370 816**	**368 118**	**490 305**	**543 216**	**608 229**	**644 259**	**700 574**	**736 734**
1100 Of individuals	74 608	87 105	189 698	219 886	300 559	340 708	393 232	418 548	453 768	489 733
1110 On income and profits	74 608	87 105	189 698	219 886	300 559	340 708	393 232	418 548	453 768	489 733
Employees tax	..	..	179 144	213 113	295 824	334 863	382 883	407 105	440 141	474 454
Employment Incentive Tax (ETI) refunds	..	..	0	0	0	-2 000	-3 349	-4 905	-4 672	-3 392
PIT Provisional tax	..	..	14 605	15 719	17 188	19 944	24 200	27 313	29 427	33 426
PIT Assessment payments	..	..	5 373	7 425	8 849	8 682	9 970	11 594	15 011	16 230
PIT Refunds	..	..	-9 425	-16 372	-21 301	-20 781	-20 474	-22 559	-26 139	-30 986
1120 On capital gains	..	..	..	..	..	..	..	..	..	..
1200 Corporate	23 464	23 987	160 235	132 275	173 738	182 022	191 348	200 765	214 316	215 939
1210 On profits	23 464	23 987	160 235	132 275	173 738	182 022	191 348	200 765	214 316	215 939
CIT Provisional tax	..	..	159 596	136 615	177 034	181 491	190 437	202 636	214 097	222 178
CIT Assessment payments	..	..	7 604	9 051	9 170	12 040	11 119	10 291	12 888	13 714
Royalties	..	..	328	161	325	276	369	544	434	676
CIT Refunds	..	..	-7 294	-13 552	-12 791	-11 784	-10 577	-12 706	-13 103	-20 630
1220 On capital gains	..	..	..	..	..	..	..	..	..	..
1300 Unallocable between 1100 and 1200	6 372	8 887	20 883	15 957	16 008	20 486	23 649	24 946	32 489	31 062
2000 Social security contributions	**0**	**0**	**10 004**	**10 975**	**14 188**	**15 599**	**17 139**	**17 787**	**18 652**	**19 163**
2100 Employees	..	..	5 071	5 598	7 233	7 931	8 725	9 051	9 483	9 635
2110 On a payroll basis	..	..	137	220	279	262	311	314	314	107
2120 On an income tax basis	..	..	4 933	5 377	6 955	7 668	8 414	8 737	9 169	9 528
2200 Employers	..	..	4 933	5 377	6 955	7 668	8 414	8 737	9 169	9 528
2210 On a payroll basis	..	..	0	0	0	0	0	0	0	0
2220 On an income tax basis	..	..	4 933	5 377	6 955	7 668	8 414	8 737	9 169	9 528
2300 Self-employed or non-employed	..	..	0	0	0	0	0	0	0	0
2310 On a payroll basis	..	..	..	..	..	..	..	..	..	..
2320 On an income tax basis	..	..	..	..	..	..	..	..	..	..
2400 Unallocable between 2100, 2200 and 2300	..	..	0	0	0	0	0	0	0	0
2410 On a payroll basis	..	..	..	..	..	..	..	..	..	..
2420 On an income tax basis	..	..	..	..	..	..	..	..	..	..
3000 Taxes on payroll and workforce	**0**	**870**	**7 023**	**8 240**	**11 900**	**13 264**	**15 111**	**15 092**	**15 891**	**17 265**
4000 Taxes on property	**2 653**	**3 829**	**33 350**	**40 108**	**51 453**	**58 303**	**59 110**	**67 554**	**74 514**	**81 967**
4100 Recurrent taxes on immovable property	0	0	23 159	31 041	41 421	46 291	44 618	51 668	58 732	65 786
4110 Households	..	..	22 566	30 533	40 896	45 807	44 169	51 133	58 234	65 243
4120 Others	..	..	593	508	525	484	449	535	498	543
4200 Recurrent taxes on net wealth	0	0	0	0	0	0	0	0	0	0
4210 Individual	..	..	..	..	..	..	..	..	..	..
4220 Corporate	..	..	..	..	..	..	..	..	..	..
4300 Estate, inheritance and gift taxes	270	436	783	855	1 266	1 519	2 065	1 832	2 667	2 740
4310 Estate and inheritance taxes	258	417	672	794	1 163	1 349	1 918	1 612	2 303	1 894
4320 Gift taxes	13	19	111	61	103	170	147	220	364	846
4400 Taxes on financial and capital transactions	686	1 094	3 863	2 912	3 617	4 098	5 069	6 081	5 248	5 967
4500 Non-recurrent taxes	1 697	2 299	5 546	5 300	5 149	6 394	7 358	7 974	7 868	7 474
4510 On net wealth	0	0	0	0	0	0	0	0	0	0
4520 Other non-recurrent taxes	1 697	2 299	5 546	5 300	5 149	6 394	7 358	7 974	7 868	7 474
4600 Other recurrent taxes on property	0	0	0	0	0	0	0	0	0	0
5000 Taxes on goods and services	**70 381**	**84 462**	**236 908**	**278 924**	**390 171**	**420 457**	**471 281**	**498 073**	**511 366**	**562 240**
5100 Taxes on production, sale, transfer, etc.	70 381	84 462	232 555	273 602	382 810	412 874	463 423	489 342	500 917	550 824
5110 General taxes	42 655	52 054	151 904	170 548	231 545	256 482	277 551	294 694	293 900	324 702
5111 Value added taxes	42 655	52 054	151 904	170 552	231 528	256 464	277 530	294 674	293 864	324 682
Domestic VAT	21 890	52 547	186 413	202 535	258 213	281 236	303 285	314 734	333 719	368 766
VAT on Imports	20 765	25 148	91 494	78 645	124 906	134 535	148 392	150 986	150 768	169 018
VAT Refunds	0	-25 641	-126 002	-110 627	-151 592	-159 307	-174 147	-171 046	-190 624	-213 103
5112 Sales tax	0	0	0	-5	16	17	21	20	36	20
5113 Other	0	0	0	0	0	0	0	0	0	0
5120 Taxes on specific goods and services	27 726	32 408	80 650	103 054	151 265	156 392	185 872	194 647	207 017	226 122

Table 5.27. **South Africa / Afrique du Sud** *(cont.)*

Details of tax revenue / Recettes fiscales détaillées

Million ZAR

	1998	2000	2008	2010	2013	2014	2015	2016	2017	2018
5121 Excises	21 480	24 341	53 981	76 239	103 156	112 440	137 859	143 337	155 062	167 389
Specific excise tax - Domestic	..	..	19 613	22 448	28 290	31 400	34 918	35 714	36 731	41 568
Ad valorem excise - Domestic	..	..	1 363	1 569	2 198	2 848	3 295	3 238	3 652	4 163
Fuel levy	..	..	24 314	32 758	42 656	46 802	56 694	61 064	68 608	74 376
Plastic bags	..	..	94	177	200	139	213	221	238	287
Electricity levy	..	..	0	5 065	8 968	8 541	8 481	8 507	8 495	8 448
Incandescent light bulb levy	..	..	0	180	116	68	52	66	62	46
CO_2 tax - motor vehicle emissions	..	..	0	205	1 669	1 591	1 429	1 177	1 347	1 376
RAF	..	..	8 596	13 837	19 058	21 051	32 778	33 350	35 336	36 379
Tyre Levy	..	..	0	0	0	0	0	0	593	744
5122 Profits of fiscal monopolies	0	0	0	0	0	0	0	0	0	0
5123 Customs and import duties	6 182	7 714	24 216	25 196	42 794	41 857	43 965	47 438	47 367	53 936
Import duties	..	..	..	..	30 708	31 616	32 130	33 855	32 742	37 649
Ad valorem Imported	..	..	..	..	8 011	7 573	8 495	8 701	5 668	10 091
Excise Imported	..	..	..	..	4 076	2 668	3 340	4 882	8 954	6 191
International Oil Pollution Levy	..	..	..	..	0	0	0	0	3	5
5124 Taxes on exports	0	0	0	61	72	118	121	116	103	62
5125 Taxes on investment goods	0	0	0	0	0	0	0	0	0	0
5126 Taxes on specific services	0	0	2 026	2 252	2 967	2 992	3 224	3 401	3 775	3 999
5127 Other taxes on internat. trade and transactions	65	353	427	-695	2 276	-1 015	703	355	709	736
5128 Other taxes	0	0	0	0	0	0	0	0	0	0
5130 Unallocable between 5110 and 5120	0	0	0	0	0	0	0	0	0	0
5200 Taxes on use of goods and perform activities	0	0	4 354	5 322	7 361	7 583	7 858	8 732	10 450	11 415
5210 Recurrent taxes	..	..	4 354	5 322	7 361	7 583	7 858	8 732	10 450	11 415
5211 Paid by households: motor vehicles	..	..	3 303	4 046	5 742	5 879	6 234	6 565	8 120	8 860
5212 Paid by others: motor vehicles	..	..	826	1 012	1 435	1 470	1 558	1 641	2 030	2 215
5213 Paid in respect of other goods	..	..	225	264	184	234	66	525	299	341
5220 Non-recurrent taxes	0	0	0	0	0	0	0	0	0	0
5300 Unallocable between 5100 and 5200	0	0	0	0	0	0	0	0	0	0
6000 Other taxes	**1 628**	**2 420**	**1 671**	**23**	**5**	**-29**	**-1**	**9**	**-17**	**-11**
6100 Paid solely by business	0	0	0	0	0	0	0	0	0	0
6200 Other	1 628	2 420	1 671	23	5	-29	-1	9	-17	-11
Stamp duties and fees	..	..	625	9	31	0	0	0	0	0
Unallocated Tax Revenue	..	..	1 047	14	-26	-29	-1	9	-17	-11

Table 5.27. **South Africa / Afrique du Sud** *(cont.)*

Details of tax revenue / Recettes fiscales détaillées

.. Not available

Note: Year ending 31st December. Some fiscal year data have been adjusted to align to calendar years. Social security contributions and taxes at provincial and local level are reported on a fiscal year basis beginning 1st April. For example, the data for 2016 represent April 2016 to March 2017. Data prior to 1995/96 were restated retrospectively to aggregate the revenues from TBVC States and Self-Governing Territories.

With the adoption of the interim Constitution in 1994, these were abolished.

-TBVC States: Transkei, Bophuthatswana, Venda and Ciskei.

-Self-Governing Territories: Gazankulu, Kangwane, Kwandebele, Kwazulu, Lebowa and Qwaqwa.

Tax revenues on national and provincial government level in South Africa are on a cash basis, while local authorities and public entities are on an accrual basis.

Tax revenues at the local and provincial levels are only available from 2003 (representing fiscal year 2003/04).

For the year 2018/19, figures for the Road Accident Fund Levy, provincial and local taxes, and contributions to the unemployment insurance funds are projected figures. This affects headings 2000, 5121, 5126, and 5200.

Headings 1110 and 1120: The figures include Capital Gains Tax (CGT). CGT cannot been listed separately under 1120 and 1220 because the data that South African Revenue Service (SARS) collated for CGT are for liability raised and not actual CGT collections received. The figures exclude interest and fines from 1994 onwards. Figures on ETI refunds, which started being collected in 2014, are now reported under 1110. These were included as part of Employees tax in previous editions.

Heading 2000: the social security contributions in South Africa consist of contributions to the Unemployment Insurance Fund (UIF). Standard practice in South Africa is to classify UIF under non-tax revenue. The methodology applied in the compilation of the data was to allocate 50% of the total social security contributions (UIF) to each of employees and employers.

Headings 2120 and 2220: 2018 figures are projections based on the previous three years of data.

Heading 4120: the figures refer to penalties and collection charges on property rates.

Headings 4110 and 5120: 2018 figures are projections based on the previous three years of data.

Heading 5111: includes interests and fines.

Heading 5121: following the OECD classification, the Road Accident Fund (RAF) is classified as an excise. The national classification of South Africa classifies this revenue as a social security contribution. Revenues from the Tyre Levy were reported for the first time in this edition of Revenue Statistics in Africa. RAF figures for 2018 are projections based on the previous three years of data.

Headings 5121 and 5123: The data for customs duties and excise include revenue on import duties plus specific and ad valorem excise duties that will be paid to Botswana, Eswatini, Lesotho and Namibia (BELN) through the revenue sharing agreement.

Heading 5123: SARS only started separately reporting ordinary custom duties on imported goods, specific excise duties on imported goods and ad valorem duties on imported goods from April 2012. From April 2014 onwards, the Customs Duty amounts for the specific tariff headings under chapter 27 (Mineral Fuels) were treated as fuel levies (5121 Excises). Some estimation was used for the year 2012 due to missing information.

Heading 5124: Revenues from the International Pollution Levy were reported for the first time in this edition of Revenue Statistics in Africa.

Heading 5126: 2018 figures are projections based on the previous three years of data.

Headings 5127 and 6200: include negative figures due to refund accounting adjustments.

Heading 5211: an 80:20 ratio was used to split provincial recurrent motor vehicle taxes based on research about South Africa's commercial and private household motor vehicle fleet.

Headings 5211, 5212, and 5213: 2018 figures are projections based on the previous three years of data.

Heading 6200: includes stamp duties and fees plus unallocated tax revenue.

Taxes that were discontinued and introduced (causing breaks in the data) include the following:

a. Ordinary levy discontinued in March 2003 (heading 5127).

b. Demutualisation charge has been included in heading 4400. There were two collections in March 1999 and August 1999.

c. Secondary Tax on Companies (STC) in heading 1300 effective from July 1993 and changed to Dividends Tax (DT) in April 2012.

d. Small business tax amnesty (heading 1300) effective from March 2007.

e. VAT (heading 5111) effective from September 1991 at a rate of 10% and increased to 14% in 1993. Prior to that, sales tax data was restated to VAT.

f. Levy on financial services (heading 4400) effective from January 1992.

g. Skills development levy (heading 3000) effective from May 2000.

h. Excises (5121)

- Plastic bags effective from June 2005.
- Electricity levy effective from August 2009.
- Incandescent light bulbs effective from March 2010.
- CO_2 tax effective from September 2010.

i. Air departure tax (heading 5126) effective from December 2000.

j. Universal services fund (heading 5213) effective from March 2006.

Source: Data on national government taxation from the South African Revenue Service (SARS); data on social security contributions, and taxes levied at the provincial and local level from the National Treasury of South Africa.

StatLink https://doi.org/10.1787/888934183351

Table 5.28. **Togo**

Details of tax revenue / Recettes fiscales détaillées

Million XOF

	1998	2000	2008	2010	2013	2014	2015	2016	2017	2018
Recettes fiscales totales	..	**99 994**	**214 083**	**250 441**	**416 628**	**471 498**	**533 556**	**586 813**	**585 660**	**576 528**
1000 Impôts sur revenu, bénéfices et gains en capital	..	**20 928**	**40 238**	**41 200**	**73 749**	**78 972**	**88 658**	**112 797**	**100 214**	**117 078**
1100 Des personnes physiques	..	9 440	18 839	18 000	28 542	22 700	30 791	39 703	40 826	44 595
1110 Sur le revenu et les bénéfices	..	9 440	18 839	18 000	28 542	22 700	30 791	39 703	40 826	44 595
Impôt sur le revenu (IR) des transporteurs routiers	..	452	530	393	204	272	379	500	366	368
Retenue sur les revenus des capitaux mobiliers	..	1 185	2 345	6 106	7 428	6 199	8 365	12 222	9 882	11 183
IR des personnes physiques	..	7 804	15 964	11 500	20 908	16 229	22 046	26 976	30 571	33 043
IR des personnes physiques (transferts aux collectivités locales)	..	..	1	1	2	0	0	5	8	0
1120 Sur les gains en capital	..	0	0	0	0	0	0	0	0	0
1200 Des sociétés	..	11 488	21 399	23 200	45 207	56 272	57 867	73 094	59 388	72 483
1210 Sur les bénéfices	..	11 488	21 399	23 200	45 207	56 272	57 867	73 094	59 388	72 483
Impôt sur les sociétés	..	8 997	16 774	18 280	42 162	50 496	51 177	64 564	52 080	64 851
Prélèvement bénéf. industriels et commerciaux (BIC)	..	2 490	4 625	4 920	3 045	5 776	6 691	8 530	7 309	7 632
1220 Sur les gains en capital	..	0	0	0	0	0	0	0	0	0
1300 Non ventilables entre 1100 et 1200	..	0	0	0	0	0	0	0	0	0
2000 Cotisations de sécurité sociale	..	..	..	..	..	..	..	..	..	..
2100 A la charge des salariés	..	..	..	..	..	..	..	..	..	..
2110 Sur la base du salaire	..	..	..	..	..	..	..	..	..	..
2120 Sur la base de l'impôt sur le revenu	..	..	..	..	..	..	..	..	..	..
2200 A la charge des employeurs	..	..	..	..	..	..	..	..	..	..
2210 Sur la base du salaire	..	..	..	..	..	..	..	..	..	..
2220 Sur la base de l'impôt sur le revenu	..	..	..	..	..	..	..	..	..	..
2300 A charge des travailleurs indép. ou sans emploi	..	..	..	..	..	..	..	..	..	..
2310 Sur la base du salaire	..	..	..	..	..	..	..	..	..	..
2320 Sur la base de l'impôt sur le revenu	..	..	..	..	..	..	..	..	..	..
2400 Non ventilables entre 2100, 2200 et 2300	..	..	..	..	..	..	..	..	..	..
2410 Sur la base du salaire	..	..	..	..	..	..	..	..	..	..
2420 Sur la base de l'impôt sur le revenu	..	..	..	..	..	..	..	..	..	..
3000 Sur salaires ou main d'oeuvre	..	**1 973**	**3 561**	**5 491**	**5 542**	**9 155**	**4 551**	**5 599**	**5 018**	**4 757**
Taxe complémentaire à l'impôt sur le revenu	..	79	203	1 220	1 598	5 887	956	1 246	1 256	1 042
Taxes/salaires	..	1 894	3 233	4 137	3 714	2 956	3 284	3 963	3 274	3 253
Taxe complémentaire à l'Impôt sur le revenu (transferts aux collectivités locales)	..	..	126	134	230	312	311	389	488	463
4000 Impôts sur le patrimoine	..	**374**	**1 627**	**1 898**	**2 729**	**3 826**	**4 360**	**4 766**	**4 256**	**4 819**
4100 Impôts périodiques sur la propriété immobilière	..	374	1 627	1 898	2 729	3 826	4 360	4 766	4 256	4 819
Taxe foncière sur les propriétés bâties	..	278	482	655	679	1 078	1 465	1 507	1 315	1 410
Droits d'immatriculation des propriétés foncières	..	96	314	335	502	521	613	783	228	334
Taxe d'enlèvement des ordures (transferts aux collectivités locales)	..	..	112	129	212	288	315	360	331	407
Taxe foncière sur les propriétés bâties (transferts aux collectivités locales)	..	..	532	553	977	1 551	1 404	1 494	1 783	2 032
4110 Ménages	..	0	188	226	359	388	563	623	599	636
Taxe d'habitation (transferts aux collectivités locales)	..	..	188	226	359	388	563	623	599	636
4120 Autres agents	..	0	0	0	0	0	0	0	0	0
4200 Impôts périodiques sur l'actif net	..	0	0	0	0	0	0	0	0	0
4210 Personnes physiques	..	..	..	..	..	..	..	..	..	..
4220 Sociétés	..	..	..	..	..	..	..	..	..	..
4300 Impôts sur mut. par décès, succ. et donations	..	0	0	0	0	0	0	0	0	0
4310 Impôts sur mut. par décès et successions	..	..	..	..	..	..	..	..	..	..
4320 Impôts sur les donations	..	..	..	..	..	..	..	..	..	..
4400 Impôts sur transact. mobilières et immob.	..	0	0	0	0	0	0	0	0	0
4500 Impôts non-périodiques	..	0	0	0	0	0	0	0	0	0
4510 Sur l'actif net	..	..	..	..	..	..	..	..	..	..
4520 Autres non-périodiques	..	..	..	..	..	..	..	..	..	..
4600 Autres impôts périodiques sur patrimoine	..	0	0	0	0	0	0	0	0	0
5000 Impôts sur les biens et services	..	**74 771**	**164 294**	**196 239**	**325 665**	**370 207**	**427 424**	**454 604**	**459 815**	**439 693**
5100 Impôts sur production, vente, transfert, etc.	..	74 662	163 817	195 813	324 810	368 570	425 367	452 380	457 429	437 006
5110 Impôts généraux	..	36 941	91 279	115 056	187 809	225 401	250 410	271 347	269 266	256 847
5111 Taxes sur la valeur ajoutée	..	36 073	87 088	110 316	179 342	213 671	236 011	255 323	253 663	237 537
Recettes TVA (douanes)	..	25 101	66 792	69 840	136 522	142 840	167 228	172 435	138 802	142 211
Recettes TVA (intérieure)	..	10 972	20 296	40 476	42 820	70 830	68 783	82 888	114 861	95 325
5112 Impôts sur les ventes	..	0	0	0	0	0	0	0	0	0

Table 5.28. **Togo** *(cont.)*

Details of tax revenue / Recettes fiscales détaillées

Million XOF

	1998	2000	2008	2010	2013	2014	2015	2016	2017	2018
5113 Autres impôts	..	868	4 191	4 740	8 468	11 731	14 399	16 024	15 602	19 311
Taxe professionnelle unique	..	146	319	334	329	381	507	515	485	537
Taxe professionnelle	..	722	1 157	1 587	3 191	4 371	6 693	7 943	5 831	7 270
Taxe professionnelle unique (transferts aux collectivités locales)	..	..	173	206	332	423	507	572	539	597
Taxe professionnelle (transferts aux collectivités locales)	..	..	2 541	2 613	4 616	6 556	6 693	6 995	8 747	10 906
5120 Impôts sur biens et services déterminés	..	37 696	72 511	80 724	137 000	143 168	174 957	181 033	188 164	180 159
5121 Accises	..	12 785	15 940	16 360	30 669	29 369	35 150	43 686	43 471	44 429
Droits d'accises/produits pétroliers	..	11 773	11 836	11 738	20 122	16 861	17 972	20 945	20 337	22 978
Autres droits d'accises	..	1 012	4 104	4 622	3 847	7 033	8 246	10 906	10 955	11 835
Prélèvement dette secteur pétrolier	..	0	0	0	6 701	5 474	8 932	11 836	12 179	9 616
5122 Bénéfices des monopoles fiscaux	..	0	0	0	0	0	0	0	0	0
5123 Droits de douane et droits à l'importation	..	22 559	51 437	61 676	93 471	99 201	122 750	119 825	127 065	117 608
Droits de douane	..	18 519	43 619	52 941	80 115	83 234	101 730	98 020	86 383	90 186
Redevance statistique	..	2 717	6 017	6 763	10 103	12 740	13 578	14 021	32 653	18 447
Timbre douanier	..	94	264	297	424	359	424	298	283	285
Cartes et vignettes	..	186	240	237	406	385	369	600	609	872
Taxe de protection et d'entretien des infrastructures	..	1 039	1 293	1 434	2 418	2 476	2 958	3 252	3 575	3 917
Produits des crédits en douane	..	2	1	2	4	6	5	9	8	8
Prélèvement national de solidarité	..	0	0	0	0	0	3 686	3 625	3 555	3 893
Remises	..	1	0	0	0	0	0	0	0	0
Entrepôts fictifs	..	1	4	2	0	1	0	0	0	0
5124 Taxes à l'exportation	..	302	1 197	1 430	1 881	2 544	2 728	2 476	2 737	2 977
Taxe spéciale de réexportation	..	302	1 197	1 430	1 235	1 947	2 260	2 015	2 156	2 685
Redevance minière (66,67%)	..	0	0	0	646	597	468	461	580	292
5125 Impôts sur biens d'équipement	..	0	0	0	0	0	0	0	0	0
5126 Impôts sur services déterminés	..	2 049	3 936	1 258	10 979	12 055	14 329	15 046	14 891	15 146
Taxe sur les produits des jeux de hasard	..	151	231	347	882	682	913	1 047	1 185	1 184
Taxe/convention d'assurance	..	227	688	815	1 405	1 396	2 035	2 365	2 205	2 158
Taxe sur les activités financières	..	1 671	2 934	0	8 536	9 793	11 140	11 372	11 204	11 508
Taxe sur les produits des jeux de hasard (transferts aux collectivités locales)	..	..	80	94	151	171	228	262	296	296
Taxe sur les spectacles (transferts aux collectivités locales)	..	..	2	2	5	13	13	0	0	0
5127 Autres impôts sur commerce et transact. internat.	..	0	0	0	0	0	0	0	0	0
5128 Autres impôts	..	0	0	0	0	0	0	0	0	0
5130 Non ventilables entre 5110 et 5120	..	25	28	33	0	0	0	0	0	0
5200 Impôts sur utilisation des biens et exerc. activites	..	108	476	426	855	1 637	2 057	2 224	2 386	2 687
5210 Impôts périodiques	..	108	476	426	855	1 637	2 057	2 224	2 386	2 687
5211 A la charge des ménages: véhicules à moteur	..	0	0	0	0	0	0	0	0	0
5212 A la charge autres agents: véhicules à moteur	..	2	0	0	3	185	287	308	311	312
5213 Autres impôts périodiques	..	106	476	426	852	1 452	1 770	1 915	2 076	2 375
Taxe spéc. sur la fabric. et le commerce des boissons	..	106	242	162	413	843	1 145	1 158	1 300	1 521
Taxe spéc. sur la fabric. et le commerce des boissons (transferts aux collectivités locales)	..	..	234	264	439	609	625	757	776	855
5220 Impôts non-périodiques	..	0	0	0	0	0	0	0	0	0
5300 Non ventilables entre 5100 et 5200	..	0	0	0	0	0	0	0	0	0
6000 Autres impôts	**..**	**1 949**	**4 363**	**5 612**	**8 943**	**9 338**	**8 563**	**9 048**	**16 356**	**10 180**
Droits de timbres	..	1 471	2 428	3 135	2 926	2 862	3 612	3 676	3 338	3 258
Droits d'enregistrement	..	478	1 896	2 436	5 953	6 469	4 949	5 158	12 498	6 553
Taxe d'enregistrement (transferts aux collectivités locales)	..	..	39	41	64	6	2	214	521	369
6100 A la charge exclusive des entreprises	..	..	..	..	..	..	..	..	..	..
6200 A la charge d'autres agents	..	..	..	..	..	..	..	..	..	..

Table 5.28. **Togo** *(cont.)*

Details of tax revenue / Recettes fiscales détaillées

.. Non disponible

Note : Année civile se terminant le 31 décembre.

Les données sont sur la base des encaissements.

Les chiffres sous les rubriques 1110, 3000, 4100, 5113, 5126, 5213, et 6000 incluent les recettes recouvrées par l'administration fiscale togolaise pour le compte des collectivités locales. Ce traitement s'applique sur la période 2008-18 et les lignes concernées sont mises en exergue avec la mention « transferts aux collectivités locales ». Ces recettes sont classifiées comme des recettes du gouvernement central conformément au guide d'interprétation de l'OCDE. Le Togo ne les comptabilise pas dans les recettes du budget de l'État.

Rubrique 1210 : Dans cette édition, les données sur les impôts sur les bénéfices n'incluent pas les montants recouvrés au cours des exercices précédents, relatifs à tout type d'impôt (TVA, impôts sur le revenu, impôt sur les sociétés, droits d'accise...), montants qu'il n'était pas possible de ventiler dans les éditions précédentes. Dans cette édition, le Togo a retraité ces données afin d'obtenir les montants exacts de chaque type d'impôts collecté au cours d'une année donnée.

Rubrique 2000 : Les données de cotisations de sécurité sociale ne sont pas disponibles.

Rubrique 5121 : Le prélèvement pour l'apurement de la dette du secteur pétrolier (PADSP) est considéré comme une recette fiscale dans cette publication comme le préconise la classification OCDE (voir le guide d'interprétation en Annexe A). La classification nationale du Togo considère ces recettes comme des recettes non fiscales.

Les données sur les remboursements de TVA ne sont pas disponibles car au Togo, les crédits de TVA ne font pas l'objet de remboursement avec les moyens classiques de paiement (virement, chèque, espèces...). Lorsqu'un contribuable dispose d'un crédit de TVA, il adresse une demande de remboursement à l'administration fiscale qui lui délivre un certificat de détaxe. Ce certificat lui permet de payer non seulement ses déclarations ultérieures de TVA mais aussi les autres impôts.

La classification nationale du Togo considère les amendes et pénalités relatives aux impôts, les confiscations et ventes en douane et les remboursements du prélèvement communautaire de solidarité comme des recettes fiscales. Ces recettes sont classifiées comme des recettes non fiscales dans cette publication comme le préconise la classification OCDE (voir le guide d'interprétation en Annexe A).

Le Soutien à la politique pétrolière (SPP) est un fond financé par un prélèvement effectué sur la TVA recouvrée par la douane, sauf pour les années 2010-12 quand le SPP était financé par une subvention de l'état. Dans les éditions précédentes, ces fonds ont été comptabilisés à tort dans les recettes de la TVA.

Source : Office Togolais des Recettes.

StatLink https://doi.org/10.1787/888934183294

Table 5.29. **Tunisia / Tunisie**

Details of tax revenue / Recettes fiscales détaillées

Million TND

	1998	2000	2008	2010	2013	2014	2015	2016	2017	2018
Recettes fiscales totales	..	**7 196**	**14 833**	**17 143**	**22 407**	**24 998**	**25 613**	**26 596**	**29 810**	**33 824**
1000 Impôts sur revenu, bénéfices et gains en capital	..	**1 624**	**4 611**	**5 091**	**6 878**	**7 955**	**7 678**	**7 384**	**8 506**	**8 979**
1100 Des personnes physiques	..	1 049	2 195	2 658	3 711	4 096	5 003	5 931	6 191	6 359
1110 Sur le revenu et les bénéfices	..	1 037	2 187	2 644	3 686	4 058	4 965	5 887	6 139	6 311
Traitements et salaires	..	742	1 606	2 006	3 068	3 260	3 549	4 107	4 029	4 054
Honoraires, commissions, courtage et loyers (personnes physiques)	..	20	143	184	205	236	364	483	541	508
Intérêts dépôts des comptes spéciaux d'épargne	..	65	66	68	102	125	159	176	199	270
Revenus des capitaux mobiliers (personnes physiques)	..	32	82	75	69	87	212	269	272	310
Avances sur les marchés (personnes physiques)	..	27	47	50	46	56	313	508	624	720
Bénéfices industriels et commerciaux	..	43	75	94	95	98	119	142	146	154
Bénéfices non commerciaux	..	17	28	49	46	71	76	79	81	98
Impôt forfaitaire	..	14	23	25	22	31	36	37	39	48
Revenus agricoles	..	5	6	8	11	15	19	22	26	26
Revenus fonciers et autres	..	5	7	8	10	12	14	22	27	30
Autres impôts sur le revenu et bénéfices	..	66	102	78	13	67	105	42	156	93
1120 Sur les gains en capital	..	12	9	13	24	38	39	45	52	48
1200 Des sociétés	..	575	2 414	2 432	3 165	3 855	2 673	1 450	2 315	2 620
1210 Sur les bénéfices	..	575	2 413	2 424	3 159	3 848	2 658	1 442	2 295	2 613
Sociétés pétrolières	..	96	1 150	813	1 438	1 575	950	346	527	709
Sociétés non-pétrolières	..	359	706	864	779	1 137	1 088	806	1 299	1 149
Avances sur les marchés (sociétés)	..	33	277	356	389	478	222	46	47	57
Avance au titre des importations	..	7	42	111	166	184	198	198	268	430
Revenus des capitaux mobiliers (sociétés)	..	58	115	113	174	215	72	27	106	226
Honoraires, commissions, courtage et loyers (sociétés)	..	16	102	125	169	183	86	2	1	5
Redevances servies aux non résidents	..	3	17	39	36	53	18	9	7	4
Autres impôts sur les bénéfices	..	3	3	3	8	22	25	9	40	33
1220 Sur les gains en capital	..	0	1	7	6	7	14	7	19	7
1300 Non ventilables entre 1100 et 1200	..	0	1	2	3	4	2	4	0	0
2000 Cotisations de sécurité sociale	..	**1 551**	**3 568**	**4 629**	**6 504**	**6 882**	**7 549**	**8 415**	**9 259**	**9 826**
2100 A la charge des salariés	..	..	..	..	..	..	..	..	..	..
2110 Sur la base du salaire	..	..	..	..	..	..	..	..	..	..
2120 Sur la base de l'impôt sur le revenu	..	..	..	..	..	..	..	..	..	..
2200 A la charge des employeurs	..	..	..	..	..	..	..	..	..	..
2210 Sur la base du salaire	..	..	..	..	..	..	..	..	..	..
2220 Sur la base de l'impôt sur le revenu	..	..	..	..	..	..	..	..	..	..
2300 A charge des travailleurs indép. ou sans emploi	..	..	..	..	..	..	..	..	..	..
2310 Sur la base du salaire	..	..	..	..	..	..	..	..	..	..
2320 Sur la base de l'impôt sur le revenu	..	..	..	..	..	..	..	..	..	..
2400 Non ventilables entre 2100, 2200 et 2300	..	1 551	3 568	4 629	6 504	6 882	7 549	8 415	9 259	9 826
2410 Sur la base du salaire	..	..	..	..	..	..	..	..	..	..
2420 Sur la base de l'impôt sur le revenu	..	..	..	..	..	..	..	..	..	..
3000 Sur salaires ou main d'oeuvre	..	**107**	**143**	**199**	**242**	**285**	**315**	**345**	**375**	**405**
Fond de promotion des logements	..	71	87	124	147	177	191	215	231	246
Taxe de formation professionnelle	..	35	56	75	95	107	124	130	143	159
4000 Impôts sur le patrimoine	..	**81**	**157**	**177**	**244**	**257**	**282**	**299**	**303**	**308**
4100 Impôts périodiques sur la propriété immobilière	..	7	11	10	8	8	11	11	12	13
4110 Ménages	..	7	11	10	8	8	11	11	12	13
4120 Autres agents	..	0	0	0	0	0	0	0	0	0
4200 Impôts périodiques sur l'actif net	..	0	0	0	0	0	0	0	0	0
4210 Personnes physiques	..	..	..	..	..	..	..	..	..	..
4220 Sociétés	..	..	..	..	..	..	..	..	..	..
4300 Impôts sur mut. par décès, succ. et donations	..	0	0	0	0	0	0	0	0	0
4310 Impôts sur mut. par décès et successions	..	..	..	..	..	..	..	..	..	..
4320 Impôts sur les donations	..	..	..	..	..	..	..	..	..	..
4400 Impôts sur transact. mobilières et immob.	..	74	146	168	236	248	271	288	291	295
4500 Impôts non-périodiques	..	0	0	0	0	0	0	0	0	0
4510 Sur l'actif net	..	..	..	..	..	..	..	..	..	..
4520 Autres non-périodiques	..	..	..	..	..	..	..	..	..	..
4600 Autres impôts périodiques sur patrimoine	..	0	0	0	0	0	0	0	0	0
5000 Impôts sur les biens et services	..	**3 729**	**6 076**	**6 768**	**8 116**	**9 099**	**9 168**	**9 523**	**10 666**	**13 444**
5100 Impôts sur production, vente, transfert, etc.	..	3 665	5 949	6 612	7 948	8 903	8 977	9 300	10 442	13 222
5110 Impôts généraux	..	1 814	3 373	3 819	4 581	5 267	5 211	5 288	5 918	7 696

Table 5.29. **Tunisia / Tunisie** *(cont.)*

Details of tax revenue / Recettes fiscales détaillées

Million TND

	1998	2000	2008	2010	2013	2014	2015	2016	2017	2018
5111 Taxes sur la valeur ajoutée	..	1 792	3 309	3 750	4 460	5 117	5 068	5 118	5 722	7 425
Recettes TVA (brute)	..	..	3 594	4 163	5 130	5 544	5 684	5 771	6 106	7 787
Remboursements de la TVA	..	..	-285	-413	-670	-427	-617	-653	-384	-362
5112 Impôts sur les ventes	..	0	0	0	0	0	0	0	0	0
5113 Autres impôts	..	21	64	69	121	150	144	170	196	271
5120 Impôts sur biens et services déterminés	..	1 851	2 576	2 793	3 367	3 637	3 765	4 012	4 523	5 527
5121 Accises	..	1 023	1 631	1 814	2 143	2 315	2 397	2 876	3 226	3 621
Tabac	..	371	736	799	1 014	1 085	1 087	1 248	1 397	1 490
Boissons alcoolisées	..	147	164	174	267	303	290	336	363	431
Essences et huiles	..	260	262	268	258	279	305	649	705	757
Voitures	..	86	161	242	251	251	289	285	333	338
Produits alimentaires	..	19	32	31	35	45	41	44	50	60
Ciment	..	11	15	17	18	20	17	15	15	17
Autres accises	..	131	261	282	299	332	369	299	362	528
5122 Bénéfices des monopoles fiscaux	..	0	0	0	0	0	0	0	0	0
5123 Droits de douane et droits à l'importation	..	654	619	620	796	882	918	742	799	1 235
Hors tabac	..	565	466	428	570	603	639	429	486	894
Redevances sur prestations douanières à l'importation	..	68	123	142	166	182	155	188	204	221
Taxe conjoncturelle sur ventes du ciment importé	..	0	0	0	18	41	61	28	0	0
Droits de douane - Tabacs	..	9	13	23	27	31	27	37	51	57
Autres droits de douane	..	0	3	4	2	2	1	0	0	0
Prèlevements à l'importation	..	12	11	20	11	18	29	45	42	46
Autres taxes et prélèvements à l'importation	..	1	2	3	3	5	7	15	16	17
5124 Taxes à l'exportation	..	11	29	27	38	38	41	30	43	72
5125 Impôts sur biens d'équipement	..	0	0	0	0	0	0	0	0	0
5126 Impôts sur services déterminés	..	162	297	330	389	401	409	363	455	599
Taxe sur les télécommunications	..	72	126	136	160	151	147	153	150	178
Taxe de compensation sur les transports	..	55	93	105	119	123	126	67	138	141
Taxe sur les assurances	..	33	76	86	109	120	129	138	156	197
Autres impôts sur services déterminés	..	2	2	3	2	8	7	5	11	82
5127 Autres impôts sur commerce et transact. internat.	..	0	0	0	0	0	0	0	0	0
5128 Autres impôts	..	0	1	1	1	1	1	0	0	0
5130 Non ventilables entre 5110 et 5120	..	0	0	0	0	0	0	0	0	0
5200 Impôts sur utilisation des biens et exerc. activites	..	64	127	156	168	196	191	223	224	222
5210 Impôts périodiques	..	55	89	103	116	124	134	160	160	167
5211 A la charge des ménages: véhicules à moteur	..	35	51	60	69	74	81	91	96	101
5212 A la charge autres agents: véhicules à moteur	..	18	35	43	46	49	53	69	64	67
5213 Autres impôts périodiques	..	1	2	0	0	0	0	0	0	0
5220 Impôts non-périodiques	..	9	38	53	52	72	57	63	64	54
5300 Non ventilables entre 5100 et 5200	..	0	0	0	0	0	0	0	0	0
6000 Autres impôts	**..**	**104**	**278**	**279**	**423**	**520**	**622**	**630**	**702**	**862**
Droits de timbres	..	25	165	133	256	288	334	350	370	447
Droits d'enregistrements	..	40	83	107	124	145	181	201	214	248
Droit sur les voyages à l'étranger	..	12	19	21	26	30	33	35	38	42
Autres impôts - divers	..	28	12	17	17	57	75	43	81	125
6100 A la charge exclusive des entreprises	..	..	..	..	..	..	..	..	..	..
6200 A la charge d'autres agents	..	..	..	..	..	..	..	..	..	..

.. Non disponible

Note : Année civile se terminant le 31 décembre.

Les données sont sur la base des encaissements.

Les chiffres n'incluent pas les données des recettes fiscales collectées par les collectivités locales car elles ne sont pas disponibles.

Les impôts affectés aux Fonds spéciaux du Trésor et aux Fonds de concours sont compris dans les données pour la période 2000-18

La rubrique 1210 exclut les redevances des compagnies pétrolières. En Tunisie, elles sont considérées comme un complément de l'impôt sur les sociétés depuis avril 2012. Les cotisations de sécurité sociale sous la rubrique 2000 ne sont pas considérées comme des recettes fiscales en Tunisie.

Les cotisations de sécurité sociale sous la rubrique 2000 ne sont pas considérées comme des recettes fiscales en Tunisie.

Source : Ministère des Finances pour toutes les données des recettes fiscales. Ministère des Affaires sociales pour les données de cotisations de sécurité sociale.

StatLink https://doi.org/10.1787/888934183313

Table 5.30. **Uganda / Ouganda**

Details of tax revenue / Recettes fiscales détaillées

Million UGX

	1998	2000	2008	2010	2013	2014	2015	2016	2017	2018
Total tax revenue	**805 542**	**999 659**	**3 204 799**	**4 252 022**	**7 220 835**	**8 065 069**	**9 761 430**	**11 042 361**	**12 431 314**	**14 067 590**
1000 Taxes on income, profits and capital gains	**124 903**	**181 905**	**919 738**	**1 340 327**	**2 578 064**	**2 744 735**	**3 387 902**	**3 854 687**	**4 308 416**	**4 821 107**
1100 Of individuals	91 540	136 806	654 014	958 294	1 757 795	1 989 167	2 382 729	2 767 373	3 070 385	3 479 276
1110 On income and profits	91 540	136 806	654 014	958 294	1 757 795	1 989 167	2 382 729	2 767 373	3 070 385	3 479 276
PAYE	48 407	83 471	451 375	657 920	1 196 504	1 397 556	1 613 243	1 803 532	2 114 995	2 396 113
Rental income tax	0	0	0	0	0	0	27 649	55 034	71 738	88 747
Other income tax (not counting WHT)	10 251	11 220	18 819	19 001	17 898	53 616	42 189	44 322	50 766	60 485
Withholding taxes (WHT) - Total	32 882	42 115	183 821	281 373	543 392	537 995	699 648	864 485	832 885	933 931
WHT on imports	17 245	23 349	58 545	68 581	154 012	131 294	152 787	165 145	154 953	179 643
WHT on general supplies	0	0	96 717	120 061	223 256	232 028	282 825	330 729	299 594	337 521
WHT on government payments	0	0	17 038	44 446	154 236	60 016	89 367	150 824	109 882	73 824
WHT management and professional fees	0	0	3 575	24 886	1 982	35 883	45 447	61 860	65 631	89 563
WHT on dividends	0	0	7 815	11 237	5 455	33 926	61 823	69 110	126 912	87 745
WHT non residents	0	0	36	1 356	4 451	44 832	57 106	79 583	69 924	152 988
Other WHT or unclassified	15 637	18 766	94	10 806	1	16	10 293	7 234	5 989	12 646
1120 On capital gains	..	..	..	..	..	..	..	..	..	..
1200 Corporate	29 246	40 891	213 361	315 379	597 635	486 636	714 772	732 159	764 273	884 802
1210 On profits	29 246	40 891	213 361	315 379	597 635	486 636	714 772	732 159	764 273	884 802
1220 On capital gains	..	..	..	..	..	..	..	..	..	..
1300 Unallocable between 1100 and 1200	4 118	4 207	52 363	66 654	222 634	268 932	290 401	355 154	473 758	457 028
2000 Social security contributions	**..**	**..**	**..**	**..**	**..**	**..**	**..**	**..**	**..**	**..**
2100 Employees	..	..	..	..	..	..	..	..	..	..
2110 On a payroll basis	..	..	..	..	..	..	..	..	..	..
2120 On an income tax basis	..	..	..	..	..	..	..	..	..	..
2200 Employers	..	..	..	..	..	..	..	..	..	..
2210 On a payroll basis	..	..	..	..	..	..	..	..	..	..
2220 On an income tax basis	..	..	..	..	..	..	..	..	..	..
2300 Self-employed or non-employed	..	..	..	..	..	..	..	..	..	..
2310 On a payroll basis	..	..	..	..	..	..	..	..	..	..
2320 On an income tax basis	..	..	..	..	..	..	..	..	..	..
2400 Unallocable between 2100, 2200 and 2300	..	..	..	..	..	..	..	..	..	..
2410 On a payroll basis	..	..	..	..	..	..	..	..	..	..
2420 On an income tax basis	..	..	..	..	..	..	..	..	..	..
3000 Taxes on payroll and workforce	**0**	**0**	**0**	**0**	**0**	**0**	**0**	**0**	**0**	**0**
4000 Taxes on property	**..**	**..**	**..**	**..**	**..**	**..**	**..**	**..**	**..**	**..**
4100 Recurrent taxes on immovable property	..	..	..	..	..	..	..	..	..	..
4110 Households	..	..	..	..	..	..	..	..	..	..
4120 Others	..	..	..	..	..	..	..	..	..	..
4200 Recurrent taxes on net wealth	..	..	..	..	..	..	..	..	..	..
4210 Individual	..	..	..	..	..	..	..	..	..	..
4220 Corporate	..	..	..	..	..	..	..	..	..	..
4300 Estate, inheritance and gift taxes	..	..	..	..	..	..	..	..	..	..
4310 Estate and inheritance taxes	..	..	..	..	..	..	..	..	..	..
4320 Gift taxes	..	..	..	..	..	..	..	..	..	..
4400 Taxes on financial and capital transactions	..	..	..	..	..	..	..	..	..	..
4500 Non-recurrent taxes	..	..	..	..	..	..	..	..	..	..
4510 On net wealth	..	..	..	..	..	..	..	..	..	..
4520 Other non-recurrent taxes	..	..	..	..	..	..	..	..	..	..
4600 Other recurrent taxes on property	..	..	..	..	..	..	..	..	..	..
5000 Taxes on goods and services	**678 406**	**815 835**	**2 295 632**	**2 861 862**	**4 623 565**	**5 301 667**	**6 350 601**	**7 184 686**	**8 062 848**	**9 213 966**
5100 Taxes on production, sale, transfer, etc.	655 709	793 285	2 236 431	2 772 331	4 504 786	5 158 322	6 201 129	7 053 042	7 920 341	9 043 466
5110 General taxes	252 568	329 755	1 099 801	1 371 561	2 411 866	2 611 779	3 150 723	3 580 634	3 933 633	4 503 033
5111 Value added taxes	252 568	329 755	1 099 801	1 371 561	2 411 866	2 611 779	3 150 723	3 580 634	3 933 633	4 503 033
VAT on imports (government taxes)	5 865	16 628	29 696	35 775	33 787	20 344	0	0	0	0
VAT on imports (non-government taxes)	144 611	178 868	655 631	763 398	1 254 531	1 404 415	1 783 518	1 952 821	2 057 107	2 416 568
VAT on phone talk time	0	0	64 419	93 277	142 033	141 352	151 747	181 944	205 342	213 549
VAT on beer	13 818	11 586	29 869	37 034	97 365	96 412	108 831	120 513	126 862	145 809
VAT on electricity	0	0	53 719	74 584	135 306	162 673	112 811	114 679	128 080	170 471
VAT on sugar	0	0	31 180	64 276	109 802	71 294	110 801	120 363	139 657	149 558
VAT on soft drinks	4 299	5 139	14 598	15 846	34 901	30 268	32 385	35 449	43 023	42 791
VAT on cement	0	0	18 615	25 161	30 237	37 356	53 086	72 014	66 491	81 095
VAT on cigarettes	7 853	6 904	1 498	1 411	2 538	6 767	16 759	9 366	9 042	9 522
Other VAT	90 349	140 630	266 819	359 821	726 989	807 772	923 754	1 117 807	1 303 951	1 407 037
VAT refunds	-14 228	-30 000	-66 242	-99 023	-155 623	-166 874	-142 970	-144 324	-145 923	-133 368

Table 5.30. **Uganda / Ouganda** *(cont.)*

Details of tax revenue / Recettes fiscales détaillées

Million UGX

	1998	2000	2008	2010	2013	2014	2015	2016	2017	2018
5112 Sales tax	0	0	0	0	0	0	0	0	0	0
5113 Other	0	0	0	0	0	0	0	0	0	0
5120 Taxes on specific goods and services	403 141	463 530	1 136 630	1 400 770	2 092 921	2 546 543	3 050 407	3 472 408	3 986 708	4 540 433
5121 Excises	116 293	132 953	212 955	275 929	610 214	700 426	834 589	878 166	1 018 677	1 122 066
Excise tax on beer	51 492	59 938	82 942	98 864	170 717	144 222	146 853	177 678	216 717	263 072
Excise tax on phone talk time	0	0	74 293	99 490	147 560	170 432	184 175	166 780	194 297	178 966
Excise tax on soft drinks	13 915	13 348	22 599	27 907	53 520	59 338	71 799	83 125	90 009	118 869
Excise tax on cigarettes	31 300	33 572	6 085	7 698	9 911	14 246	14 979	12 617	12 072	15 591
Excise tax on spirits / waragi	1 474	915	11 249	10 376	34 240	45 555	53 331	58 203	98 886	157 512
Excise on international calls	0	0	0	0	0	68 162	65 142	34 230	33 971	33 341
Excise tax on sugar	0	0	10 073	17 187	7 351	7 479	17 854	18 220	37 973	30 277
Excise tax on cement	1	1	8 050	8 228	13 179	15 729	17 773	20 784	23 729	26 741
Other excise taxes	18 111	25 180	66 648	84 179	173 737	175 262	262 684	306 530	311 024	282 714
Tax refunds due to diesel tax exemption	0	0	-68 986	-77 999	0	0	0	0	0	14 982
5122 Profits of fiscal monopolies	0	0	0	0	0	0	0	0	0	0
5123 Customs and import duties	286 623	330 339	918 635	1 122 850	1 475 304	1 831 978	2 188 774	2 522 234	2 886 974	3 333 021
Petroleum duty	188 272	197 202	579 108	716 234	794 836	984 245	1 197 749	1 382 952	1 609 602	1 811 817
Surcharge on used imports	0	0	16 030	38 621	61 213	72 889	95 895	136 280	164 612	209 782
Non-oil imports	2 857	5 301	16 193	21 651	20 780	27 702	0	0	0	0
Commission on imports	17 441	22 746	0	2	0	0	0	0	0	0
Infrastructure Levy	0	0	0	0	0	0	57 268	62 936	69 107	87 669
Other import duties	78 054	105 090	307 563	346 621	598 735	747 533	841 381	940 066	1 043 652	1 223 753
Fixed duty drawbacks	0	0	-260	-280	-260	-390	-3 520	0	0	0
5124 Taxes on exports	0	0	4 073	122	1	3 126	13 186	15 878	13 968	12 442
5125 Taxes on investment goods	0	0	0	0	0	0	0	0	0	0
5126 Taxes on specific services	225	238	967	1 869	7 401	11 012	13 858	56 130	67 089	72 904
Casino and lottery tax	225	238	967	1 869	7 401	11 012	13 858	17 416	26 590	29 216
Bank charges	0	0	0	0	0	0	0	38 714	40 499	43 688
Levy on mobile money	0	0	0	0	0	0	0	0	0	0
Tax on over-the-top internet services	0	0	0	0	0	0	0	0	0	0
5127 Other taxes on internat. trade and transactions	0	0	0	0	0	0	0	0	0	0
5128 Other taxes	0	0	0	0	0	0	0	0	0	0
5130 Unallocable between 5110 and 5120	0	0	0	0	0	0	0	0	0	0
5200 Taxes on use of goods and perform activities	22 697	22 551	59 201	89 531	118 779	143 345	149 472	131 645	142 507	170 499
5210 Recurrent taxes	20 027	17 890	39 998	64 096	69 983	92 857	91 886	73 351	80 344	98 194
5211 Paid by households: motor vehicles	20 027	17 890	39 998	64 096	69 983	92 857	91 886	73 351	80 344	98 194
Fees and licences	20 027	17 890	39 998	64 096	69 983	92 857	91 886	73 351	80 344	98 194
Road user charges	0	0	0	0	0	0	0	0	0	0
5212 Paid by others: motor vehicles	0	0	0	0	0	0	0	0	0	0
5213 Paid in respect of other goods	0	0	0	0	0	0	0	0	0	0
5220 Non-recurrent taxes	2 670	4 660	19 203	25 434	48 796	50 488	57 586	58 294	62 164	72 305
5300 Unallocable between 5100 and 5200	0	0	0	0	0	0	0	0	0	0
6000 Other taxes	**2 233**	**1 919**	**-10 571**	**49 833**	**19 205**	**18 668**	**22 927**	**2 988**	**60 050**	**32 518**
6100 Paid solely by business	0	0	0	0	0	0	0	0	0	0
6200 Other	2 233	1 919	-10 571	49 833	19 205	18 668	22 927	2 988	60 050	32 518
Stamp duties and embossing fees	1 886	1 919	17 009	26 256	26 620	39 558	48 557	60 129	88 019	73 945
Coffee stabilisation tax	346	0	0	0	0	0	0	0	0	0
Government payments on behalf of private companies	0	0	0	0	15 059	0	0	0	0	0
Agricultural products	0	0	0	0	0	0	0	0	0	0
Un-allocated revenue	0	0	0	29 457	2 046	0	0	0	0	0
Tax refunds	0	0	-27 580	-5 880	-24 520	-20 890	-25 630	-57 141	-27 968	-41 428
Memo items:										
Total gross VAT revenue	266 796	359 755	1 166 043	1 470 584	2 567 489	2 778 653	3 293 693	3 724 958	4 079 555	4 651 383
Gross domestic VAT	116 319	164 259	480 717	671 411	1 279 171	1 353 894	1 510 175	1 772 137	2 022 448	2 234 815
VAT on imports (non-government taxes)	144 611	178 868	655 631	763 398	1 254 531	1 404 415	1 783 518	1 952 821	2 057 107	2 416 568
VAT on imports (government taxes)	5 865	16 628	29 696	35 775	33 787	20 344	0	0	0	0

Table 5.30. **Uganda / Ouganda** *(cont.)*

Details of tax revenue / Recettes fiscales détaillées

.. Not available

Note: Data are reported on a fiscal year basis beginning 1st July. For example, the data for 2018 represent July 2017 to June 2018.

The data are on a cash basis.

Figures exclude tax revenues collected by sub-national governments as the data are not available.

Heading 4000: Property tax is levied annually by local authorities. Revenue from property tax is not available.

Heading 5121: The "other excises taxes" category combines excise revenues from bottled water, cosmetics and mobile money transfers (all three in the "Indirect Domestic Taxes: excises" section of the Uganda Revenue Authority's budget document) with revenue from the excise duty (in the "taxes on international trade" section) and the excise duty (in the "government taxes" section).

Revenue from driver permits are considered non-tax revenue under the OECD classification, as set out in the Interpretative Guide in Annex A. The national classification of Uganda classifies this revenue as tax revenue.

Source: Uganda Revenue Authority.

StatLink https://doi.org/10.1787/888934183332

Chapter 6

Non-tax revenue levels and structures, 1998-2018

Chapitre 6

Tableaux des recettes non fiscales, 1998-2018

Chapter 6 / Chapitre 6

Non-tax revenue tables, 1998-2018

In all of the following tables a ("..") indicates not available or not applicable. The main series in this volume cover the years 1990 to 2018.

Figures referring to 1999, 2001-07, 2009 and 2011-12, in Table 6.1 and Tables 6.4 to 6.34 have been omitted because of lack of space. Complete series are, however, available on line at http://dx.doi.org/10.1787/93add7a4-en.

Tableaux des recettes non fiscales, 1998-2018

Dans tous les tableaux suivants le symbole («..») signifie que l'information n'est pas disponible ou qu'elle n'est pas applicable. La principale série dans ce volume couvre les années 1990 à 2018.

Les années 1999, 2001-07, 2009 et 2011-12 dans le tableau 6.1 et les tableaux 6.4 à 6.34 ont été omis en raison du manque d'espace. Les séries complètes sont cependant disponibles en ligne sur http://dx.doi.org/10.1787/ef1bbbc4-fr.

Table 6.1. **Total non-tax revenue as percentage of GDP, 1998-2018**
Tableau 6.1. **Total des recettes non fiscales en pourcentage du PIB, 1998-2018**

	1998	2000	2008	2010	2013	2014	2015	2016	2017	2018
Botswana	..	..	23.0	19.1	22.3	22.8	18.4	18.2	18.8	15.6
Burkina Faso	..	7.6	4.4	5.1	6.8	5.6	5.0	4.4	4.2	4.5
Cabo Verde	13.0	7.6	6.8	9.7	6.2	5.3	7.6	7.1	7.7	5.6
Cameroon / Cameroun	3.2	7.3	8.1	4.3	4.5	3.9	3.9	2.6	3.1	3.3
Chad / Tchad	..	..	..	5.2	5.2	6.4	5.2	3.9	6.7	6.2
Congo[1]	0.3	20.7	47.2	33.6	39.3	35.9	15.1	16.6	14.2	20.0
Congo, Dem. Rep. / Congo, Rép. dém.	..	..	..	6.2	3.6	6.4	4.7	4.1	3.5	3.3
Côte d'Ivoire	0.9	0.8	2.7	1.2	1.8	1.9	2.4	1.4	1.6	1.5
Egypt / Égypte	..	..	10.2	8.5	5.9	10.1	7.2	5.6	6.6	5.1
Equatorial Guinea / Guinée équatoriale	..	..	26.5	18.8	16.3	14.7	15.0	10.3	11.2	13.1
Eswatini	12.6	12.5	23.5	8.1	16.4	16.5	14.4	12.0	14.2	11.7
Ghana	..	1.6	3.2	3.7	4.7	4.1	4.7	3.2	3.2	3.2
Kenya[2]	..	..	3.2	1.1	1.4	1.5	1.9	1.8	2.1	2.3
Lesotho	..	..	42.9	31.9	34.4	32.1	29.0	23.3	27.0	25.2
Madagascar	0.0	2.8	3.2	3.0	1.3	2.2	1.5	1.9	2.3	2.9
Malawi	..	..	10.2	11.0	10.8	4.9	4.3	4.5	4.8	2.6
Mali	1.9	5.8	3.5	4.9	4.2	3.2	2.5	2.1	3.5	2.4
Mauritania / Mauritanie	..	..	..	6.3	7.3	6.0	6.4	4.8	4.7	7.2
Mauritius / Maurice[3]	3.6	2.7	2.9	3.7	3.1	2.9	2.8	3.2	3.7	3.8
Morocco / Maroc	..	2.2	3.3	3.6	4.1	3.8	3.9	3.5	3.5	3.7
Namibia	..	..	15.2	9.4	14.8	15.6	14.0	10.9	13.9	12.0
Niger	..	4.1	6.1	4.7	7.2	6.1	5.7	5.1	6.0	7.2
Nigeria / Nigéria	..	..	..	7.7	5.1	4.8	2.9	2.1	2.5	3.1
Rwanda	6.0	11.8	12.3	12.2	11.2	9.4	8.9	7.8	7.3	7.9
Senegal / Sénégal	2.4	1.6	2.7	2.5	3.3	4.0	3.5	4.6	4.1	3.5
Seychelles	..	..	1.0	5.7	7.8	8.3	6.0	7.8	4.7	5.6
South Africa / Afrique du Sud	0.6	0.4	0.7	0.6	0.6	0.5	0.4	0.5	0.5	0.6
Togo	..	1.8	8.3	11.2	5.3	4.3	4.2	4.3	4.9	7.3
Tunisia / Tunisie	..	2.5	3.6	2.9	3.6	2.4	2.1	1.7	2.9	3.1
Uganda / Ouganda	4.7	5.3	2.6	2.0	1.4	1.0	1.2	1.4	1.1	1.0
Africa (30) average / Moyenne Afrique (30)[4]	**..**	**..**	**..**	**8.3**	**8.7**	**8.2**	**6.8**	**6.0**	**6.5**	**6.5**

.. Not available

Note: The figures include sub-national government tax revenues for Eswatini, Kenya (for the years 2014-18), Mauritania (for 2009-18), Mauritius, Morocco, Nigeria (only state revenues) and South Africa (for 2002-18). Sub-national government tax revenues are not available in other countries.

1. Data on non-tax revenues were only available for oil revenues and grants.
2. The data are incomplete for 2011 and 2012 and a figure for total non-tax revenue is not included for these years.
3. Data for Mauritius are on a July-June fiscal year basis except for the years 2010-15 when they were reported on a calendar year basis. Please see Chapter 5 for more details.
4. Represents an unweighted average of the 30 African countries in this publication.

.. Non disponible

Note : Les chiffres incluent les recettes fiscales collectées par les administrations infranationales pour l'Afrique du Sud (pour les années 2002 à 2018), Eswatini, le Kenya (pour les années 2014-18), le Maroc, Maurice, la Mauritanie (pour les années 2009 à 2018) et le Nigéria (recettes des administrations régionales). Les données des recettes fiscales collectées par les administrations infranationales ne sont pas disponibles pour les autres pays.

1. Seules les données des recettes non fiscales relatives aux recettes pétrolières et aux dons sont disponibles.
2. Les données sont incomplètes pour 2011 et 2012 et le montant des recettes non fiscales totales n'a pas été calculé pour ces années.
3. Les données pour Maurice sont sur la base de l'année fiscale juillet-juin sauf pour les années 2010-15 où elles ont été déclarées sur la base de l'année civile. Veuillez consulter le chapitre 5 pour plus de détails.
4. Représente une moyenne non pondérée des 30 pays africains inclus dans cette publication.

StatLink https://doi.org/10.1787/888934183066

Table 6.2. **Non-tax revenue of main headings as percentage of GDP, 2018**
Tableau 6.2. **Recettes non fiscales sous les principales rubriques en pourcentage du PIB, 2018**

	Grants / Dons	Property income / Revenus de la propriété				Sales of goods and services / Ventes de biens et de services	Fines, penalties and forfeits / Amendes, pénalités et confiscations	Miscellaneous and unidentified revenue / Recettes diverses et non identifiées
		Total	Rents and royalties / Loyers et redevances	Interest and dividends / Intérêts et dividendes	Other property income / Autres revenus de la propriété			
Botswana	0.1	8.3	3.1	5.2	0.0	0.6	0.0	9.8
Burkina Faso	2.4	1.1	0.7	0.4	0.0	0.5	0.0	0.2
Cabo Verde	3.6	0.6	..	..	..	3.0	0.3	0.3
Cameroon / Cameroun	0.3	2.0	1.9	0.0	0.0	0.1	0.2	0.5
Chad / Tchad	4.0	2.1	2.1	0.0	0.1	0.1	0.0	0.4
Congo[1]	0.6	13.6	13.5	0.0	0.1	0.0	0.0	0.0
Congo, Dem. Rep. / Congo, Rép. dém.	2.0	1.1	1.0	0.1	0.0	0.3	0.1	0.0
Côte d'Ivoire	0.9	0.5	0.4	0.1	0.0	0.1	0.0	0.1
Egypt / Égypte	0.6	3.1	0.4	2.4	0.2	1.4	0.0	1.5
Equatorial Guinea / Guinée équatoriale	0.0	10.5	6.8	3.4	0.2	0.3	0.0	0.4
Eswatini	0.3	1.7	0.1	1.5	0.1	0.3	0.1	11.9
Ghana	0.6	1.3	0.5	0.7	0.0	1.3	0.0	0.0
Kenya	0.6	0.4	0.0	0.4	0.1	0.6	0.0	0.4
Lesotho	3.1	4.5	3.8	0.7	0.0	0.5	0.0	18.9
Madagascar	2.0	0.3	0.0	0.2	0.0	0.0	0.0	0.0
Malawi	3.5	0.5	0.0	0.5	0.0	0.5	0.0	0.3
Mali	1.8	1.3	0.9	0.4	0.0	0.2	0.1	0.1
Mauritania / Mauritanie	0.5	3.9	3.4	0.5	0.0	0.2	0.2	0.1
Mauritius / Maurice	0.7	1.0	0.2	0.1	0.7	0.9	0.1	1.1
Morocco / Maroc	0.0	0.8	0.4	0.4	0.0	1.6	0.3	0.8
Namibia	0.0	1.8	1.0	0.8	0.0	0.6	0.1	11.4
Niger	5.3	0.4	0.2	0.2	0.0	0.1	0.1	0.1
Nigeria / Nigéria	0.1	2.4	2.4	0.0	0.0	0.0	0.0	0.0
Rwanda[2]	4.7	..	..	..	..	..	..	2.6
Senegal / Sénégal	2.2	0.7	0.3	0.4	0.0	0.0	0.0	1.3
Seychelles	0.8	2.0	0.7	1.3	0.0	1.7	0.0	0.2
South Africa / Afrique du Sud	0.0	0.3	0.2	0.1	0.0	0.1	0.1	0.0
Togo	3.2	1.1	0.1	1.0	0.0	0.3	0.0	0.2
Tunisia / Tunisie	0.2	1.7	1.3	0.4	0.0	0.0	0.7	0.2
Uganda / Ouganda	0.9	0.0	0.0	0.0	0.0	0.3	0.0	0.0
Africa (30) average / Moyenne Afrique (30)[3]	**1.5**	**2.4**	**1.6**	**0.8**	**0.1**	**0.5**	**0.1**	**2.1**

.. Not available

Note: The figures include sub-national government tax revenues for Eswatini, Kenya (for the years 2014-18), Mauritania (for 2009-18), Mauritius, Morocco, Nigeria (only state revenues) and South Africa (for 2002-18). Sub-national government tax revenues are not available in other countries.

1. Data on non-tax revenues were only available for oil revenues and grants.
2. Data for property income, sales of goods and services and fines, penalties and forfeits are included in miscellaneous and unidentified revenue.
3. Represents an unweighted average of the 30 African countries in this publication.

.. Non disponible

Note : Les chiffres incluent les recettes fiscales collectées par les administrations infranationales pour l'Afrique du Sud (pour les années 2002 à 2018), Eswatini, le Kenya (pour les années 2014-18), le Maroc, Maurice, la Mauritanie (pour les années 2009 à 2018) et le Nigéria (recettes des administrations régionales). Les données des recettes fiscales collectées par les administrations infranationales ne sont pas disponibles pour les autres pays.

1. Seules les données des recettes non fiscales relatives aux recettes pétrolières et aux dons sont disponibles.
2. Les données relatives aux revenus de propriété, les ventes de biens et de services, les amendes, les pénalités et les confiscations sont incluses dans la rubrique « recettes diverses et non identifiées ».
3. Représente une moyenne non pondérée des 30 pays africains inclus dans cette publication.

StatLink https://doi.org/10.1787/888934183085

Table 6.3. **Non-tax revenue of main headings as percentage of total non-tax revenues, 2018**
Tableau 6.3. **Recettes non fiscales sous les principales rubriques en pourcentage du total des recettes non fiscales, 2018**

	Grants / Dons	Property income / Revenus de la propriété				Sales of goods and services / Ventes de biens et de services	Fines, penalties and forfeits / Amendes, pénalités et confiscations	Miscellaneous and unidentified revenue / Recettes diverses et non identifiées
		Total	Rents and royalties / Loyers et redevances	Interest and dividends / Intérêts et dividendes	Other property income / Autres revenus de la propriété			
Botswana	0.5	43.9	16.4	27.5	0.0	3.4	0.1	52.0
Burkina Faso	56.3	25.2	15.6	9.7	0.0	11.8	0.9	5.8
Cabo Verde	46.2	7.3	..	..	..	38.7	3.7	4.1
Cameroon / Cameroun	10.3	63.6	62.0	1.6	0.0	3.5	6.9	15.6
Chad / Tchad	60.2	31.5	30.7	0.0	0.8	0.9	0.7	6.7
Congo[1]	4.0	95.6	94.6	0.0	1.0	0.2	0.0	0.2
Congo, Dem. Rep. / Congo, Rép. dém.	56.0	29.9	27.6	2.3	0.0	9.3	3.8	0.9
Côte d'Ivoire	56.7	28.8	25.4	3.4	0.0	5.9	0.0	8.5
Egypt / Égypte	8.6	46.1	5.8	36.7	3.6	21.5	0.5	23.3
Equatorial Guinea / Guinée équatoriale	0.0	93.4	61.0	30.7	1.7	2.5	0.1	4.0
Eswatini	2.0	12.1	0.9	10.5	0.7	1.8	0.5	83.5
Ghana	18.7	39.8	16.4	23.4	0.0	41.5	0.0	0.0
Kenya	26.8	21.7	0.4	17.9	3.4	29.7	0.7	21.1
Lesotho	11.4	16.6	14.2	2.4	0.0	1.9	0.0	70.0
Madagascar	86.9	11.6	0.9	10.7	0.0	0.5	0.0	1.0
Malawi	73.0	11.3	0.0	11.3	0.0	10.2	0.0	5.6
Mali	51.3	36.9	26.0	10.7	0.2	6.4	2.3	3.1
Mauritania / Mauritanie	9.6	81.5	71.3	10.1	0.0	3.9	3.2	1.9
Mauritius / Maurice	17.6	27.6	5.8	3.2	18.6	23.4	1.8	29.7
Morocco / Maroc	0.0	23.3	12.4	10.9	0.0	45.7	8.1	22.9
Namibia	0.0	12.7	7.1	5.6	0.0	4.6	0.4	82.3
Niger	88.1	7.4	4.1	3.2	0.1	1.2	1.9	1.3
Nigeria / Nigéria	4.9	95.1	95.1	0.0	0.0	0.0	0.0	0.0
Rwanda[2]	64.6	..	..	..	..	..	..	35.4
Senegal / Sénégal	52.7	16.8	6.6	10.2	0.0	0.0	0.0	30.5
Seychelles	17.5	42.5	14.1	28.4	0.0	35.4	0.0	4.6
South Africa / Afrique du Sud	5.9	58.6	36.1	22.5	0.0	12.1	22.0	1.3
Togo	65.2	23.0	3.0	19.9	0.0	6.4	1.0	4.5
Tunisia / Tunisie	7.2	58.6	45.2	13.4	0.0	1.5	25.5	7.1
Uganda / Ouganda	76.6	1.4	1.4	0.0	0.0	22.0	0.0	0.0
Africa (30) average / Moyenne Afrique (30)[3]	**32.6**	**36.7**	**25.0**	**11.6**	**1.1**	**11.9**	**2.9**	**17.6**

.. Not available

Note: The figures include sub-national government non-tax revenues for Eswatini, Kenya (for the years 2014-17), Mauritius and Morocco. Sub-national government non-tax revenues outside of revenues collected by central governments on behalf of subnational governments are not available in other countries.

1. Data on non-tax revenues were only available for oil revenues and grants.
2. Data for property income, sales of goods and services and fines, penalties and forfeits are included in miscellaneous and unidentified revenue.
3. Represents an unweighted average of the 30 African countries in this publication.

.. Non disponible

Note : Les chiffres incluent les recettes non fiscales des administrations infranationales pour l'Eswatini, le Kenya (pour les années 2014-17), le Maroc et Maurice. Les recettes non fiscales des administrations infranationales en dehors des recettes collectées par les administrations centrales pour le compte des administrations infranationales ne sont pas disponibles dans les autres pays.

1. Seules les données des recettes non fiscales relatives aux recettes pétrolières et aux dons sont disponibles.
2. Les données relatives aux revenus de propriété, les ventes de biens et de services, les amendes, les pénalités et les confiscations sont incluses dans la rubrique « recettes diverses et non identifiées ».
3. Représente une moyenne non pondérée des 30 pays africains inclus dans cette publication.

StatLink https://doi.org/10.1787/888934183104

Table 6.4. **Total non-tax revenue in millions of US dollars at market exchange rates, 1998-2018**

Tableau 6.4. **Totale des recettes non fiscales en millions de dollars américains au taux de change du marché, 1998-2018**

	1998	2000	2008	2010	2013	2014	2015	2016	2017	2018
Botswana	..	..	2 490	2 561	3 403	3 596	2 709	2 922	3 336	2 182
Burkina Faso	..	225	420	514	914	776	594	569	594	725
Cabo Verde	75	46	122	161	115	99	122	118	137	111
Cameroon / Cameroun	338	720	2 152	1 134	1 462	1 351	1 220	860	1 078	1 293
Chad / Tchad	..	..	..	561	673	899	572	395	675	685
Congo	6	667	4 827	4 128	5 507	5 064	1 289	1 292	1 271	2 335
Congo, Dem. Rep. / Congo, Rép. dém.	..	..	..	1 340	1 169	2 300	1 788	1 504	1 322	1 554
Côte d'Ivoire	152	121	913	414	771	905	1 108	677	808	868
Egypt / Égypte	..	..	15 716	18 302	16 599	29 943	22 853	18 543	18 878	12 458
Equatorial Guinea / Guinée équatoriale	..	..	5 262	3 062	3 577	3 199	1 978	1 157	1 369	1 785
Eswatini	225	211	791	365	745	717	578	479	639	414
Ghana	..	178	1 225	1 612	2 943	2 179	2 293	1 733	1 884	2 069
Kenya	..	..	1 089	430	764	880	1 224	1 199	1 530	1 941
Lesotho	..	..	749	781	836	785	648	541	671	467
Madagascar	0	128	344	297	166	272	172	229	298	402
Malawi	..	..	877	1 110	1 355	604	511	491	558	343
Mali	64	173	348	519	552	461	334	297	537	406
Mauritania / Mauritanie	..	..	..	356	535	394	397	310	322	505
Mauritius / Maurice	155	128	267	372	381	376	323	386	475	518
Morocco / Maroc	..	873	3 055	3 323	4 407	4 153	3 961	3 592	3 809	4 330
Namibia	..	..	1 306	1 088	1 799	1 890	1 572	1 219	1 762	1 201
Niger	..	93	442	363	728	662	548	528	669	920
Nigeria / Nigéria	..	..	..	28 431	26 031	27 414	14 055	8 508	9 392	12 205
Rwanda	116	203	608	712	853	754	736	661	670	756
Senegal / Sénégal	151	96	459	412	617	800	621	882	862	811
Seychelles	..	..	10	55	104	112	83	111	72	88
South Africa / Afrique du Sud	837	596	1 975	2 211	2 112	1 837	1 406	1 375	1 630	2 097
Togo	..	27	276	384	231	197	174	193	234	392
Tunisia / Tunisie	..	529	1 617	1 257	1 664	1 121	891	716	1 145	1 229
Uganda / Ouganda	344	367	449	437	408	311	360	400	346	323

.. Not available

Note: This table is derived by dividing the total non-tax revenue figures for each country (in millions of national currency) in Table 6.1 by the exchange rate figures shown in Table 4.19.

.. Non disponible

Note : Ce tableau est obtenu en divisant les chiffres des recettes non fiscales en millions de monnaie nationale du tableau 6.1 pour chaque pays par les taux de change du tableau 4.19.

StatLink https://doi.org/10.1787/888934183123

Table 6.5. **Botswana**

Details of non-tax revenue / Recettes non fiscales détaillées

Million BWP

	1998	2000	2008	2010	2013	2014	2015	2016	2017	2018
Total non-tax revenue	**..**	**..**	**17 090**	**17 412**	**29 081**	**33 197**	**27 953**	**31 412**	**34 363**	**29 941**
Grants	..	..	84	210	125	316	74	1	170	1
Grants	..	..	84	210	125	316	74	1	170	1
IMF Gold Sales	..	..	0	0	0	0	0	0	0	0
Property income	..	..	8 220	9 914	14 967	16 402	11 152	18 424	15 092	14 171
Rents and royalties	..	..	1 605	2 071	3 228	3 775	3 223	3 320	5 648	3 403
Mineral Royalties	..	..	1 594	2 057	3 221	3 766	3 215	3 307	5 638	3 383
Royalties and Dividends	..	..	0	0	0	0	0	0	0	0
Rent of Land	..	..	10	14	7	9	8	13	10	20
Interest and dividends	..	..	6 616	7 842	11 739	12 627	7 929	15 104	9 444	10 768
Mineral Dividends	..	..	5 136	7 054	9 032	10 267	6 766	11 976	7 740	9 905
Bank of Botswana Revenue	..	..	1 302	700	1 900	2 079	1 133	2 842	1 573	740
Profits From Public Enterprises	..	..	137	61	13	48	18	67	107	117
Interest: Parastatals (DDF)	..	..	25	20	790	229	8	215	19	1
Interest: Local Authorities	..	..	0	0	0	0	0	0	0	0
Interest: Deposits	..	..	15	8	4	4	4	4	4	5
Other property income	..	..	0	0	0	0	0	0	0	0
Sales of goods and services	..	..	989	1 047	768	715	811	1 137	1 183	930
Motor vehicle revenues	..	..	252	363	52	49	50	40	44	36
Petrol, Oil and Lubricants - Revenue	..	..	110	182	235	158	231	259	184	217
Water revenues	..	..	194	42	1	1	2	2	2	2
Fees and charges	..	..	110	107	127	133	129	123	599	123
Rent of Buildings & Equipment	..	..	78	86	93	93	97	95	97	97
Sale of Livestock	..	..	3	5	2	2	2	1	4	2
Registrations, licences and certificates	..	..	19	22	37	37	33	34	29	33
Other sales of goods and services	..	..	223	242	221	242	269	583	225	419
Fines, penalties and forfeits	..	..	45	31	46	67	93	65	46	42
Traffic fines	..	..	0	0	0	0	44	25	1	0
Court fines	..	..	32	20	32	52	38	23	22	22
Bond revenues	..	..	1	1	2	1	1	3	3	1
Income tax penalty	..	..	0	0	0	0	0	0	0	0
Other fines, penalties and forfeits	..	..	11	10	12	14	11	14	20	19
Miscellaneous and unidentified revenue	..	..	7 753	6 210	13 175	15 697	15 823	11 784	17 871	14 797
SACU Revenue	..	..	7 750	6 207	13 170	15 691	15 818	11 773	17 864	14 789
Recovery of Arrears of Revenue	..	..	1	3	4	6	5	10	6	8
Revenue from Local Authorities	..	..	0	0	0	0	0	0	0	0
Reimbursement of Medical Claims (Revenue)	..	..	1	1	1	0	1	1	1	1
Total tax and non-tax revenue	..	..	29 797	31 712	48 204	55 357	47 285	55 551	56 833	53 229

.. Not available

Note: Fiscal year begins 1st April. For example, the data for 2018 represent April 2018 to March 2019.

Data are on a cash basis.

Figures exclude non-tax revenues collected by sub-national governments as the data are not available.

Source: Botswana Ministry of Finance and Economic Development, and Statistics Botswana.

StatLink https://doi.org/10.1787/888934183731

Table 6.6. **Burkina Faso**

Details of non-tax revenue / Recettes non fiscales détaillées

Millions XOF

	1998	2000	2008	2010	2013	2014	2015	2016	2017	2018
Total des recettes non fiscales	..	**160 511**	**187 428**	**254 019**	**451 523**	**382 954**	**351 209**	**337 426**	**345 257**	**402 658**
Dons	..	143 716	146 918	198 940	324 364	256 447	230 041	180 190	194 303	215 091
Revenus de la propriété	..	6 326	10 604	15 447	58 336	66 261	57 875	74 704	87 166	104 718
Loyers et redevances	..	411	2 593	12 453	36 759	36 225	37 938	45 182	53 727	65 780
Droits sur les titres miniers et redevances minières	..	324	2 593	12 453	36 759	36 225	37 938	45 182	53 727	65 780
Redevance surété	..	87	0	0	0	0	0	0	0	0
Intérêts et dividendes	..	5 915	8 011	2 993	21 577	30 036	19 937	29 522	33 438	38 937
Intérêts en douane	..	42	86	40	87	223	493	295	212	124
Portefeuille de l'Etat et plus value	..	5 873	7 925	2 954	21 490	29 813	19 443	29 227	33 227	38 813
Autres revenus de la propriété	..	0	0	0	0	0	0	0	0	0
Ventes de biens et de services	..	6 408	18 102	24 510	38 594	41 957	39 979	44 358	40 816	38 088
Diverses prestations de services	..	2 364	7 162	10 831	16 807	22 054	19 016	20 865	15 311	11 448
Location de biens	..	8	22	398	220	159	76	57	222	254
Frais douanes	..	2 493	7 875	6 667	12 206	9 166	9 795	12 533	14 121	14 173
Frais visas, papiers d'identite et permis de conduire	..	431	1 686	2 986	3 320	4 605	4 582	5 201	5 072	4 793
Autres frais administratifs	..	1 113	1 358	3 629	6 041	5 971	6 511	5 702	6 089	7 421
Amendes, pénalités et confiscations	..	1 272	2 976	4 505	5 692	6 153	8 863	19 025	3 033	4 225
Recettes diverses et non identifiées	..	2 790	8 827	10 618	24 538	12 137	14 451	19 148	19 939	40 536
Reversement des intérêts	..	2 382	4 711	3 618	3 209	3 570	2 534	785	5 309	4 133
Autres produits	..	408	4 117	7 000	21 328	8 568	11 917	18 363	14 629	36 404
Total des recettes fiscales et non fiscales	..	376 181	692 552	960 572	1 546 276	1 439 047	1 420 469	1 549 895	1 733 125	1 918 240
Pour mémoire :										
Prélèvement communautaire de solidarité (UEMOA)	..	1	13	6	10 681	9 003	9 855	11 433	11 884	11 035
Prélèvement communautaire (CEDEAO)	..	1 144	3 585	4 243	7 622	6 734	7 018	7 504	8 705	9 504

.. Non disponible

Note : Année civile se terminant le 31 décembre.

Les données sont sur la base des encaissements.

Les chiffres n'incluent pas les recettes non fiscales collectées par les collectivités locales car elles ne sont pas disponibles. Cependant, ils incluent des recettes collectées par l'administration centrale au profit des collectivités locales.

Les recettes provenant de la taxe de location de biens, des droits sur les titres miniers, redevances minières et des frais administratifs sont incluses dans les recettes non fiscales comme le préconise la classification OCDE (voir le guide d'interprétation en Annexe A). La classification nationale du Burkina Faso les comptabilise comme des recettes fiscales.

Source : Ministère de l'Économie, des Finances et du Développement du Burkina Faso.

StatLink https://doi.org/10.1787/888934183712

Table 6.7. **Cabo Verde**

Details of non-tax revenue / Recettes non fiscales détaillées

Million CVE

	1998	2000	2008	2010	2013	2014	2015	2016	2017	2018
Total des recettes non fiscales	**7 324**	**5 372**	**9 204**	**13 396**	**9 574**	**8 211**	**12 116**	**11 777**	**13 405**	**10 368**
Dons	5 369	3 931	6 236	9 440	4 024	2 787	3 958	4 507	6 193	2 265
Transferts courants de gouvernements étrangers	5 369	0	0	0	254	228	370	461	278	851
Aide budgétaire	0	..	..	..	0	0	0	0	0	0
Aide alimentaire	907	..	..	..	0	0	0	0	0	0
Dons directs	4 398	..	..	..	253	228	353	449	266	846
Autre transfert courants	64	..	..	..	1	0	17	13	12	5
Transferts en capital de gouvernements étrangers	0	3 931	6 236	9 440	3 769	2 559	3 588	4 046	5 914	1 414
Aide budgétaire	..	0	1 640	3 085	1 199	1 041	1 282	1 312	2 701	1 103
Aide alimentaire	..	672	217	338	329	17	0	60	283	154
Dons directs	..	3 259	3 884	6 018	2 235	1 501	2 048	2 542	2 930	158
Autre dons en capital	..	0	494	0	6	0	259	132	0	0
Revenus de la propriété	428	364	604	316	476	209	1 022	1 083	976	1 793
Loyers et redevances	..	..	..	..	..	..	..	..	..	..
Intérêts et dividendes	..	..	..	..	..	..	..	..	..	..
Autres revenus de la propriété	..	..	..	..	..	..	..	..	..	..
Ventes de biens et de services	551	592	1 840	3 077	3 897	4 010	4 652	5 042	5 189	5 509
Taux	287	448	1 788	3 003	3 734	3 823	4 492	4 738	4 995	5 293
Ventes	264	144	52	74	163	187	160	303	194	216
Amendes, pénalités et confiscations	96	54	309	376	511	706	404	679	498	369
Recettes diverses et non identifiées	881	431	215	187	666	499	2 079	467	550	431
Autres transferts	256	413	44	41	32	128	36	35	28	24
Autres recettes diverses et non spécifiées	625	18	171	146	635	371	2 043	432	521	407
Total des recettes fiscales et non fiscales	15 700	16 346	37 783	38 948	36 875	34 299	41 783	42 833	48 290	49 526
***Pour mémoire :** Prélèvement communautaire de la CEDEAO*	0	67	236	245	266	258	254	290	317	324

.. Non disponible

Note : Année civile se terminant le 31 décembre.

Les données sont sur la base des encaissements.

Les chiffres n'incluent pas les données des recettes non fiscales collectées par les administrations infranationales car elles ne sont pas disponibles.

La présente publication n'inclut pas le produit de la vente d'actifs non financiers rapporté dans les documents budgétaires du Cabo Verde. La classification nationale du Cabo Verde compte le produit de la vente d'actifs non financiers comme une recette non fiscale. Selon la classification de l'OCDE (voir le guide d'interprétation en Annexe B), le produit de la vente d'actifs n'est pas considéré comme une recette (fiscale ou non fiscale) car il ne représente pas une augmentation de la valeur nette résultant d'une transaction.

Le prélèvement communautaire de la CEDEAO (Communauté économique des États de l'Afrique de l'Ouest) n'est pas compris dans le total des recettes non fiscales ou fiscales et est présenté à titre de rubrique « Pour mémoire ». Le prélèvement communautaire de la CEDEAO est considéré comme une recette fiscale au Cabo Verde. Selon la classification de l'OCDE (voir le guide d'interprétation en Annexe A § 4), ce paiement n'est pas compris parmi les impôts.

Source : Ministère de Finance et du Plan du Cabo Verde.

StatLink https://doi.org/10.1787/888934183826

Table 6.8. **Cameroon / Cameroun**

Details of non-tax revenue / Recettes non fiscales détaillées

Million XAF

	1998	2000	2008	2010	2013	2014	2015	2016	2017	2018
Total des recettes non fiscales	**199 568**	**527 053**	**959 970**	**560 690**	**722 010**	**666 820**	**721 082**	**509 962**	**626 311**	**717 707**
Dons	0	6 900	193 393	78 805	75 879	23 813	18 089	54 100	64 800	86 700
Revenus de la propriété	135 900	404 500	721 834	442 296	577 877	580 497	465 541	396 033	398 521	510 077
Loyers et redevances	135 900	404 500	711 058	437 650	568 962	570 574	445 587	376 734	388 483	499 042
Redevance pétrolière	131 100	399 300	685 925	418 971	538 732	517 040	384 630	316 005	319 434	413 325
Droits de passage du pipeline	0	0	8 749	9 080	8 802	24 675	36 201	31 953	27 891	29 543
Autres loyers et redevances	4 800	5 200	16 384	9 599	21 428	28 860	24 756	28 776	41 158	56 175
Intérêts et dividendes	..	..	10 776	4 646	8 915	9 922	19 954	19 299	10 038	11 035
Autres revenus de la propriété	..	..	0	0	0	0	0	0	0	0
Ventes de biens et de services	26 300	33 500	32 588	37 732	62 682	52 990	188 402	29 094	21 737	48 055
Amendes, pénalités et confiscations	0	0	2 580	1 857	5 362	3 975	26 849	15 487	43 386	57 334
Recettes diverses et non identifiées	37 368	82 153	9 575	0	211	5 546	22 201	15 248	97 867	15 541
Total des recettes fiscales et non fiscales	877 185	1 337 553	2 441 829	2 132 385	2 980 748	3 152 865	3 409 008	3 253 870	3 561 490	3 864 201

.. Non disponible

Note : Année civile se terminant le 31 décembre.

Les données sont sur la base des encaissements.

Les chiffres n'incluent pas les recettes non fiscales collectées par les administrations infranationales car elles ne sont pas disponibles.

Revenus de la propriété: Cette rubrique inclut les taxes domaniales, la taxe à l'extraction des carrières et la redevance à la production des eaux comme le préconise la classification OCDE (voir le guide d'interprétation en Annexe B). La classification nationale du Cameroun les comptabilise comme des recettes fiscales.

Recettes diverses et non identifiées: Y compris transferts de capitaux non compris ailleurs et transferts volontaires autres que les dons.

Source : Ministère des Finances du Cameroun.

StatLink https://doi.org/10.1787/888934183769

Table 6.9. **Chad / Tchad**

Details of non-tax revenue / Recettes non fiscales détaillées

Million XAF

	1998	2000	2008	2010	2013	2014	2015	2016	2017	2018
Total des recettes non fiscales	..	..	..	**277 272**	**332 534**	**443 756**	**337 889**	**233 894**	**392 097**	**380 332**
Dons	..	..	..	68 799	144 795	135 891	221 884	175 497	235 922	199 244
Revenus de la propriété	..	..	..	193 129	169 263	281 907	87 733	35 039	123 555	149 077
Loyers et redevances	..	..	..	190 753	166 992	279 795	86 094	34 208	120 357	146 899
Redevances et dividendes pétroliers	..	..	..	185 445	166 646	231 676	86 094	14 044	42 699	58 653
Autres recettes pétrolières	..	..	..	5 308	346	48 119	0	20 164	77 659	88 246
Intérêts et dividendes	..	..	..	0	0	0	0	0	0	0
Autres revenus de la propriété	..	..	..	2 377	2 271	2 112	1 639	831	3 198	2 178
Ventes de biens et de services	..	..	..	4 162	5 405	10 304	10 591	6 837	3 694	2 393
Amendes, pénalités et confiscations	..	..	..	6 474	5 505	5 347	1 513	3 721	2 700	5 971
Recettes diverses et non identifiées	..	..	..	4 708	7 566	10 308	16 168	12 801	26 226	23 648
Total des recettes fiscales et non fiscales	..	..	..	1 054 998	1 314 874	1 205 773	707 707	479 359	737 810	817 437

.. Non disponible

Note : Année civile se terminant le 31 décembre.

Les données sont sur la base des encaissements.

Les chiffres n'incluent pas les recettes fiscales collectées par les collectivités locales car elles ne sont pas disponibles.

Les données des dons sont issues du FMI.

Les recettes provenant des amendes fiscales, des valeurs mobilières de l'État et de la redevance audiovisuelle sont incluses dans les recettes non fiscales comme le préconise la classification OCDE (voir le guide d'interprétation en Annexe A). La classification nationale du Tchad les comptabilise comme des recettes fiscales. Les recettes provenant des amendes fiscales sont comptabilisées dans la rubrique amendes, pénalités et confiscations. Les recettes provenant des valeurs mobilières de l'État et de la redevance audiovisuelle sont comptabilisées dans la rubrique de la vente de biens et de services.

Source : Ministère des Finances et du Budget du Tchad; FMI, *Perspectives de l'économie mondiale*, avril 2020.

StatLink https://doi.org/10.1787/888934184187

Table 6.10. **Congo**

Details of non-tax revenue / Recettes non fiscales détaillées

Million XAF

	1998	2000	2008	2010	2013	2014	2015	2016	2017	2018
Total des recettes non fiscales	**3 600**	**474 909**	**2 153 036**	**2 040 807**	**2 719 805**	**2 499 550**	**762 263**	**765 612**	**738 435**	**1 296 197**
Dons	3 600	6 800	35 436	4 100	26 900	31 100	41 400	40 400	29 600	10 800
Revenus de la propriété	..	468 109	2 117 600	2 034 514	2 690 859	2 466 650	713 099	720 025	705 842	1 282 018
Loyers et redevances	..	468 109	2 117 600	2 034 462	2 685 688	2 463 172	707 304	704 803	698 460	1 269 611
Recettes pétrolières	..	468 109	2 117 600	2 032 755	2 678 972	2 456 307	699 478	699 937	679 323	1 259 497
Redevance pétrolière	..	..	..	0	53	15	70	118	71	77
Redevance minière	..	..	..	2	1 534	405	60	12	42	1
Redevance forestière	..	..	..	1 705	5 129	6 445	7 696	4 735	19 024	10 035
Intérêts et dividendes	..	..	..	0	0	0	0	0	0	0
Autres revenus de la propriété	..	..	..	53	5 171	3 478	5 796	15 223	7 382	12 407
Ventes de biens et de services	..	..	..	780	1 135	864	794	776	1 183	812
Amendes, pénalités et confiscations	..	..	..	0	0	0	0	0	0	0
Recettes diverses et non identifiées	..	..	..	1 412	911	936	6 969	4 411	1 810	2 567
Total des recettes fiscales et non fiscales	84 342	573 593	2 466 349	2 494 717	3 488 145	3 353 628	1 661 223	1 562 737	1 443 270	1 846 744

.. Non disponible

Note : Année civile se terminant le 31 décembre.

Les données sont sur la base des encaissements

Les données des dons et des recettes pétrolières sont issues de la base de données de la publication PEM 2020 (*Perspectives de l'économie mondiale*, avril 2020) pour les dons et PEM 2019 pour les données des recettes pétrolières.

Les données de 2010-2018 ont été revisées et de nouvelles données ont été integrées.

Source : Ministère des Finances et du Budget de la République du Congo, Publication du FMI (*Perspectives de l'économie mondiale* 2019 et 2020).

StatLink https://doi.org/10.1787/888934183807

Table 6.11. **Congo, Dem. Rep. / Congo, Rép. dém.**

Details of non-tax revenue / Recettes non fiscales détaillées

Million CDF

	1998	2000	2008	2010	2013	2014	2015	2016	2017	2018
Total des recettes non fiscales	..	..	..	**1 213 982**	**1 075 255**	**2 127 683**	**1 656 103**	**1 539 532**	**1 956 028**	**2 523 427**
Dons	..	0	35 499	656 421	522 072	1 444 380	1 108 062	1 050 733	1 095 000	1 292 812
Revenus de la propriété	..	0	0	397 774	415 292	464 141	330 992	259 619	585 379	795 108
Loyers et redevances	..	..	..	358 125	345 027	400 379	292 678	237 299	540 068	713 030
Royalties des sociétés pétrolières	..	..	..	39 705	40 763	38 717	19 050	15 218	29 084	41 483
Redevance et royalty minières	..	..	..	65 476	110 013	148 882	138 244	114 681	279 414	387 478
Droits superficie annuels	..	..	..	25 340	20 788	20 172	20 102	14 522	28 232	12 840
Bonus de signature - renouvellement (hydrocarbures)	..	..	..	4 566	521	820	624	1 015	31 462	736
Redevance annuelle sur l'exploitation et autres	..	..	..	50 599	33 755	37 086	38 632	50 465	55 095	53 356
Autorisation de concessions, extractions et autres autorisations	..	..	..	9 126	137	18 639	5 789	102	30	131 631
Permis ressources forestières et faune	..	..	..	3 541	1 487	1 730	387	638	6 566	771
Marge distribuable (recettes pétrolières)	..	..	..	84 491	132 450	123 433	52 694	34 918	102 933	83 408
Redevances superficiaires sur permis d'exploration et sur concession	..	..	..	10	13	4 197	8 791	4 280	5 878	30
Autres loyers	..	..	..	75 272	5 099	6 703	8 365	1 461	1 374	1 297
Intérêts et dividendes	..	..	..	39 301	69 526	62 272	37 159	22 228	45 162	40 811
Dividendes on shore (recettes pétrolières)	..	..	..	8 068	21 846	17 375	14 665	3 916	5 867	10 994
Participations off shore (recettes pétrolières)	..	..	..	25 347	39 726	36 372	15 806	10 463	30 839	24 271
Autres dividendes et participations	..	..	..	5 886	7 953	8 524	6 688	7 848	8 457	5 546
Autres revenus de la propriété	..	..	..	348	740	1 490	1 155	92	149	41 266
Ventes de biens et de services	..	158	360	123 659	96 777	146 328	164 250	159 225	182 127	331 986
Vente des imprimés	..	158	360	1 106	1 312	1 881	690	218	52	219
Taxe de numérotation	..	..	..	16 464	17 414	21 121	26 110	26 898	40 126	51 014
Taxe de régulation et taxe de modification des titres obtenus / télécommunications	..	..	..	13 180	22 433	28 709	36 198	38 820	21 884	20 191
Passeport, visa et carte de travail	..	..	..	20 344	18 917	26 288	30 957	26 053	32 248	45 943
Taxes sur le gardiennage par la Police Nationale Congolaise	..	..	..	4 247	3 346	10 346	11 337	10 597	16 059	23 016
Contrôle des produits d'origine toxique, soporifique et stupéfiante	..	..	..	647	1 582	7 699	7 328	6 862	6 248	7 736
Redevance sur la désinfection et le contrôle sanitaire des friperies	..	..	..	3 828	64	2 292	3 111	2 586	3 081	14 156
Agréments	..	..	..	1 359	278	1 340	1 045	404	783	1 479
Autres	..	..	..	62 483	29 562	44 827	44 950	45 686	59 315	163 763
Loyers, Institut National de Sécurité Sociale (CNSS)	..	..	..	0	1 868	1 825	2 524	1 101	2 331	4 468
Amendes, pénalités et confiscations	..	420	742	35 378	36 630	71 428	50 772	64 953	75 139	101 256
Amendes et pénalités (Direction générale des impôts)	..	418	176	15 455	30 848	42 138	15 160	40 058	18 504	65 525
Amendes et pénalités (DGDA)	..	2	566	1 561	1 424	1 615	4 093	2 525	3 492	1 910
Amendes et pénalités (DGRAD)	..	..	..	18 363	4 358	27 676	31 518	22 369	53 144	33 821
Recettes diverses et non identifiées	..	..	..	750	4 483	1 407	2 027	5 002	18 382	2 266
Total des recettes fiscales et non fiscales	..	7 551	941 657	2 833 206	4 108 543	5 283 953	5 078 045	4 729 472	5 792 838	8 293 209

.. Non disponible

Note : Année civile se terminant le 31 décembre.

Les données sont sur la base des encaissements.

Les chiffres n'incluent pas les données des recettes non fiscales collectées par les collectivités locales car elles ne sont pas disponibles.

Les données des dons sont issues de la base de données de la publication PEM 2020 (*Perspectives de l'économie mondiale 2020*) publiée par le FMI.

Les données autres que les dons sont disponibles qu' à partir de 2010. Pour la période 2010-18, 5 % en moyenne des recettes considérées comme non fiscales par la République Démocratique du Congo ont été classifiées comme recettes fiscales dans cette publication comme le préconise la classification OCDE (voir le guide d'interprétation en Annexe A). Ces recettes collectées par la DGRAD (Direction Générale des Recettes Administratives, Judiciaires, Domaniales et de Participations) sont entre autres les redevances sur produits spécifiques, les droits proportionnels sur les S.A.R.L, la taxe ad valorem sur les gains des parieurs, les autorisations d'exportation et d'importation, la taxe d'implémentation des établissements dangereux/insalubres/incommodes et diverses autorisations.

Source : Ministère des Finances de la République Démocratique du Congo; Publication du FMI (*Perspectives de l'économie mondiale*, avril 2020).

StatLink https://doi.org/10.1787/888934183788

Table 6.12. **Côte d'Ivoire**

Details of non-tax revenue / Recettes non fiscales détaillées

Million XOF

	1998	2000	2008	2010	2013	2014	2015	2016	2017	2018
Total des recettes non fiscales	**89 854**	**86 004**	**407 061**	**205 073**	**380 736**	**447 046**	**654 836**	**401 313**	**469 133**	**481 966**
Dons	50 500	33 500	183 300	106 540	201 460	303 989	282 200	253 518	266 126	246 158
Revenus de la propriété	3 654	4 204	195 977	76 308	149 233	91 828	285 955	68 211	135 029	139 032
Loyers et redevances	3 654	4 204	167 008	44 902	119 015	82 046	255 515	57 736	119 272	115 311
Revenus du domaine	0	0	689	283	941	1 363	2 111	2 972	2 152	2 160
Taxe d'exploitation pétrolière	0	0	150 351	27 275	60 764	39 595	30 851	23 555	27 595	36 888
Taxes domaniales (hors taxe ad valorem 2012-2018)	3 654	4 204	4 020	7 696	37 395	31 737	37 224	25 697	24 251	31 812
Autres loyers et redevances	0	0	11 947	9 647	19 915	9 351	185 329	5 512	65 273	44 451
Intérêts et dividendes	0	0	28 932	27 981	29 973	9 693	30 440	10 475	15 757	23 721
Autres revenus de la propriété	0	0	37	3 426	245	89	0	0	0	0
Ventes de biens et de services	0	0	16 515	21 700	28 097	31 556	35 414	43 920	27 870	47 111
Redevance Radiodiffusion Télévision Ivoirienne (RTI)	..	..	3 281	4 107	5 568	6 021	6 244	7 275	8 270	8 587
Taxe audiovisuelle	..	..	72	0	0	0	0	0	0	0
Autres ventes de biens et de services	..	..	13 162	17 592	22 529	25 535	29 170	36 645	19 600	38 524
Amendes, pénalités et confiscations	0	0	208	173	219	291	0	0	0	0
Recettes diverses et non identifiées	35 700	48 300	11 061	353	1 727	19 382	51 267	35 664	40 108	49 664
Total des recettes fiscales et non fiscales	1 275 414	1 255 611	2 241 395	2 240 541	3 102 515	3 393 148	4 069 253	4 137 767	4 452 815	4 671 094

.. Non disponible

Note : Année civile se terminant le 31 décembre.

Les données sont sur la base des encaissements.

Les chiffres n'incluent pas les données des recettes non fiscales collectées par les collectivités locales car elles ne sont pas disponibles.

Les recettes des taxes domaniales, la taxe ad valorem et la taxe d'exploitation sont considérées comme des recettes non fiscales selon la classification OCDE (voir le guide d'interprétation en Annexe B). La classification nationale de la Côte d'Ivoire les compte comme des recettes fiscales.

Les recettes des taxes domaniales sont hors taxe ad valorem pour la période 2012 à 2018, période pour laquelle il a été possible de distinguer ces recettes.

La taxe audiovisuelle et la redevance radiodiffusion télévision ivoirienne (RTI) sont considérées comme des recettes non fiscales selon la classification OCDE (voir le guide d'interprétation en Annexe B). La classification nationale de la Côte d'Ivoire les compte comme des recettes fiscales.

Source : Ministère de l'Économie et des Finances.

StatLink https://doi.org/10.1787/888934183750

Table 6.13. **Egypt / Égypte**

Details of non-tax revenue / Recettes non fiscales détaillées

Million EGP

	1998	2000	2008	2010	2013	2014	2015	2016	2017	2018
Total non-tax revenue	..	..	**88 051**	**101 032**	**103 534**	**201 296**	**163 927**	**143 795**	**205 018**	**202 374**
Grants	..	..	1 463	4 333	5 208	95 856	25 437	3 543	17 683	3 194
Property income	..	..	53 772	55 890	58 039	58 856	83 412	71 503	94 498	74 266
Rents and royalties	..	..	3 216	7 216	4 903	3 898	8 252	6 890	11 917	18 262
Royalties on petroleum	..	..	1 444	2 750	2 933	1 737	5 964	4 139	7 372	11 610
Royalties on Suez Canal	..	..	1 454	1 354	1 617	1 867	1 945	2 059	3 360	5 163
Other royalties	..	..	318	3 112	353	293	343	693	1 185	1 489
Interest and dividends	..	..	47 444	47 115	52 770	54 709	74 894	64 264	75 244	55 608
SCA	..	..	15 098	12 729	16 375	18 084	19 214	14 755	29 381	23 718
C.B.E.	..	..	32	205	11 317	9 283	13 417	29 462	19 427	5 233
Economic authorities	..	..	3 047	1 431	1 915	1 630	10 093	7 820	10 989	8 297
Public and private companies and enterprises	..	..	2 648	3 272	3 539	3 157	3 295	3 433	5 230	6 867
EGPC	..	..	25 282	25 546	18 785	21 809	25 414	7 820	5 944	8 144
Other dividends and interests	..	..	1 337	3 930	839	747	3 460	974	4 273	3 350
Other property income	..	..	3 113	1 559	366	250	265	350	7 337	396
Sales of goods and services	..	..	16 960	24 037	13 433	20 624	25 722	28 481	44 150	58 364
Administrative fees	..	..	2 569	2 681	3 705	3 745	4 482	4 453	7 559	10 437
Development fees	..	..	868	841	751	742	931	920	534	403
Service fees	..	..	1 738	3 505	2 564	10 001	6 620	7 168	9 010	11 588
Capital revenues	..	..	11 743	16 962	6 264	6 029	13 610	15 824	26 934	35 803
Other sales of goods and services	..	..	42	49	150	108	80	116	113	134
Fines, penalties and forfeits	..	..	153	234	213	285	422	671	935	574
Miscellaneous and unidentified revenue	..	..	15 704	16 538	26 642	25 674	28 934	39 597	47 753	65 977
Current revenues from special accounts and funds	..	..	9 393	12 268	18 946	17 052	17 797	19 627	26 223	35 732
Voluntary transfers other than grants	..	..	557	684	612	1 061	901	1 455	2 956	2 143
Current revenues	..	..	5 457	3 312	6 721	7 215	9 827	17 968	17 964	27 576
Other revenues	..	..	297	275	363	346	408	547	610	525
Total tax and non-tax revenue	..	..	241 402	292 524	389 355	503 366	520 022	534 828	731 759	863 983

.. Not available

Note: Fiscal year ends on 30 June. For example, the data for 2018 represent July 2017 to June 2018.

The data are on a cash basis.

Figures exclude non-tax revenues collected by sub-national governments as the data are not available.

Royalties on the Suez Canal as well as other royalties and administrative fees are reported as tax revenues in Egypt. In accordance with the OECD classification, as set out in the Interpetative Guide in Annex A, these revenues are considered non-tax revenues.

Source: Ministry of Finance.

StatLink https://doi.org/10.1787/888934183845

Table 6.14. **Equatorial Guinea / Guinée équatoriale**

Details of non-tax revenue / Recettes non fiscales détaillées

Million XAF

	1998	2000	2008	2010	2013	2014	2015	2016	2017	2018
Total non-tax revenue	..	..	**2 346 772**	**1 515 259**	**1 766 895**	**1 579 336**	**1 169 328**	**685 668**	**794 644**	**991 641**
Grants	..	..	0	0	0	0	0	0	0	0
Property income	..	..	2 333 915	1 489 017	1 722 012	1 524 837	1 087 688	649 765	742 191	962 877
Rents and royalties	..	..	1 620 031	957 200	1 194 154	1 028 514	688 968	421 568	484 757	604 305
Petroleum royalties	..	..	1 616 633	951 507	1 186 798	1 022 254	680 217	415 597	478 744	590 596
Surface royalties	..	..	248	844	1 887	766	1 842	619	530	1 794
Fishing and concessional royalties	..	..	3 149	4 850	5 469	5 493	6 909	5 352	5 483	11 915
GEOGAM gas sales	..	..	0	0	0	0	0	0	0	0
Interest and dividends	..	..	543 553	437 662	521 844	491 591	380 575	206 307	244 266	328 453
Shareholder participation in oil revenues	..	..	307 420	257 392	257 064	325 264	237 800	103 899	99 609	134 422
Oil dividends	..	..	173 250	146 345	242 261	144 237	134 965	84 190	132 925	185 706
Non-oil dividends	..	..	12 258	17 314	12 555	15 601	7 538	17 339	11 522	7 794
Interest on reserve funds	..	..	32 484	6 977	4 346	489	43	45	12	498
Other interest (banking, deferrals)	..	..	18 140	9 635	5 312	5 674	52	43	8	1
INSESO: Interest and dividends	..	..	0	0	306	326	178	792	191	32
Other property income	..	..	170 331	94 155	6 014	4 732	18 145	21 889	13 168	30 119
Contributions of public companies and independent entitites	..	..	227	1 624	3 854	3 773	4 149	21 889	9 744	26 104
Other oil-related property income	..	..	170 104	92 531	2 160	959	13 997	0	3 424	4 015
Sales of goods and services	..	..	9 316	15 935	28 643	26 515	24 901	27 212	20 154	17 470
Administrative fees and government services	..	..	8 006	13 975	22 335	21 821	19 669	19 335	15 052	14 234
Consular fees	..	..	1 025	1 357	1 387	906	973	875	561	1 694
Tolls	..	..	193	458	2 194	1 000	2 714	509	0	383
Rentals of government buildings	..	..	92	145	292	189	132	191	69	139
INSESO: Medical goods and services	..	..	0	0	2 334	2 491	1 355	6 042	1 147	875
INSESO: Other goods and services	..	..	0	0	101	108	59	262	139	144
INSESO: Provincial medical fees	..	..	0	0	0	0	0	0	3 186	0
Fines, penalties and forfeits	..	..	0	0	272	269	258	199	462	451
INSESO: Sanctions, arrears and penalties	..	..	0	0	272	269	258	199	462	451
Miscellaneous and unidentified revenue	..	..	3 541	10 307	15 968	27 716	56 481	8 492	31 837	10 843
Total tax and non-tax revenue	..	..	3 035 407	2 127 636	2 733 390	2 629 588	2 105 235	1 157 882	1 265 740	1 471 741

.. Not available

Note: Year ending 31st December.

The data are on a cash basis

For the first time, non-tax revenues collected by the Instituto Nacional de Seguridad Social de Guinea Ecuatorial (INSESO) are reported in this edition. This affects interest and dividends; sales of goods and services; fines, penalties and forfeits; and miscellaneous and unidentified revenue over the years 2013-18.

Source: Ministry of Finance, Economy and Planning.

StatLink https://doi.org/10.1787/888934183883

Table 6.15. **Eswatini**

Details of non-tax revenue / Recettes non fiscales détaillées

Million SZL

	1998	2000	2008	2010	2013	2014	2015	2016	2017	2018
Total non-tax revenue	**1 279**	**1 546**	**6 566**	**2 668**	**7 409**	**8 092**	**7 641**	**6 856**	**8 552**	**7 420**
Grants[1]	0	0	0	1	101	134	99	122	174	123
Property income	158	95	273	553	173	353	494	1 196	1 038	1 069
Rents and royalties	0	0	0	3	4	56	72	75	81	81
Land concession rents, postal revenue	0	0	0	0	0	0	0	0	0	0
Rents attributed to social security funds	0	0	0	3	4	56	72	75	81	81
Interest and dividends	138	91	271	548	161	283	391	878	896	919
Local interest collected by central government	47	21	132	538	24	0	60	7	-30	28
Central bank profit	5	0	120	0	110	214	245	287	244	0
External interest and interest on capital	81	69	10	0	5	11	0	2	4	3
Dividends	4	1	10	8	13	0	11	115	115	106
Interest and dividends collected by social security funds	0	0	0	1	10	58	75	467	564	783
Other property income	20	4	1	1	8	13	31	244	62	69
Quitrents	0	0	0	0	0	0	0	0	0	0
Local government property income	20	4	1	1	8	13	31	244	62	69
Sales of goods and services	42	40	162	115	76	71	73	216	154	325
Sundry fees	18	13	89	38	22	6	6	144	64	246
Passports, citizenship and resident permits	5	5	18	25	23	25	25	29	35	33
Rental of government real estate	2	3	7	7	10	10	11	12	13	13
Driver's licences, motor vehicle certification	1	1	5	8	7	8	11	15	14	15
Hospital and medical services	2	5	6	6	7	7	6	7	7	8
Hire of government plants and vehicles	0	0	19	21	0	0	0	0	0	0
Aviation fees	11	12	1	0	0	0	0	0	0	0
Sale of government furniture and vehicles	0	0	15	6	0	6	7	1	10	2
Sale of agricultural products and services	2	2	1	1	2	3	2	3	3	3
Public service transport fees	1	0	1	1	1	2	1	1	1	1
Sale of government publications	0	0	1	1	1	1	1	2	1	1
Prison industry sales	0	0	0	0	0	0	0	0	0	0
Local government sales of goods and services	0	0	1	1	2	2	2	3	5	5
Fines, penalties and forfeits	3	4	17	28	30	32	33	42	43	46
Traffic fines	2	2	6	15	15	15	13	14	15	15
Judicial fines and other penalties	0	1	7	10	12	15	18	22	24	24
Interest and penalties on late tax payments	0	0	3	1	2	2	2	5	5	4
PAYE penalties[2]	0	1	1	1	0	0	0	0	0	0
Fines, penalties and forfeits (local non-tax revenue)	0	0	0	0	0	0	0	0	0	3
Miscellaneous and unidentified revenue	1 076	1 407	6 114	1 972	7 029	7 502	6 942	5 280	7 143	5 856
SACU revenue	1 076	1 406	6 111	1 969	7 025	7 487	6 931	5 252	7 109	5 844
SACU penalties	0	0	1	2	0	14	9	12	18	9
Miscellaneous and unidentified revenue (local non-tax revenue)	0	0	2	2	4	1	3	16	16	3
Total tax and non-tax revenue	2 372	2 872	10 167	7 256	13 605	15 396	15 562	16 016	18 653	18 311

Note: Data are reported on a fiscal year basis beginning 1st April. For example, the data for 2018 represent April 2018 to March 2019.

The data are on a cash basis.

Revenues from motor vehicle licences, the change of ownership fees and the registration of new motor vehicles are considered as tax revenue under the OECD classification as set out in the Interpretative Guide in Annex A and are classified under heading 5211 (Recurrent taxes paid by households: motor vehicles). The national classification of Eswatini classifies these revenues as non-tax revenues.

Revenues from business and sundry licences are considered as tax revenue under the OECD classification, as set out in the Interpretative Guide in Annex A and are classified under heading 5211 (Recurrent taxes paid on use of goods and perform activities other than on motor vehicles). The national classification of Eswatini classifies these revenues as non-tax revenues.

Revenues from the registrations of specific goods (e.g. firearms) are considered as tax revenue under the OECD classification, as set out in the Interpretative Guide in Annex A and are classified under heading 5220 (Non-recurrent taxes on use of goods and perform activities). The national classification of Eswatini classifies these revenues as non-tax revenues.

Revenues from the education loans' repayments do not represent an increase of net worth resulting from a transaction and therefore are not considered as revenues under the OECD classification, as set out in the Interpretative Guide in Annex B.

1. The data are not available up to 2011.
2. Revenue from PAYE Penalties, tax interests and penalties on taxes are considered as non-tax revenue under the OECD classification, as set out in the Interpretative Guide in Annex A. The national classification of Eswatini classifies it as tax revenues.

Source: Eswatini Revenue Authority.

StatLink https://doi.org/10.1787/888934184149

Table 6.16. **Ghana**

Details of non-tax revenue / Recettes non fiscales détaillées

Million GHS

	1998	2000	2008	2010	2013	2014	2015	2016	2017	2018
Total non-tax revenue	..	**97**	**1 296**	**2 306**	**5 751**	**6 369**	**8 512**	**6 777**	**8 199**	**9 493**
Grants	..	57	821	1 080	739	814	2 689	1 141	1 535	1 135
Project grants	..	24	402	591	374	787	1 744	1 034	1 535	1 121
Programme grants	..	34	257	288	158	27	945	106	0	14
International debt relief	..	0	162	201	207	0	0	0	0	0
Property income	..	7	63	347	2 123	2 727	2 628	1 803	3 263	4 639
Rents and royalties	..	0	0	0	748	1 075	908	757	1 346	1 969
Mineral royalties (aside from oil)	..	..	..	..	408	517	518	578	749	744
Oil revenues	..	..	..	..	339	554	384	176	589	1 213
Lodgements to MDAs and MMDAs: surface rentals from oil/PHF interest	..	..	..	..	2	4	6	3	8	12
Lodgements to MDAs and MMDAs: fees from granting of new stability agreements	..	..	..	..	0	0	0	0	0	0
Revenue from oil companies (includes corporate tax)	..	..	..	..	0	0	0	0	0	0
Interest and dividends	..	7	63	347	1 375	1 653	1 720	1 046	1 916	2 670
Lodgements to MDAs and MMDAs: dividend, interest and profits from oil companies	..	0	0	0	875	1 435	995	491	1 586	2 531
Lodgements to MDAs and MMDAs: dividend, interest and profits aside from oil companies	..	7	63	347	500	218	726	556	331	139
Other property income	..	0	0	0	0	0	0	0	0	0
Sales of goods and services	..	32	412	879	2 888	2 827	3 195	3 833	3 401	3 719
Retentions by MDAs and MMDAs	..	23	308	685	2 516	2 497	2 531	3 368	2 849	3 165
Lodgements to MDAs and MMDAs: fees and charges	..	10	104	194	372	330	663	466	553	555
Lodgements to MDAs and MMDAs: gas receipts	..	0	0	0	0	0	2	0	0	0
Fines, penalties and forfeits	..	0	0	0	0	0	0	0	0	0
Miscellaneous and unidentified revenue	..	0	0	0	0	0	0	0	0	0
Total tax and non-tax revenue	..	584	5 608	9 001	19 789	25 312	32 104	36 272	43 499	51 842

.. Not available

Note: Year ending 31st December.

The data are on a cash basis.

Revenues for MDAs (Municipalities, Departments and Agencies) and MMDAs (Metropolitan, Municipal and District Assemblies) contain a mixture of revenues collected at the local level and revenues collected at the federal level. These are reported as revenues to the central government.

Source: Ghana Statistical Service.

StatLink https://doi.org/10.1787/888934183864

Table 6.17. **Lesotho**

Details of non-tax revenue / Recettes non fiscales détaillées

Million LSL

	1998	2000	2008	2010	2013	2014	2015	2016	2017	2018
Total non-tax revenue	**..**	**..**	**6 421**	**5 668**	**8 669**	**9 171**	**8 978**	**7 458**	**8 787**	**8 691**
Grants	..	..	569	1 306	1 175	635	966	1 229	1 005	1 373
Property income	..	..	827	1 583	1 278	1 296	1 394	1 449	1 457	1 613
Rents and royalties	..	..	465	897	1 172	984	993	1 088	1 244	1 294
Water royalties	..	..	324	432	717	740	740	837	941	937
Mining and other royalties	..	..	141	465	455	244	252	251	304	357
Interest and dividends	..	..	362	686	106	312	401	362	213	319
Other property income	..	..	0	0	0	0	0	0	0	0
Sales of goods and services	..	..	123	149	160	203	216	256	169	166
Fines, penalties and forfeits	..	..	1	2	2	3	4	4	3	0
Miscellaneous and unidentified revenue	..	..	4 901	2 628	6 055	7 034	6 398	4 519	6 154	5 538
SACU revenue	..	..	4 901	2 628	6 055	7 034	6 398	4 519	6 154	5 538
Total tax and non-tax revenue	..	..	8 952	8 945	13 091	14 353	14 839	13 446	14 777	15 675
Total non-tax revenue excluding grants	..	..	5 852	4 362	7 494	8 536	8 012	6 229	7 783	7 317

.. Not available

Note: Data are on a fiscal year basis beginning 1st April. For example, the data for 2018 represent April 2018 to March 2019.
Data are reported on a cash basis.

Source: Lesotho Revenue Authority

StatLink https://doi.org/10.1787/888934183902

Table 6.18. **Kenya**

Details of non-tax revenue / Recettes non fiscales détaillées

Million KES

	1998	2000	2008	2010	2013	2014	2015	2016	2017	2018
Total non-tax revenue	..	..	**74 381**	**33 643**	**65 179**	**76 497**	**113 760**	**119 549**	**156 955**	**198 572**
Grants	..	..	53 427	14 060	26 155	27 397	29 501	37 452	42 110	49 772
Grants from foreign governments - Capital	..	..	22 954	0	5 459	7 355	2 644	2 641	1 831	2 431
Grants from foreign governments - Current	..	..	0	0	0	0	0	0	0	65
Grants from foreign governments - Cash through exchequer	..	..	13 056	3 108	2 566	514	1 383	1 573	1 423	2 431
Grants from foreign governments - Direct payments treated as Appropriations in Aid (AIA)	..	..	9 898	6 107	2 893	6 841	16 098	16 275	12 840	17 658
Grants from International orgs - Capital	..	..	3 759	0	0	0	5 533	5 914	11 514	10 543
Grants from International orgs - Current	..	..	0	0	4	0	3 843	4 757	6 440	6 100
Grants from International orgs - Cash through Exchequer	..	..	3 759	4 845	2 622	5 205	0	6 293	8 062	10 543
Grants from International orgs - Direct payments-Treated as Appropriations in Aid (AIA)	..	..	0	0	12 611	7 482	0	0	0	0
Property income	..	..	5 073	9 921	18 508	11 876	16 216	22 309	34 049	62 843
Rents and royalties	..	..	1 368	1 184	1 887	1 694	695	743	665	2 460
Rent of land	..	..	1 297	1 108	1 789	1 588	8	25	38	1 725
Kenya Airports Authority (KAA) concession fees	..	..	71	77	99	106	113	114	127	131
Base titanium royalty	..	..	0	0	0	0	338	356	295	407
Mining royalties	..	..	0	0	0	0	136	143	118	143
Royalties from soda ash	..	..	0	0	0	0	100	105	87	55
Interest and dividends	..	..	3 705	8 736	16 621	5 865	10 781	18 225	28 053	55 112
Profits and dividends	..	..	3 133	8 354	15 264	5 865	9 002	15 919	26 022	52 580
Interests	..	..	572	382	1 356	0	1 779	2 306	2 032	2 532
Other property income	..	..	0	0	0	4 317	4 740	3 341	5 330	5 271
Surplus funds from regulatory authority	..	..	0	0	0	4 317	4 740	3 341	5 330	5 271
Sales of goods and services	..	..	1 894	2 302	12 479	28 990	45 303	47 042	46 601	47 870
Work permits	..	..	0	0	4 277	900	4 098	5 226	5 363	4 384
Road transit toll	..	..	352	457	546	495	562	674	737	766
Immigration visas and other consular fees	..	..	0	0	2 751	606	2 822	3 063	3 144	4 898
Fees under traffic act	..	..	913	1 188	548	108	0	0	0	1 254
Land administration fees	..	..	0	0	64	148	1 826	586	915	829
Motor driver's licences	..	..	627	656	762	0	0	0	1 270	0
Passport fees	..	..	0	0	502	125	570	845	867	1 021
Rent of government buildings and housing	..	..	1	0	274	54	135	213	332	376
Other fees for administrative services	..	..	0	0	2 606	128	556	542	556	829
Hire of security service fees	..	..	0	0	9	18	372	321	330	372
Registration of organisations, professionals and agreements	..	..	0	0	70	46	296	360	369	387
Registration of births, deaths and marriages	..	..	0	0	71	62	214	193	198	254
Other non-tax revenue collected by local government	..	..	..	..	..	26 300	33 850	35 020	32 520	32 500
Fines, penalties and forfeits	..	..	159	229	1 465	1 443	1 459	1 470	1 098	2 733
Miscellaneous and unidentified revenue	..	..	13 828	7 131	6 572	6 792	21 281	11 275	33 097	35 354
Contribution from government employees to social and welfare schemes within government	..	..	1 062	341	0	204	871	462	390	0
National Social Security Fund	..	..	5 363	6 790	6 572	6 588	9 210	9 486	9 491	9 988
Other Miscellaneous	..	..	7 402	0	0	0	11 200	1 327	23 216	25 365
Total tax and non-tax revenue	..	..	512 751	573 806	877 075	1 053 411	1 198 979	1 351 320	1 556 612	1 648 759

.. Not available

Note: Data are reported on a fiscal year basis beginning 1st July. For example, the data for 2018 represent July 2017 to June 2018.

The data are on a cash basis.

Detailed non-tax revenue data are not readily available for 2001, 2002, 2003, 2004, 2006, 2011 and 2012. Figures exclude non-tax revenues collected by sub-national governments as the data are not available

The national classification of Kenya classifies revenues from the airport revenue, aviation revenue, petroleum development levy, FMV, road maintenance levy, sugar levy, petroleum regulatory levy, merchant superintendent shipping levy, railway development levy, revenue Stamps, KEBS and land rates as non-tax revenues. They are considered in this publication as tax revenues under the OECD classification, as set out in the Interpretative Guide in Annex A.

Source: Kenya Revenue Authority Statistical Service.

StatLink https://doi.org/10.1787/888934183921

Table 6.19. **Madagascar**

Details of non-tax revenue / Recettes non fiscales détaillées

Million MGA

	1998	2000	2008	2010	2013	2014	2015	2016	2017	2018
Total des recettes non fiscales	**0**	**172 677**	**586 983**	**619 717**	**366 032**	**656 663**	**504 711**	**726 921**	**929 098**	**1 340 511**
Dons	0	153 554	537 304	351 388	295 535	592 127	423 925	611 340	806 948	1 207 985
Dons - programmes des gouvernements étrangers	..	0	100 682	0	0	206 018	39 869	226 095	292 600	410 118
Dons - projets des institutions internationales	..	153 554	420 831	336 704	295 535	386 109	384 056	385 245	514 348	797 867
Ressources PPTE	..	0	15 791	14 684	0	0	0	0	0	0
Revenus de la propriété	0	17 649	31 401	266 340	52 892	50 097	59 980	94 467	107 633	109 916
Loyers et redevances	..	5 649	14 962	241 311	11 999	16 061	14 064	12 024	8 634	14 663
Intérêts et dividendes	..	12 000	16 439	25 029	40 893	34 036	45 916	82 443	98 999	95 253
Autres revenus de la propriété	..	0	0	0	0	0	0	0	0	0
Ventes de biens et de services	0	1 474	7 595	1 989	12 128	12 228	5 225	20 389	4 886	3 778
Amendes, pénalités et confiscations	0	0	0	0	0	0	0	0	0	0
Recettes diverses et non identifiées	0	0	10 683	0	5 477	2 211	15 581	725	9 631	18 832
Total des recettes fiscales et non fiscales	403 760	775 877	2 675 397	2 600 566	2 913 549	3 358 580	3 650 753	4 507 907	5 416 139	6 623 565

.. Non disponible

Note : Année civile se terminant le 31 décembre.

Les données sont sur la base des encaissements.

Les chiffres n'incluent pas les recettes non fiscales collectées par les administrations infranationales car elles ne sont pas disponibles.

Source : Ministère de l'Économie et des Finances de Madagascar.

StatLink https://doi.org/10.1787/888934183959

Table 6.20. **Malawi**

Details of non-tax revenue / Recettes non fiscales détaillées

Million MWK

	1998	2000	2008	2010	2013	2014	2015	2016	2017	2018
Total non-tax revenue	..	..	**69 671**	**105 601**	**189 222**	**112 961**	**124 112**	**159 138**	**202 474**	**126 362**
Grants	..	..	59 806	78 448	175 765	79 183	79 392	131 007	147 706	70 155
Grants from foreign governments - Current	..	..	9 439	18 782	69 840	25 055	20 769	12 323	8 962	0
Grants from foreign governments - Capital	..	..	24 271	25 844	34 679	41 046	47 519	49 542	73 505	44 300
Grants from international orgs - Current	..	..	26 096	33 822	67 068	13 083	10 711	67 302	65 239	25 855
Grants from international orgs - Capital	..	..	0	0	4 178	0	393	1 840	0	0
Property income	..	..	0	3 466	325	20 638	32 815	13 653	22 837	20 083
Rents and royalties	..	..	..	0	0	0	0	0	0	0
Interest and dividends	..	..	..	3 466	325	20 638	32 815	13 653	22 837	20 083
Parastatal dividends	..	..	..	3 466	325	20 638	32 815	13 653	22 837	20 083
Other property income	..	..	..	0	0	0	0	0	0	0
Sales of goods and services	..	..	8 629	13 724	10 927	10 667	11 397	14 478	20 607	34 639
Fertiliser sales revenue	..	..	4 349	736	0	0	0	0	0	0
Receipts from fertiliser option	..	..	0	0	0	0	0	0	0	0
Maize sales	..	..	0	0	0	0	0	0	0	0
Departmental receipts	..	..	4 280	12 988	10 927	10 667	11 397	14 478	20 607	34 639
Fines, penalties and forfeits	..	..	206	205	1 204	2 472	509	0	0	1 485
Penalties	..	..	206	205	1 204	2 472	509	..	..	1 485
Miscellaneous and unidentified revenue	..	..	1 030	9 758	1 000	0	0	0	11 325	0
Other current transfers not elsewhere classified	..	..	1 030	9 758	1 000	0	0	..	11 325	..
Total tax and non-tax revenue	..	..	169 300	258 346	473 391	522 419	609 438	763 359	998 258	1 007 257

.. Not available

Note: Data are on a fiscal year basis beginning 1st July. For example, the data for 2018 represent July 1, 2017 to June 30, 2018.

Figures exclude non-tax revenues collected by sub-national governments as the data are not available.

Source: Ministry of Finance, Economic Planning and Development of Malawi

StatLink https://doi.org/10.1787/888934184035

Table 6.21. **Mali**

Details of non-tax revenue / Recettes non fiscales détaillées

Million XOF

	1998	2000	2008	2010	2013	2014	2015	2016	2017	2018
Total des recettes non fiscales	**37 652**	**122 795**	**155 081**	**256 632**	**272 661**	**227 378**	**197 471**	**175 908**	**311 733**	**225 401**
Dons	25 163	102 481	118 736	190 540	206 507	162 500	112 124	98 310	159 914	136 049
Dons - gouvernements étrangers	0	0	54 625	22 263	10 006	18 188	20 665	8 639	14 208	6 129
Dons - institutions internationales	25 163	102 481	51 335	160 368	171 019	127 529	79 066	71 942	127 477	110 927
Ressources PPTE	0	0	12 776	7 909	11 313	12 909	12 393	17 729	18 229	18 993
Ressources exceptionnelles: reconversion dette monétaire fonds de concours	0	0	0	0	14 169	3 874	0	0	0	0
Revenus de la propriété	2 120	9 669	18 454	34 564	38 062	35 055	46 966	33 747	115 029	48 426
Loyers et redevances	157	358	71	650	564	756	1 735	750	81 041	21 023
Concessions ordinaires	115	336	71	262	378	401	1 315	276	80 510	20 425
Redevances superficiaires	42	22	0	388	153	263	262	240	421	371
Taxe d'extraction	0	0	0	0	33	92	158	234	110	107
Autres loyers et redevances - extrabudgétaires	0	0	0	0	0	0	0	0	0	121
Intérêts et dividendes	1 963	9 311	18 210	32 873	37 159	34 118	44 810	32 544	33 252	25 157
Revenus des valeurs mobilières, des titres et des dividendes	1 939	9 296	16 958	30 500	34 169	30 745	41 261	29 761	8 059	7 201
Autres intérêts et dividendes (budget d'état)	24	15	0	0	0	0	0	0	21 563	15 726
Interêts des comptes bancaires (INPS)	0	0	1 252	2 373	2 990	3 373	3 549	2 783	3 630	2 230
Autres revenus de la propriété	0	0	174	1 041	338	181	420	453	736	2 246
Autres revenus de la propriété (CMSS)	..	..	0	0	88	48	140	142	87	47
Autres revenus de la propriété (INPS)	..	..	174	1 041	250	133	281	311	649	2 199
Ventes de biens et de services	3 351	3 897	7 437	13 188	13 893	12 053	22 825	23 951	19 919	21 806
Prestations, évacuations, importations, exportations - extrabudgétaires	0	0	0	0	0	0	0	0	0	3 351
Droits de chancellerie	584	886	2 228	2 152	2 455	2 225	4 310	3 033	3 914	4 255
Passeports et cartes d'identités,	369	473	2 326	2 609	3 239	3 487	2 680	1 494	1 352	3 251
Recettes sur rôles (Trésor - BN)	1 247	981	0	91	0	0	0	0	0	0
Frais d'administration, voitures	376	497	684	813	960	1 021	1 200	1 342	1 355	1 137
Ventes en douanes	1	15	18	117	15	12	26	66	18	19
Location des immeubles de l'état	1	393	6	0	0	0	0	29	0	0
Autres ventes de biens et de services (budget d'état)	773	652	523	6 440	5 139	3 663	12 574	14 531	8 178	6 521
Recettes de la Caisse Malienne de Sécurité Sociale (CMSS) - hors cotisations	0	0	587	699	1 150	999	995	1 672	1 146	779
Recettes de l'Institut National de Prévoyance Sociale (INPS) - hors cotisations	0	0	1 064	267	935	646	1 040	1 784	3 956	1 436
Location des immeubles de l'état - extrabudgétaires	0	0	0	0	0	0	0	0	0	517
Autres ventes de biens et de services - extrabudgétaires	0	0	0	0	0	0	0	0	0	540
Amendes, pénalités et confiscations	3 227	2 786	7 117	8 010	9 661	9 782	12 764	15 196	7 289	8 753
Pénalités sur impots directs	1 356	352	1 321	3 939	5 592	4 742	4 753	7 580	3 529	2 983
Pénalités sur impôts indirects	1 175	1 528	1 970	1 418	1 792	2 729	3 101	3 794	1 247	1 800
Amendes et confiscations	575	710	1 797	1 268	937	1 292	2 738	2 357	1 301	1 487
Transactions forestières, pêche et chasse	55	98	57	153	121	137	0	0	0	0
Frais et amendes judiciaires	66	98	326	249	229	258	397	386	302	296
Autres pénalités (budget d'état)	0	0	484	77	85	87	624	69	51	50
Pénalités et frais contentieux (INPS)	0	0	1 162	906	905	537	1 151	1 010	859	2 137
Recettes diverses et non identifiées	3 791	3 962	3 337	10 329	4 537	7 988	2 793	4 705	9 582	10 367
Compensations des moins values de recettes	0	0	675	0	0	0	0	0	0	0
Amendes arbitrées	222	268	39	66	127	112	41	80	94	60
Autres recettes diverses	3 569	3 694	2 623	10 263	4 410	7 876	2 752	4 625	9 488	8 162
Autres recettes diverses - extrabudgétaires	..	..	..	..	..	..	..	..	..	2 145
Total des recettes fiscales et non fiscales	267 852	362 157	740 722	1 004 877	1 203 547	1 216 339	1 372 331	1 547 057	1 803 523	1 554 390
Pour mémoire : Redevances Statistiques (taxe UEMOA)	2 484	1 394	0	0	0	0	0	0	0	0

.. Non disponible

Note : Année civile se terminant le 31 décembre.

Les données sont sur la base des encaissements.

Les chiffres n'incluent pas les recettes non fiscales collectées par les collectivités locales car elles ne sont pas disponibles.

Les données pour 2018 incluent des recettes extrabudgétaires. Les recettes extrabudgétaires incluent les recettes des budgets annexes et les recettes des comptes spéciaux du trésor. Les catégories affectées sont indiquées avec la note " - extrabudgétaires".

Certaines données classées comme recettes non fiscales dans les éditions précédentes ne sont plus classées comme des recettes dans cette édition.

Source : Ministère de l'Économie et des Finances et la Direction Nationale du Trésor et de la Comptabilité Publique du Mali.

StatLink https://doi.org/10.1787/888934183978

Table 6.22. **Mauritania / Mauritanie**

Details of non-tax revenue / Recettes non fiscales détaillées

Million MRU

	1998	2000	2008	2010	2013	2014	2015	2016	2017	2018
Total des recettes non fiscales	..	..	..	**9 833**	**15 841**	**11 877**	**12 868**	**10 914**	**11 469**	**18 008**
Dons	..	..	..	830	874	0	1 988	1 600	1 096	201
Dons courants états étrangers	..	..	..	0	874	0	1 988	1 600	1 096	0
Dons courants organismes	..	..	..	830	0	0	0	0	0	201
Revenus de la propriété	..	..	..	8 164	13 500	10 823	9 551	7 936	9 343	15 148
Loyers et redevances	..	..	..	6 835	8 512	6 965	8 112	6 900	8 180	13 840
Accords de pêche	..	..	..	3 945	6 251	3 263	4 068	4 966	5 048	5 859
Droits d'accès pêche	..	..	..	208	268	236	318	850	1 524	1 643
Licences télécom et sanctions	..	..	..	3	608	544	1 906	451	464	452
Mine : permis d'exploitation et de recherche	..	..	..	1 562	758	797	635	613	620	615
Pétrole : bonus de signature	..	..	..	65	0	60	0	0	460	5 141
Pétrole : redevances et autres	..	..	..	1 035	600	2 037	1 150	11	24	85
Redevances et concessions domaniales	..	..	..	16	27	28	35	10	39	45
Intérêts et dividendes	..	..	..	1 329	4 988	3 858	1 439	1 035	1 161	1 308
Autres revenus de la propriété	..	..	..	0	0	0	0	0	3	0
Ventes de biens et de services	..	..	..	106	557	410	486	468	447	508
Visas	..	..	..	0	0	67	150	231	162	179
Passeport	..	..	..	0	215	134	102	86	149	167
Carte grise et permis de conduire	..	..	..	0	64	51	54	34	24	40
Frais administratifs	..	..	..	106	277	159	181	118	92	98
Frais universités, instituts et centres nationaux	..	..	..	0	0	0	0	0	20	24
Amendes, pénalités et confiscations	..	..	..	206	393	389	393	458	366	519
Amendes de pêche	..	..	..	75	22	69	57	57	130	80
Autres amendes	..	..	..	131	371	320	336	401	236	439
Recettes diverses et non identifiées	..	..	..	526	516	255	450	453	218	1 632
Total des recettes fiscales et non fiscales	..	..	12 587	24 386	44 088	41 139	40 592	41 585	45 500	57 212

.. Non disponible

Note : Année civile se terminant le 31 décembre.

Les données sont sur la base des encaissements

Les données de cette édition sont en monnaie MRU, devise officielle de la Mauritanie depuis le 1er janvier 2018. Elle remplace la monnaie MRO, devise utilisée dans les éditions précédentes.

Les chiffres n'incluent pas les recettes des droits de conservation foncière . Elles sont incluses dans les recettes fiscales comme le préconise la classification OCDE (voir le guide d'interprétation en Annexe A) mais considérées comme des recettes non fiscales en Mauritanie.

Source : Ministère des Finances de la Mauritanie

StatLink https://doi.org/10.1787/888934183997

Table 6.23. **Mauritius / Maurice**

Details of non-tax revenue / Recettes non fiscales détaillées

Million MUR

	1998	2000	2008	2010	2013	2014	2015	2016	2017	2018
Total non-tax revenue	**3 494**	**3 293**	**7 944**	**11 458**	**11 688**	**11 517**	**11 331**	**13 645**	**16 627**	**17 719**
Grants	217	161	454	1 991	1 416	940	1 202	345	2 920	2 635
Grants from foreign governments	..	..	..	2	121	569	183	122	1 915	2 248
Grants from international organizations	..	..	..	1 989	1 295	371	1 019	223	1 005	387
Property income	2 639	2 370	5 119	5 020	5 315	5 193	3 604	5 048	4 583	4 996
Rents and royalties	0	0	358	1 284	1 219	1 087	752	961	960	1 171
Interest and dividends	0	0	1 861	979	1 827	1 404	873	679	534	1 051
Interest	..	..	362	392	408	461	382	360	236	271
Dividends	..	..	1 499	587	1 418	943	492	319	298	780
Other property income	2 639	2 370	2 900	2 756	2 269	2 701	1 979	3 408	3 089	2 773
Other property income - Budgetary	1 874	1 692	1 458	1 549	1 066	1 437	1 392	2 289	1 810	1 039
Other property income - Extra-budgetary	31	58	162	349	272	170	33	22	63	170
Other property income - Social security funds	679	544	1 172	777	756	1 038	529	1 058	1 169	1 531
Other property income - Regional	0	0	7	11	14	11	5	5	13	12
Other property income - Local	56	76	102	71	161	46	20	34	34	20
Sales of goods and services	495	626	1 952	2 028	3 002	3 738	3 644	3 800	3 889	3 503
Work/occupational permits	0	0	60	95	163	205	194	203	205	266
Extra-budgetary fees, charges, and non-industrial sales	97	177	704	543	689	1 118	1 219	1 054	1 180	1 118
Fees, charges, and non-industrial sales by social security funds	27	20	80	51	234	140	78	156	159	0
Regional government sales of goods and services	0	0	7	5	7	7	4	4	9	11
Local government sales of goods and services	40	60	123	113	419	691	353	713	678	445
Other sales of goods and services	332	370	979	1 222	1 489	1 577	1 797	1 669	1 658	1 663
Fines, penalties and forfeits	54	65	178	272	313	332	292	247	305	253
Budgetary fines, penalties and forfeits	54	65	176	269	308	326	290	244	251	238
Extra-budgetary fines, penalties and forfeits	0	0	0	0	1	2	0	0	49	2
Regional government fines, penalties and forfeits	0	0	1	3	4	4	2	2	5	5
Local government fines, penalties and forfeits	0	0	0	0	0	0	0	0	0	8
Miscellaneous and unidentified revenue	89	70	241	2 147	1 642	1 314	2 588	4 205	4 931	6 332
Budgetary miscellaneous and unidentified revenue	1	10	24	1 803	144	139	157	167	250	242
Extra-budgetary miscellaneous and unidentified revenue	77	44	215	293	280	1 173	1 092	1 771	4 460	1 173
Miscellaneous and unidentified revenue for social security funds	2	4	0	3	0	0	0	0	0	0
Regional government miscellaneous and unidentified revenue	0	0	0	1	2	1	0	1	52	1
Local government miscellaneous and unidentified revenue	0	0	0	1	2	1	0	1	52	1
Transfers from special funds	0	0	0	0	1 216	1	1 339	2 266	171	4 914
Total tax and non-tax revenue	20 687	25 439	58 383	69 862	83 179	87 294	90 555	95 983	105 211	113 428

.. Not available

Note: Data for years prior to 2010 and subsequent to 2015 are on a fiscal year basis beginning 1st July. For example, the data for 2009 represent July 2008 to June 2009 and 2018 represents July 2017 to June 2018. The data for years 2010-15 are on a calendar year (January-December) basis.

Mauritius budget statements cover January-June 2015 and July 2015 to June 2016, but neither the fiscal nor the calendar year for 2015. Figures for 2015 are therefore estimated using quarterly revenue figures at the aggregate level and fiscal year revenue data.

Data for the central government budgetary tax prior to 2007 and all extra-budgetary, regional and local data were classified according to the IMF Government Finance Statistics Manual. The 1986 manual was used for data up to 2009 and the 2001 manual for data up to 2009 onwards. Data from 2007 onwards are classified under the OECD classification, as set out in the Interpretative Guide in Annex A.

Revenues reported as "Transfers from special funds" in fact represent funds raised from various sources, including tax revenues, non-tax revenues, and inter-governmental transfers which not properly classified as revenues. Special Funds are special purpose vehicles set up by way of legislation for a specific purpose, i.e., to finance a dedicated programme or projects. Funds are transferred to the Fund from the Consolidated Fund through an appropriate expenditure item in the budget. Such Funds also generate their own revenue in terms of, for example, a levy imposed on petroleum products or contributions from international institutions and friendly countries. As such, once the dedicated programme or projects are completed, the available balance in the Special Funds are transferred to the Consolidated Fund and reported as revenues in budget documents for Mauritius.

Mauritius Revenue Authority for the central government budgetary tax data from 2007 to 2017; Statistics Mauritius for extra-budgetary, local government, regional government and social security revenues from 1990 to 2018, as well as for budgetary central government tax revenues up to 2006; Ministry of Finance budget estimates for detailed revenue figures for the periods July 2005-June 2008, for 2016-18, and for the figures used to estimate calendar year 2015 revenues.

Source: Mauritius Revenue Authority for the central government budgetary tax data from 2007 to 2017; Statistics Mauritius for extra-budgetary, local government, regional government and social security revenues from 1990 to 2018, as well as for budgetary central government tax revenues up to 2006; Ministry of Finance budget estimates for detailed revenue figures for the periods July 2005-June 2008, for 2016-18, and for the figures used to estimate calendar year 2015 revenues.

StatLink https://doi.org/10.1787/888934184016

Table 6.24. **Morocco / Maroc**

Details of non-tax revenue / Recettes non fiscales détaillées

Million MAR

	1998	2000	2008	2010	2013	2014	2015	2016	2017	2018
Total des recettes non fiscales	..	**9 278**	**23 676**	**27 970**	**37 039**	**34 913**	**38 673**	**35 225**	**36 921**	**40 642**
Dons	..	2	2	199	7	0	0	0	0	0
Revenus de la propriété	..	3 125	6 563	9 786	13 063	10 938	8 934	9 425	8 604	9 896
Loyers et redevances	..	1 507	3 674	3 868	5 360	5 387	5 192	4 237	4 583	4 787
Redevance gazoduc	..	298	1 748	1 442	2 327	2 438	1 765	999	1 016	1 538
Redevances et contributions pour licence de pêche en haute mer	..	94	412	329	177	538	520	593	739	235
Redevances pour l'occupation du domaine public	..	132	192	331	566	279	281	195	257	273
Autres redevances	..	7	13	63	9	3	6	10	8	6
Loyers et redevances reçues par les collectivités locales	..	977	1 310	1 703	2 281	2 128	2 620	2 440	2 563	2 735
Intérêts et dividendes	..	1 618	2 888	5 918	7 702	5 551	3 742	5 188	4 021	5 109
Dividendes des monopoles	..	1 008	2 615	5 584	7 378	4 970	3 236	4 675	3 526	4 650
Intérêts sur placements et avances	..	419	57	96	73	322	195	199	174	119
Interêts et dividendes reçus par collectivités locales	..	191	216	239	251	259	311	315	322	340
Autres revenus de la propriété	..	0	0	0	0	0	0	0	0	0
Ventes de biens et de services	..	4 573	11 125	10 286	14 244	14 417	16 009	14 746	16 890	17 731
Cartes d'identités, passeports et documents divers	..	453	471	567	489	220	498	718	759	950
Produits de certains établissements publics	..	1 544	4 940	2 990	5 410	4 551	5 462	3 149	4 432	4 425
Revenus des immeubles domaniaux (loyers, charges locatives, etc.)	..	137	238	250	239	217	265	312	302	335
Autres produits et divers	..	175	1 354	646	801	864	965	791	1 199	1 661
Ventes de biens et de services par collectivités locales	..	2 265	4 123	5 832	7 304	8 566	8 819	9 777	10 198	10 360
Amendes, pénalités et confiscations	..	398	2 002	2 802	2 526	2 690	2 994	3 179	2 973	3 963
Amendes et condamnations pécuniaires	..	17	27	21	46	56	61	68	63	66
Amendes transactionnelles	..	36	89	130	485	893	706	593	471	481
Autres (produits des confiscations, pénalités et amendes autres que fiscales)	..	6	1	1	1	1	0	0	0	0
Majorations et pénalités	..	339	1 885	2 650	1 994	1 740	2 226	2 518	2 439	3 416
Recettes diverses et non identifiées	..	1 180	3 984	4 897	7 200	6 868	10 736	7 875	8 454	9 053
Fonds de concours	..	147	3 310	3 597	4 441	2 564	3 453	2 187	2 250	1 944
Recettes en atténuation des dépenses de la dette	..	801	68	480	1 024	2 230	4 386	1 894	691	963
Reversements sur traitements et salaires	..	55	122	99	96	63	62	60	1 300	957
Créances sur le trésor prescrites	..	30	50	39	112	78	97	163	260	305
Autres (divers remboursement à l'Etat)	..	7	108	6	281	396	254	254	46	11
Recettes diverses et non identifiées des collectivités locales	..	139	327	677	1 246	1 536	2 484	3 316	3 907	4 873
Total des recettes fiscales et non fiscales	..	106 504	240 185	244 956	285 992	296 682	299 642	311 309	330 537	348 765

.. Non disponible

Note : Année civile se terminant le 31 décembre.

Les données sont sur la base des encaissements.

Majorations et pénalités (DGI): Les recettes des majorations et pénalités relatives aux impôts sont considérées comme des recettes non fiscales. La classification nationale du Maroc les compte comme des recettes fiscales.

Source : Ministère de l'Économie et des Finances.

StatLink https://doi.org/10.1787/888934183940

Table 6.25. **Namibia**

Details of non-tax revenue / Recettes non fiscales détaillées

Million NAD

	1998	2000	2008	2010	2013	2014	2015	2016	2017	2018
Total non-tax revenue	**..**	**..**	**10 843**	**7 948**	**17 909**	**21 342**	**20 781**	**17 447**	**23 812**	**21 336**
Grants	..	..	83	24	278	110	152	0	1	72
Property income	..	..	1 719	1 373	1 820	2 334	2 568	2 474	3 026	2 571
Rents and royalties	..	..	662	1 015	471	1 377	1 482	1 477	1 691	1 869
Diamond royalties	..	..	452	602	108	1 043	1 060	978	1 203	1 255
Other mineral royalties	..	..	93	280	185	201	309	391	343	347
Fishing quota levies	..	..	118	133	178	133	113	108	145	267
Interest and dividends	..	..	1 056	358	1 349	957	1 086	997	1 335	702
Other property income	..	..	0	0	0	0	0	0	0	0
Sales of goods and services	..	..	503	534	1 029	734	628	835	1 092	1 228
Fines, penalties and forfeits	..	..	36	43	55	47	78	67	95	90
Miscellaneous and unidentified revenue	..	..	8 502	5 975	14 727	18 117	17 355	14 071	19 598	17 375
SACU Revenue Pool Share	..	..	8 502	5 975	14 727	18 117	17 355	14 071	19 598	17 375
Total tax and non-tax revenue	..	..	23 447	23 377	41 910	49 957	52 218	50 943	58 657	55 883

.. Not available

Note: Data are on a cash basis.

Data are on a fiscal year basis beginning 1st April. For example, the data for 2018 represent April 2018 to March 2019.

Figures exclude tax revenues collected by sub-national governments as the data are not available.

Source: Ministry of Finance of Namibia.

StatLink https://doi.org/10.1787/888934184054

Table 6.26. **Niger**

Details of non-tax revenue / Recettes non fiscales détaillées

Million XOF

	1998	2000	2008	2010	2013	2014	2015	2016	2017	2018
Total des recettes non fiscales	..	**65 671**	**197 013**	**179 681**	**359 601**	**326 622**	**323 732**	**313 103**	**388 363**	**510 606**
Dons	..	59 240	169 300	130 144	304 855	222 124	232 611	270 255	342 117	428 900
Revenus de la propriété	..	4 751	17 961	28 436	35 440	42 838	40 249	31 921	28 929	47 496
Loyers et redevances	..	4 673	11 117	14 977	20 173	34 589	32 963	19 974	16 095	38 235
Bonus de signature	..	0	0	0	0	16 082	17 044	0	0	22 974
Redevance minière (RM)	..	4 519	10 311	14 381	18 526	13 195	11 323	13 105	8 850	7 214
Redevance superficaire pétrole	..	0	0	0	0	3 064	2 776	3 093	3 138	3 046
Publicité foncière	..	50	485	429	979	1 024	950	1 476	2 149	2 650
Redevance superficaire mine	..	0	0	0	0	396	449	1 001	1 117	1 463
Retenue pour logements	..	6	0	25	193	276	173	165	228	139
Concessions provisoires	..	0	220	86	299	212	164	740	190	288
Permis de coupe de bois	..	65	45	42	125	277	52	358	295	191
Bornage de terrains	..	4	7	9	14	32	20	23	23	190
Concessions définitives	..	29	49	5	37	31	12	12	103	82
Intérêts et dividendes	..	0	6 692	13 166	15 018	7 990	6 996	11 613	12 459	8 864
Dividendes	..	..	6 692	12 081	9 663	2 994	2 990	3 990	7 542	5 263
Bénéfices pétroliers	..	..	0	0	5 190	4 857	3 577	3 674	4 042	3 430
Intérêts créditeurs	..	..	0	1 084	165	140	430	3 949	876	170
Autres revenus de la propriété	..	78	153	293	249	259	290	334	375	398
Droits d'occupation du domaine public	..	78	153	293	249	259	290	334	375	398
Ventes de biens et de services	..	85	1 709	289	3 568	39 120	36 492	2 730	4 733	15 429
Vente de licence de téléphonie cellulaire	..	0	0	0	0	34 000	34 000	0	0	10 000
Commission sur transferts banque centrale (BCEAO)	..	0	1 094	42	2 002	3 691	1 090	799	3 093	3 905
Vente passeports/visa interpol	..	0	0	0	669	288	469	961	760	731
Vaccination internationale	..	0	0	0	215	201	239	275	217	179
Emission cartes grises/transport	..	0	0	0	125	141	143	121	180	3
Recettes des régies forestières	..	30	178	159	280	263	127	46	26	20
Ventes imprimés DGI/DGD	..	0	0	0	70	90	104	51	74	43
Droit de chancellerie	..	0	4	3	12	4	76	8	10	17
Location d'immeubles	..	9	348	63	41	22	9	27	21	29
Autres ventes de biens et services	..	46	85	21	155	419	235	442	352	503
Amendes, pénalités et confiscations	..	1 348	2 419	3 816	6 040	6 653	6 744	4 215	7 433	9 612
Amendes et pénalités de la DGI	..	1 188	1 065	2 296	4 108	4 289	4 035	2 281	5 167	7 727
Amendes et frais de police	..	0	483	482	655	916	1 230	820	895	909
Amendes et confiscations	..	159	252	214	414	478	842	628	602	561
Amendes, frais et pénalités (gendarmerie et police)	..	0	570	769	807	861	595	428	707	266
Amendes et saisies forêts et chasse	..	1	40	45	47	84	26	9	8	32
Amendes et frais de justice	..	0	7	8	3	18	9	42	42	85
Amendes et saisies sur contrôle des prix-poids-mesure	..	0	2	1	5	7	8	7	13	32
Recettes diverses et non identifiées	..	248	5 624	16 995	9 698	15 887	7 635	3 983	5 151	9 168
Autres recettes diverses - Trésor National	..	0	5 138	16 461	9 241	15 155	4 921	3 021	3 681	8 539
Autres recettes diverses	..	248	285	420	457	732	779	962	1 269	251
Reversements UEMOA et produits divers ARC	..	0	201	114	0	0	1 935	0	0	0
Commissariat à l'Organisation du Hadjj et de la Oumra (COHO)	..	0	0	0	0	0	0	0	201	378
Total des recettes fiscales et non fiscales	..	181 490	490 530	553 142	1 001 009	989 793	1 044 271	958 003	1 003 807	1 265 802
Pour mémoire :										
Prélèvement communautaire de la CEDEAO	..	448	1 999	5 302	3 893	4 433	4 893	3 961	0	0
Prélèvement communautaire UEMOA	..	866	0	0	0	0	0	4 518	0	0

Table 6.26. **Niger** *(cont.)*

Details of non-tax revenue / Recettes non fiscales détaillées

.. Non disponible

Note : Année civile se terminant le 31 décembre.

Les données sont sur la base des encaissements.

Les chiffres n'incluent pas les données des recettes non fiscales collectées par les collectivités locales car elles ne sont pas disponibles.

Les données des dons sont issues de la base de données de la publication PEM 2020 (*Perspectives de l'économie mondiale* 2020) publiée par le FMI.

Les données pour la période 2000-04 doivent être interprétées avec prudence car les données non fiscales collectées par la Direction Générale du Trésor et de la Comptabilité Publique (DGTCP) ne sont pas disponibles pour cette période. Selon la classification OCDE (voir le guided'interprétation en Annexe B), le produit de la vente d'immeuble bâtis n'est pas considéré comme une recette (fiscale ou non fiscale) car il ne représente pas une augmentation de la valeur nette résultant d'une transaction. La classification du Niger compte ces recettes comme des recettes non fiscales.

Selon la classification OCDE (voir le guided'interprétation en Annexe B), le produit de la vente d'immeuble bâtis n'est pas considéré comme une recette (fiscale ou non fiscale) car il ne représente pas une augmentation de la valeur nette résultant d'une transaction. La classification du Niger compte ces recettes comme des recettes non fiscales.

1. Le prélèvement communautaire de la CEDEAO (Communauté économique des États de l'Afrique de l'Ouest) et le prélèvement communautaire de solidarité de l'UEMOA (Union Economique et Monétaire Ouest Africaine) ne sont pas compris dans le total des recettes fiscales ou des recettes non fiscales comme le préconise la classification OCDE (voir le guide d'interprétation en Annexe A) et est présenté ici à titre de rubrique « Pour mémoire ». La classification du Niger les compte comme des recettes.

Source : Ministère des Finances; FMI, *Perspectives de l'économie mondiale*, avril 2020

StatLink https://doi.org/10.1787/888934184073

Table 6.27. **Nigeria / Nigéria**

Details of non-tax revenue / Recettes non fiscales détaillées

Million NGN

	1998	2000	2008	2010	2013	2014	2015	2016	2017	2018
Total non-tax revenue	..	..	..	**4 273 105**	**4 095 036**	**4 346 522**	**2 716 478**	**2 156 625**	**2 872 115**	**3 957 081**
Grants	..	..	..	335	35 406	8 912	49 288	125 059	141 055	196 901
Property income	..	..	..	4 266 330	4 037 340	4 309 750	2 622 660	2 007 436	2 731 060	2 636 270
Rents and royalties	..	..	..	4 266 330	4 037 340	4 309 750	2 622 660	2 007 436	2 731 060	2 636 270
Revenue from oil	..	..	..	3 574 420	3 069 250	3 320 800	2 059 110	1 607 090	2 100 870	1 395 650
Revenue from royalties	..	..	..	691 910	968 090	988 950	563 550	400 346	628 690	1 235 200
Revenue from fees and licences	..	..	..	0	0	0	0	0	1 500	5 420
Interest and dividends	..	..	..	0	0	0	0	0	0	0
Other property income	..	..	..	0	0	0	0	0	0	0
Sales of goods and services	..	..	..	0	0	0	0	0	0	0
Fines, penalties and forfeits	..	..	..	0	0	0	0	0	0	0
Miscellaneous and unidentified revenue	..	..	..	6 440	22 290	27 860	44 530	24 130	0	1 123 910
Total tax and non-tax revenue	..	..	..	8 296 702	10 822 856	11 232 659	8 477 903	7 570 536	9 419 129	12 124 118

.. Not available

Note: Year ending 31st December.

The data are on a cash basis

Grant revenues were not available for 2018, so the revenues reported for that year are projections based on the last three years of revenues.

"Revenue from oil" refers to government share of revenues from revenue sharing agreements with oil and exploration companies.

"Revenue from fees and licenses" refers to government fees collected in exchange for granting Oil Prospecting Licenses (OPL) and Oil Mining Leases (OML).

"Revenue from royalties" includes royalties charged to oil and mineral exploration companies.

Miscellaneous and unidentified revenue includes some revenues from dividends and issued profits from state-owned enterprises.

Source: Federal Inland Revenue Service

StatLink https://doi.org/10.1787/888934184092

Table 6.28. **Rwanda**

Details of non-tax revenue / Recettes non fiscales détaillées

Million RWF

	1998	2000	2008	2010	2013	2014	2015	2016	2017	2018
Total non-tax revenue	**36 371**	**79 888**	**332 060**	**415 465**	**551 411**	**514 565**	**529 400**	**520 541**	**556 992**	**650 724**
Grants	32 967	76 710	279 775	397 352	459 200	421 821	374 600	339 336	359 731	398 686
Property income	..	..	..	..	..	..	..	..	..	..
Rents and royalties	..	..	..	..	..	..	..	..	..	..
Interest and dividends	..	..	..	..	..	..	..	..	..	..
Other property income	..	..	..	..	..	..	..	..	..	..
Sales of goods and services	..	..	..	..	..	..	..	..	..	..
Fines, penalties and forfeits	..	..	..	..	..	..	..	..	..	..
Miscellaneous and unidentified revenue	3 404	3 178	52 284	18 113	92 211	92 745	154 800	181 205	197 261	252 038
Total tax and non-tax revenue	101 634	148 797	685 056	856 189	1 311 569	1 380 119	1 526 632	1 636 177	1 805 009	2 052 226

.. Not available

Note: Year ending 31st December.

The data are on a cash basis.

Figures exclude non-tax revenues collected by sub-national governments as the data are not available.

Figures exclude fines related to tax revenues as it is not possible to split these out from tax revenues. Revenues from fines related to taxes are now classified as non-tax revenues following a change in the OECD classification. Rwanda considers these revenues as tax revenues.

Miscellaneous and unidentified revenue: This category includes non-tax fines, administrative fees and revenue from public property and public assets for Rwanda. These data could not be disaggregated to allocate revenue to the relevant non-tax revenue categories.

Source: Rwanda Revenue Authority.

StatLink https://doi.org/10.1787/888934184111

Table 6.29. **Senegal / Sénégal**

Details of non-tax revenue / Recettes non fiscales détaillées

Million XOF

	1998	2000	2008	2010	2013	2014	2015	2016	2017	2018
Total des recettes non fiscales	**88 640**	**68 000**	**204 600**	**203 550**	**304 935**	**394 700**	**366 943**	**522 831**	**500 930**	**450 211**
Dons	81 800	64 000	139 700	161 850	187 540	253 500	232 034	244 348	264 000	256 420
Revenus de la propriété	0	0	58 500	39 600	88 795	81 300	84 990	83 413	84 230	97 691
Loyers et redevances	..	..	5 800	20 300	45 420	25 200	35 790	31 943	33 200	53 591
Intérêts et dividendes	..	..	52 700	19 300	43 375	56 100	49 200	51 470	51 030	44 100
Autres revenus de la propriété	..	..	0	0	0	0	0	0	0	0
Ventes de biens et de services	0	0	0	0	0	0	0	0	0	0
Amendes, pénalités et confiscations	0	0	0	0	27 100	49 000	28 220	0	0	0
Recettes diverses et non identifiées	6 840	4 000	6 400	2 100	1 500	10 900	21 700	195 070	152 700	96 100
Recettes exceptionnelles (Swapp et Sonatel)	0	0	0	0	0	0	0	139 770	0	24 000
Divers reversements	6 840	4 000	6 400	2 100	1 500	10 900	21 700	55 300	152 700	72 100
Total des recettes fiscales et non fiscales	545 720	627 295	1 343 731	1 471 349	1 744 344	1 981 565	2 090 075	2 443 175	2 488 028	2 573 716

.. Non disponible

Note : Année civile se terminant le 31 décembre.

Les données sont sur la base des encaissements.

Les chiffres n'incluent pas les données des recettes fiscales collectées par les collectivités locales car elles ne sont pas disponibles.

Amendes, pénalités et confiscations: Les recettes des amendes et les pénalités sur impôts et taxes sont considérées comme des recettes non fiscales. Cependant, il n'a pas été possible de séparer le versement des amendes et pénalités des recettes correspondant aux impôts auxquels ces amendes et pénalités se rattachent et sont donc exlues de cette rubrique. La classification nationale du Sénégal les compte comme des recettes fiscales.

Recettes diverses et non identifiées: y compris transferts de capitaux non compris ailleurs.

Source : Ministère de l'Économie, des Finances et du Plan.

StatLink https://doi.org/10.1787/888934184130

Table 6.30. **Seychelles**

Details of non-tax revenue / Recettes non fiscales détaillées

Million SCR

	1998	2000	2008	2010	2013	2014	2015	2016	2017	2018
Total non-tax revenue	..	..	**93**	**668**	**1 256**	**1 425**	**1 103**	**1 475**	**986**	**1 227**
Grants	..	..	0	101	343	532	144	271	173	281
Property income	..	..	93	300	518	391	528	595	419	579
Rents and royalties	..	..	93	93	117	108	141	133	139	152
Fishing licence fees	..	..	93	93	0	0	0	0	0	0
Annual EU fishing licence fees to access Seychelles EEZ	..	..	0	0	53	47	43	36	37	42
EU fishing licence: vessel fee	..	..	0	0	14	21	37	33	29	35
Non EU fishing licence fees	..	..	0	0	49	40	60	64	72	72
Local fishing licence fees	..	..	0	0	0	0	1	1	0	2
Interest and dividends	..	..	0	206	401	283	386	462	280	426
SIBA and FSA fees	..	..	0	0	0	133	158	158	0	0
Other income from interest and dividends	..	..	0	206	401	151	228	304	280	426
Other property income	..	..	0	0	0	0	0	0	0	0
Sales of goods and services	..	..	0	191	297	347	322	428	349	335
Fines, penalties and forfeits	..	..	0	0	0	0	0	0	0	0
Miscellaneous and unidentified revenue	..	..	0	77	98	155	110	182	45	32
Total tax and non-tax revenue	..	..	2 439	4 108	5 816	6 478	6 362	7 373	7 448	8 365

.. Not available

Note: Year ending 31st December.

The data are on a cash basis.

Figures exclude non-tax revenues collected by sub-national governments as the data are not available.

Heading "Rents and royalties" : This category includes fishing licence fees considered as non-tax revenues in accordance with the OECD classification, as set out in the Interpretative Guide in Annex A. The Seychelles classifies these revenues as tax revenues.

Heading "Interest and dividends" : The SIBA and FSA fees refer to dividends paid by the Financial Services Authority to the government. They are the regulatory bodies for the financial sector excluding banks consisting mainly of Corporate Services Providers.

Source: Ministry of Finance, Ministry of Environment, Natural Resources and Transport.

StatLink https://doi.org/10.1787/888934184168

Table 6.31. **South Africa / Afrique du Sud**

Details of non-tax revenue / Recettes non fiscales détaillées

Million ZAR

	1998	2000	2008	2010	2013	2014	2015	2016	2017	2018
Total non-tax revenue	**4 632**	**4 135**	**16 296**	**16 192**	**20 382**	**19 922**	**17 934**	**20 234**	**21 711**	**27 761**
Grants	521	637	1 993	1 012	2 335	1 960	1 467	1 800	1 283	1 332
Property income	1 959	1 378	7 525	8 170	11 172	12 102	10 113	11 189	12 726	16 845
Rents and royalties	191	0	978	4 448	6 648	5 489	3 772	5 948	7 834	9 049
Interest and dividends	1 768	1 378	6 547	3 721	4 524	6 613	6 341	5 240	4 891	7 796
Interest	851	714	4 961	2 524	2 585	4 467	4 487	3 981	3 485	6 834
Dividends	917	664	1 586	1 197	1 939	2 146	1 853	1 259	1 406	963
Other property income	0	0	0	0	0	0	0	0	0	0
Sales of goods and services	1 616	2 006	3 393	2 335	1 671	1 663	2 159	2 592	2 629	2 321
Fines, penalties and forfeits	79	114	3 094	4 425	4 782	3 647	3 665	4 206	4 786	6 877
Interest on overdue tax: individuals	..	..	846	1 225	1 009	918	993	1 301	1 698	1 991
Interest on overdue tax: companies	..	..	1 769	1 744	2 306	1 554	1 707	2 239	2 622	3 135
Other fines, penalties and forfeits	79	114	479	1 457	1 466	1 174	965	667	466	1 752
Miscellaneous and unidentified revenue	456	0	292	251	422	550	531	448	287	386
Total tax and non-tax revenue	183 739	215 696	676 070	722 579	978 404	1 070 731	1 188 804	1 263 007	1 342 691	1 445 120
Memo items: *SACU expenditure*	..	..	28 921	17 905	43 374	51 738	51 022	39 448	46 542	56 921

.. Not available

Note: Data are reported on a fiscal year basis beginning 1st April. For example, the data for 2018 represent April 2018 to March 2019

The data are on a cash basis.

Figures exclude non-tax revenues collected by sub-national governments as the data are not available.

The grants data represent total grants and donations received mainly from foreign governments and multilateral institutions. Moreover, this flow does not go through the Government Revenue fund, it is earmarked for specific projects implemented across government (by line departments). Data on grants was missing for fiscal year 2018/19 and so projected figures were used instead. 2018 figures are projections based on the previous three years of data.

Memo items: the Southern African Customs Union (SACU) expenditure records the difference between South Africa contributions to the SACU pool and the South Africa revenue share from the SACU pool that includes the balance of the "surplus/deficit" for that fiscal year and allocations to the SACU secretariat. The figures for 2013/14 figures differ from numbers published in South African tax statistics since some Fuel Levy imports were included in that year. 2018/19 figures are unaudited.

Source: National Treasury of South Africa. Data for grants are from the financial statements of the Reconstruction and Development Fund Programme (RDP) Fund administered by the office of Accountant General.

StatLink https://doi.org/10.1787/888934184263

Table 6.32. **Togo**

Details of non-tax revenue / Recettes non fiscales détaillées

Million XOF

	1998	2000	2008	2010	2013	2014	2015	2016	2017	2018
Total des recettes non fiscales	..	**18 987**	**123 311**	**189 745**	**114 019**	**97 064**	**102 957**	**114 513**	**135 695**	**217 448**
Dons	..	4 292	29 261	80 357	73 511	45 762	57 238	75 601	88 527	105 895
Dons projets	..	4 292	15 499	62 257	62 786	45 762	47 539	64 333	40 208	72 712
Dons programmes	..	0	13 762	18 100	10 725	0	9 699	11 267	48 319	33 183
Revenus de la propriété	..	10 040	49 755	92 473	30 852	29 585	25 555	21 201	31 185	41 010
Loyers et redevances	..	5 548	42 950	42 400	6 368	8 468	3 837	3 640	4 125	3 426
Redevances minières	..	0	0	0	3 181	7 367	1 270	1 372	1 850	2 322
Redevances de réhabilitation de l'Aéroport International Gnassingbé Eyadéma (AIGE)	..	5 548	0	0	35	1 101	2 240	1 819	1 828	665
Redevance contour global	..	0	0	0	0	0	0	408	447	332
Autres recettes domaniales	..	0	42 950	42 400	3 152	0	327	42	0	106
Intérêts et dividendes	..	4 492	6 805	50 073	24 484	21 117	21 718	17 560	27 061	37 584
Dividendes	..	2 416	800	6 745	16 453	13 172	16 179	11 335	21 784	31 592
Intérêts de placement	..	771	515	985	301	7 507	4 307	307	1	1
Produits divers (commissions, transferts BCEAO et intérêts)	..	0	0	0	0	190	201	4 642	4 649	5 234
Autres produits financiers	..	1 304	5 490	42 344	7 729	248	1 032	1 276	627	758
Autres revenus de la propriété	..	0	0	0	0	0	0	0	0	0
Ventes de biens et de services	..	1 365	2 631	140	6 450	17 690	7 692	9 017	8 623	57 659
Loyers d'immeuble	..	0	0	0	0	428	201	1 626	267	386
Redevances téléphoniques	..	0	0	0	2 000	11 949	2 000	1 500	1 573	51 000
Recettes de services	..	1 365	2 631	140	3 710	4 261	4 752	5 286	6 047	6 064
Recettes consulaires	..	0	0	0	740	1 052	739	605	736	210
Amendes, pénalités et confiscations	..	1 222	1 185	495	1 033	2 131	1 359	953	1 318	1 148
Amendes et pénalités (recettes fiscales)	..	955	630	262	409	912	989	754	1 129	821
Amendes et penalités (recettes douanières)	..	267	555	232	624	1 219	369	199	189	326
Recettes diverses et non identifiées	..	2 069	40 480	16 280	2 173	1 895	11 114	7 741	6 042	11 737
Confiscations et ventes en douane	..	0	0	0	0	385	954	4 226	2 459	9 616
Ordre de recettes (gestion antérieure)	..	0	0	0	166	0	6	262	53	43
Ordre de recettes (gestion courante)	..	0	0	0	0	85	95	53	65	175
Divers reversements	..	785	0	0	1 923	1 271	9 754	2 985	3 207	1 114
Autres recettes non fiscales	..	1 284	40 480	16 280	85	154	305	216	259	789
Total des recettes fiscales et non fiscales	..	118 981	337 395	440 185	530 648	568 562	636 513	701 326	721 355	793 976

.. Non disponible

Note : Année civile se terminant le 31 décembre.

Les données sont sur la base des encaissements.

Les recettes non fiscales incluent les recettes des autres ministères ou directions, autres que le Ministère de l'économie et des finances.

Les chiffres n'incluent pas des autres recettes collectées par les collectivités locales pour leur propre compte, car elles ne sont pas disponibles. La classification nationale du Togo considère le Prélèvement pour apurement de la dette du secteur pétrolier (PADSP) comme une recette non fiscale. Cette recette est considérée comme une recette fiscale dans cette publication comme le préconise la classification OCDE (voir le guide d'interprétation en Annexe A).

Amendes et pénalités (recettes fiscales): Ces recettes sont classifiées comme des recettes non fiscales dans cette publication comme le préconise la classification OCDE (voir le guide d'interprétation en Annexe B). La classification nationale du Togo comptabilise ces recettes comme des recettes fiscales.

Confiscations et ventes en douane: Cette rubrique comprend les recettes provenant des confiscations et ventes en douane et les reversements du prélèvement communautaire de solidarité qui sont classifiés comme des recettes non fiscales dans cette publication comme le préconise la classification OCDE (voir le guide d'interprétation en Annexe B. La classification nationale du Togo considère ces recettes comme des recettes fiscales douanières. Avant 2014, ces recettes étaient comptabilisés dans la rubrique « Amendes et pénalités (recettes douanières) ».

Source : Office Togolais des Recettes.

StatLink https://doi.org/10.1787/888934184206

Table 6.33. **Tunisia / Tunisie**

Details of non-tax revenue / Recettes non fiscales détaillées

Million TND

	1998	2000	2008	2010	2013	2014	2015	2016	2017	2018
Total des recettes non fiscales	..	**725**	**1 993**	**1 799**	**2 704**	**1 903**	**1 749**	**1 539**	**2 770**	**3 254**
Dons	..	7	192	54	225	368	292	130	201	236
Revenus de la propriété	..	525	1 442	1 299	1 514	976	863	915	1 623	2 105
Loyers et redevances	..	185	387	435	372	357	350	388	1 251	1 353
Redevances pétrolières et du gaz	..	177	370	415	353	337	328	366	1 224	1 324
Loyers	..	8	17	19	18	20	22	23	27	29
Intérêts et dividendes	..	341	1 055	864	1 143	618	513	527	372	752
Intérêts	..	56	71	56	31	42	41	8	53	72
Transferts des entreprises publiques et bénéfices de la Banque Centrale	..	274	977	796	1 070	503	430	447	262	631
Remises sur crédit	..	3	3	2	2	3	3	4	4	4
Autres intérêts et dividendes non compris ailleurs	..	9	4	10	39	70	39	68	53	44
Autres revenus de la propriété	..	0	0	0	0	0	0	0	0	0
Ventes de biens et de services	..	22	42	40	26	24	28	32	42	72
Ventes de produits divers	..	21	41	38	25	22	26	30	40	70
Frais administratifs	..	1	1	2	2	2	2	2	2	2
Amendes, pénalités et confiscations	..	87	144	186	730	346	378	273	708	532
Recettes diverses et non identifiées	..	85	174	220	208	188	189	190	197	309
Total des recettes fiscales et non fiscales	..	7 922	16 826	18 942	25 112	26 901	27 362	28 135	32 580	37 078

.. Non disponible

Note : Année civile se terminant le 31 décembre.

Les données sont sur la base des encaissements.

Les chiffres n'incluent pas les données des recettes non fiscales collectées par les administrations infranationales car elles ne sont pas disponibles.

Dons: Les dons affectés pour les Fonds spéciaux du Trésor et les Fonds de concours sont compris dans les données des dons des gouvernements et institutions étrangères.

Recettes diverses et non identifiées: Les recettes diverses et non identifiées incluent entre autres des recettes accidentelles à divers titres et des recettes non fiscales des Fonds spéciaux du Trésor et des Fonds de concours.

Source : Ministère des Finances.

StatLink https://doi.org/10.1787/888934184225

Table 6.34. **Uganda / Ouganda**

Details of non-tax revenue / Recettes non fiscales détaillées

Million UGX

	1998	2000	2008	2010	2013	2014	2015	2016	2017	2018
Total non-tax revenue	**399 372**	**568 523**	**773 362**	**921 459**	**1 039 054**	**827 086**	**1 109 069**	**1 400 151**	**1 239 490**	**1 191 569**
Grants	397 552	566 605	738 588	863 608	936 181	702 488	930 809	1 147 209	949 743	774 198
Budget support	193 411	255 205	475 227	467 338	198 668	191 442	258 151	339 676	259 263	154 513
Project grants	204 141	311 400	263 360	396 270	737 513	511 046	672 658	807 533	690 480	619 684
Property income	0	0	3 906	4 061	7 442	8 237	8 684	10 914	16 930	17 766
Rents and royalties	..	..	3 906	4 061	7 442	8 237	8 684	10 914	16 930	17 766
Mining royalties	..	..	3 906	4 061	7 442	8 237	8 684	10 914	16 930	17 766
Interest and dividends	..	..	0	0	0	0	0	0	0	0
Other property income	..	..	0	0	0	0	0	0	0	0
Sales of goods and services	1 820	1 919	30 869	53 790	95 431	116 361	169 575	242 029	272 818	399 605
Driver's permits[1]	1 820	1 919	5 501	12 373	13 655	14 147	15 921	18 245	33 561	37 335
Migration fees	..	..	14 948	23 317	41 740	49 993	90 913	123 251	121 892	140 196
Passport fees	..	..	3 241	4 614	7 980	10 413	12 800	21 660	21 065	25 950
Uganda Registration Services Bureau	..	..	0	0	0	20 490	23 470	24 417	32 549	21 461
Other administrative fees	..	..	7 179	13 486	32 056	21 317	26 472	54 456	63 750	174 663
Fines, penalties and forfeits	0	0	0	0	0	0	0	0	0	0
Miscellaneous and unidentified revenue[2]	0	0	0	0	0	0	0	0	0	0
Total tax and non-tax revenue	1 204 914	1 568 183	3 978 161	5 173 480	8 259 888	8 892 155	10 870 499	12 442 513	13 670 804	15 259 159

.. Not available

Note: Data are reported on a fiscal year basis beginning 1st July. For example, the data for 2018 represent July 2017 to June 2018.

The data are on a cash basis.

Figures exclude non-tax revenues collected by sub-national governments as the data are not available.

1. Revenue from drivers permits are considered as non-tax revenue according the OECD classification described in the Interpretative Guide. The national classification of Uganda classifies it as tax revenues.
2. This category includes non-tax fines, administrative fees and revenue from public property and public assets. These data could not be disaggregated to allocate revenue to the relevant non-tax revenue categories.

Source: Uganda Revenue Authority.

StatLink https://doi.org/10.1787/888934184244

Revenue Statistics in Africa 1990-2018/Statistiques des recettes publiques en Afrique 1990-2018

ANNEX A

The OECD classification of taxes and interpretative guide[1]

Table of contents

A.1. The OECD classification of taxes

1. 1000 Taxes on income, profits and capital gains
   - 1100 Taxes on income, profits and capital gains of individuals
     - 1110 On income and profits
     - 1120 On capital gains
   - 1200 Corporate taxes on income, profits and capital gains
     - 1210 On income and profits
     - 1220 On capital gains
   - 1300 Unallocable as between 1100 and 1200
2. 2000 Social security contributions
   - 2100 Employees
     - 2110 On a payroll basis
     - 2120 On an income tax basis
   - 2200 Employers
     - 2210 On a payroll basis
     - 2220 On an income tax basis
   - 2300 Self-employed or non-employed
     - 2310 On a payroll basis
     - 2320 On an income tax basis
   - 2400 Unallocable as between 2100, 2200 and 2300
     - 2410 On a payroll basis
     - 2420 On an income tax basis
3. 3000 Taxes on payroll and workforce
4. 4000 Taxes on property
   - 4100 Recurrent taxes on immovable property
     - 4110 Households
     - 4120 Other
   - 4200 Recurrent taxes on net wealth
     - 4210 Individual
     - 4220 Corporate
   - 4300 Estate, inheritance and gift taxes
     - 4310 Estate and inheritance taxes
     - 4320 Gift taxes
   - 4400 Taxes on financial and capital transactions
   - 4500 Other non-recurrent taxes on property
     - 4510 On net wealth
     - 4520 Other non-recurrent taxes
   - 4600 Other recurrent taxes on property

5. 5000 Taxes on goods and services

5100 Taxes on production, sale, transfer, leasing and delivery of goods and rendering of services

5110 General taxes

5111 Value added taxes

5112 Sales taxes

5113 Other general taxes on goods and services

5120 Taxes on specific goods and services

5121 Excises

5122 Paid by other than business or unidentifiable

5123 Paid by other than business or unidentifiable

5124 Paid by other than business or unidentifiable

5125 Taxes on investment goods

5126 Taxes on specific services

5127 Other taxes on international trade and transactions

5128 Other taxes on specific goods and services

5130 Unallocable as between 5110 and 5120

5200 Taxes on use of goods, or on permission to use goods or perform activities

5210 Recurrent taxes

5211 Paid by households in respect of motor vehicles

5212 Paid by others in respect of motor vehicles

5213 Other recurrent taxes

5220 Non-recurrent taxes

5300 Unallocable as between 5100 and 5200

6. 6000 Other taxes

6100 Paid solely by business

6200 Paid by other than business or unidentifiable

A.2. Coverage

General criteria

1. In the OECD classification the term "taxes" is confined to compulsory unrequited payments to general government. Taxes are unrequited in the sense that benefits provided by government to taxpayers are not normally in proportion to their payments.

2. The term "tax" does not include fines, penalties and compulsory loans paid to government. Borderline cases between tax and non-tax revenues in relation to certain fees and charges are discussed in §11–14.

3. General government consists of the central administration, agencies whose operations are under its effective control, state and local governments and their administrations, certain social security schemes and autonomous governmental entities, excluding public enterprises. This definition of government follows that of the 2008 *System of National Accounts* (SNA).[2] In that publication, the general government sector and its sub-sectors are defined in Chapter 4, paragraphs 4.117 to 4.165.

4. Extra-budgetary units are part of the general government system. These are general government entities with individual budgets that are not fully covered by the main or general budget. These entities operate under the authority or control of a central, state, or local government. Extra-budgetary entities may have their own revenue sources, which may be supplemented by grants (transfers) from the general budget or from other sources. Even though their budgets may be subject to approval by the legislature, similar to that of budgetary accounts, they have discretion over the volume and composition of their spending. Such entities may be established to carry out specific government functions, such as road construction, or the nonmarket production of health or education services. Budgetary arrangements vary widely across countries, and various terms are used to describe these entities, but they are often referred to as "extra-budgetary funds" or "decentralised agencies."

5. Compulsory payments to supra-national bodies and their agencies are no longer included as taxes as from 1998, with some exceptions. However, custom duties collected by EU member states on behalf of the European Union are still identified as memorandum items and included in overall tax revenue amounts in the country tables of the country in which they are collected (See §99). In countries where the church forms part of general government church taxes are included, provided they meet the criteria set out in §1 above. As the data refer to receipts of general government, levies paid to non-government bodies, welfare agencies or social insurance schemes outside general government, trade unions or trade associations, even where such levies are compulsory, are excluded. Compulsory payments to general government earmarked for such bodies are, however, included, provided that the government is not simply acting in an agency capacity.[3] Profits from fiscal monopolies are distinguished from those of other public enterprises and are treated as taxes because they reflect the exercise of the taxing power of the state by the use of monopoly powers (see §65–67), as are profits received by the government from the purchase and sale of foreign exchange at different rates (see §74).

6. Taxes paid by governments (e.g., social security contributions and payroll taxes paid by governments in their capacity as an employer, consumption taxes on their purchases or taxes on their property) are not excluded from the data provided. However, where it is possible to identify the amounts of revenue involved,[4] they are shown in Chapter 4.2 of this Report.

7. The relationship between this classification and that of the System of National Accounts (SNA) is set out in Sections A.9 and A.11 below. Because of the differences between the two classifications, the data shown in national accounts are sometimes calculated or classified differently from the practice set out in this guide. These and other differences are mentioned where appropriate (e.g., in §30 below) but it is not possible to refer to all of them. There may also be some differences between this classification and that employed domestically by certain national administrations (e.g., see §12 below), so that OECD and national statistics data may not always be consistent: any such differences, however, are likely to be very slight in terms of amounts of revenues involved.

Social security contributions

8. Compulsory social security contributions, as defined in §39, and paid to general government, are treated here as tax revenues. Being compulsory payments to general government they clearly resemble taxes. They may, however, differ from other taxes in that the receipt of social security benefits depends, in most countries, upon appropriate contributions having been made, although the size of the benefits is not necessarily related to the amount of the contributions. Better comparability between countries is obtained by treating social security contributions as taxes, but they are listed under a separate heading so that they can be distinguished in any analysis.

9. The strict dividing line between tax revenues (compulsory unrequited payments to general government) and non-tax compulsory payments (NTCPs) (payments that are either requited or made to other institutions) is clearly defined. However, within the range of different compulsory payments to governments existing across countries, it is not always straightforward in practice to decide whether specific payments are either taxes or NTCPs. For example, compulsory pension savings that are controlled by general government and that accumulate on an individual account earning a market return or a rate that compensates for inflation would at first sight be categorised as NTCPs as opposed to taxes. However, even these payments might still be 'unrequited' and therefore classify as taxes instead of NTCPs (for example if these pension savings are not paid out when the taxpayer dies before reaching the pension age and the funds are then used to provide a minimum pension to all taxpayers that are insured). These issues result in the social security revenue figures reported for most countries being based on the premise that all types of compulsory payments to general government are judged to some extent to have a re-distributional element. It should be noted that this conclusion is based on a typically broad interpretation of the term 'unrequited' in the tax definition.

10. Social security contributions which are either voluntary or not payable to general government (see §1) are not treated as taxes, though in some countries, as indicated in the country footnotes, there are difficulties in completely eliminating voluntary contributions and certain compulsory payments to the private sector from the revenue figures. Imputed social security contributions are also not treated as taxes.

Fees, user charges and licence fees

11. Apart from vehicle licence fees, which are universally regarded as taxes, it is not easy to distinguish between those fees and user charges which are to be treated as taxes and those which are not, since, whilst a fee or charge is levied in connection with a specific service or activity, the strength of the link between the fee and the service provided may vary considerably, as may the relation between the amount of the fee and the cost of providing

the service. Where the recipient of a service pays a fee clearly related to the cost of providing the service, the levy may be regarded as requited and under the definition of §1 would not be considered as a tax. In the following cases, however, a levy could be considered as 'unrequited':

a. where the charge greatly exceeds the cost of providing the service;

b. where the payer of the levy is not the receiver of the benefit (e.g., a fee collected from slaughterhouses to finance a service which is provided to farmers);

c. where government is not providing a specific service in return for the levy which it receives even though a licence may be issued to the payer (e.g., where the government grants a hunting, fishing or shooting licence which is not accompanied by the right to use a specific area of government land);

d. where benefits are received only by those paying the levy but the benefits received by each individual are not necessarily in proportion to his payments (e.g., a milk marketing levy paid by dairy farmers and used to promote the consumption of milk).

12. In marginal cases, however, the application of the criteria set out in §1 can be particularly difficult. The solution adopted — given the desirability of international uniformity and the relatively small amounts of revenue usually involved — is to follow the predominant practice among tax administrations rather than to allow each country to adopt its own view as to whether such levies are regarded as taxes or as non-tax revenue.[5]

13. A list of the main fees and charges in question and their normal[6] treatment in this publication is as follows:

- *Non-tax revenues:* court fees; driving licence fees; harbour fees; passport fees; radio and television licence fees where public authorities provide the service.
- *Taxes within heading 5200:* permission to perform such activities as distributing films; hunting, fishing and shooting; providing entertainment or gambling facilities; selling alcohol or tobacco; permission to own dogs or to use or own motor vehicles or guns; severance taxes.

14. In practice it may not always be possible to isolate tax receipts from non-tax revenue receipts when they are recorded together. If it is estimated that the bulk of the receipts derive from non-tax revenues, the whole amount involved is treated as a non-tax revenue; otherwise, such government receipts are included and classified according to the rules provided in §32 below.

Royalties

15. The ownership of subsoil assets in the form of deposits of minerals or fossil fuels (coal, oil, or natural gas) depends upon the way in which property rights are defined by law and also on international agreements in the case of deposits below international waters. In some cases, either the ground below which the mineral deposits are located, the deposits themselves or both may belong to a local or central government unit.

16. In such cases, these general government units may grant leases to other institutional units that permit them to extract these deposits over a specified period of time in return for a payment or series of payments. These payments are often described as 'royalties' but they are essentially rent that accrues to owners of natural resources in return for putting these assets at the disposal of other units for specified periods of time. The rent may take the form of periodic payments of fixed amounts, irrespective of the rate of extraction, or, more commonly, they may be a function of the quantity, volume, or value of the asset extracted. Enterprises engaged in exploration on government land may make payments to general government units

in exchange for the right to undertake test drilling or otherwise investigate the existence and location of subsoil assets. Such payments are also recorded as rents even though no extraction may take place. These payments are therefore classified as non-tax revenues.

17. The same principles apply when other institutional units are granted leases that permit them to fell timber in natural forests on land owned by general government units. These payments are also classified as non-tax revenues.

18. These rents or royalties paid to general government should not be confused with taxes on income and profits, severance taxes, business licenses, or other taxes. If the payments are levied on the profits from the extraction activity, then they should be classified as taxes on incomes, profits and gains (1000). In addition, any severance payments that are imposed on the extraction of minerals and fossil fuels from reserves owned privately or by another government should be classified as taxes. Payments related to the gross value of production should be classified as other taxes on goods and services (5128). Payments for a license or permit to conduct extraction operations should be classified as taxes on use of goods and on permission to use goods or perform activities (5213).

Fines and penalties

19. In principle, fines and penalties charged on overdue taxes or penalties imposed for the attempted evasion of taxes should not be recorded as tax revenues. However it may not be possible to separate payments of fines or other penalties from the revenues from the taxes to which they relate. In this case the fines and penalties relating to a particular tax are recorded together with the revenues from that tax and fines and penalties paid with revenue from unidentifiable taxes are classified as other taxes in Category 6000. Fines not relating to tax offences (e.g., for parking offences), or not identifiable as relating to tax offences, are also not treated as tax revenues.

A.3. Basis of reporting

Accrual reporting

20. The data reported in this publication for recent years are predominantly recorded on an accrual basis, i.e. recorded at the time that the tax liability was created. Further information is provided in the footnotes to the country table in Chapter 4 of the Report.

21. However, data for earlier years are still predominantly recorded on a cash basis, i.e. at the time at which the payment was received by government. Thus, for example, taxes withheld by employers in one year but paid to the government in the following year and taxes due in one year but actually paid in the following year are both included in the receipts of the second year. Corrective transactions, such as refunds, repayments and drawbacks, are deducted from gross revenues of the period in which they are made.

22. Data on tax revenues are recorded without offsets for the administrative expenses connected with tax collection. Similarly, where the proceeds of tax are used to subsidise particular members of the community, the subsidy is not deducted from the yield of the tax, though the tax may be shown net of subsidies in the national records of some countries.

23. As regards fiscal monopolies (heading 5122), only the amount actually transferred to the government is included in government revenues. However, if any expenditures of fiscal monopolies are considered to be government expenditures (e.g., social expenditures undertaken by fiscal monopolies at the direction of the government) they are added back for the purpose of arriving at tax revenue figures (see §65 below).

The distinction between tax and expenditure provisions[7]

24. Because this publication is concerned only with the revenue side of government operations, no account being taken of the expenditure side, a distinction has to be made between tax and expenditure provisions. Normally there is no difficulty in making this distinction as expenditures are made outside the tax system and the tax accounts and under legislation separate from the tax legislation. In borderline cases, cash flow is used to distinguish between tax provisions and expenditure provisions. Insofar as a provision affects the flow of tax payments from the taxpayer to the government, it is regarded as a tax provision and is taken into account in the data shown in this publication. A provision which does not affect this flow is seen as an expenditure provision and is disregarded in the data recorded in this publication.

25. Tax allowances, exemptions and deductions against the tax base clearly affect the amount of tax paid to the government and are therefore considered as tax provisions. At the other extreme, those subsidies which cannot be offset against tax liability and which are clearly not connected with the assessment process, do not reduce tax revenues as recorded in this publication. Tax credits are amounts deductible from tax payable (as distinct from deductions from the tax base). Two types of tax credits are distinguished, those (referred to here as wastable tax credits) which are limited to the amount of the tax liability and therefore cannot give rise to a payment by the authorities to the taxpayer, and those (referred to as non-wastable tax credits) which are not so limited, so that the excess of the credit over the tax liability can be paid to the taxpayer.[8] A wastable tax credit, like a tax allowance, clearly affects the amount of tax paid to the government, and is therefore considered as a tax provision. The practice followed for non-wastable tax credits[9] is to distinguish between the 'tax expenditure component',[10] which is that portion of the credit that is used to reduce or eliminate a taxpayer's liability, and the 'transfer component', which is the portion that exceeds the taxpayer's liability and is paid to that taxpayer. Reported tax revenues should be reduced by the amount of the tax expenditure component but not by the amount of the transfer component. In addition, the amounts of the tax expenditure and transfer components should be reported as memorandum items in the country tables. Countries that are unable to distinguish between the tax expenditure and transfer components should indicate whether or not the tax revenues have been reduced by the total of these components, and provide any available estimates of the amounts of the two components. Further information is given in of the Report, which illustrates the effect of alternative treatments of non-wastable tax credits on tax to GDP.

Calendar and fiscal years

26. National authorities whose fiscal years do not correspond to the calendar year show data, where possible, on a calendar year basis to permit maximum comparability with the data of other countries. There remain a few countries where data refer to fiscal years. For these the GDP data used in the comparative tables also correspond to the fiscal years.

A.4. General classification criteria

The main classification criteria

27. The classification of receipts among the main headings (1000, 2000, 3000, 4000, 5000 and 6000) is generally governed by the base on which the tax is levied: 1000 income, profits and capital gains; 2000 and 3000 earnings, payroll or number of employees; 4000 property; 5000 goods and services; 6000 multiple bases, other bases or unidentifiable bases. Where a

tax is calculated on more than one base, the receipts are, where possible, split among the various headings (see §32 and §81). The headings 4000 and 5000 cover not only taxes where the tax base is the property, goods or services themselves but also certain related taxes. Thus, taxes on the transfer of property are included in 4400[11] and taxes on the use of goods or on permission to perform activities in 5200. In headings 4000 and 5000 a distinction is made in certain sub-headings between recurrent and non-recurrent taxes: recurrent taxes are defined as those levied at regular intervals (usually annually) and non-recurrent taxes are levied once and for all (see also §47 to §50, §53, §54 and §79 for particular applications of this distinction).

28. Earmarking of a tax for specific purposes does not affect the classification of tax receipts. However, as explained in §39 on the classification of social security contributions, the conferment of an entitlement to social benefits is crucial to the definition of the 2000 main heading.

29. The way that a tax is levied or collected (e.g., by use of stamps) does not affect classification.

Classification of taxpayers

30. In certain sub-headings distinctions are made between different categories of taxpayers. These distinctions vary from tax to tax:

a. *Between individuals and corporations in relation to income and net wealth taxes*

The basic distinction is that corporation income taxes, as distinct from individual income taxes, are levied on the corporation as an entity, not on the individuals who own it, and without regard to the personal circumstances of these individuals. The same distinction applies to net wealth taxes on corporations and those on individuals. Taxes paid on the profits of partnerships and the income of institutions, such as life insurance or pension funds, are classified according to the same rule. They are classified as corporate taxes (1200) if they are charged on the partnership or institution as an entity without regard to the personal circumstances of the owners. Otherwise, they are treated as individual taxes (1100). Usually, there is different legislation for the corporation taxes and for the individual taxes.[12] The distinction made here between individuals and corporations does not follow the sector classification between households, enterprises, and so on of the System of National Accounts for income and outlay accounts. The SNA classification requires certain unincorporated businesses[13] to be excluded from the household sector and included with non-financial enterprises and financial institutions. The tax on the profits of these businesses, however, cannot always be separated from the tax on the other income of their owners, or can be separated only on an arbitrary basis. No attempt at this separation is made here and the whole of the individual income tax is shown together without regard to the nature of the income chargeable.

b. *Between households and others in relation to taxes on immovable property*

Here the distinction is that adopted by the SNA for the production and consumption expenditure accounts. The distinction is between households as consumers (i.e. excluding non-incorporated business) on the one hand and producers on the other hand. However, taxes on dwellings occupied by households, whether paid by owner-occupiers, tenants or landlords, are classified under households. This follows the common distinction made between taxes on domestic property versus taxes on business property. Some countries are not, however, in a position to make this distinction.

c. *Between households and others in relation to motor vehicle licences*

Here the distinction is between households as consumers on the one hand and producers on the other, as in the production and consumption expenditure accounts of the SNA.

d. *Between business and others in relation to the residual taxes (6000)*

The distinction is the same as in c) above between producers on the one hand and households as consumers on the other hand. Taxes which are included under the heading 6000 because they involve more than one tax base or because the tax base does not fall within any of the previous categories but which are identifiable as levyable only on producers and not on households are included under 'business'. The rest of the taxes which are included under the heading 6000 are shown as 'other' or non-identified.

Surcharges

31. Receipts from surcharges in respect of particular taxes are usually classified with the receipts from the relevant tax whether or not the surcharge is temporary. If, however, the surcharge has a characteristic which would render it classifiable in a different heading of the OECD list, receipts from the surcharge are classified under that heading separately from the relevant tax.

Unidentifiable tax receipts and residual sub-headings

32. A number of cases arise where taxes cannot be identified as belonging entirely to a heading or sub-heading of the OECD classification and the following practices are applied in such cases:

a. The heading is known, but it is not known how receipts should be allocated between sub-headings: receipts are classified in the appropriate residual sub-heading (1300, 2400, 4520, 4600, 5130, 5300 or 6200).

b. It is known that the bulk of receipts from a group of taxes (usually local taxes) is derived from taxes within a particular heading or sub-heading, but some of the taxes in the group whose amount cannot be precisely ascertained may be classifiable in other headings or sub-headings: receipts are shown in the heading or sub-heading under which most of the receipts fall.

c. Either the heading nor sub-heading of a tax (usually local) can be identified: the tax is classified in 6200 unless it is known that it is a tax on business in which case it is classified in 6100.

A.5. Commentaries on items of the list

1000 — Taxes on income, profits and capital gains

33. This heading covers taxes levied on the net income or profits (i.e. gross income minus allowable tax reliefs) of individuals and enterprises. Also covered are taxes levied on the capital gains of individuals and enterprises, and gains from gambling.

34. Included in the heading are:

a. taxes levied predominantly on income or profits, though partially on other bases. Taxes on various bases which are not predominantly income or profits are classified according to the principles laid down in §32 and §81;

b. taxes on property, which are levied on a presumed or estimated income as part of an income tax (see also §47(a), (c) and (d));

c. compulsory payments to social security fund contributions that are levied on income but do not confer an entitlement to social benefits. When such contributions do confer an entitlement to social benefits, they are included in heading 2000 (see §39);

d. receipts from integrated scheduler income tax systems are classified as a whole in this heading, even though certain of the scheduler taxes may be based upon gross income and may not take into account the personal circumstances of the taxpayer.

35. The main subdivision of this heading is between levies on individuals (1100) and those on corporate enterprises (1200). Under each subdivision a distinction is made between taxes on income and profits (1110 and 1210), and taxes on capital gains (1120 and 1220). If certain receipts cannot be identified as appropriate to either 1100 or 1200, or if in practice this distinction cannot be made (e.g., because there are no reliable data on the recipients of payments from which withholding taxes are deducted) they are classified in 1300 as not-allocable.

Treatment of credits under imputation systems

36. Under imputation systems of corporate income tax, a company's shareholders are wholly or partly relieved of their liability to income tax on dividends paid by the company out of income or profits liable to corporate income tax. In countries with such systems,[14] part of the tax on the company's profits is available to provide relief against the shareholders' own tax liability. The relief to the shareholder takes the form of a tax credit, the amount of which may be less than, equal to, or more than the shareholder's overall tax liability. If the tax credit exceeds this tax liability the excess may be payable to the shareholder. As this type of tax credit is an integral part of the imputation system of corporate income tax, any payment to the shareholders is treated as a repayment of tax and not as expenditure (compare the treatment of other tax credits described in §25).

37. As the tax credit under imputation systems (even when exceeding tax liability) is to be regarded as a tax provision, the question arises whether it should be deducted from individual income tax receipts (1110) or corporate income tax receipts (1210). In this Report, the full amount of corporate income tax paid is shown under 1210 and no imputed tax is included under 1110. Thus, the full amount of the credit reduces the amount of 1110 whether the credit results in a reduction of personal income tax liability or whether an actual refund is made because the credit exceeds the income tax liability. (Where, however, such tax credits are deducted from corporation tax in respect of dividends paid to corporations the amounts are deducted from the receipts of 1210).

1120 and 1220 — Taxes on capital gains

38. These sub-headings comprise taxes imposed on capital gains, 1120 covering those levied on the gains of individuals and 1220 those levied on the gains of corporate enterprises, where receipts from such taxes can be separately identified. In many countries this is not the case and the receipts from such taxes are then classified with those from the income tax. Heading 1120 also includes taxes on gains from gambling.

2000 — Social security contributions

39. Classified here are all compulsory payments that confer an entitlement to receive a (contingent) future social benefit. Such payments are usually earmarked to finance social benefits and are often paid to institutions of general government that provide such benefits. However, such earmarking is not part of the definition of social security contributions

and is not required for a tax to be classified here. However, conferment of an entitlement is required for a tax to be classified under this heading. So, levies on income or payroll that are earmarked for social security funds but do not confer an entitlement to benefit are excluded from this heading and shown under personal income taxes (1100) or taxes on payroll and workforce (3000). Taxes on other bases, such as goods and services, which are earmarked for social security benefits are not shown here but are classified according to their respective bases because they generally confer no entitlement to social security benefits.

40. Contributions for the following types of social security benefits would, *inter alia*, be included: unemployment insurance benefits and supplements, accident, injury and sickness benefits, old-age, disability and survivors' pensions, family allowances, reimbursements for medical and hospital expenses or provision of hospital or medical services. Contributions may be levied on both employees and employers.

41. Contributions may be based on earnings or payroll ('on a payroll basis') or on net income after deductions and exemptions for personal circumstances ('on an income tax basis'), and the revenues from the two bases should be separately identified if possible. However, where contributions to a general social security scheme are on a payroll basis, but the contributions of particular groups (such as the self-employed) cannot be assessed on this basis and net income is used as a proxy for gross earnings, the receipts may still be classified as being on a payroll basis. In principle, this heading excludes voluntary contributions paid to social security schemes. When separately identifiable these are shown in the memorandum item on the financing of social security benefits. In practice, however, they cannot always be separately identified from compulsory contributions, in which case they are included in this heading.

42. Contributions to social insurance schemes which are not institutions of general government and to other types of insurance schemes, provident funds, pension funds, friendly societies or other saving schemes are not considered as social security contributions. Provident funds are arrangements under which the contributions of each employee and of the corresponding employer on his/her behalf are kept in a separate account earning interest and withdrawable under specific circumstances. Pension funds are separately organised schemes negotiated between employees and employers and carry provisions for different contributions and benefits, sometimes more directly tied to salary levels and length of service than under social security schemes. When contributions to these schemes are compulsory or quasi-compulsory (e.g., by virtue of agreement with professional and union organisations) they are shown in the memorandum item (refer to Chapter 4.2 of the Report).

43. Contributions by government employees and by governments in respect of their employees, to social security schemes classified within general government are included in this heading. Contributions to separate schemes for government employees, which can be regarded as replacing general social security schemes, are also regarded as taxes.[15] Where, however, a separate scheme is not seen as replacing a general scheme and has been negotiated between the government, in its role as an employer, and its employees, it is not regarded as social security and contributions to it are not regarded as taxes, even though the scheme may have been established by legislation.

44. This heading excludes 'imputed' contributions, which correspond to social benefits paid directly by employers to their employees or former employees or to their representatives (e.g., when employers are legally obliged to pay sickness benefits for a certain period).

45. Contributions are divided into those of employees (2100), employers (2200), and self-employed or non-employed (2300), and then further sub-divided according to the basis on which they are levied. Employees are defined for this purpose as all persons engaged in activities of business units, government bodies, private non-profit institutions, or other paid employment, except the proprietors and their unpaid family members in the case of unincorporated businesses. Members of the armed forces are included, irrespective of the duration and type of their service, if they contribute to social security schemes. The contributions of employers are defined as their payments on account of their employees to social security schemes. Where employees or employers are required to continue the payment of social security contributions when the employee becomes unemployed these contributions, data permitting, are shown in 2100 and 2200 respectively. Accordingly, the sub-heading 2300 is confined to contributions paid by the self-employed and by those outside of the labour force (e.g., disabled or retired individuals).

3000 — Taxes on payroll and workforce

46. These consist of taxes payable by enterprises assessed either as a proportion of the wages or salaries paid or as a fixed amount per person employed. They do not include compulsory social security contributions paid by employers or any taxes paid by employees themselves out of their wages or salaries

4000 — Taxes on property

47. This heading covers recurrent and non-recurrent taxes on the use, ownership or transfer of property. These include taxes on immovable property or net wealth, taxes on the change of ownership of property through inheritance or gift and taxes on financial and capital transactions. The following kinds of tax are excluded from this heading:

a. taxes on capital gains resulting from the sale of a property (1120 or 1220);

b. taxes on the use of goods or on permission to use goods or perform activities (5200); see §76;

c. taxes on immovable property levied on the basis of a presumed net income which take into account the personal circumstances of the taxpayer. They are classified as income taxes along with taxes on income and capital gains derived from property (1100);

d. taxes on the use of property for residence, where the tax is payable by either proprietor or tenant and the amount payable is a function of the user's personal circumstances (pay, dependants, and so on). They are classified as taxes on income (1100);

e. taxes on building in excess of permitted maximum density, taxes on the enlargement, construction or alteration of certain buildings beyond a permitted value and taxes on building construction. They are classified as taxes on permission to perform activities (5200);

f. taxes on the use of one's own property for special trading purposes like selling alcohol, tobacco, meat or for exploitation of land resources (e.g., United States severance taxes). They are classified as taxes on permission to perform activities (5200).

4100 — *Recurrent taxes on immovable property*

48. This sub-heading covers taxes levied regularly in respect of the use or ownership of immovable property.

- these taxes are levied on land and buildings;
- they can be in the form of a percentage of an assessed property value based on a national rental income, sales price, or capitalised yield; or in terms of other characteristics of real property, (for example size or location) from which a presumed rent or capital value can be derived.
- such taxes can be levied on proprietors, tenants, or both. They can also be paid by one level of government to another level of government in respect of property under the jurisdiction of the latter.
- debts are not taken into account in the assessment of these taxes, and they differ from taxes on net wealth in this respect.

49. Taxes on immovable property are further sub-divided into those paid by households (4110) and those paid by other entities (4120), according to the criteria set out in §30(*b*) above.

4200 — *Recurrent taxes on net wealth*

50. This sub-heading covers taxes levied regularly (in most cases annually) on net wealth, i.e. taxes on a wide range of movable and immovable property, net of debt. It is sub-divided into taxes paid by individuals (4210) and taxes paid by corporate enterprises (4220) according to the criteria set out in §30(*a*) above. If separate figures exist for receipts paid by institutions, the tax payments involved are added to those paid by corporations.

4300 — *Estate, inheritance and gift taxes*

51. This sub-heading is divided into taxes on estates and inheritances (4310) and taxes on gifts (4320).[16] Estate taxes are charged on the amount of the total estate whereas inheritance taxes are charged on the shares of the individual recipients; in addition the latter may take into account the relationship of the individual recipients to the deceased.

4400 — *Taxes on financial and capital transactions*

52. This sub-heading comprises, *inter alia*, taxes on the issue, transfer, purchase and sale of securities, taxes on cheques, and taxes levied on specific legal transactions such as validation of contracts and the sale of immovable property. The heading does not include:

a. taxes on the use of goods or property or permission to perform certain activities (5200);
b. fees paid to cover court charges, charges for birth, marriage or death certificates, which are normally regarded as non-tax revenues (see §11);
c. taxes on capital gains (1000);
d. recurrent taxes on immovable property (4100);
e. recurrent taxes on net wealth (4200);
f. once-and-for-all levies on property or wealth (4500).

4500 — *Other non-recurrent taxes on property*[16]

53. This sub-heading covers once-and-for-all, as distinct from recurrent, levies on property. It is divided into taxes on net wealth (4510) and other non-recurrent taxes on property (4520). Heading 4510 would include taxes levied to meet emergency expenditures, or for

redistribution purposes. Heading 4520 would cover taxes levied to take account of increases in land value due to permission given to develop or provision of additional local facilities by general government, any taxes on the revaluation of capital and once-and-for-all taxes on particular items of property.

4600 — Other recurrent taxes on property

54. These rarely exist in OECD member countries, but the heading would include taxes on goods such as cattle, jewellery, windows, and other external signs of wealth.

5000 — Taxes on goods and services

55. All taxes and duties levied on the production, extraction, sale, transfer, leasing or delivery of goods, and the rendering of services (5100), or in respect of the use of goods or permission to use goods or to perform activities (5200) are included here. The heading thus covers:

a. multi-stage cumulative taxes;

b. general sales taxes — whether levied at manufacture/production, wholesale or retail level;

c. value-added taxes;

d. excises;

e. taxes levied on the import and export of goods;

f. taxes levied in respect of the use of goods and taxes on permission to use goods, or perform certain activities;

g. taxes on the extraction, processing or production of minerals and other products.

56. Borderline cases between this heading and heading 4000 (taxes on property) and 6100 (other taxes on business) are referred to in §47, §52 and §78. Residual sub-headings (5300) and (5130) cover tax receipts which cannot be allocated between 5100 and 5200 and between 5110 and 5120, respectively; see §32.

5100 — Taxes on the production, sale, transfer, leasing and delivery of goods and rendering of services

57. This sub-heading consists of all taxes, levied on transactions in goods and services on the basis of their intrinsic characteristics (e.g., value, weight of tobacco, strength of alcohol, and so on) as distinct from taxes imposed on the use of goods, or permission to use goods or perform activities, which fall under 5200.

5110 — General taxes on goods and services

58. This sub-heading includes all taxes, other than import and export duties (5123 and 5124), levied on the production, leasing, transfer, delivery or sales of a wide range of goods and/ or the rendering of a wide range of services, irrespective of whether they are domestically produced or imported and irrespective of the stage of production or distribution at which they are levied. It thus covers value-added taxes, sales taxes and multi-stage cumulative taxes. Receipts from border adjustments in respect of such taxes when goods are imported are added to gross receipts for this category, and repayments of such taxes when goods are exported are deducted. These taxes are subdivided into 5111 value-added taxes, 5112 sales taxes, 5113 turnover and other general taxes on goods and services.

59. Borderline cases arise between this heading and taxes on specific goods (5120) when taxes are levied on a large number of goods, for example, the United Kingdom purchase tax

(repealed in 1973) and the Japanese commodity tax (repealed in 1988). In conformity with national views, the former United Kingdom purchase tax is classified as a general tax (5112) and the former Japanese commodity tax as excises (5121).

5111 — *Value-added taxes*

60. All general consumption taxes charged on value-added are classified in this sub-heading, irrespective of the method of deduction and the stages at which the taxes are levied. In practice, all OECD countries with value-added taxes normally allow immediate deduction of taxes on purchases by all but the final consumer and impose tax at all stages. In some countries the heading may include certain taxes, such as those on financial and insurance activities, either because receipts from them cannot be identified separately from those from the value-added tax, or because they are regarded as an integral part of the value-added tax, even though similar taxes in other countries might be classified elsewhere (e.g., 5126 as taxes on services or 4400 as taxes on financial and capital transactions).

5112 — *Sales taxes*

61. All general taxes levied at one stage only, whether at manufacturing or production, wholesale or retail stage are classified here.

5113 — *Turnover and other general taxes on goods and services*

62. These are multi-stage cumulative taxes and taxes where elements of consumption taxes are combined with multistage taxes. These taxes are levied each time a transaction takes place without deduction for taxes paid on inputs. Multi-stage taxes can be combined with elements of value-added or sales taxes.

5120 — *Taxes on specific goods and services*

63. Excises, profits generated and transferred from fiscal monopolies, and customs and imports duties as well as taxes on exports, foreign exchange transactions, investment goods and betting stakes and special taxes on services, which do not form part of a general tax of 5110, are included in this category.

5121 — *Excises*

64. Excises are taxes levied as a product specific unit tax on a predefined limited range of goods. Excises are usually levied at differentiated rates on nonessential or luxury goods, alcoholic beverages, tobacco, and energy. Excises may be imposed at any stage of production or distribution and are usually assessed as a specific charge per unit based on characteristics by reference to the value, weight, strength, or quantity of the product. Included are special taxes on individual products such as sugar, sugar beets, matches, and chocolates; taxes levied at varying rates on a certain range of goods; and taxes levied on tobacco goods, alcoholic drinks, motor fuels, and hydrocarbon oils. If a tax collected principally on imported goods also applies, or would apply, under the same law to comparable domestically produced goods, then the revenue from this tax is classified as arising from excises rather than from import duties. This principle applies even if there is no comparable domestic production or no possibility of such production. Taxes on the use of utilities such as water, electricity, gas, and energy are regarded as excises rather than taxes on specific services (5126). Excises exclude those taxes that are levied as general taxes on goods and services (5110); profits of fiscal monopolies (5122); customs and other import duties (5123); or taxes on exports (5124).

5122 — *Profits of fiscal monopolies*

65. This sub-heading covers that part of the profits of fiscal monopolies which is transferred to general government or which is used to finance any expenditures considered to be government expenditures (see §23). Amounts are shown when they are transferred to general government or used to make expenditures considered to be government expenditures.

66. Fiscal monopolies reflect the exercise of the taxing power of government by the use of monopoly powers. Fiscal monopolies are non-financial public enterprises exercising a monopoly in most cases over the production or distribution of tobacco, alcoholic beverages, salt, matches, playing cards and petroleum or agricultural products (i.e. on the kind of products which are likely to be, alternatively or additionally, subject to the excises of 5121), to raise the government revenues which in other countries are gathered through taxes on dealings in such commodities by private business units. The government monopoly may be at the production stage or, as in the case of government-owned and controlled liquor stores, at the distribution stage.

67. Fiscal monopolies are distinguished from public utilities such as rail transport, electricity, post offices, and other communications, which may enjoy a monopoly or quasi-monopoly position but where the primary purpose is normally to provide basic services rather than to raise revenue for government. Transfers from such other public enterprises to the government are considered as non-tax revenues. The traditional concept of fiscal monopoly is not generally extended to include state lotteries, the profits of which are usually accordingly regarded as non-tax revenues. However, they can be included as tax revenues if the prime reason for their operation is to raise revenues to finance government expenditure. Fiscal monopoly profits are distinguished from export and import monopoly profits (5127) transferred from marketing boards or other enterprises dealing with international trade.

5123 — *Customs and other import duties*

68. Taxes, stamp duties and surcharges restricted by law to imported products are included here. Also included are levies on imported agricultural products which are imposed in member countries of the European Union and amounts paid by certain of these countries under the Monetary Compensation Accounts (MCA) system.[17] Starting from 1998, customs duties collected by European Union member states on behalf of the European Union are no longer reported under this heading in the country tables (in Chapter 4 of the Report). Excluded here are taxes collected on imports as part of a general tax on goods and services, or an excise applicable to both imported and domestically produced goods.

5124 — *Taxes on exports*

69. In the 1970s, export duties were levied in Australia, Canada and Portugal as a regular measure and they have been used in Finland for counter-cyclical purposes. Some member countries of the European Union pay, as part of the MCA system, a levy on exports (see note 16 to §68). Where these amounts are identifiable, they are shown in this heading. This heading does not include repayments of general consumption taxes or excises or customs duties on exported goods, which should be deducted from the gross receipts under 5110, 5121 or 5123, as appropriate.

5125 — *Taxes on investment goods*

70. This sub-heading covers taxes on investment goods, such as machinery. These taxes may be imposed for a number of years or temporarily for counter-cyclical purposes. Taxes

on industrial inputs which are also levied on consumers [e.g., the Swedish energy tax which is classified under (5121)] are not included here.

5126 — *Taxes on specific services*

71. All taxes assessed on the payment for specific services, such as taxes on insurance premiums, banking services, gambling and betting stakes (e.g., from horse races, football pools, lottery tickets), transport, entertainment, restaurant and advertising charges, fall into this category. Taxes levied on the gross income of companies providing the service (e.g., gross insurance premiums or gambling stakes received by the company) are also classified under this heading. Tax revenues from bank levies and payments to deposit insurance and financial stability schemes are provisionally included here for the 2012 edition. The detailed classification is set out in §108.

72. Excluded from this sub-heading are:

a. taxes on services forming part of a general tax on goods and services (5110);

b. taxes on electricity, gas and energy (5121 as excises);

c. taxes on individual gains from gambling (1120 as taxes on capital gains of individuals and non-corporate enterprises) and lump-sum taxes on the transfer of private lotteries or on the permission to set up lotteries (5200);[18]

d. taxes on cheques and on the issue, transfer or redemption of securities (4400 as taxes on financial and capital transactions).

5127 — *Other taxes on international trade and transactions*

73. This sub-heading covers revenue received by the government from the purchase and sale of foreign exchange at different rates. When the government exercises monopoly powers to extract a margin between the purchase and sales price of foreign exchange, other than to cover administrative costs, the revenue derived constitutes a compulsory levy exacted in indeterminate proportions from both purchaser and seller of foreign exchange. It is the common equivalent of an import duty and export duty levied in a single exchange rate system or of a tax on the sale or purchase of foreign exchange. Like the profits of fiscal monopolies and import or export monopolies transferred to government, it represents the exercise of monopoly powers for tax purposes and is included in tax revenues.

74. The sub-heading covers also the profits of export or import monopolies, which do not however exist in OECD countries, taxes on purchase or sale of foreign exchange, and any other taxes levied specifically on international trade or transactions.

5128 — *Other taxes on specific goods and services*

75. This item includes taxes on the extraction of minerals, fossil fuels and other exhaustible resources from deposits owned privately or by another government together with any other unidentifiable receipts from taxes on specific goods and services. Taxes on the extraction of exhaustible resources are usually a fixed amount per unit of quality or weight, but can be a percentage of value. The taxes are recorded when the resources are extracted. Payments from the extraction of exhaustible resources from deposits owned by the government unit receiving the payment are classified as rent.

5200 — *Taxes on use of goods or on permission to use goods or perform activities*

76. This sub-heading covers taxes which are levied in respect of the use of goods as distinct from taxes on the goods themselves. Unlike the latter taxes – reported under 5100 –, they are

not assessed on the value of the goods but usually as fixed amounts. Taxes on permission to use goods or to perform activities are also included here, as are pollution taxes not based upon the value of particular goods. It is sometimes difficult to distinguish between compulsory user charges and licence fees which are regarded as taxes and those which are excluded as non-tax revenues. The criteria which are employed are noted in §11–12.

77. Although the sub-heading refers to the 'use' of goods, registration of ownership rather than use may be what generates liability to tax, so that the taxes of this heading may apply to the ownership of animals or goods rather than their use (e.g., race horses, dogs and motor vehicles) and may apply even to unusable goods (e.g., unusable motor vehicles or guns).

78. Borderline cases arise with:

a. taxes on the permission to perform business activities which are levied on a combined income, payroll or turnover base and, accordingly, are classified following the rules in §81;

b. taxes on the ownership or use of property of headings 4100, 4200 and 4600. The heading 4100 is confined to taxes on the ownership or tenancy of immovable property and – unlike the taxes of 5200 – they are related to the value of the property. The net wealth taxes and taxes on chattels of 4200 and 4600 respectively are confined to the ownership rather than the use of assets, apply to groups of assets rather than particular goods and again are related to the value of the assets,

5210 — *Recurrent taxes on use of goods and on permission to use goods or perform activities*

79. The principal characteristic of taxes classified here is that they are levied at regular intervals and that they are usually fixed amounts. The most important item in terms of revenue receipts is vehicle licence taxes. This sub-heading also covers taxes on permission to hunt, shoot, fish or to sell certain products and taxes on the ownership of dogs and on the performance of certain services, provided that they meet the criteria set out in §11–12. The sub-divisions of 5210 are user taxes on motor vehicles paid by households (5211) and those paid by others (5212). Sub-heading 5213 covers dog licences and user charges for permission to perform activities such as selling meat or liquor when the levies are on a recurring basis. It also covers recurrent general licences for hunting, shooting and fishing where the right to carry out these activities is not granted as part of a normal commercial transaction (e.g., the granting of the licence is not accompanied by the right to use a specific area which is owned by government).

5220 — *Non-recurrent taxes on use of goods and on permission to use goods or perform activities*

80. This section covers non-recurrent taxes levied on the use of goods or on permission to use goods or perform activities and taxes levied each time goods are used. It includes taxes levied on the emission or discharge into the environment of noxious gases, liquids or other harmful substances.

- Payments for tradable emission permits issued by governments under cap and trade schemes should be recorded here at the time the emissions occur. No revenue should be recorded for permits that governments issue free of charge. The accrual basis of recording means that there can be a timing difference between the cash being received by government for the permits and the time the emission occurs. In the national accounts, this timing gives rise to a financial liability for government during the period.

- Payments made for the collection and disposal of waste or noxious substances by public authorities should be excluded as they constitute a sale of services to enterprises.

81. Other taxes falling under heading 5200 that are not levied recurrently are also included here. Thus, once-and-for-all payments for permission to sell liquor or tobacco or to set up betting shops are included provided they meet the criteria set out in §11–12.

6000 — Other taxes

82. Taxes levied on a base, or bases, other than those described under headings 1000, 3000, 4000 and 5000, or on bases of which cannot be considered to be related to any one of these headings, are included here. Where taxes are levied on a multiple base and it is possible to estimate the receipts related to each base the separate amounts are included under the appropriate headings. If separate amounts cannot be estimated and it is known that most of the receipts are derived from one base, the whole of the receipts are classified according to that base. Otherwise, they are classified here. Other revenues included here are presumptive taxes not included elsewhere in the classification system, taxes on individuals in the form of a poll tax or capitation tax, stamp taxes not related to financial and capital transactions nor falling exclusively on a single category of transaction, expenditure taxes where personal deductions or exemptions are applied and unidentifiable tax receipts. A subdivision is made between taxes levied wholly or predominantly on business (6100) and those levied on others (6200).

A.6. Conciliation with National Accounts

83. This section of the tables provides a re-conciliation between the OECD calculation of total tax revenues and the total of all taxes and social contributions paid to general government as recorded in the country's National Accounts. Where the country is a member of the European Union (EU), the comparison is between the OECD calculation of total tax revenues and the sum of tax revenues and social contributions recorded in the combination of the general government and the institutions of the EU sectors of the National Accounts.

A.7. Memorandum item on the financing of social security benefits

84. In view of the varying relationship between taxation and social security contributions and the cases referred to in §39 to §45, a memorandum item collects together all payments earmarked for social security-type benefits, other than voluntary payments to the private sector. Data are presented as follows (refer to Chapter 4.2 of the Report):

a. Taxes of 2000 series.

b. Taxes earmarked for social security benefits.

c. Voluntary contributions to the government.

d. Compulsory contributions to the private sector.

Guidance on the breakdown of (a) to (d) above is provided in §39 to §45.

A.8. Memorandum item on identifiable taxes paid by government

85. Identifiable taxes actually paid by government are presented in a memorandum item classified by the main headings of the OECD classification of taxes. In the vast majority of countries, only social security contributions and payroll taxes paid by government can

be identified. These are, however, usually the most important taxes paid by governments (refer to Chapter 4.2 of the Report).

A.9. Relation of OECD classification of taxes to national accounting systems

86. A system of national accounts (SNA) seeks to provide a coherent framework for recording and presenting the main flows relating respectively to production, consumption, accumulation and external transactions of a given economic area, usually a country or a major region within a country. Government revenues are an important part of the transactions recorded in SNA. The final version of the 2008 SNA was jointly published by five international organisations: the United Nations, the International Monetary Fund, the European Union, the Organisation for Economic Co-operation and Development, and the World Bank in August 2009. The *System* is a comprehensive, consistent and flexible set of macroeconomic accounts. It is designed for use in countries with market economies, whatever their stage of economic development, and also in countries in transition to market economies. The important parts of the SNA's conceptual framework and its definitions of the various sectors of the economy have been reflected in the OECD's classification of taxes.

87. There are, however, some differences between the OECD classification of taxes and SNA concepts that are listed below. They arise because the aim of the former is to provide the maximum disaggregation of statistical data on what are generally regarded as taxes by tax administrations.

a. OECD includes compulsory social security contributions paid to general government in total tax revenues. Imputed and voluntary contributions plus those paid to private funds are not treated as taxes (§8 and §10 above);

b. there are different points of view on whether or not some levies and fees are classified as taxes (§11 and §12 above);

c. OECD excludes imputed taxes or subsidies resulting from the operation of official multiple exchange rates or from the central bank paying a rate of interest on required reserves that is different from other market rates;

d. there are differences in the treatment of non-wastable tax credits

88. As noted in §1 and §2, headings 1000 to 6000 of the OECD list of taxes cover all unrequited payments to general government, other than compulsory loans and fines. Such unrequited payments including fines, but excluding compulsory loans can be obtained from adding together the following figures in the 2008 SNA

- value-added type taxes (D.211);
- taxes and duties on imports, excluding VAT (D.212);
- export taxes (D.213);
- taxes on products, excluding VAT, import and export taxes (D.214);
- other taxes on production (D.29);
- taxes on income (D.51);
- other current taxes (D.59);
- social contributions (D.61), excluding voluntary contributions;
- capital taxes (D.91).

A.10. The OECD classification of taxes and the International Monetary Fund (GFS) system

89. The coverage and valuation of tax revenues in the GFS system and the 2008 SNA are very similar. Therefore, the differences between the OECD classification and that of the 2008 SNA (see §87 above) also apply to the GFS. In addition the International Monetary Fund subdivides the OECD 5000 heading into section IV (Domestic Taxes on Goods and Services) and section V (Taxes on International Trade and Transactions). This reflects the fact that while the latter usually yield insignificant amounts of revenue in OECD countries, this is not the case in many non-OECD countries.

A.11. Comparison of the OECD classification of taxes with other international classifications

90. The table below describes an item by item comparison of the OECD classification of taxes and the classifications used in the following:

a. System of National Accounts (2008 SNA);

b. European System of Accounts (2010 ESA);

c. IMF *Government Finance Statistics Manual* (GFSM2014).

91. These comparisons represent those that would be expected to apply in the majority of cases. However in practice some flexibility should be used in their application. This is because in particular cases, countries can adopt varying approaches to the classification of revenues in National Accounts.

OECD Classification	2008 SNA	2010 ESA	GFSM2014
1000 Taxes on income, profits and capital gains			
1100 Individuals			
1110 Income and profits	D51-8.61a	D51A	1111
1120 Capital gains	D51-8.61c, d	D51C, D	1111
1200 Corporations			
1210 Income and profits	D51-8.61b	D51B	1112
1220 Capital gains	D51-8.61c	D51C	1112
1300 Unallocable as between 1100 and 1200			1113
2000 Social security contributions			
2100 Employees	D613-8.85	D613	1211
2200 Employers	D611-8.83	D611	1212
2300 Self-employed, non-employed	D613-8.85	D613	1213
2400 Unallocable as between 2100, 2200 and 2300			1214
3000 Taxes on payroll and workforce	D29-7.97a	D29C	112
4000 Taxes on property			
4100 Recurrent taxes on immovable property			
4110 Households	D59-8.63a	D59A	1131
4120 Other	D29-7.97b	D29A	1131
4200 Recurrent net wealth taxes			
4210 Individual	D59-8.63b	D59A	1132
4220 Corporations	D59-8.63b	D59A	1132
4300 Estate, inheritance and gift taxes			
4310 Estate and inheritance taxes	D91-10.207b	D91A	1133
4320 Gift taxes	D91-10.207b	D91A	1133
4400 Taxes on financial and capital transactions	D59-7.96d; D29-7.97e	D214B, C	114114; 1161
4500 Other non-recurrent taxes on property	D91-10.207a	D91B	1135
4600 Other recurrent taxes on property	D59-8.63c	D59A	1136

OECD Classification	2008 SNA	2010 ESA	GFSM2014
5000 Taxes on goods and services			
5100 Taxes on production, sale and transfer of goods and services			
5110 General taxes on goods and services			
5111 Value-added taxes	D211-7.89	D211; D29G	11411
5112 Sales taxes	D2122-7.94a; D214-7.96a	D21224; D214I	11412
5113 Other general taxes on goods and services	D214-7.96a	D214I	11413
5120 Taxes on specific goods and services			
5121 Excises	D2122-7.94b; D214-7.96b	D21223; D214A, B, D	1142
5122 Profits of fiscal monopolies	D214-7.96e	D214J	1143
5123 Customs and other import duties	D2121-7.93	D2121; D21221, 2	1151
5124 On exports	D213-7.95a	D214K	1152-4
5125 On investment goods			
5126 On specific services	D2122-7.94c; D214-7.96c	D21225; D214E, F, G, H; D29F	1144; 1156
5127 Other taxes on international trade and transactions	D2122-7.94d D29-7.95b D29-7.97g D59-8.64d	D21226; D29D; D59E	1153; 1155-6
5128 Other taxes on specific goods and services			1146
5130 Unallocable between 5110 and 5120			
5200 Taxes on use of goods and on permission to use goods or perform activities			
5210 Recurrent taxes on use of goods and on permission to use goods or perform activities			
5211 Motor vehicle taxes households	D59-8.64c	D59D	11451
5212 Motor vehicles taxes others	D29-7.97d	D214D; D29B	11451
5213 Other recurrent taxes on use of goods and on permission to use goods or perform activities	D29-7.97c, d, f D59-8.64c	D29B, E, F; D59D	11452
5220 Non-recurrent taxes on permission to use goods or perform activities			11452
5300 Unallocable as between 5100 and 5200			
6000 Other taxes			
6100 Payable solely by business			1161
6200 Payable by other than business, or unidentifiable	D59-8.64a, b	D59B, C	1162

A.12. Attribution of tax revenues by sub-sectors of general government

92. The OECD classification requires a breakdown of tax revenues by sub-sectors of government. The definition of each sub-sector and the criteria to be used to attribute tax revenues between these sub-sectors are set out below. They follow the guidance of the 2008 SNA and GFSM 2014.

Sub-sectors of general government to be identified

a) Central government

93. The central government sub-sector includes all governmental departments, offices, establishments and other bodies which are agencies or instruments of the central authority whose competence extends over the whole territory, with the exception of the administration of social security funds. Central government therefore has the authority to impose taxes on all resident and non-resident units engaged in economic activities within the country.

b) State, provincial or regional government

94. This sub-sector consists of intermediate units of government exercising a competence at a level below that of central government. It includes all such units operating independently of central government in a part of a country's territory encompassing a number of smaller

localities, with the exception of the administration of social security funds. In unitary countries, regional governments may be considered to have a separate existence where they have substantial autonomy to raise a significant proportion of their revenues from sources within their control and their officers are independent of external administrative control in the actual operation of the unit's activities.

95. At present, federal countries comprise the majority of cases where revenues attributed to intermediate units of government are identified separately. Spain is the only unitary country in this position. In the remaining unitary countries, regional revenues are included with those of local governments.

c) Local government

96. This sub-sector includes all other units of government exercising an independent competence in part of the territory of a country, with the exception of the administration of social security funds. It encompasses various urban and/or rural jurisdictions (e.g., local authorities, municipalities, cities, boroughs, districts).

d) Social security funds

97. Social security funds form a separate sub-sector of general government. The social security sub-sector is defined in the 2008 SNA by the following extracts from paragraphs 4.124 to 4.126 and 4.147:

> *"Social security schemes are social insurance schemes covering the community as a whole or large section of the community that are imposed and controlled by government units. The schemes cover a wide variety of programmes, providing benefits in cash or in kind for old age, invalidity or death, survivors, sickness and maternity, work injury, unemployment, family allowance, health care, etc. There is not necessarily a direct link between the amount of the contribution paid by an individual and the benefits he or she may receive." (Paragraph 4.124).*

> *"When social security schemes are separately organised from the other activities of government units and hold their assets and liabilities separately from the latter and engage in financial transactions on their own account they qualify as institutional units that are described as social security funds." (Paragraph 4.125).*

> *"The amounts raised, and paid out, in social security contributions and benefits may be deliberately varied in order to achieve objectives of government policy that have no direct connection with the concept of social security as a scheme to provide social benefits to members of the community. They may be raised or lowered in order to influence the level of aggregate demand in the economy, for example. Nevertheless, so long as they remain separately constituted funds, they must be treated as separate institutional units in the SNA. (Paragraph 4.126).*

> *"The social security funds sub-sector (of general government) consists of the social security funds operating at all levels of government. Such funds are social insurance schemes covering the community as a whole or large section of the community that are imposed by government units." (Paragraph 4.147).*

98. This definition of social security funds is followed in the OECD classification with the two following exceptions which are excluded

- Schemes imposed by government and operated by bodies outside the general government sector, as defined in §3 of this manual; and
- Schemes to which all contributions are voluntary.

Supra-national Authorities

99. This sub-sector covers the revenue-raising operations of supra-national authorities within a country. In practice, the only relevant supra-national authority in the OECD area is that of the institutions of the European Union (EU). As from 1998, supra-national authorities are no longer included in the *Revenue Statistics*, to achieve consistency with the SNA definition of general government which excludes them. For example, income taxes and social security contributions collected by European Institutions and paid by European civil servants who are resident of EU member countries should not be included. However the specific levies paid by the member states of the EU continue to be included in total tax revenues and they are shown under this heading.

Criteria to be used for the attribution of tax revenues

100. When a government collects taxes and pays them over in whole or in part to other governments, it is necessary to determine whether the revenues should be considered to be those of the collecting government which it distributes to others as grants, or those of the beneficiary governments which the collecting government receives and passes on only as their agent. The criteria to be used in the attribution of revenues are set out in §101 to §104 which replicate paragraphs 3.70 to 3.73 from the 2008 SNA.

101. In general, a tax is attributed to the government unit that

a. exercises the authority to impose the tax (either as a principal or through the delegated authority of the principal),

b. has final discretion to set and vary the rate of the tax

102. Where an amount is collected by one government for and on behalf of another government, and the latter government has the authority to impose the tax, and set and vary its rate, then the former is acting as an agent for the latter and the tax is reassigned. Any amount retained by the collecting government as a collection charge should be treated as a payment for a service. Any other amount retained by the collecting government, such as under a tax-sharing arrangement, should be treated as a current grant. If the collecting government was delegated the authority to set and vary the rate, then the amount collected should be treated as tax revenue of this government.

103. Where different governments jointly and equally set the rate of a tax and jointly and equally decide on the distribution of the proceeds, with no individual government having ultimate overriding authority, then the tax revenues are attributed to each government according to its respective share of the proceeds. If an arrangement allows one government unit to exercise ultimate overriding authority, then all of the tax revenue is attributed to that unit.

104. There may also be the circumstance where a tax is imposed under the constitutional or other authority of one government, but other governments individually set the tax rate in their jurisdictions. The proceeds of the tax generated in each respective government's jurisdiction are attributed as tax revenues of that government.

Levies paid by member states of the European Union

105. The levies paid by the member states of the EU take the form specific levies which include

a. custom duties and levies on agricultural goods (5123),

b. gross monetary compensation accounts (5123 if relating to imports and 5124 if relating to exports); and

c. Steel, coal, sugar and milk levies (5128).

106. The custom duties collected by member states on behalf of the EU are recorded

- on a gross of collection fee basis;
- using figures adjusted so that duties are shown on a 'final destination' as opposed to a 'country of first entry' basis where such adjustments can be made. These adjustments concern in particular duties collected at important (sea) ports. Although the EU duties are collected by the authorities of the country of first entry, when possible these duties should be excluded from the revenue of the collecting country and be included in the revenue of the country of final destination

107. This is the specific EU levy that most clearly conforms to the attribution criterion described in §99 above. Consequently as from 1998, these amounts are footnoted as a memorandum item to EU member state country tables and no longer shown under heading 5123. However the figures are included in the total tax revenue figures on the top line for all the relevant years shown in the tables.

A.13. Provisional classification of revenues from bank levies and payments to deposit insurance and financial stability schemes

108. The OECD have adopted the following interim approach to reporting revenue from bank levies plus deposit insurance and stability fees for the 2012 and subsequent editions of *OECD Revenue Statistics*. It is recommended that the amounts should be recorded under category 5126.

- Compulsory payments of stability fees, bank levies and deposit insurance should generally be treated as tax revenues where the payments are made to General Government and allocated to the governments' consolidated or general funds so that the Government is free to make immediate use of the money for the purposes that it chooses. This principle would apply regardless of whether the Government is promising to make payments to guarantee the banks' customer deposits in some future contingency.
- If the compulsory payments are made to general government and placed in funds that are earmarked to be entirely channelled back to the sector of the economy that comprises the companies that are subject to the payment, they would still generally be treated as tax revenues on the grounds that the funds would be available for the government and would reduce its budget deficit, the fee is unrequited for an individual entity and the amounts raised could be unrelated to any eventual pay out to depositors or expenditure on wider support for the financial sector.
- Payments to made to the smaller long-standing schemes for insuring 'retail' deposits, where the payment levels are consistent with the costs of insurance should be classified as fee for service.
- Any payments which involve governments realising the assets of a failed institution or receiving a priority claim on its assets in liquidation in order to fund payments of compensation to customers for their lost deposits would be treated as a fee for a service as opposed to tax revenues.
- Compulsory payments that are made to funds operated outside the government sector and non-state institutions backed by the deposit takers and all payments to voluntary schemes should not be treated as tax revenues.

Notes

1. References in this OECD Interpretative Guide to Sections or Parts of "this Report" refer to OECD (2019), Revenue Statistics 2019, OECD Publishing, Paris
2. All references to SNA are to the 2008 edition.
3. See section A.12 of this guide for a discussion of the concept of agency capacity.
4. It is usually possible to identify amounts of social security contributions and payroll taxes, but not other taxes paid by government.
5. If, however, a levy which is considered as non-tax revenue by most countries is regarded as a tax — or raises substantial revenue — in one or more countries, the amounts collected are footnoted at the end of the relevant country tables, even though the amounts are not included in total tax revenues.
6. Names, however, can frequently be misleading. For example, though a passport fee would normally be considered a non-tax revenue, if a supplementary levy on passports (as is the case in Portugal) were imposed in order to raise substantial amounts of revenue relative to the cost of providing the passport, the levy would be regarded as a tax under 5200.
7. A more detailed explanation of this distinction can be found in the special feature, 'Current issues in reporting tax revenues', in the 2001 edition of the *Revenue Statistics*.
8. Sometimes the terms 'non-refundable' and 'refundable' are used, but it may be considered illogical to talk of 'refundable' when nothing has been paid.
9. A different treatment, however, is accorded to non-wastable tax credits under imputation systems of corporate income tax (§36–38).
10. This is not strictly a true tax expenditure in the formal sense. Such tax expenditures require identification of a benchmark tax system for each country or, preferably, a common international benchmark. In practice it has not been possible to reach agreement on a common international benchmark.
11. Unless based on the profit made on a sale, in which case they would be classified as capital gains taxes under 1120 or 1220.
12. In some countries the same legislation applies to both individual and corporate enterprises for particular taxes on income. However, the receipts from such taxes are usually allocable between individuals and enterprises and can therefore be shown in the appropriate sub-heading.
13. For example, "...sufficiently self-contained and independent that they behave in the same way as corporations.......(including) keeping a complete set of accounts" (2008 SNA, section 4.44).
14. In Canada — a country also referred to as having an imputation system — the (wastable) tax credit for the shareholder is in respect of domestic corporation tax deemed to have been paid whether or not a corporation tax liability has arisen. As there is no integral connection between the corporation tax liability and the credit given against income tax under such systems, these credits for dividends are treated, along with other tax credits, on the lines described in §25.
15. This may also apply where a scheme for government employees existed prior to the introduction of a general social security scheme.
16. In the 2008 SNA these are regarded as capital transfers and not as taxes (see section A.8).
17. This is the system by which the European Union adjusts for differences between the exchange rates used to determine prices under the Common Market Agricultural Policy and actual exchange rates. Payments under the system may relate to imports or exports and where these amounts are separately identifiable they are shown under the appropriate heading (5123 or 5124). In this Report, these amounts are shown gross (i.e. without deducting any subsidies paid out under the MCA system).
18. Transfers of profits of State lotteries are regarded as non-tax revenues (see also §67).

Revenue Statistics in Africa 1990-2018/Statistiques des recettes publiques en Afrique 1990-2018

ANNEXE A

Classification des impôts de l'OCDE et Guide d'interprétation[1]

Table des matières

A.1. Classification des impôts de l'OCDE

1. 1000 Impôts sur le revenu, les bénéfices et les gains en capital

    1100 Impôts sur le revenu, les bénéfices et les gains en capital des personnes physiques

        1110 Sur le revenu et les bénéfices

        1120 Sur les gains en capital

    1200 Impôts sur le revenu, les bénéfices et les gains en capital des sociétés

        1210 Sur le revenu et les bénéfices

        1220 Sur les gains en capital

    1300 Non ventilables entres les rubriques 110 et 1200

2. 2000 Cotisations de sécurité sociale

    2100 A la charge des salariés

        2110 Sur la base du salaire

        2120 Sur la base de l'impôt sur le revenu

    2200 A la charge des employeurs

        2210 Sur la base du salaire

        2220 Sur la base de l'impôt sur le revenu

    2300 A la charge des travailleurs indépendants ou des personnes n'occupant pas d'emploi

        2310 Sur la base du salaire

        2320 Sur la base de l'impôt sur le revenu

    2400 Non ventilables entre les rubriques 2100, 2200 et 2300

        2410 Sur la base du salaire

        2420 Sur la base de l'impôt sur le revenu

3. 3000 Impôts sur les salaires et la main-d'œuvre

4. 4000 Impôts sur le patrimoine

    4100 Impôts périodiques sur la propriété immobilière

        4110 Ménages

        4120 Autres agents

    4200 Impôts périodiques sur l'actif net

        4210 Personnes physiques

        4220 Sociétés

    4300 Impôts sur les mutations par décès, les successions et les donations

        4310 Impôts sur les mutations par décès et les successions

        4320 Impôts sur les donations

    4400 Impôts sur les transactions mobilières et immobilières

    4500 Autres impôts non périodiques sur le patrimoine

        4510 Impôts sur l'actif net

        4520 Autres impôts non périodiques

    4600 Autres impôts périodiques sur le patrimoine

5. 5000 Impôts sur les biens et services

5100 Impôts sur la production, la vente, le transfert, la location et la livraison des biens et la prestation de services

5110 Impôts généraux

5111 Taxes sur la valeur ajoutée

5112 Impôts sur les ventes

5113 Impôts sur le chiffre d'affaires et autres impôts généraux sur les biens et services

5120 Impôts sur des biens et des services déterminés

5121 Accises

5122 Bénéfices des monopoles fiscaux

5123 Droits de douane et autres droits à l'importation

5124 Taxes à l'exportation

5125 Impôts sur les biens d'équipement

5126 Impôts sur des services déterminés

5127 Autres impôts sur les transactions et les échanges internationaux

5128 Autres impôts sur des biens et services déterminés

5130 Non ventilables entre les rubriques 5110 et 5120

5200 Impôts sur l'utilisation des biens ou l'autorisation d'utiliser des biens ou d'exercer des activités

5210 Impôts périodiques

5211 A la charge des ménages au titre de véhicules à moteur

5212 A la charge d'autres agents au titre de véhicules à moteur

5213 Autres impôts périodiques

5220 Impôts non périodiques

5300 Non ventilables entre les rubriques 5100 et 5200

6. 6000 Autres impôts

6100 A la charge exclusive des entreprises

6200 A la charge d'autre agents que les entreprises ou non identifiables

A.2. Champ couvert

Principes généraux

1. Dans la classification de l'OCDE, le terme « impôts » désigne uniquement les versements obligatoires effectués sans contrepartie au profit des administrations publiques. Les impôts n'ont pas de contrepartie en ce sens que, normalement, les prestations fournies par les administrations au contribuable ne sont pas proportionnelles à ses versements.

2. Le terme « impôts » ne couvre pas les amendes, les pénalités, ni les prêts obligatoires aux administrations. Les cas dans lesquels la délimitation entre recettes fiscales et non fiscales est délicate à tracer, pour certains droits et taxes d'utilisation, sont examinés dans les § 11 à 14.

3. Les administrations publiques comprennent l'administration centrale et les organismes dont les opérations sont sous son contrôle effectif, les administrations régionales et locales et leurs services, les organismes de sécurité sociale et les entités publiques autonomes, à l'exception des entreprises publiques. Cette définition des administrations est calquée sur celle du Système de comptabilité nationale 2008 (SCN)[2]. Dans cette publication, les administrations publiques et leurs sous-secteurs sont décrits dans le chapitre 4, paragraphes 4.117 à 4.165.

4. Les unités extrabudgétaires sont des composantes du système des administrations publiques. Il s'agit d'entités d'administration publique dotées de budgets distincts, qui ne sont pas intégralement financés par le budget central ou général. Ces organismes fonctionnent sous l'autorité ou le contrôle d'une administration centrale, d'un État fédéré ou d'une collectivité locale. Les entités extrabudgétaires peuvent disposer de leurs propres sources de recettes, qui peuvent être complétées par des dotations (transferts) provenant du budget général ou d'autres sources. Même si leurs budgets peuvent être soumis à l'approbation du corps législatif, comme les comptes budgétaires, elles disposent d'une certaine latitude quant au volume et à la composition de leurs dépenses. Ces entités peuvent être mises en place pour exercer des fonctions spécifiques des administrations publiques, telles que la construction de routes ou la production non marchande de services de santé ou d'éducation. Les dispositions budgétaires peuvent varier grandement suivant les pays, et différents termes sont utilisés pour décrire ces entités, mais elles sont souvent qualifiées de « fonds extrabudgétaires » ou d'« organismes autonomes ».

5. Les paiements obligatoires à des organismes supranationaux et aux organismes qui en dépendent ne sont plus compris depuis 1998 parmi les impôts sauf quelques exceptions. En effet, les droits de douane collectés par les États membres de l'Union européenne pour le compte de celle-ci sont toujours présentés à titre de rubrique « Pour mémoire » et compris dans le total des recettes fiscales (voir § 99). Dans les pays où les églises font partie des administrations publiques, les impôts sur les cultes sont inclus dans ces paiements, à condition qu'ils répondent aux critères énoncés au § 1 ci-dessus. Comme les données se réfèrent aux montants encaissés par les administrations publiques, les contributions versées à des organismes privés, aux organismes sociaux ou régimes de sécurité sociale extérieurs aux administrations publiques, aux syndicats ou aux associations professionnelles sont exclues, même si elles sont obligatoires. Sont toutefois inclus les versements obligatoires aux administrations publiques dont le montant est affecté à ces organismes, à condition que l'administration ne fasse pas simplement office d'agent collecteur[3]. On a distingué les bénéfices des monopoles fiscaux de ceux d'autres entreprises publiques et on les a considérés comme des impôts parce qu'ils reflètent l'exercice du pouvoir d'imposition de l'État par l'intermédiaire du monopole (voir § 65 à 67), comme le sont les bénéfices de l'État provenant de l'achat et de la vente de monnaies étrangères à des taux différents (voir § 74).

6. Les impôts payés par les administrations elles-mêmes (tels que les cotisations de sécurité sociale et les impôts sur les salaires payés par les administrations en tant qu'employeurs (2200 et 3000), les impôts sur la consommation qu'elles acquittent à l'occasion de leurs achats ou les impôts sur leur patrimoine) sont inclus dans les données présentées. Toutefois, lorsqu'il est possible de les isoler, les montants provenant de ces impôts[4] sont indiqués dans le chapitre 4.2 de cette publication.

7. Les rapports entre cette classification et celle du Système de comptabilité nationale (SCN) sont indiqués dans les sections A.9 et A.11. À cause des différences qui existent entre les deux classifications, les statistiques de la comptabilité nationale ne sont pas toujours établies ou classées suivant la pratique adoptée dans le présent guide. Ces différences et d'autres encore sont mentionnées dans les cas appropriés (voir par exemple § 30), mais il est impossible de toutes les signaler. Il peut y avoir aussi certaines différences entre cette classification et celle utilisée par certaines administrations nationales (voir par exemple § 12), aussi les statistiques nationales et celles de l'OCDE ne peuvent pas toujours être compatibles ; ces différences, cependant, sont vraisemblablement très insignifiantes dans les montants des recettes en cause.

Cotisations de sécurité sociale

8. Les cotisations obligatoires de sécurité sociale, définies au § 39, qui sont versées aux administrations publiques, font partie des recettes fiscales. Elles sont évidemment assimilables à des impôts puisqu'il s'agit de versements obligatoires à des administrations publiques. Mais elles peuvent différer toutefois des autres impôts du fait que le paiement des prestations de sécurité sociale dépend dans la plupart des pays du versement des cotisations appropriées, encore qu'il n'y ait pas forcément un lien entre l'importance des prestations et le montant des cotisations. La comparabilité entre les pays sera meilleure si on considère les cotisations de sécurité sociale comme des impôts ; elles figurent cependant sous une rubrique distincte de façon à permettre un traitement séparé pour n'importe quelle analyse.

9. La distinction stricte entre les recettes fiscales (qui sont des paiements obligatoires sans contrepartie aux administrations publiques) et les prélèvements obligatoires non fiscaux (PONF) (qui sont soit des paiements avec contrepartie aux administrations publiques, soit des paiements destinés à d'autres organismes) est clairement définie. Néanmoins, dans la palette des divers prélèvements obligatoires destinés aux administrations publiques qui existent dans les différents pays, il n'est pas toujours évident de déterminer en pratique si tel ou tel prélèvement est un impôt ou un PONF. Ainsi, l'épargne-retraite obligatoire qui est placée sous le contrôle des administrations publiques et qui s'accumule sur un compte individuel rémunéré à un taux correspondant au rendement du marché ou destiné à compenser l'inflation semble, à première vue, constituer une forme de PONF, et non d'impôt. Toutefois, ces paiements peuvent encore être considérés comme « sans contrepartie » et, par conséquent, être classés dans les impôts et non dans les PONF (par exemple si cette épargne-retraite n'est pas remboursée au cas où le contribuable décède avant d'atteindre l'âge de la retraite, et si les fonds en question sont utilisés ensuite pour verser une pension minimale à tous les contribuables qui sont assurés). En conséquence, les chiffres relatifs aux recettes de sécurité sociale indiqués pour la plupart des pays reposent sur l'hypothèse que l'on considère que tous les types de prélèvements obligatoires destinés aux administrations publiques comportent, dans une certaine mesure, un élément redistributif. Il convient de noter que cette conclusion découle d'une interprétation généralement large du terme « sans contrepartie » dans la définition de l'impôt.

10. Les cotisations de sécurité sociale qui sont facultatives ou qui ne sont pas versées à des administrations publiques (voir § 1) ne sont pas considérées comme des impôts, bien que dans certains pays (comme il est indiqué dans les notes correspondantes), il soit difficile d'éliminer complètement les cotisations facultatives et certains versements obligatoires au secteur privé des statistiques relatives aux recettes publiques. Les cotisations de sécurité sociale imputées ne sont pas considérées comme des impôts.

Droits, taxes d'utilisation et droits de licence

11. Si l'on excepte les droits perçus sur les permis de circulation des véhicules à moteur, qui sont universellement considérés comme des impôts, il n'est pas facile de distinguer les droits et taxes d'utilisation qui doivent être traitées comme des impôts de celles qui ne doivent pas l'être. Si, en effet, un droit ou une taxe est perçu au titre d'un service ou d'une activité déterminée, le lien entre ce prélèvement et la prestation fournie peut être plus ou moins important, de même que la relation entre le montant du prélèvement et le coût de la prestation. Lorsque le bénéficiaire d'une prestation acquitte un droit dont le montant est clairement lié au coût de la prestation fournie, on peut considérer que le prélèvement comporte une contrepartie, et d'après la définition donnée au § 1, il ne sera pas traité comme un impôt. Toutefois, dans les cas suivants, les prélèvements seraient 'sans contrepartie':

a. lorsque le prélèvement est très supérieur au coût de la prestation fournie ;
b. lorsque le redevable de la contribution n'est pas le bénéficiaire de la prestation correspondante (par exemple, un droit perçu sur l'abattage du bétail pour financer un service qui est fourni aux agriculteurs) ;
c. lorsque l'État ne fournit pas un service déterminé en contrepartie du droit qu'il perçoit, même si un permis est délivré à celui qui acquitte le droit (par exemple, lorsque l'État délivre des permis de chasse, de pêche ou de port d'armes qui ne sont pas assortis du droit d'utiliser une parcelle déterminée de terres appartenant à l'État) ;
d. lorsque les bénéficiaires de la prestation sont les personnes qui ont acquitté le droit, mais que la prestation dont chacun bénéficie n'est pas nécessairement en rapport avec le montant de ses propres versements (par exemple, le droit de commercialisation du lait acquitté par les fermiers qui sert à promouvoir la consommation de lait.

12. Dans des cas limites, cependant, l'application des critères énoncés au § 1 peut être particulièrement difficile. La solution adoptée, dans un souci d'uniformité entre les pays et eu égard aux montants relativement faibles des recettes en cause, consiste à s'en tenir à la pratique prépondérante des administrations fiscales plutôt que de laisser chaque pays décider si ces prélèvements sont des impôts ou des recettes non fiscales[5].

13. On trouvera ci-après la liste des principaux droits et taxes en question et leur traitement normal[6] dans la présente publication :

- *Recettes non fiscales* : frais de justice ; droits de délivrance de permis de conduire ; droits portuaires ; redevances de passeport ; redevances de radio et de télévision lorsque le service est assuré par les pouvoirs publics.
- *Impôts du sous-groupe 5200*: autorisation d'exercer certaines activités telles que : distribution de films ; chasse, pêche et utilisation d'armes à feu ; organisation de spectacles ou de jeux et paris ; vente de boissons alcoolisées ou de tabacs ; autorisation de posséder des chiens et d'utiliser ou posséder des véhicules à moteur ou des armes à feu ; taxes d'extraction.

14. Dans la pratique, il se peut qu'il ne soit pas toujours possible d'isoler les recettes fiscales des recettes non fiscales quand elles sont enregistrées ensemble. Si l'on estime qu'il s'agit surtout de recettes non fiscales, l'ensemble sera traité comme tel ; dans le cas contraire, les recettes seront comptabilisées et classées conformément aux règles énoncées au § 32.

Redevances

15. La propriété des gisements prenant la forme de minéraux ou de combustibles fossiles (charbon, pétrole ou gaz naturel) dépend de la façon dont les droits de propriété sont définis par la loi, et aussi par les conventions internationales quand les gisements sont situés sous les eaux internationales. Dans certains cas, soit le terrain sous lequel les gisements sont situés, soit les gisements eux-mêmes, soit les deux peuvent appartenir à une administration publique centrale ou locale.

16. Ces unités des administrations publiques peuvent alors consentir un bail à d'autres unités institutionnelles en les autorisant à exploiter ces gisements pendant une période déterminée, en contrepartie d'un paiement ou d'une série de paiements. Ces paiements sont souvent qualifiés de redevances (« royalties »), mais ils n'en constituent pas moins essentiellement des loyers, qui reviennent aux propriétaires des ressources naturelles considérées parce qu'ils mettent ces actifs à la disposition d'autres unités institutionnelles pour des durées déterminées. Ces loyers peuvent prendre la forme de versements périodiques d'un montant fixe, indépendant du rythme d'extraction ; plus vraisemblablement, ils peuvent être fonction de la quantité, du volume ou de la valeur des actifs extraits. Les entreprises engagées dans des activités de prospection sur des terrains publics peuvent effectuer des paiements aux unités de l'administration publique concernées, en contrepartie de l'autorisation de procéder à des forages d'essai ou de réaliser par d'autres moyens des recherches concernant l'existence et la localisation de gisements. Ces paiements sont également considérés comme des loyers, même en l'absence d'extraction. Ils sont donc classés dans les recettes non fiscales.

17. Les mêmes principes s'appliquent lorsque d'autres unités institutionnelles se voient consentir un bail leur permettant de couper du bois dans des forêts naturelles sur des terrains appartenant à des unités des administrations publiques. Ces paiements sont également classés dans les recettes non fiscales.

18. Ces loyers ou redevances versés aux administrations publiques ne doivent pas être confondus avec les impôts sur le revenu et les bénéfices, les taxes d'extraction, les taxes professionnelles ou d'autres impôts. Si ces paiements sont prélevés sur les bénéfices tirés des activités d'extraction, ils doivent être classés dans les impôts sur le revenu, les bénéfices et les gains en capital (1000). En outre, toute taxe d'extraction relative à des minéraux ou des combustibles fossiles extraits de réserves privées ou appartenant à d'autres administrations publiques doit être classée dans les impôts. Les paiements liés à la valeur brute de la production doivent être classés dans les autres impôts sur des biens et services déterminés (5128). Les paiements effectués en contrepartie d'une autorisation ou d'un permis d'extraction doivent être classés dans les impôts sur l'utilisation des biens ou l'autorisation d'utiliser des biens ou d'exercer des activités (5200).

Amendes et pénalités

19. En principe, les amendes et pénalités portant sur les impôts impayés ou les pénalités appliquées en cas de tentative d'évasion fiscale ne doivent pas être enregistrées comme des recettes fiscales. Cependant, il se peut qu'il ne soit pas possible de séparer le versement des amendes et pénalités des recettes correspondant aux impôts auxquels ces amendes et

pénalités se rattachent. Dans ce cas, les amendes et pénalités associés à un impôt particulier sont enregistrées avec les recettes correspondant à cet impôt alors que les amendes et pénalités liées à des recettes correspondant à des impôts non-identifiés sont classées comme autres impôts dans la catégorie 6000. Les amendes qui ne concernent pas des infractions fiscales (comme les infractions au stationnement), ou qui ne sont pas identifiables en tant que telles, ne sont pas non plus considérées comme des recettes fiscales.

A.3. Bases de comptabilisation

Droits constatés

20. Les données enregistrées dans cette publication pour les années récentes sont essentiellement indiquées en droits constatés, c'est-à-dire qu'elles sont enregistrées au moment du fait générateur de l'impôt. D'autres informations sont fournies dans les notes des tableaux par pays au chapitre 4 de ce rapport.

21. Toutefois, les données des années antérieures sont encore principalement comptabilisées sur la base des décaissements, c'est-à-dire au moment où l'administration reçoit le versement. Ainsi, les impôts retenus à la source par les employeurs au cours d'un exercice, mais versés à l'administration au cours de l'exercice suivant, et les impôts dus au titre d'une année mais effectivement versés l'année suivante, figurent les uns et les autres dans les recettes du second exercice. Les restitutions, remboursements et retraits résultant d'opérations rectificatives sont déduits des recettes brutes de la période au cours de laquelle ces opérations sont effectuées.

22. Les données relatives aux recettes fiscales sont comptabilisées, sans déduction compensatoire des dépenses administratives liées au recouvrement de l'impôt. De même, lorsque le produit d'un impôt sert à subventionner certains membres de la collectivité, la subvention n'est pas déduite du rendement de l'impôt, encore que certains pays fassent figurer dans leurs données l'impôt après déduction des subventions.

23. Pour les monopoles fiscaux (sous-groupe 5122), seul le montant effectivement transféré à l'État est inclus dans les recettes publiques. Toutefois, les dépenses des monopoles fiscaux qui sont considérées comme des dépenses publiques (par exemple, des dépenses de caractère social engagées par les monopoles fiscaux à l'instigation de l'État) sont ajoutées après coup pour calculer le montant des recettes fiscales (voir § 65).

La distinction entre dispositions fiscales et dépenses directes[7]

24. Étant donné que la présente publication ne vise que les recettes publiques en faisant abstraction des dépenses, il convient de distinguer entre les dispositions fiscales et les dépenses directes. Normalement, cette distinction ne soulève aucune difficulté, car les dépenses directes sont effectuées en dehors du système fiscal et des comptes fiscaux et en vertu de dispositions législatives distinctes. Dans les cas limites, on recourt, pour établir la distinction, au principe de la comptabilisation sur la base des paiements. Dans la mesure où une disposition affecte le montant des paiements du contribuable à l'État, elle est considérée comme une disposition fiscale dont il est tenu compte dans les données figurant dans cette publication. Une disposition qui n'affecte pas ce montant est considérée comme une dépense directe dont il n'est pas tenu compte dans les données reproduites dans cette publication.

25. Il est clair que les abattements fiscaux, exonérations et déductions de l'assiette de l'impôt modifient le montant de l'impôt acquitté à l'État ; il s'agit donc de dispositions fiscales. Inversement, les formes d'aides qui ne sont pas imputables sur l'impôt et n'ont

donc aucun lien avec le processus d'imposition, ne réduisent pas les recettes publiques qui sont consignées dans ce volume. Les crédits d'impôt sont des montants déductibles de l'impôt à acquitter (par opposition aux déductions, qui sont opérées sur l'assiette de l'impôt). On distingue deux catégories de crédits d'impôt : ceux (que l'on qualifiera ici de 'non récupérables') qui sont limités au montant de l'impôt à acquitter et ne peuvent donc donner lieu à un versement de l'administration au contribuable, et ceux (qualifiés ici de 'récupérables') qui n'ont pas cette limite, de sorte que l'excédent du crédit sur l'impôt peut être versé au contribuable[8]. Le crédit d'impôt non récupérable, comme un abattement fiscal, affecte évidemment le montant de l'impôt acquitté à l'État ; aussi est-il considéré comme une disposition fiscale. La solution adoptée pour les crédits d'impôts récupérables[9] consiste à distinguer l'élément de « dépense fiscale »[10], qui est la part du crédit utilisée pour réduire ou supprimer l'impôt dû par le contribuable, et l'« élément de transfert », qui correspond à la part excédant l'impôt dû par le contribuable et qui lui est reversée. Les recettes fiscales rapportées doivent être diminuées du montant de l'élément de dépense, mais non de l'élément de transfert. En outre, les montants de l'élément de dépense fiscale et de l'élément de transfert doivent être indiqués pour mémoire dans les tableaux par pays. Les pays qui ne sont pas en mesure de faire la distinction entre l'élément de dépense fiscale et l'élément de transfert doivent indiquer si leurs recettes fiscales ont été ou non diminuées du montant total de ces éléments, et fournir toutes les estimations dont ils disposent concernant les montants de ces deux éléments. Des informations complémentaires figurent dans le chapitre 1 de ce Rapport, qui fait apparaître les effets des différents traitements possibles des crédits d'impôts récupérables sur les ratios impôt rapportant les impôts au PIB.

Année civile et année fiscale (exercice budgétaire)

26. Les autorités nationales dont l'exercice budgétaire ne correspond pas à l'année civile fournissent, autant que possible, leurs données sur la base de l'année civile afin de faciliter au maximum la comparaison avec les données des autres pays. Les données d'un petit nombre de pays se réfèrent à l'exercice budgétaire. Pour ceux-ci, les statistiques de PIB utilisées dans les tableaux comparatifs portent aussi sur les exercices budgétaires.

A.4. Principes généraux de classification

Les fondements essentiels de la classification

27. Les recettes sont classées par groupes principaux (1000, 2000, 3000, 4000, 5000, 6000) suivant l'assiette de l'impôt : 1000 revenus, bénéfices et gains en capital ; 2000 et 3000 salaires et nombre d'employés ; 4000 patrimoine ; 5000 biens et services ; 6000 assiettes diverses, autres ou non identifiables. Lorsqu'un impôt est calculé en fonction de plusieurs assiettes, les recettes sont, chaque fois que c'est possible, réparties entre les divers groupes (voir § 32 et § 81). Les groupes 4000 et 5000 ne comprennent pas seulement les impôts ayant pour assiette le patrimoine, les biens ou les services eux-mêmes, mais aussi certains impôts connexes. Ainsi, les impôts sur les mutations du patrimoine sont classés dans le groupe 4400[11] et les impôts sur l'utilisation des biens, ou l'autorisation d'exercer une activité, dans le groupe 5200. Dans les groupes 4000 et 5000, une distinction est faite dans certains sous-groupes entre impôts périodiques et impôts non périodiques : on entend par impôts périodiques ceux qui sont perçus à intervalles réguliers (ordinairement tous les ans) et par impôts non périodiques ceux qui ne sont perçus qu'une seule fois (voir aussi les § 47 à 50, § 53, § 54, et § 79 pour une application particulière de cette distinction).

28. L'affectation spéciale de certaines recettes fiscales n'influe pas sur leur classification. Toutefois comme explicité au § 39 sur la classification des cotisations de sécurité sociale, l'octroi d'un droit aux prestations sociales est crucial dans la définition de la rubrique principale 2000.

29. La manière selon laquelle un impôt est perçu ou recouvré (par exemple, au moyen de timbres) n'affecte pas sa classification.

Classification des contribuables

30. Dans certains sous-groupes, des distinctions sont faites entre les différentes catégories de contribuables. Ces distinctions varient d'un impôt à l'autre :

a. Ventilation des impôts sur le revenu et sur l'actif net entre personnes physiques et sociétés

La distinction fondamentale entre les impôts sur le revenu des sociétés et les impôts sur le revenu des personnes physiques est que les premiers sont perçus sur la société en tant qu'entité et non sur les personnes physiques qui en sont propriétaires, donc sans tenir compte de la situation personnelle de celles-ci. La même distinction est applicable aux impôts sur l'actif net des sociétés et des personnes physiques. Les impôts perçus sur les bénéfices des sociétés de personnes et sur le revenu de certaines institutions comme les caisses d'assurance-vie ou de retraite, sont classés selon le même principe. Ils sont compris dans les impôts sur les sociétés (1200) lorsqu'ils sont perçus sur la société de personnes ou l'institution en tant qu'entité sans que la situation personnelle des propriétaires entre en ligne de compte ; dans les autres cas, ils sont considérés comme des impôts sur les personnes physiques (1100). Ordinairement, les impôts sur les sociétés et les impôts sur les personnes physiques sont régis par des dispositions législatives différentes[12]. La distinction qui est faite ici entre personnes physiques et sociétés ne reprend pas la classification par secteur (ménages, entreprises, etc.) adoptée dans les comptes de revenus et de dépenses du SCN. Cette dernière classification exclut du secteur des ménages certaines entreprises non constituées en sociétés[13] et les fait figurer parmi les entreprises non financières et les institutions financières. Toutefois, l'impôt sur les bénéfices de ces entreprises ne peut pas toujours être isolé de l'impôt sur les autres revenus des propriétaires de ces entreprises, ou ne peut l'être que d'une façon arbitraire. On n'a pas cherché ici à faire la distinction et l'impôt sur le revenu des personnes physiques figure globalement, quelle que soit la nature du revenu imposable.

b. Ventilation des impôts sur les biens immobiliers entre ménages et autres agents

En l'occurrence, la distinction est celle qui a été adoptée par le SCN dans les comptes de production et de consommation. On distingue, en effet, les ménages en tant que consommateurs d'une part (c'est-à-dire à l'exclusion des entreprises individuelles), et les producteurs d'autre part. Cependant, les impôts sur les logements occupés par les ménages, qu'ils soient à la charge des propriétaires qui les occupent, du locataire ou du propriétaire, sont classés comme étant à la charge des ménages. C'est la distinction faite habituellement entre les impôts sur les biens des personnes et les impôts sur les biens des entreprises. Toutefois, certains pays ne sont pas en mesure d'établir cette distinction.

c. Ventilation des permis de circuler des véhicules à moteur entre taxes à la charge des ménages et à la charge d'autres agents

On distingue ici les ménages en tant que consommateurs d'une part, et producteurs d'autre part, comme dans les comptes de production et de consommation du SCN.

d. Ventilation des autres impôts (6000) entre les entreprises et les autres agents

Il est fait la même distinction qu'au point (c) ci-dessus entre les producteurs, d'une part, et les ménages consommateurs d'autre part. Les impôts qui figurent dans le groupe 6000 parce qu'ils ne comportent pas une assiette unique ou parce que leur assiette ne relève d'aucune des catégories précédentes, mais qui ne sont manifestement perçus que sur les producteurs et non sur les ménages, sont classés comme étant 'à la charge des entreprises'. Les autres impôts du groupe 6000 figurent sous la rubrique 'à la charge d'autres agents' ou 'non identifiés'.

Surtaxes

31. Les recettes des surtaxes relatives à des impôts particuliers sont classées ordinairement avec les recettes de l'impôt correspondant, que la surtaxe ait ou non un caractère temporaire. Toutefois, si l'une des caractéristiques de la surtaxe permet de la classer sous une rubrique différente de la classification de l'OCDE, les recettes de cette surtaxe sont classées sous cette rubrique et non pas avec les recettes de l'impôt correspondant

Recettes fiscales non identifiables et sous-groupes résiduels

32. Il arrive parfois qu'on ne puisse déterminer si des impôts relèvent entièrement d'un groupe ou d'un sous-groupe de la classification de l'OCDE ; dans ces cas on applique les méthodes suivantes :

a. le groupe est connu, mais on ne sait pas comment répartir les recettes entre les sous-groupes ; les recettes sont alors classées dans le sous-groupe résiduel approprié (1300, 2400, 4520, 4600, 5130, 5300 ou 6200) ;

b. on sait que l'ensemble des recettes d'un groupe d'impôts (ordinairement des impôts locaux) provient d'impôts relevant d'un groupe ou sous-groupe particulier, mais certains impôts du groupe, dont le montant ne peut être déterminé avec précision, peuvent être classés dans d'autres groupes ou sous-groupes ; dans ce cas les recettes sont comptabilisées dans le groupe ou sous-groupe dont relève l'essentiel des recettes ;

c. il est impossible d'identifier le groupe ou le sous-groupe d'un impôt (ordinairement un impôt local) ; l'impôt est alors classé dans le groupe 6200, à moins qu'il ne s'agisse d'un impôt manifestement à la charge des entreprises, auquel cas il est classé dans le sous-groupe 6100.

A.5. Commentaires sur les postes de la liste

1000 — Impôts sur le revenu, les bénéfices et les gains en capital

33. Ce groupe couvre les impôts prélevés sur le revenu ou le bénéfice net (c'est-à-dire le revenu brut déduction faite des abattements autorisés) des personnes physiques et des entreprises. Sont aussi couverts les impôts prélevés sur les gains en capital des personnes physiques et des entreprises et sur les gains provenant de jeux.

34. Ce groupe comprend :

a. les impôts perçus principalement sur les revenus ou les bénéfices, bien qu'ils puissent l'être partiellement sur d'autres bases. Les impôts qui ont une autre assiette principale que le revenu ou les bénéfices sont classés selon les principes énoncés aux § 32 et § 81 ;

b. les impôts sur la propriété immobilière, qui sont perçus sur la base d'un revenu présumé ou estimé faisant partie de l'assiette de l'impôt sur le revenu (voir aussi § 47 (a), (c) et (d)) ;

c. les versements obligatoires aux caisses de sécurité sociale qui sont prélevés sur les revenus mais ne donnent pas droit à des prestations sociales. Lorsque ces contributions donnent droit à des prestations sociales, elles figurent à la rubrique 2000 (voir § 39) ;

d. les recettes provenant d'impôts cédulaires sur le revenu intégrés dans le régime général qui sont globalement classés dans ce groupe, bien que certains de ces impôts soient sur le revenu brut et ne tiennent pas toujours compte de la situation personnelle du contribuable.

35. Les impôts figurant dans ce groupe sont subdivisés en deux grands sous-groupes, les impôts sur le revenu des personnes physiques (1100) et les impôts sur le revenu des sociétés (1200), une ventilation étant faite dans chacun d'eux entre les impôts sur le revenu et les bénéfices (1110 et 1210) et les impôts sur les gains en capital (1120 et 1220). Si certaines recettes ne peuvent être identifiées comme relevant soit du sous-groupe 1100, soit du sous-groupe 1200, ou si cette distinction ne peut être faite dans la pratique (parce qu'il n'y a pas de données fiables sur les bénéficiaires des paiements sur lesquels la retenue à la source est faite), elles sont classées dans le sous-groupe 1300 (non ventilables).

Traitement des crédits d'impôt dans les systèmes d'imputation

36. Dans les régimes d'imputation de l'impôt sur les bénéfices des sociétés, les actionnaires bénéficient d'une compensation totale ou partielle d'imposition sur les dividendes que la société leur a versés et pour lesquels elle a acquitté l'impôt sur le revenu des sociétés. Dans les pays qui appliquent un tel régime, une fraction de l'impôt sur les bénéfices des sociétés sert à alléger l'impôt dû par l'actionnaire. Cet allégement prend la forme d'un crédit d'impôt, dont le montant peut être inférieur, égal ou supérieur au montant total de l'impôt dont il est redevable. Si le crédit d'impôt dépasse ce montant, l'excédent peut être versé à l'actionnaire. Comme ce type de crédit d'impôt fait partie intégrante des systèmes d'imputation de l'impôt sur le revenu des sociétés, tout paiement à l'actionnaire est considéré comme un remboursement d'impôt et non comme une dépense (se référer au traitement des autres crédits d'impôt exposé au § 25).

37. Puisque, dans les systèmes d'imputation, le crédit d'impôt (même lorsqu'il dépasse l'impôt dû) est censé être une disposition fiscale, on peut se demander s'il doit être déduit des recettes de l'impôt sur le revenu des personnes physiques (1110) ou de celles de l'impôt sur les bénéfices de sociétés (1210). Dans ce Rapport le montant intégral de l'impôt acquitté sur les bénéfices des sociétés figure sous le poste 1210 et aucun impôt imputé n'est inclus dans le poste 1110. Le montant total du crédit d'impôt réduit donc le montant des recettes du poste 1110, que ce crédit se traduise par une réduction de l'impôt dû sur le revenu des personnes physiques ou par un remboursement réel du fait que le crédit dépasse le montant de l'impôt. (Cependant, lorsque ces crédits sont déduits de l'impôt sur les sociétés au titre de dividendes versés à des sociétés, le montant est déduit des recettes du poste 1210).

1120 et 1220 — Impôts sur les gains en capital

38. Ces postes comprennent les impôts perçus sur les gains en capital, le sous-groupe 1120 comptabilisant les impôts prélevés sur les gains des personnes physiques et le sous-groupe 1220 ceux qui sont perçus sur les gains des entreprises constituées sous forme de sociétés,

lorsque ces recettes peuvent être ventilées. Ce n'est pas le cas dans de nombreux pays et les recettes de ces impôts sont alors classées avec celles de l'impôt sur le revenu. Les impôts sur les gains provenant de jeux sont aussi classés sous le poste 1120.

2000 — Cotisations de sécurité sociale

39. Figurent dans ce groupe tous les versements obligatoires qui donnent le droit de bénéficier d'une prestation sociale future (éventuelle). Ces versements sont généralement affectés au financement de prestations sociales et souvent effectués au profit d'institutions ou d'administrations publiques qui fournissent de telles prestations. Cependant, cette affectation n'entre pas dans la définition des cotisations de sécurité sociale et n'est pas nécessaire pour qu'un impôt soit classé dans cette rubrique. Cependant, il faut qu'un impôt confère un droit pour être classé dans cette rubrique. Par conséquent, les prélèvements sur les revenus ou la masse salariale qui sont affectés aux caisses de sécurité sociale mais ne donnent aucun droit à des prestations sont exclus de cette rubrique et figurent à celle des impôts sur le revenu des personnes physiques (1100) ou des impôts sur les salaires et la main-d'œuvre (3000). Les impôts assis sur d'autres bases, telles que les biens et services, qui sont affectés à des prestations de sécurité sociale, ne sont pas indiqués ici, mais sont classés en fonction de leurs bases respectives parce qu'en général ils ne donnent pas droit à des prestations de sécurité sociale.

40. Seraient entre autres incluses les cotisations au titre des catégories suivantes de prestations de sécurité sociale : les allocations d'assurance-chômage et les compléments, les allocations pour accidents, blessures et maladie, les pensions de retraite, d'invalidité et de survivant, les allocations familiales, les remboursements de dépenses médicales et d'hospitalisation ou la fourniture de services médicaux ou hospitaliers. Les cotisations peuvent être collectées à la fois auprès des employés et des employeurs.

41. Les cotisations peuvent être assises sur les gains ou la masse salariale (« sur la base du salaire ») ou sur le revenu net après déductions et exemptions en fonction de la situation personnelle (« sur la base de l'impôt sur le revenu ») et les recettes correspondant à ces deux bases doivent être identifiées séparément si possible. Cependant, lorsque les cotisations à un régime général de sécurité sociale sont assises sur la masse salariale, mais que les cotisations de groupes particuliers (tels que les travailleurs indépendants) ne peuvent être évaluées sur cette base et que le revenu net est utilisé comme valeur rapprochée des gains bruts, les recettes peuvent encore être considérées comme assises sur la masse salariale. En principe, cette rubrique exclut les cotisations facultatives à des régimes de sécurité sociale. Lorsqu'elles peuvent être identifiées séparément, elles figurent pour mémoire dans le tableau indiquant le financement des prestations de sécurité sociale. Toutefois, en pratique, elles ne peuvent pas toujours être distinguées des cotisations facultatives, et dans ce cas elles figurent à cette rubrique.

42. Les cotisations à des régimes d'assurance sociale qui ne relèvent pas des pouvoirs publics et à d'autres régimes d'assurance ou de prévoyance, aux caisses de retraite, sociétés de secours mutuel ou autres systèmes d'épargne, ne sont pas considérées comme des cotisations de sécurité sociale. Les caisses de prévoyance résultant d'arrangements aux termes desquels les cotisations de chaque salarié et celles que l'employeur verse en son nom sont comptabilisées séparément dans un compte productif d'intérêts d'où elles peuvent être retirées dans des conditions biens déterminées. Les caisses de retraite sont des régimes autonomes organisés par négociations entre salariés et employeurs, qui comportent diverses contributions et prestations, parfois liées plus directement au salaire et à la durée

d'activité que dans les régimes de sécurité sociale. Lorsque les cotisations à ces régimes sont obligatoires ou quasi obligatoires (par exemple en vertu d'un accord entre organisations professionnelles et syndicales), elles sont comptabilisées dans le poste pour mémoire (voir le chapitre 4.2 du rapport).

43. Les cotisations versées par les agents des administrations et par les administrations au titre de leurs agents à des régimes de sécurité sociale relevant des pouvoirs publics sont incluses dans ce groupe. Sont aussi assimilées à des impôts les cotisations à des régimes particuliers réservés aux agents des administrations qui sont censés remplacer un régime général de la sécurité sociale[14]. Par contre, lorsqu'un régime distinct n'est pas censé remplacer un régime général et résulte de négociations entre l'administration, agissant en qualité d'employeur, et ses agents, il n'est pas considéré comme un régime de sécurité sociale et les cotisations à ce titre ne sont pas assimilées à des impôts, même si le régime a été institué par des dispositions législatives.

44. Cette rubrique ne comprend pas les cotisations 'imputées', qui correspondent aux prestations sociales versées directement par les employeurs à leurs salariés, ou anciens salariés, ou à leurs représentants (par exemple, lorsque des employeurs sont légalement tenus de verser des prestations maladies pendant une certaine période).

45. Le groupe comprend les cotisations à la charge des salariés (2100), à la charge des employeurs (2200), et à la charge des travailleurs indépendants ou des personnes n'occupant pas d'emploi (2300). À cet effet, on entend par salariés toutes les personnes qui exercent une activité dans des entreprises, des administrations, des institutions privées sans but lucratif, ou qui occupent d'autres emplois rémunérés, à l'exception des propriétaires et des membres de leur famille non rémunérés dans le cas d'entreprises individuelles. Sont également compris les membres des forces armées, quelle que soit la durée et la nature de leurs services, s'ils cotisent à un régime de sécurité sociale. Par cotisations à la charge des employeurs, on entend les versements qu'ils effectuent au régime de sécurité sociale pour le compte de leurs salariés. Si, en cas de chômage, les salariés ou employeurs sont tenus de continuer à effectuer ces versements, ces derniers doivent figurer respectivement dans les sous-groupes 2100 et 2200. En conséquence, le sous-groupe 2300 est réservé aux cotisations versées par les travailleurs indépendants et par ceux qui n'appartiennent pas à la population active (comme les handicapés ou les retraités).

3000 — *Impôts sur les salaires et la main-d'œuvre*

46. Il s'agit d'impôts que doivent acquitter les entreprises, déterminés en proportion des salaires et des traitements payés, ou d'après un montant fixe par personne employée. Ils ne comprennent pas les cotisations obligatoires de sécurité sociale payées par les employeurs, ni les impôts payés par les salariés sur leurs traitements et leurs salaires.

4000 — *Impôts sur le patrimoine*

47. Ce groupe couvre les impôts périodiques et non périodiques sur l'utilisation, la propriété ou la mutation des biens. Sont comptabilisés ici les impôts sur la propriété immobilière et sur l'actif net, les impôts sur les mutations par décès, les successions et les donations, et les impôts sur les transactions mobilières et immobilières. Sont exclus de ce groupe :

a. les impôts sur les gains en capital provenant de la vente d'un bien (1120 ou 1220) ;

b. les impôts sur l'utilisation des biens ou l'autorisation d'utiliser des biens ou d'exercer des activités (5200) [voir § 76] ;

c. les impôts immobiliers perçus sur la base d'un revenu net présumé qui tiennent compte de la situation personnelle du contribuable. Ces impôts sont classés dans le groupe 1100 en tant qu'impôts sur le revenu, avec les impôts sur le revenu et les gains en capital provenant des biens immobiliers ;

d. les impôts sur l'utilisation de biens immobiliers aux fins d'habitation qui sont à la charge du propriétaire ou du locataire et dont le montant est fonction de la situation personnelle de l'utilisateur (salaire, personnes à charge, etc.). Ils sont classés dans le groupe 1100 en tant qu'impôts sur le revenu ;

e. les impôts sur les constructions dépassant la densité autorisée, les impôts sur l'extension, la construction ou la modification de certains immeubles au-delà d'une valeur autorisée et les impôts sur la construction d'immeubles. Ces impôts sont classés dans le poste 5200 en tant qu'impôts sur l'autorisation d'exercer certaines activités ;

f. les impôts sur l'utilisation de biens immobiliers par le propriétaire à des fins commerciales particulières, comme la vente de boissons alcoolisées, de tabac, de viande, ou pour l'exploitation de sols ou terrains (par exemple aux États-Unis, les taxes d'extraction). Ils sont classés dans le poste 5200 en tant qu'impôts sur l'autorisation d'exercer certaines activités.

4100 — *Impôts périodiques sur la propriété immobilière*

48. Ce sous-groupe comprend les impôts prélevés régulièrement au titre de l'utilisation ou de la propriété de biens immobiliers.

- ces impôts sont prélevés sur les terrains et les bâtiments ;
- ces impôts sont calculés en pourcentage de la valeur du bien évalué d'après un revenu locatif fictif, le prix de vente ou le rendement capitalisé, ou en fonction d'autres caractéristiques du bien, comme sa dimension ou son emplacement, d'où l'on peut déduire une valeur locative présumée ou la valeur du capital.
- ces impôts sont à la charge du propriétaire, du locataire ou des deux. Ils peuvent également être payés par une administration à une autre administration au titre d'un bien relevant de la compétence de cette dernière.
- il n'est pas tenu compte des dettes pour la détermination de l'assiette de ces impôts, contrairement aux impôts sur l'actif net.

49. Les impôts sur la propriété immobilière sont en outre subdivisés en impôts acquittés par les ménages (4110) et impôts acquittés par d'autres agents (4120), suivant les critères exposés au § 30(*b*) ci-dessus.

4200 — *Impôts périodiques sur l'actif net*

50. Ce sous-groupe comprend les impôts prélevés régulièrement (dans la plupart des cas annuellement) sur l'actif net, c'est-à-dire les impôts perçus sur un large éventail de biens mobiliers et immobiliers, endettement déduit. Il est subdivisé en impôts acquittés par des personnes physiques (4210), et en impôts acquittés par des sociétés (4220) selon les critères exposés plus haut au § 30(a). Si les recettes provenant des institutions sont comptabilisées à part, 66res doivent être ajoutées aux impôts des entreprises.

4300 — Impôts sur les mutations par décès, les successions et les donations

51. Ce sous-groupe comprend les impôts sur les mutations par décès et les successions (4310) et les impôts sur les donations (4320). Les impôts sur les mutations par décès sont calculés soit sur l'ensemble de la masse successorale, soit en fonction de la part de chacun des bénéficiaires (« part héréditaire ») ; en outre, ces derniers impôts peuvent tenir compte du degré de parenté entre chacun des bénéficiaires et le défunt.

4400 — Impôts sur les transactions mobilières et immobilières

52. Sont compris, entre autres, dans ce sous-groupe les impôts sur l'émission, le transfert, l'achat et la vente de valeurs mobilières, les impôts sur les chèques, ainsi que les droits perçus à l'occasion d'actes juridiques déterminés, comme la validation de contrats et la vente de biens immobiliers. Sont exclus :

a. les impôts sur l'utilisation de biens, mobiliers ou immobiliers, ou l'autorisation d'exercer certaines activités (5200) ;
b. les droits acquittés au titre de frais de justice, ou pour la délivrance de certificats de naissance, de mariage ou de décès, car ces droits sont considérés comme des recettes non fiscales (voir § 11) ;
c. les impôts sur les gains en capital (1000) ;
d. les impôts périodiques sur la propriété immobilière (4100) ;
e. les impôts périodiques sur l'actif net (4200) ;
f. les prélèvements sur le patrimoine ou sur l'actif net effectués une fois pour toutes (4500) ;

4500 — Autres impôts non périodiques sur le patrimoine[16]

53. Ce sous-groupe comprend les prélèvements sur le patrimoine effectués une fois pour toutes (par opposition aux prélèvements périodiques). Il est subdivisé en impôts sur l'actif net (4510) et en autres impôts non périodiques sur le patrimoine (4520). Le poste 4510 inclurait les impôts perçus pour couvrir des dépenses exceptionnelles ou à des fins de redistribution. Le poste 4520 comprendrait les impôts prélevés pour tenir compte d'une plus-value prise par les terrains du fait que les administrations publiques ont autorisé l'extension ou l'aménagement d'installations locales, ainsi que les impôts sur la réévaluation du capital ou les impôts perçus une seule fois sur certains biens déterminés.

4600 — Autres impôts périodiques sur le patrimoine

54. Ils sont rares dans des pays Membres de l'OCDE ; ce sous-groupe comprendrait les impôts sur des biens tels que le cheptel, les bijoux, les fenêtres et les signes extérieurs de richesse.

5000 — Impôts sur les biens et services

55. Ce poste couvre tous les impôts et droits perçus sur la production, l'extraction, la vente, le transfert, la location ou la livraison de biens et la prestation de services (5100), ou sur l'utilisation ou l'autorisation d'utiliser des biens ou d'exercer des activités (5200). Ce groupe comprend donc :

a. les taxes cumulatives en cascade ;
b. les taxes générales sur les ventes — perçues au stade de la production ou de la fabrication, du gros ou du détail ;

c. les taxes sur la valeur ajoutée ;
d. les accises ;
e. les taxes perçues à l'importation et à l'exportation de biens ;
f. les impôts perçus sur l'utilisation de biens et sur l'autorisation d'utiliser des biens ou d'exercer certaines activités ;
g. les impôts sur l'extraction, le traitement ou la production de minéraux et autres produits.

56. Les cas douteux de délimitation entre ce groupe et le groupe 4000 (impôts sur le patrimoine) et le sous-groupe 6100 (autres impôts à la charge des entreprises) sont examinés aux § 47, § 52 et § 78. Des postes résiduels (5300 et 5130) ont été prévus pour comptabiliser les recettes fiscales qui ne peuvent être ventilées respectivement entre les postes 5100 et 5200 et entre les postes 5110 et 5120 (voir § 32).

5100 — *Impôts sur la production, la vente, le transfert, la location et la livraison de biens et la prestation de services*

57. Ce sous-groupe comprend tous les impôts perçus sur les transactions afférentes à des biens ou services, en fonction de leurs caractéristiques propres (comme la valeur, le poids du tabac, le degré d'alcool, etc.), à la différence des impôts perçus au titre de l'utilisation ou de l'autorisation d'utiliser des biens ou d'exercer des activités, qui entrent dans le sous-groupe 5200.

5110 — *Impôts généraux sur les biens et services*

58. Ce sous-groupe comprend tous les impôts, autres que les droits à l'importation et à l'exportation (5123 et 5124), perçus sur la production, la location, le transfert, la livraison ou la vente d'une gamme de biens ou la prestation d'une gamme de services, qu'ils soient produits dans le pays ou importés, et quel que soit le stade de la production ou de la distribution aux quel ils sont perçus. Il couvre ainsi les taxes sur la valeur ajoutée, les taxes sur les ventes et les taxes de caractère cumulatif en cascade. On a ajouté aux recettes brutes de cette catégorie les recettes provenant de la compensation à la frontière de ces impôts lorsque les biens sont importés, et déduit les remboursements d'impôts effectués lorsque les marchandises sont exportées. Ces impôts sont ventilés en : taxes sur la valeur ajoutée (5111), impôts sur les ventes (5112), impôts sur le chiffre d'affaires et autres impôts généraux sur les biens et services (5113).

59. Certains cas se trouvent à la limite entre ce sous-groupe et celui des impôts sur des biens et services déterminés (5120) lorsque ces impôts sont perçus sur un grand nombre de biens, comme dans le cas de la « *purchase tax* » au Royaume-Uni (abrogée en 1973) et l'impôt japonais sur les biens marchands (abrogé en 1988). Conformément aux options nationales, la « *purchase tax* » britannique est classée impôt général (5112) et l'impôt japonais dans les accises (5121).

5111 — *Taxes sur la valeur ajoutée*

60. Sont classés dans ce sous-groupe tous les impôts généraux sur la consommation prélevée sur la valeur ajoutée, quels que soient le mode de déduction et les stades auxquels ils sont perçus. En pratique, tous les pays de l'OCDE où existe une taxe sur la valeur ajoutée autorisent normalement la déduction immédiate des taxes sur les achats par tous les redevables, à l'exception du consommateur final, et imposent la taxe à tous les stades. Dans certains pays, le poste peut inclure aussi certains impôts, comme les taxes sur les activités

financières et les assurances, soit parce que les recettes correspondantes ne peuvent être dissociées de celles de la taxe sur la valeur ajoutée, soit parce qu'elles sont considérées comme faisant partie intégrante de la taxe sur la valeur ajoutée, même si les taxes similaires qui existent dans d'autres pays peuvent être classées autrement (par exemple, sous le poste 5126 comme impôts sur les services ou sous le poste 4400 comme impôts sur les transactions mobilières et immobilières).

5112 — *Impôts sur les ventes*

61. Sont classés ici tous les impôts perçus à un stade unique, que ce soit celui de la fabrication, de la production, du gros ou du détail.

5113 — *Impôts sur le chiffre d'affaires et autres impôts généraux sur les biens et services*

62. Il s'agit des taxes cumulatives en cascade et des taxes qui combinent des éléments de taxe sur la consommation et des taxes en cascade. Ces impôts sont prélevés sur chaque transaction sans déduction des taxes acquittées en amont. Les taxes en cascade peuvent être combinées avec des éléments de taxe sur la valeur ajoutée ou d'impôts sur les ventes.

5120 — *Impôts sur des biens et des services déterminés*

63. Ce sous-groupe couvre les accises, les bénéfices engendrés et transférés par les monopoles fiscaux, et les droits de douane et à l'importation, ainsi que les taxes à l'exportation, les opérations de change, les biens d'équipement et les paris, et aussi les impôts spéciaux sur les services qui ne font pas partie d'un impôt général du sous-groupe 5110.

5121 — Accises

64. Les accises sont des impôts spécifiques perçus par unité produite sur une gamme limitée de biens prédéfinie. Les accises sont généralement prélevées à des taux différenciés sur des biens non essentiels ou de luxe, les boissons alcoolisées, les produits à base de tabac et l'énergie. Les accises peuvent être perçues à un stade quelconque de la production ou de la distribution et sont calculées généralement sur la base d'un prélèvement spécifique par unité correspondant aux caractéristiques du produit considéré, par référence à sa valeur, son poids, son degré ou son volume. Cette subdivision couvre ainsi les impôts spéciaux sur certains produits tels que le sucre, la betterave, les allumettes et le chocolat ; les impôts prélevés à des taux variables sur une gamme déterminée de produits ; ainsi que les impôts perçus sur les produits à base de tabac, les boissons alcoolisées, les combustibles et les hydrocarbures. Si un impôt frappant principalement des produits importés doit ou devrait également être perçu sur des produits nationaux comparables, suivant la même législation, les recettes de cet impôt doivent alors être classées dans la catégorie des accises et non dans celle des droits à l'importation. Ce principe vaut également même s'il n'existe pas, ou ne peut exister, de production nationale comparable. Les impôts prélevés sur la consommation de services d'utilité publique (eau, électricité, gaz et autres formes d'énergie) sont considérés comme des accises, et non comme des impôts sur des services déterminés (5126). Ne sont pas inclus dans les accises les prélèvements entrant dans les catégories des impôts généraux sur les biens et services (5110), des bénéfices des monopoles fiscaux (5122), des droits de douane et autres droits à l'importation (5123) ou des taxes à l'exportation (5124).

5122 — *Bénéfices des monopoles fiscaux*

65. Ce sous-groupe couvre la fraction des bénéfices des monopoles fiscaux qui est transférée aux administrations publiques ou qui sert à financer des dépenses considérées comme

dépenses publiques (voir § 23). Les montants sont comptabilisés lorsqu'ils sont transférés aux administrations publiques ou utilisés pour effectuer des dépenses considérées comme des dépenses publiques.

66. Les monopoles fiscaux reflètent l'exercice du pouvoir d'imposition de l'État par l'intermédiaire du monopole. Les monopoles fiscaux sont des entreprises publiques non financières, qui exercent dans la plupart des cas un monopole sur la production ou la distribution du tabac, des boissons alcoolisées, du sel, des allumettes, des cartes à jouer et des produits pétroliers ou agricoles (c'est-à-dire, sur le genre de produits qui peuvent être soumis, principalement ou accessoirement, aux accises du poste 5121), pour procurer des recettes publiques qui, dans d'autres pays, sont obtenues par le biais d'impôts frappant les transactions sur ces produits d'entreprises privées. Le monopole d'État peut être exercé au stade de la production, ou au stade de la distribution comme dans le cas des magasins de vente de boissons alcoolisées qui appartiennent à l'État et sont contrôlés par lui.

67. Les monopoles fiscaux sont différents des services publics, comme les chemins de fer, l'électricité, les postes et autres moyens de communication, qui peuvent avoir une position de monopole ou de quasi-monopole, mais dont l'objet principal est, normalement, de fournir des services essentiels et non pas de procurer des recettes à l'État. Les transferts à l'administration de ces autres entreprises publiques sont considérés comme des recettes non fiscales. La notion traditionnelle de monopole fiscal n'a généralement pas été élargie pour inclure les loteries nationales, dont les bénéfices sont habituellement considérés comme des recettes non fiscales. Cependant, ces bénéfices peuvent être considérés comme des recettes fiscales quand la raison principale de la mise en œuvre de ces loteries est l'augmentation des recettes pour financer les dépenses publiques. On distingue les bénéfices des monopoles fiscaux des bénéfices des monopoles d'exportation et d'importation (5127), qui sont transférés des offices de commercialisation ou d'autres entreprises s'occupant du commerce international.

5123 — *Droits de douane et autres droits à l'importation*

68. Figurent ici les taxes, droits de timbre et surtaxes qui, selon la loi sont perçus exclusivement sur des produits importés. Sont aussi inclus dans ce poste les droits perçus sur l'importation de denrées agricoles dans les pays Membres de l'Union Européenne et les montants acquittés par certains de ces pays en vertu du Système de Montants Compensatoires[15]. À partir de 1998 les droits de douane collectés par les États membres de l'Union européenne pour le compte de l'Union européenne ne sont plus reportés sous cette rubrique dans les tableaux par pays (chapitre 4 de ce rapport). Sont exclues ici les taxes perçues sur les importations au titre d'un impôt général sur les biens et les services ou d'une accise applicable aussi bien aux produits importés qu'aux produits fabriqués dans le pays.

5124 — *Taxes à l'exportation*

69. Pendant les années 70, les droits à l'exportation étaient perçus normalement en Australie, au Canada et au Portugal, et ils étaient utilisés en Finlande à des fins conjoncturelles. Certains pays Membres de l'Union Européenne acquittent, dans le cadre du système des montants compensatoires, une taxe sur les exportations (voir la note 16 du § 68). Lorsque ces montants sont identifiables, ils sont inclus dans ce poste. Ce dernier ne comprend pas les remboursements effectués au titre d'impôts généraux sur la consommation d'accises ou de droits de douane sur des biens exportés, qui doivent être déduits des recettes brutes comptabilisées, selon le cas, sous le poste 5110, 5121 ou 5123.

5125 — Impôts sur les biens d'équipement

70. Ce sous-groupe comprend les impôts perçus sur les biens d'équipement, comme les machines. Ils peuvent exister depuis un certain nombre d'années ou avoir un caractère temporaire et être prélevés à des fins conjoncturelles. Ne sont pas inclus les impôts sur les 'inputs' industriels qui frappent aussi les consommateurs (comme l'impôt suédois sur l'énergie qui est classé sous le poste 5121).

5126 — Impôts sur des services déterminés

71. Sous ce poste figurent tous les impôts calculés sur la rémunération de services spécifiques, comme les taxes sur les primes d'assurance, les taxes sur les services bancaires, sur les jeux et paris (par exemple : courses de chevaux, pronostics de football, billets de loterie nationale), les transports, les spectacles, les restaurants et la publicité. Les impôts prélevés sur le revenu brut des sociétés prestataires d'un service (exemple : primes d'assurance brutes, mises de jeux encaissées par les sociétés) sont classés sous ce poste. Les recettes fiscales provenant des prélèvements sur les banques et des contributions aux mécanismes de garantie des dépôts et de stabilité financière sont provisoirement classés ici pour l'édition 2012. La classification détaillée est présentée au § 108.

72. Ne figurent pas sous ce poste :

a. les impôts sur les services qui font partie d'un impôt général sur les biens et services et sont classés sous le poste 5110 ;

b. les taxes sur l'électricité, le gaz et l'énergie (classées sous le poste 5121 en tant qu'accises) ;

c. les taxes sur les gains personnels tirés de jeux et paris (qui sont classées sous le poste 1120, en tant qu'impôts sur les gains en capital des personnes physiques et entreprises individuelles) et les montants forfaitaires perçus sur le transfert de loteries privées ou sur l'autorisation de créer des loteries (5200)[16] ;

d. les impôts sur les chèques et sur l'émission, le transfert ou le remboursement de valeurs mobilières, (qui sont classés sous le poste 4400, en tant qu'impôts sur les transactions mobilières et immobilières).

5127 — Autres impôts sur les transactions et les échanges internationaux

73. Ce sous-groupe couvre les recettes perçues par l'État sur l'achat et la vente de monnaies étrangères à des taux différents. Lorsque l'État exerce le privilège exclusif dont il dispose pour s'assurer une marge entre le prix d'achat et le prix de vente de devises qui ne se réduit pas à la simple couverture des frais administratifs, ce bénéfice représente un prélèvement obligatoire imposé dans des proportions indéterminées à l'acheteur et au vendeur des monnaies étrangères. Il équivaut normalement au droit à l'importation et au droit à l'exportation perçus dans un système de taux de change unique, ou à une taxe sur la vente ou l'achat de monnaies étrangères. Comme les bénéfices des monopoles fiscaux et des monopoles d'importation ou d'exportation transférés à l'État, il représente l'exercice d'un monopole aux fins d'imposition et est inclus dans les recettes fiscales.

74. Ce sous-groupe comprend aussi les bénéfices des monopoles d'exportation ou d'importation, bien qu'il n'en existe pas dans les pays de l'OCDE, les impôts sur l'achat ou la vente de devises et tous les autres impôts perçus spécifiquement sur les opérations ou les échanges internationaux.

5128 — *Autres impôts sur des biens et services déterminés*

75. Cette rubrique comprend les impôts sur l'extraction de minéraux, combustibles fossiles et autres ressources non renouvelables provenant de gisements privés ou détenus par une autre administration, ainsi que toute autre recette non ventilable provenant des impôts sur des biens et services déterminés. Les impôts sur l'extraction de ressources non renouvelables correspondent généralement à un montant forfaitaire par unité de qualité ou de poids, mais peuvent être calculés ad valorem. Les impôts sont comptabilisés à la date d'extraction des ressources. Les versements tirés de l'extraction de ressources non renouvelables issues de gisements appartenant à l'administration publique qui perçoit ces versements sont classés en tant que loyers.

5200 — *Impôts sur l'utilisation des biens ou l'autorisation d'utiliser des biens ou d'exercer des activités*

76. Ce sous-groupe comprend les taxes prélevées en raison de l'utilisation de biens, indépendamment des impôts frappant les biens eux-mêmes. Contrairement à ceux-ci (5100), les impôts du sous-groupe 5200 ne sont pas calculés d'après la valeur des biens, mais ordinairement d'après un montant forfaitaire. Sont aussi couverts les impôts perçus au titre du droit d'utiliser des biens ou d'exercer des activités, comme les taxes sur la pollution qui ne reposent pas sur la valeur de biens déterminés. Il est parfois difficile de distinguer les taxes d'utilisation et droits de licence obligatoires, qui sont considérés comme des impôts, de ceux qui ne le sont pas parce qu'ils sont assimilés à des recettes non fiscales ; les critères appliqués sont ceux indiqués aux § 11 et 12.

77. Bien que le sous-groupe se réfère à l'utilisation des biens, le fait générateur de l'impôt peut être aussi bien l'enregistrement de la propriété, de sorte que les impôts relevant de ce sous-groupe peuvent viser la possession d'animaux ou de biens plutôt que leur utilisation (par exemple, les chevaux de course, les chiens, les véhicules à moteur) et même s'appliquer à des biens inutilisables (comme les véhicules à moteur ou les fusils inutilisables).

78. Les cas limites concernent :

a. les impôts sur l'autorisation d'exercer des activités commerciales, qui sont classés selon les règles exposées au § 81 lorsqu'ils ont une assiette mixte associant le revenu, les salaires versés ou le chiffre d'affaires ;

b. les impôts sur la propriété ou l'utilisation de la propriété de biens visés par les postes 4100, 4200 et 4600. Le poste 4100 ne vise que les impôts sur la propriété ou la location de biens immobiliers et, contrairement aux impôts du sous-groupe 5200, ils sont fonction de la valeur du bien. Les impôts sur l'actif net et les impôts sur les biens meubles des sous-groupes 4200 et 4600 visent la propriété et non pas l'utilisation des biens, couvrent un groupe d'actifs et non pas de biens particuliers et sont aussi fonction de la valeur du bien.

5210 — *Impôts périodiques sur l'utilisation de biens ou sur l'autorisation d'utiliser des biens ou d'exercer certaines activités*

79. Ces impôts ont pour principale caractéristique d'être perçus à intervalles réguliers et de représenter ordinairement des montants forfaitaires. Le poste le plus important, du point de vue du volume des recettes, est constitué par les permis de circulation des véhicules. Ce sous-groupe inclut aussi les taxes perçues lors de la délivrance de permis de chasse, de tir ou de pêche, ou l'autorisation de vendre certains produits, ainsi que les taxes sur la possession de chiens et sur la prestation de certains services à condition qu'elles

répondent aux critères définis aux § 11 et 12. Les subdivisions du poste 5210 comprennent les taxes d'utilisation de véhicules à moteur à la charge des ménages (5211) et à la charge d'autres agents (5212). Le poste 5213 couvre les plaques de chiens et les taxes perçues pour l'autorisation d'exercer certaines activités, comme la vente de viande et d'alcool, lorsque les prélèvements ont un caractère périodique. Il couvre aussi les permis généraux de chasse, de port d'armes et de pêche, lorsque le droit d'exercer ces activités n'est pas accordé au titre d'une opération commerciale normale (par exemple, la délivrance du permis ne comporte pas le droit d'utiliser une parcelle déterminée de terrain appartenant à l'État).

5220 — Impôts non périodiques sur l'utilisation de biens ou sur l'autorisation d'utiliser des biens ou d'exercer certaines activités

80. Cette rubrique recouvre les taxes non périodiques perçues sur l'utilisation de biens ou sur l'autorisation d'utiliser des biens ou d'exercer certaines activités et celles qui sont prélevées chaque fois que des biens sont utilisés.

- Les impôts prélevés sur l'émission ou le rejet dans l'environnement de gaz toxiques, liquides nocifs ou autres substances dangereuses figurent ici. Les paiements au titre des permis d'émission négociables délivrés par les administrations publiques dans le cadre des dispositifs de plafonnement et d'échange doivent également être comptabilisés sous cette rubrique au moment où les émissions sont produites. Les permis délivrés gratuitement par les administrations ne donnent lieu à aucun enregistrement comptable de recettes.
- La comptabilisation en droits constatés implique un éventuel délai entre la date à laquelle l'administration perçoit le règlement des permis et la date à laquelle les émissions sont produites. Dans les comptes nationaux, ce délai se traduit pour l'administration par un engagement financier sur la période.
- Il convient d'exclure les paiements effectués au titre de la collecte et de l'élimination de déchets ou de substances nocives par les autorités publiques, étant donné qu'il s'agit là de vente de services aux entreprises.

81. D'autres impôts non périodiques qui relèvent du poste 5200 sont aussi classés dans cette rubrique. Ainsi figurent les paiements uniques effectués au titre de l'autorisation de vendre des boissons alcoolisées ou des tabacs ou d'ouvrir des guichets de « paris mutuels », à condition qu'ils répondent aux critères définis aux § 11 et 12.

6000 — Autres impôts

82. Ce groupe couvre les impôts prélevés sur une ou plusieurs assiettes différentes de celles qui sont indiquées pour les groupes 1000, 3000, 4000 et 5000, ou sur des assiettes qui ne peuvent être considérées comme liées à l'une de celles afférentes à ces groupes. Lorsque des impôts sont perçus sur plusieurs assiettes différentes, et qu'il est possible d'évaluer les recettes liées à chaque assiette, les montants correspondants sont inclus dans le groupe approprié. S'il est impossible d'évaluer le montant correspondant à chaque assiette, et si l'on sait que l'essentiel des recettes provient des impôts perçus sur une assiette donnée, la totalité des recettes est classée en fonction de cette assiette. Sinon, les impôts sont classés dans le présent groupe. Sont également inclus dans ce groupe les impôts forfaitaires non inclus ailleurs dans le système de classification, les impôts prélevés sur les personnes physiques sous la forme de taxe civique ou d'impôt de capitation, les droits de timbre qui ne sont pas liés à des transactions mobilières ou immobilières et qui n'entrent pas exclusivement dans une catégorie de transactions, les impôts sur les dépenses dès lors qu'ils s'accompagnent

d'abattements et d'exonérations individuels, ainsi que les recettes fiscales non identifiables. Ce poste est divisé en impôts exclusivement ou principalement à la charge des entreprises (6100) et en impôts à la charge d'autres contribuables (6200).

A.6. Conciliation avec les comptes nationaux

83. Cette section des tableaux permet de concilier les calculs des recettes fiscales totales de l'OCDE et l'ensemble des impôts et cotisations sociales versés aux administrations publiques qui sont enregistrés dans les comptes nationaux par pays. Lorsque le pays en question est membre de l'Union européenne (UE) la comparaison est effectuée entre les calculs des recettes fiscales totales des pays de l'OCDE et la somme des recettes fiscales et cotisations de sécurité sociale perçues par les administrations publiques et les institutions des secteurs de l'Union européenne des comptes nationaux.

A.7. Poste pour mémoire relatif au financement des prestations de sécurité sociale

84. Le rapport entre les impôts et les cotisations de sécurité sociale étant variable, et en raison des problèmes évoqués aux § 39 à 45, on a réuni dans un poste pour mémoire l'ensemble des versements affectés à des prestations du type sécurité sociale, en dehors des versements facultatifs au secteur privé. Les données sont présentées de la façon suivante (voir le chapitre 4.2)

a. impôts du groupe 2000 ;
b. impôts affectés aux prestations de sécurité sociale ;
c. cotisations facultatives à l'administration ;
d. cotisations obligatoires au secteur privé.

Les § 39 à 45 ci-dessus contiennent des directives pour la ventilation entre ces quatre catégories

A.8. Poste pour mémoire relatif aux impôts identifiables payés par les administrations

85. Les impôts effectivement payés par les administrations elles-mêmes et que l'on peut identifier sont indiqués dans un poste pour mémoire et classés suivant les grandes rubriques de la classification des impôts de l'OCDE. Dans la très grande majorité des pays, seuls peuvent être identifiées en l'occurrence les cotisations de sécurité sociale et les impôts sur les salaires, mais il s'agit là en général des impôts les plus importants acquittés par les administrations (voir le chapitre 4.2 de cette publication).

A.9. Rapport de la classification des impôts de l'OCDE avec les systèmes nationaux de comptabilité nationale

86. Un système de comptabilité nationale (SCN) tend à fournir un cadre cohérent pour enregistrer et présenter les principaux flux relatifs à la production, à la consommation, à l'accumulation et aux transactions extérieures d'une zone économique donnée, d'ordinaire un pays ou une grande région d'un pays. Les recettes publiques sont une partie importante des transactions enregistrées dans le SCN. La version finale du SCN 2008 a été diffusée conjointement par cinq organisations internationales : les Nations Unies, le Fonds Monétaire International, l'Union européenne, l'Organisation de Coopération et de Développement Économiques et la Banque Mondiale, en août 2009. Le Système est un ensemble complet,

cohérent et souple de comptes macro-économiques. Il est élaboré pour être utilisé dans les pays à économie de marché quel que soit leur niveau de développement économique ainsi que dans les pays en transition vers l'économie de marché. De larges extraits du cadre théorique ainsi que les définitions des divers secteurs de l'économie du SCN figurent dans la classification des impôts de l'OCDE.

87. Il existe cependant un certain nombre de différences entre la classification des impôts de l'OCDE et les concepts du SCN qui sont indiqués ci-dessous. Ils proviennent du fait que l'objectif de cette classification est de permettre une ventilation aussi large que possible des données statistiques pour ce que les administrations fiscales conviennent de considérer de manière générale comme des impôts.

a. l'OCDE inclut les cotisations obligatoires de sécurité sociale payées aux administrations publiques dans les recettes fiscales totales. Les cotisations sociales facultatives et imputées ainsi que celles versées aux caisses privées ne sont pas considérées comme des impôts (§ 8 et 10 ci-dessus) ;
b. les avis diffèrent sur la question de savoir s'il y a lieu de classer certains prélèvements et redevances dans les impôts (§ 11 et 12 ci-dessus) ;
c. l'OCDE exclut les impôts imputés ou les subventions résultant d'opérations de taux de change officiels multiples et ceux résultant du fait que la banque centrale paye un taux d'intérêt sur les réserves obligatoires différent des autres taux du marché ;
d. il existe des différences dans le traitement des crédits d'impôt récupérables.

88. Comme on l'a noté aux § 1 et 2, les groupes 1000 à 6000 de la classification de l'OCDE comprennent tous les versements sans contrepartie aux administrations publiques, à l'exclusion des prêts obligatoires et des amendes. On peut obtenir le total de ces versements sans contrepartie, amendes incluses, mais prêts obligatoires exclus, en additionnant les postes suivants du SCN 2008 :

- impôts du type valeur ajoutée (D.211) ;
- droits et taxes sur les importations à l'exclusion de la TVA (D.212) ;
- droits sur les exportations (D.213) ;
- taxes sur les produits, à l'exclusion de la TVA, des droits sur les importations et les exportations (D.214) ;
- autres impôts sur la production (D.29) ;
- impôts sur le revenu (D.51) ;
- autres impôts périodiques (D.59) ;
- cotisations de sécurité sociale (D.61) à l'exclusion des cotisations facultatives ;
- impôts sur le capital (D.91).

A.10. La classification des impôts de l'OCDE et le système du Fonds monétaire international (SFP)

89. Le périmètre et l'évaluation des recettes fiscales dans le système de statistiques de finances publiques (SFP) et dans le système de comptabilité nationale de 2008 (SCN 2008) sont très proches. Par conséquent, les différences entre la classification de l'OCDE et celle du SCN 2008 (voir § 87 ci-dessus) sont également valables pour les SFP. En outre, le Fonds monétaire international subdivise le groupe 5000 de la classification de l'OCDE en une section iv (Taxes intérieures sur les biens et services) et une section v (Taxes sur

les transactions et les échanges internationaux). Cela tient à ce que le rendement de ces dernières taxes représente généralement des sommes infimes dans les pays de l'OCDE ce qui n'est pas le cas dans beaucoup de pays non membres.

A.11. Comparaison de la classification des impôts de l'OCDE et des autres classifications internationales des recettes publiques

90. Le tableau ci-dessous décrit point par point la comparaison entre la classification des impôts de l'OCDE et les classifications suivantes :

a. Système des comptes nationaux (SCN 2008) ;

b. Système européen des comptes (SEC 2010) ;

c. Manuel de statistiques des finances publiques du Fonds monétaire international (MSFP 2014).

91. Ces comparaisons correspondent à celles qui devraient s'appliquer dans la majorité des cas. Toutefois, en pratique il faut faire preuve d'une certaine souplesse dans leur application. En effet, dans certains cas, les pays peuvent adopter des méthodes diverses de classification des recettes dans les comptes nationaux.

OECD Classification	2008 SNA	2010 ESA	GFSM2014
1000 Taxes on income, profits and capital gains			
1100 Individuals			
1110 Income and profits	D51-8.61a	D51A	1111
1120 Capital gains	D51-8.61c, d	D51C, D	1111
1200 Corporations			
1210 Income and profits	D51-8.61b	D51B	1112
1220 Capital gains	D51-8.61c	D51C	1112
1300 Unallocable as between 1100 and 1200			1113
2000 Social security contributions			
2100 Employees	D613-8.85	D613	1211
2200 Employers	D611-8.83	D611	1212
2300 Self-employed, non-employed	D613-8.85	D613	1213
2400 Unallocable as between 2100, 2200 and 2300			1214
3000 Taxes on payroll and workforce	D29-7.97a	D29C	112
4000 Taxes on property			
4100 Recurrent taxes on immovable property			
4110 Households	D59-8.63a	D59A	1131
4120 Other	D29-7.97b	D29A	1131
4200 Recurrent net wealth taxes			
4210 Individual	D59-8.63b	D59A	1132
4220 Corporations	D59-8.63b	D59A	1132
4300 Estate, inheritance and gift taxes			
4310 Estate and inheritance taxes	D91-10.207b	D91A	1133
4320 Gift taxes	D91-10.207b	D91A	1133
4400 Taxes on financial and capital transactions	D59-7.96d; D29-7.97e	D214B, C	114114; 1161
4500 Other non-recurrent taxes on property	D91-10.207a	D91B	1135
4600 Other recurrent taxes on property	D59-8.63c	D59A	1136
5000 Taxes on goods and services			
5100 Taxes on production, sale and transfer of goods and services			
5110 General taxes on goods and services			
5111 Value-added taxes	D211-7.89	D211; D29G	11411
5112 Sales taxes	D2122-7.94a; D214-7.96a	D21224; D214I	11412
5113 Other general taxes on goods and services	D214-7.96a	D214I	11413

OECD Classification	2008 SNA	2010 ESA	GFSM2014
5120 Taxes on specific goods and services			
5121 Excises	D2122-7.94b; D214-7.96b	D21223; D214A, B, D	1142
5122 Profits of fiscal monopolies	D214-7.96e	D214J	1143
5123 Customs and other import duties	D2121-7.93	D2121; D21221, 2	1151
5124 On exports	D213-7.95a	D214K	1152-4
5125 On investment goods			
5126 On specific services	D2122-7.94c; D214-7.96c	D21225; D214E, F, G, H; D29F	1144; 1156
5127 Other taxes on international trade and transactions	D2122-7.94d; D29-7.95b D29-7.97g; D59-8.64d	D21226; D29D; D59E	1153; 1155-6
5128 Other taxes on specific goods and services			1146
5130 Unallocable between 5110 and 5120			
5200 Taxes on use of goods and on permission to use goods or perform activities			
5210 Recurrent taxes on use of goods and on permission to use goods or perform activities			
5211 Motor vehicle taxes households	D59-8.64c	D59D	11451
5212 Motor vehicles taxes others	D29-7.97d	D214D; D29B	11451
5213 Other recurrent taxes on use of goods and on permission to use goods or perform activities	D29-7.97c, d, f D59-8.64c	D29B, E, F; D59D	11452
5220 Non-recurrent taxes on permission to use goods or perform activities			11452
5300 Unallocable as between 5100 and 5200			
6000 Other taxes			
6100 Payable solely by business			1161
6200 Payable by other than business, or unidentifiable	D59-8.64a, b	D59B, C	1162

A.12. Répartition des recettes fiscales par sous-secteurs d'administration publique

92. La classification de l'OCDE appelle une ventilation des recettes fiscales par sous-secteurs d'administration. On trouvera ci-après la définition de chaque sous-secteur et les critères à utiliser pour répartir entre eux les recettes fiscales. Ces définitions et critères suivent les orientations qui figurent dans le SCN 2008 et le MSFP 2014.

Sous-secteurs des administrations publiques à identifier

a) Administration centrale

93. Le sous-secteur des administrations centrales groupe tous les ministères, bureaux, établissements et autres organismes qui sont des services ou des moyens d'action du pouvoir central et dont la compétence s'étend à la totalité du territoire, à l'exception de l'administration des caisses de sécurité sociale. L'administration centrale a donc le pouvoir de prélever des impôts sur toutes les unités résidentes et non résidentes exerçant des activités économiques à l'intérieur du pays.

b) Administration d'un État fédéré, d'une province ou d'une région

94. Ce sous-secteur comprend les unités administratives intermédiaires et inclut toutes les unités administratives dont la compétence s'exerce indépendamment de l'Administration centrale sur une partie du territoire englobant un certain nombre de petites localités, à l'exception des caisses de sécurité sociale. Dans les pays unitaires, les administrations régionales peuvent être considérées comme dotées d'une existence distincte lorsqu'elles

disposent d'une autonomie substantielle pour percevoir une part importante de leurs recettes de sources placées sous leur contrôle et lorsque leurs agents ne sont pas soumis à un contrôle administratif externe dans l'exercice des activités de l'unité.

95. Actuellement, les pays à structure fédérale représentent la majorité des cas dans lesquels les recettes attribuées aux unités administratives intermédiaires sont identifiées séparément. L'Espagne est le seul pays à structure unitaire qui se trouve dans cette situation. Dans les autres pays unitaires, les recettes des administrations régionales sont incluses dans celles des administrations locales.

c) Collectivités locales

96. Ce sous-secteur comprend toutes les autres unités administratives exerçant une compétence indépendante sur une partie du territoire d'un pays, à l'exception des administrations des caisses de sécurité sociale. Il englobe les diverses circonscriptions urbaines et/ou rurales (par exemple les collectivités locales, les municipalités, les villes, les bourgs ou les districts).

d) Caisses de sécurité sociale

97. Les caisses de sécurité sociale constituent un sous-secteur distinct des administrations publiques. Le sous-secteur de la sécurité sociale est défini dans le SCN de 2008 par les extraits suivants des paragraphes 4.124 à 4.126 et 4.147 :

> *« Les systèmes de sécurité sociale sont des systèmes d'assurance sociale qui couvrent l'ensemble de la collectivité ou d'importants sous-ensembles de la collectivité : ces systèmes sont imposés et contrôlés par les administrations publiques. Ces systèmes couvrent une grande variété de programmes qui consistent à fournir des prestations, en espèces ou en nature, au titre des circonstances suivantes : vieillesse, invalidité ou décès, survie, maladie et maternité, accident du travail, chômage, allocations familiales, soins de santé etc. Il n'existe pas nécessairement de lien direct entre le montant de la cotisation versée par un particulier et les prestations qu'il est susceptible de recevoir » (paragraphe 4.124).*

> *« Lorsque les systèmes de sécurité sociale ont une organisation distincte des autres activités des administrations publiques et détiennent des actifs et des engagements indépendamment de ces dernières et effectuent des opérations financières pour leur propre compte, ils peuvent être considérés comme des unités institutionnelles désignées sous le nom de caisses de sécurité sociale » (paragraphe 4.125).*

> *« Il est possible de faire varier de façon discrétionnaire les montants prélevés et versés sous forme de cotisations de sécurité sociale et de prestations afin d'atteindre des objectifs de politique publique qui n'ont pas de lien direct avec la notion de sécurité sociale en tant que système visant à fournir des prestations à des membres de la collectivité. Ainsi, ces cotisations ou prestations peuvent être augmentées ou diminuées afin d'influer sur le niveau de la demande globale au sein de l'économie. Néanmoins, tant que ces caisses restent indépendantes, elles doivent être traitées comme des unités institutionnelles distinctes dans le SCN ». (paragraphe 4.126).*

> *« Le sous-secteur des administrations de sécurité sociale comprend les administrations de sécurité sociale opérant à tous les niveaux des administrations publiques. Les administrations de sécurité sociale sont des systèmes couvrant l'ensemble de la collectivité ou d'importants sous-ensembles de la collectivité qui sont rendus obligatoires et contrôlés par des administrations publiques » (paragraphe 4.147).*

98. Cette définition des administrations de sécurité sociale est suivie dans la classification de l'OCDE à l'exception des régimes suivants :

- Les régimes imposés par l'administration et exploités par des organismes extérieurs au secteur des administrations publiques, tel qu'il est défini au § 3 de ce manuel et
- Les régimes qui perçoivent des cotisations facultatives.

Autorités supranationales

99. Ce sous-secteur s'applique aux activités de collecte de recettes publiques des autorités supranationales sur le territoire d'un pays. En pratique, le seul cas d'autorité supranationale de la zone de l'OCDE est celui des institutions de l'Union européenne (UE). Depuis 1998, les autorités supranationales ne figurent plus dans les Statistiques des recettes publiques dans un souci de cohérence avec la définition du SCN des administrations publiques qui les exclut. Par exemple, les impôts sur le revenu et des contributions de sécurité sociale rassemblées par des Institutions européennes et payé par les fonctionnaires européens qui sont résidents de pays membres de l'Union européenne ne devraient pas être inclus. Toutefois, les prélèvements spécifiques versés par les États membres à l'Union européenne continuent à être inclus dans les recettes fiscales totales et ils sont indiqués sous cette rubrique.

Critères à utiliser pour l'attribution des recettes fiscales

100. Lorsqu'une administration collecte l'impôt et le reverse, en totalité ou en partie, à d'autres administrations, il est nécessaire de déterminer si ces recettes doivent être considérées comme étant celles de l'administration qui les perçoit et les répartit entre d'autres administrations ou celles des administrations bénéficiaires auxquelles l'administration qui les a perçues les a transférées en simple qualité d'agent. Les critères à utiliser dans l'attribution des recettes sont indiqués aux § 101 à 104, qui reprennent les paragraphes 3.70 à 3.73 du SCN 2008.

101. En général, un impôt est attribué à l'Unité administrative qui :

a. exerce le pouvoir de percevoir l'impôt (soit en tant que détenteur de ce pouvoir soit par délégation de l'autorité qui le détient),

b. dispose du pouvoir discrétionnaire final de fixer et de faire varier le taux de l'impôt.

102. Lorsqu'une somme est collectée par une administration au profit d'une autre administration et en son nom, et que cette dernière a le pouvoir de percevoir l'impôt et de fixer et de faire varier son taux, la première intervient comme agent pour le compte de la dernière et l'impôt est réaffecté. Toute somme retenue par l'administration collectrice au titre des frais de recouvrement doit être considérée comme la rémunération d'un service rendu. Toute autre somme conservée par l'administration collectrice, notamment dans le cadre d'un accord de partage d'impôt, doit être considérée comme une subvention courante. Si l'administration collectrice s'est vu déléguer le pouvoir de fixer et de faire varier le taux, le montant recouvré doit être considéré comme une recette fiscale de cette administration.

103. Lorsque des administrations différentes fixent conjointement et sur un pied d'égalité la répartition du produit de cet impôt, aucune administration ne disposant d'un pouvoir prépondérant en dernier ressort, les recettes fiscales sont attribuées à chaque administration en fonction de sa part respective du produit de l'impôt. Si un accord permet à une unité administrative d'exercer un pouvoir prépondérant en dernier ressort, la totalité des recettes fiscales est attribuée à cette unité.

104. Dans certains cas aussi, un impôt est perçu dans le cadre des compétences d'une administration qui résulte de la constitution ou d'autres dispositions mais d'autres administrations fixent individuellement le taux d'imposition sur leurs territoires. Le produit de l'impôt généré sur les territoires respectifs de chaque administration est attribué à l'administration en question comme constituant ses recettes fiscales.

Versements effectués par les États membres de l'Union européenne

105. Les versements effectués par les États membres de l'Union européenne prennent la forme de prélèvements spécifiques qui comprennent :

a. les droits de douane et les prélèvements agricoles (5123),
b. les montants compensatoires monétaires bruts (5123 si relatifs aux importations et 5124 si relatifs aux exportations), et
c. les prélèvements de la CECA, les cotisations sucre et les taxes de coresponsabilité sur le lait (5128).

106. Les droits de douane collectés par les États membres pour le compte de l'Union européenne sont comptabilisés :

- sur une base qui ne tient pas compte des droits d'encaissement,
- en utilisant des chiffres corrigés de manière à exprimer les droits sur la base de la « destination finale » et non du « pays de première entrée » lorsque de telles corrections sont possibles. Ces corrections concernent en particulier les droits prélevés dans des ports (maritimes) importants. Bien que les droits de l'UE soient prélevés par les autorités du pays de première entrée, ces droits doivent être dans la mesure du possible déduits des recettes du pays qui les recouvre et inclus dans les recettes du pays de destination finale.

107. Ces droits de l'UE sont le plus clairement conformes au critère d'attribution décrit au § 99 ci-dessus. En conséquence, à partir de 1998, ces montants sont mentionnés dans une note de bas de page à titre de rubrique « Pour mémoire » dans les tableaux des États membres de l'UE (chapitre 4 du Rapport) et ne figurent plus sous la rubrique 5123. Toutefois, ces montants sont inclus dans les grands totaux des recettes fiscales à la ligne supérieure pour toutes les années indiquées dans les tableaux.

A.13. Classification provisoire des recettes provenant des prélèvements sur les banques et des contributions aux mécanismes de garantie des dépôts et de stabilité financière

108. L'OCDE a provisoirement adopté, depuis l'édition 2012 de ses *Statistiques des recettes publiques*, le principe suivant concernant l'enregistrement comptable des recettes issues des prélèvements sur les banques ainsi que des redevances acquittées au titre de la garantie des dépôts et de la stabilité financière. Il est recommandé que les montants concernés soient comptabilisés à la rubrique 5126.

- Les redevances de stabilité, les prélèvements sur les banques et les contributions à la garantie des dépôts, qu'il est obligatoire d'acquitter, doivent généralement être traitées comme des recettes fiscales lorsque les versements sont effectués au profit de l'administration publique et affectés au budget consolidé ou général des administrations de sorte que les pouvoirs publics soient libres d'utiliser les fonds sans délai aux fins qu'ils jugent opportunes. Ce principe s'appliquerait indépendamment du fait que l'administration promette ou non d'effectuer des versements pour garantir les dépôts des clients des établissements bancaires si la situation l'exigeait à l'avenir.

- Si les paiements obligatoires sont effectués au profit de l'administration publique et imputés à des budgets dont les ressources doivent être entièrement réaffectées au secteur de l'économie qui englobe les entreprises assujetties à ces paiements, ceux-ci seront toujours traités, en règle générale, comme des recettes fiscales étant donné que les fonds seraient disponibles pour l'administration et réduiraient son déficit budgétaire, que la redevance est sans contrepartie pour les entités individuelles et que les montants collectés pourraient être dissociés de tout versement en faveur des déposants ou de toute dépense visant à soutenir plus largement le secteur financier.
- Les contributions aux mécanismes traditionnels de moindre envergure destinés à garantir les dépôts de détail, contributions dont le montant est aligné sur le coût de la garantie, doivent être classées en tant que redevances pour services rendus.
- Tout versement au titre de la réalisation par une administration des actifs d'un établissement en faillite ou du recouvrement par cette administration d'une créance prioritaire sur les actifs de l'établissement en cours de liquidation, effectué en vue de financer l'indemnisation des clients ayant perdu leurs dépôts, serait traité comme une redevance par opposition aux recettes fiscales.

Les contributions obligatoires aux fonds administrés en-dehors du secteur public et aux organismes non étatiques bénéficiant du soutien des institutions collectrices de dépôts ainsi que toutes les contributions aux mécanismes facultatifs ne doivent pas être traitées comme des recettes fiscales.

Notes

1. « Les références dans cette annexe aux chapitres ou aux sections de « ce rapport » sont issues de OCDE (2019), Statistiques des recettes publiques 2019, Éditions OCDE, Paris. »
2. Toutes les références au SCN concernent l'édition de 2008.
3. Se reporter à la section A.12 de ce manuel pour l'examen de cette notion.
4. Il est en général possible d'identifier les montants des cotisations de sécurité sociale et les impôts sur les salaires, mais pas les autres impôts payés par les administrations.
5. En revanche, si un ou plusieurs pays considèrent comme un impôt un droit que la plupart des pays font entrer dans les recettes non fiscales ou qui procure des recettes substantielles, les montants ainsi perçus figureront dans une note de renvoi à la fin des tableaux par pays correspondants, même s'ils ne sont pas inclus dans le total des recettes fiscales.
6. Les appellations peuvent cependant être souvent trompeuses. Ainsi, une redevance de passeport sera normalement considérée comme une recette non fiscale, alors qu'un prélèvement additionnel sur les passeports (comme c'est le cas au Portugal), qui a pour but de procurer un montant substantiel de recettes eu égard au coût de délivrance du passeport, sera considéré comme un impôt du sous-groupe 5200.
7. On trouvera des précisions sur cette distinction dans l'étude spéciale intitulée « L'information sur les recettes fiscales : problèmes actuels », de l'édition de 2001 des *Statistiques des recettes publiques*.
8. On utilise parfois les expressions « non remboursable » et « remboursable » mais il peut paraître illogique de parler de « remboursement » lorsque rien n'a été versé.
9. Toutefois, dans les systèmes d'imputation de l'impôt sur les sociétés, les crédits d'impôts récupérables sont traités différemment (§ 36 à 38).
10. Il ne s'agit pas d'une véritable dépense fiscale au sens strict. De telles dépenses fiscales supposent que l'on identifie un système fiscal de référence pour chaque pays ou, de préférence, une norme internationale commune. En pratique, il n'a pas été possible de parvenir à un accord sur une norme internationale commune.
11. Sauf s'ils sont calculés sur le bénéfice résultant de la vente, auquel cas ils seraient classés parmi les impôts sur les gains en capital dans le sous-groupe 1120 ou 1220.

12. Dans certains pays, la même législation est applicable aux personnes physiques et aux entreprises dans le cas d'impôts sur le revenu particulier. Cependant, les recettes procurées par ces impôts peuvent, en général, être ventilées et figurent donc dans les deux sous-groupes appropriés.
13. Ainsi, « celles qui sont suffisamment autonomes et indépendantes pour que leur fonctionnement soit comparable à celui d'une société... (y compris) la tenue de comptes complets » (2008 SCN section 4.44).
14. Il peut en être ainsi lorsqu'un régime en faveur des administrations existait avant l'instauration d'un régime général de sécurité sociale.
15. Système selon lequel l'Union Européenne ajuste les effets des différences entre les taux de change utilisés pour fixer les prix des produits agricoles dans le cadre de la politique agricole commune, et le taux de change réel. Les paiements effectués selon ce système portent sur les importations ou les exportations; lorsqu'ils sont identifiables, ces montants figurent dans la rubrique appropriée (5123 ou 5124). Dans ce guide, sont inclus les montants bruts, c'est-à-dire sans déduction d'aucune prime payée dans le cadre du système des montants compensatoires.
16. Les transferts de bénéfices de loteries d'État sont considérés comme des recettes non fiscales (voir aussi § 67).

Annex B

Interpretative guide to non-tax revenue in Revenue Statistics in Africa

Table of contents

B.1. Coverage

The definition of non-tax revenues and the main subcategories identified in this publication generally correspond to the concepts laid out in the 2014 IMF Government Finance Statistics Manual (GFSM). Non-tax revenues refer to increases in government net worth resulting from transactions other than tax revenues. They exclude funds arising from the repayment of previous lending by governments or from borrowing, or proceeds derived from sales of fixed capital assets, stocks, land and intangible assets or private gifts.

Non-tax revenues are made up of the following elements.

B.2. Grants

The GFSM 2014 states "Grants are transfers receivable by government units from non-resident government units or international organisations without the receipt of any goods, services, or assets in return. Grants are normally receivable in cash, but may also take the form of the receipt of goods or services (in kind)". These transfers are un-refundable and unrequited. Grants encompass reparations and gifts given for particular projects or programmes. The term "grants" is not used to refer to transfers to or from non-governmental units and excludes inter-governmental transfers. The remission of funds collected by one government for another in an agency capacity should not be shown as receipt of a grant by the beneficiary government but as its direct receipt of revenue.

B.3. Property income

This category includes income to government arising from their ownership of property, enterprises, financial assets, or intangible assets when government units place them at the disposal of other units. Sales of non-financial assets such as the sales of lands are not recorded as revenue because disposal of such an asset does not increase the net worth. Similarly, repayments on loans and loan disbursements are not revenue. Property income may take the form of dividends, interest, land rents, royalties, or withdrawals from entrepreneurial income. The main components are:

- Interest and dividends: Interest is the revenue earned by the government unit from a financial asset by putting it at the disposal of another institutional unit. Dividends are the revenue earned by placing equity funds at the disposal of a corporation (resident or non-resident corporation). This category also consists of profits of state-owned enterprises except those classified as fiscal monopolies (see §62-§64 of the OECD Interpretative Guide to tax revenue in Annex A), export and import monopoly profits (see §70-§71 of the same document) or those providing public utilities such as rail transport, electricity, post offices and other communications. In this category are included revenue from public financial institutions such as the central banks' profits, profits transferred or distributed from the operation of monetary authority functions outside the central bank and the profits of state lotteries transferred to the government. Transfers from public utilities enterprises are recorded as non-tax revenue under "sales of goods and services" whereas profits for fiscal, export or import monopolies are classified as tax revenue.
- Rents or royalties: Rent is the revenue generated from natural resources, such as land, mining, or oil resources, when a government unit places these at the disposal of private or foreign entities. The rents received relate to a resource lease-giving agreement for the exploitation and extraction of a natural resource by the lessee in return for a payment.

Payments for exploration rights are also treated as rent. Rents should not be confused with other payments a government may receive related to the exploitation of subsoil and similar assets, such as severance taxes, business licenses, or other taxes (e.g. value added taxes, excises, taxes on exports, etc.). They should also not be taken to mean incomes from the rental of buildings and equipment, which are treated as sales of goods and services. Revenues from rents and royalties are in some cases difficult to establish and depend on the agreement between the government unit and the lessee. For example rents, royalties and taxes such as corporate income taxes and VAT are sometimes encompassed in a single payment to the general government. In such cases the revenue should be classified under the category to which the majority of revenue belongs (see §71 of Annex A for further explanation.)

- Other property income: This includes revenue earned by a government unit placing funds at a disposal of quasi-corporations.[1] Conceptually this source of revenue is equivalent to that of dividends from a corporation but by definition, quasi-corporations cannot distribute income in the form of dividends. This category of "other property income" also includes retained or reinvested earnings, i.e. the percentage of distributable revenue not paid out as dividends, but retained by the corporation or quasi-corporation on foreign investment; property income from investment income disbursements and unidentified property income.

B.4. Sales of goods and services

Revenue under the category "sales of goods and services" is generally reported on a gross basis, without deduction of costs. Since these costs can represent a significant proportion of revenues, they cannot be regarded in total as funds available for governments to finance their general activities. This contrasts with tax revenues, where the collection costs are usually a small proportion of revenue. This difference implies that it may not be meaningful to sum tax and non-tax revenues as part of a calculation of generally available funds.

The proceeds of sales of nonfinancial assets such as the sale of buildings or lands are not classified as revenues since their disposal does not increase the net worth.

Sales of goods and services consist of:

- Sales by market establishments.[2]
- Administrative fees for services (i.e. fees for drivers' licences, passports, visas, court fees, harbour fees, fees for birth, marriage or death certificates, patent registrations, radio and television licenses when public authorities provide general broadcasting services).
- Administrative fees that are sales of services associated with a regulatory function of government (such as fees for the inspection of premises before delivering a business licence) and considered to be proportional to the cost of producing the service are included in this category. If the fee in return for the service provided by the government unit is disproportionate, then the fee will be classified as a tax. Specific examples of fees that are considered taxes include fees for permission to perform activities such as hunting, fishing and shooting; and fees for business registration where this is a legal requirement for the business to operate.
- Sales by nonmarket establishments such as fees at government hospitals, tuition fees at government schools and admission fees to museums and parks.
- Leasing of buildings and equipment.

B.5. Fines, penalties and forfeits

The GFSM 2014 states "Fines and penalties are compulsory transfers imposed by courts of law or bodies for violations of laws or administrative rules. Out-of-court agreements are also included (...). Forfeits are amounts deposited with a general government unit pending a legal or administrative proceeding, and that will be transferred to the unit upon resolution". For example traffic fines are included here. Fines and penalties charged on overdue taxes or penalties imposed for the evasion of taxes should be recorded in this category and not as taxes. However if it is not possible to separate the amounts paid in taxes and fines, the whole amount should be classified under the tax to which the fine relates (see §14 of Annex A for further explanation).

B.6. Other social contributions

This category includes the actual and imputed contributions to social insurance schemes operated by governments as employers on behalf of their employees that do not create a future defined liability. This category also includes the sum of the total voluntary contributions.[3] Excluded from this category are any contributions to funds in which the contributions of each participant and of his employer on his behalf are kept in a separate account earning interest and withdrawable under specified circumstances or any contributions to a pension fund autonomous to the general government. This category is not included in this publication.

B.7. Miscellaneous and unidentified revenue

This category consists of unidentified non-tax revenues or those that do not fit into any of the other categories listed above. It includes revenue such as gifts and transfers from individuals, private non-profit institutions, nongovernmental foundations, corporations, or sources other than governments and international organisations. Major non-recurrent payments receivable in compensation for extensive damages or serious injuries not covered by insurance policies are also included, such as payments of compensation for damages caused by major explosions; oil spillages; or payments receivable for damage to property other than payments from an insurance settlement.

Notes

1. Quasi-corporations are unincorporated enterprises that exercise some functions of corporations, but have not been granted separate legal personality by statute.
2. A market establishment is an establishment that charges economically significant prices.
3. The IMF includes these contributions as part of their total of social security contributions.

Revenue Statistics in Africa 1990-2018/Statistiques des recettes publiques en Afrique 1990-2018

ANNEXE B

Guide d'interprétation des recettes non fiscales dans les Statistiques des recettes publiques en Afrique

Table des matières

B.1. Champ couvert

La définition des recettes non fiscales et des principales sous-catégories décrites dans la présente publication coïncident en grande partie avec les notions retenues dans le manuel des statistiques de finances publiques du FMI de 2014 (manuel SFP 2014). Les recettes non fiscales désignent des augmentations de la valeur nette résultant d'une transaction et qui ne sont pas des recettes fiscales. Elles excluent les fonds relatifs au remboursement de prêts consentis antérieurement par les administrations ou liés à des emprunts, ainsi que le produit de la cession d'actifs immobilisés, d'éléments de stocks, de terrains, d'actifs immatériels et les dons à titre privé.

Les recettes non fiscales se composent des éléments suivants.

B.2. Dons

Selon le manuel SFP 2014, les dons sont des transferts qu'une administration publique reçoit d'une autre administration publique étrangère ou d'une organisation internationale, sans recevoir de cette dernière un bien, un service ou un actif en contrepartie directe. Les dons sont habituellement reçus en espèces, mais peuvent aussi prendre la forme de biens ou de services (en nature). Ces transferts sont non remboursables et sans contrepartie. Les dons recouvrent les réparations et dons assignés à des projets ou programmes particuliers. Le terme de « dons » n'est pas employé pour désigner les transferts réalisés par des entités autres que des administrations publiques ou effectués en leur faveur et exclut les transferts entre administrations. Le versement de fonds collectés par une administration qui agit en qualité de mandataire ne devrait pas entrer dans la catégorie des dons perçus par l'administration bénéficiaire, mais bien s'ajouter aux recettes directement perçues par cette dernière.

B.3. Revenus de la propriété

Cette catégorie regroupe les recettes publiques découlant de la détention de biens fonciers, de parts de sociétés, d'actifs financiers ou d'actifs immatériels que certaines unités administratives ont mis à la disposition d'autres unités administratives. Les cessions d'actifs non financiers comme la vente de terrains ne sont pas enregistrées en tant que recettes parce que la cession de tels actifs n'a pas d'effet sur la valeur nette. De même, les remboursements de prêts et les prêts octroyés ne sont pas des recettes. Les revenus de la propriété peuvent prendre la forme de dividendes, d'intérêts, de revenus fonciers, de redevances, ou de prélèvements sur des revenus d'entreprises. Les principales composantes en sont les suivantes :

- Intérêts et dividendes : Les intérêts sont les revenus perçus par une unité administrative au titre d'un actif financier qu'elle met à la disposition d'une autre unité institutionnelle. Les dividendes sont les recettes perçues par une unité qui met des capitaux à la disposition d'une société (qu'elle soit ou non un résident du pays concerné). Cette catégorie recouvre également les bénéfices d'entreprises détenues par une administration, en excluant les monopoles fiscaux (voir paragraphes 62 à 64 du Guide d'interprétation de l'OCDE en Annexe A), les monopoles d'exportation et d'importation (voir paragraphes 70 et 71 du même document) ainsi que les entreprises qui fournissent des services publics comme les chemins de fer, l'électricité, les postes et autres moyens de communication. Sont regroupés dans cette catégorie les revenus provenant d'institutions financières publiques comme les bénéfices de la banque centrale, les bénéfices transférés ou distribués au titre de fonctions de l'autorité monétaire exercées en dehors de la banque centrale et les bénéfices liés aux loteries nationales qui sont transférés à l'administration. Les transferts émanant d'entreprises qui assurent des services publics sont comptabilisés dans la rubrique « ventes de biens et de services » alors que les bénéfices des monopoles fiscaux, d'exportation ou d'importation constituent des recettes fiscales.

- Loyers et redevances : Les loyers sont des revenus générés lorsqu'une unité administrative met à la disposition d'autres entités privées ou étrangères des ressources naturelles, comme des terrains ou des gisements de minéraux ou de pétrole. Les loyers perçus sont liés à des accords de concession relatifs à l'exploitation et à l'extraction d'une ressource naturelle par un concessionnaire en contrepartie d'un paiement. Les paiements en échange de droits de prospection doivent également être traités comme des loyers. Les loyers sont à distinguer des autres paiements qu'une administration publique peut recevoir pour l'exploitation d'actifs du sous-sol et d'autres actifs du même type, par exemple les paiements de taxes d'extraction, patentes ou autres impôts (taxes sur la valeur ajoutée, accises, taxes à l'exportation, etc.). Il ne faut pas non plus confondre loyers et revenus de la location de bâtiments et d'équipements, par exemple, qui sont classés dans les ventes de biens et de services. Les revenus liés aux loyers et redevances sont parfois difficiles à déterminer car ils dépendent de la nature de l'accord conclu entre l'unité administration et le concessionnaire. À titre d'exemple, un versement unique effectué en faveur des administrations publiques peut regrouper le paiement de loyers, de redevances et d'autres obligations fiscales comme l'impôt sur les bénéfices des sociétés ou la TVA. Dans un tel cas, le paiement est classé dans la catégorie qui correspond à la majeure partie du versement considéré (voir paragraphe 71 en Annexe A pour plus de précisions).
- Autres revenus de la propriété : Cette catégorie inclut les recettes perçues par une unité administrative qui met des capitaux à la disposition de quasi-sociétés[1]. Cette source de recettes est en substance équivalente à des dividendes versés par une société mais, par définition, les quasi-sociétés ne distribuent pas de bénéfices sous forme de dividendes. Cette catégorie englobe de plus les bénéfices non distribués ou réinvestis, à savoir la fraction du bénéfice distribuable qui n'a pas été versée sous forme de dividendes, mais conservée par la société ou quasi-société sur des investissements étrangers ; les revenus de la propriété provenant de versements de revenus d'investissements et revenus de la propriété non identifiés.

B.4. Ventes de biens et de services

Les recettes qui entrent dans cette catégorie sont enregistrées en valeur brute, sans déduction de coûts. Dans la mesure où les coûts peuvent représenter une part importante des recettes, le montant total des ventes biens et de services ne peut pas être considéré comme un montant dont l'administration dispose dans son intégralité pour financer ses activités générales. C'est une différence notable avec les recettes fiscales, auxquelles sont associés des coûts de recouvrement qui ne représentent le plus souvent qu'une faible part des recettes. De ce fait, le montant obtenu par addition des recettes fiscales et non fiscales ne fournit pas forcément une bonne évaluation des fonds généralement disponibles.

Le produit généré par la cession d'actifs non financiers tels que des bâtiments ou des terrains n'est pas enregistré en tant que recettes étant donné que la cession de tels actifs n'a pas d'effet sur la valeur nette.

Les ventes de biens et de services se composent des éléments suivants :

- les ventes des établissements marchands[2].

- les droits administratifs pour services fournis (droits sur les permis de conduire, sur les passeports, sur les visas ; droits de procédure ; droits portuaires ; droits pour l'établissement d'actes de naissance, de mariage, de décès ; frais de dépôt de brevet ; licences de radio et télévision lorsque les autorités publiques fournissent des services généraux de radiodiffusion).
- Les droits administratifs qui sont des ventes de biens et de services associés à une fonction régulatrice des administrations publiques (comme les droits perçus au titre d'une inspection d'installations menée en vue de la délivrance d'un permis d'exploitation) sont inclus lorsqu'ils sont considérés comme étant proportionnels au coût de production du service en question. Lorsque les droits perçus en contrepartie d'un service fourni par l'administration sont disproportionnés par rapport aux coûts, ils sont considérés comme des impôts. Parmi les droits ainsi classés dans la catégorie des recettes fiscales figurent notamment les droits perçus pour l'octroi de permis d'exercer des activités telles que la chasse, la pêche et l'utilisation d'armes à feu ; et les droits d'enregistrement d'une société dès lors que les entreprises sont tenues par la loi de procéder à un tel enregistrement pour pouvoir exercer leur activité.
- les ventes par les établissements non marchands, comme les droits prélevés par les hôpitaux publics, les droits de scolarité des écoles publiques et les droits d'entrée aux musées et parcs.
- la location de bâtiments et d'équipements.

B.5. Amendes, pénalités et confiscations

Le manuel des statistiques de finances publiques du FMI de 2014 définit les amendes et pénalités comme des transferts obligatoires imposés aux unités par des tribunaux ou des organismes pour infraction à la loi ou aux règlements administratifs. Les accords extra-judiciaires sont également inclus. Les confiscations sont les montants déposés auprès d'une unité d'administration publique pendant le déroulement d'une procédure judiciaire ou administrative puis transférés à cette unité au moment du règlement de celle-ci. À titre d'exemple, les amendes sanctionnant les contraventions au code de la route entrent dans cette catégorie. Les amendes et pénalités appliquées au titre d'arriérés d'impôts ou les pénalités pour fraude fiscale devraient également être comptabilisées ici et non comme des recettes fiscales. Toutefois, s'il est impossible de distinguer les montants qui correspondent respectivement à l'impôt et aux pénalités, la somme totale est rattachée aux recettes générées par l'impôt qui a motivé l'application des pénalités (voir paragraphe 14 en Annexe A pour plus de précisions).

B.6. Autres cotisations sociales

Cette catégorie englobe les cotisations sociales effectives et imputées aux régimes d'assurance sociale gérés par des administrations publiques en qualité d'employeurs pour le compte de leurs employés qui ne génèrent pas de passif défini dans des périodes futures. Cette catégorie inclut également la somme des contributions volontaires totales[3]. Toutefois, sont exclues les cotisations à des fonds dans lesquels les cotisations de chaque salarié et celles que l'employeur verse en son nom sont comptabilisées séparément dans un compte productif d'intérêts d'où elles peuvent être retirées dans des conditions biens déterminées, ainsi que les cotisations à des fonds de pension autonomes vis-à-vis des administrations publiques. Cette catégorie n'est pas incluse aux fins de la présente publication.

B.7. Recettes diverses et non identifiées

Cette catégorie regroupe toutes les recettes non fiscales qui ne peuvent être identifiées ou qui n'entrent dans aucune des catégories décrites précédemment. Elle englobe des dons et transferts provenant de personnes physiques, d'institutions privées sans but lucratif, de fondations non gouvernementales, de sociétés ou de sources autres que les administrations publiques et les organisations internationales. Les paiements non récurrents d'un montant élevé reçus par les administrations publiques en compensation de dommages importants non couverts par des polices d'assurance sont également inclus, ainsi que des paiements d'indemnités en compensation de dommages causés par des explosions de grande ampleur, le déversement d'hydrocarbures, ou des paiements exigibles en cas de dommages matériels autres que les paiements au titre d'une indemnisation par une assurance.

Notes

1. Les quasi-sociétés sont des entreprises non constituées en sociétés qui exercent certaines de leurs activités comme des sociétés, mais n'ont pas reçu de personnalité juridique distincte en vertu de la loi.
2. Un établissement marchand est une entité qui pratique des prix économiquement significatifs.
3. Le FMI comptabilise ces cotisations dans le total des cotisations de sécurité sociale.

www.ingramcontent.com/pod-product-compliance
Ingram Content Group UK Ltd.
Pitfield, Milton Keynes, MK11 3LW, UK
UKHW051457290926
15471UKWH00008B/1245

9 789264 952003